the middle east
fourteen islamic centuries

third edition

GLENN E. PERRY
Indiana State University

Prentice Hall, Upper Saddle River, New Jersey 07458

Library of Congress Cataloging-in-Publication Data

Perry, Glenn E. (Glenn Earl)
    The Middle East : fourteen Islamic centuries / Glenn E. Perry.—
3rd ed.
        p.   cm.
    Includes bibliographical references and index.
    ISBN 0–13–266339–2
    1. Middle East—History—1517–   2. Islamic Empire—History.
I. Title.
DS62.4.P46   1997   96-33631
956—dc20   CIP

Acquisitions editor: Sally Constable
Editorial/production supervision: Alison D. Gnerre
Cover design: Bruce Kenselaar
Manufacturing buyer: Lynn Pearlman

To the memory of

Jackson Tedders (1876–1956)
and
Barbara Tedders (1878–1966)

Printed in the United States of America
10   9   8   7   6   5   4   3

ISBN 0-13-266339-2

Prentice-Hall International (UK) Limited, *London*
Prentice-Hall of Australia Pty. Limited, *Sydney*
Prentice-Hall Canada Inc., *Toronto*
Prentice-Hall Hispanoamericana, S.A., *Mexico*
Prentice-Hall of India Private Limited, *New Delhi*
Prentice-Hall of Japan, Inc., *Tokyo*
Simon & Schuster Asia Pte. Ltd., *Singapore*
Editora Prentice-Hall do Brasil, Ltda., *Rio de Janeiro*

contents

LIST OF MAPS

preface

This book is intended as a survey of the history of the Middle East—concentrating heavily on Egypt, the Arabian Peninsula, the Fertile Crescent, Turkey, and Iran, with only occasional mention of areas such as the Maghrib or what we used to call Soviet Central Asia—from the rise of Islam to the present. In keeping with the concerns of most people who want to understand the region better and with the needs of many who teach introductory Middle Eastern history courses (and other courses on the area, for which a concise historical account may constitute an indispensable background), it provides a substantial but relatively telescoped account of the early centuries and then devotes a disproportionate number of pages to the modern period, particularly the post-1914 decades. As in the second edition (but not the first, to which I refer any reader who wants a more detailed version), I have limited my treatment of the pre-Islamic background in Chapter 1 to the minimum necessary to allow the reader to see the Islamic centuries in the context of the earlier predominance and later subordination of the region and to understand the emergence of and interrelationships among various peoples and sects, especially those that remain a part of the Middle Eastern "mosaic."

The overwhelmingly favorable responses the earlier editions received from reviewers, as well as from professors and students in the many colleges and universities where it was used, indicate that it has served its purpose. But this also—in light of the many dramatic developments that have occurred since mid-February 1991, when the second edition was completed—points to the need to bring it up to date.

Besides the obvious updating, the third edition incorporates considerable revisions, taking into account findings of various researchers. While retaining the same organization as before, I have added considerable elaboration at various points.

As in the second edition, I have followed much scholarly practice in matters of transliterating Arabic names. In particular, I have generally used reverse apostrophes to represent the medial *ayn* and ordinary apostrophes for the *hamzah* in similar positions. As in earlier editions, I have avoided indicating either *ayn* or *hamzah* at the beginnings and ends of words. I have also omitted dots and diacritical marks while otherwise staying close to the consonantal and vowel structure of most Arabic words. In a few cases, I have opted for popular spellings, as in the omission of the reverse apostrophe from "Saudi Arabia" but not from "Sa'udi" when it clearly refers to the family rather than to the state.

The bibliographical essay represents the continuing veritable publication explosion in this field during the past two decades. As in the previous edition, I had to omit many items, sometimes fairly arbitrarily, in order to avoid unduly lengthening the essay. With much reluctance, I have continued to drop a lot of older works that are still of value.

I appreciate the many valuable suggestions made by two reviewers, Ronald Davis of Western Michigan University and Mehrdad Kia of the University of Montana. I also wish to thank Sally Constable and Alison D. Gnerre for their important contributions to the process of completing this edition.

Glenn E. Perry
Terre Haute, Indiana

1

setting and prelude
the beginnings to a.d. 610

The term *Middle East,* which I employ here only because of the lack of a better alternative, reveals a European-centered perspective of the world. The fact that Middle Easterners themselves now use this name for their own terrain provides testimony concerning the extent to which the West[1] (i.e., Europe and regions such as North America that have been settled mainly by Europeans) recently has been the center of world civilization and power.

Western preponderance vis-à-vis the Islamic world and the other great civilizations of Eurasia, which goes back at least to the eighteenth century A.D. (and extends back another quarter of a millennium on the seas and in the Western Hemisphere), is the consequence of transformations in much of the West that often are labeled "modernization," of which the Industrial Revolution is the most salient aspect. Non-Western regions did not share in the early stages of modernization (except for

---

[1] While usage varies, I will use the term *West* to include the Greco-Roman world (minus its Middle Eastern conquests) and both its Orthodox Christian (Byzantine-Russian) and its Far Western offshoots. The historian Arnold Toynbee, among others, reserves the word *Western* for the latter, but he recognizes the "affiliation" of the three, making the disagreement a semantic one. One should, of course, approach such classifications of civilizations with caution, as there are arguments for including the ancient Greeks as an integral part of the Middle (or Near) East and indeed for thinking of them as forebears of Islamic as much as of modern Western civilization. Needless to say, our references to *East* and *West* bear no relationship to the so-called East-West conflict in the twentieth-century cold war sense and indeed coincides much more closely to what today we usually call the North-South division.

experiencing a negative impact, ranging from the annihilation experienced by some peoples in the Americas following their "discovery" to the less obvious but nevertheless insidious incorporation of what we now know more generally as the Third World into a world economy that assigned an underdeveloped, deindustrialized, peripheral status to it), and most of them have now discovered that there is a gap between their societies and the modernized West that they cannot easily bridge.

The present situation is atypical of the whole course of history. For a much longer period, as William McNeill shows in *The Rise of the West,* Europe, the Middle East, India, and the Far East were relatively equal centers of civilization. Europe and the Middle East alternately stood in each other's shadow from about 500 B.C. to about A.D. 1700, but their levels of technical development and long-range military capability were about the same. For many centuries in premodern times it was India and China more often than Europe that sometimes tended temporarily to outshine the Middle East in creativity. For even more millennia before 500 B.C., the Middle East clearly was ahead of the rest of humanity, as the advances initiated there slowly spread elsewhere.

To point to a distinction between two broad culture areas, Europe and the Middle East, is not to endorse invidious distinctions. Edward Said, a prominent Palestinian-American scholar, argues that the aim of domination has inspired Occidental scholarship on the "Orient" (including the Middle East) and that Orientalists have portrayed the latter ("the other") in such a manner as to justify this domination. Indeed, various Western writers have presented prejudiced, uninformed, even racist pictures of "Oriental" countries—that they share a common proclivity to "Oriental despotism" because of governmental control over irrigation, that there is a distinctive "Asiatic mode of production," and so forth—that real specialists on the Orient (that is, Orientalists in the original sense of the word) often have assiduously rejected. The reality is that despotism historically has cut across the East-West divide and that even if some of the particular institutions in the West during various periods—such as freehold ownership of land, feudalism based on contract and a nobility in a position to balance royal power, incorporated cities, and an independent bourgeoisie—sometimes did not exist to the same extent or in the same form in the Middle East, other seeds of pluralism have been present there. And indeed careful scholarship suggests that the kind of absolutism we often see today, far from being inherent in Middle Eastern culture, represents a facet of the impact of the West. As for the alleged natural proclivity to backwardness, the area's leadership in the field of civilization over so many millennia would seem to speak for itself.

THE PHYSICAL SETTING: LOCATION, LAND, AND SEAS

The most lasting determinant of Middle Eastern society has been its physical setting. The region's central location, incorporating parts of Africa, Asia, and Europe,[2] has

---

[2] Asia is, of course, only a residual term for the Eurasian continent minus its European subcontinent. The terms *Asia* and *Europe* nevertheless make sense as geographical divisions from the perspective of the Mediterranean, the Aegean, the Turkish Straits, and the Black Sea.

given it a crucial role in world history. It has alternated between being a leading center of cultural florescence and economic and military might—the world's hub—and a weak and "backward" area—merely a crossroads or bridge—that even then is a key object of contention among outside powers.

The unique intertwining of lands and seas in the Middle East has enhanced its position. Only a narrow isthmus, now traversed by the Suez Canal, historically interrupted water communications between the oceans. The great number of seas, gulfs, and straits provide a network of ready-made highways.

The proximity of Europe to the Middle East via the Mediterranean has decreed a particularly intimate, if often adverse, relationship between these two regions. This has made for a similarity in their civilizations, even though their mutual distinctiveness is epitomized by the millennia-old appellations "East" and "West." The spread of Islam to the Indian subcontinent incorporated much of the latter into the sphere of Middle Eastern civilization, but India's distance from the main centers of Middle Eastern history produced a wider dichotomy between these two regions' civilizations in their formative stages. And yet, although modernization in recent centuries has set the West off from a residual "non-West," the civilizations of Europe, India, and the Middle East show a family resemblance that separates them from their more distant Far Eastern relative.

Geography has also dictated close relationships with the rest of Africa and with the central core of the Eurasian continent. Middle Eastern culture spread into both of these places, and movements of people and commerce have been recurrent in each direction. The ease with which horse-borne nomads could cross the arc of flat, arid grasslands (steppes) extending across central Eurasia from Manchuria to Hungary allowed them in premodern times again and again to overrun the Middle East and other civilized lands on Eurasia's periphery. The steppes also provided a link for slow cultural diffusion and trade between the Middle East and China.

TOPOGRAPHY

Topographically, the Middle East can be divided into northern and southern zones. The former, consisting of Turkey and Iran, tends to be a rugged, mountainous area. In Anatolia (i.e., today's Turkey in Asia) the Pontic and Taurus Mountains roughly parallel each other from west to east. In Iran the Zagros Mountains cross the south, while the crescent-shaped Alborz range, reaching as high as 18,500 feet, lies south of the Caspian Sea. Several smaller chains rise in the extreme east and northeast. High plateaus form the central portions of both Anatolia and Iran.

Though generally much flatter, the southern zone contains scattered mountain regions. Two parallel chains extend from north to south at the eastern end of the Mediterranean. These mountains taper off in Palestine but rise as high as 8,644 feet in Sinai. While western Egypt is known for its depressions rather than its mountains, a modest chain divides the Nile Valley from the Red Sea coast. Another chain, known by different names locally, stretches down the western side of the Arabian Peninsula. At the southern end, these mountains' height exceeds 10,000 feet in the interior of

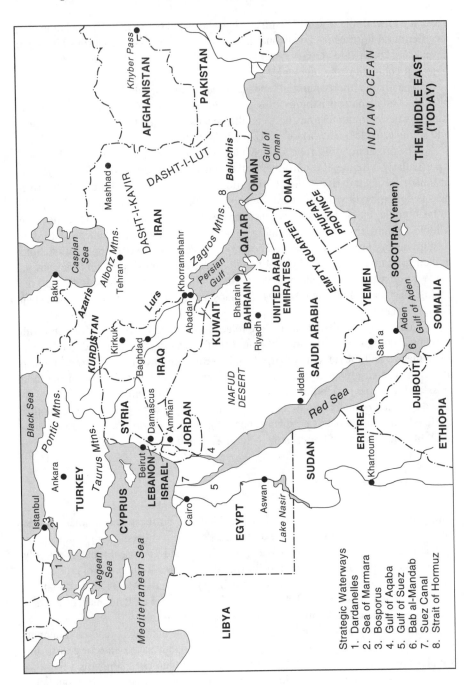

Strategic Waterways
1. Dardanelles
2. Sea of Marmara
3. Bosporus
4. Gulf of Aqaba
5. Gulf of Suez
6. Bab al-Mandab
7. Suez Canal
8. Strait of Hormuz

MAP 1

Yemen. The peninsula generally slopes from the south toward the low-lying region near the Persian Gulf, but the sudden, towering mountains of Oman provide a major exception to this picture.

CLIMATE

The Middle East is a region of hot summers. Daytime temperatures sometimes shoot up well past 120°F in parts of the Middle East, such as southern Egypt and the Persian Gulf. Mountains and some coastal areas are cooler, and nighttime temperatures drop drastically in most places. The effects of heat are partly counteracted by dryness, although some areas, such as coastal Arabia, also suffer from high levels of humidity.

Differences of latitude and altitude make for diverse winter temperatures. The southern region is generally semitropical, although considerable amounts of snow occasionally fall as far south as Jerusalem. But much of the northern zone experiences severe winters, with blizzards raging at high elevations. Temperatures have dropped as low as –35°F in central Anatolia.

The area's most salient geographic characteristic is its aridity. Most of the region is uncultivable desert or is steppeland that receives only enough rainfall to support nomadic life. In most of the Middle East, rainfall is limited mainly to fall and winter and is erratic from year to year. Rare cloudbursts in some deserts account for networks of dry riverbeds and for ground water that feeds wells and oases. Conversely, areas that normally receive the minimum of about seven inches of precipitation a year necessary for cultivation sometimes experience disastrously dry years.

Overall, the northern zone is less desertlike. This is particularly true for most of Anatolia and northwestern Iran. Some areas receive over a hundred inches of precipitation annually. The Persian word *jangal* (cognate of the English "jungle" but meaning "forest") is used to describe the dense vegetation of Iran's Gilan Province, at the southern end of the Caspian Sea. However, Iran's climate is mostly arid too, and a prominent feature of its agriculture is dependence on underground aqueducts (*qanats*) that bring ground water from high in the mountains. Large parts of Iran, such as the Dasht-i-Lut and the Dasht-i-Kavir of the east, are as barren as central Arabia, and much of central Anatolia is steppeland or even true desert.

The southern region includes large expanses of desert. The Nafud Desert and the greater Empty Quarter, an almost impenetrable sea of shifting sand dunes, occupy much of the interior of Arabia. Aside from some important oases fed by underground water and areas of the south and extreme east that get more rain, the peninsula is steppeland at best, Egypt, especially in the south, is virtually devoid of rainfall.

There are exceptions to the aridity of the southern area. The Yemeni highlands and some adjacent areas of southern Saudi Arabia, as well as a smaller region in Oman, lie on the edge of the monsoon zone, with its summer rains fed by winds from the Indian Ocean. Thus Yemen, with its nonnomadic agriculture, historically has accounted for perhaps a majority of the peninsula's population. Syria (that is, geographical Syria, since it includes Lebanon and Palestine) provides a better-known exception, as its coastal region gets enough rain to turn it green for part of the year and to water nonirrigated crops.

Irrigated river valleys form a different kind of exception. The Tigris and Euphrates Rivers rise from rain and melted snow in the Anatolian highlands to surge southeast toward the Persian Gulf. They merge to form the Shatt al-Arab in southern Iraq. These rivers historically have made Iraq (or Mesopotamia)[3] a major center of population and civilization. A much smaller river, the Karun, which rises in the Zagros Mountains of Iran, discharges into the Shatt al-Arab.

The Tigris-Euphrates Valley converges with geographic Syria to form a "Fertile Crescent." A steppe-desert region, the Syrian Desert, fits between the two horns of the Crescent and has offered an age-old starting point for nomadic infiltration into the settled lands.

The Nile provides Egypt unrivaled means for irrigation. This river forms in the Sudan from branches that rise in the Ethiopian highlands and in the tropical rain belt of central Africa. Until the Aswan High Dam tamed it in the 1960s, the annual inundation covered the Nile Valley and Delta during much of the year. Without the Nile, the narrow Valley of Upper (southern) Egypt, which averages about four miles in width, would be part of the empty desert, as is 95 percent of the country. Lower (northern) Egypt, the fan-shaped delta formed by the accumulation of silt, would be part of the Mediterranean Sea.

NATURAL RESOURCES

Water is not the only natural resource that is scarce in the Middle East. There is also a limited amount of tillable soil, although areas such as the Nile Valley and Delta are extremely fertile. Forests always were restricted mainly to the highland regions, and even these tended to become casualties of civilization. Various minerals have been mined in many places, but supplies of most of these appear to be small. In general, the northern zone, particularly Anatolia, has greater quantities of materials such as copper, tin, lead, coal, and iron than does the rest of the Middle East.

There is one glaring exception to this. Over 65 percent of the world's proven oil reserves—and also large reserves of natural gas—today are located in the countries bordering on the Persian Gulf. But this resource was largely irrelevant until the twentieth century. Moreover, most of the Middle Eastern countries have only modest amounts of oil or none at all.

---

[3] The two names will be used interchangeably and refer roughly to the area within the boundaries of the twentieth-century state of Iraq without regard to the distinction Arabs historically made between "al-Jazirah" and "al-Iraq."

THE NEOLITHIC REVOLUTION

In past millennia, large parts of the Middle East possessed another rich resource in their unusual combination of wild flora and fauna, the ancestors of wheat and barley and of sheep, pigs, and cows, to mention a few examples. This provided the answer to the challenge of encroaching aridity ten thousand years ago, leading to the development of agriculture. Instead of continuing to depend on scouring the earth for the now less plentiful wild plants and on hunting game with crude stone weapons, people in geographic Syria, northern Mesopotamia, and parts of Iran and Anatolia began to domesticate plants and animals.

A chain reaction of innovations ensued. Agriculture brought about settled village life, increased trade, and the invention of pottery, baskets, weaving, and spinning. Another development was the improved stone tools, such as the hoe and the sickle, that gave the subsequent era the designation "Neolithic" (New Stone) Age. Despite occasional innovations in later periods (including a major cluster of innovations in Mesopotamia about five thousand years later), the basic nature of largely self-sufficient agricultural life endured to modern times.

NOMADISM

In addition to settled agriculture, the Neolithic Revolution also gave birth to the lifestyle of the nomadic herder, pursued by perhaps 5 percent of the Middle Eastern population as late as the mid-twentieth century A.D. People drove their sheep, goats, and donkeys (and later camels) in regular circuits that took them to water holes near the "sown" areas during the dry summers and to points farther into the desert or steppe when winter rains made vegetation shoot up there. In mountain regions tribes—sometimes called "vertical" nomads—drove their flocks into the high areas during the summer and back into the valleys for winter. Governed by tribal councils and elective chiefs who were only first among equals and sharing property on a communal basis, the relatively democratic, classless character of nomadic life—within each kinship unit, but not on an intertribal level, as some tribes claimed greater "nobility" than others—contrasted with autocratic, exploitative, settled societies.

The feud between desert and sown dominated much of Middle Eastern history. The relationship was a symbiotic one, as nomads traded animals for grain and other village produce. But nomadic tribes, who knew no moral obligations transcending the tribe (sometimes even after nominally adhering to a universal religion) and were restrained only by the threat of retaliation, also raided one another and plundered, conquered, or exacted tribute from the less militaristic villagers.

Blood ties among nomads provided the unrivaled social solidarity within each tribal community that made desert life possible. The nomads' style of life made for mobility and discipline, and their tribal ethos emphasized military valor. All this made them a terror for villagers, and although the proud, freedom-loving nomads had contempt for those who tilled the soil, material rewards repeatedly lured them from the desert. As the fourteenth-century Arab historian ibn-Khaldun showed, such nomadic incursions periodically brought new dynasties to power and renewed the vitality of settled societies. New languages and corresponding ethnic identities also tended to rise with each conquest.

THE BIRTH OF CIVILIZATION

Long before the Neolithic Revolution caught on in most of Eurasia and Africa, the fourth millennium B.C. brought accelerated change with the emergence, again in the Middle East, of a style of life called civilized. This went a step beyond the Neolithic transformations, with greater agricultural productivity relieving a portion of the population of the need to raise its own food. This nonagricultural population concentrated in cities, where occupations became specialized, and a ruling class took its toll of the peasants' produce to support luxuries, warfare, and works of art and architecture. A few people learned the art of writing, without which such a complicated society, with its need to keep records and transmit messages, would have hardly been viable.

The first breakthrough to this kind of society came with the Sumerians, a southern Mesopotamian people whose language seems to be unrelated to any others. Possibly originating in the Iranian highlands, the Sumerians were newcomers to Mesopotamia.

Egypt followed in the wake of Sumer and soon surpassed it. Linguistically, the ancient Egyptians belonged to what was traditionally called the Hamitic family of languages, which also includes the Berber tongues of North Africa and other languages extending today from Nigeria to Somalia. Modern scholars, however, consider these languages to constitute several distinct groups belonging to a larger Hamito-Semitic (or Afro-Asian) family that also includes the Semitic peoples, that is, those whose languages belong to the Semitic subfamily. Thus the Egyptians were linguistically related to the Semites, who then were limited to Southwest Asia (but may have crossed from East Africa to Arabia during earlier millennia). Besides this original kinship, the Egyptian people and their language seem to have acquired some Semitic overlay as a result of an early influx of Semites from Arabia via Syria. If so, this provides one of the earliest examples of migration by Semitic tribes who periodically, at least according to a widely accepted theory, overflowed from the increasingly desiccated Arabian Peninsula into more fertile lands. But while the Fertile Crescent was almost fully Semiticized by the second millennium B.C., Egypt retained its Hamitic character until it adopted a Semitic language (Arabic) and identity (Arab) during Islamic times.

In the twenty-fourth century B.C., the Akkadians, Semitic people from farther north, led by Sargon, ruler of the city of Akkad, overran Sumeria. Under Sargon and his successors, the Akkadians began a process whereby Semites eventually absorbed the Sumerians but preserved their civilization. A related Semitic people, the Amor-

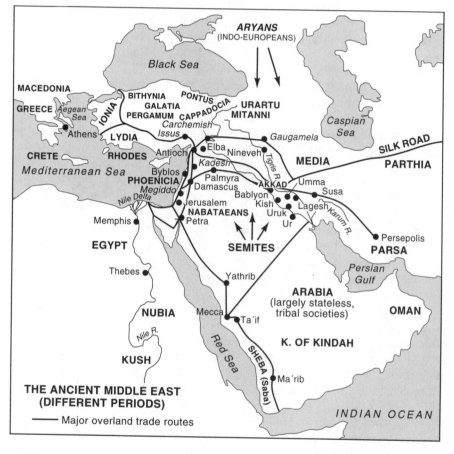

**THE ANCIENT MIDDLE EAST
(DIFFERENT PERIODS)**
—— Major overland trade routes

MAP 2

ites, centered in the city of Babylon, unified Mesopotamia during the early part of the next millennium but preserved the Akkadian language and civilization.

From Mesopotamia, civilization spread into adjacent areas. Excavations in northern Syria in 1974 revealed remains of the city of Ebla, which was the center of a flourishing civilization and empire in the mid–third millennium B.C. The Eblaite language is the oldest known Semitic tongue. The third millennium B.C. also saw the rise of civilization in Elam, in southwestern Iran. Both Ebla and Elam borrowed Sumer's cuneiform script and became outlying areas of Mesopotamian civilization.

Although bronze tools and other products of advanced culture came into use over a wider area, civilization had not spread farther than the adjacent corners of Europe (Crete) and India (the Indus Valley) by 2000 B.C. Both of these civilizations seemingly developed under Middle Eastern inspiration.

The early part of the second millennium B.C. witnessed a movement of peoples that profoundly influenced the course of history. Middle Eastern civilizations succumbed to "barbarian" conquerors, and lengthy interludes preceded revival.

Central Eurasia played a key role in this process, as Aryan (Indo-European) nomads from west of the Caspian Sea overran the continent's periphery. The Aryans' acquisition of bronze weapons from the Middle East helped to make them formidable, but they also made a basic breakthrough of their own in about 3000 B.C. by domesticating the horse. They now bred varieties of this animal strong enough to pull war chariots, and, according to recent archaeological evidence that contradicts what we once thought, also for riding. The Aryans also invented a new kind of two-wheeled chariot by 1700 B.C. This, together with these people's nomadic habits and the ease of traversing vast distances of steppeland, put civilized lands, with their tempting riches, at the Aryans' mercy. The horse may have spread to the Fertile Crescent region by the time of Sargon.

The ethnic pattern of the world was changing. By 2000 B.C., Aryan peoples were established in Anatolia. Farther east, the new ethnic-linguistic pattern emerging from the invasion earned a vast region the name "Land of the Aryans," or Iran.

The exhaustion of Egypt and the defeat of the Hittite Empire, centered in Anatolia, by the "Peoples of the Sea" (refugees from the Aegean) permitted a new wave of Semitic tribes to enter Syria. These groups joined some of their predecessors, particularly the Canaanites of Palestine and Lebanon, in making spectacular contributions to world civilization. Mountains protected the northernmost Canaanites, the Phoenicians, from new Semitic invasions and allowed them to continue their earlier seaborne commerce from city-states such as Byblos, Sidon, and Tyre.

The new wave of Semites included Aramaeans in the north and Hebrews in the south. The Aramaeans established numerous small states, such as Damascus and Aleppo, and specialized in overland trade that extended throughout the Middle East. The Aramaic language later became the spoken tongue of the entire Fertile Crescent and replaced Akkadian as the *lingua franca* (common language) of the Middle East.

The main group of Hebrews was the Israelites, who conquered eastern Palestine and part of Transjordan. Organized in twelve tribes, the Israelites may have entered Palestine as early as the nineteenth century B.C. Then they (or some of them) migrated to Egypt but later invaded Palestine from the east. At first establishing several enclaves, they exterminated part of the Canaanite population but presumably assimilated others. They adopted a Canaanite dialect as the "Hebrew" language. Some modern scholars argue that they were mainly Canaanites in the hill country who were joined by a few invaders.

The Israelite invasion of Palestine came shortly after the Philistines—Peoples of the Sea—had entered the land from the west. Defeat by the Philistines' iron weapons, an innovation that had emerged in the Hittite Empire, eventually induced the Israelite tribes to unite under a monarchy.

Tribal divisions ended the Israelite empire after the death of Solomon in 922 B.C. The northern tribes broke away but continued to be called the Kingdom of Israel. Solomon's descendants retained control over a small region in the south, mainly their own tribe of Judah, and thus the southern kingdom, still centered at Jerusalem, was called Judah (Judea). Its people, as well as heterogeneous people who later converted to their religion, eventually came to be known as Jews, while the northern Israelites—with Samaria as their capital city—took the name Samaritans.

The day of small powers now made way for the rise of the empire of the Assyrians—a Semitic people in northern Mesopotamia—that surpassed all its predecessors in size and brutality. Known by the name of their god of war, Assur, the Assyrians were perhaps the most militaristic people in ancient times. Further advances in horse breeding and the use of saddles, bridles, and bits in the Eurasian steppe spread to them by the eighth century B.C., enabling them to introduce cavalry forces into Middle Eastern warfare.

Conquered peoples suffered a terrible fate under the Assyrians. Mass uprooting was common, especially of skilled craftspeople and potentially troublesome upper classes. The deported northern Israelites (Samaritans) provide the best known example, while the remaining Samaritans absorbed diverse peoples who settled in the former kingdom.

Militarism exhausted the Assyrian people, and they increasingly depended on restive subjects as troops. A new wave of Semitic peoples, the Chaldeans, took control of Babylon in 626 B.C., while the Medes were a rising power in the Iranian highlands. Now Medes, Chaldeans, and others formed a great coalition that destroyed the Assyrian Empire.

The fall of Assyria left southwest Asia divided mainly into two empires. The Medes ruled the area north of the Tigris and continued to expand into Anatolia. Farther south, the Neo-Babylonian (Chaldean) empire defeated Egypt at the Battle of Carchemish in 605 B.C. and established its hold on Syria.

Now another people came to the fore in the empire of the Medes and gave it new vitality. The Persians, originally from a part of southern Iran called Parsa (now "Fars," or Persia),[4] spoke a language related to that of the Medes and other Iranian peoples. The Persian rulers, the Achaemenid house, were vassals of the Medes until

[4] Westerners, including some leading scholars, conventionally use the name Persia for Iran as a whole.

Cyrus II ("the Great") gained control of the empire in 550 B.C. Within the following two decades he overran southwest Asia, including the Chaldean empire in 539 B.C. A theoretically absolute "king of kings" (*shahanshah*) kept the empire unified, ruling through his twenty satraps, a system of royal roads, and a postal service.

Belief in one God climaxed the emergence of the increasingly cosmopolitan Middle Eastern world. Prophets, that is, individuals believed to be messengers of a god, long had existed among the Semitic peoples. Now Hebrew prophets in particular began to speak of Yahweh as the one God of the whole world, although the Israelites were still his chosen people. At about the same time, Iran provided the soil for growth of another monotheistic and transcendent religion, Zoroastrianism. Zoroaster, apparently one of the Iranian priests or Magi, attacked many older practices and emphasized that there was one God, Ahura Mazda ("the Knowing Lord"), whose Good Spirit was constantly opposed to the spirit of evil. Zoroastrianism was only one of many Iranian cults and did not predominate until much later.

THE EAST OVERRUN

By the late sixth century B.C., the emerging classical civilization of Greece loomed on the Middle Eastern horizon. The Greeks had sunk into illiteracy after invasion by new tribes in about 1200 B.C., but another Middle Eastern transfusion occurred as the Greeks belatedly adopted the Phoenician alphabet in about 750 B.C. Most of the foundations of Greek (Hellenic) civilization came from the Middle East, but it was one of the most creative civilizations that ever existed. It was distinctive in many ways, with its city-states (*poleis;* singular, *polis*) whose governments were based on citizen participation, with a worldliness unknown farther east, and with a spirit of inquiry that sought natural laws to explain all phenomena.

Hellenic civilization increasingly touched the Middle East. The favorable terms of trade commanded by Greek exports compared with, say, Egyptian grain provided a basis for the prosperity of a wide segment of Hellenic society. There were Greek commercial colonies in various parts of the Mediterranean and Black Sea regions. The Twenty-sixth Egyptian Dynasty increasingly recruited Greek mercenaries, as did the Persian Empire. But even in 500 B.C. the East superficially seemed preponderant. A key part of the Greek world, the Ionian cities of western Anatolia, was subject to the king of kings, and the other Greek city-states seemed insignificant in comparison with the great Persian Empire, whose attempt to conquer Greece nevertheless failed in the early fifth century B.C.

The vitality of Hellenic civilization began to contrast with the stagnation prevailing in the lands to the east, as the Achaemenid Empire began to disintegrate. There was no fundamental gap, certainly not of a technical nature, in development between the two regions comparable to that which emerged in the eighteenth century A.D. Yet a social gap was present, as the tightly governed Greek *polis,* with its citizen participation and its intense feeling of civic solidarity that had parallels elsewhere only on a tribal level, vied with the autocratic but less effective governmental pattern of the Achaemenid Empire.

The partially Hellenized kingdom of Macedon, north of Greece, finally provided the unity needed for an offensive in the East after King Philip II's forces defeated a coalition of Greek states in 338 B.C. The *polis* rarely enjoyed full independence from now on, although participation in its institutions remained a hallmark of Hellenism that set it off from Eastern cultures in the Hellenistic age, as subsequent centuries came to be known. Philip was ready to inaugurate what was in effect the first age of Western colonialism, but his untimely death in 336 B.C. left the task for his nineteen-year-old son, Alexander II ("the Great").

Alexander led armies that overran the whole Persian Empire and more. He had transformed the Middle East, but it had also transformed him. He began to wear Eastern clothing, and at one point he demanded that his Macedonian officers prostrate themselves, like the subjects of a Persian king, in his presence. His role as the successor of the Achaemenids rather than as their conqueror began taking hold. It is unclear whether such policies as encouraging his soldiers to marry Iranian women were mainly a pragmatic response to governing a vast empire or whether they represented an idealistic furtherance of the brotherhood of the human race.

Alexander's death brought a struggle for power in the army that left separate kingdoms headed by Macedonian generals. Despite political disunity, the Hellenistic world remained a cultural whole. Ideas and commerce flowed freely across frontiers, facilitated by a *lingua franca, koine* (common) Greek. The Hellenes, eventually including many Hellenized Easterners, were the ruling class throughout the Hellenistic world.

The incorporation of the Middle East (excluding Iran—ruled by the Parthian Empire for about four centuries—and Arabia and usually Mesopotamia and Armenia) into the Roman Empire is sometimes considered the end of the Hellenistic period. In reality, the Roman is an extension of the Hellenistic age, which lasted until the Arab Muslims displaced Roman rule in Egypt and Syria in the seventh century A.D. (and longer in the case of Anatolia). Just as Hellenic civilization continued to predominate in the East, the *lingua franca* there continued to be Greek. This resulted in a new split of the Hellenic world into a Latin West and a Greek "East" (both Greece and the East proper) that later was perpetuated by a division of the Empire into eastern and western halves and eventually by a schism of the main body of the Christian Church along Latin (Roman Catholic) and Greek (Orthodox) lines. Yet this overlooks the basic cultural unity of Greece and Rome that makes them both "Western" in the broad sense, in contrast to the Middle East.

If Egypt was the most exploited province, Judea proved to be the most troublesome area for the Romans. For Toynbee, Judea's Roman client King Herod became the prototype of the ruler who chooses to emulate a dominant, intrusive civilization, though (unlike some later "Herodians," who intended to learn from intruders in order to resist them) this king of Judea collaborated willingly with the occupiers.

A new, uncompromising Jewish faction, the Zealots, emerged. Their approach was to devote themselves increasingly to the traditions that their foreign rulers and native collaborators violated. For Toynbee, the Zealots became the prototype of a more general "zealot" approach that rejects the influence of an intruding civilization. Although some zealots in the Toynbeean sense have been politically docile, the original ones were not; with an unparalleled nationalistic fanaticism they suicidally hurled themselves against the occupiers. Judea and the newly Judaized Galilee were scenes of revolt with little letup from the time the Romans first arrived.

The Jewish revolt reached its zenith in A.D. 66–70. After a long siege by Roman forces, Zealot-held Jerusalem finally succumbed. Many thousands of Jews died, while the Romans sold others into slavery and destroyed Herod's Temple. Zealots in the mountain fortress of Masada held out for three more years and chose to commit mass suicide rather than to surrender.

A Zealot named Simon Bar Kokhba, hailed as the Messiah, led another revolt in 132–135. Suppression ended with the exile of the remaining Jews from Judea, although some Jews remained in other parts of Palestine. Galilee in particular retained a substantial Jewish minority for a while. With periodic conversion adding to the widespread Jewish community, whose membership came generally to be defined in religious terms, the national connection of the Jews with their ancient coreligionists became a moot point, but they continued to identify themselves as the "People of Israel," whom a future Messiah would restore to the "Land of Israel."

The Middle East was the scene of remarkable intellectual activity during the Hellenistic-Roman era. Yet the flowering was among Hellenes, who were alien to the indigenous culture of the region. Although some of them were Hellenized Easterners rather than the Greek colonists, the vast majority of the Easterners were at most little affected by the dominant Greek civilization. Only in parts of western Anatolia did everyday Greek speech displace native languages.

While the Middle East remained submerged politically and intellectually, its religions spread westward. From Syria came the cult of the Invincible Sun, while Roman emperors built temples to Isis in the capital. Anatolia contributed the cult of Cybele, and the worship of Mithras came from Iran, as did the doctrine of Manichaeism, whose name derived from its founder, Mani, believed to be the "seal of the prophets." The Manichaean dualism that stressed the polarity of Ahura Mazda and the evil Ahriman was an outgrowth of Zoroastrianism, but in combination with Christian, Buddhist, and other influences. Judaism also proved attractive, as some Jews engaged in widespread proselytism, and a large semi-Judaized group, called the Reverent Ones, existed in cities throughout the Mediterranean region.

Christianity was the most successful Oriental religion. It started as a Jewish sect but soon outgrew the parent religion as missionaries turned to the conversion of the world. The small group of Christians who insisted on remaining a sect of Judaism, observing the Mosaic Law, soon withered away. Following a long period of rivalry by other Oriental religions and periodic outbreaks of anti-Christian persecution, the Emperor Constantine gave Christianity recognition in 313, and he later was baptized. This religion now was clearly displacing paganism, especially in the Roman Middle East and somewhat more slowly in the West. Thus, paradoxically, from the period of Hellenic dominance came a strong Oriental strain that transformed Hellenism and became a fundamental part of subsequent European civilizations.

The East-West interaction was nevertheless a reciprocal one. In becoming the religion of a Hellenic-dominated world, Christianity was put in Hellenic dress. To make their religion meaningful to those with Greek education, the Christians explained that Christ was the "Word [*Logos*] of God." The *Logos,* a polestar of Greek thought, described the concept of a rational order of the universe. Thus the divine nature of Christ came to be identified with the impersonal God of the philosophers. On this point, the Jewish Philo of Alexandria, a contemporary of Jesus, had prepared the way by identifying the *Logos* as the Word (and, figuratively, the Son) of God. The gospel was spread by a New Testament written, not in Aramaic or Hebrew, but in Greek, and thinkers continued to reconcile their Hellenic and Christian heritages.

In 330 Constantine moved the capital of the Roman Empire to a "New Rome"—Constantinople—on the site of the old Greek town of Byzantium. With the practice of appointing a coemperor for the largely peripheral western provinces, which eventually were overrun by "barbarian" Germanic tribes, the unity of the empire came to be a legal fiction. What west Europeans called the "Byzantine" Empire was thus the continuation of the state of the first Caesars, although in many ways it was increasingly transformed.

The basic Hellenic character of the empire remained intact. The capital had only moved closer to the original home of Hellenism. Although the sixth-century Emperor Justinian temporarily restored imperial control over most of the western Mediterranean coast, the empire that continued to subordinate the Orient was increasingly a Greek rather than a Latin one.

But Oriental influences increasingly infiltrated the empire's Hellenic character. The government absorbed forms such as prostration before the ruler from Eastern monarchies even before the capital was moved to the Bosporus. The Christian art and architecture of the period shows heavy Eastern, particularly Iranian and Armenian, influences. Literary and artistic activity largely took place in the non-European parts of the empire, and indigenous forces were bound to show through.

Religious schisms within Christianity provided an outlet for the assertion of Eastern distinctiveness. The great issue of the age was the nature of Christ: that is, whether he was divine or human and, if both, how the two attributes could belong to the same being. In what seems to have been largely an ideological disguise for nationalistic and cultural dissatisfaction, doctrines eventually determined to be heretical by a Hellenic-dominated church invariably gained overwhelming support in Egypt, Syria, and the less Hellenized parts of Anatolia.

Fourth-century Antioch produced the doctrine that Christ has the two completely separate natures of God and human. Nestorianism, as this belief is known, was rejected by the Third Ecumenical Council in 431. Now persecuted by the Roman government, many Nestorians fled to the Sassanian (Persian) Empire and organized their own church hierarchy, with Syriac (a form of Aramaic) as its liturgical language. This became the predominant form of Christianity in the Persian Empire, with many adherents particularly in the Mesopotamian region.

Then another movement, Monophysitism, appeared. According to this doctrine, Christ has only one nature, the divine, which has completely displaced the human aspect. This swept through the Eastern part of the Roman Empire and continued to prevail there even after the Fourth Ecumenical Council, meeting in Chalcedon, rejected it in 451 in favor of a declaration that Christ has two inseparable natures, that is, the Western—or Chalcedonian—form of Christianity that encompasses Greek Orthodoxy, Catholicism, and Protestantism today. While some emperors sought Eastern support by espousing either Monophysitism or a compromise doctrine, the Monophysites knew only persecution after Justinian's death in 565 and were ready to greet a foreign deliverer.

Separate Monophysite churches came into being. The Egyptian (Coptic) Church was the largest, and eventually predominated in Ethiopia too. In Syria, the Monophysites, sometimes known as the Jacobites, established the Syriac Church, although a few Syrians followed Constantinople's lead. The church in Armenia, which had become the world's first Christian land in the early fourth century, mistakenly often has been labeled "Monophysite," although it took an intermediate position in the dispute.

Religious divisions were not the only signs of weakness. Wars exhausted the economy, and the government's consequent fiscal problems led to heavier taxes and more suffering. An outbreak of the plague in the 540s depopulated whole cities. Corruption and anarchy ate at the heart of the empire.

SASSANIAN IRAN

The third century saw a resurgence of Iran under a new dynasty, the Sassanians. Ruling from Mesopotamia to northern India, they posed as restorers of the empire of the Achaemenids. And in many ways this was an assertion of Iranian traditions vis-à-vis Hellenism, although there was no attempt to uproot the influence of the latter. As late as the sixth century, the Sassanians gave refuge to Greek philosophers, whose school in Athens was closed, and Greek as well as Sanskrit works were translated into Pahlavi (that is, Middle Persian). A new Pahlavi literature also emerged.

Zoroastrianism became the Sassanian state religion. What was in effect a Zoroastrian Church came into existence for the first time. Adherents to other religions sometimes met severe persecution. Native Iranian heresies, including Manichaeism and the sixth-century communist doctrine of Mazdakeanism, faced particularly harsh measures that forced them underground.

By the sixth century, signs of decay were evident. The many wars sapped the empire's strength, and increasingly high taxes bore down on the poor. Society had become rigid, with a caste system of priests, soldiers, scribes, and commoners that undermined the loyalty of the masses to the state. Mazdakeanism was one reaction to social injustice. The rich agricultural land of southern Mesopotamia, long the economic mainstay, became less productive, and the cultivation of silkworms in the

Roman Empire reduced Sassanian revenues from the formerly lucrative Silk Road. Rigid rules of behavior and a backward-looking attitude epitomized the period's stagnation. Rivals fought for the throne of an empire that now hardly offered viable hope for an Eastern upsurge.

Rome and Iran, the two greatest empires west of China, faced each other in perennial combat. The two armies sometimes seesawed from Syria to western Iran. In 602 Shah Khushru Parvis started the last Sassanian offensive against the Romans. For a time it seemed that the enemy would be completely overrun. But as the two giants exhausted themselves, their common nemesis soon was to come from an unsuspected direction.

TURKS ON THE HORIZON

Central Eurasia might have seemed to be a potential source of a reorganized Middle East. Instead of the Aryan tribes that had predominated since 2000 B.C., a new ethnic, linguistic element appeared from farther east. These different peoples spoke languages that modern scholars call Altaic or Ural-Altaic, from their location between the Ural and Altai Mountains. Turks dominated the steppe by the sixth century and began to penetrate the area just north of the Oxus River. They eventually were to transform the Middle East, just as tribes from both Central Eurasia and the Arabian Peninsula had done so often before. But the turn of the latter region came first, and it is there that one must look for an alternative to the two dying empires.

ARABIA: CRADLE OF EASTERN RESURGENCE

Because of its size and desert climate, the Arabian Peninsula had been the area least affected by Middle Eastern civilization or by Hellenism. Tribes of Arabian origin had established empires, but Arabia itself never had been the seat of a major empire. Neither had outsiders controlled large parts of the peninsula for long. Still, an image of ancient Arabia as a civilizational vacuum inhabited only by nomads would be highly inaccurate, as recent archaeological findings make ever more clear. The Persian Gulf coast in particular was the site of sophisticated commercial centers on the route to the Indus Valley in the period of the Sumerians.

Southern Arabia was the home of an elaborate civilization from at least the eighth century B.C. Of the various southern Arabian kingdoms, Saba (Sheba) was the largest and tended to dominate the others. Dams and terraced mountains supported an agricultural society. The Sabaeans also provided an important link in world commerce by bringing Indian spices by sea to Southern Arabia and exporting them, together with Arabian frankincense and myrrh, along caravan routes to the Mediterranean world.

Southern Arabia was in decline as a new dynasty, the Himyarites, dominated the country from the second century B.C. to the sixth century A.D. While legend attributes this to the breaking of the vital Ma'rib Dam, the more complex set of reasons for decline included Roman commercial competition, recurrent Ethiopian invasions, the rise of feudal challenges to royal power, and nomadic encroachments from the north. Many South Arabians turned nomadic and formed a diaspora throughout the peninsula.

The rest of Arabia was the home of nomadism *par excellence*. The tribes in the north were classified, often without much factual basis, as northern (Adnani) and southern (Qahtani) Arabs—that is, those indigenous to the area and those who had migrated from the south. These bedouin (literally, desert people) were essentially like the earlier, non-Arab Semitic nomads that appeared in the Fertile Crescent. Although Arabic was the last Semitic language committed to writing, it may in some ways be older than the others. It spread south by the seventh century to supplant the ancient South Arabian language.[5] Thus if language is the criterion, the South Arabians were only belatedly Arabized, although legend reverses the distinction between northern and southern tribes. The latter, supposedly descendents of Qahtan, a great-great-great-grandson of Noah, were known as "Arab Arabs," while the former, who traced their lineage to Adnan and his father, Ishmael (Isma'il), the son of Abraham (Ibrahim), were called "Arabized [i.e., assimilated as] Arabs."

Several Arab kingdoms emerged in the steppelands adjacent to the Fertile Crescent. Arab tribes known as the Nabataeans established the Kingdom of Petra, in southern Transjordan, in the sixth century B.C. Astride the north-south trade route, Petra became a flourishing center of commerce and civilization. At their zenith, the Nabataeans ruled much of the Syrian interior, including Damascus, and resisted attacks by several Hellenistic rulers. But they eventually became a client state of Rome, providing a convenient way for the empire to maintain order on its desert frontier. Vassal status gave way to complete absorption into the Roman Empire as Provincia Arabia in 195 A.D.

Another Arab client state of Rome was based in Palmyra, an oasis in the Syrian Desert. The Palmyrans controlled a trade route that connected Mesopotamia with the Mediterranean, and protection for the caravans provided a lucrative source of income. In the third century, King Udaynath became vice-emperor of the Roman Empire, but the excessive ambitions of his widow, Queen Zenobia, who later temporarily drove the Roman legions out of most of the Middle East, ended with the downfall of Palmyra in 272.

At least three other Arab kingdoms should be mentioned. The Byzantines relied on a buffer state, the Ghassanids, allegedly of South Arabian origin, in the Syrian interior to guard the Arabian frontiers until the early seventh century. The Ghassanids became Christians, as did another "Southern" group, the Lakhmids, who performed a similar buffer role on the Sassanian frontier. In Central Arabia, other

---

[5] The South Arabian language has been preserved in some local vernaculars, particularly on the Yemeni island of Socotra.

South Arabian tribes formed the Kingdom of Kindah for a while during the fifth century as allies of the decaying Himyarites.

Three cities—Mecca, Ta'if, and Yathrib (later called Madina)—emerged in the Hijaz, the coastal region[6] north of Yemen. The largest of these, Mecca, was located at the intersection of the Yemen-to-Syria route and a less important east-west route. After centuries of decline, the north-south route gained a renewed role in the sixth century, as Roman commerce on the Red Sea dwindled and as Roman-Sassanian warfare interrupted the northern routes. Mecca's brackish well of Zamzam made the city a convenient stop for parched caravans. The clans of the tribe of Quraysh, which settled there during the sixth century, became the predominant element of the population. Qurayshi merchants avidly engaged in commerce and came to control a major part of the caravan traffic, especially on the Mecca-to-Syria link. A council of clan chiefs governed the city.

Mecca was also a religious center. A cube-shaped building, the Ka'bah, housed a black stone venerated by pilgrims from all over Arabia, and idols of various tribes were placed there. According to tradition, Adam first built this sanctuary, and Abraham and Ishmael restored it. The Arabs' lunar year included the month of Dhu'l-Hijjah, during which worshippers performed prescribed rites (the *hajj* or Greater Pilgrimage) that included a procession to the nearby Plain of Arafat and slaughtering sheep for a feast. A distinct ritual, the Lesser Pilgrimage (*umrah*) included the circumambulation of the Ka'bah and kissing the black stone. Unlike the *hajj*, the *umrah* could be performed at any time of the year. Both pilgrimages later became part of the religion of Islam, which also made the ceremonies at the Ka'bah a part of the Greater Pilgrimage itself.

Animistic religious concepts still predominated in most of Arabia. Invisible humanlike, and usually evil, spirits called *jinn* (singular, *jinni*) were believed to share the world with people and sometimes to possess their bodies.

Other religions gradually gained favor. Christianity percolated into Arabia from the Ghassanids and the Lakhmids, as well as from Ethiopia. Judaism also had footholds at Khaybar Oasis, in the north, and at Mecca's rival city, Yathrib. The latter was founded by Jewish tribes, although pagan tribes, mainly the Aws and the Khazraj (both known as southern Arabs), later settled there. Unlike Mecca, Yathrib was a cluster of separate agricultural communities sharing a large oasis, without much unity. Yemen also underwent partial Judaization, and the last Himyarite kings converted to this religion.

The concept of one God was familiar to many Arabs. Mecca's main deity was known simply as the God (to translate literally the Arabic word *Allah,* which is used by all Arabic-speaking monotheists). According to Arab tradition, the Ka'bah originally had been devoted to the worship of God alone. While there were people called *Hanifs* who preached a local form of monotheism, pre-Islamic Arabs normally com-

---

[6] Strictly speaking, the Hijaz does not refer to the immediate coastal region but only to the nearby mountain "barrier."

bined the idea of God with the concept of many lesser gods that included his daughters, Allat ("the goddess"), Manat, and Uzzah.

Later Arabs—and Muslims generally—called the pre-Islamic period, particularly the sixth and the early seventh centuries in Arabia, the *Jahiliyyah,* literally "the Age of Ignorance." With the decline of South Arabia, the peninsula had relatively little civilization, but while literacy was somewhat rare, a city such as Mecca can hardly be called barbarian. Still, from a Muslim point of view, this was an age of ignorance of "true religion." Certain pre-Islamic customs also seem barbaric to Muslims, a case in point being the practice of burying unwanted baby girls alive, a survival of the infanticide that was common elsewhere in ancient times.

Poetry experienced a remarkable development, and the verses of this Heroic Age—"the Days of the Arabs"—never have ceased to reverberate from Arab tongues. This poetry presented vivid, if romanticized, images of Arabia at the time and of the bedouin culture and its values. Courage, eloquence, unquestioning loyalty to the tribe, undying revenge against enemies, help for the weak, idealization of the hard life, extremes of hospitality, pride in noble ancestry and the virtues of one's people, and glorification of romantic love and sexual prowess are recurring themes.

Poetry was no avocation of the cultured few. Poets were great popular heroes, believed to possess magic gained from the *jinn* that inhabited their bodies. And indeed the words, repeated by professional reciters, seemed to work magic on the listeners. The verses not only related tales of intertribal vendettas but were seen as veritable weapons in these conflicts, as there existed a belief that satires and lampoons actually would wound the enemy against which they were directed. Poetry contests highlighted the annual twenty-day fair at Ukaz, near Mecca, with fighting forbidden as representatives of all tribes came together in a fantastic expression of Arab cultural unity.

Poetry achieved its zenith in the form of the highly stylized *Qasidah,* or Ode. The *Qasidahs* of seven poets have come down to us as the Suspended Poems, or the Golden Odes, since they are said to have won the annual prize and, inscribed in gold letters, to have hung on the door of the Ka'bah.

Arabia increasingly was involved in world politics. Cities such as Mecca played the Romans and the Sassanians off against each other. From the fourth century on, international rivalry took on a religious coloring, with Jews and Nestorians favoring the Persians. Despite the Monophysites' persecution in the Roman Empire, Constantinople supported them elsewhere against Nestorians and non-Christians. By the early sixth century, religious intolerance appeared on all sides. While the Christian town of Najran persecuted those who would not adopt its faith, the Jewish King Dhu al-Nuwas of the Himyarites persecuted the Christians, allegedly incinerating some of them alive. Ethiopia invaded Yemen to help its coreligionists as well as to gain control of the trade routes, and Ethiopian rule there lasted for half a century.

In a war started because of rivalry between his new church and the Ka'bah as religious centers, an Ethiopian governor named Abraha sent elephant-borne troops to attack Mecca in about 570. According to legend, Abraha failed to enter the helpless city only because of a remarkable set of events, notably the appearance of a flock of birds that dropped stones from the sky and thus decimated his troops. In the same year a future prophet, Muhammad, of the Hashimite clan of the Quraysh tribe, was born there. But Ethiopian control of Yemen soon gave way to a Sassanian invasion of that country, which became a loosely governed satrapy of the shah.

CONCLUSIONS

Beginning with the Neolithic Revolution, which started about ten thousand years ago, the Middle East was continuously in the forefront of human progress. After the Middle East went on to invent civilized life about five thousand years ago, it was the central stage of world history for the next two and a half millennia. During this time, separate Middle Eastern societies gradually merged on both the political and the civilizational levels, while non–Middle Eastern civilizations caught up.

Certain aspects of Hellenic civilization enabled it to dominate the Middle East for about a millennium, beginning in the fourth century B.C. Hellenism became the elite culture of the area and left an indelible imprint. Still, this was only a veneer over the largely dormant cultures of the East, which had in the meantime left their own permanent marks on the West.

At the beginning of the seventh century, the Middle East still had not regained the role it held in the ancient world. A limited Eastern reaction against Hellenism had taken place in Iran under the Sassanians, but internal decay eventually set in. Sectarian divisions within Christianity provided outlets for Syrian and Egyptian distinctiveness vis-à-vis the West, but these countries offered neither the military means nor the cultural creativity necessary to lead an overall Eastern upsurge. Instead, a lasting revival of Middle Eastern civilization and power was destined to come from outside the old centers of civilization, from among tribes possessing intense solidarity and a fresh approach. The Turkish tribes of Central Eurasia already loomed on the horizon. Of more immediate importance was the Arabian Peninsula, with its Arab tribes, who now showed an exceptional cultural effervescence. With leadership and inspiration the Arabs could climax the ancient process of invasion and renewal by Semitic tribes.

2

the east reborn
610–750

Sassanian armies were pushing fast into Roman (Byzantine) territories in A.D. 610. The Roman military governor of northwestern Africa, Heraclius, had already taken upon himself the task of stemming the empire's decline and launched a revolt that Roman forces in other provinces soon joined. But as Heraclius occupied Constantinople and began a new imperial dynasty, the Sassanian advance accelerated. Wracked by Monophysite dissatisfaction with Orthodox doctrines that reflected the age-old dichotomy between East and West, Syria, and Egypt rapidly succumbed to the invading army. Persian forces in Jerusalem destroyed the Church of the Holy Sepulchre and carried the "True Cross" to Ctesiphon, the Sassanian winter capital. Another Sassanian army fought its way across Anatolia and encamped across the Bosporus from Constantinople in 614.

In a brilliant offensive, Heraclius's forces sailed to the eastern end of the Black Sea in 622. They invaded Sassanian domains via the Caucasus and reached the outskirts of Ctesiphon in 628. After Shah Khushru Parviz was murdered by his own men, a succession of short-lived rulers sat on the shaky Persian throne. Later legends of visions and signs portending disaster carry a ring of poetic truth. A peace settlement of 630 restored the conquered provinces to Constantinople and the "True Cross" to Jerusalem.

The two great empires were left exhausted by this veritable fast-motion replay of earlier encounters between the Eastern and Hellenic worlds. And Heraclius was

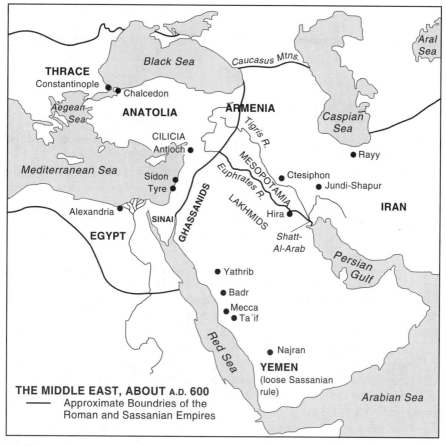

THE MIDDLE EAST, ABOUT A.D. 600
—— Approximate Boundries of the
Roman and Sassanian Empires

MAP 3

not destined to repeat the feats of Alexander, for seemingly unimportant events in a heretofore remote Arabia combined with the weakened condition of the two empires to make way for a new Middle Eastern order that would destroy the Sassanian Empire and leave the Roman Empire truncated almost beyond recognition. Arab client states that had stabilized the desert frontier were vanishing as the Sassanians abolished the Lakhmid kingdom in 602, and the Romans could no longer afford to restore their subsidies to the Ghassanids following the repulsion of the Persians. As early as 611, greater events to come were presaged when Arab tribes defeated a Sassanian force in southern Iraq. But few would have guessed that Arabia was to provide a new synthesis for Middle Eastern culture and lead the region in a reassertion of its pre-Hellenistic primacy.

MUHAMMAD'S MESSAGE

A renewed Middle East began to form in 610 as a voice,[1] afterward identified as that of the angel Gabriel, commanded a forty-year-old Meccan, Muhammad, to "Recite!" The scene of this event, which in the long run would dwarf the significance of the change of dynasty in Constantinople the same year, was a mountain outside Mecca where Muhammad had sometimes sought quiet and privacy in order to contemplate matters that troubled him. His familiarity with Christians and Jews (subsequently known by Muslims as "People of the Book"), together with his serious, reflective nature, had perhaps brought Muhammad to see the need of the still largely animistic Arabs for a holy book of their own, in the Arabic language. Himself an orphan reared by his grandfather and later by his uncle, Abu Talib, Muhammad was sensitive to the plight of the unfortunate and was sickened by the money-grubbing practices of the large merchants, whose prosperity caused them to forget their former egalitarian tribal values.

Although active in commerce, Muhammad's Hashimite clan was one of the relatively poor and uninfluential divisions of the Quraysh tribe that dominated the city. Muhammad is said to have accompanied his uncle's caravan to Syria at the age of twelve, and of the many legends about his early life, one of the most quoted is that of the Syrian Christian monk who noticed that a cloud moved with the boy to protect him from the sun and who found the signs of a prophet on his back. Muhammad's profound intelligence and admirable character, which earned him the nickname Amin ("Trustworthy"), eventually brought him success in the business world, leading caravans to and from Syria. One employer, a forty-year-old widow named Khadijah, was so impressed with Muhammad, who was fifteen years her junior, that she asked him to marry her. Not only did the marriage give Muhammad the economic security that permitted him to devote his mind to religious matters, but as a woman

---

[1] It is not for the historian to say whether such a statement is literally true. The non-Muslim, in particular, may choose a rational explanation, but no fair-minded person believes that Muhammad was insincere.

of elevated character, Khadijah was subsequently one of her husband's greatest sources of strength. Muhammad was deeply devoted to Khadijah and took no other wife as long as she lived.

At first Muhammad was confused by the voice. He feared that he was mad, and thoughts of suicide kept passing through his mind. One of Khadijah's cousins, who probably was a *Hanif,* advised her that the revelations were like those of the biblical prophets, and she reassured her husband. Indeed, she became his first convert, followed by his ten-year-old cousin, Ali, who lived in Muhammad's house and ever remained one of his most devout followers. Others who heeded Muhammad's warnings included persons who lacked the protection that only kinship ties could provide in this tribal society, as well as members of weak clans and even some less influential members of the leading units. Uthman ibn Affan, of the dominant Umayyad clan, is an example of the latter. The mild-mannered Abu Bakr, a successful merchant, was another of Muhammad's early followers.

Muhammad's prophetic experiences continued at irregular intervals. Sometimes he heard a voice, accompanied by a "ringing of bells"; at other times he had visions or even felt intense pain and fell to the ground in a trance. Following these occurrences, he conveyed passages of rhymed prose to his followers, who committed them to memory. Sometimes these passages (the Qur'an, or "recitation," as they are collectively known) were written down on whatever material was at hand, and only after the Prophet's death were they collected in one book. The non-Muslim reader may find translations of the Qur'an dull and sometimes incomprehensible. The later arbitrary arrangement of 114 *suras,* or chapters (except for the short "Opening" one) in order of length, with some *suras* consisting of separate, unrelated revelations, makes a cover-to-cover reading as unrewarding as, say, reading a Christian hymnal in the same fashion. And, in fact, the Qur'an is a book of separate devotional readings. Perhaps more than any other literary work, the Qur'an loses its impact in translation, and most Muslims reject the very possibility of translating it. Even if non-Arabic-speaking Muslims sometimes use another language version to explain the meaning of the passages that they "read" (pronounce) in the original, the translation is not, in their view, really the Qur'an. Muslim doctrine holds that the chapters of the Arabic Qur'an are taken letter-for-letter from a book in Heaven.

In the original Arabic the Qur'an's effect is almost hypnotic. It was the only "miracle" that Muhammad produced as proof of his prophethood. It was said that all "people and *jinn*" together could not compose such a work, and indeed no person since has succeeded in producing a piece of literature with the same impact or one that is read and recited so much. For Muslims, who today number about one-fifth of the inhabitants of the Earth, a final proof that the book came by way of revelation is the alleged fact that Muhammad did not even know how to read and write, which skeptics question in view of his business activity.

The essentials of a new monotheistic faith were taking shape. It was in the tradition of Judaism and Christianity, and Muslims ("those who submit") do not see their religion, Islam ("Submission" to God), as starting with Muhammad, who is rather the "seal" (last) of a series of prophets or messengers (only a few of the prophets have the latter designation) and, of course, only a man. (Many Muslims resent uninformed references to them as "Muhammadans," which may incorrectly imply that they worship Muhammad the way Christians worship Christ.) Submission included prayer, although the requirement of five daily prayers at specified times was not fixed at the beginning. Earlier prophets, such as Adam, Abraham, Moses, and Jesus, and those who submitted to the messages conveyed by God through them are also considered to have been Muslims. Just as the nonbeliever may conclude that many passages in the Qur'an are garbled versions of biblical stories, the devout Muslim believes that the Christian and Jewish scriptures were revealed to earlier prophets but have been tampered with since their revelation. To a great extent, Christian and Muslim doctrines are similar. Thus, Muslims believe that Jesus was not only a prophet but also the Messiah, was born of a virgin, ascended to Heaven without dying (the doctrine of the crucifixion is regarded as demeaning to such a great prophet), and will come again. But the idea that Jesus was the Son of God is adamantly rejected, and Muslims, who stress the oneness of God, view the Christian doctrine of the Trinity as smacking of polytheism.

Muhammad's early messages were particularly reminiscent of biblical concepts. The Last Judgment, he warned, was near, with human beings to be resurrected and rewarded in Paradise or punished in the flames of Hell. God is all-powerful and righteous, to be feared, but "beneficent and merciful." In return for God's goodness people are expected to be generous toward the needy, and, seemingly with the rich in mind, the Prophet warned against pride and ungratefulness. People are to worship God, and the ritual of prayer—involving a repeated sequence of kneeling and prostration until the forehead touches the ground—was evolving. (Box 2–1 on page 28 outlines the most basic duties, known as the Pillars of Islam, some of which we have already touched on.)

From the beginning, Islam incorporated indigenous Arabian features. Not unlike other local monotheists, the Muslims performed the pilgrimage to the Ka'bah. Belief in *jinn*—some of whom are said to have also converted to Islam at one point—joined with Judeo-Zoroastrian-Christian concepts of angels, Satan (the leader of the evil *jinn* or *shaytans*), and the like. Although he later pushed numerous social reforms, Muhammad took for granted many of the practices of his people.

Most Meccans, particularly the leaders of the influential merchant families, rejected Muhammad's message and became increasingly hostile. They disliked attacks on their selfish behavior. They also resented claims of prophethood made by a person of modest social status and even feared that acceptance of his message would give him a position of political leadership. Some Meccans were offended by attacks on their ancestral practices. Muhammad's frank admission, after being put on the spot by a clever opponent, that his own grandfather would be punished in Hell, was used against him. But perhaps economic motives were more important in creating opposition, as many feared that the pagan shrines, a major factor in Mecca's prosperity, would lose their attraction if the new doctrine gained acceptance. For a brief time—according to some sources—Muhammad temporized. A new revelation proclaimed "God's three daughters"—deities central to the profitable pilgrimage—to be intermediaries between God and humans. But Muhammad soon announced that "Satanic verses" had deceived him on this matter and henceforth stuck to his original strict monotheism.

Muhammad's increasing attacks on polytheism met still greater opposition. Islamic doctrines, such as that of the resurrection, evoked ridicule. Muslims were harassed and sometimes even murdered, especially if they lacked blood ties or their own kin disowned them and they were unable to find a clan to guarantee their protection. Meccan society still was stateless, and law and order rested on the threat of retaliation by a clan against a person who wronged one of its members or someone else given its protection. Possibly with the aim of starting a new commercial center to rival Mecca, one group of Muslim families migrated to Ethiopia. Muhammad was fortunate in having the Hashimite clan's protection as long as Abu Talib headed it, and for two years this clan even weathered an economic boycott by the others. New converts kept entering the fold, the most notable being Umar ibn al-Khattab, a tall, austere man of commanding mien who had once beaten his own sister for accepting Islam but afterwards became one of the most devoted Muslims. Among Muhammad's experiences in his last years in Mecca was his ascent in a dream to the "Seventh Heaven," transported on a winged horse via the site of Solomon's Temple in Jerusalem. This would lead future Muslims to consider Jerusalem's Temple Mount, which they call the Haram al-Sharif (Noble Sanctuary), one of the holiest places. But in 619 Abu Talib died and his successor as head of the clan was bitterly opposed to the new religious movement. The death of Khadijah in the same year was another personal blow to Muhammad. He traveled to Ta'if in the hope of being given refuge there, only to have stones hurled at him as he left.

MUHAMMAD IN POWER

A turning point for the Muslims came in 620, when six men from Yathrib came to Mecca for a pilgrimage. These Yathribis were impressed with Muhammad's message, and they apparently hoped that he could provide leadership for their anarchy-ridden city in which no one had authority over the separate tribes. Two years later (in 622), a larger group of Yathribis pledged to obey Muhammad and to fight with him. Thus, about the time of the Roman offensive against the Persians, the way became clear for the Prophet to move his activities to Yathrib, from that point on called Madina (*Madinat al-Nabi,* "the City of the Prophet").

The Emigration (*hijrah*) of the Muslims—literally a breaking of kinship ties and the establishment of new bonds—took place gradually and at first gained little notice. By September of the same year, only Muhammad and his close associates, Ali and Abu Bakr, remained behind. Now the Meccan leaders realized that something was happening and plotted to kill Muhammad, who, with Abu Bakr, slipped out at night and hid in a cave for three days before proceeding nine more days by camel to Madina. With the Prophet himself aiding in the work, the Emigrants (*Muhajirun,* as those who left Mecca were termed) and the Helpers (*Ansar,* as those Madinan

Box 2-1: The Pillars of Islam

The term *Five Pillars of Islam* sums up what Sunni Muslims consider to be their most basic duties. The Shi'ite list of basic duties[*] is somewhat different; it includes *jihad* (see Box 2–2), which is the Kharijites' Sixth Pillar. The First Pillar is the *shahadah* (bearing witness), that is, testifying sincerely that "There is no god but God, and Muhammad is the Messenger of God." Muslims normally take such profession at face value and accept the person so testifying as a fellow Muslim even if he or she is negligent about the other duties; and many people (for example, in countries once under Communist rule) are born into Muslim families, as is the case with other religions, who hardly take their faith seriously at all but whose membership in the community—which is relevant to, say, marriage or burial—no one ordinarily disputes as long as they do not embrace another religion.

The Second Pillar is *salat* (prayer). This occurs at five specific times each day—starting before dawn and ending during midevening—that in predominantly Muslim countries a muezzin (*mu'adhdhin,* announcer) announces from a minaret (tower) that is a characteristic feature of mosques. The Muslim may perform his or her prayer wherever he or she is (typically using a rug), but Muslim men are supposed to attend congregational prayer in a mosque at least once a week, that is, each Friday (Day of Congregation) at midday, with an *imam* (leader; literally, the one in front) praying in front of the others to provide guidance. If women choose to participate in congregational prayer, they go to a part of the mosque that will give them privacy from the men. Wherever prayer occurs, it involves a set of rituals that includes praising God and reciting Qur'anic verses and bowing and prostrating oneself until one's forehead touches the floor, while facing in the direction of Mecca. Before prayer, one has to be in a state of ritual purity, which involves washing the feet, hands, face, and mouth. Muslims may also choose to pray at additional times.

The Third Pillar, which actually applies only to those who have the economic means, is the payment of *zakat* (usually translated as alms) for the benefit of the poor. When there exists an Islamic government to collect a fixed rate from members of the community, this amounts to a tax rather than alms in the ordinary sense of the word, but of course the making of such contributions to the poor remains a religious duty even if the state does not require it. Islamic law specifies certain rates of pay-

[*]See the articles on "Pillars of Islam" (by Mahmoud M. Ayoub) and "Ithnā 'Asharīyah" (by Abdulaziz Sachedina) in John L. Esposito, ed., *The Oxford Encyclopedia of the Modern Islamic World,* 4 vols. (New York and Oxford: Oxford University Press, 1995).

ment on various kinds of wealth, such as cattle of different types, but this typically amounts to about 2.5 percent of all assets each year. The Muslim's religion also encourages him or her to make other, purely voluntary contributions to the poor, known as *sadaqah*. Many Muslims today see this as a set of provisions designed to ensure social justice and argue that extremes of wealth and poverty never could have emerged if everyone had observed such obligations over the centuries.

The Fourth Pillar—also sometimes said to relate to social justice by requiring everyone to experience the kind of temporary hardship that will give him or her empathy with the less fortunate—is fasting throughout the month of Ramadan, during which time one is also supposed to make a special effort to be pious in other ways. During the daylight hours, obviously a long time when this ninth lunar month (the one that includes the Night of Power, when the Prophet received his first revelation) occurs during the summer, the Muslim is obligated absolutely to abstain from all food and drink (as well as sexual activity). Religious authorities in each place determine the exact moment the fast begins and ends each day (based on whether there is enough light to distinguish a black thread from a white thread), with a long-awaited daily *iftar* (breakfast) starting as soon as the daytime ordeal is over. Although night is a time for catching up, with people typically getting up just before daybreak to fill their stomachs before the fast begins, even the least religious people in most Muslim countries usually do not dare face the social disapproval that would come from being seen violating the fast. The Qur'an provides flexibility by allowing travelers and sick people to observe this obligation at another time. The end of Ramadan marks one of the major celebrations of the Islamic year, the Feast of Breaking the Fast (*Id al-Fitr*).

The Fifth Pillar of Islam, although one that is incumbent only on those who can afford to observe it, is performance of the *hajj* (pilgrimage) at least once during a person's lifetime. (Any Muslim may make the Lesser Pilgrimage or *umrah* at any time of the year, but the *hajj* is a set of ceremonies that occurs on a specific annual occasion.) Every year since the time of the Prophet, Muslims have arrived in Mecca and its immediate hinterland during the month of Dhu'l-Hijjah proclaiming, "I am here, Lord. I am here," with rulers historically sponsoring caravans that converged in such cities as Damascus and proceeded to the Hijaz. Today the pilgrims come by air and by sea from virtually every country of the world. The number of participants in each *hajj* during recent decades has grown to two million, about half of whom come from outside the peninsula. Not only does this provide a symbol of the worldwide unity of

(continued)

Box 2–1: The Pillars of Islam (*continued*)

the Muslim community without regard to nationality or race, but also the state of purity that each individual enters into at the beginning of the pilgrimage, which includes shaving or cropping one's hair and wearing the same simple dress—two white sheets in the case of men—symbolizes the equality of all.

The ritual starts with everyone walking around the Ka'bah seven times and attempting to kiss or touch the black stone and then includes several other ceremonies, including running back and forth between the hills of Safa and Marwa in remembrance of Ishmael's mother, Hagar's, struggle to find water, as well as again circumambulating the Ka'bah seven times. Later the whole mass of pilgrims proceed together to the Valley of Arafat, where the companions of the Prophet assembled to hear him deliver his farewell sermon. Ceremonies the next day include throwing pebbles at a rock at Mina that symbolizes the devil before carrying out the annual slaughter of animals for the great Feast of the Sacrifice (*Id al-Adha*) in emulation of Abraham's obedience to God. Muslims throughout the world—not just those participating in the *hajj*—engage in this great feast at the same time, with each family supposed to give to the poor what meat it cannot consume. The *hajj* is one of the greatest events in many people's lives, whereupon the word *Hajj* or *Hajji* often is added to one's name.

Muslims came to be known) constructed Muhammad's modest brick house, whose courtyard became the center of congregational prayers, that is, the first mosque (*masjid*, "place of prostration").

With the *hijrah*, the Muslims were transformed from a persecuted minority into an autonomous religio-political community (*ummah*). The importance assigned to this development—epitomized by the fact that the Muslims soon designated the year of the *hijrah* as the Year One of the Islamic calendar—points to an important difference between Islam and Christianity. From the start, the concept of a division between religious and political authority ("God and Caesar") would have been foreign to Muhammad's thinking. According to the Muslim concept, all believers form a separate community (*ummah*) whose ties with one another are more basic than are any tribal, ethnic, or racial divisions. This *ummah* must have its own government, whose purpose is to enforce God's law (the *shari'ah*, literally, "the path"), to pursue God's purposes, and to help the members to find salvation.

The *ummah* was analogous to a new tribe, based on religion rather than kinship ties. Headed by Muhammad, the Emigrants were in effect one clan of the tribe. The so-called Constitution of Madina may not have existed in full at the beginning, but it shows some of the principles that form the basis of the *ummah*. The Constitution clearly enunciated the primacy of the whole community by providing that—unlike the old kinship system, in which each clan protected its members against outsiders—an offender against a member of another clan would be turned over for punishment.

This does not mean that a centralized government under Muhammad's rule existed at first. His chief political function for the whole *ummah* was that of arbitrating interclan disputes. Muhammad ruled his own "clan," although more as a democratic tribal *shaykh* than as a despot of a more advanced state. The Helpers accepted his authority when it was in the form of Qur'anic revelation. Most of the non-Jewish Madinan clans at least nominally embraced the new faith. But certain individuals called the "Hypocrites" remained hostile to Islam and the influence of the newcomers.

The Jewish clans found themselves in an anomalous position in Madina. The Constitution made them part of the *ummah* and forbade any molestation of those who sided with the Muslims. Since they were already worshippers of one God, it probably did not occur to Muhammad to ask them to convert to Islam. Instead, he assumed that they would welcome him as a carrier of their common monotheistic message to the Arabs. His teachings underwent so much Jewish influence for a while that, in retrospect, one can imagine that Islam might have evolved into the status of a Jewish sect. The Muslims adopted the Jewish feast of Yom Kippur, as well as the Jewish practice of facing Jerusalem in prayer.

Instead of confirming Muhammad's message, the Madinan Jews recognized discrepancies between it and their own scriptures. By ridiculing his doctrines, they appeared as a threat to the new religion, and thus Muhammad emphasized the idea of Islam as the primordial religion of Abraham that preceded Judaism. Some Jewish elements in Islam were dropped, although Muslim scholars deny that this resulted from the break with the Jews. In any case, instead of Yom Kippur, the Muslims adopted the month of Ramadan (when Muhammad's first revelation occurred) as a period of fasting and turned to pray toward Mecca rather than Jerusalem. Although Islam does not require a weekly day of rest, Friday became the day of congregational noon prayer.

The Jewish clans became increasingly hostile to Muhammad and began to collaborate with his enemies. Accused of treason, they received harsh treatment that contrasts with the relatively favorable position of Jews and other People of the Book under Islamic rule generally, although some Muslims and some Jews would seize on this incident in the context of the conflict over Palestine during the twentieth century as alleged evidence of the other side's long tradition of perfidy. The Muslims allowed those small clans of Jews that they did not perceive as a threat to continue to live in Madina (although eventually they excluded nonbelievers from most of the peninsula), while they expelled two main clans, whose land the Emigrants took over. Men of another clan were executed and their women and children enslaved.

Muhammad continued to receive revelations in Madina. Those *suras* are generally distinguishable from the earlier, Meccan ones by being longer, often dealing with practical matters of the moment, and lacking an apocalyptic character. Reflecting Muhammad's responsibility as head of a political community, some of the Madinan *suras* are of a legislative type. While the revelations did not modify most customary rules, a number of changes emerged in family law and other matters improving the status of women.

Some of the Qur'anic reforms were radical for the time, although their realistic compromises with tradition make the same rules objectionable to many today. Thus, while daughters previously had been excluded from inheritance, the Qur'an provided that they would receive half as much as sons. Although a variety of marriage customs had coexisted in pre-Islamic Arabia, there had often been no limit to the number of wives a man could have at one time. But now the Qur'an set four as a maximum. Even that was on the condition, labeled an impossibility, of completely equal treatment that some modernists now reread as a veiled prohibition. A man was permitted an unlimited number of sexual relationships with his own unmarried, willing slave girls, each of whom gained a special status and eventual freedom after bearing a child. Actually, Muhammad received a revelation excepting himself from the four-wife limitation and married several women after Khadijah's death, but one can explain most of these unions either as a charitable way of looking after the widows of Muslims killed in battle or else in terms of political connections with leading personalities and families. While Uthman married two of Muhammad's daughters and Ali married another (Fatimah), the Prophet wedded Abu Bakr's daughter, A'ishah, who at first was so young that she still played with dolls but later became his favorite wife.

Soon after the *hijrah,* Muhammad and the Emigrants began to make war on their native city. After all, raiding was an old tribal practice. More than that, the Emigrants had reason for revenge. In addition, they needed a new source of livelihood; they saw the attractive prospect not only of acquiring booty but possibly of taking control of the trade route. And they surely realized that their movement could not be a true success without incorporating Mecca and places beyond into the realm of Islam.

Before two years had passed, Muslim raiders met their first success. Members of a small party, having opened sealed instructions from the Prophet after their departure from Madina, attacked a Meccan caravan. This was during the annual truce, violation of which caused uneasiness in the *ummah* at first. But for Muhammad the old pagan customs were no longer binding, and this symbolized his break with the past. Besides, newly revealed verses approved the raid on the grounds that it was against those who persecuted the Muslims.

Soon afterward, a bigger victory ensued at Badr, south of Madina. A three-hundred-member Muslim force, including Helpers, intercepted a large Meccan caravan led by the Umayyad chief, Abu Sufyan. Another Meccan, Abu Jahl, brought an army out of his city to join in the caravan's defense, and the Muslims were grossly outnumbered. But Muhammad planned the battle astutely, posting his forces at wells where the caravan would have to replenish its water supply. According to Muslim tradition, Muhammad's force did not have a numerical disadvantage at all, as legions of angels fought by his side. The Muslims routed the Meccans, thus acquiring vast amounts of booty and, more important, evidence that God's help had made them invincible.

In 625 a Meccan force that sought revenge for Badr shook Muslim confidence. Enticed out of Madina by the Meccans pasturing their horses and camels in vital fields of unharvested grain, the Muslims again stood outnumbered—ten to one, it is said, in addition to a lack of horses and armor—at the foot of the hill of Uhud. Although the Muslims prevailed at first, a tough, bloodthirsty Meccan cavalryman named Khalid ibn al-Walid took advantage of temporary confusion in one section of their army. Khalid broke through the weak spot to attack the Muslims from the other direction and inflicted severe casualties. Yet the Meccans, seemingly satisfied by avenging their earlier losses, departed from the field without pressing their victory. They knew that the complete defeat of the Muslim forces, now positioned on the hill, was beyond their capability, and the Muslim challenge to Mecca remained unbroken.

Then, at the Battle of the Trench (627), the Muslims frustrated a final attempt of Meccan-led tribes. A huge army, said to have numbered 10,000, headed for the Prophet's city. To hold back such a force, a former Persian slave proposed a defense tactic previously unknown in Arabia: to dig a deep ditch around the part of Madina that was not already protected by hills. The Muslims tried the proposal, and it worked. The Meccan mainstay, the cavalry, could not cross, and after two weeks the entire army, now tired and running low on provisions, returned home.

The Meccan challenge was broken, and Meccan caravans no longer dared move to Syria. More and more tribes moved over to Muhammad's side, and his position in Madina was increasingly like that of a monarch. Even some Meccans wondered whether they should come to terms with their challenger, especially when they saw that Islam would not be a threat to the city's religious importance. Meanwhile Muhammad apparently realized that the administrative and commercial assets of his enemies would be valuable to the *ummah.* When Muhammad led a large group of Muslims toward Mecca in March 628 to celebrate the Lesser Pilgrimage, another battle appeared imminent, but envoys met the pilgrims just outside the city. The two sides worked out a compromise whereby the Muslims would go back to Madina this time but would be allowed to make the pilgrimage a year later.

A ten-year truce was agreed upon, but Muslim power became increasingly irresistible. Expeditions to northwest Arabia imposed the Muslims' will on various tribes. A treaty with the Jews at Khaybar Oasis providing for tribute to Madina in return for protection became a precedent for subsequent toleration of People of the Book. Opportunistic Meccans such as Khalid and the crafty Amr ibn al-As came over to the Muslim side and were soon to be in command of Muslim armies. Even Abu Sufyan softened (the marriage of his daughter, an early Muslim, to Muhammad may have been helpful) and came to Madina to work out terms of surrender. When Muhammad led a large force into Mecca in 630 (the year Heraclius retook Jerusalem), he met scarcely any resistance and proceeded to grant amnesty to his former foes, who at least nominally accepted Islam, and to destroy all the idols in the Ka'bah.

The submission of Mecca accelerated the momentum of Muslim success. Ta'if soon surrendered too, and a large Muslim force broke a confederation of tribes east of Mecca. A "Year of Delegations" followed, as representatives of tribes or factions of tribes as far away as the Persian Gulf offered their fealty to Muhammad, but his effective rule never extended much farther than western Arabia, and most of the tribes did not truly convert to Islam. Even the Persian governor of Yemen submitted, although a revolt soon broke out there. Other challenges to Islam arose, notably the emergence of rival claimants to prophethood.

The seeds of bigger things to come could be seen. As the tribes joined together in one *ummah,* they were to turn their tradition of internecine raids outward into an ever wider circle of conquests. In late 630, Muhammad mustered a force of 30,000 fighters for a campaign in northwestern Arabia. A smaller force had already gone farther north for an unsuccessful encounter with Roman forces on the border of Syria, and the Prophet was preparing for a return engagement. While the story that Muhammad sent messages to Constantinople and Ctesiphon demanding submission may be apocryphal, such was the emerging challenge to the old empires in 632 when the Prophet suddenly became ill with a fever. He spent his last days in the apartment of A'ishah, where his breath stopped as his head lay on her lap.

ABU BAKR, THE CALIPHATE, AND CONSOLIDATION

Some Muslims could hardly believe that the Prophet was dead. But Abu Bakr reminded them that God was the object of their worship and that he was still alive. The community held to its faith, and before the irreplaceable Prophet was buried (at the spot of his death), the question of leadership arose. All the old divisions came to the surface. The Helpers, who resented the newcomers' position in Madina, met and proposed one of themselves as the new leader, and someone even suggested the possibility of separate leaders for themselves and the Emigrants, but the Aws and Khazraj were also jealous of each other. Then a group of Emigrants joined the meeting, and one of them, Abu Bakr, nominated Umar and Abu Ubaydah as alternative candidates. But when both of these men said "no" and insisted that Abu Bakr was the worthiest among them, the others went along.

During his illness, Muhammad had authorized Abu Bakr to lead prayers, an act symbolic of leadership in a religio-political community, although it is uncertain how much weight this act carried at the time. The seeds of a permanent sectarian division in Islam appeared, as some Muslims, possibly at this time but mainly later, believed that the youthful Ali, as Muhammad's son-in-law (he had no surviving son) and because of his inherently superior qualifications, was the rightful successor. Actually, the concept of hereditary monarchy was unfamiliar to most Arabs at that time, but Ali's supporters—citing a statement made by Muhammad that other Muslims also accept as authentic but interpret in a less specific way—later maintained that Muhammad had designated him for the succession.

The sixty-year-old Abu Bakr became the first "successor [*Khalifah;* "caliph"] of the Messenger of God." He was the successor in all capacities except that of prophethood; that is, he assumed political leadership of the *ummah.* In the predominant concept that eventually emerged, each caliph was to be chosen by the *ummah,* though in an informal kind of election. Each man theoretically was able to withhold the *bay'ah,* a touch on the hand that signified allegience. The caliph was also known as the *imam* ("leader")[2] and, after Abu Bakr, as commander of the faithful.

When Abu Bakr took office, the greatest challenge came from nomadic tribes throughout the peninsula. Conventionally termed "Apostates," the tribes renounced their loyalty to Madina, which they considered to be terminated with the Prophet's death. They stopped sending their *zakat* (alms payable to the state and one of the requirements of Islam) and sometimes expelled the envoys that had been sent. Claimants to prophethood proliferated. Only Mecca and Ta'if, together with a few neighboring tribes, remained loyal to Madina, and the Apostates seemed to pose a mortal danger to the capital itself.

Then after a two-month delay caused by Abu Bakr's decision to go ahead with the plans for an expedition to Syria, the campaign to subdue the tribes began. These "Wars of Apostasy," the label subsequently given to the struggle against tribes that had mainly never been Muslim in the first place, were conducted by eleven separate armies, and more than a year elapsed before every corner of the peninsula fell under the caliph's rule. The most notable commanding role was played by Khalid, in northern and eastern Arabia, and with a degree of inhumanity that shocked such people as Umar. Characteristically, Khalid barely waited for some of his victims to die before marrying their widows and consummating the marriages on the blood-soaked battlefields. Yet this "Sword of Islam," a title bestowed by a sometimes disapproving Muhammad, proved himself such an effective general that the scandalized Abu Bakr could not afford to do more than reprimand him.

Even before the Muslims fully subdued Arabia, the conquests began to overflow into Sassanian and Roman lands that internecine conflict had already weakened. Armed with swords, lances, and bows and with siege engines that hurled stones or fire, Arab cavalry and infantry moved on. Khalid joined with the powerful Bakr tribe in the region of Arabia next to Iraq and defeated the wobbly Sassanians in several engagements during 634. Hira, the old Lakhmid capital, submitted to the Muslim forces and agreed to pay tribute. Other columns sent from Madina entered Syria, and, as Heraclius sent in massive reinforcements, Abu Bakr conveyed orders to Khalid to join the fight there. In a legendary, seemingly incredible feat, Khalid crossed the Syrian Desert with about five hundred fighters in eighteen days, allegedly sustained by water from the stomachs of slain camels, to begin a series of victories on the Romans' eastern frontier. This was the state of affairs when death ended the two-year rule of Abu Bakr, who had already nominated Umar as his successor.

UMAR AND THE CONQUESTS

During the ten-year caliphate of Umar, the Arab tribes swept in all directions to create a vast empire. On his deathbed in 644, after being stabbed by a Persian Christian slave who was angry over the caliph's failure to take his side in a dispute with his

---

[2] The word *imam* is used in several contexts, particularly for the leader of prayers in the mosque.

owner, Umar selected a five-member council to choose his successor. The electors finally settled on Uthman as the third caliph, and the conquests continued until growing conflict within the *ummah* temporarily halted them.

After Khalid and his warriors reached the Syrian front, the Arab forces quickly crushed larger Roman armies there. The Romans depended on mercenaries, including members of Syrian Arab tribes, some of whom quickly changed allegiance. So poor was the morale of many Roman fighters—as of the Sassanians—that at times they were chained together in battle to prevent desertion. The local population often faced the change of overlords with indifference and even saw the Arabs as deliverers from the high taxes and the religious intolerance of the Romans. Heraclius had attempted to impose a Monothelite compromise doctrine—that Christ has two natures but only one will—to bridge the gap between the Orthodox Hellenic population and the Monophysite Orient, but with little success, although the Maronites of Lebanon (who later embraced orthodoxy) may have accepted the new position. Also, the Jewish minority, whose forcible conversion to Christianity Heraclius had decreed in 634, foresaw a new kind of toleration and collaborated with their Arab cousins against Christian Roman rule. The conquest, in effect the final rollback of a millennium of Hellenic domination from the East, appeared as a disaster mainly to the Greek-speaking upper crust, many of whom fled with the Roman armies to Anatolia.

With all the solidarity of the Arab tribes channeled outward, the armies of their enemies stood no chance. Religion was a contributing factor; at least some of the Arabs saw themselves engaged in a *jihad* (endeavor) in the path of God and were willing to sacrifice their lives with the assurance given by Islam to those who die in this manner that they would pass directly into Paradise. (See Box 2–2, pp. 38–39.) Yet one may make too much of this. Many were Muslims in name only, and for that matter Christian Arab tribes joined in this greatest of all onslaughts of the desert against "the sown." Inspiration also came from a mundane consideration, the prospect of booty. The Arabs, after all, had started out by merely raiding and had turned to outright conquest as an afterthought. Once the outflow started, it gained its own momentum, and no central authority could have changed its course.

Syria was soon in Arab hands. The Arabs' defeat of a large Roman army in Palestine soon after Khalid's arrival and their acceptance of him as the overall commander in the area (until Umar dismissed him) left much of the area open to them. Damascus soon surrendered, although the Arabs later withdrew to the Yarmuk River (an eastern tributary of the Jordan) as Heraclius's brother launched a large Roman offensive. The Roman army, allegedly numbering 140,000, was almost decimated by 36,000 Arabs on horseback in the Battle of the Yarmuk in 636. Umar came up from Madina to help organize the new territories. Typical of his magnanimity toward the conquered was his refusal to enter the Church of the Holy Sepulchre lest other Muslims follow him and eventually turn it into a mosque.

Syria provided a staging point for further expansion. One force moved eastward across the Euphrates and soon invaded Armenia. Also, despite Umar's misgivings, Amr ibn al-As led 3,500 warriors, later reinforced, on to Egypt, where the Coptic population was embittered by Roman rule, and a series of easy victories fol-

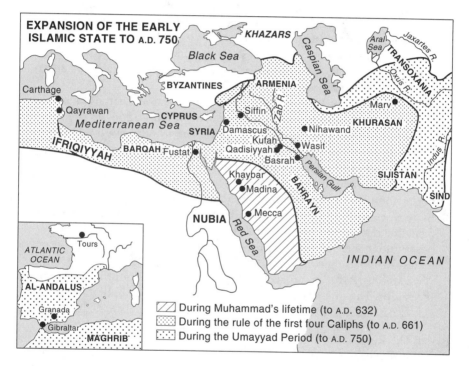

EXPANSION OF THE EARLY ISLAMIC STATE TO A.D. 750

During Muhammad's lifetime (to A.D. 632)
During the rule of the first four Caliphs (to A.D. 661)
During the Umayyad Period (to A.D. 750)

MAP 4

Box 2–2: *Jihad*

Among the duties of the Muslim, but one that most Muslims have not elevated to the status of a Sixth Pillar, is *jihad*—endeavor or striving—in the path of God. Muslim writers have always said that the Greater *Jihad* is the effort to combat evil, as in one's own heart, and relegate military struggle to the status of the Lesser *Jihad*. In the latter sense (and the one which jurists have given most attention to), *Jihad* refers to the obligation of the *ummah* in general to endeavor to defeat the enemy and sometimes to the personal obligation of the individual to contribute to the effort. This is a religious duty because the community is a religious one, committed to Islam as an ideology (to make a comparison with modern secular states, which similarly articulate the obligation of the government and the citizen individually to struggle, militarily or otherwise, for national causes).

Non-Muslims have conventionally understood that *jihad* means holy war, but that at best represents an oversimplification. As the historian Bernard Lewis points out, the phrase *holy war* did not even exist in Classical Arabic, although to some extent *jihad* might loosely be translated that way and might be understood as the Muslim equivalent of the Christian crusade. But some careful scholars suggest that *jihad* is better understood as the equivalent of the medieval Christian idea of *Just War.* In a sense, *jihad* serves as a euphemism in a religion that rejects war in principle but calls on the Muslim to struggle militarily for the right purposes under the right conditions—but only against unbelievers or renegades—while using a different word for it.

Medieval Muslim jurists saw the world divided mainly into two hostile camps. The first was the House of Peace (*dar al-Islam*), that is, the ter-

---

lowed. The Roman fort of Babylon (inside what later became Cairo) fell, and the Bishop of Egypt soon surrendered Alexandria. Although the Roman navy later retook the city, the Arabs' setback proved temporary, and soon they advanced westward into North Africa, to take Barqah (Cyrenaica) and temporarily to occupy part of Tunisia by 647.

Control of Alexandria and the Syrian coast brought ships and experienced sailors into Arab hands, and Arab naval domination ensued in much of the Mediterranean. As governor of Syria, Uthman's cousin and Abu Sufyan's son, Mu'awiyyah, assumed the leadership in this field. Raiding as far west as Sicily, the new fleet seized several islands, including Cyprus in 649, and in a decisive encounter wreaked havoc on the Roman navy off the southern coast of Anatolia in 655.

By this time, the Arabs had occupied almost all of the Sassanian Empire. The Persians at first laughed at the Arabs' small spears, and stories abound depicting the tribespeople's simplicity amidst the splendors of the lands they overran. Terrorized ritories under Islamic rule. Aside from a few neutral territories (mainly Ethiopia, which had given refuge to the early Muslims who fled there from Mecca), the rest of the world was described as the House of War (*dar al-harb*), with which, except for temporary truces modeled on the Prophet's agreement with the Meccans, a continuous state of *jihad* would exist until the whole world came to be incorporated into the House of Peace, with the conquered People of the Book (*ahl al-kitab*) either accepting Islam or taking on the status of *ahl al-dhimma* (or *dhimmis*, protected people) under Islamic rule and allowed to practice their own religion and live under their own law while paying the poll tax (*jizyah*). Such writers as Shafi'i also recognized an intermediate status, the House of the Covenant (*dar al-ahd*), that described non-Muslim territories which remained in control of their own affairs but entered into a treaty arrangement with the House of Peace providing for payment of tribute.

Although modern Muslims do not ordinarily invoke such medieval juristic concepts, the idea of *jihad* remains alive in the specifically military sense as well as the broader endeavor to resist evil. The label *jihad* has regularly been used to describe the struggle against foreign colonialism or other invasion, as in the case of those who fought against the French in Algeria or, more recently, the USSR in Afghanistan, and even participants in some basically secular anticolonial movements call themselves *Mujahidin* (literally, Endeavorers). Paralleling the early Kharijites, it has become commonplace during the late twentieth century for militant opposition groups to declare what they consider to be oppressive rulers to be enemies of Islam, against which they have the obligation to wage *jihad*.

by the Sassanians' war elephants, the invaders met a setback in the "Battle of the Bridge" on the Euphrates in 634 but then, under the command of Sa'd ibn Abi-Waqqas, an early convert to Islam and one of the Emigrants, proceeded from victory to victory. Defeating a Persian force at Qadisiyyah in 637, the Arabs quickly took control of Ctesiphon, as the new shah, Yazdagird III, took flight. With the rich yet declining agricultural land of Iraq falling to the Arabs, the Iranian highlands did not suffice to support the empire, although the rough terrain and a certain amount of popular resistance slowed the Arab advance. But a Sassanian defeat in 642 at Nihawand in western Iran—the Arabs' "Victory of Victories"—brought the end near. As the local nobility came to terms with the conquerors, the shah fell at the hands of one of his own satraps at the northeastern corner of his domain.

Umar now confronted the problem of administering the vast empire. Each province had a governor, appointed by and responsible to the caliph. Except at the top levels, the government of the provinces remained largely as it had been before the conquest. Greek and Pahlavi long continued as the languages of the administration, with the same officials in charge. Each conquered religious community had its own law and courts. Any idea of converting non-Arabs to Islam hardly took high priority.

The newcomers remained aloof from the conquered populations. Except for some Syrian cities, where they took over the property of the departed Hellenic upper class, the Arabs confined themselves to their own garrison towns (*amsar*), such as Kufah and Basrah in Iraq and Fustat in Egypt. Each was located on the margins of the familiar desert, where the conquerors could retreat if necessary. According to a decision made by Umar, Arabs did not become landowners in the new domains. While the former state lands and unclaimed land became the collective property (*fay*) of the *ummah*, tilled by the same peasants as before, other land retained its original ownership. The non-Muslim landowners paid a land tax (*kharaj*), in addition to a poll tax (*jizyah*) that the new rulers levied on those male adults who were able to pay, although the clear distinction between the two taxes only emerged gradually. Special terms for towns that submitted without resistance led to a lack of uniformity in such matters at first. Muslim landowners in Arabia paid a smaller tax, the *ushr* (tithe), in addition to the *zakat*.

Rules emerged to govern the distribution of the new wealth. Movable property at the time of conquest had the status of booty (*ghanimah*), to be divided on the spot after the conquering forces sent one-fifth to the caliph. Similarly, a fifth of the tax revenue went to the caliph. In both cases, the fifth was intended to be used for general matters, especially for distribution among the poor, not solely for the ruler's private purposes. From the remainder of the tax revenue were deducted local administrative and military expenses. What remained belonged to the Faithful as a body. Umar organized a *diwan* (register) of the Muslims, providing annual stipends whose sizes depended on each person's rank in the community. Thus each of the Prophet's widows, at the head of the list, received 12,000 dinars; most Helpers and Emigrants got 3,000; and those Meccans who had held out until Muhammad's conquest of their city got 2,000.

THE FIRST CIVIL WAR

Under Uthman, the *ummah* underwent increasing strains that culminated in Islam's First Civil War (*fitnah*, literally "trial" or "testing," as by fire, also connoting sedition, straying from the right path, or temptation). Most accounts have attributed much of the problem to Uthman's weak leadership, although in some ways the opposite is true, for this third caliph attempted to tighten up the loose, sometimes almost negligible, control of Madina over the *amsar*. Weakness in leadership seemed apparent in his reliance on members of his Umayyad clan to fill top positions. It was not that there was so much objection to nepotism per se. Rather it was the fact that these were the very people who had persecuted the Prophet for such a long time that was so galling to the Madinans. Governors who tried to counter the centrifugal forces made many enemies for the caliph in the *amsar*. Terminated officials, particularly

Amr, the dismissed governor in Egypt, became embittered. On the other hand, the loyalty that Mu'awiyyah gained among the Arab tribes in Syria made that province a bastion of the Umayyad clan. There was also much criticism of Uthman's alleged arbitrariness when he established a standard version of the Qur'an and ordered those copies with minor variations burned. Although some writers have portrayed Uthman as too busy reading the Qur'an to govern, there was also opposition to his government becuase it seemed to have strayed from Muhammad's example. Ali, in particular, was emerging as a focus of pious dissatisfaction.

The underlying problem had little to do with Uthman's qualities. The quantity of booty, even with continuing expansion, could not equal the riches that had so quickly fallen into Arab hands during the first conquests. In addition, ever growing numbers of tribespeople, including former Apostates, were settling in the *amsar* and decreasing the slice of the pie for those who won these territories and considered them rightfully their own.

With Madina already wracked by disturbances, five hundred people from Fustat came to the capital to present their grievances. Taking Uthman at his word, the petitioners believed that he had given in to them. But on their return to Egypt, they discovered they had been betrayed and that punishment awaited them. Returning to Madina, a small group broke into the unprotected home of the caliph and thrust a dagger into his back as he was praying. For the first time, internecine bloodshed threatened to tear the *ummah* apart.

Although accused of complicity in Uthman's murder, Ali succeeded to the caliphate. But he met violent opposition, including, for personal reasons, that of some of Muhammad's closest companions and Uthman's most avid opponents. Two Emigrants, Talhah and Zubayr, returned to Mecca to establish an opposition movement. There they joined forces with A'ishah, who demonstrated a violent hatred for her stepson-in-law, perhaps dating back to an earlier time when he was receptive to an accusation that she had been unfaithful to her husband. From Mecca, the three proceeded to Basrah with a small party, while Ali, in what turned out to be the end of Madina as the capital of the Islamic state, moved to Kufah. Ali's forces met the rebels outside Basrah in 656 and crushed them in the Battle of the Camel, named for A'ishah's presence inside a curtained litter on the back of a camel at the center of the fight. Talhah and Zubayr, as well as many of their followers, died in this clash, while A'ishah received Ali's forgiveness.

Ali's greatest threat came from Syria, where Mu'awiyyah remained in control and demanded punishment for his uncle's murder. Ali led troops toward Syria, and the two armies met on the Euphrates at Siffin. After months of facing each other, the two sides began to battle, and Ali's forces seemed to be prevailing. But on the clever suggestion of Amr, who had now become one of the leading Umayyad supporters, Mu'awiyyah saved the day by having his soldiers march toward the enemy with pages from the Qur'an attached to their lances. In effect, Ali's opponent was asking him to allow the question of leadership to be arbitrated on the basis of the principles of the Qur'an. Ali had misgivings, as he had nothing to gain and would only undermine his own authority by putting himself on par with a rebel. But some of the caliph's pious supporters fell for the scheme. With each side choosing a member of the arbitral tribunal, Ali went along with the spirit of the agreement and chose an impartial man. Mu'awiyyah stacked the cards in his own favor by picking his friend Amr. Although there are varied accounts of the details of the arbitration, that which comes through clearly is Amr's success in duping his colleague into agreeing that both Ali and Mu'awiyyah were unfit for the caliphate. But after they announced that Ali was deposed, Amr reneged on the part of the agreement relating to Mu'awiyyah.

Seeing what had happened, Ali rejected the decision. But the balance of opinion was clearly shifting in his opponent's favor. Ali had lost the support both of those who opposed arbitration and of those who thought that he was obligated to accept the decision. Mu'awiyyah immediately extended his territorial base, as Amr reconquered Egypt for him.

Ali's acceptance of arbitration had met bitter rejection from one group of his supporters. These tribespeople, who came to be known as Kharijites ("seceders"), withdrew from his camp and proclaimed themselves the only true Muslims. Ali sent a force to defeat them, but the *ummah* would hear from these fiercely egalitarian Muslim purists again and again as they proclaimed the necessity of making war on— that is, directing *jihad* against—the alleged pseudo-Muslims. A Kharijite avenged the massacre of members of his rebellious sect by assassinating Ali in 661, a year after the conclave of Mu'awiyyah's troops had proclaimed their leader to be the new caliph. Now Mu'awiyyah proceeded to gain control of the Islamic domains. The Kufans accepted Ali's son Hasan as the new caliph, but he was interested in his own personal pleasure far more than in politics and gladly accepted Mu'awiyyah's offer of a handsome pension in return for withdrawing his claim.

Although the First Civil War was over, its imprint never faded. Aside from the Kharijites (who have become extinct except for a few from their most moderate branch, mainly in Oman), the Islamic world continues even today to be divided into two main sects, the Sunnis or Sunnites[3] (as the majority of Muslims later became known) and diverse groups of Shi'ites (Shi'is) or followers of the party (Shi'ah) of Ali. Differences later took on other dimensions, but although there is no longer a caliph (and few give much thought to restoring the office), the issue of succession remains the main theoretical problem. The Sunnites came to accept the principle of a caliph "elected" from the Quraysh tribe, whereas the Shi'ites believe in a succession of hereditary leaders starting with Ali. The Kharijites say that no caliph is necessary, but that if one is to be chosen, lineage is irrelevant—that "even an African slave" may qualify.

MU'AWIYYAH AND
THE UMAYYAD DYNASTY

From a later perspective, the accession of Mu'awiyyah to the caliphate marked a sharp turn in the life of the *ummah*. No longer was the person in command one of

---

[3] The full name is "People of Custom (*Sunnah*) and Community."

Muhammad's close associates, as the first four (so-called *Rashidun,* "Rightly Guided") caliphs had been. In their place were Muhammad's longstanding enemies, the sincerity of whose conversion was suspect. The seat of government was now located in a sophisticated ancient center of civilization, Damascus, instead of in simple Madina. The Rightly Guided caliphs had been the epitome of unpretentiousness; Abu Bakr, for example, continued for several months to go to the marketplace. But now this simplicity gave way to pomp and splendor befitting successors of emperors and shahs. Instead of personal ties of freedom-loving tribespeople to the chief of their "supertribe," who was only the first among equals, an elaborate bureaucracy emerged. The mainstay of the regime was now the Arab tribes of Syria, including those whose residence there had predated Islam. Other provinces became virtual subjects of Syria and, especially in the case of Iraq, the government was able to keep control largely through force. Some of the Syrian Arabs were still Christians, and they and other Christians often enjoyed high positions in the government. For pious Muslims, the godly order seemed to be giving way to a secular state, or as the accusation went, there was no longer a caliphate but merely a "kingdom."

Mu'awiyyah started an Umayyad dynasty whose rule would last nine decades. Admittedly, hereditary succession remained a matter of practice rather than a normative principle, and for a while the scions of the Umayyad house had rivals for succession. Only with the coming in the 680s of another branch of the Umayyads, the Marwanids, did the fact of a dynasty become clear. The theory of "election" by the leaders of the *ummah* continued to persist in Sunni Islam, but Mu'awiyyah made this a legal fiction when long before his death he cajoled the notables to accept his son Yazid as his successor. This precedent would be followed again and again.

During his nineteen-year reign, Mu'awiyyah kept the *ummah* on a steady course. The manner in which he induced Hasan to give up his claims is characteristic of the caliph's pragmatic dealing with all former or potential opponents. Known for his adeptness at using persuasion whenever possible and coercion only as a last resort, Mu'awiyyah demonstrated his mastery of the art of government. A corps of skillful and loyal provincial governors included Amr in Egypt and Ziyad ibn Abi Sufyan for Kufah and Basrah (and the eastern half of the empire generally). Many people knew the latter, because of his illegitimate birth, simply as "Ziyad, the Son of His Father," but he was glad to trade his support for recognition as the caliph's half-brother. With a large measure of harshness, Ziyad prevented the resurgence of opposition in Iraq and kept his half of the empire stable.

Under Mu'awiyyah, Muslim armies moved on to still more conquests. From Egypt, Amr sent forces deep into North Africa. They established a base at Qayrawan (in Tunisia) and Arab forces reached the Atlantic Ocean in 682, although a subsequent Berber revolt temporarily pushed them back. While the First Civil War had brought the temporary loss of eastern Iran, Ziyad sent forces east as far as the Oxus. Each summer, Islamic armies launched an expedition against Anatolia, but they made no long-term conquests in the high Anatolian country (the "Land of Rome," as it came to be known). On the sea the Arab fleet temporarily occupied Crete and Rhodes, as well as bases in the Straits near Constantinople. Two campaigns sent against the Roman capital nearly succeeded, first from a base established just across the Bosporus in

668–669 and again in the form of annual expeditions during 674–680 from a point on the Sea of Marmara. On the latter occasion, "Greek fire," a newly invented form of petroleum that burned on water, held back the would-be conquerors.

THE SECOND CIVIL WAR
AND THE MARWANIDS

Mu'awiyyah's death in 680 brought new disorder, the Second Civil War of Islam. Ali's second son, Husayn, rushed from the Hijaz to Kufah to lead his father's old supporters. But deserted by the fear-ridden Kufans, Husayn and his small band of followers were massacred outside the city at a place called Karbala. Husayn's severed head was sent triumphantly to Damascus. But instead of being the end of the Shi'ite movement, the martyrdom of Husayn—perhaps comparable to the Crucifixion for Christians—marked the real beginning. It became an event that evoked continuous calls for revenge, rallying the downtrodden against those in power, although until the late twentieth century the Shi'ite religious establishment tended to portray it as evidence that revolt is futile and thus to bolster the status quo. To this day, Husayn's grave at Karbala remains a holy spot for Shi'ites, who mourn the martyrdom with passion plays and ceremonies of self-flagellation, while Mu'awiyyah's son, the evil caliph Yazid, remains the symbol of tyranny.

In the short run, a bigger challenge to the Umayyads emerged in the Hijaz, led by Abdullah, the son of Zubayr. Umayyad forces besieged Mecca, where Abdullah set up his headquarters, but the death of Yazid in 682 (and then of his teenage son), brought a crisis of succession that gave Abdullah's challenge a new lease on life. The army was ready to recognize him as caliph, but only if he would move his capital to Damascus, which he was unwilling to do. Although later tradition labeled him the "anti-caliph," he at one point gained acclaim everywhere except in Syria.

Then a new Umayyad candidate came to the fore. This was Marwan, from another branch of the clan. The Marwanids were able to provide an uninterrupted succession of rulers until 750. The first challenge met by Marwan was in Syria, where the tribes that once had united in support of the Umayyads now formed two rival groups, the Qays and the Kalb, labeled respectively as "northern" and "southern" Arabian in origin. The Qays, backers of Abdullah, met defeat by the pro-Marwanid Kalb in 684. Once established in Syria, the new caliph soon also gained control over Egypt, but his death left the task of conquering the rest of the empire to his successor, Abd al-Malik. To complicate the picture, a man named Mukhtar emerged in Kufah as the leader of a new Shi'ite movement, proclaiming his revolt in the name of Muhammad ibn al-Hanafiyyah, a son of Ali (but not by Fatimah, and thus not the Prophet's grandson).

With Ali's son acclaimed as the Mahdi—that is, the "guided one" who would establish justice—the movement took on messianic tones and drew support from new, non-Arab converts who sought equality in an Arab-dominateed *ummah*. Some Shi'ites, called *Ghulat* ("exaggerators") by their opponents, accepted the concept of a succession of rightful *imams* possessing divine qualities. Although Abdullah's supporters in Basrah suppressed Mukhtar's revolt in 687, it nevertheless became another important part of Shi'ite tradition. For a while, claimants to the caliphate had to deal with Kharijites and other rebels, but then Abd al-Malik sent an army headed by a former schoolteacher, the brutal Hajjaj, to the Hijaz. After a seven-month siege during which Abd al-Malik's troops bombarded Mecca with catapults and destroyed the Ka'bah, Hajjaj captured the city and killed Abdullah in 692.

Abd al-Malik, who ruled for twenty years (until 705), eventually restored order to the Islamic lands. A newly established postal service enabled the ruler's will to emanate quickly to the empire's four corners. A unified, Arabicized bureaucracy emerged, and what the late Marshall Hodgson has called the "High Caliphate" replaced the more primitive earlier government. Abd al-Malik's success was a consequence of his reliance on Hajjaj, whom he named governor of rebellion-wracked Iraq after his success in the Hijaz. Appearing in the Kufah mosque incognito, the new governor removed his mask and issued blood-curdling threats against anyone who might think of opposing him. Indeed, 120,000 people were executed at his command. He established his headquarters at a place called Wasit (literally, "Middle"), halfway between Kufah and Basrah, in order to be close enough to both places to suppress any rebellion. Ruling with an iron hand throughout the east, he snuffed out rebellions of Kharijites and others, and all who opposed him succumbed to his reign of terror. At the same time, Hajjaj directed his military leaders eastward, while in Iraq he devoted attention to restoring agricultural productivity. Never forgetting his teaching days, he still had time to make some permanent improvements in the Arabic alphabet.

The reigns of the early Marwanids (including Abd al-Malik and four of his sons) brought the borders of the Arab kingdom to its farthest limits. Except for the survival of Roman Anatolia and the failure of another Arab attempt to take Constantinople in 716–717, the conquerors swept up everything before them. One of Hajjaj's generals, Qutaybah ibn Muslim, penetrated deep into Central Asia to Turkish lands that had adopted Buddhism and had come under the suzerainty of an expanding Chinese empire ruled by the T'ang dynasty. The realm of Islam reached the Jaxartes, and Arab armies came into contact with the Chinese. Many wars ensued with the Turkish tribes of Central Asia and their relatives west of the Caspian, the eventually Judaized Khazars.[4] Another Arab force occupied Sind, the Indus region of the Indian subcontinent.

From Qayrawan a general named Musa ibn Nusayr reached the Atlantic again. Now the pagan Berbers, whose tribal organization and culture were reminiscent of the pre-Islamic Arabs, rapidly accepted the religion of their conquerors and gave Islamic expansionism in the far west a new lease on life. In 711 one of Musa's subordinates, a freedman named Tariq, crossed to what has since been known as Jabal ("the mountain of") Tariq, corrupted in European languages to "Gibraltar," and the

---

[4]There has been much speculation, especially by twentieth-century opponents of Zionism, that the European Jews today are primarily of Khazar origin. It is unlikely that this can ever be proved or disproved.

Visigothic-dominated Iberian Peninsula (which the Arabs called al-Andalus, "the land of the Vandals") quickly fell under the caliph's rule. Before long, the Arabs had crossed the Pyrenées to occupy parts of France for a few years. The minor defeat (not the great decisive battle so often imagined) by the Frankish Charles Martel in 732 near Tours and Poitiers, not far from Paris, marks the farthest extent of raids by the Islamic East into Europe's western flank, after which the tide slowly receded.

RIVAL VISIONS OF THE NEW EAST

Among the several issues that began to tear the *ummah* apart, the greatest one was, in effect, whether this was to be an Arab or an Islamic state. Should the Arabs as an ethnic group be the dominant caste, or should all Muslims, Arab and non-Arab alike, fill this role? The equality of Believers is a prime postulate of Islam, and yet many people seemingly took for granted that the faith was revealed especially for the Arabs. Although the Muslims forcibly converted pagan Arab tribes, the People of the Book, a term that eventually proved broad enough to include most religions, were allowed to keep their faiths. When non-Arabs embraced Islam, they had to attach themselves to Arab tribes as Clients (*mawali;* singular, *mawla*), just as individuals, particularly freedmen, had come under the protection of a tribe in pre-Islamic times.

During the Umayyad period, the Clients generally failed to gain equal status with the Arab Muslims. This is part of the reason for the charge that the Umayyad caliphate was merely an "Arab kingdom." On the other hand, ethnic discrimination was far from complete, for while some Arabs failed to attain elite status, the Persian aristocracy quickly and opportunistically converted to Islam and joined the new ruling class. And although the Arab conquerors tried to stay in the *amsar,* apart from the conquered population, the line of separation began to blur as some Arabs acquired large estates (officially leased from the state) and as Clients began to settle in the *amsar* and to outnumber the Arabs.

Also, new converts could gain the same exemptions from the land tax that Arabs enjoyed, a situation that began to deprive the state of important revenue. It was the caliph Abd al-Malik and his viceroy, Hajjaj, who took action to stem this development by forcing the Clients back from the *amsar* to the land and by requiring continuous payment of the land tax after conversion, although the Clients remained exempt from the *jizyah.* In effect, the government was discouraging conversion. Only with the accession of Umar II (717–720), whose piety sets him apart from the other members of his dynasty, was an attempt made to remedy this situation. Umar II again exempted the Clients from payment of the land tax, but with the provision that transferring land to a nontaxable status could not occur after the Islamic year 100 (A.D. 719). He also entered the names of Client soldiers in the *diwan* to allow them to draw pensions. The corollary to this policy was the application of previously neglected restrictions on the *dhimmis* (protected people, that is, non-Muslims), such as requiring distinctive clothing, banning the construction of new houses of worship, and forbidding them to ride horses (rules that were rarely enforced during Islamic history). But while the forces of assimilation were irresistible in the long run, little of Umar's policy of nondiscrimination against Clients outlasted his short reign.

Most of the later Marwanids gained a reputation for a moral degeneration that put pious Muslims to shame. One caliph is said to have swum in a pool of wine, but the obvious exaggeration that he drank enough to lower noticeably the level of the pool so strains credibility that one is warned not to take all the polemical accounts of later anti-Umayyad historians too seriously. In any case, devout people doubted whether their rulers were Muslims at all.

Conflict between rival Arab tribes helped to tear the state apart. Described in terms of particular tribes and clans, such as the Qays and the Kalb in Syria, belonging to the northern (Adnani) and southern (Qahtani or Yemeni) groupings respectively (see Chapter 1), the rivalry has conventionally been understood simply in terms of mutual prejudice. But some modern scholars believe that profound ideological issues were at stake, with the alliance actually cutting across the southern-northern division. A recent writer, M. A. Shaban (whose ideas admittedly have not convinced most scholars), maintains that the so-called southern tribes were those who were established in the conquered territories, who developed roots in these lands, who resented the continuing wars of expansion that disrupted their lives, and who wanted to merge with the non-Arab Muslims population and allow the Islamic identity to predominate. The northern Arabs, as this theory goes, were simply newcomers who supported expansion and who wanted to keep themselves apart from the local people. Whichever the case, successive Marwanid caliphs were unable to stay above the fray and aligned themselves with one group or the other, with the northern tribes favored at the end.

The Alid party (that is, supporters of Ali's line) became a focus for pious opposition to the Umayyads. Clients increasingly rallied to Alid banners, and partly as a result of resentment against Syrian domination, Iraq remained a Shi'ite stronghold. Separate Alid movements initiated sporadic revolts as various descendants of Ali or other relatives of the Prophet claimed to be the "designated" one. Thus one of Husayn's grandsons, Zayd, rose in 740 in Kufah, and his short-lived revolt began a subsect of the Shi'ah, the one nearest to the Sunnite position, that lives on today in Yemen. The majority of the later Shi'ites accepted a line of *imams* that included Muhammad al-Baqir (brother of Zayd) and his son Ja'far al-Sadiq. Of more immediate importance was the so-called Hashimite movement of Abu Hashim, son and successor to Muhammad ibn al-Hanafiyyah. And by stretching the legitimist concept a little, members of the Abbasid house (descendents of Muhammad's uncle, Abbas) also began to claim the right to lead the *ummah*. One Abbasid reported that Abu Hashim had willed his rights to him, and so this family, which could also invoke the prestige of membership in the Hashimite clan, now took up the leadership of the opposition to the Umayyads. A secret organization came into being in Kufah (ca. 718) and sent missionaries to spread the party's propaganda in all directions. Propagandists stationed at strategic points on caravan routes were able to reach large audiences. The greatest success came in Khurasan.

When the twenty-year reign of Caliph Hisham ended in 743, the Islamic world found itself in a Third Civil War. Rebellion was rampant, with peoples such as Berbers and Copts rising up at different times. Conflict within the Syrian army and palace coups within the Marwanid house undermined the foundations of the regime. A Shi'ite revolt flared in Iraq and western Iran. As ever, Kharijites proved to be a thorn in the side of the established order.

When the Abbasids sent a former Persian slave, the awe-inspiring, austere Abu Muslim, as their representative to Khurasan in 746, the condition of the Islamic world was rapidly coming to a head. A man of mysterious origin, Abu Muslim was uniquely qualified to unite different Arab tribes and Iranian Clients. A capable, ruthless general, he led them to victory over the disintegrating regime that even the relatively able Marwan II, who took the helm in 744, could not save. In 747, before an assembly of his supporters near Marv, Abu Muslim unrolled the black flag that became the symbol of the Abbasid movement. Having started as the Prophet's standard, the black banner had been used by various rebel movements. It now conveyed an eschatological sort of symbolism. The Ummayads yielded to the ever-increasing numbers rallying behind Abu Muslim throughout the east. Kufah fell to the advancing force in 749, and there the latest scion of the Abbasid house, Abu al-Abbas (who was nicknamed al-Saffah, "the Bloodletter"), was proclaimed caliph in the Great Mosque. A battle fought on the Great Zab, a river in northern Iraq, left the way to Syria open to the new claimant, and in the spring of 750, the end came to the Umayyads as Damascus fell and the members of the family fled, with nearly invariable futility, from the exterminating hands of the new regime. The last Umayyad caliph to sit in Damascus was caught and killed in Egypt, while the graves of his predecessors, Umar II's being a notable exception, were desecrated.

BIRTH OF A CIVILIZATION

The Arabs' unification of the Middle East and lands beyond left many facets of life largely unaffected. The peasant majority might at times have hardly known that their rulers had changed, although the taxes generally were less oppressive than before. The people in conquered territories were governed by their bishops or, in Iran, by *dihqans* (nobles), with Arabs replacing only the top echelons of the old empires. The man that Heraclius had appointed as governor of Damascus still held the post under Mu'awiyyah and, although remaining a Christian, became the head of financial matters for the empire. The bureaucracy long continued to be non-Arab, and it was not until the reign of Abd al-Malik that Arabic became the administrative language. Neither did an Islamic currency replace Roman and Sassanian coins until the time of Abd al-Malik. There were as yet mere beginnings of a two-pronged process of Islamization and Arabicization. Only gradually did a new civilization emerge, a synthesis of ancient Middle Eastern and Hellenistic heritages, with Islam—itself a synthesis of Jewish, Christian, and Arabian traditions—providing the unifying element. However important in providing building blocks, the older Aramaic, Coptic, and even Pahlavi incarnations of Eastern civilization—above the folk level of culture—were far too weak as a whole to rival the newly rising structure.

Starting from the architectural barrenness of pre-Islamic Arabia, the new faith developed its own styles, which emulated and rivaled Hellenistic and Persian patterns. The mosque became a vehicle of Islamic architectural distinctiveness. The courtyard of Muhammad's house in Madina, where the faithful lined up to perform their rituals of kneeling and prostration before God, became a model for numerous crude mosques in the *amsar;* these soon made way for monumental buildings. Besides being places of worship, mosques also served as schools where children began their training by reading and memorizing the Qur'an.

By Marwanid times there was the dazzling splendor of such structures as the Umayyad Mosque (formerly the Cathedral of St. John the Baptist and even earlier a pagan temple) in Damascus and the Dome of the Rock, built over the stone on which—according to Muslim beliefs—an angel will stand while blowing the last trumpet at the Resurrection and from which Muhammad ascended into Heaven. Both this and al-Aqsa Mosque are parts of the Haram al-Sharif in Jerusalem. In each, the *qiblah* (direction of prayer) was marked by a semicircular niche in the wall, the *mihrab,* while other characteristic features included the high *minbar* ("pulpit"), whose steps a preacher ascended to deliver the Friday noon sermon, and the high tower (*minarah,* "minaret") above the mosque, from which a *muezzin* announced the time of prayer five times each day. Thus came into existence some of the permanent features of mosque architecture.

There were already other splendid architectural achievements. Examples included the Umayyad Palace in Damascus and the many "hunting lodges" scattered over the desert. Fine frescoes decorated the walls of secular buildings, but the likenesses of human and animal figures were avoided in mosques, although such prohibitions do not seem to have become fixed in Islamic doctrine at first.

Busy with conquests and inhibited by restraints against continuing pagan tradition, the Arab were slow to make new literary contributions. The Qur'an so overwhelmed one poet, Labid, that he decided to give up his vocation and indeed lived thirty more years without composing another verse. Although poetry was suspect in Islamic eyes, some poets devoted their talents to the Prophet's cause even during his lifetime. Recitations of poetry sometimes rallied the Arab conquerors before battles. During the Umayyad period, several schools of poetry flourished. Some followed the *Jahiliyyah* tradition, while others modified these forms. Poets such as the Christian bedouin, al-Akhtal, Abd al-Malik's poet laureate who allegedly appeared in his patron's presence wearing a large gold cross and with wine dripping from his beard, exemplify the secular, irreverent trends, as do many writers of verses glorifying drink and free love. At least one poet dared to compare Paradise unfavorably with earthly pleasure. Love lyrics began to abound in Mecca, whose reputation for wine and dancing women exasperated pious Muslims. Love ballads flourished, and those of Qays ibn al-Mulawwah (Majnun, "the Demented"), who described his insanity as coming from unrequited love for a woman named Layla, would be repeated in the literature of many Islamic languages.

Rudimentary beginnings of Arabic prose literature appeared. Early writings on the life of the Prophet, commentaries on the Qur'an, and histories of the conquests have disappeared, except insofar as later authors quoted them. A special body of literature was developing in the form of stories (*hadiths;* literally "news reports") about the life and sayings of the Prophet. Each story included a chain (*isnad*) of oral transmitters (telling who heard it from whom, and so on).

As Islamic concepts of a legal system inseparable from religion later matured, *hadiths* were to be accepted as the basis of the *sunnah* (practice; literally, "trodden path") of the Prophet, a body of rules second in authority only to the Qur'an. Indeed, pious Muslims already looked to *hadiths* as guides to ideal behavior, and there was a faction, the People of Hadith (Traditionalists), that demanded their systematic use. But modern scholarship demonstrates that Islamic law (the *shari'ah*, "the Way," originally meaning, "the path to a water hole") was then still rudimentary. Judges (*qadis*) appointed by the Umayyads' provincial governors enforced some distinctively Islamic rules, such as the few found in the Qur'an. Otherwise, they relied on caliphal decrees, personal judgment (*ra'y*, "opinion"), local or tribal custom, and rules borrowed from Sassanian, Roman, Jewish, or Christian law. Such judicial practice contributed to the content of Islamic law in its later form. By the late Umayyad period, groups of pious legal scholars in cities such as Madina and Kufah—the "ancient schools of law"—were developing their own concepts. But this had little to do with judicial practice, although the tendency for rulers to appoint religious specialists as judges already had some beginnings. The ancient schools called their extra-Qur'anic body of rules "the *sunnah* of the Prophet," but theirs was a "living tradition" without any real attempt to base it on *hadiths.*

Partly resulting from the staying power of Hellenism, the beginnings of theological debate were visible. Contact with such Christian leaders as St. John of Damascus, an influential person in the Umayyad court, was commonplace. And avid, seemingly friendly religious disputes with these Christians led Muslims to think about new questions. Apparently influenced by the Hellenic concept of *Logos,* Muslims always referred to the Qur'an as the "Word" of God.

An early debate among Muslims centered around whether a person who commits a major sin can be considered a Muslim at all. In response to the Kharijites' "no," a more moderate theological school, the Murji'ites, said that only God could make such a judgment. This was a question of great political relevance, since a decision that the Umayyads, who were so obviously sinful, were not Muslims would mean that their rule was illegitimate.

A third theological position, first associated with a devout preacher and judge, Hasan al-Basri, and then with a group known as the Mu'tazilites, held that sinners who professed Islam occupied an intermediate position between true believers and complete unbelievers. Another Mu'tazilite doctrine borrowed from Hasan was that of free will, a rejection of other Muslims' belief that God directs all human acts. This and other Mu'tazilite doctrines would later take on great significance during an age of more intense Hellenic impact.

CONCLUSIONS

As the Roman and Sassanian empires fought each other to exhaustion, events in little-noticed Mecca made way for a new religious, political, and cultural order for the Middle East and much of the world. With their new faith enabling them to make a long-lasting transformation, Semitic tribes from Arabia again overran and renewed the civilization of the area. The conquerors did not immediately create a new civilization, but they provided a thread that would tie together diverse elements of ancient Middle Eastern civilizations and some aspects of the Hellenism whose encroachment they repelled.

The new Muslim state's conquest of the Sassanian Empire and its expulsion of the Romans from all Eastern lands except Anatolia allowed it to resume the career of the Achaemenids, which decay and Hellenic conquest had interrupted for more than a millennium. Now again, the reincarnated East was on the offensive against the remaining Roman lands and had extended westward, via North Africa, as far as France and eastward to occupy part of India and to border on China. The Arabic language assumed more successfully the ancient role of Aramaic as the *lingua franca,* and Islam began to displace Christianity and Zoroastrianism, providing the region with its first overall religious unity. The dichotomy between East and West would thereafter coincide at least roughly with a Muslim-Christian confrontation.

Even as it spread, the Islamic community underwent a series of internal crises that threatened its existence. The Abbasid Revolution now promised to resolve the problems. Whether or not it would succeed, the new civilization was on the threshold of maturity. Admittedly, as William McNeill points out, the absolute primacy that the Middle East had enjoyed before 500 B.C. was not destined to reappear. Possibly more than Islam, T'ang China inherited the mantle of creativity that Hellenism and Gupta India had successively held. But for a while the reborn Middle East would have no other real rival in either the politico-military or the cultural sphere.

3

the east florescent
750–1260

The Abbasid Revolution inaugurated a new era for the Islamic world. The classical period of Islam emerged in full splendor at a time when Christian Europe was in the "Dark Ages." Paradoxically, the only real center of European, if somewhat Orientalized, civilization was largely in the Middle East in a Roman (Byzantine) Empire that conquests by Arabs and others had reduced mainly to Balkan and Anatolian territories. And the only civilization of consequence in western Europe was a Middle Eastern one, in Spain. For centuries, the civilization of the Middle East dazzled the world, particularly Europe.

Even though the unity of the Islamic world would give way to political fragmentation, the florescence of Islam was to increase. Geographic expansion—military, religious, and cultural—gained periodic momentum on several fronts. But the century following 750, when the descendants of Abbas—caliphs such as al-Saffah (749–754), Mansur (754–775), Mahdi (775–785), Hadi (785–786), Harun al-Rashid (786–809), Amin (809–813), Ma'mun (813–833), Mu'tasim (833–842), Wathiq (842–847), and Mutawakkil (847–861)—still effectively ruled much of the Atlantic-to-China region, was always to be regarded as a Golden Age.

THE ABBASID REGIME

Completing the process that was already apparent under the Marwanids, the Islamic state no longer remained the simple, unpretentious, and in some ways democratic regime of the early caliphate. It had now assimilated the autocratic patterns of earlier civilized Middle Eastern—and Western—empires. A burgeoning bureaucracy of clerks (*katibs*), organized in separate bureaus (*diwans*) and supervised by the vizier (*wazir,* "prime minister"), carried out the ruler's will. Exalted caliphs bore titles such as "the shadow of God on Earth" and "caliph of God," rather than, as before, merely "caliph of the Prophet of God." (Admittedly, a few scholars recently have argued that the shortened title, "caliph of God" with its more absolutist implications, gained some currency at an early date.)

Posing as the executor of God's eternal law, and seeking the support of the religious scholars (*ulama*) and the pious in general, the new rulers in effect claimed divine right. The Abbasids were not more devout than their predecessors, for they had their share of drunkards and worse, but their hypocrisy quotient was higher, as was their reliance on brute force (exemplified by the executioner), when their claim to religious authority failed to suffice.

SHIFT TO THE EAST

Some earlier writers often represented the Abbasid Revolution as the displacement of Arab by Persian dominance, but this is at best a half-truth. The Abbasid family based its privileged status on its place in the Arab Hashimite clan alongside the Prophet. Often mothered by non-Arab slaves, the Abbasid caliphs might have less and less Arab blood in their veins, but in a patrilineal society that did not matter much.

The Abbasids brought the Iranians and other non-Arabs fully into the Islamic fold. The core of the army became the Khurasanian guard, which consisted of both Persians and Arabs who had settled in Khurasan. Persians filled high posts in the government. One Central Asian Persian family in particular, the aristocratic Barmakids, was at the center of the power structure in the early Abbasid period, beginning with Khalid ibn al-Barmak, al-Saffah's secretary, and continuing with a series of Barmakid viziers. This family finally lost favor during the reign of Harun, who catapulted Ja'far, the then-prominent scion of the house, from the vizierate into the hands of the executioner. One could only expect such a demise for anyone whose power potentially threatened the position of an autocrat. Although the Barmakids never regained influence, other Persians continued to be important.

Persian ways began to predominate at the court. From wines to high cone-shaped hats, the Arabs emulated the sophistication of an older civilization. A literary movement known as the Shu'ubiyyah ("of the peoples"), which flourished especially among the Persians but also among the other non-Arabs, flaunted these peoples' allegedly superior heritage. Also, during the late eighth century some important Persian officials who technically were Muslims held Manichaean doctrines and attacked

Islam. But, while Zoroastrians were treated as one of the People of the Book, those accused of being *zindiqs* (Manichaeans) faced severe persecution. The term came to mean heretics in general.

The Abbasid Revolution ended Syria's role as the center of the Islamic empire. The capital was henceforth in Iraq, first at Kufah or nearby and then, starting during Mansur's reign, in the newly established "City of Peace," always better known as Baghdad. Located where the Tigris and Euphrates come close together and in the vicinity of Ctesiphon (and the even earlier Babylon), the new capital was made defensible by the two rivers and a network of canals. These waterways also provided an intersection for waterborne commerce that extended eastward to China and for the overland traffic that connected the Mediterranean with regions farther east. With the move of the capital, the Islamic empire's orientation was to be away from the old Roman lands, and it appeared more as a new incarnation of its Sassanian and Achaemenid predecessors.

Baghdad was perhaps the greatest city of its age. Enclosed by a double round wall, its main part centered around the caliph's palace; other royal residences were built outside the walls. On four sides, gates opened to the highways over which the caliph's postal system connected the empire to the capital.

Military expansionism decreased, although war with the Byzantines sputtered on from time to time. Dramatic success for an Islamic offensive occurred under Harun's generalship during the reign of Mahdi, but that proved to be temporary. Harun's army reached the Bosporus but withdrew in return for payment of tribute. An offensive during Harun's reign brought Muslim troops deep into Anatolia, but it ended in the same way. Sometimes the Romans invaded parts of Syria, and sometimes the Muslims temporarily penetrated Anatolia. With their string of fortifications, a frontier society of *ghazis* ("warriors for the faith") and their Christian counterparts on the other side alternated between friendly contact and warfare for centuries, but no more major shifts in the border occurred until the late eleventh century.

THE ECONOMIC FOUNDATION

A flourishing economy provided the basis for the imposing civilization of early Abbasid times. Trade was not limited to the usual luxury items. There was a wide variety of industries, such as Egyptian linens, Syrian and Iraqi silk, and paper from Samarkand; these and agricultural products, such as Egyptian grain and Iraqi dates, found their way to many parts of the Islamic world and beyond. A merchant class gained importance; a banking system evolved, with the use of checks (significantly, a word of Arabic origin) and letters of credit. Urbanization was on the upsurge. Political unity facilitated trade, which continued after the gradual breakup of caliphal power. The flow of gold from Nubia and the western Sudan (which includes such present-day states as Mali and Niger) gave a boost to the Middle Eastern economy, but also brought a rise in prices.

Trade with other areas was of major importance. The concurrent flowering of T'ang China allowed the two regions to reinforce each other's prosperity. Chinese ships sailed to Baghdad, and there were Middle Eastern merchant settlements in eastern China. Besides sea traffic, caravans carried goods along the ancient Silk Road, and major Middle Eastern–Indian trade also followed both land and sea routes. Recent studies have pointed to the extent the Islamic world helped transform the way of life of its own people and of the whole Mediterranean region (and beyond) by introducing crops such as cotton, rice, and citrus fruits from southern and eastern Asia. Trade with sub-Saharan Africa was especially vigorous, with gold and slaves exchanged for a variety of Middle Eastern goods.

Despite sporadic warfare, there was much trade with Byzantium. Christian western Europe, however, long remained a dark, unknown region. Still, there was some overland traffic across Russia as far as the Baltic region, partly through Jewish intermediaries, with Europeans exporting Slavic slaves to the Middle East.

SOCIAL DIVISIONS

As in other civilizations, social classes developed in the Islamic world. Various medieval writers offered their own classifications. Sometimes they divided society into people of the pen, people of the sword, people of negotiation (including merchants and artisans), and people of husbandry, but these divisions are largely of a vertical nature rather than representing purely horizontal strata. Another medieval writer speaks of four categories, ranging from the ruler to the cultured middle class, and dismisses all the rest as "mere scum." Others speak of the ruling elite and the masses, with the latter term including everyone from vagabonds to rich merchants. Some writers specify that a function of government is to keep the classes in their places.

Using modern terminology, we might warily divide medieval society into upper, middle, and lower classes. Starting with the latter, the bulk of the population of course tilled the soil, as in all premodern societies except in nomadic areas. In early Abbasid times, the peasants tended to own their own land, but landlordism later became more common, with the person furnishing only labor typically getting a fifth of the crops and with another fifth going to the provider of each of the following: land, animals, seed, and water.

Islamic law and practice—although this in part is a later development—allow for several types of ownership of the soil, including *miri* land, which the state technically owns but with particular individuals having the right to cultivate it. This was the most widespread pattern, at least in later periods, as far as agricultural land was concerned. In what is called the *musha* system (common only in some areas), the families of a village redistribute the various strips of land from year to year. Then there are endowments administered for charitable or other purposes (i.e., *waqfs*). Finally, there is strictly private—that is, freehold—land (*mulk*), which, at least in post-Abbasid times, mostly was limited to orchards and such. However, even when the state held the formal title to the land, the cultivator possessed a hereditary, salable right to it (that is, usufruct) that in some ways was analogous to ownership. And people had the right to use their village pasture land.

Most nomads, even those belonging to "noble" tribes, would have to be grouped generally with peasants in the lower classes, as would most craft workers, who were often organized in guilds, at least during the latter part of this period. In an altogether different category were the beggars, persons performing disreputable jobs (e.g., usurers), criminals, and others at the bottom of urban society.

At the opposite extreme was the small upper class, which might be defined as including the ruling families, high officials in the government, tribal elites, and leading establishment-oriented *ulama,* as well as wealthy merchants and large landholders. Power, wealth, family antecedents, religious learning, and other matters were marks of upper-class status from the perspective of those possessing each one. But social scientists who have defined the premodern upper strata in terms of power (which also led to wealth) are basically correct.

Besides the central ruling class, there were always the "notables," including *ulama,* merchants, and heads of traditionally prominent families on a local level. Such people not only had their mass followings but also acted as intermediaries— "patrons" obtaining favors for their "clients" and in turn making it possible for the rulers to rule—between the masses and the central elite. But, when the central government was weak, the notables tended to become independent rulers.

There was a wide gulf between the luxurious life of a few and the meager existence of the many. However, relative to other preindustrial societies, a commercial middle class was fairly large in early Abbasid times, and the term "middle classes" might also describe the bulk of government officials and *ulama.* Aside from their low ranking by medieval writers with a ruling-class bias, some artisans and shopkeepers would seem to fit properly in the middle classes, and even some medieval classifications deemed them "respectable."

In contrast with the caste systems of other areas and sometimes of the pre-Islamic Middle East, there was in theory no barrier to social mobility. Perhaps this was one concrete result of Islam's emphasis of the equality of Believers, distinguished only by degrees of piety. And indeed this theory converged with the reality of political instability to bring many individuals from the bottom of society to the top, while others lost their privileged positions. Aside from the prestige of descendants of the Prophet, called *sayyids* or *sharifs,* no hereditary aristocracy emerged.

Slavery was widespread, and although slaves were inherently at the bottom of society, it has already become apparent that slavery was often a road to ruling-class status. Aside from those purchased for training as soldiers, slaves were used mainly as domestic servants and were treated as subordinate members of the family. They sometimes were able to purchase their freedom. Despite notable exceptions, slaves were rarely used in agriculture or other labor on a large scale.

There were slaves of all races, but one important source was sub-Saharan Africa. Prejudice against both Nordic and Negroid racial features was always discernible, but Islamic society has possibly been the least race-conscious of any in history. No kind of racial segregation ever existed in the Islamic world, and blacks have tended to melt into the general population rather than to be singled out as a distinct ethnic group. Historically, members of the most prestigious families tended to have slave mothers, African or otherwise.

Religious divisions overshadowed racial ones. We have already described the Islamic pattern of autonomy for *dhimmis*. Living under their own law, their position contrasted with the widespread persecution of religious minorities in the Christian world, even in the few instances in which Islamic governments made an effort to apply the most overt discriminatory rules that existed in theory. *Dhimmis* had their own law and courts and could worship freely, although they were second-class citizens in some ways. For example, in case of conflict between a *dhimmi* and a Muslim, the law of the latter prevailed, Christians and Jews, however, often held high positions in the society and government.

A pattern of male supremacy is one of the best-known aspects of the Middle East. Even here, a comparison with other nonmodern societies—with such practices as Hindu suttee (the death of a widow on her husband's funeral pyre) and Chinese foot binding—may put the matter in a different perspective. Some aspects of Islamic practice were drawn from Sassanian and Byzantine customs. Feminists would applaud some of the rights of women in Islamic society; for example, women keep their maiden names after marriage, and Islamic law gives them the right to own property and to keep control of it. But polygamy (although the exception in practice), the seclusion of women in the harem (private, literally "forbidden" quarters of the house), and the largely urban practice of veiling (i.e., covering the face) have been important aspects of Islamic culture. The face covering is an example of a sometimes strongly entrenched custom that goes beyond the requirement that women cover their heads, exposing only hands and faces in public. (However, the Arabic word, *hijab,* which describes the required covering, often is translated as "veil" even when it does not include a face cover, thus causing some confusion in the West.) Men's almost exclusively one-sided right to divorce their wives at will is another characteristic of Islamic law. However, Islamic law and practice require each man to provide a dowry to his bride. Sometimes she does not get the whole amount at the time of marriage, in which case an additional amount is reserved for payment if her husband divorces her; the prospect of such a financial loss may constitute an important inhibition to terminating the union. While Islam guarantees many rights to a woman, such as inheriting half as much as her brother's share (a radical reform when first instituted), the Islamic heritage is such that calls for sexual equality have been a key part of modern reform movements.

THE SHI'ITE OPPOSITION

The Shi'ites who helped bring the Abbasids to power soon experienced intense disillusionment. The Shi'ites had expected a descendant of Ali to ascend the throne and were not impressed with the Abbasids' claims to rule. Understandably, the divergent intentions of the anti-Umayyad coalition now came into the open. Abu Salama, a leader of the Abbasid Revolution who insisted on an Alid caliph, was soon executed, and Abu Muslim's turn was not long in coming. Early Abbasid caliphs often saw the Alids as a threat and sometimes harshly suppressed them. The Alid proclivities of Kufah were a main reason for building the new capital at Baghdad. Ma'mun was an exception; he designated Ali al-Rida, the eighth recognized Shi'ite *imam,* descended from Ali, as his successor. But the non-Shi'ite majority was horrified, and so he eventually gave up the idea.

Shi'ite doctrines crystallized during the early Abbasid period. The earlier vague concept of succession belonging to Ali's descendants (or even his relatives' descendants) gave way to a recognized line of *imams.* (Shi'ites have tended to emphasize this title but also use the term caliph.) Thus all Shi'ites came to agree on a common list of four successors to the Prophet, that is, Ali, Hasan, Husayn, and Ali Zayn al-Abidin.

But the name of the rightful fifth *imam* is a matter of contention. A few, known as Zaydis and eventually concentrating in Yemen, recognized Zayd and a subsequent line of *imams* who are theoretically elected from among the descendants of the Prophet. Among Shi'ites, the Zaydis' doctrines of the imamate come closest to Sunnism.

Most Shi'ites recognized Zayd's brother Muhammad al-Baqir as the fifth and Ja'far al-Sadiq as the sixth *imam.* From here on, another division occurred, as Ja'far outlived his designated successor, wine-imbibing Isma'il. One group, which came to be known as Isma'ilis (or Seveners), insisted that Isma'il and his son belonged next in line (as sixth and seventh respectively, since Ali in this case is given an even more exalted title and not considered one of the *imams*). The other group accepted another son of Ja'far and a line that ends with the twelfth *imam,* Muhammad al-Muntazar ("the Expected One"). This subsect, which is now dominant in Iran and southern Iraq (as well as in much of Lebanon), is known as the Twelvers, Ja'faris, or Imamis.

Acceptance of these men as *imams* does not mean that they actually ruled or even necessarily aspired to do so. Some of them were politically inactive, but from a Shi'ite point of view, they were the rightful rulers. The moderate Zaydis apart, Shi'ites attribute a far more exalted role to the *imam,* who is deemed infallible, than do Sunni Muslims to their caliph.

Shi'ites (again excepting Zaydis) share an emphasis on messianism. Twelvers believe that the twelfth *imam*—or the Absent Imam—disappeared in 874 but ultimately will return as the Mahdi, who will restore justice to the world. Twelvers believe that he was in touch with his community during the first phase of the Absence, which ended in 941. Isma'ilis hold that their seventh *imam* became invisible to all but a few of his purest followers and that he or, in the doctrine of most factions, one of his descendants will emerge (or already has emerged) as the Mahdi. Both Isma'ilis and Twelvers agree that the universe could not exist without an *imam.* They also accept the principle of *taqiyyah* ("dissimulation"); that is, that it is permissible to deny one's real beliefs if necessary.

The Isma'ilis adopted other distinctive ideas. There was a hierarchy of missionaries (*da'is*) engaged in propagating an elaborate view of history, with the Mahdi to provide the climax. In addition to the apparent meaning of the Qur'an, Isma'ilis developed the doctrine that a hidden, allegorical meaning awaited discovery by the few. Some extreme Isma'ilis place the *imam* higher than the Prophet or deify Ali, but they are not typical.

DEVELOPMENT OF ISLAMIC LAW

The Islamic system of jurisprudence (*fiqh*) took shape during the early Abbasid period. As it eventually developed, this body of law, called the *shari'ah* ("the Way" or "Path"), is considered to be God's eternal set of rules, and governs all aspects of a pious Muslim's life. Rules require or forbid certain acts; other kinds of behavior are merely recommended or are declared reprehensible but still permitted (divorce is an example). The law even expresses its indifference in some matters. The *shari'ah* includes everything from criminal law to rules of worship, and some rules are not even theoretically enforceable by governments. The degree to which rulers applied the *shari'ah* has varied from field to field. The constitutional rules (qualifications for the caliphate, etc.) rarely limited powerful rulers; however, the law of personal status (marriage, divorce, inheritance, and charitable endowments or *waqfs*) has generally been a relatively sacrosanct area. Even in matters of personal status, local custom (*adah*) sometimes prevails over the *shari'ah*. But from an Islamic point of view, the *shari'ah* is always the ideal, true law.

Islamic jurisprudence generally—and especially the Sunnite version—came to recognize four main sources of law (roots of jurisprudence). The Qur'an is the most authoritative, but it provides only a handful of legal rules. Second comes the *sunnah* (tradition), a body of rules based on the *hadith*s (reports) of the Prophets (the *hadith*s as such do not constitute a separate source of jurisprudence), whose words and actions Muslims accept as having provided an ideal human model. One may derive rules not explicitly stated in the Qur'an or the *sunnah* through the use of *qiyas* (analogical reasoning), which is the third source of law. For instance, the Qur'an forbids drinking wine. Why? Because it causes one to be intoxicated. By analogy, any substance that intoxicates must also be forbidden. Finally, whatever the Islamic community—in practice, the *ulama,* although arguably others should participate in the process too—agrees on must be right; this is the principle of *ijma* (consensus), the name for the fourth source of jurisprudence (and one that is not clearly subordinate to the others, for only through consensus can the Qur'an itself be interpreted or the content of the *sunnah* established). There has never been anything comparable to a church council in Islam, for Islam has no church; no formal organization distinct from the state, no sacraments that require priests, and in fact no priests, for any Muslim can perform such religious tasks as leading prayer. *Ijma* could only emerge informally (somewhat like, say, modern scientific opinion), and its failure to attain universality—this is not a matter of proponents of any position simply being in the majority—within the Islamic community on important points provides the basis for sectarianism. A possible fifth source of law, personal judgment (*ra'y*), which was so important for early Islamic judges, came to be rejected by Sunnis or else restricted to a minor role under other names, such as the public interest (*maslahah*).

At least two factors in the early Abbasid period brought this concept of law into the form just described. First, the Abbasid posture as a truly religious state required the appointment of specialists in religious law as judges, which enabled a theoretical body of law to take on the character, at least to a large extent, of positive law almost for the first time. But as the previous chapter shows, the concepts of the ancient schools of law during the Umayyad period were quite unsystematic. The second factor in the development of the law was the contribution of a jurist, Muhammad ibn-Idris al-Shafi'i, who died in 820. Al-Shafi'i's stress on the necessity of basing the entire *sunnah* strictly on *hadiths* (often collectively called "the *Hadith*") meticulously documented by uninterrupted chains (*isnads*) of authorities going back to the Prophet eventually won out over less rigorous practices.

To a large extent (at least in the opinion of some modern Western scholars, whose views, however, Muslims often see as denigrating to Islam), this meant finding *hadiths* to support a body of rules that had already evolved in the "ancient schools." There was no shortage of *hadiths,* as anyone wanting to push particular views on any matter could invent a story and a spurious *isnad.* This required the development of a whole science of *hadiths,* with scholars separating the weak from the sound. Since the character of the people in the *isnad* was the key factor in evaluation, scholars put great emphasis on collecting biographical information. Collections of *hadiths* came into existence; of six main ones accepted by the Sunni Muslims, those compiled by two ninth-century scholars, Bukhari and Muslim, are of special significance. Often described as canonical, they (not the Qur'an, the "Word of God") are the rough equivalent of the Christian Gospels.

Sunni Islam came to be divided into so-called schools (*madhhabs*) of law. This reflects the fact that consensus did not develop on some minor points except in the sense that everyone agreed, in effect, that the disagreements were unimportant and accepted one another's ideas as orthodox. There are even some disagreements within each school, and it would be inaccurate to describe the separate schools as subsects. One of the schools—the Shafi'ite—was founded by al-Shafi'i and predominates today in Lower Egypt, much of the Red Sea region, and Southeast Asia. The Hanafite school, which is dominant in the Indian subcontinent, all Sunni Turkish areas, and parts of the Fertile Crescent, is not only the most widespread but also the most liberal in its use of the roots of jurisprudence, even giving a limited role to personal judgment. Both the Hanafites and the Malikites, the group found in most Islamic parts of the African continent (including Upper Egypt), grew out of earlier legal schools after taking over al-Shafi'i's emphasis on *hadiths.* The most strictly *hadith*-minded school is that of the Hanbalites, founded in the ninth century by the zealous Ahmad ibn-Hanbal. It rejected the validity of *ijma* except for that of the Prophet's generation (later extended to the first three centuries) and at first disfavored the principle of *qiyas.* The Hanbalites' strict opposition to theological speculation made them much more than just another school of jurisprudence. Lacking official backing, the Hanbalite school later almost disappeared, but sponsorship by the Sa'udi family, which embraced the strict "Wahhabi" movement, gave it a new lease on life in Central Arabia during the eighteenth century.

Much the same is true of the Shi'ites. The *sunnahs* of the various Shi'ite sub-sects differ from the Sunni *sunnah* in only a few details. For example, sanction for temporary marriage—from one day to ninety-nine years—is perhaps the most unusual feature of Twelver Shi'ite law. A distinctive feature of the Shi'ite theory of law is that no *hadith* is valid unless one of the recognized *imams* is included in the *isnad.* Since the *imams* are infallible as a source of law, the principle of *ijma* became relevant only after the disappearance of the Twelfth Imam, and Shi'ites have never emphasized it as much as have Sunnites. Also, most Shi'ites (the Zaydis are an exception) reject *qiyas* in favor of an at least theoretically less restrictive principle, the use of "intellect" (*aql*).

Originally a flexible body of law, the *shari'ah* gradually took on a rigid character. Until the tenth century, religious scholars claimed the right to exercise *ijtihad* (literally, "striving" for the truth), which meant a continuous rethinking of the rules. A learned Muslim might choose to reinterpret a *hadith* or a passage in the Qur'an or to apply analogy in a different way, and a new *ijma* could conceivably evolve as jurists come to see issues in the light of new circumstances. But gradually the idea took hold that the "door of *ijtihad*" was closed, cracked open only for a "relative *ijtihad*" on minor points. Now the principle of *taqlid* ("imitation") prevailed; that is, whatever issues early Muslims scholars agreed on could not be reopened.

Perhaps this was a necessary means for the *ulama* to resist future pressure from tyrants to exercise *ijtihad* arbitrarily, but a law that could not evolve with the times later came to be blamed by Islamic modernists for inhibiting progress. This may be a case of backward looking that points to the waning creativity and ultimate decline of Islamic civilization. Admittedly, Shi'ite legal theory continued to recognize a few *mujtahids* ("ones practicing *ijtihad*"); and Hanbalites, such as the fourteenth-century Damascene scholar Ibn Taymiyyah, being less restricted by existing *ijma,* asserted the same right. But this did not make much difference in practice.

There continued to be some development in the *shari'ah* on points where no previous consensus existed, as legal authorities known as *muftis* responded to individual inquiries in the form of *fatwas*. Sometimes attached to courts, *muftis* provided decisions on points of law, which judges applied to the cases in question. Also, sometimes there has been a resort to tricks (*hiyal,* literally "devices") to enable the letter of the law to be followed while effectively evading its spirit in matters such as the rule against usury.

DECLINE OF CALIPHAL POWER: THE MAMLUKS

Long before Islamic legal institutions fully evolved, the actual power of the caliphs had begun to wane. The unified Islamic realm split apart as local dynasties sprang up in province after province. At the same time, army commanders became the real rulers in the capital itself.

To begin with the latter phenomenon, important changes emerged in the composition of the army. Of unexcelled military proclivity, Turkish tribespeople from the Eurasian steppes appeared as an alternative to Khurasani troops. For the next thousand years one of the most important phenomena in Islamic history would be Turks as soldiers—and as rulers. Later they came in as tribes, but the predominance of Turks in the Islamic army originated in another, equally enduring form.

Such soldiers, particularly Turks during the Abbasid period but also including members of the other ethnic groups, were known as *mamluks.* Literally, this means "those who are owned," that is, slaves. Boys were bought in the slave markets of the steppes, given military training and simultaneously Islamized, and then freed. Having lost their ties with their own kin, such children developed intense familial loyalty to those who became their first masters and then their patrons. The recruitment of slaves as troops was not unusual in itself; what was unique in the Islamic world is that, over the centuries, *mamluks* became generals, usurped power, and continued to recruit more *mamluks,* some of whom would also rise to the top and perpetuate the process. A military oligarchy of slave origin thus recurrently took hold of the Islamic world.

While we hear of Turkish troops early in the Abbasid caliphate, the beginning of *mamluk* predominance came during the reign of Mu'tasim. His newly established 60,000-soldier *mamluk* force, loyal to him alone, provided an unsurpassed means of control over the empire. But to the populace of the capital, the *mamluks* were crude and overbearing, so much so that in 836 Mu'tasim moved the seat of government sixty miles northward to the newly established Samarra. While Baghdad remained the cultural center, the caliphs and their *mamluks* remained at a distance for over half a century.

Even during the Samarra period, the *mamluks,* sometimes in league with a caliph's slave mother, began to take control. Throughout the late ninth and early tenth centuries, caliph after caliph was assassinated or deposed by the Turkish troops. Attempts to balance the Turks with *mamluks* of other ethnic backgrounds and to play them off against one another failed to restore caliphal authority. The real rulers continued to give largely figurehead caliphs recognition by having their names mentioned in the Friday prayers and struck on coins. Even this honor was shared with the *mamluk* general who held the title of commander of commanders beginning in 936. Anarchy prevailed as the various *mamluk* commanders struggled for supremacy.

THE BREAKUP OF ISLAMIC POLITICAL UNITY

By the mid-tenth century, the central government's power did not extend far from the capital. Taking advantage of the difficulty of controlling such a vast empire, opportunistic commanders set themselves up as de facto rulers, usually acknowledging the formal authority of and being officially accredited by the caliph, and began their own dynasties.

The breakup of Islamic political unity dates back to the Abbasid Revolution, for Spain never came under the sway of the new regime. A young Umayyad prince, Abd al-Rahman, fled from the Abbasids. After a harrowing five-year trek, he reached Spain and rapidly gained the support of Syrian Arab troops there. This was the beginning of an independent Umayyad amirate that rejected even the titular authority of Baghdad. Beginning in 929, these Umayyad rulers assumed the title of caliph. One of the most dynamic regions of Islamic civilization, Muslim Spain later split into numerous small states and sometimes came under the control of North African dynasties. Although the last Muslim kingdom in Spain finally succumbed in 1492, with the Muslim population eventually expelled or forcibly Christianized, indelible Arab imprints have remained on the Spanish and Portuguese languages and cultures.

In the face of Berber separatism, sometimes Kharijite-inspired, Abbasid control over the Maghreb proved tenuous and short-lived. In part of Algeria a local dynasty, the Rustamids, asserted its independence in 761. Fleeing after the failure of his rebellion in Madina, Idris ibn-Abdullah set up a Shi'ite dynasty in Morocco in 789 that would survive for two centuries. The region between Morocco and Egypt—then known simply as *Ifriqiyyah* (Africa) and centering on Qayrawan—gained de facto independence under the Aghlabid dynasty, starting with the governor sent by Harun in 800. The Aghlabids, who lasted until 909, dominated the western Mediterranean and even extended the realm of Islam by conquering Sicily and other islands.

BREAKUP IN THE EAST

Closer to Baghdad, numerous rebellions threatened the new Abbasid order from the beginning. Several extreme Shi'ite movements, sometimes with Iranian national overtones, were suppressed. The Ibadis, a highly moderate Kharijite subsect, established themselves during the late 700s in Oman, where they remain today.

Violent conflict sometimes raged within the Abbasid house. The most notable case of this was a Fourth Islamic Civil War, between two of Harun's sons. Harun left the caliphate to the degenerate, weak Amin, with the able half-Persian Ma'mun in Khurasan in charge of the eastern part of the empire and designated as his brother's ultimate successor. Amin broke the agreement in 810 and named his own son as his successor. But Ma'mun's forces, commanded by the Persian general Tahir, pushed back all the armies that Amin could send. After a year-long siege in which Amin's loyal followers endured severe hardships and the city suffered greatly from catapults and "Greek fire," Baghdad finally succumbed to Tahir's army, and Ma'mun became the new caliph. Again, during Ma'mun's pro-Shi'ite period, a rival Abbasid claimant was proclaimed caliph in Baghdad, and two years passed before Ma'mun's forces restored control in 819.

With Ma'mun belatedly moving his residence from Khurasan back to Baghdad, the east began to assert its independence. Appointed governor of Khurasan in 821, Tahir founded a separate dynasty that did not always bother to give the caliph formal recognition. In the late ninth century, the Tahirids made way for another Per-

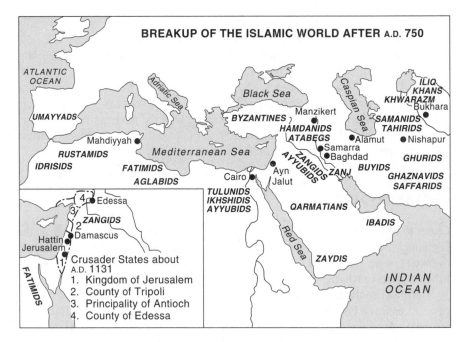

BREAKUP OF THE ISLAMIC WORLD AFTER A.D. 750

ATLANTIC OCEAN

Adriatic Sea

Black Sea

Caspian Sea

ILIQ KHANS

KHWARAZM

Bukhara

UMAYYADS

BYZANTINES

Manzikert

SAMANIDS

TAHIRIDS

Mahdiyyah

Mediterranean Sea

HAMDANIDS

ATABEGS

Alamut

Nishapur

RUSTAMIDS

Samarra

Baghdad

GHURIDS

IDRISIDS

FATIMIDS

AGLABIDS

Cairo

ZANGIDS

AYYUBIDS

Ayn Jalut

ZANJ

BUYIDS

GHAZNAVIDS

SAFFARIDS

TULUNIDS
IKHSHIDIS
AYYUBIDS

QARMATIANS

IBADIS

4 Edessa

Red Sea

ZAYDIS

INDIAN OCEAN

3

2 ZANGIDS

Damascus

Hattin

Jerusalem

1

Crusader States about
A.D. 1131
1. Kingdom of Jerusalem
2. County of Tripoli
3. Principality of Antioch
4. County of Edessa

FATIMIDS

MAP 5

sian dynasty, the Saffarids, founded by a popular brigand, Ya'qub ibn al-Saffar ("the coppersmith"). Then Iranian particularism reached a high point under the Samanid dynasty, named for an ancestor of Nasr I, who established his rule over all of Transoxania in the late ninth century. The Samanids ruled from Bukhara as amirs under the titular authority of the Abbasid caliph. Relying heavily on Turkish *mamluk* troops whose source was close at hand, the Samanids united most of eastern Iran under their control by the mid-tenth century to form one of the Islamic world's most powerful and culturally brilliant states.

REVOLUTIONARY MOVEMENTS IN THE EAST

Heterodox parties challenged Baghdad's power in Iraq and Arabia during the late ninth and early tenth centuries. A fierce revolt that espoused Kharijite doctrines and brought the deaths of perhaps a half million people occurred in southern Iraq and spread to adjacent parts of Iran from 870 to 883. This movement found its main following among the largely East African (Zanj) slaves, who had suffered harsh treatment in that region, but it also drew some Arab support. Its leader was an Iranian, Ali ibn-Muhammad, supposedly a descendant of Ali. Protection by almost impenetrable marshes made the Zanj rebels seem nearly invincible. At one point they captured and looted Basrah and came close to Baghdad. They committed merciless massacres and received similar treatment at the hands of Abbasid forces that finally overcame them.

Soon it was the turn of a new Isma'ili movement called the Qarmatians ("Carmathians") after its founder, the Iraqi Hamdan Qarmat. As was the case with other Isma'ili movements, a network of missionaries carried their message far and wide. Drawing support from bedouin tribes and idealistic young people from the cities who aspired to end injustice, the Qarmatians were initiated into an exclusive society and an early kind of welfare state that enabled their enemies and later historians to portray them inaccurately as communists who shared all property and (even more ludicrous) wives. Organized in the Syrian desert at the end of the ninth century, the Qarmatians raided the Fertile Crescent lands for several years before being suppressed. Another Qarmatian movement appeared on the Persian Gulf coast of the Arabian Peninsula, where a "republic" came into existence in the region then called Bahrayn, now al-Hasa. They invaded or raided much of Arabia, snatching the black stone away from Mecca at one point, and no one managed fully to uproot them until the eleventh century.

Among other heterodox regimes, a Zaydi state emerged in Yemen in 897. Another dynasty that eventually adopted Shi'ism was the Hamdanids, of bedouin origin, who established themselves in northern Iraq in 890 and later conquered northern Syria. Ruling from Aleppo after 944, the Hamdanids vigorously resisted Roman offensives that sometimes penetrated far into Syria, and they also provided a flourishing center of civilization.

Claiming Sassanian descent, the Persian Twelver Shi'ite Buyids established their rule in the early tenth century in the rugged region south of the Caspian. After expanding into other parts of western Iran, they took Baghdad in 945, thus ending whatever power the *mamluk*-surrounded caliphs could sporadically exercise. Ruling from Shiraz, the Buyids pragmatically chose not to abolish the figurehead Abbasid caliphs. They preferred instead to be the real power as "commander of commanders" and eventually adopted the Old Persian title "king of kings." After all, one implication of the doctrine of the Absent Imam is that one should not bother with even trying to establish a truly legitimate regime before his return. The Buyids split into several branches ruling different areas well before the end of the century. They also increasingly relied on and then were dominated by *mamluk* troops.

EGYPT AND THE FATIMIDS

A series of separatist dynasties gained control of Egypt. The process began when the caliph sent a Turkish *mamluk* general, Ahmad ibn-Tulun, to Fustat in 868. Ibn-Tulun soon quit sending tax revenues to Samarra and thereafter hardly paid more than the usual formal allegiance to the Abbasids. Soon adding Syria to their patrimony, ibn-Tulun and his descendants ruled a prosperous, powerful, and culturally florescent amirate with an army of African and Turkish *mamluks* until 905, when Baghdad restored its control.

Another Turkish *mamluk* general, Muhammad ibn-Tughj, repeated ibn-Tulun's defiance of the caliphate in 935. This was the beginning of a short-lived regime known as the Ikhshidis, so-called from the Persian title awarded by the caliph. In reality, a black African general named Abu al-Misk Kafur ruled the Ikhshidi domain (including Syria and Hijaz most of the time), first as regent and finally assuming the formal title, from Muhammad ibn-Tughj's death in 946 until Egypt fell to the armies of a rising North African power, the Fatimids, in 969.

Established in Tunisia as a new caliphate rivaling the Abbasids, the Fatimids had deep roots in the Isma'ili movement. The dynasty began with one who later took the name al-Mahdi, a claimant to descent from the seventh Isma'ili *imam,* and the dynasty itself acquired the name Fatimid after his ancestress, Fatimah, wife of Ali and daughter of the Prophet. After extensive propaganda activity in various parts of the Islamic world, his chief missionary went to North Africa and rapidly gained support among Berbers. After this preparation, al-Mahdi left his headquarters in Syria and made a perilous trek to North Africa. By 909, he had taken over the Aghlabid territories and established his capital near Qayrawan. The Qarmatians seemingly accepted the Fatimids' nominal authority at first, and sporadically thereafter, despite the latter's moderate, pragmatic policies.

The Fatimids soon became the dominant power throughout North Africa. Their great military leader, the Sicilian ex-Christian *mamluk* Jawhar, overran Egypt in 969 and ended Ikhshidi rule. The Fatimid capital moved to the newly acquired land and to a new city named al-Qahirah ("the Victorious," corrupted to "Cairo" in Western languages).

Cairo became the greatest Islamic city and the center of possibly the most powerful state in the Islamic world. Egypt's agricultural wealth combined with an upsurge of commerce that now extended to western Europe, with the country's fabrics and other exports, as well as the Egyptian route between the oceans, achieving renewed prominence. Cairo was now the center of a great ideological movement, with the chief missionary one of the top officials in the government and with the newly established al-Azhar Mosque-University training a missionary army. Paradoxically, the regime normally also was highly tolerant of other religions and apparently never made any serious dent in the overwhelmingly Sunni character of the population.

An old process repeated itself as the Fatimid state began to decline by the eleventh century. Weak rulers lost control to the heterogeneous *mamluk* forces, whose various ethnic elements, particularly blacks, Turks, and Berbers, vied for supremacy.

The Fatimid caliph al-Hakim (996–1021) proved to be one of the most unusual monarchs of any dynasty. His capriciousness extended to banning honey and grapes. He alternately put *dhimmis* in high positions and then, in violation of Islamic law, persecuted them. He even ordered the destruction of the Church of the Holy Sepulchre but later rebuilt it. He remained an ally of Constantinople all the while. No one ever found out what happened after he suddenly rode a mule into the desert, although one man later proudly claimed to have killed him. Contrary to conventional accounts, al-Hakim may not actually have proclaimed himself an incarnation of God (a highly un-Islamic concept). But the Druzes, a small sect that emerged in Syria, accept his alleged divine status even today.

TURKISH DYNASTIES
AND THE SUNNI UPSURGE

Contact with the Samanids had brought about the conversion of Central Asian Turks to Sunni Islam. By the eleventh century, Turkish dynasties began to champion the Sunni cause and to reverse the previous Shi'ite tide.

The first Turkish dynasty, the Ghaznavids (from their capital, Ghaznah, in Afghanistan) was founded by a *mamluk* named Alptigin in the service of the Samanids. The Ghaznavids displaced the Samanids in most of their territories except in Transoxania, where another Turkish dynasty, the Ilek-Khans, took over. The third member of the Ghaznavid dynasty, Mahmud of Ghaznah (998–1030), conquered large parts of northern India, much of which thus was permanently Islamized, and he raided and plundered even farther. The caliph awarded Mahmud such titles as "ghazi" and "sultan" ("the one with power"), henceforth a common designation for independent rulers who paid formal obeisance to a caliph.

It fell to other Turkish tribes, led by the house of Saljuq, to unite most of southwest Asia in the name of Sunnism and the Abbasid caliph. Known from the name of one of their ancestors, the new dynasty displaced the Ilek-Khans and moved south in 1040 to vanquish the armies of the Ghaznavids, whose rule afterward survived only in Afghanistan and India. In 1055 the Saljuq Tughril Beg entered Baghdad and liberated the caliph from the Buyids. Recognized as "sultan" and "king of East and West," Tughril restored control after a Buyid army returned to establish the short-lived nominal authority of the Fatimids in Baghdad. On an intellectual level, the Saljuq championship of Sunnism soon involved the establishment of institutions of higher education, called *madrasahs,* in cities such as Baghdad and Nishapur. While this was the beginning of a widespread kind of university, these in particular acquired the designation *Nizamiyyahs* after the name of Sultan Alp Arslan's and his successor, Sultan Malikshah's, brilliant Persian vizier, Nizam al-Mulk, who was mainly responsible for them.

In 1071, Alp Arslan achieved a success that matched that of the Ghaznavids in India by defeating the Byzantines at the Battle of Manzikert in eastern Anatolia. Already, during the previous thirty years, the Saljuqs had directed the aggressiveness of unruly Turkoman tribes into Anatolia, and parts of the peninsula had come under their control. But only after Manzikert did large-scale Turkish settlement begin, although the subsequent Turkification of what is now the Republic of Turkey (and parts of Iran, including Azarbayjan) probably owes more to assimilation than to immigration. The newcomers did not displace the local population, and non-Chalcedonian Christians such as the Armenians were delighted to have the tolerant Turks replace their former Orthodox master. Indeed, the process of Islamization remained incomplete until the twentieth-century exodus of Greeks and Armenians, while the Muslim Indo-European Kurds still prevail in southeast Anatolia. This westernmost peninsula of geographic Asia, that had been largely Hellenized for a millennium and thus culturally a part of Europe, was being incorporated into the Middle East.

Reaching its height under Sultan Malikshah, the Saljuq empire was divided among rival members of the house after his death in 1092. Of these, the Sultanate of Rum ("Rome"), whose effective independence in Anatolia had already emerged soon after Manzikert, was to play an important role as a link between the Saljuq empire and the later Ottomans. A second branch, centered in Hamadan, in western Iran, long dominated the caliph. Another Saljuq, Sultan Sanjar, prevailed in all the eastern territories.

For a while, Sanjar was able to keep a restive Turkish dynasty, the shahs of Khwarazm, south of the Aral Sea, under control. He also bore the brunt of other Turkish tribes moving westward along the Central Asian steppes. Rebellious Turkish tribes captured Sanjar in 1154, after which the eastern Saljuqs were so weakened that the Khwarazm-shah now took over their territories and became the main power in that region.

In the southwest Saljuq territories, local dynasties proliferated. In most cases nominally headed by Saljuq princes, the real powers in each were usually Turkish freedmen officers known as *atabegs* (literally, "father-lords"). One *atabeg* dynasty that provided the seed for greater things in the future was founded in Mosul by Imad al-Din Zangi in 1127 and soon expanded into northern Syria.

During the late twelfth century, especially after 1194, when the Hamadan-centered Saljuqs succumbed to the Khwarazm-shahs, the Abbasid caliphs were able to assert some real power again. Caliph Nasir (1180–1225) astutely entered into the interdynastic rivalries of the region by playing off various rulers against the Khwarazm-shahs. He also found an effective base of political support in Baghdad in the chivalrous Futuwwah brotherhood, an organization that was widespread in Middle Eastern cities during this period. Aside from his importance as the formal head of Sunni Islam, his political control extended over most of Iraq and some small parts of southwestern Iran. However, in 1216 the Khwarazm-shah Muhammad was preparing to occupy Baghdad and set up a descendant of Ali as caliph. Nasir saved the Abbasid dynasty for a short time but invited its ultimate destruction, which may have been inevitable anyway, by appealing for help from the rising power of Chingiz Khan, whose rumbles could already be heard across the great distance separating Baghdad from Mongolia.

A NEW ISMA'ILI MOVEMENT: THE "ASSASSINS"

In reaction to the firm Sunni order of the Saljuqs, a new Isma'ili movement gained importance at the end of the eleventh century. Led by their chief missionary, the Persian Hasan ibn al-Sabbah, these revolutionaries took control of the impregnable mountain citadel of Alamut, in northwest Iran. From this main base other scattered fortresses in Iran and Syria came under their control. A corps of missionaries spread the doctrine, while trained *fida'iyin* ("self-sacrificers") took the lives of political leaders, beginning with Nizam al-Mulk, who posed a threat to the movement.

Hasan's followers broke with the Fatimids over a question of succession. They are properly called the Nizari Isma'ilis because they accepted Nizar as the rightful Fatimid caliph-*imam* after the death of his father in 1094. But they are better known as *Hashshashin* ("takers of hashish," corrupted in English to "Assassin") as a result of a set of seemingly apocryphal stories about the *fida'iyin*'s being given the drug before their missions.

The Nizari strongholds lasted until the late 1200s. Though eventually losing its original revolutionary character, this branch of Isma'ilism survived as a small minority. Headed by their *imam,* the Agha Khan, most of the members now live in the Indian subcontinent.

WESTERN OFFENSIVE: THE CRUSADES

By the eleventh century, still largely semibarbaric western Europe was flexing its muscles. Venice and other Italian city-states that had grown up in the light of Byzantine civilization were taking over the Muslims' former naval dominance in the Mediterranean. Towns, crafts, and trade were growing in other parts of Europe. Norman adventurers wrested Sicily from Muslim control in 1071. Christians had already retaken about half of the Iberian Peninsula and were slowly pushing the Muslims southward. With Christians responding to calls by their Spanish coreligionists for help, the Latin Christian version of holy war, later known as the Crusades, took form.

Although the rapid breakup of Saljuq unity left the Islamic world vulnerable, Constantinople was too weak to take advantage of the situation. One tactic of the Byzantine emperor was to ask for help from the Latin West. Byzantium and the Far West had little affection for each other, and the break between the Christendom of the remaining imperial territories (the Greek Orthodox) and that led by the pope in the Far West (the Roman Catholic) had been finalized in 1054. Still, the emperor hoped that some knights would enter his service as mercenaries, but the surprising response was so immense that it frightened him.

The western Europeans had their own reasons for marching to Palestine. There had been stories of mistreatment of pilgrims by Turkish rulers. As always, the facts are complicated. Large bands of pilgrims, sometimes heavily armed, had often aroused popular resentment. The Saljuqs had facilitated pilgrimages, but with the breakup of the empire, the visitors often endured a degree of anarchy or else resented paying taxes to every petty prince whose domains they entered. Hakim's destruction of the Church of the Holy Sepulchre was also fresh in some Christian minds, and few understood that this was an aberration and that Muslims, even Hakim himself, had repudiated it.

This was a spiritual age, in which a call to fight for one's faith was compelling. Still, materialistic motives may have been more important, as nobles hoped to find principalities for themselves and as the bored, poverty-ridden masses sought excitement and plunder. Cities such as Venice had an eye on commercial gains in territories conquered by Christendom. The papacy may have hoped to reunify the Church under its authority. In any case, when Pope Urban II called for a crusade in 1095, cries of "It is the will of God" rang out in the conclave and echoed from the British Isles of Italy.

The First Crusade reached Constantinople in 1097. It joined imperial forces in recovering much of Anatolia for Byzantium, although the Sultanate of Rum survived in the interior. As city after city in Syria fell to the crusaders and as the Venetian and Genoese fleets took coastal towns for them, Muslims and Jews were massacred, although the people in the countryside, among whom Christians were still quite numerous, survived and remained a majority in crusader territory. The blood of the Muslim dead in Jerusalem allegedly was ankle deep as the crusaders took control from the Fatimids in 1099, while the small Jewish community was burned alive in the chief synagogue.

Crusader leaders established kingdoms for themselves. Technically owing fealty to Constantinople, a king of Jerusalem ruled a state that included nearly all of Palestine and part of Transjordan all the way to the Gulf of Aqaba. The Counties of Tripoli and Edessa and the Principality of Antioch owed nominal allegiance to Jerusalem.

The uncultured crusaders disgusted both Byzantines and Muslims with their cruelties and their manners. One Arab writer compared them to animals, but they gradually absorbed the refinement of the area, even Middle Eastern food and clothing. Those who returned to Europe may have helped to introduce more cultivated ways there. With Muslim rulers reacting pragmatically from the start, the Latin states also began to enter into alliances with them as their interests dictated, and thus tended gradually to become part of the interstate politics of the area.

Despite their quick victories, the crusaders—or "Franks," as the Muslims indiscriminately called them—scarcely extended their sway beyond the Mediterranean coast. They were never more than a pinprick for the Islamic world as a whole. They could survive only as long as naval domination by the Italian states (which became important intermediaries for the Middle East and Europe) allowed the flow of reinforcements to continue, and as long as no other strong Muslim powers rose to fill the vacuum resulting from Saljuq disintegration.

THE EAST RECOVERING:
ZANGIDS AND AYYUBIDS

By the mid-twelfth century, the Muslim East began to repel the Western intrusion. With his army of Turkish *mamluks* and Kurdish tribes, the *atabeg* Zangi had created the first Muslim state able to confront the Franks. He dealt them a serious blow in 1144 by taking Edessa; some Franks, but not Eastern Christians, were massacred. In response, a Second Crusade was organized, but it ended with the unsuccessful siege of Damascus. By this time, Zangi was dead, and his capable son Nur al-Din, who ruled from Damascus, beleaguered the crusaders. He finished off the County of Edessa and won some victories against the remaining Latin states.

Under the tottering Fatimid dynasty, Egypt provided the vigorous Zangids with a field from which the countercrusade would gain force. The last Egyptian-held enclave on the Palestinian coast fell to the Franks in 1153, and they raided the Nile Delta and exacted tribute. Shawar, a former Fatimid vizier who lost to a rival, took refuge in Syria and sought aid from Nur al-Din.

The Zangid ruler's right-hand man, a Kurdish general named Shirkuh, took an army to Egypt and restored Shawar to power. But the ungrateful Egyptian refused to pay the compensation that he had promised and called on the king of Jerusalem to help get rid of the Syrian army, whose only alternative was to return empty-handed. The crusader-Fatimid alliance also foiled a return campaign to Egypt by Shirkuh. But Shawar implored Nur al-Din to send help again, as the crusaders, who on one occasion carried out an indiscriminate masacre of both Muslims and Copts, again tried to take control of Egypt. This time (in 1169), Shirkuh's strong army assured his success, and the crusaders withdrew from the country. With Shawar beheaded before he could carry out another plot, Shirkuh became the new vizier, but he died two months later. The vizierate passed on to his nephew, Salah al-Din Yusuf ibn-Ayyub (corrupted by Westerners to "Saladin"), a studious, intensely religious young man who had participated ably, if at first reluctantly, in his uncle's three expeditions.

Salah al-Din's leadership of the Islamic world's upsurge was to make his father and the Zangids a mere prelude. For eighteen years he worked to consolidate his position before pursuing the drive against the crusaders. Soon after he became vizier, a joint Frankish-Byzantine expedition descended on Egypt by land and sea. But a shortage of provisions, and finally a storm, put an end to the invasion. Salah al-Din battled occasionally with the crusaders, and his forces repelled a Norman Sicilian naval invasion of Alexandria, but he gave more attention to other matters for several years.

Symbolizing the Sunni restoration, Salah al-Din dropped the name of the figurehead Fatimid caliph from the Friday sermon in 1171 in favor of his Abbasid rival. Aside from *jihad* against the Franks, Salah al-Din's passion was Sunnism, and he strove to let the *shari'ah* guide his government. Following the Saljuq example, he supported the establishment of Sunni *madrasahs* that temporarily replaced al-Azhar, itself later to be transformed into the greatest training ground for Sunni Islam.

The abolition of the Fatimid caliphate was an anticlimactic end for the previous Isma'ili political upsurge. Isma'ilis became a small minority even among Shi'ites. The few who still accepted the leadership of the last Fatimid caliphs soon vanished. Aside from the Nizaris, the main group of Isma'ilis was to be the Tayyibis, who recognized a different branch of the Fatimid family from 1130 on and who survive mainly in Yemen and India as a commercially oriented Bohora ("trader") community.

Salah al-Din was in an anomalous relationship with the Zangids. Egypt was naturally the main base of Muslim power in the eastern Mediterranean region, but he continued to submit to some control from Damascus. The relationship was already tense when Nur al-Din died in 1174, after which several weak members of the Zangid family set up virtually independent states. Salah al-Din had extended his control to the Hijaz, Barqah, and Yemen, while a number of internal threats, ranging from plots to restore the Fatimids to a mutiny of black African troops, were suppressed. From Nur al-Din's death until 1186, Salah al-Din was busy with a series of military campaigns in Syria and northern Iraq that essentially brought the former Zangid territories under his control. Syrian-Egyptian unity created a ring around the crusaders, who were now wracked by internecine conflict as well.

Salah al-Din put diplomacy to work in preparation for the coming battle. Commercial relations with the Italian states enhanced Egyptian prosperity and decreased the crusaders' usefulness to the Italians. A Cairo-Constantinople treaty of 1181 encouraged the growing Byzantine-Frankish breach. Then the crusaders attacked a Muslim caravan in 1187, in violation of a peace treaty concluded two years earlier.

Salah al-Din had been waiting for just such provocation. The war resumed with an immediate blow to the crusader movement. In the Battle of Hattin, in northern Palestine, the Franks suffered severe losses; the 20,000 who survived, including the king of Jerusalem, fell into captivity. Within the next six months, the Muslims took city after city, including Jerusalem. The crusaders retained only a few enclaves on the coast north of Palestine. While not all of his commanders rose above the cruelty expected in this age, Salah al-Din earned a reputation in East and West for magnanimity by freeing thousands of Frankish captives who could not pay the customary ransom. While Frankish settlers fled, the new rules respected indigenous Christians, who sometimes appeared to welcome the change of regime, and the Muslims allowed Jews to settle in Jerusalem again.

Latin Europe, led by its greatest monarchs, responded with a Third Crusade. After a two-year siege, the Frankish forces took Acre, followed by the massacre of 2,700

Muslim prisoners. Then, after this modest achievement, the crusaders were willing to accept a peace settlement in 1192 that limited them to a narrow strip extending from Jaffa to Acre but gave their unarmed pilgrims the right to visit Jerusalem.

From his death in 1193 until the mid-thirteenth century, Salah al-Din was followed by a series of sultans from his family, the Ayyubids. The Syrian part of the empire tended to break up as various Ayyubids established their own principalities. While Egypt was able to maintain a tenuous hegemony for a while, it later lost control.

The Franks even regained some of their earlier position. Although those domiciled in the East seemed to lose their crusading zeal and devoted their energies to internal squabbling, reinforcements renewed the old spirit. In 1219 and 1249 the Fifth and Sixth Crusades struck at the Egyptian Delta with some initial success but got bogged down each time in the floods and networks of canals. In the Sixth Crusade, the army of King Louis IX of France suffered disaster, and the king was captured. (The Fourth Crusade never reached the Islamic lands, as the crusaders diverted their energy to the conquest of Constantinople in 1204.)

Ayyubids sometimes demonstrated pragmatic policies in these matters. Sultan Kamil disgusted the Islamic world in 1229 when he let his alliance with a Holy Roman emperor who agreed not to organize a new crusade induce him to cede Jerusalem and a corridor connecting with Acre to the Franks, who however were hardly a force to contend with a newly unified Egypt and Syria.

EMERGENCE OF THE MAMLUK SULTANATE

The seed of such revised power—and for the end of the Ayyubids—was planted by Sultan Malik al-Salih (1240–1249). Instead of the Ayyubids' previous heavy reliance on Kurdish troops, al-Salih turned to the more traditional basis of an Islamic army, Turkish *mamluks*. The largest group of al-Salih's *mamluks* was stationed on the island of Rawdah in the River (*Bahr*; literally, "sea") Nile; along with their successors, who provided a series of sultans, they were consequently known as the Bahri *mamluks*. It was these soldiers, foremost of whose commanders was Baybars, who defeated King Louis IX in 1250.

Already, a remarkable series of events was bringing the *mamluks* to power. When Malik al-Salih died in 1249, his widow, Shajar al-Dur (a former slave), strove to prevent a struggle for power in the army by keeping the death a secret until the return of his son, Turan Shah, from a military campaign. In the meantime, she managed to rule in the late sultan's name. When the son returned, he soon antagonized the Bahri *mamluks* by showing partiality for other troops. Conniving with Shajar al-Dur, the Bahris murdered Turan Shah and made this woman "sultan." Taunted by a letter from the caliph offering to send a man to rule if none was available in Egypt, the *mamluks* got Shajar to marry one of their commanders, Aybak, who now assumed the sultanate jointly with a six-year-old Ayyubid puppet. But Shajar continued to be in effective charge of the government.

Set afire with jealousy when Aybak decided to take another wife, Shajar had him murdered in his bath in 1257. In turn, she was beaten to death, and another *mamluk* commander, Qutuz, soon became the new ruler.

The so-called Mamluk[1] dynasty thus emerged. In fact, it was not a dynasty, as succession was not mainly hereditary (and sons of *mamluks* were mostly barred from the elite corps), but often emerged from struggles among the army commanders. Following the general pattern begun under the Abbasids, the *mamluk* oligarchy in Cairo perpetuated itself over the centuries through the continuous purchase of slaves.

MUSLIM RECOVERY IN ANATOLIA

The Saljuq sultans of Rum eventually recovered from the blow of the First Crusade and paralleled the Ayyubids' success against Christendom. For a while another Anatolian dynasty, the Danishmendids dominated the sultans, but Sultan Mas'ud asserted his primacy in the remaining Turkish territories of Anatolia by the mid-twelfth century and began to expand at Byzantine expense. When the Second Crusade tried to cross Anatolia in 1147, Turkish forces defeated it. Those who could not afford to continue their journey to Palestine by ship became the recipients of Turkish charity, and some converted to Islam. The last Byzantine attempt to restore control in Anatolia ended in utter failure in 1176.

With subsequent expansion extending its rule over most of Anatolia, the Sultanate of Rum reached its height in the 1220s and 1230s. Its armies defeated crusaders, Khwarazmis, and Ayyubids at different times. The Kingdom of Lesser Armenia, which had emerged in southern Anatolia, came under the sultan's hegemony. However, the incompetent sultans who followed as well as a revolt led by the Turkish chieftain and "prophet" Baba Ishaq, whose suppression in 1240 required great effort, left the state weakened in the face of an emerging threat from Mongolia. But now it is time for us to turn from politics and war to cultural developments.

ISLAMIC CIVILIZATION

The period from the eighth to the thirteenth century was one of cultural florescence. During the early Abbasid period a prosperous empire poured vast amounts of wealth into the capital, and the government lavished it on patronizing artists, writers, and scholars. Then, rather than dimming as the empire fell apart, the light of Islamic civilization glowed brightly and in sundry colors from new centers, as rival dynasties vied with each other culturally and politically.

The early Abbasid period saw a convergence of the world's heritages that enriched a civilization whose core was Islamic and Arab. To take one example, a

---

[1] The word "Mamluk" is capitalized here when it refers to this specific state or regime, but not when it refers to members of the freedman military and ruling class in this and other regimes.

clash of Islamic and Chinese armies in 751 resulted in the capture of Chinese paper makers and the consequent use of paper in the Middle East and the West. Scholars translated Sanskrit mathematical texts into Arabic, while others translated works from Pahlavi. Perhaps the best known was the Persian government official ibn-Muqaffa's version of the book of animal fables called *Kalilah and Dimnah,* which was originally written in Sanskrit. The popular stories that were evolving into *The Thousand and One Nights* also exemplify the diversity of sources, particularly Indian. But no other alien culture had as much of an impact on Islamic civilization as did the Hellenic.

The usual division of fields of intellectual endeavor into "Arab" and "foreign" (primarily Greek, secondarily Indian) sciences epitomizes the two strains in medieval Islam. The "Arab sciences" were those connected with Islam and the Arabic language, of which we have already seen the study of jurisprudence and *hadith.* Aside from theology, which was largely in response to Hellenism, other fields of literature connected with Islam were the commentaries on the Qur'an, including that of the ninth- to tenth-century al-Tabari, or the biographies of the Prophet, such as that of ibn-Hisham. Al-Tabari was perhaps the most important medieval Islamic historian. He is reputed to have written forty pages a day for forty years. The *History of al-Tabari,* which survives only in a condensed version now published in ten large volumes (the now-ongoing English translation will constitute 38 volumes), provides the typical chronological account, mainly of Islamic history, but it also presents divergent versions of the same stories and the author's source for each. Unlike the usual annalists was the tenth-century al-Mas'udi, whose descriptions of different countries, including those in the one surviving fragment called *Meadows of Gold,* has earned him comparison with Herodotus. Conquests, pilgrimages, trade, and the postal service also inspired many writers to produce important geographical works.

Since the study of religion involved an Arabic Qur'an, a body of literature emerged in the related fields of grammar and lexicography. While Arabs were more likely to take their own language for granted, the conversion of Persians gave a special fillip to these studies.

The rules of literary (classical) Arabic took permanent form. The models were the Qur'an and pre-Islamic poetry. Arabic has evolved into many "colloquial" dialects that vary from country to country about as much as Italian differs from Spanish, both of which developed in a similar way from Latin. But the literary language that educated Arabs read and write or use in formal lectures (and which even non-Arab Muslims use as a religious language) is the same everywhere and has not basically changed since early Islamic times.

BELLES-LETTRES

Literature came to be associated with a kind of sophisticated, well-mannered society, particularly that of the high bureaucracy. A refined person (*adib*) was supposed to possess broad knowledge, especially about the Arab heritage and Arabic literature, and to be able to quote from it extensively. The ornate, artistic essays on subjects ranging from animals to the alleged superiority of the black race that came from the pen of the ninth-century Amr al-Jahiz, whose grandfather was a black African slave, set the standard for a kind of literary polish for the *adib* to match. *Adab,* an Arabic word that might originally have been translated as "urbanity," came to mean "literature" or *belles-lettres.*

The Arabic language's endemic genius for poetry reached its zenith at the Abbasid and Hamdanid courts. Freeing themselves from long-lasting rigid conventions developed by what one writer now contemptuously called "bedouin vagabonds," countless poets nevertheless continued their predecessors' tradition of irreverence. There was the part-Persian Abu Nuwas, whom Harun al-Rashid patronized and befriended but sometimes imprisoned. One of Abu Nuwas's hedonistic wine poems proclaimed his unhappiness with ever having to be sober and advocated enjoying as many sins as possible in the belief that God would be forgiving. And there was one nicknamed "al-Mutanabbi" ("the Pretender to be a Prophet," once imprisoned for this light-hearted sacrilege), whose eulogies at the court of the tenth-century Hamdanid ruler, Sayf al-Dawlah, led many Arabs subsequently to deem him to be their greatest poet.

The blind Abu al-Ala al-Ma'ari also received Sayf al-Dawlah's favors for a while but spent most of his life as a recluse and a vegetarian in his small Syrian hometown. Abu al-Ala cynically described the evils of a world into which he resented having been born. He denounced all conventional religion, Islam included, as superstition and sought refuge in a rationalistic concept of God and an ethic of love and compassion. When he failed in an attempt to prove that a mere human could imitate the Qur'an, he insisted that this must be because so many readers had edited it to perfection for centuries.

Rhymed prose became another important Arabic literary medium. In the tenth and eleventh centuries, the pens of the Persian Badi al-Zaman ("the Wonder of the Age") Hamadhani and the Basran Abu Muhammad al-Hariri developed a genre known as *maqamat* ("the assemblies," so-called because the storyteller usually performed before the assembly of men after Friday prayers). In a highly ornate style that tends to make use of linguistic gymnastics, the *maqamat* vividly portray the life of the age as they relate stories of the narrator and a clever, eloquent trickster that he continuously meets during his travels. Some aspects of the *maqamat* exerted a strong influence on works of Italian and Spanish literature, such as *Don Quixote.*

THE HELLENIC IMPACT

The impact of Hellenic civilization on the Islamic world increased after 750. Moving the center of the empire away from the Mediterranean coast did not make Hellenic influence more distant, for it had survived in places far removed from the original source. Nestorian and Monophysite Christians, as well as the pagan "Sabians" in northern Iraq, had absorbed much of Hellenic civilization, and many Greek writings had been translated into Syriac and Pahlavi. Jundi-Shapur, in western Iran, had been a major center of Greek learning (with emphasis on medicine) since Shah Khusraw Nushirwan welcomed the arrival of Nestorian Christian scholars in the sixth century. For that matter, both Indians and Central Asian Buddhists, who had never completely shaken off Alexander's cultural legacy, provided sources of indirect Hellenic influences. This time Greek civilization came, not as before like a blow to moribund ancient Middle Eastern civilizations, but as welcome food for one that was vigorous and self-confident. And just as the ancient East provided the West's spiritual element, the still-glowing coals of the ancient West strengthened the Islamic East's rational, scientific side. Like ancient Jews and Christians, Muslims also struggled with the problem of integrating the two parts.

The first stage, which gained full speed soon after 750, was the translation into Arabic of Greek philosophy—a term used broadly to include fields such as medicine and mathematics. Manuscripts were eagerly sought out, and the "House of Wisdom" in Baghdad stored them and served as a center for translation and instruction. A corps of translators turned Plato, Aristotle, Plotinus, Galen, Claudius Ptolemy, Euclid, and a host of others into Arabic, sometimes directly but mostly from Syriac versions. While indeed Constantinople and the lands it controlled also preserved ancient Greek civilization, much would have disappeared except for the Muslims, and it is paradoxical that the dose of Hellenism that later inspired the western European Renaissance came largely by way of the Islamic world, particularly through Spain.

ISLAMIC SCIENCE AND PHILOSOPHY: CARRYING THE HELLENIC TORCH

Islamic scholars proceeded from translations to original contributions in the Hellenic and Hindu traditions. A few examples of Islamic science will show that this was a high point of creativity, perhaps overshadowed only by the burst of discovery that occurred much later in Europe. Medieval cities such as Baghdad and Cairo had pharmacies and hospitals; and medical researchers, whose religion forbade the dissection of human bodies, sought apes as the best substitute. Among the many medical treatises, those of the eighth- to ninth-century Persian physician al-Razi remained standard texts in western Europe until the sixteenth century. Advances occurred in many fields of mathematics; the word "algebra" is a corruption of part of the title of a book by the ninth-century Iranian mathematician, Muhammad al-Khwarazmi, whose receptivity to the Hindu-invented zero initated the use of "Arabic" numerals in the West. As early as the reign of Ma'mun an observatory existed in Baghdad. Islamic astronomers knew that the earth is round, and another eleventh-century Khwarazmi, al-Biruni, was familiar with the still-disfavored idea that it rotates on its axis. Enjoying the successive patronage of the Samanids and of Mahmud of Ghaznah, al-Biruni also wrote penetrating treatises on many subjects, including Sanskrit philosophy and Indian society.

This was also an age of philosophical writing in a more specialized sense. Such names as the ninth-century Arab al-Kindi, the tenth-century al-Farabi (of Turkish origin, patronized by the Hamdanids), and the eleventh-century Persian ibn-Sina (who served the Buyids as vizier) deserve prominence in any truly worldwide history of philosophy. Absorbing the writings of Plato and Aristotle and drawing heavily on neo-Platonic writers such as Plotinus, Islamic philosophers strove to combine and reconcile Hellenic concepts with Islam. To cite some typical ideas, the philosophers came to identify the concept of God with the philosophical notion of "First Cause," taken from Hellenic cosmological doctrines, with the universe "emanating" from it via such phenomena as "absolute reason" and "active intellect." A prophet—equated with Plato's Philosopher King—was one who used "imaginative faculties" to provide the same truths obtainable through reason, but in a symbolic form understandable by the masses. Such philosophical activity was anathema to people with conventional religious ideas and generally withered after the twelfth century, although new kinds of "philosophical theology" flourished long afterward.

DEVELOPMENT OF THEOLOGY

Islamic theology emerged largely in response to the philosophical movement. One group of scholars began to turn Hellenic methods to the defense of Islam and developed the theological school of Mu'tazilism, which was infused with rationalism. Sometimes misunderstood as being "free-thinkers," the Mu'tazilites nevertheless were ardent Muslims who carried monotheism to great lengths.

One Mu'tazilite doctrine related to God's not determining human acts. To the horror of many Muslims, who stressed God's absolute power (and thus the inapplicability of human concepts of justice to him), the Mu'tazilites conceived of a God of justice, who would not arbitrarily punish people for acts that he had forced on them. Thus they insisted on the doctrine of free will.

Other Mu'tazilite concepts are related to a stress on the oneness of God. The Mu'tazilites objected to the anthropomorphic idea that God literally has hands and other parts mentioned in the Qur'an and insisted that to treat the ninety-nine Qur'anic names of God ("the Beneficent," "the Victorious," and so on) as "attributes" was contrary to the fact of his unity. Of special importance in this regard, the Mu'tazilites rejected the idea that the Qur'an is uncreated (i.e., that it has always existed) as meaning that God has a partner. Instead, they argued that the Qur'an was created when it was revealed to Muhammad. The more literalist Muslims, known as "people of *hadith,*" or Traditionalists, whose most ardent exponents were the Hanbalites, bitterly rejected such speculation, as did later schools of theology.

For a while, beginning with the era of Ma'mun, Mu'tazilism was in official favor. A *mihnah* ("inquisition"), the only example of such an institution in Islamic history, was set up to test the doctrines of teachers, judges, and such. The acid test was to ask whether the Qur'an was created. Ahmad ibn-Hanbal's resolute refusal to accept the Mu'tazilite doctrine, despite imprisonment, beatings, and threats of execution, earned him the admiration of later ages of Muslims. But soon afterward, the state turned away from Mu'tazilism, which, without official support and in the face of new theological formulas, eventually died out among the Sunnis. However, Shi'ites have preserved some of its doctrines.

It was in reaction to Mu'tazilism that orthodox Sunni theology took shape. Among the conservative theologians who turned this kind of disputation against the Mu'tazilites was Abu al-Hasan al-Ash'ari, an early tenth-century Basran who once embraced the doctrine himself but turned away from it after the Prophet Muhammad appeared to him, so it is said, in a series of dreams. For al-Ash'ari, the Qur'an is un-created, and anthropomorphic passages, though inexplicable, cannot be treated as merely metaphorical. He rejected free will too, saying that God alone determines our acts, because a person's "free will" itself is predetermined. It is the choice put in the mind by God, although he somehow allows us to "acquire" the responsibility. In the Ash'arite conception, sometimes described as "atomistic," God recreates every phe-nomenon in the universe separately every instant, and no one has control over his or her future. Other theologians, notably the more liberal al-Maturidi, a Central Asian contemporary of al-Ash'ari, were to have less influence on the Islamic mainstream. Of course, the Hanbalites, with their total rejection of Hellenic rationalism, also sur-vived, and not just as a school of jurisprudence.

Although this may be an oversimplification, it is sometimes suggested that the Muslim's resignation to God's will, following al-Ash'ari's theory, has held back progress. Ash'arite theology does seem to typify a rejection of innovation and gener-ally of Hellenic and other influences that contributed to the Islamic world's early flowering. But it is doubtful that such a doctrine has affected people's efforts in any area of life. In any case, great achievement by Muslims did not end with Ash'arism.[2]

SUFISM

Another strain of thought that began early in Islam has so far escaped mention. Known as Sufism, apparently from the plain wool (*suf*) clothing that its originators wore, the movement provided an alternative to an intellectualism that few under-stood and to the legalistic rules of the *ulama* and their concept of a stern, remote God. Stressing the mercy and love of God and their love for him, Sufis renounced the world in favor of voluntary poverty. And, citing a Qur'anic verse that declared God to be as close to each person as one's own jugular vein, the dervishes (*darvish*, "poor," in Persian; *faqir* in Arabic) turned to mystical communion with the Divine. From there they sometimes turned to the goal of drowning their own independent ex-istence in union with him. Ceremonies developed in which constant repetition of words and body movements put devotees in trances.

Sufism produced many examples of sainthood. Rabi'ah al-Adawiyyah, a late ninth-century Basran whom some Sufis consider their greatest saint, epitomized the

---

[2] Also, the later transition to modernity was unique to parts of the West (and paradoxically some-times attributed to Calvinist predestinationism). It is not the failure of the Middle East, along with most of the world, to undergo such abnormal developments that requires explanation.

spirit of the movement by declaring her love of God to be so overwhelming that she had no time even for hating the devil and by asking God to send her to Hell if she worshipped him only for the sake of Paradise. She refused all offers of marriage on the ground that she did not exist apart from God. When another Sufi, al-Hallaj, told of his attainment of union with the Deity by saying "I am the Truth" (one of the Qur'anic names of God), the authorities of Baghdad took this as blasphemy and crucified him in 927. Following the example of Jesus, a figure especially revered by many Sufis, Hallaj asked God to forgive his executioners, whose actions he described as natural for people who had not been favored by what had been revealed to him.

A vast Sufi theological literature emerged that included some of Islam's most lofty poetry. The *Epistles* of the eleventh-century al-Qushairi outlined forty-five stations (stages) on the Sufi way that ended with incessant desire to be with God. Other writers identified as many as a hundred stations. The concept of a hierarchy of saints emerged. The voluminous esoteric writings of the tenth-century Spanish-born ibn-al-Arabi, who apparently claimed to be the "Seal of the Saints," were of particular importance. Another example of Sufi writing was that of the great Persian poet Jalal al-Din al-Rumi, who lived in the Sultanate of Rum during the thirteenth century.

Begun in individual practice, Sufism soon developed into monastic orders (*tariqahs,* "ways") with networks of meeting places or monasteries. Groups such as the Mevlevya (or Mawlawa), which claimed Rumi as its founder and was famous for its "whirling dervishes," had leaders (*shaykhs,* Persian *pirs*) whom they accorded the status of saints. Practices varied widely from order to order, with a few groups practicing celibacy. Large numbers of lay members were attached to each lodge and participated in its ceremonies.

This became a popular form of religion that seemed increasingly at variance with official Islam. Not only did such Sufi corruptions as snake handling, drug taking, and saint worship pose dilemmas for all who understood Islam, but even moderate Sufism seemed alien to most of the *ulama* and perhaps threatened to displace orthodox obsei ances. While several people tried to reconcile the two divergent approaches, the success of such an attempt awaited the writings of Abu al-Hamid al-Ghazali, who died in 1111.

AL-GHAZALI: "RENEWER OF THE FAITH"

In the tradition that Islam has a renewer every hundred years, some Muslims consider al-Ghazali to be the one who rose at the beginning of the sixth Muslim century. Already one of the most highly recognized scholars of his time, the thirty-seven-year-old professor of Shafi'i law and the head of the Nizamiyyah Madrasah in Baghdad underwent a spiritual crisis in 1095. He had already written several important books, including the *Incoherence of the Philosophers* (later answered by the leading Spanish Muslim philosopher ibn-Rushd's book, the *Incoherence of Incoherence*), which struck a blow at the recent wave of Greek-inspired writing while using much

Greek philosophy in the process. But now he was dissatisfied with striving for wealth and recognition in the academic world and became so obsessed with the danger of hell that he developed a speech defect and could not teach.

Al-Ghazali told how he had already turned to philosophy, Isma'ilism, and theology but found each inadequate. For a while he lost all faith. Now, in 1095, he left his family and position behind him to make pilgrimages to Jerusalem and Mecca and finally to take up a life of mysticism in his native town in Khurasan. It was ten years before he agreed to take a professorship in the Nishapur Madrasah. In works such as *The Revival of Religious Sciences* he demonstrated convincingly to Islamic scholars that orthodoxy and Sufism, at least if not carried to extremes, need not be opposed, how indeed rituals such as prayer were the foundation but that mysticism can provide a deeper meaning. It is to al-Ghazali that much of the credit is due for the continued, if sometimes uneasy, coexistence of the two approaches to Islam.

THE RISE OF THE NEW PERSIAN

The emergence of independent dynasties in Iran brought a linguistic and literary revival that perpetuated the Persian national identity and put the Persian tongue alongside Arabic as a supranational Islamic language. The older Pahlavi (Middle Persian) survived only as a language read by Zoroastrian priests, whose religion gradual Islamization reduced to a small minority by the tenth century. (About 20,000 Zoroastrians still live in Iran today, but there are more in India, where they are known as Parsis.)

Persians had long written a disproportionate share of Arabic literature, and even the Shu'ubiyyah movement had used Arabic as its medium. Arabic was to remain an important language for Persians in the religious field, but, aside mainly from the southwestern province of Khuzistan, the language of Arabia would never displace the local forms of speech, which include several minor regional languages such as Kurdish and Baluchi.

Beginning with the Tahirids and the Saffarids, a body of literature developed that transformed a post-Pahlavi patois into the Iranian national language, New Persian. The Samanids, who nevertheless still used Arabic as the official language, accelerated this trend through their generous patronage of Persian poetry. The linguistic legacy of the Arab conquest remained in the form of the Arabic alphabet, which, with minor adjustments, became the vehicle for New Persian writing. Also, much like the Latin contribution to English, the vocabularies of New Persian and other languages of Islamic peoples have borrowed many Arabic words, particularly in matters relating to religion and government.

The rise of Turkish dynasties gave new momentum to Persian culture, as Turkish rulers eagerly sought Persian sophistication in their courts. The Turks who entered the Middle East did not produce any written literature in their own language during this period, but a host of writers earned Persian poetry, and, to a lesser extent, prose, an unexcelled place in world literature.

It was the pen of Firdausi who brought the rhymed couplet and Persian poetry to a climax with his monumental *Book of Kings* (*Shah Namah*). Writing for Mahmud of Ghaznah, Firdausi set the standard for the Persian language and, with his immortal portrayal of ancient Persian heroes, kept the country's pre-Islamic past alive in the memory of Iranians.

The Islamic conquest caused a break with the Iranian heritage in the sense that Pahlavi literature was subsequently known only in the form of translations into New Persian. Paradoxically, conversion to Islam was eventually nearly universal in Iran, whereas large Christian groups continued to exist in Syria and Egypt. But the survival of Iranian ethnic and linguistic distinctiveness—and thus of a separate national identity—would be in contrast to the nearly total Arabicization of the Fertile Crescent and Egypt.

Under the Saljuqs the geographic realm of Persian literature extended into most Islamic regions north and east of the Fertile Crescent. Nizam al-Mulk's *Book of Government* provides a prime example of the "mirror for princes" genre, dealing with the art of government. Its keen insight deserves an important place in political thought. Strangely, it is the great mathematician, astronomer, and masterful amateur poet Omar Khayyám whose quatrians *(Ruba'iyat)* are best known in the English-speaking world. The mystical writings of Rumi and his contemporary, Sa'di, represent a poetry that continued to flourish for centuries.

ART AND ARCHITECTURE

With the Abbasids' shift of the capital to Iraq, the Eastern features of art and architecture became more evident, as Sassanian influence emerged in mosques and palaces. While few of the spectacular examples have survived, the Great Mosque of Samarra, with its spiraling minaret, even reflects the historically remote example of the Sumerian ziggurat. The Mosque of ibn-Tulun in Egypt also shows remarkable similarities to this. Indeed, the Samarran style of enormous fortified palaces and mosques using ornamental stucco over burnt brick became widespread. A great deal of carved stucco and carved wood ornamented the doors and walls, typically the rosette and vine leaf designs. The Samanids, in the tomb of Isma'il at Bukhara, built in 907, contributed the overhanging niche (stalactite), which fills in the space wherever a circular dome rests on a square frame. This is an exclusively Islamic development and remained in use throughout the period.

Despite its short life Samarra produced artistic results that served as models for the entire Islamic realm. Not only was its stucco famous, but Islamic pottery styles were first found here. Especially noticeable during this period is the impact of T'ang Chinese porcelains on Muslim ceramics. The Samarrans imitated the Chinese techniques, and from this emerged the exclusively Middle Eastern polychrome luster-ware pots and vases. Most of the figures on this pottery were Central Asian, depicting even the Bactrian (two-humped) camel rather than its Middle Eastern one-humped relative.

Indicative of the great diversity of styles are the many varieties of minarets. Spain showed a preference for square shapes, while Central Asia opted for cylinders. Conical ones existed in Iran, and something resembling a candle snuffer appeared at the top of some minarets in Anatolia. Of course, climate had a great deal to do with the shape and materials of buildings. Tops of Anatolian structures had to be built to shed the rain, and it was more practical to work with brick than with stucco. The Saljuqs used bricks in their mausoleums, mosques, and *madrasahs.* Covering an entire wall with glazed tile is considered one of their innovations.

Islamic strictures against portraying human or animal figures diverted art to the prolific use of foliated inscriptions, begun in Kufah and perfected by artists in Fatimid Egypt. Fancy calligraphy was used in an artistic, geometric Kufic script, with final letters ending in elaborate shapes of palms or flowers. Within the paintings were often hidden different animals, and a sharp eye could sometimes pick out a human form. The combination of people and animals cleverly formed a message, often verses of the Qur'an. European Christian cathedrals sometimes copied this work without realizing that it contained Qur'anic inscriptions.

While diverse dynasties built their mosques, palaces, mausoleums, and *madrasahs,* artisans throughout the Islamic world showed their creativity in working with metals, pottery, and even cloth. Damascus and Mosul became famous centers for intricate inlaid metal work. Weapons, trays, and vases were much sought after. Along with this, the art of inlaid wood carving developed, using mother-of-pearl and ivory. Mosiac techniques taken from the Byzantines emerged in Islamic tiles. In addition to their use of glazed tiles, the Saljuqs brought carpet making into the Middle East. Originating in Central Asia, this art, like other forms, turned up in Iran and Egypt. The pattern in the carpet was usually geometric, with Kufic writing around the borders. Most of the printed textiles produced in Fatimid Egypt employed this kind of pattern.

ECONOMIC DECLINE

While the expensive monuments to this civilization took form, economic deterioration made way for a long-range decline of the Middle East. Agriculture in particular became less productive, as irrigation brought salinization in some places and as governments became increasingly lax in maintaining complicated irrigation systems. There may even have been geological changes that caused the Tigris, Euphrates, and their tributaries to flow faster, aggravating the problem. The decline of Iraq is notable after the early Abbasid period and helps to account for the shift of the centers of power and civilization to Egypt and other sites in the Islamic world. Nomadic incursions sometimes devastated agricultural land, although the primary example of such a phenomenon occurred with the Hilali tribes' invasion of North Africa in the eleventh century. In any case, well before the thirteenth century the decline of agriculture was widespread, both absolutely and relative to developments in Europe such as the use of new kinds of harnesses or the windmill (the latter ironically invented and formerly used in Iran). Some villages were deserted, and governmental revenues fell dramatically.

Administrative patterns gave impetus to decline. With revenues harder to come by, governments turned collection over to tax-farmers, who, being allowed to keep all above a fixed sum for themselves, gouged the peasantry. Corruption became increasingly commonplace. The use of property sometimes became immobilized as perpetual trusts (*waqfs*) were set up either for the support of mosques, schools, and the like or simply for members of the family as a way of avoiding confiscation. From Buyid times on, and increasingly under the Saljuqs, Ayyubids, and Mamluks, a kind of feudalism emerged, but it was unlike the European version in many ways, and careful writers often reject the use of the term "feudal" in reference to it. In the Middle East, holders of fiefs (*iqta*) lived in the cities, not on self-sufficient manors, and holdings were rarely hereditary and were often rotated. This gave fief-holders little identification with the land and little incentive to make improvements; rather, it gave them every reason to squeeze all they could from the land. Thus while European feudalism may have provided a transition for recovery from the Germanic onslaught, the Middle Eastern variant portended stagnation and decay. And by not producing a stable nobility whose position vis-à-vis the ruler was defined by a contract, as in Europe, Middle Eastern "feudalism" allegedly failed to create the kind of dispersion of authority that eventually brought parliaments and constitutionalism into existence in Europe. But now it is time to return to our political narrative and to the final blow that was to fall on the classical age.

THE MONGOL INVASION

As the Christian tide receded in Syria and Anatolia, a more serious threat rose in the northeast. At the beginning of the thirteenth century the tribes of Mongolia were welded together by a chieftain subsequently known as Chingiz Khan. Within a half century he and his successors led their armies, which included Mongols, Turks, and Chinese engineers and artillery, as far west as central Europe and as far east as the Sea of Japan. When they came to the Islamic Middle East, they demonstrated a ferocity that apparently represented both calculated terror and sheer sadism. In Middle Eastern eyes, they were monsters who threatened all civilization and human life.

Some Christians had a different reaction. They hoped that Chingiz, whose people included a few Nestorians, would prove to be the legendary Far Eastern Christian Prester John, or at least would convert to their faith and join Europe in a pincers movement against Islam. Although Christian Europe was not spared the Mongol scourge, Christian kingdoms such as Armenia and Georgia collaborated with the new power, which sometimes favored the Christian population of conquered territories in the Middle East.

Chingiz at first overestimated Khwarazmi power and sought an alliance rather than conquest. But Shah Muhammad was angered by a letter from Chingiz addressing him as his "son," and the Mongol emissaries were killed. What was inevitable in the long run thus came quickly as the angry Chingiz led his troops westward in 1219 and overran Khwarazm. His forces destroyed cities such as Bukhara, Samarkand, Marv, and Nishapur, and they never fully recovered. The Mongols strove to wipe out the conquered population, although some whose skills as artisans could be used were taken to Mongolia. Mounds of human skulls remained, and estimates of the number killed ran as high as 15 million. Hordes of refugees loosely designated as Khwarazmis poured westward. Some were welcomed as mercenary troops in various places and even helped the Ayyubids recover Jerusalem in 1243, but more often they excited fear in the lands where they sought refuge.

A respite for the Middle East followed as Chingiz returned home weighted down with booty. His successor busied himself with the conquest of China, but Anatolia felt the storm in 1242 as the Mongols defeated the Saljuqs and then penetrated deep into the peninsula. Although facing increasing Mongol domination, the Saljuqs of Rum avoided extermination by agreeing to pay tribute.

In 1253 Great Khan Mengu sent an army commanded by Hulagu, grandson of Chingiz, to finish the conquests in the Middle East. After a three-year siege, Alamut fell, and the power of the "Assassins" was uprooted. When Baghdad's turn came in 1258, the conquerors sacked it and massacred a large proportion of its population. The caliph and other members of the Abbasid house were killed, and for a while Sunni Islam lacked a head. While Arabia was spared, Hulagu, named *il-khan* ("viceroy") for the Middle Eastern territories with loyalty to a great khan soon to rule from Beijing, swept through Syria.

Egypt proved to be the only power west of Japan capable of stopping the Mongols. After Sultan Qutuz executed the emissaries sent to ask for his submission, Baybars defeated an advance unit at Gaza and proceeded to northern Palestine, where the Mongol army was encamped at a place called Ayn Jalut ("Goliath's Spring"). By this time, Hulagu had left for the Far East to involve himself in a struggle for power after Mengu's death. The troops Hulagu had left behind in Palestine were greatly outnumbered by the *mamluks,* who were themselves ferocious children of the Eurasian steppe. On the other hand, the Mongols had never in memory lost a major battle. But, pursuing the Egyptian attackers in the decisive Battle of Ayn Jalut in September 1260, the Mongols were then decimated by the *mamluk* horsemen and quickly withdrew from Syria.

CONCLUSIONS

The five centuries following the Abbasid Revolution saw one of history's golden ages. As the Middle East again played a leading global role, its rich, multifaceted civilization reached maturity. Its own creativity was matched by an early receptivity to outside ideas. While the contemporary West had little to offer, the ghost of ancient Hellenic civilization provided the renewed Orient its greatest cross-fertilization. A new ethnic group, the Turks, entered the area and gave Islamic expansion a new lease on life from separate centers, while the New Persian language provided another important form of literary expression.

Several signs of decline were visible long before the thirteenth century. While Islam provided for a system of universal government in principle, centrifugal forces made this largely theoretical. Sometimes rival concepts of legitimacy, posed in religious terms, were at stake. More often, the unworkability of the ideal left the field open to a sheer struggle for power among alien troops that had no ties to the society.

The receptivity to new ideas had yielded to certain kinds of rigidity. A divine law was no longer susceptible to new interpretation, and "innovation" became a term of reproach. The Hellenic impact had largely given way to a theology that feared reason and even denied human beings' control of their own actions in the face of an all-determining God. At the same time, long-term economic forces and a pattern of society that in some ways resembled feudalism undermined Middle Eastern greatness, while a western Europe that had seemed to be destined for perpetual backwardness began to catch up.

A Western military thrust into central Islamic lands proved temporarily successful but was gradually being repulsed. The crusaders reassured the East of its superiority and perhaps in the long run contributed to dangerous complacency. Finally, the Mongols dealt the Middle East a harsh blow. While the Egyptian-based Mamluk army stopped the invaders, the survival of Islamic civilization may have seemed in doubt.

4

recovery, new zenith, and decline 1260–1774

The aftermath of the Battle of Ayn Jalut in 1260 saw the Middle East divided into Mamluk and Mongol realms. For a quarter of a millennium, a series of Mamluk sultans ruled in Cairo. Besides Egypt and Syria, they soon controlled the Hijaz, parts of the Sudan and Cyrenaica, and sometimes Cyprus and parts of southeast Anatolia.

At first ruling technically only as *il-khans* ("viceroys") of the great khan in Beijing, Hulagu and his line—which we continue to refer to as the Il-Khans or as the Il-Khanid dynasty long after the subordinate status that the name implied had vanished—predominated east of the Euphrates. This basically comprised Iraq and Iran, although some parts of the region were only under loose Il-Khanid overlordship most of the time. The Saljuq sultan of Anatolia also fell under Il-Khanid suzerainty for a while.

Middle Eastern civilization survived the ravages of the Mongols. The conquerors soon were absorbed by the region and patronized some of its greatest cultural achievements. Furthermore, this period made way for larger empires that renewed the momentum of Islamic power. Despite Europe's overseas expansion and renewed cultural vigor, it still often found itself in the shadow of the Middle East, and this relationship between the two regions did not fundamentally end until the eighteenth century.

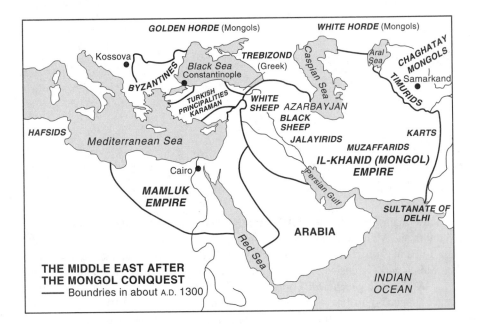

THE MIDDLE EAST AFTER
THE MONGOL CONQUEST
—— Boundries in about A.D. 1300

MAP 6

THE MAMLUK SULTANATE

On their return to Egypt after defeating the Mongols, a group of *mamluks* assassinated Sultan Qutuz. Baybars, whose treacherous kiss provided the signal for the attack, became the new ruler. He proved to be as capable in charge of an empire as he had been in battle and may be considered a founder of the Mamluk state. The hereditary principle sometimes was followed, as Qalawun, a commander who rose to power after Baybars's death, started a line of real or nominal sultans that lasted off and on until the late fourteenth century. But the *mamluk* army was the real arbiter, periodically bringing new freedmen commanders to power. The sons of *mamluks* were allowed to serve only in secondary military units, while the purchase of Turkish boys by both the sultan and fief-holders continuously renewed the warrior class.

The *mamluks* were an alien ruling group. Except for the *ulama* who held offices of an educational or legal nature, the indigenous people were excluded from public positions. Tribal rebellion against such an order was recurrent, particularly in Syria and Upper Egypt, and there were other popular revolts. Still, recent studies show that the *mamluks* did not rule through force alone but through a pattern of patronage extending to the *ulama* (who tended to represent local interests) and other notables, and even to potential opposition groups in the general population.

A member of the Abbasid family escaped from the Mongols and found refuge in Cairo to perpetuate the ghost of the caliphate. In fact, the position of the subsequent titular caliphs hardly compared with that of their predecessors, not even with those during the century or so before 1258. But as had often happened in Baghdad, figurehead caliphs provided some religious legitimacy to the Mamluk sultans, although most of the Islamic world ignored this claim.

The Mamluks tightened their grip on the crusaders. Baybars and Qalawun took several of their remaining strongholds and also finished off the Syrian Nizaris ("Assassins"), who had joined forces with them. The Mamluks' siege engines brought the capitulation of Acre, the last Frankish coastal enclave, in 1293. Thus ended western Europe's early thrust into the Middle East.

The early Mamluk period was one of prosperity. Egypt was a burgeoning emporium of East-West commerce, and customs duties on Indian goods, including spices sold to Italian merchants, enriched the government. An attempt by the Pope to get a Christian boycott of the Muslims failed. Gold from present-day Mali and silver from Europe flowed into the Mamluk treasury, paying for canals, bridges, hospitals, and impressive mausoleum-mosques. Prosperity and relative stability, plus an influx of refugees from Mongol-occupied lands, brought an upsurge in the size of the population.

Only with the appearance of a new enemy, the plague, in the mid-1300s did this prosperity end. Even the devastation that the Mongols inflicted had been small in comparison. According to some estimates, as much as a third of the population of Egypt and Syria died during this one epidemic. Although some survivors, such as the skilled laborers, made economic gains as a result of the deaths of so many of their associates, the overall impact was disastrous, and agriculture and trade were disrupted.

New ethnic elements began to predominate among the *mamluks*. As a counterweight to the Turkish Bahris, Sultan Qalawun began the practice of keeping another group of *mamluks* in the towers of the Cairo Citadel. These were ethnically diverse but mainly Circassians, a people of the Caucasus region known for their military qualities. The second phase of Mamluk rule, that of the Burjis (literally, those from the tower [*burj*]), began with Sultan Barquq in 1382. Most of the remaining sultans were Circassians, although two were Greeks. The hereditary principle was henceforth almost completely disregarded and made way for a rapid succession of unrestrained power struggles and of sultans who sometimes maintained only a precarious hegemony over their fellow commanders.

THE IL-KHANS

As for the Mamluks' enemies, Chingiz Khan's descendants split his patrimony into virtually independent realms. The great khan, in China, retained only nominal control over his viceroy, Hulagu, in southwest Asia. These two Mongols maintained a close mutual alliance against their cousin of the Golden Horde, who ruled in Russia, and another cousin in Transoxania. The Il-Khans fought many wars with their northern neighbors, especially with the Golden Horde over the Caucasus region.

Inter-Mongol conflict meshed with a broader pattern of rivalries. For the crusader states, the Il-Khans were allies against the Mamluks. The Il-Khans established friendly diplomatic contact with the Pope and various western European capitals, but offers to join in a concerted drive against the Islamic world never materialized. The Mamluks, on the other hand, found allies in the Golden Horde, not only because the Il-Khans were their common enemy but also because of a traffic in slaves that was as lucrative for the Mongol exporters as it was essential for the Mamluks to perpetuate their army and regime. The Golden Horde's early conversion to Islam facilitated the emergence of an alliance with the Mamluks and even the formal recognition of the sultan in Cairo as overlord. The Saljuqs looked to Baybars for support in overthrowing Il-Khanid hegemony. He entered central Anatolia in 1277 to occupy the Saljuq throne but soon withdrew as the enemy prepared for another offensive.

The Il-Khans continued to press on Syria. They took Damascus in 1300 but withdrew to deal with threats on other frontiers. The last of many unsuccessful Il-Khanid crossings of the Euphrates came in 1313, and a peace treaty with the Mamluks soon followed.

The early Il-Khans repressed the Sunni Muslim majority in favor of religious minorities, including Christians and Shi'ites. A few Mongols were Nestorian Christians even before the conquest, while others were Buddhists, which was also the faith of some of Hulagu's successors.

The early Il-Khanid period was one of economic decline. Unprecedented slaughter left the region severely underpopulated, a trend that may have preceded the Mongol invasion to some extent. Nomadic incursions and exactions by tax-farmers that forced many peasants to flee the villages were severe blows to agriculture.

Seemingly unlike anything in earlier Islamic periods, a pattern of binding peasants to the soil emerged. Some formerly great cities shrank almost to the status of villages, and many artisans who were not killed or carried away were reduced to slavery. On top of all this, in 1294 one Il-Khan blindly introduced a radical innovation from China, paper money, and decreed death for anyone refusing to accept it. The result was that for a while merchants stopped selling altogether, and complete disaster was avoided only by revoking the thoughtless policy.

Still, the Mongol conquests encouraged international trade. Silk and other products from China moved across the steppe to Il-Khanid lands and beyond. Iranian silk also occupied a central place in trade with Italian merchants via Mediterranean and Black Sea ports of Anatolia. Indian spices came to Hormuz, at the opening to the Persian Gulf, and went overland to Tabriz—thus bypassing Iraq and accelerating its decline—and on through Anatolia. Russian furs and Turkish slaves met sugar and other products from the Arab world along trans-Anatolian routes or on the Italian-dominated sea lanes. Direct Chinese shipping to the Persian Gulf gained importance briefly in the early fifteenth century.

The Mongols increasingly converted to Islam and melted into the Middle East. The distinction between Mongols and Turks tended to fade, while Persian remained the chief language of high culture.

With the accession of Ghazan to the throne in 1295, the Il-Khans became a Muslim dynasty. Symbolically, the Mongols replaced their brimmed hats with turbans, while they dropped their formal allegiance to Beijing. Ghazan also introduced reforms, particularly in taxation, that brought economic improvements. Non-Muslims underwent persecution for a short period: Buddhism vanished from the Middle East, while Nestorian Christians shrank to a small minority.

The Il-Khanid realm slowly disintegrated during the fourteenth century. There was a severe famine in 1318 as well as a series of bitter rivalries among leading officials. Later *il-khans* were mere tools of one faction or another. While the Golden Horde encroached on northwestern Iran, local dynasties proliferated, including the Muzaffarids, who eventually ruled from Shiraz. The Jalayirid family, of Mongol origin, established its rule in Baghdad and held sway over parts of western Iran for a while. Such minor dynasties tended to be heavily exploitative, and their emphasis on "feudalism" (the kind that, as we explained in the previous chapter, greatly diverged from the European pattern) brought further agricultural decline. The great outbreak of the plague in the mid-fifteenth century may have decimated the population here as it did in Mamluk lands.

THE RISE OF THE OTTOMANS

In the last quarter of the thirteenth century, the Saljuq sultans of Rum fell under increasing Il-Khanid domination and eventually disappeared. In turn, the decline of the Il-Khans left a power vacuum in Anatolia. This made way for the rise of what was to be in some ways the greatest of all Islamic states.

Nomadic Turkish tribes (Turkomans) began to pour westward into Anatolia in the eleventh century. Founding little ghazi principalities on the Saljuq frontier, they warred against Byzantium for the sake of Islam and for land and booty. In the mid-thirteenth century, one Turkoman chief, Ertogrul, established his control over a small area of northwest Anatolia, perhaps as a vassal of the Saljuq sultan. Ertogrul's son, Osman, succeeded in 1280 and gave his name to the Osmanli (Ottoman) dynasty. During his forty-four years of ghazi warfare, Osman extended the new state's sway over a much larger chunk of northwest Anatolia, including the city of Bursa.

Osman's son, Orhan (1324–1359), not only expanded his territory in Anatolia but also crossed the Straits to Gallipoli. At first merely intervening by invitation in an intradynastic squabble in Constantinople in 1346, the Ottoman forces stayed on in the fragmented Balkans.

Murad I (1360–1389), who took the titles "sultan" and "emperor," pushed his boundary into north-central Anatolia and then concentrated on the Balkans. Amidst calls in Rome for a crusade, the armies of Hungary and several smaller states suffered disastrous defeats. Some Balkan rulers, including the Byzantine emperor, accepted tributary status at least temporarily. So did the Ottomans' longstanding rivals, the central Anatolian amirate of Karaman, after suffering defeat in 1387. In a renewed campaign, Christian Balkan rulers, aided by troops from Hungary and Poland, had some initial success but were crushed at Kosova in 1389. Most of the area south of the Danube came under Ottoman aegis. With their capital at Edirne (Adrianople), the Ottomans' center of gravity was long to be in their European lands, which they called Rumelia.

Bayezid I (1389–1402) was nicknamed Yildirim ("lightning") because of the speed of his conquests on two distant fronts. The state now had lost its original simplicity, and the ruler was no longer merely the first among a group of equal chieftains. Feudal cavalrymen, slave troops, and auxiliaries contributed by Christian vassal states had already supplemented the Turkoman tribes. The ghazi spirit was making way for assimilation to Byzantine imperial forms and even for the use of Christian advisors. The conquests in the Balkans were rounded out, and the Byzantine emperor, now controlling little more than the city of Constantinople, was forced to establish a Muslim quarter. Another crusade met defeat by the Ottomans at Nicopolis in 1396. But while the ghazi tradition of the Turkomans limited their value largely to use against non-Muslims, the availability of other forces allowed Bayezid to concentrate on the conquest of Anatolia. During the 1390s his forces subdued Karaman and several eastern Anatolian states. All this warfare against fellow Muslims instead of unbelievers stirred up resentment among the Turkomans and made them look hopefully to another Muslim conqueror.

TIMUR'S SWEEP OVER EURASIA

In 1369 a Turkish Muslim warrior, Timur Leng ("Timur the Lame," "Tamerlane"), came to power in Samarkand. Then the "Great Wolf," as the crippled but magnetic "conqueror of the world" called himself, led hundreds of thousands of tribespeople to conquer areas as far apart as India and Russia. As he moved on, pyramids of human skulls or prisoners buried alive en masse perpetuated the terror that bolstered his invincibility.

A decade after Timur came to power, his armies swept through Iran and Iraq to subdue the petty dynasties that had succeeded the Il-Khans. A Mamluk sultan executed the emissary from Timur, who then sent forces into Syria. Now weakened by epidemics, famine, and high taxes, the Mamluks fell back south of Damascus in 1400. Fortunately for Egypt, Timur turned in another direction.

The Great Wolf entered Anatolia and repeatedly defeated the Ottomans. Turkoman disaffection with Bayezid's policies played into his hands. The Timurid host utterly routed the Ottomans at Ankara in 1402 and carried Bayezid around in a cage as a trophy of war. Before long the conqueror reached the Aegean coast. Local rulers, including two of Bayezid's sons and also some former victims of Ottoman conquests, became vassals of Timur. A third son of Bayezid ruled in Rumelia.

Timur returned to Samarkand, where he died in 1405 as he was preparing for a campaign to China. His descendants ruled until 1469 in Transoxania and Iran, while another Timurid continued the line at Herat, in Afghanistan, during the late fifteenth century.

The Jalayirids restored their control in Baghdad for a while but soon succumbed to a Turkish Shi'ite tribal confederation known as the Black Sheep (Kara-Koyunlu). Based in Mosul, the Black Sheep controlled Iraq and adjacent areas. A second Turkish confederation, the Sunni White Sheep (Ak-Koyunlu) of eastern Anatolia, which formed an alliance with Venice against the newly resumed expansion of the Ottomans, reached its height in the mid-fifteenth century by conquering the Black Sheep and the Iranian Timurids but then soon disintegrated. All of this proved to be a transition to the rise of two great states, a revived Ottoman Empire and a new dynasty, the Safavids, in Iran. Meanwhile, important cultural developments were taking place.

RENEWED VITALITY OF ISLAMIC CIVILIZATION

There is a widespread idea that Islamic civilization virtually ended with the advent of the Mongols. In reality, the next three centuries brought cultural accomplishments that in some ways surpassed those of the former, "classical" age. Admittedly, Mongol decimation set back an already declining Iraq, but Egypt was able to increase its previously emerging cultural primacy in the Arab world.

The post-1260 period saw a growing dichotomy between the Arabic and the Persian cultural zones. Fields closely connected with religion, including law, continued to use the Arabic medium throughout the Islamic world. But otherwise the language of high culture in non-Arab-inhabited regions was Persian. This was true in later realms as far apart as those of the Ottomans and the Moguls of India, with the semi-Persianized forms of local languages, Ottoman and Urdu, only slowly gaining recognition.

The notion that Islamic cultural greatness was in serious decline is a result of giving one's main attention to the Arab zone. With some spectacular exceptions, such an assessment is valid for that region. This is paradoxical in light of the fact that the Arab world, with the sad exception of Iraq, either avoided Mongol conquest or, as was true of Syria, experienced it only for short periods. The regenerative consequences of nomadic conquest of declining civilizations in the case of the thirteenth-century Mongols hardly seems comparable to that of, say, the seventh-century Arabs; but its savagery notwithstanding, it does help explain some of the Persian-based culture of the age. What decreasing momentum one can discern in Islamic civilization was due to tendencies at work in the region before the Mongol eruption more than to the destruction caused by the invasion.

The ecumenical sweep of the Mongols threw all the great civilizations, including those of the Middle East and the Far East, against each other. The conquerors took captured Middle Eastern Muslim artisans and craftspeople to the Far East, while Chinese scientists, engineers, and administrators appeared in the Il-Khanid lands. Chinese inventions, including gunpowder and printing, spread and ultimately had a revolutionary impact on both the Middle East and the West. Far Eastern influences permeated Islamic art.

Hulagu had hardly finished destroying before he began to pick up the pieces. He established an observatory in 1259 in western Iran, where a great scholar who had entered his service, Nasir al-Din Tusi, made important astronomical discoveries. Besides the natural sciences, history was a field that benefited from both Il-Khanid patronage and the wider world view of the age. The Persian Ata Malik al-Juwayni's *History of the World Conqueror,* an account of Chingiz Khan and of the Mongols generally, is of particular note. Another writer who stands out was Ghazan Khan's court physician, Rashid al-Din, whose two-volume *Collection of Histories* some scholars deem the nearest thing to an authentic world history before the twentieth century and the greatest of all Persian prose works. The author dealt with peoples from the Far East to the usually neglected western Europe and used informants and source material from all these regions.

Some of Persian poetry's revered geniuses appeared during the era of the Il-Khans or of their petty successor states. The poetry of the fourteenth-century mystic, pantheistic Hafiz of Shiraz, who wrote at the Muzaffarid and Jalayirid courts, represents another high point in Persian literature.

The Mongols sparked a renewal of the Middle East's creative spirit in the visual arts by enhancing trade and cultural contact with the Far East. The motifs of the Chinese lotus, Chinese-looking faces, dragons, phoenixes, and cloud scrolls entered Middle East art patterns but were stylized in an Islamic way. The many miniature paintings produced to decorate manuscripts provide particularly striking examples of this.

The Il-Khanid mausoleums were octagonal, with minarets at each corner, reminiscent of the great Mongol tents. Blue faience tiles or bricks decorated their exterior. Like the Saljuqs, the Mongols also used stucco for decoration. The most significant building of the Il-Khans probably was the Congregational Mosque east of Isfahan. Built in the fourteenth century, it has the typical four aisles opening onto a courtyard, an octagonal dome, and a single cylindrical minaret.

Islamic arts blossomed even more extensively during the Timurid period, which some writers have compared to the simultaneous Italian Renaissance. Timur himself was intent on making Samarkand the showplace of the world. Persian architectural style soon reached its zenith. The fantastic mausoleum at Samarkand demonstrated a new dome style, involving lobes and tile work. Landscapes predominated in the new painting style. Shiraz became the manuscript center where paintings were collected for illustrating copies of classic books. Herat claimed the greatest Islamic painter, Bihzad, who was the first to begin a practice of signing miniatures.

Timurid accomplishments extended to the field of literature. Several of the rulers of the dynasty were poets, and they eagerly patronized other writers. The last of the great medieval Persian poets, Jami of Herat, lived until 1492 at the Timurid court. Jami used the highly ornate style that increasingly became the norm in Persian writing. A member of the Naqshabandi order of dervishes, he expressed his mysticism in symbolic erotic terms.

Architecture flowered in the Mamluk sultanate. The Mamluks built ornamental mosques and many mausoleums which demonstrated the influence of their Fatimid predecessors as well as of Turkish styles. Also, the stained glass of European churches was adapted to the many stucco lattice windows to soften the brightness of the Cairo sun. Mamluk mosques were characterized by six-aisled sanctuaries and central courtyards. Ornate decorations typified this period, which was also famous for the use of elaborate geometric patterns. Another innovation brought to Mamluk buildings was the ever-present beautiful sunken fountains.

Aside from architecture, the Mamluks were successful in Cairo and Syria with the minor arts, such as glassmaking and pottery. Metalwork and woodcarving also flourished, while textile weaving was unsurpassed. Damask cloth and fine linens were much sought after in Europe.

In general, this was not an age of greatness in science and letters in the Arab world, but intellectual effort never ceased in any field. The Mamluk sultans patronized learning, and students came from distant lands to study at al-Azhar and other mosque-colleges. Historians in Egypt, such as the fifteenth-century al-Maqrizi, continued to write valuable chronicles in the traditional style, and the massive biographical encyclopedia of ibn-Khallikan in the late thirteenth century has preserved important information. In the field of popular literature, Mamluk Egypt saw the final development of *The Thousand and One Nights*. In the natural sciences, a remarkably overlooked name is that of the fourteenth-century Damascene astronomer, ibn-Shatir, who made some of the discoveries that Copernicus repeated a century afterward.

The most spectacular exception to the picture of an Arab civilization in decline was ibn-Khaldun, who died in 1406 after a career as royal advisor, chief judge, and teacher in his native North Africa, Spain, and Egypt. Having traveled to Damascus shortly before Timur entered the city, he met with the conqueror. He is usually described as a historian, but his lengthy chronological account, mainly of North Africa, is not what made him distinctive. What reveals his greatness is the three-volume *Introduction (Muqaddimah)* to his history, which in effect was a pioneer work in social science. Among his many other generalizations about human society, ibn-Khaldun explained history in terms of the social solidarity *(asabiyyah)* of tribal communities based on kinship. He said that it is groups with intense solidarity, especially when they supplement this with a religion, that found new states through conquest. Each dynasty, according to ibn-Khaldun's analysis, lives out a natural life lasting for three generations (120 years), during which solidarity erodes to make way for the state's downfall and then for a repetition of the cycle as other tribes that have retained their *asabiyyah* fill the resultant void.

Brilliant exceptions notwithstanding, Islamic civilization in both the Arabic and the Persian zones was now less creative in one sense than before. As Marshall Hodgson stresses, this was an age beset by a "conservative spirit," that is, one that focused on working within classic patterns. Although new ideas sometimes slipped in, people generally assumed that the early Islamic period had been the high point of history and that the most one could do now was to ward off decline. There was suspicion of innovation, and education consisted mainly of having students memorize the works of the past.

The Islamic receptivity to innovation provided a mixed story during these centuries. Aside from Far Eastern influences in the fine arts, the same Chinese inventions that helped European Christendom gather momentum on its road to modernization (after an early start partly resulting from Arab influences in the twelfth century) provide especially instructive examples in the case of the Middle East. Gunpowder was adopted by Muslim armies in some cases, notably by the Ottoman infantry at an early date (Muslims in Spain also were using it in warfare as early as the 1320s). Those troops that rejected the new weaponry, mainly cavalry forces, may have been evincing an instinctive conservatism (and indeed were able to point out that such an innovation was a deviation from the Prophet's path), but this was largely a matter of protecting their own kind of warfare. No one seems truly to have rejected gunpowder weapons on the ground that Islam did not permit them, and the *ulama* were not the center of opposition. In the case of the printing press, the *ulama* did resist this innovation, seemingly to protect vested interests of copyists and calligraphers. Although printing was known in the Islamic world in the Mongol period and continued to be used by some Middle Eastern Jews and Christians, it was forbidden to Muslims in the Ottoman Empire until the eighteenth century. By contrast, the pre-Mongol Islamic world had readily adopted such Chinese inventions as the compass.

OTTOMAN RESTORATION
AND RENEWED OFFENSIVE

As for the Ottomans after their defeat by Timur, the restoration of the empire required a complicated, decade-long process. But in the struggle with three other sons of Bayezid, Mehmed I became the sultan of a newly restored empire by 1413. The Ottoman state now resumed the momentum of conquest. Mehmed I (1413–1421) and Murad II (1421–1451) suppressed numerous revolts and warred in Europe and Asia. They restored control over much of the Balkan peninsula, and Ottoman forces raided as far as Hungary. Wars with Venice, Hungary, Serbia, and Wallachia (which, with Moldavia, later formed Romania) were recurrent, and all these states periodically became Ottoman tributaries. The most troublesome problem in the Balkans was the revolt of the indomitable Skanderbeg of Albania. Alternately resisting and paying tribute was the little remnant of the Byzantine Empire. Murad II besieged Constantinople and nearly destroyed it, but troubles across the Straits diverted his attention.

Ottoman control of Anatolia immediately after the restoration was limited to a small area in the west. Numerous principalities that Bayezid I had ruled were now independent. Some of these gradually fell under Ottoman dominion during the second quarter of the fifteenth century, while Karaman remained a major challenge.

An offensive by Christian Europe in the 1440s severely tested the Ottoman mettle. King Ladislaus of Poland and Lithuania ascended the throne of Hungary as well, and a great Hungarian general, János Hunyadi, led a crusade that brought together armies from much of Christendom. Advancing southward from Hungary, Hunyadi repeatedly defeated the Ottomans while Murad II dealt with Karaman. In a ten-year truce, agreed to in 1444, the Ottomans relinquished control over Serbia and Wallachia. But when the Pope convinced Hunyadi that a treaty with an "infidel" was not binding, the crusade soon resumed. Now the tide turned, as the Ottomans utterly routed the crusaders at the great battle of Varna (1444). Another crusade led by Hunyadi was demolished at Kosova in 1448.

Far from being turned back, the Eastern tide gained a new impetus that was to leave the West long on the defensive. For Byzantium, time was about to run out, and the desperate attempt by the ruling class to unite the Greek Orthodox Church with Roman Catholicism in the face of the Turkish threat did it no good. Such had been the Greeks' hatred of the Latins since the crusader sacking of Constantinople in 1204 that the slogan of the day in that city was "Better the turban of the Prophet than the tiara of the Pope."

The accession of the courageous, able twenty-three-year-old Mehmed II ("the Conqueror") in 1451 ushered in a period of accelerated expansion. His most dramatic achievement was to fulfill the centuries-old Islamic dream of wresting Constantinople from Christendom. After a fifty-four-day siege and one of the first large-scale uses of gunpowder in warfare, the Ottomans breached the walls of a city defended mainly by unpopular auxiliaries from the Latin West. Following the customary looting, a period of reconstruction began as the new rulers encouraged diverse peoples to settle in a long-declining, underpopulated metropolis. While the Byzantine emperor chose to perish in battle rather than to endure defeat, the general reaction of the populace was one of relief that a tolerant Islamic empire, which nominated a new Greek Orthodox patriarch and protected the Church, had saved it from the Latins. But now the Hagia Sophia was to be a mosque, and Constantinople—or Istanbul, a Turkish variant on the city's name—became the Ottoman capital.

Mehmed II's forces advanced in all directions. He defeated the White Sheep and took much of their territory, and he completely subdued and annexed Karaman in 1474. He clashed with Karaman's ally, the Mamluk Sultanate. Genoa's outpost in the Crimea fell, and the Crimean Tatar khan, representing a surviving branch of the

Golden Horde, accepted a vassal status that was to endure for three centuries. There were clashes with the Kingdom of Poland and Lithuania, wars with Hungary and Venice, and another crusade in 1464. Except for the failure to take Belgrade from the Hungarians, the Conqueror rounded out his holdings in the Balkans, and outright Ottoman rule superseded looser arrangements as far away as the Danube. Mehmed II expanded the Ottoman navy, which took much of Greece and several Aegean islands. His forces finally subdued Skanderbeg, bringing the Ottomans to the Adriatic coast. Ottoman armies penetrated to the outskirts of Venice, which accepted tributary status. With the dream of conquering Italy in Mehmed's mind, Ottoman troops landed at Otranto, at the "heel" of the peninsula in 1480, and the Pope prepared to flee. Only the sultan's death the next year brought withdrawal from Italy.

Mehmed II's death led to a struggle between his two sons, Bayezid II and Jem. The former, an ascetic, scholarly man backed by slave troops and other forces favoring a less active policy of expansion for a while, prevailed over his more warlike brother. After taking refuge in Rhodes, where he expected to lead another expedition against Bayezid II, Jem found himself a virtual prisoner. He was tossed from one Christian ruler to another for thirteen years, with the hosts receiving handsome payments from Bayezid II in return for not unleashing him.

Bayezid II was a weak ruler who preferred to leave matters of state to his grand vizier. But even now, victories and minor territorial acquisitions continued in wars in Europe. Rivalry for control of Turkoman border principalities brought war with the Mamluk Sultanate from 1485 to 1489. An Ottoman naval buildup was underway. War with Venice, which got support from crusading forces, ended that city's supremacy on the seas. Instead, "sea *ghazis*" asserted Ottoman domination of the western Mediterranean.

RISE OF THE SAFAVIDS

By now, a new empire, that of the Safavids, had arisen in Iran and was to remain for two centuries a second Middle Eastern power alongside the Ottomans. Fiercely devoted to Twelver Shi'ite Islam, the Safavid dynasty imposed the doctrine on a hitherto largely Sunni land. Henceforth, Iran was to be an overwhelmingly Twelver country, with about 90 percent of its population adhering to this doctrine today. This became an important fact in setting Iran off from the countries around it and particularly in providing ideological coloring for its relationship with the Sunni Ottomans. The subversive nature of the Safavids' creed dictated a fierce, almost unremitting struggle between the two.

Suggestions that there was something in Iran's ancient heritage that caused it to adopt a relatively distinct form of Islam are fanciful. After all, earlier Islamic dynasties there had tended to be staunchly Sunni. Actually, the Safavids were Turkish in origin; early members of the dynasty wrote Turkish poetry while their Ottoman contemporaries paradoxically composed verses in Persian. The language of the Safavid court continued to be Turkish into the seventeenth century. One should also keep in mind that some Arab areas adjacent to Iran are predominantly Shi'ite; the early Safavids actually had to bring in Shi'ite *ulama* from the Arab world. But, while we should avoid projecting back the expectations of our own age of "nation-states" that often are ethnically and linguistically distinct from one another, the Safavids increasingly took on the appearance of an Iranian dynasty. By uniting the country under one monarchy, they reasserted its ancient identity in a way that made them heirs to the pre-Islamic Sassanians.

Not born until the first decade of the sixteenth century, the Safavid state had undergone a two-century period of gestation. The Safavid movement, as a Sufi order rather than as a state, emerged at about the same time as the Ottoman dynasty from the disorder ensuing in the aftermath of Hulagu's conquests. The proliferation of Shi'ite and other heterodox Sufi orders was a characteristic feature of this period, although ironically the Safavids seem originally to have been Sunnis.

The Safavid movement took its name from Shaykh Safi al-Din, who was born in the late thirteenth century. An intensely devout young man, he found guidance from the elderly *shaykh* of a Sufi order in the northwestern Iranian town of Ardabil and later became the head of the group. Ardabil remained the center of a movement that directed Shi'ite propaganda over wide areas during the next century. Turkoman tribes tended especially to heed the Safavid appeals. Opposed by the local power, the Black Sheep, the Safavids moved their activities to the territory of the White Sheep, with whom a series of intermarriages occurred.

Following a period of disorder after the White Sheep decline, the leadership of the Safavid family fell to the inspiring young Isma'il at the end of the century. Establishing a base in Gilan, he attacked and overwhelmed the decaying White Sheep state in 1501. Assuming the title of *shahanshah*, the Safavid ruler soon extended his control over all of Iran and Iraq. Another Turkoman dynasty, the Shaybanis, who now headed a new Uzbek state centered in Transoxania, was driven from eastern Iran but not from the region farther north. The Uzbeks remained a hostile Sunni power on the Safavids' northeastern flank.

OTTOMAN-SAFAVID WARS

The Safavid-Ottoman showdown was not long in coming. In Anatolia, thousands of Shi'ite Turkomans, known as *Kizilbash* ("Red Heads") from the red hats that symbolized their movement, rose up against the Ottomans. Their leader was one who called himself Shah Kuli ("The Slave of the Shah") but whose foes called him Shaytan Kuli ("the Slave of Satan"). Many Ottoman soldiers joined in the revolt.

Sultan Bayezid II's forces suppressed the rebels, but there was widespread demand for a more warlike ruler to take the helm against the Safavid threat. Such was Bayezid's son, Salim I ("the Grim"), who succeeded in a palace coup in 1512. The fanatical but capable Salim I proceeded with ruthless cruelty to exterminate Shi'ites in his territory. As Shah Isma'il prepared to overthrow the sultan in favor of another member of the Ottoman family, Salim initiated *jihad* against the Safavids. The Mamluks sealed their own fate by a policy of nonintervention that was inevitably to put them at the mercy of a newly preponderant victor, as Salim led a great army of 100,000 soldiers to northwestern Iran.

Meeting the foe at Calderan in 1514, Salim's army was well equipped with cannon, which the Safavids lacked. The Safavid army was mainly cavalry and had long resisted firearms, as did the Ottoman *sipahis*. Following some initial successes by the Safavids on one side, the superior Ottoman forces repulsed them on the other side, and this decisive battle soon turned into a disaster for the shah, himself now wounded. Some of his fanatical followers had believed he possessed divine qualities; their faith in him had been so great that they sometimes dispensed with armor in battle. But now his invincibility was gone. The anticlimactic remaining decade of his reign saw him succumb to military inactivity and to alcoholism. After Calderan, Salim entered Tabriz, Isma'il's capital, but soon left with plans to return and conquer Iran in the spring. Dissatisfaction among his troops prevented him from carrying through with this second campaign, but Shah Isma'il's defeat brought about the absorption of most of eastern Anatolia into the empire and paved the way for expansion into Syria and Egypt.

CONQUEST OF THE MAMLUK SULTANATE

A series of blows to the Mamluk state in the fifteenth century contributed to its fall into Ottoman hands. Many Syrians and Egyptians were ready to welcome a more stable and, it was hoped, a more just ruler with open arms, and dissatisfied factions of *mamluks* also were eager to collaborate with an outside force. The Burji sultans were oppressive, and political chaos prevailed. Famines and the plague, which seems to have decimated the *mamluks* more than the indigenous people, had severely reduced the population, and wars further drained the economy. Christian European pirates raided Mamluk seaports several times. Inflation got out of hand as demand for silver in Europe resulted in the substitution of copper coins in the Mamluk Sultanate. The *mamluks* were unwilling to adopt new military techniques that might have helped them to survive. Mounted on horseback, they were wedded to a kind of warfare that artillery seemed to threaten, and they scorned such weapons as worthy only of weaklings. They acquired only a few cannon and entrusted them to low-prestige units.

The first phase of modern European overseas expansion also helped to undermine the Mamluks. The Portuguese imposed a crushing blow on the Egyptian economy by rounding the Cape of Good Hope in 1498 to begin direct commercial relations with India that bypassed Mamluk territory. Receiving Ottoman assistance, partly because the Safavids and the Portuguese were working together, the Mamluk navy defeated the latter in one engagement. But a Portuguese victory in 1513 sealed the Mamluks' fate.

The Portuguese success did not represent any decisive superiority of Europe over the Middle East as a whole. The Indian spice trade did not completely bypass this area for another two centuries. Portugal could occupy relatively primitive or underpopulated areas, as in the Americas, and was supreme on the seas for a while, but it was hardly a serious menace to the great land empires of the Far or Middle East. The beneficiary of the economic damage it did to the Mamluks was to be the Ottomans, who in turn continued on the offensive against Christian Europe. Still, a process was in motion that would subordinate the Middle East to the West two centuries later.

Salim's incorporation of some Anatolian Turkoman principalities that had been tributaries of Cairo brought strains in Ottoman-Mamluk relations. The Mamluks were suspected of working with the shah, and such actions as giving sanctuary to Jem also antagonized Istanbul. When Salim led an army eastward in 1516, the Mamluk sultan feared that it would turn south in his direction. And so a Mamluk army advanced to northern Syria. Even supposing that Salim's real purpose was to march on Iran again, he could not do so with the Mamluks in a position to attack him from the rear.

Salim confirmed Mamluk fears when he turned south into Syria. The Mamluk governor of Aleppo, Khayr Bey, who was secretly in league with the enemy, pulled his forces back, and the largely pregunpowder Mamluk army suffered a crushing defeat in the vicinity of Aleppo. As the last Mamluk sultan refused to submit to Ottoman suzerainty, Salim moved on to defeat his force again near Cairo in 1517 and to annex the Mamluk realm.

Salim did not establish direct control over all of the new territories. He left an Ottoman force in Egypt but did not destroy the *mamluks*, and Khayr Bey became an Ottoman vassal there. The next three centuries saw an ever-shifting rivalry between Ottoman governors and the *mamluks*. While southern Syria remained under its own local notables, an Ottoman governor took charge of the north.

The end of the Mamluk Sultanate also terminated the line of titular Abbasid caliphs. Salim took the last of them to Istanbul, and a story emerged centuries later that the right to the office was turned over to the Ottoman house. In the nineteenth century, this was to be the basis for the dynasty's claim to a special position in the Islamic world. In fact, this purely apocryphal story was contrary to the Sunni theory, according to which the caliph had to be elected and be of Qurayshi descent. Except for the occasional use of the title in a loose sense (not unique to the Ottomans), no one seems to have laid claim to the caliphate for centuries after the Ottoman conquest of Egypt.

THE OTTOMANS AS A GREAT WORLD POWER

The conquests of Salim I heralded the zenith of the Ottoman Empire. The next sultan, Sulayman (variously surnamed "the Great," "the Magnificent," "the Law-giver," and "the Lord of His Age"), who reigned from 1520 to 1566, came to be synonymous with a period of Islamic glory that in some ways surpassed that of the early Abbasid era. The momentum of conquest and the power of the Ottoman state and its efficient military force in relation to the other kingdoms of the time were enough to guarantee this. But Sulayman's wise leadership and his devotion to justice—although he also could be merciless, as in having his own son assassinated—provided new ingredients for imperial success.

As he led great armies alternately to his eastern and western frontiers, Sulayman remained the great ruler of the age. He was at the center of a pattern of international politics that extended at least from western Europe to India, and he found himself the arbiter in conflicts among the others. To the northwest of Sulayman's Rumelian domains lay one of his persistent enemies, the Hapsburg ruler of Austria and head of the Holy Roman Empire, who had also inherited the throne of Spain. The Ottomans' former foe, Hungary, was now reduced to the position of being a mere object of Ottoman-Hapsburg competition. A second great Christian European ruler was the king of France, whose rivalry with the Hapsburgs dictated that periodic professions of Christian solidarity would be mere window dressing for an alliance, sometimes tacit and sometimes more or less open, with Istanbul. Venice was, as before, alternately to join anti-Ottoman Christian coalitions and then to come to terms with its great Eastern neighbor.

Christian naval expansion notwithstanding, Islamic states constituted the great land powers of the sixteenth century. Contrary to the widespread image of Western supremacy that dates back half a millennium, Hodgson rates most Christian kingdoms in this period alongside the lesser Islamic states of southern India, and points out that Persian was the nearest thing to a world language.

The Safavids, under the strong leadership of Shah Tahmasp during much of this period, were the Ottomans' great Islamic enemy. Perhaps more than the equal of any Christian European power, the Safavids were natural allies of the Hapsburgs, while both the Ottomans and the Uzbeks constituted a threat. The early sixteenth century also saw the establishment of another major Islamic empire. The "Moguls" were founded by Babur, a refugee Transoxanian Timurid prince who had lost in the struggle at home with the Uzbeks. The Moguls sometimes were allied with either the Safavids or the Uzbeks but tended to stay out of these conflicts.

Though still only irritants to the Islamic powers, Europeans were outflanking the Middle East. Portuguese naval power in the Indian Ocean still was not an insuperable threat, but the emergence of the Dutch and English in the same waters during the following century was to pose a more serious challenge.

Completing Europe's encirclement of the Islamic world, Russia advanced eastward at the expense of Muslim khanates. The Russians were eventually to look toward the Black Sea and the Straits as an outlet to the Mediterranean. Having adhered to Orthodox Christianity and in some ways representing an extension of the Byzantine version of European civilization, they posed as protectors of their coreligionists. After the fall of Constantinople to the Ottomans, one Russian ruler married a Byzantine princess and took the title czar (caesar). The "Third Rome" (Moscow) devoted itself to liberating Constantine's city from the "infidel." But, while the czars sometimes clashed with the Ottomans' Crimean vassals during the time of Sulayman, they were only beginning to cause worry in Istanbul.

Sulayman's reign began with a drive deeper into Europe. The two places where Mehmed II's forces had failed, Belgrade and Rhodes, quickly fell into his hands. Though the Ottomans at first directed their eyes to a projected conquest of Italy, French calls for aid against the Hapsburgs channeled efforts northward. The Hapsburgs had placed their own favorite on the Hungarian throne, and Sulayman entered on behalf of the Hungarian peasants and Prince Zapolya, who represented resistance to Austrian control. The Ottomans also came as protectors of a widespread Hungarian Protestant movement, which they generally favored against the Catholics throughout Europe. They crushed the Hapsburgs at Mohacs in 1526 and occupied the Hungarian cities of Buda and Pest (today's Budapest) but then left Zapolya as their vassal. With the subsequent restoration of the pro-Hapsburg candidate, Sulayman entered Hungary again three years later with a quarter of a million soldiers. And, while some of his troops raided deep into Germany, the sultan proceeded to besiege Vienna. This city nearly succumbed but was saved when Sulayman's troops demanded to return to Istanbul for the winter. In 1541, as a result of Sulayman's fourth Hungarian campaign, most of the country acquired the status of Ottoman provinces, and the Hapsburgs had to pay tribute to the sultan. It was in his final campaign in Austria that the aging Sulayman died in 1566.

Meanwhile, religious and military conflict with the Safavids continued. Another *Kizilbash* revolt in eastern Anatolia was suppressed, and Sulayman led several major campaigns into western Iran. A pattern emerged in which Shah Tahmasp withdrew to allow the invader to enter areas of scorched earth. Tahmasp generally eluded Sulayman's army, which eventually withdrew each time in order to get home for the winter. But Iraq and some parts of Armenia and Kurdistan fell under Ottoman rule. In order to concentrate on repelling a simultaneous Uzbek invasion, the shah concluded a peace treaty with Istanbul in 1555 that accepted the new Ottoman conquests.

The Ottomans derived both strength and weakness from the practice whereby the sultan led the whole army on each campaign. With some exceptions, conquest was not left to subordinates, who could have established their de facto independence, and not many years passed before the sultan himself appeared on opposite frontiers in Europe and Iran. Within that sweep, the Ottoman Empire retained an unusual degree of central control. However, the troops liked to spend the winter in Istanbul, and so campaigns were limited to the period from April to September of each year. An enemy army that could evade the sultan until the end of the fighting season had succeeded, in effect, in defending its territory. Another potential drawback of the Ottoman practice was that it required one quiet front while a campaign proceeded on the other side of the empire and a combination of skill and luck to prevent the Hapsburgs and the Safavids from acting in concert.

Despite its primary concern with expanding on land, the Ottoman Empire was also a great sea power. A Turkish privateer, Khayr al-Din, entered the service of the sultan and became the grand admiral of the empire. Khayr al-Din's forces established tenuous Ottoman control over the whole North African coast except for the then-vigorous Kingdom of Morocco. Parts of the newly acquired coast had previously fallen under the control of Spain, which itself had only recently (in 1492) ended the Muslim Kingdom of Granada. Muslim refugees from Spain were especially avid sea ghazis in the Ottoman navy. Most of the Aegean Islands were now under Ottoman control.

Though Khayr al-Din failed to take Malta, he made Ottoman naval power dominant in the Mediterranean throughout most of the sixteenth century. Crusader fleets met defeat on several occasions, and the Ottoman navy, whose maps even dared to label the new World one of the empire's provinces, raided the coasts of Spain and Italy.

Ottoman naval forces based in Egypt and Basrah also challenged the Portuguese east of Suez. The Ottoman admiral Piri Ra'is drove the Portuguese from Socotra and established the sultan's control over Aden, much of Yemen, and parts of the Horn of Africa. There were Ottoman expeditions to India and as far away as Sumatra. But the Portuguese were able to hold onto Hormuz, at the entrance to the Persian Gulf, thus preventing Ottoman egress from that waterway.

INTERNATIONAL TRADE

The sixteenth century saw active commerce crisscrossing the Middle East. Bursa, near the Sea of Marmara, was long a main center of international trade. There Italian merchants traded various European products, such as woolens, for Iranian silk, Anatolian iron, Indian spices, and Chinese porcelain, all of which were funneled along the regular caravan routes through Anatolia. Silk and other Iranian goods were also exported via Russia, while the Black Sea provided important routes for Ottoman trade with the Crimea and Russia. Indian spices reached Bursa by way of the Red Sea and Damascus, and products such as sugar from the Arab lands paid for Anatolian timber and the like.

Iranian silk remained a basic item of trade. Heavily taxed, it provided the Safavids with a major source of revenue, and the silk trade even became a royal monopoly under Shah Abbas. This business was later to fall almost entirely into the hands of an Armenian community, whose ancestors Shah Abbas transplanted to the Isfahan area. By the end of the sixteenth century, English merchants and the Dutch East India Company were taking Iranian silk from ports on the Persian Gulf.

PATTERNS OF OTTOMAN RULE

Now that we have traced the rise of the Safavid and Ottoman empires, it is necessary to look at their internal dynamics. Both represented a marriage of older Islamic patterns with Turkish and Mongol traditions. Both took on new forms in response to the great technological development of the age, gunpowder, which they ardently accepted. In keeping with older patterns of the Islamic world, each "gunpowder empire," as Hodgson calls them, developed a military and political elite continuously replenished through slavery but with new characteristics.

In each state, an emperor (*padishah,* a Persian title that largely superseded the term "sultan" in Ottoman usage) ruled through a vast household. Although both dynasties survived for centuries, rival members of the family, who served as provincial governors during their father's lifetime, repeatedly struggled to succeed to the throne. In the Ottoman Empire, this developed into a pattern in which the victorious member of the dynasty had his brothers strangled to prevent further struggle; backed by a religious legal ruling (*fatwa*), Mehmed II officially condoned this seemingly quite un-Islamic procedure.

Those whose luck brought them close to the emperor were able to exert vast influence. The harem (i.e., female quarters) was often the real center of power. This was where the sultan's mother and other female and young male relatives, his concubines (picked by the queen mother), potential wives of important officials, and female servants lived and received their own exclusive kind of education. During much of Sulayman the Magnificent's reign, his Russian concubine, Hurrem Sultan (Roxelana) was perhaps the most powerful person in the empire, but the queen mother always outranked the other women and wielded the greatest influence during her lifetime.

Besides the harem, the Ottoman sultan's slave household was divided into an "inner" and an "outer" service. The former, dealing with purely internal matters of the palace, was a small, potentially influential group of "white eunuchs." It included garment carriers, cupbearers, and the like and was in charge of educating pages, who were young slaves of the sultan destined for high office. The larger outer service included religious functionaries; court physicians; astrologers; guards; and officers in charge of the garden, the kitchen, the mint, the education of princes, and so on.

The Ottoman sultan headed the formal structure of government. He governed through an imperial council (*divan,* the Turkish variant on the Arabic *diwan*), to which cases of miscarriage of justice could be appealed. The sultan originally presided over the council but later left this duty to his grand vizier (prime minister). The "Sublime Porte" (or "Porte"), which came to be a common term in the West for the Ottoman government, at first referred to the high doorway in which the sultan conducted state affairs and then later to the grand vizier's residence. Other members of the council included the imperial treasurer, the chancellor (who prepared documents, certificates, and so on), chief judges for Rumelia and Anatolia, the commander of the Janissaries (*yeni cheri,* "new troops," who were slaves of the sultan), the chief admiral, governors (*beylerbeys*) of important provinces (*eyalets,* including several *sanjaks*), and the *shaykh al-Islam* (Mufti of Istanbul and head of the *ulama*).

Europeans called the Ottoman Empire "Turkey," a term that would have been incomprehensible to the Ottomans. Admittedly, Europeans sometimes inaccurately described all Muslims as "Turks" (and "to turn Turk" meant to become a Muslim), and only with this even more distorted meaning in mind did the word properly describe the Ottoman Empire, which besides being a dynastic state, was a Sunni Muslim one. This was not an empire in which the Turks as such ruled over others. With their slave mothers, the sultans' Turkish blood increasingly diminished to the vanishing point. A form of Turkish was used as the court language, and the whole ruling class as well as the dynasty was known as Ottoman. But admission to the Ottoman class did not require Turkish background. When this class was open to free-born Muslims, such peoples as Arabs were equally eligible and provided some high officials almost to the last days of the empire. Paradoxically, the ruling class—"people of the sword" and "people of the pen"—used the word "Turk" pejoratively for tribespeople, peasants, and other persons of low status. In Ottoman terminology, the nonelite people of whatever ethnic background—though sometimes with specific reference to non-Muslims—were the "flock" (*ra'aya*).

In the earliest Ottoman period, Turkoman chieftains made up the ruling class. These evolved into a body of fief-holders whose expansionistic enthusiasm could still be directed mainly against non-Muslims. But such chiefs were not malleable subjects of a lofty autocrat, and they resisted centralization.

Increasingly clashing with and eventually replacing the tribal leaders were the "slaves of the Porte" (*kapi kulus*). Such individuals, recruited as youths and hence lacking competing family or regional ties, were intensely loyal to their master. Most notable among the slave institutions was the Janissary corps, first created during the fourteenth century. The Janissaries, who maintained a close interrelationship with the ultraheterodox Bektashi dervish order, with its shades of Shi'ism and Christianity, were outnumbered by other troops but long remained the elite fighting force.

Although slavery had been the route to military and ruling-class status for centuries, the pattern in the Ottoman Empire was different. Unlike the *mamluks,* who were manumitted after being trained, the slaves of the Porte remained the property of the sultan throughout their lives. Also, unlike the *mamluk* horsemen, the Janissaries were infantrymen and evolved in response to the need for artillery forces, although there were *kapi kulu* cavalrymen, called *sipahis* of the Porte, in the Ottoman army too. Also unlike previous freedmen regimes, the Ottoman slave oligarchy remained subject, if sometimes later only formally, to a dynastic sultanate.

By the time of Sulayman the Magnificent, the victory of the slave element was nearly complete. The grand vizier in particular came almost invariably to be a slave of the sultan. Likewise, nonslaves, including the descendants of the slave-elite, were ineligible for all offices except those of a basically religious nature, which *ulama* filled.

Another innovation in the Ottomans' slave-elite class was the method of recruitment. The main route to slave status was through a practice known as the *devshirme.* This was a pattern whereby (in violation of Islamic rules that forbid enslavement of Muslims or *dhimmis*) rural Christian boys within the empire, typically in their teens, were periodically taken as a tax on their families. Most of these boys were sent to serve provincial governors and other officials and, after receiving physical, military, and vocational training and learning to speak Turkish, generally became Janissaries. The most promising group became pages in the palace, received a rigorous education, and at the age of twenty-five began to occupy important offices.

Naturally, Christian families were of a mixed mind with regard to the *devshirme.* Some religious people were surely heartbroken to have their sons invariably turned into Muslims, although technically there was no forced conversion. But this meant access to high positions. Sometimes Christian peasants would learn years later that their son was the grand vizier. The *devshirme* was often regarded as a privilege, and some Muslims are known to have disguised their sons as Christians in order to get in on this opportunity.

Besides the Janissaries, "feudal" cavalrymen (*sipahis*) were an important (and numerically significant) part of the Ottoman army. Although some provinces, such as Egypt, were turned over to tax-farmers (whose image of mercilessly bleeding the populace at least one recent study has put in question), the most common arrangement was for land to be divided into fiefs (*timars* in the case of the typical small ones). But this differed so much from Western feudalism that the use of the term "feudal" is misleading at best. Taxes from such lands supported and provided homes for *sipahis,* who were called into the service of the sultan when he needed them for a military campaign. The fiefs were sometimes—but not always—hereditary, but unlike the medieval European pattern, they remained under the effective control of the central government and helped to mobilize the agricultural wealth of the empire to support a massive war machine. Other state officials, notably judges, exercised power in the same areas as the *timar*-holders and acted as a check on them.

The surplus produced by the largely self-sufficient peasants was what supported the *sipahis,* usually in the form of a tithe and other taxes paid in kind, as well as certain types of labor. In addition, the fief-holder collected taxes based on both Islamic law and decrees by the sultan. Peasants were tied to the land and, if they left it, could legally be forced to return any time within the following fifteen years. Nearly all the land they tilled was technically owned by the state (that is, it was of the *miri* type). However, the lot of the Ottoman peasant during the period of military expansion was clearly enviable compared to that of European serfs. Many cases are recorded in which the latter crossed into Ottoman territories, and they generally welcomed the conquering armies of the sultan. The changed conditions of the Balkan peasantry under the Ottomans has been described by both Turkish and Western historians as a social revolution. Recent scholarship points to an Ottoman peasantry whose rights to the land did not differ much from outright ownership in practice. Indeed, the old idea in the West that the Ottomans and the "East" generally represented the epitome of despotism rested on the fact that no truly feudal landed class existed to challenge the sultan's power.

While the *devshirme* class predominated in one sphere, free Muslims filled the religious elite. The latter category meant those *ulama* employed in schools, colleges, and mosques and as judges and muftis. Although in large part supported by pious endowments (*waqfs*), they too were part of the government. The judges (*qadis*) who applied religious law were also generally in charge of their districts, which were the smallest administrative units.

The *shari'ah* was the supreme law in the Ottoman realm, perhaps more than in any previous major Islamic state. The sultan issued decrees (*qanuns*), and some rulers, such as Mehmed II, enacted collections of imperial rules when they came to the throne. But these rules were valid only if the *shaykh al-Islam,* the highest religious authority, issued a ruling (*fatwa*) confirming that they were not in violation of the *shari'ah.* In practice, the *shaykh al-Islam* was usually able to exercise much power only when he was backed by powerful cliques. He was an appointee of and normally subservient to the sultan.

The millet (religious community) system provided a framework for toleration and sectarian self-government. Besides the Muslim millet, headed by the *shaykh al-Islam,* the Grand Rabbi headed the Jewish community, and separate patriarchs were appointed for the Greek Orthodox and Armenian Christians. The Armenian patriarch also had loose jurisdiction over such miscellaneous sects as Copts and Nestorians. As in all Islamic systems, each religion had its own law and courts governing relations among its members. The millet head was the intermediary between the sultan and the members of his flock in such matters as collecting taxes. The clergy's control over their communities long gave them a vested interest in perpetuating Ottoman rule. In the cities each sect normally inhabited its own quarter. Some Christian areas, such as Moldavia and Wallachia, were vassal principalities—they are often referred to simply as "the Principalities"—not under direct Ottoman control.

Despite being second-class subjects, the Christian and Jewish population enjoyed a kind of toleration rarely known by religious minorities in other parts of the world. Non-Muslim groups naturally preferred to be ruled by people of their own persuasions, but their second choice tended to be incorporation into a Muslim state. Invariably, Greek Orthodox Christians looked to the Ottomans as liberators from Roman Catholic rule. Also, thousands of Jews fleeing Christian persecution in Spain found refuge in Ottoman territories. Both Jews and Christians were especially important in industry and commerce and sometimes served as tax collectors. One group of Greeks, called the Phanariotes from the name of the district they inhabited in Istanbul, gained a key role as translators and mediators in Ottoman dealings with Europeans. Perhaps the greatest case of intolerance was the treatment of Shi'ites and Sunnis in the Ottoman and Safavid empires respectively, but even that was a matter of suppressing rebellions that took on sectarian form.

In the cities, guilds of artisans and merchants were a central aspect of life. Each craft guild allocated raw materials and labor and controlled standards and levels of production, prices, training of apprentices, admission to master status, and the right to open shops. Within limits set by some degree of state control (including, as in all Islamic states, the employment of a supervisor of the market), the guilds provided an important arena for local self-government in an Islamic world that lacked corporate municipalities. The masters in each guild elected several officers, including a *shaykh,* and all the guilds of the city chose an overall *shaykh.* Both these guild leaders and the *ulama* provided vital intermediaries between the state and the populace.

The Muslim guilds doubled as *futuwwah* brotherhoods, with their codes of chivalry. They also had close links with dervish orders, such as the Naqshabandis, whose lodges provided another nucleus of life, urban and village alike. In fact, for a Muslim not to be a member of such an order was a rarity.

SAFAVID INSTITUTIONS
AND SOCIETY

The Safavid shahs ruled much like their Ottoman counterparts in some ways. The main difference was the near divine status given to early Safavids. Although more orthodox Shi'ite influences eventually wore this away, the shah's claim to represent the Absent Imam—in addition to a mythical descent from another one of the twelve imams—exemplified a continuing theocratic tendency.

The Safavid pattern of division between basically governmental and essentially religious offices evolved in a distinctive way. The early shahs ruled through a Turkoman vicegerent (*wakil*), whose authority in both religious and secular matters obliterated any possible distinction between the two spheres. The position of vicegerent eventually vanished, leaving the grand vizier (*sadr-i azam*), who was always a Persian, as the main person in charge of the bureaucracy. In part, this change represented the gradual ascendancy of Persians, whose coexistence with the Turkoman leaders had long been uneasy.

Another Persian official appointed by the shah, the *sadr,* was the counterpart of the Ottoman *shaykh al-Islam.* The *sadr* continued to have some control over mosque-colleges, pious endowments, the judiciary, and the like. But religious leadership began to take on a different form in the sixteenth century, although this did not fully develop until the late 1700s. The most influential religious authorities came to be a group of *mujtahids,* each of whose authority to exercise *ijtihad* depended on general acceptance by a body of followers rather than on official appointment. *Mujtahids* apparently did not challenge the principle of monarchy or assert a right to rule directly; however, they claimed that they, not the shahs, had the right to act in the name of the Absent Imam. Thus there arose a separate center of authority, quite unlike the religious bureaucracy subservient to the Ottoman ruler. The Iranian *mujtahids* sometimes exercised great influence at the court but were also often in active opposition. This was the beginning of a kind of pluralism of state and *ulama* (themselves far from monolithic) that ultimately—in the late twentieth century—would allow one faction of religious scholars actually to take over the state in Iran.

During the sixteenth century, the Turkoman tribes were a powerful force who intermittently became the real rulers of the state. They repeatedly decided who would ascend the throne as their puppets, though sometimes destined eventually to turn against them. Only after a nine-year interregnum of *Kizilbash* domination was Shah Tahmasp able to assert his power in 1533 and to become the second great ruler of his house. In 1588 an eleven-year period of *Kizilbash* control made way for the accession of another strong ruler, Shah Abbas the Great.

The Safavids increasingly depended on a slave elite, or *ghulams.* Consequently, the shahs were able to free themselves from the influence of independent-minded Turkoman tribes. The process started with Tahmasp and was more fully implemented by Abbas. The *ghulams,* though at least superficially converted to Islam, were mainly of Georgian, Circassian, and Armenian origin, usually prisoners of war. While Turkoman cavalry were retained and supplemented by Iranian peasant musketeers, the elite group in the Safavid army became a corps of *ghulams*. Slaves of the same origin also gained top governmental posts such as governorships. They predominated in the harem and occupied influential roles as queen mothers and concubines, the latter vying in turn to gain the throne for their sons. But Persians always occupied most of the posts in the bureaucracy.

Agricultural land, generally—as in other Islamic countries—of the *miri* (technically, state-owned) type, was administered and taxed in two ways. One part, known as state provinces, was in the hands of governors who supported tribal forces and local militias and also sent part of the agricultural produce to the shah. The second division, the demesnes, was under the direct control of the royal household, through agents, compensated by enfeoffment, who had the right connections or paid bribes at the court. Paralleling the emergence of a centralized slaveocracy, the latter pattern increasingly predominated.

Typically, the old pattern prevailed: A person who provided only the labor got one-fifth of the produce; if he used his own oxen, he received another fifth. But while conditions naturally varied, some European travelers presented a picture of an unusually prosperous peasantry in Iran.

The guilds seemingly performed the same functions as those in Ottoman lands. One unique feature was that they had to provide certain kinds of free labor for the palace. Also, there was a large element of state capitalism in crafts such as weaving, with many artisans working in royal workshops.

OTTOMAN AND SAFAVID CULTURE

Almost as though time was dimming the glow of creativity, the rise of large, relatively stable empires paradoxically was accompanied by a drop in some cultural fields. Thus it was a deeper malaise in Islamic civilization that made way for eventual political and military decline as well. Arnold Toynbee blamed this on the bifurcation of the "Iranic" world into the mutually hostile sectarian empires and the subsequent "collision" between the Ottomans and the "Arabic" zone. Indeed, with no independent courts to patronize intellectual and artistic efforts, the already-diminished creativity of the Arab Middle East dipped further during the next three hundred years, as did the size of a population ravaged by tax-farmers.

The termination of the political chaos of the Mongol-Timurid age coincided with the relative decline of literary florescence in Iran. This has been attributed to the Safavids' opposition to mysticism, formerly a basic inspiration for poetry. It is ironic in light of the dynasty's origin as a Sufi order. However, a recent study argues that the extent of the literary vacuum has been exaggerated and points out that the Safavids sometimes patronized poets. Also, poets of Iranian origin continued to flourish in India at the Mogul court. Hodgson extends the period of "Persianate flowering" to include the sixteenth century. But excluding the visual arts, it was mainly in the field of philosophical theology—with the elaborate ideas of the early seventeenth-century Mulla Sadra in particular—that the Safavids left much of note.

Although the Ottomans produced a major body of fine literature, little of it could be called great. Originally limited to Persian, later poets also employed Ottoman Turkish. Commonly labeled *"divan"* poetry because of the collections (*divans*) in which they were gathered, the verses of numerous poets such as the sixteenth-century Muhammad Ahmad al-Baki followed all the classic Persian forms and the ornate styles. There was also a body of folk literature, such as Dede Korkut's epics, in the Turkish vernacular. But the great age of Islamic world power failed to produce another Hafiz or ibn-Khaldun.

Partly representing Byzantine influence, the Ottomans created a new architectural style. A central dome with a series of connecting buildings and smaller domes dominated Ottoman structures. The sixteenth-century Sinan was the great Ottoman architect who devised this type of interconnecting structure, which was both functional and visually striking. Such buildings contained the mosque, mosque-college, library, hospital, and rooms for the students. Decorative tiles covered the exterior. The seventeenth-century Sultan Ahmad Mosque (or Blue Mosque), with six tall minarets, exemplifies this style and is in fact regarded as the last truly great monument of the dynasty.

The famous Isnik tiles were unique. The design was painted on first, and then a transparent lead glaze was applied. Isnik potters imitated Chinese porcelain by using the popular blue and white; turquoise and green later became more common.

The floral drawings that dominated the tile paintings also were subjects for cloth design. The Ottoman artists imitated the designs on imported Italian silks and velvets. Book illustrators, however, used the Persian miniaturists as their models.

While Safavid art and architecture do not show any great originality, they were productive and magnificent. Popularly described as "half the world," Isfahan had many mosques, mosque-colleges, caravanserais (inns), and at least two hundred baths. The showplace of the period was the seventeenth-century Shah Abbas Mosque. It included the typical four halls (*iwans*), which opened onto a central outdoor court where the fountain was located. The entrance was strikingly beautiful, with faience tiles and mosaics in blue. The Safavids encouraged painting and succeeded in bringing the great Bihzad from Herat to Tabriz. The Safavid-Ottoman era certainly was one of great artistic accomplishments.

OTTOMAN DECLINE
AFTER SULAYMAN

The death of Sulayman the Magnificent in 1566 marks the beginning of a long period of gradual decline for the Ottoman Empire. The roots of weakness may go back even earlier, but some should be mentioned here, starting with more or less superficial ones.

Among the obvious reasons for decline was a degeneration in the quality of rulers. The first ten members of the dynasty had been exceptionally capable leaders. But now Sulayman made way for his only surviving son, Salim II, whose most revealing nickname was "the Sot." Salim II did not bother to lead his armies, as his predecessors had done, and preferred to leave matters of state to the grand vizier. Luckily for the Ottomans, Sulayman's able grand vizier, Muhammad Sokullu, stayed on for more than a decade and provided some continuity.

For the most part, Ottoman rulers continued to fit into this new pattern. Sometimes a child, a lunatic, or some other totally incompetent prince ascended the throne, and the real rulers were the shifting cliques of courtiers, military commanders, queen mothers, and concubines. Overlooking the fact that some of the most capable figures in Islamic history were women and that men provided their share of bad rulers, past writers mistakenly treated the influence of the harem as a major factor in the Ottomans' decline. The relevant point is that the sultan had always been the keystone of the state; and a bad one, who relied on cliques of either sex, weakened the whole structure.

The way the dynasty resolved the problem of succession aggravated the problem of leadership. The early Ottoman method of letting the sons of the dead sultan fight it out and for the victor to have the others executed had its practical as well as moral drawbacks. However, this system did allow the princes to gain important experience as provincial governors during their fathers' lifetimes. While fratricide continued sporadically throughout the seventeenth century, now the accepted rule was that the eldest male member of the royal family would succeed, thus avoiding a struggle. Instead of holding governorships, potential successors to the throne were kept confined in a "cage" in the palace, in effect as prisoners. The mid-seventeenth century Sultan Ibrahim ("the Mad"), who turned out to be one of the most tyrannical and incapable rulers, had been in the "cage" so long that when a delegation appeared to inform him that he was to take the throne he thought his executioners had arrived and tried to keep them out.

The *devshirme* system began to break down. Levies of boys became less common over the years and completely stopped in the late 1600s. Sons of Janissaries enrolled in the corps, as did other unqualified persons. Unlike the earlier pattern, Janissaries in active service could marry and engage in business. They were no longer the disciplined crack force intensely devoted to the sultan. Hardly an army at all any more, the Janissaries proved uncontrollable. As early as 1622, a sultan met his end when the Janissaries heard of his secret plan to create a Kurdish tribal force for use against them.

The *timar* system also degenerated. In many cases fief-holders evolved into mere tax-farmers or their lands became pious endowments. The timars no longer served to support a cavalry of high quality or to manage the economy efficiently. Corruption became commonplace. Offices were regularly bought and sold without regard to ability. To many Ottomans, corruption seemed to be the real villain.

Economic problems undermined the empire. Silver of Mexican origin poured into Ottoman lands in the late sixteenth century, and the consequent severe inflation had devastating effects on the society and its institutions. Also, the increasing diversion of trade by Dutch and English merchants to sea routes furthered Ottoman economic decline. Perhaps even more basic was the fact that conquest—with its accompanying booty and opportunities to acquire new fiefs—had reached its limits, and war now was an expensive rather than a lucrative activity. A decline in sources of revenue brought excessive, arbitrary taxation and debased coinage. An upsurge of population growth produced a shortage of land in some areas and brought an influx of unemployable people into the cities. All these factors fed the rebellions that flared up more and more frequently throughout Anatolia.

Ottoman control over the Arab regions was weak. North African provinces became virtually independent, and their corsairs raided as far away as Iceland. *Mamluk* beys became the real powers in Egypt and periodically overthrew Ottoman viceroys who tried to exercise power. However, a viceroy restored considerable control over the mutually hostile *mamluk* factions in the 1660s. In the Lebanese mountain region, the Ma'ans, a local Druze dynasty, were under only nominal central authority during the early 1600s, as was a newly dominant family, the Shihabs, later in the century. The Lebanese chieftains sometimes asserted control over adjacent regions. Military commanders repeatedly revolted in Baghdad, nullifying the governors' authority. A local dynasty dominated Basrah from 1567 until 1668. Tribes in southern Iraq resisted Ottoman control in the late seventeenth century and even occupied Basrah for a while.

From time to time strong individuals attempted to restore Ottoman grandeur. Several sultans were helpless in the face of opposition from *ulama* and Janissaries, but some carried out campaigns of reform through ruthless cruelty toward corrupt people. Sultan Murad IV brought an upturn in Ottoman fortunes with large-scale executions that became more and more arbitrary, allegedly claiming 100,000 victims.

From 1656 to 1661 an octogenerian "slave" strongman, Mehmed Koprulu, became grand vizier. He accepted the office only on the condition that the sultan and the *shaykh al-Islam* give approval in advance to all his actions. Again a campaign on behalf of honesty and austerity was pursued through bloodthirsty means. Much of this was repeated by a series of Koprulu's descendants, who gave the grand vizierate a nearly dynastic character throughout the rest of the century. But no reformer at this time sought to make any basic changes in the Ottoman system. The assumption was always that the machine of government had simply to be restored so that it would work again as in the days of Sulayman the Magnificent.

THE MIDDLE EAST AND EUROPE:
A REVERSAL OF ROLES

One cannot understand the gradual decline of the Ottoman state after the late sixteenth century and the subsequent rapid deterioration of the Safavids simply in terms of incompetent individuals and misdirected institutions. Rather, it basically reflected the ebbing fortune of Islamic civilization while Christian Europe's edge grew to indisputable predominance by the late eighteenth century.

The emergence of a fundamental gap between the capabilities of the West and the world at large was a product of abnormal vitality in European civilization. For centuries all spheres of life in much of the West were transformed at ever faster rates, eventually making each generation primitive in comparison with the next. The conventional term for this has become "modernization," with "modern," mainly Western, societies contrasted with more "traditional" ones in which human control over nature is less accelerated. Indeed, the West's industrialization was to have an adverse impact on the Middle East by undermining the latter's age-old industries and crafts (a process already initiated by Mongol devastation) and turning it into a producer of raw materials for the new "world market." In effect, it created a kind of "underdevelopment" that previously did not exist.

When Europe was undergoing these changes, the Middle East found itself in a relatively unflorescent period. The basic conservatism of Islamic society at the time of its post-Mongol zenith—or even earlier—may have provided the seed for decline, and the dazzling nature of recent politico-military achievements may have blinded Middle Easterners to long-term dangers.

Receptivity to imported innovation waned. In the fifteenth and sixteenth centuries, the Ottomans often were aware of Europe's most recent military technology and geographic findings, but such new knowledge ceased to be of interest to Middle Easterners just as it was mushrooming.

To a certain extent mutual insularity was normal for two different civilizations. Ideas and styles did not usually percolate freely across civilizational lines. Scholars who wrote in Persian and Arabic and in terms of their own cultural tradition simply lived in a different intellectual world from their Christian European counterparts.

Everyday things crossed civilizational lines more freely. The introduction of maize, potatoes, tomatoes, and other Western Hemisphere plants met no resistance. Even tobacco gained acceptance after some initial opposition. Spreading from Ethiopia and Southern Arabia in the sixteenth century, coffee drinking rapidly became a conspicuous feature of Middle Eastern life, and the *ulama* did not hold out against it for long.

Military innovations were usually acceptable to the *ulama* on the grounds that they would help in the defense and expansion of Islam. Even here, Islamic efforts eventually lagged. The Ottoman navy, which had previously kept astride of the newest developments in Europe, belatedly found its galleys outclassed by European "tall ships" in the late sixteenth century. By the next century, it was commonplace for Ottoman and Safavid weapons to be outdated. Shah Abbas's acceptance of help from English military experts shows a receptivity to new ideas but also demonstrates that the Safavid army had fallen behind.

Middle Eastern Christian minorities were less aloof from European developments. Trade with Europe came to be almost exclusively in their hands. Missionaries in the eighteenth century soon learned that the conversion of Muslims almost always was out of the question and instead concentrated on local Christians. Missionary schools were an early channel of transmission for European civilization to a few. Some Middle Eastern Christian groups—mostly fragments of older sects—kept their own liturgies while merging with the Roman Catholic Church. The most notable example of such "Uniate" churches is the Maronites of Lebanon, some of whom studied in Rome even in the sixteenth century. The impact of modernity thus got a head start among many Christians, and the Maronites in particular have recently some-times fancifully regarded themselves as an island of "Westerners."

Islamic creativity reached its nadir in the eighteenth century. Even the revi-sionist historians who have rightly refuted overstated versions of this statement are unable to deny its essential accuracy. Indeed, the Islamic world never knew a "Dark Age"; its civilization was alive but now lacked much vitality. Mosque schools and colleges continued to transmit old religious and legal learning by memorization. Books were written in traditional patterns, with few signs of originality, although some new styles emerged in a still-flowering Ottoman poetry. None of the mosques and palaces being constructed compared with the great earlier ones. The "conserva-tive spirit" had just about spent itself. Only in the last part of the century were there signs—pointed to in one study—of a slow intellectual revival in some places, partic-ularly Egypt. Western supremacy in the economic, cultural, political, and military fields had still left Middle Eastern empires largely intact. Although its logical conse-quences were not fully obvious until the end of the century, it seemed to immobilize a civilization whose internal dynamics had already reduced its creativity.

SLOWED MILITARY MOMENTUM

Returning to the story of Ottoman wars with Christian Europe after the death of Su-layman the Magnificent, we find setbacks beginning to occur, but the days of expan-sion were not yet over. The reign of Salim II witnessed the failure of an ambitious plan to push the Russians back and to dig a canal between the Don and the Volga to provide a waterway to the Caspian and permit an attack on the Safavids from a new direction. Soon afterwards, the Ottomans' Tatar vassals raided Moscow, but in the long run they could not stop czarist expansion.

War in the Mediterranean brought mixed results in the 1570s. Venetian-held Cyprus fell to the Ottomans, but the sultan's navy suffered its first major setback in 1571 at the hands of a crusader armada at Lepanto, near the Greek coast. Still, an in-tense building program restored the decimated Ottoman fleet within a year. As it pro-ceeded to raid southern Europe, the prospect of a landing and conquest seemed likely, but Christian naval domination of the Mediterranean soon became a basic reality.

A "Long War" (1593–1606) with the Hapsburgs provided another indication of relative decline in Ottoman power. With several Balkan peoples revolting against Is-tanbul's rule, the fortunes of war alternated, but the Ottomans were able to hold their own. A peace treaty generally restored the territorial status quo ante. But Vienna's former tribute to Istanbul ended, and for the first time the Ottomans recognized the Hapsburg ruler as a fellow emperor instead of a mere king.

The only enemy capable of posing a dire threat to the Ottoman heartland was still the Safavids. This was because the Safavid zenith, under Abbas the Great's new slave armies, came at a time when the Ottomans were already in decline.

The Ottomans went on the offensive in the east during the struggle for power in Iran after Shah Tahmasp's death. The Uzbeks compounded the Safavids' problem by invading eastern Iran. When Shah Abbas took the throne, he needed peace with the Ottomans in order to deal with the peril from the north. And so, in a peace treaty in 1590, the Safavids acquiesced in Ottoman conquests as far east as the Caspian. But after driving the Uzbeks back at the end of the century, Abbas moved westward again and soon restored the old boundary. He continued to advance, taking Iraq in 1623 and then penetrating Anatolia. It was not until 1638 that the Ottomans, strengthened by Murad IV's reforms, were able to roll the Iranians back, after which the peace treaty of 1639 established a frontier that generally corresponds to Iran's western boundary today.

A rapid deterioration of Safavid strength after the death of Abbas saved the day for the Ottomans. Almost all subsequent Safavid rulers virtually duplicated the vices and weaknesses of their worst Ottoman counterparts. Most were victims of alcoholism. In part, this was a result of confining princes in the palace—at least those who were not killed or blinded by their fathers and brothers—for fear that they would usurp power. Rulers with this kind of preparation were content to be mere instruments of intrigue involving concubines, queen mothers, eunuchs, and other people around them. Only the *ulama* and tribes sometimes challenged the degenerate, corrupt order that ate into the military power and prosperity of the realm.

The last half of the seventeenth century saw a mixture of victories and setbacks for the Ottomans. They took Crete from Venice, but in another Ottoman-Hapsburg war started in 1663, they were unable to resume the offensive on that front, and Christian Europe was heartened. However, the Ottomans made new advances in their campaign against Poland in the 1670s. A peace treaty with Poland in 1676 left the Ukraine divided into areas of direct Ottoman control and of Ottoman suzerainty. But Russia was able to hold the Ottomans back and force them to accept the Dnieper River as their northern frontier.

A new offensive in Europe began in the 1680s. Grand Vizier Kara Mustafa led a huge army into Hungary and took the Hapsburg-ruled part of the country. With the Pope calling for a crusade, armies from various European states eventually joined in a War of the Holy League against the Ottomans. Vienna came under a three-month Ottoman siege in 1683, and the city undoubtedly could have been taken by storm if Kara Mustafa had not so confidently planned for it to surrender without a fight. When the Polish king led in a relief force, the Ottomans neglected to intercept it in time. An Ottoman force diverted to meet the Poles was defeated, and the sultan's army fell back from Vienna, never to return.

The rest of the war was largely one of Ottoman losses. The Hapsburgs drove their foe from the region north of the Danube. With Muslim refugees pouring out of the lost territories, the Ottomans' economic problems multiplied. Venice conquered southern Greece and part of the Adriatic coast; the Russians, under Peter the Great, occupied Azov, on the northern coast of the Black Sea; and Poland held the Ukraine.

Ottoman defeats, confirmed in the Treaty of Karlowitz (1699), marked a watershed in the relationship between Christian Europe and the Islamic world. The fearful Ottoman government had no choice but to accept its losses of territory. A separate treaty with Russia the next year confirmed the boundary changes on that front. Al-

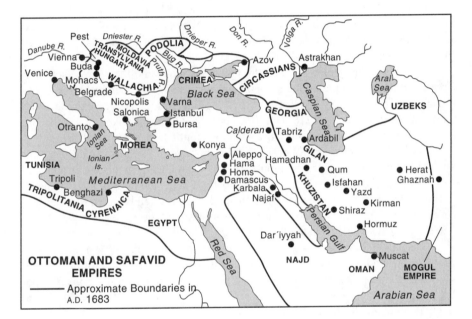

**OTTOMAN AND SAFAVID
EMPIRES**

—— Approximate Boundaries in
A.D. 1683

MAP 7

though the Ottomans were still too strong for almost any single European state and actually reversed some of the territorial changes a few years later, the trend generally became one of slow withdrawal from Europe. The old fear of an Islamic onslaught ceased to haunt Christendom.

EIGHTEENTH-CENTURY OTTOMANS: REFORM AND DEFEAT

The early eighteenth century brought considerable success to the Ottomans. In another Russo-Ottoman war, czarist troops entered Moldavia in 1710, but they moved too far ahead of their supplies and failed to get the active help they expected from the Moldavians. Suffering from famine, the Russians tried to withdraw but were trapped at the River Pruth. The two powers concluded the Treaty of Pruth (1711), whereby Russia relinquished the gains it made in 1700.

In a war with Venice in 1713 the Ottomans recovered the Morea (southern Greece). But Austria entered the struggle and soon made considerable gains, occupying the rest of Hungary and large slices of the Balkans, including Belgrade. Then the Treaty of Passarowitz (1718) confirmed both the Ottomans' losses to Austria and their gains on the Venetian front. In still another conflict, in 1736, the Russians met setbacks in the Crimea, again because of the shortage of supplies, while the Tatar khan raided deep into the czar's empire. Austria's initial gains in this war brought an Ottoman offensive and, according to the Treaty of Belgrade (1739), a regaining of territories lost twenty-one years earlier. This separate peace endangered Russian successes in Moldavia, and a Russo-Ottoman treaty restored the earlier frontier and excluded Russian vessels from the Black Sea.

Despite their sporadic successes and a certain continuing self-confidence, the post-Karlowitz Ottomans realized for the first time that they could profit from learning some of Europe's secrets. Not only did western Europe now prove powerful, but Peter the Great's eager emulation of this region had seemingly worked for Russia and might do the same for Islam. Thus a series of Westernizing reforms initiated a recurrent, later to be accelerated, Herodian pattern whereby Middle Eastern rulers selectively imitated those European powers that defeated them, if only to ward off further losses.

The years from 1718 to 1730 in the Ottoman Empire came to be known as the "tulip era," as gardens in which that plant was cultivated became the rage among the ruling class. Along with this came an aping of European buildings, furniture, clothing, and other superficial matters that would have been inconceivable in former times. Only a century before, awe for the East had induced King Charles II of England pretentiously to adopt Persian dress at his court for a short time. Even now the notion of Eastern inferiority was not so completely jelled in the West as to prevent some craze for Ottoman styles and for tulips.

Not all reforms of the tulip era were so superficial, although the idea still prevailed that no basic changes in Islamic civilization need accompany the adoption of specific European techniques. The Ottoman ambassador to Paris was instructed to seek out useful knowledge, and he wrote in approving tones about some of the exotic social customs there, including the appearance of women in public. A few individuals bothered for the first time to learn French. Among numerous Western-inspired reforms, the most notable was the establishment of a printing press on the initiative of Ibrahim Muteferrika, a Hungarian convert to Islam. A ruling from the *shaykh al-Islam* approved this innovation, but only on the condition that books on religion be excluded from such reproduction. In turn, Western science and ideas seeped in faster by way of printed translations. Another convert to Islam, a French renegade, the Comte de Bonneval, was instrumental in bringing about several reforms in the army, including the establishment of schools for teaching modern mathematics and medicine for military use. Even a conservative reaction, which brought a Janissary revolt and the fall of Sultan Ahmad and his modernizing grand vizier in 1730, could not stop the Herodian trend in the long run.

Neither could the piecemeal eighteenth-century reforms so easily contain the tide of decline and defeat. More wars weakened the economy. Taxes became unbearable, and the coinage was debased. There were numerous popular rebellions and cases of flight of peasants from the land.

Control over the provinces weakened further during the eighteenth century. In Egypt from 1711 on, rule by particular factions of *mamluk* beys alternated with times of anarchy during which *mamluks,* Janissaries, and sometimes rebellious tribes and peasants struggled for power. After 1757, one *mamluk,* Ali Bey, became the ruler of an essentially independent state. His control even extended to the Hijaz. In an alliance with Shaykh Zahir Al Umar, a Galilean notable who established another de facto state in northern Palestine, Egypt's ruler marched through Syria and held Damascus for a while. One of his *mamluks,* Abu-Dhahab, overthrew him in 1772 and defeated him the next year in his attempted comeback from exile in Shaykh Zahir's territory.

In Baghdad, an Ottoman governor, Hasan Pasha, founded a de facto dynasty in 1704. Then, after 1747, a rapid succession of *mamluk* rulers ensued amidst an intermittent series of coups.

Even in Anatolia and eventually in Rumelia, local notables asserted their control during the early eighteenth century. The Ottoman army became heavily dependent on the contingents they contributed. Anatolia was lucky in comparison with most Arab provinces in that its *derebeys* ("valley lords"), as the notables there were known, had local roots and had the welfare of their own regions at heart. But the sultan enjoyed little control over what the map now so misleadingly showed to be his empire.

The third quarter of the eighteenth century demonstrated European supremacy still more convincingly. With Istanbul objecting to Russian encroachment on Poland and the resultant shift in the eastern European balance of power, war broke out again in 1768. Although the Tatars once more raided Russia, the Russians soon prevailed and established a puppet regime in the Crimea. Other Russian forces crushed the Ottomans in 1770 and sliced through the northeastern part of the Balkans. The prospect that they would reach Istanbul seemed real for a while. At the same time the Russian navy, with English help, sailed from the Baltic to the Mediterranean to destroy the Ottoman fleet and join forces with Ali Bey and Shaykh Zahir. Only civil strife and other problems in Russia, plus the pressures of European countries who realized that excessive gains for the czar would strengthen him too much relative to themselves, saved the Ottomans from disaster.

The Treaty of Kuchuk Kaynarja ended the state of war in 1774. The two powers recognized the independence of the Crimean khanate, over which the Ottoman rulers would retain the title of caliph in a purely religious capacity. This distinction, inexplicable in terms of Islamic political theory, was seemingly the first of a series of Ottoman rulers' attempts to assert their weak claims to the caliphate. While Russia was to withdraw from much of the conquered territory, the Ottomans ceded it several fortresses, the district of Azov, and the area between the Bug and the Dnieper. Russia, whose ruler was also dignified by recognition as a *padishah,* thus became a Black Sea coastal power. The right of its merchants to use this sea and the Straits was guaranteed. The treaty also gave Russia the right to build and keep under its protection a church in Istanbul and to remonstrate in favor of Christians in the evacuated areas, rights which the czars later succeeded in stretching to mean a general role as protector of the Greek Orthodox Church in the Ottoman Empire. Thus began a now nearly inexorable process, restrained only by the jealousies of other European powers, of czarist encroachment on former Ottoman lands. More broadly, this was a world in which Islamic lands increasingly were subject to the whims of European Christendom.

IRANIAN INTERREGNUM

Unlike the Ottomans' more gradual decline, the disintegration of the Safavid Empire took place in the early eighteenth century. It began in 1711, when two groups of Afghan tribespeople rebelled and established their independence. Safavid forces sent against the Ghalzay Afghans, led by Mahmud, were decimated eight years later after mistakenly firing cannon on their own troops. And actions of the incompetent Husayn Shah, such as having his grand vizier's eyes torn out before discovering that charges of treachery against him were false, helped to ripen the Safavid Empire for conquest. Following earlier raids, Mahmud reached Isfahan in 1722, a city now reduced by disease and famine to cannibalism. The large Safavid army quickly fell apart in its encounter with a small group of tribespeople, and few Persians had the will to resist Mahmud as he ascended the throne.

The Afghan conquest of Iran brought anarchy and economic decline. Magnificent Isfahan nearly vanished, and other great cities shrank to little more than villages.

Both the Ottomans and the Russians saw a chance to gain territory and agreed in 1724 to partition much of the old Safavid territory between themselves. While Peter the Great occupied parts of the north, the Ottomans incongruously posed as supporters of the deposed Safavids against their fellow Sunni Afghans and conquered much of western Iran, which the Afghan dynasty ceded to Istanbul.

A Safavid claimant, Tahmasp II, gained the support of some large tribes whose importance went back to their *Kizilbash* days. These included the Qajars and the Afshars. A dauntless warrior of the latter tribe, Nadir Khan Afshar, soon became the leader of the Safavid restorationist camp. Nadir repulsed the Afghans in 1729 and proceeded to win a series of battles that rapidly brought about their demise. With Iran now seemingly getting hold of itself, the Russians agreed to withdraw from the conquered territory, and victories over Ottoman forces in the early 1730s led to a treaty restoring the status quo ante. A year later, the Afshar strongman ended all pretense by declaring himself Nadir Shah.

The new shah obscured Iran's fundamental decline with a whirlwind of military victories. He took Iranian armies deep into Central Asia to defeat the khanates that had succeeded in some of the Uzbek lands. Another drive took Nadir into Afghanistan and on through the Khyber Pass to rout the forces of a declining Mogul Empire. Although Iranian forces occupied Delhi in 1739, Nadir did not try to hold India permanently. Nadir also inflicted another serious defeat on the Ottomans in 1745. Within Iran he tended to centralize the state by avoiding feudal grants and by confiscating pious foundations, as well as through the forcible settlement of some tribes.

But the Afshar dynasty's success proved ephemeral. Nadir imposed high taxes. Moreover, victory seemingly evoked sadism in him, and his style of rule soon came to be symbolized by the pyramids of suspected Iranians' heads, which only intensified opposition to him. In a country where chaos—which he admittedly ameliorated—had brought so much economic loss, the shah simply hoarded the wealth he took from India and other conquered areas. The masses suffered from famine.

The shah's religious innovation proved to be another important source of resentment as he attempted to turn Iran again to Sunnism. Perhaps calculating that this would help win acceptance for his leadership in the larger Islamic world, he tried to get Iran's Twelver form of Shi'ism accepted as a fifth (Ja'fari) *madhhab* (school) of Sunni law. Few Shi'ite *ulama* were willing to accept such an idea except under the threat of death.

With Nadir Shah's assassination in 1747, anarchy returned. Other members of his dynasty were able to hold some areas, but not for long. By the 1750s the benevolent and politically adept Karim Khan of the Zand tribe prevailed in most of Iran and ruled from Shiraz as the vicegerent of a figurehead Safavid shah. For now he subdued his main rival, the later ascendant Turkoman Qajar tribe. Although Karim Khan brought some improvement, the country was economically exhausted, and recurrent starvation, disease, emigration, and war had halved the population of some cities. The Ottomans, who were retreating on other fronts, were in no position to take advantage of Iran's misfortune, but European penetration was evident as the Russians gradually gained preponderance in Georgia and as the English East India Company became active in the Persian Gulf.

THE CAPITULATIONS

Western economic power furthered the decline of lagging Middle Eastern economies. European merchants became increasingly active, and their products began to
undermine those of local manufacturers and put artisans out of work, although the
decline did not nearly reach the serious proportions of the next century. Trade and
shipping between Christian Europe and the Islamic world were entirely in the hands
of the Europeans, whose merchants were also active in trade between different Ottoman ports.

Agreements known as capitulations enhanced European economic penetration.
Islamic states had always not only allowed religious minorities to live under their
own law but also granted non-Muslim outsiders (*harbis,* "people of the house of
war") special permission to enter Islamic territory with guarantees of security. The
Ottoman Empire concluded agreements with Italian city-states allowing their subjects such rights in the fourteenth century, and they extended a similar arrangement
to France in the sixteenth century. In a related matter, France began to pose as the
protector of the sultan's Catholic subjects, and other powers claimed responsibility
for their own chosen minorities.

Over the centuries, both the Ottomans and the Safavids concluded such capitulation agreements with various European states. In general, the agreements provided for trading privileges, including low customs duties, and exempted merchants
from local jurisdiction (i.e., provided extraterritoriality). Even in cases involving Ottoman or Safavid subjects, the foreign merchant acquired certain privileges, such as
trial on criminal charges only in special courts outside the regular judicial system.

At first the capitulations did not involve submission to somebody more powerful. The word *capitulation* originated in reference to the "chapters" (Latin, *capitula*)
into which each treaty was divided and only later took on its present connotation in
keeping with what the treaties had come to represent. A powerful Ottoman Empire
had entered into its first capitulation agreements in a somewhat condescending spirit
toward Europeans, and there were provisions for reciprocal rights for the sultan's
subjects. But as the empire weakened, the extraterritorial provisions, which European powers could even extend to local people, particularly *dhimmis,* increasingly
belied the Ottomans' and Iranians' control over their own territory.

REVIVAL IN ARABIA

Central Arabia, or Najd, had never fallen under Ottoman control, although Istanbul
claimed a vague overlordship. Instead, various nomadic tribes maintained their independence, as did small amirates centered on the villages and towns that oasis agriculture and trans-Arabian commerce and pilgrimage traffic supported. As with many
bedouin, Islamization tended to be more or less superficial. Widespread Sufi practices such as pilgrimages to saints' tombs smacked of idolatry to some. Reverence for
sacred trees and the like may have been carry-overs from pre-Islamic days.

In this situation, a movement arose in the eighteenth century that in some ways presaged other attempts at reform during the next two hundred years. A pious young Najdi, Muhammad ibn-Abd al-Wahhab, who pursued religious studies in Madina and Basrah, embraced the strict Hanbali school of law and the teachings of the fourteenth-century Syrian Hanbali theologian, ibn-Taymiyyah, with such ardor that he was expelled from several places. In 1745 he took refuge in the hitherto petty amirate of Dar'iyyah, ruled by the house of Sa'ud. He converted Amir Muhammad ibn-Sa'ud to his doctrine and, marrying the latter's daughter, became a virtual coruler; the descendants of the two men have since been closely intertwined. Ibn-Abd al-Wahhab's "Unitarian" movement—or the "Wahhabis," to use a term originally adopted by detractors and still often resented by its adherents—now had the backing of Sa'udi political and military power, and it began a career of enforced purification and expansionism that, following one abortive mushrooming in the early nineteenth century, finally culminated in the creation of the Kingdom of Saudi Arabia in the twentieth.

"Wahhabism" was a radical rejection of then-current trends in Islam and of all un-Islamic practices. In keeping with Hanbali doctrine, these Unitarians demanded the reopening of the gates of *ijtihad,* unrestrained by the consensus of the Islamic community after the first three centuries. Otherwise, only the Qur'an and the *sunnah* were to be accepted without question, with the idea that this would lead not to a freer but rather to a stricter interpretation as part of a return to a long-corrupted faith. Tobacco, jewelry, silk, and the like were banned, as were domed tombs of saints and other objects of veneration. By 1774 the Sa'udi-"Wahhabi" state was well on its way to uniting Central Arabia. But it had still hardly attracted the attention of the wider Islamic world.

CONCLUSIONS

The devastation inflicted by the Mongols proved to be a prelude to continuing cultural greatness under Mongol and Turkish dynasties. This was particularly true of the northern Middle East, the zone of Persian culture; but even the Arab region under the Mamluk Sultanate showed some flashes of creativity. Still, a general wariness about innovation tended to bring a diminution of florescence in the long run, although the acceptance of Chinese influence brought by the Mongols provided a brilliant exception.

Then a network of mutually hostile Islamic states, including the Ottoman and Safavid Empires, became the greatest centers of world power. The Ottomans in particular outdid all other Middle Eastern conquerors in invading and ruling much of Europe. But two paradoxes accompanied this great eruption of Middle Eastern power. First, it came just as the civilizational flowering of the anarchical Mongol age began to fade. Second, it came at a time when Europeans were encircling the region by virtue of their supremacy on the oceans—including, in the case of the Russians, the "dry sea" of the Eurasian steppe—and expanding into underpopulated lands.

Using their not-yet-abnormal cultural florescence as a base, Europeans began a takeoff incomparable to anything since the Middle East–nurtured Neolithic Revolution ten millennia earlier. By the eighteenth century, Europe was indisputably ahead of where it had been two centuries earlier and equally in advance of its contemporaries elsewhere. Not only did the world at large remain outside the positive impact of this economic, politico-military, and cultural revolution, but the developing "world market" produced by Europe's Industrial Revolution was already undermining Middle Eastern industries. The Islamic world had reached a low point in relation to its former achievements. Internal disintegration and defeats by European powers, including the beginning of the Ottomans' slow retreat from Europe by 1774, provided telling signs of the emerging relationship between the West and the Middle East. So far, the Middle East had made only minor attempts to learn Europe's secrets, but drastic efforts were to follow as increasingly unbearable blows and the insufficiency of selective borrowing eventually awakened more Middle Easterners to a sense of their civilization's fundamental inadequacy.

5

the european tide
1774–1914

From the late eighteenth century on, a Europe whose cultural vitality and military and economic power knew no rivals began to close in on the Middle East. The latter, like the other civilizations of Asia, had more often than not previously been at least the equal of the West, whose abnormal transformations now however put the rest of the world increasingly at its mercy. Only the condition of an enfeebled Iran exceeded that of the Ottoman "sick man of Europe," leaving Europeans bedeviled by the "Eastern question"—how to dispose of such once-powerful empires without upsetting the European balance of power. Unlike most of the non-Western world, the two major Middle Eastern states retained their formal independence throughout the period. For that matter, the Ottomans only slowly relinquished their colonial Christian territories in the Balkans, a curious relic of an age when the relative capabilities of the Islamic and Christian worlds had been radically different. Yet, especially by the latter half of the nineteenth century, Ottoman and Iranian sovereignty had become empty shells preserved only by the mutual rivalries of European powers.

Russia recurrently encroached on both Middle Eastern states. But other European governments' concern for the balance of power always frustrated St. Petersburg's greater ambitions. Great Britain, the dominant imperial power of the age, was usually not much interested in annexing Middle Eastern territories as long as other powers did not threaten its "road to India." And so such powers as Britain, though sometimes carving out de facto colonies for themselves, served as a check against czarist expansionism.

Besides the specter of European political and military power, the issue of westernization engrossed Middle Easterners during this period. Rulers saw that Western military techniques were their only hope for salvation. Once introduced, such innovations produced demands for westernization in other spheres of life. While the zealots' loyalty to their own heritage remained at one pole, Middle Eastern nationalists increasingly adopted a Herodian stance that called for further westernization to save themselves. Some began to claim that the wholesale adoption of Western civilization provided the only alternative to weakness and backwardness; others took a new look at Islamic ideals to legitimize the selective adoption of some of the secrets of European power.

AFTER KUCHUK KAYNARJA: MORE PRESSURES AND REFORM

The immediate aftermath of the Treaty of Kuchuk Kaynarja saw accelerated reform in the sultan's realm in the face of continuing danger from European, particularly Russian, encroachment. Some earlier innovations such as the printing press were now reinstated. In the early 1780s under Sultan Abd al-Hamid I's reformist grand vizier, Halil Hamid Pasha, there were several attempts to modernize the army and navy, including the establishment of a new school of mathematics. Even before the peace treaty was signed, one significant departure from traditional reform was the employment of Christian French army officers as advisors. In turn, the opposition of conservative Janissaries and *ulama* led to the execution of the grand vizier in 1785 and the interruption of the trend.

The youthful Sultan Salim III (1789–1807) initiated a more radical stage of reform as soon as a respite from still another war with Russia permitted him to concentrate on internal matters. The New Order (*Nizam-i Jadid*), which the sultan pronounced in 1792, included a variety of attempts to reform the administration of the Empire, but the centerpiece was an infantry corps that reflected despair with proposals to improve existing troops. Modeled on European armies, even in matters of clothing, the New Order troops required numerous other innovations, such as a medical service and Western-style schools for officers. These schools used French books, not all of which were devoted to purely military matters, and French officers provided instruction and enjoyed a kind of informal personal relationship with Ottoman subjects that Westerners had not experienced before. What started as an attempt to learn from the West in the military field brought a long train of unexpected consequences in other aspects of life.

Another channel for westernization was diplomacy. In 1793, for the first time in Ottoman history, Salim III established permanent diplomatic relations with several European countries. The ambassadors received instructions to seek useful information, and young men were sent specifically to learn the languages of the host countries.

As the growth of provincial independence continued and as both Russia and Austria demonstrated expansionist designs, the Ottomans' international position deteriorated further. Istanbul was helpless as the czar violated the peace treaty by annexing the Crimean Khanate in 1779. Catherine the Great of Russia was soon working to implement a project to restore the Byzantine Empire, with her grandson prepared for the role of emperor in the Second Rome from the day of his baptism as Constantine. War with both Russia and Austria began in 1787, and the allies advanced rapidly into the sultan's European territories. With a war against revolutionary France forcing Austria to withdraw from the conflict in 1791, Russia continued to press on and to impose the humiliating Treaty of Jassy on the Ottomans the next year. The treaty legitimized the annexation of the Crimea and other territories, while the Russians withdrew from the Balkans.

The old Franco-Ottoman friendship eroded somewhat in the 1780s as it proved unable to prevent Russian encroachment on the sultan's lands. Still, it survived the French Revolution of 1789, which precipitated a series of wars between France and shifting groups of European powers that lasted until 1815. Then, in 1797, France and Austria concluded a peace treaty that partitioned the Venetian territories between them. As part of this deal, France got control of the Ionian Islands—near the western coast of Greece—and some enclaves on the Albanian coast. This put the French too close for Istanbul's comfort, as some rebellious notables in the sultan's Balkan territories began to connive with French agents and as Paris gazed greedily toward other Ottoman lands.

BONAPARTE IN THE EAST

General Napoleon Bonaparte, whose conquests in Italy had recently buoyed his popularity in the French Republic, pushed for acceptance of his characteristically grandiose proposal for an invasion of Egypt. Bonaparte, then in his late twenties, had been assigned to lead an assault on Britain, the only major country then in the enemy camp. But he saw the establishment of a French colony in Egypt as a more feasible alternative, one that would allow him to cut Britain's communications with its empire in India, where the French had lost out in the early 1760s. French commercial interests in Egypt had recently grown in importance, while British dealings with Ibrahim and Murad, the duumvirate of *mamluk* beys now in power there, posed a threat. Also, the arbitrary exaction of taxes by the beys provided an official justification for the invasion. But Bonaparte's dreams carried him far beyond Egypt. His reading of ancient history told him that the "East" was where all the great "glory" had been won, and he once proclaimed Europe a mere "molehill" unworthy of his effort. He hoped to march on to India much like Alexander the Great—even, in his wild dreams, to ride an elephant and found a new religion. Presumably he would then reduce both the Ottomans and the Iranians to the status of French vassals. The five-member Directory, which then ruled France, eventually accepted Bonaparte's plan, perhaps in part to get rid of a dangerous threat to the Directory's power.

Stopping to take Malta on the way, a great armada of four hundred ships carried Bonaparte and the 50,000 people in his army to their top-secret destination in 1798. The British knew something was underway, and their superior fleet, commanded by Lord Nelson, now was in the Mediterranean after a recent absence. It took a measure of good luck for the French armada to reach Alexandria. The *mamluks* received the news of the landing with derision, for they assumed that they could easily defeat "Frankish" armies, which, after all, had not dared attack the Islamic heartland for so many centuries. But the invaders were able to push on to Cairo during the same month they landed and to defeat the *mamluks* decisively at the Battle of the Pyramids. Still, the ease with which the French won can be exaggerated, for the *mamluks* withdrew to Upper Egypt, where Bonaparte's troops never fully subdued them.

Bonaparte's expedition in many ways was a turning point in relations between the West and the Middle East. For one thing, the Western world learned a great deal about Egypt, as Bonaparte aped Alexander the Great to the extent of taking a corps of five hundred scholars with him. Constituting the Institute de l'Égypte, they represented virtually every field of study, from zoology to Eastern languages. Their findings appeared years later in the twenty-four-volume *Déscription de l'Égypte*, a work of unprecedented thoroughness. One notable discovery was the Rosetta stone, with its parallel inscriptions in Greek and ancient Egyptian demotic and hieroglyphic characters, which provided modern scholars the key to deciphering hieroglyphics and thus gave birth to the science of Egyptology, the study of ancient Egypt.

More important for our purposes was the beginning of the modern Western impact on the Arab East. The area could no longer remain confident of its own superiority, and it was inevitable that future rulers of Egypt would seek what the militarily superior West had to offer. *Ulama* from al-Azhar visited the French scholars and in some cases were highly impressed with their scientific procedures. The printing press is an example of what the French expedition introduced to Egypt for the first time.

Bonaparte soon began to experience setbacks. Lord Nelson found the French armada soon after it reached Egypt. A great naval battle ensued, which ended in the devastation of the French fleet. A British naval blockade virtually isolated the French forces from their home base. Also, Bonaparte seriously miscalculated Sultan Salim III's response to his occupation of Egypt, which was, after all, an Ottoman province, though not under the central government's actual control. Bonaparte's claim that he was there as a friend of the sultan and to suppress the latter's enemies failed to impress anyone. There was great anger among the people of Istanbul because of this "unbeliever's" encroachment and also because the disruption of imports from Egypt produced a food shortage. The sultan entered into alliances with both Britain and Russia and declared war on France. Enthusiastic Turkish crowds applauded as a Russian fleet passed through the Straits.

As for the Egyptians, Bonaparte announced that he was there to deliver them from *mamluk* oppression. In what he later privately admitted to be pure "charlatanry," he even proclaimed that he was a "true Muslim." He offered his conflict with the Pope and with the Knights of Malta, whose centuries-old piracy against the Muslims was a holdover from the crusades, as weak evidence. The stilted, faulty Arabic in his proclamation—composed by one of the French scholars—added ridicule to the Egyptian people's hatred of their conqueror. In any case, his heavy taxation and other oppressive policies soon turned the *ulama*-led populace against him. A series of rebellions and repression followed. Admittedly, the *mamluks* were a despotic ruling group, and Bonaparte made the innovation of encouraging the Egyptians to help to govern themselves through representative councils but failed to convince them that the French were an improvement over even the worst Muslim rulers. Bonaparte, perhaps inspired by Alexander's worship of Amon and seeing the advantages he might gain in the East, seems to have flirted with the idea of converting to Islam, but he told a group of leading *ulama* that his men would never agree to be circumcised or to give up wine. Again imitating Alexander, Bonaparte once tried Eastern clothes but dropped the idea after evoking ridicule from his troops.

Cut off from France by sea, the "great sultan," as Bonaparte sometimes was dubbed, opted to break out of isolation by moving overland into Syria. He still hoped to go on to India and dreamed of returning home via Istanbul. A Bosnian soldier, Ahmad al-Jazzar, had come to dominate much of Syria, nominally as an Ottoman governor, and was about to move on Egypt. Also, the "great sultan" may have hoped to escape from the bubonic plague, which threatened his men in Egypt but which then continued to strike at them as they moved on. He defeated some Turkish forces in Palestine, carrying out a massacre of over three thousand prisoners in Jaffa and piling up their bodies to form a barricade. But Jazzar thwarted the conquest of Acre with the aid of the British fleet and with his defenses actually organized by a French renegade (a former classmate that Bonaparte detested for his better marks). Finally giving up the siege of the city, Bonaparte retreated to Egypt. Before long, he deserted his men by slipping through the British blockade—again with amazing luck—and returned to France to compete in the renewed struggle for power there. Within months, he carried out a coup d'etat and eventually became the Emperor Napoleon.

After the Syrian debacle, the French still easily defeated two Ottoman forces sent against them. But Bonaparte's successors in command—General Jean-Baptiste Kléber and later General Jacques Abdallah Menou, who at least pretended to convert to Islam—were concerned mainly with getting their demoralized army out of its hopeless predicament. A Franco-Ottoman agreement allowing the French to evacuate Egypt was concluded but fell apart after the British demanded that they first surrender and become prisoners of war. Then, in 1801, British and Ottoman armies landed near Alexandria and, after a series of engagements, forced the French to surrender. The French were allowed to return home according to the terms of the earlier agreement. Their mission accomplished, the British also left two years later to allow local and Ottoman forces to pursue their own internecine struggle for control of Egypt.

The Ottomans—and also the British and Russians, though only temporarily—soon made peace with France. By 1806 the Ottomans had resumed their traditional role as an ally of the French, now against both Britain and Russia, with the latter invading the Principalities (Moldavia and Wallachia). Then, in 1807, Napoleon concluded a separate peace with the czar at Tilsit and for a while even considered a plan to partition Ottoman territories. He still dreamed of returning to Egypt and marching on to India. Now increasingly concerned about the possibility of Russian control of the Straits, Britain made peace with the sultan in 1809. Napoleon's invasion of Russia in 1812 made it imperative for the latter to have peace on its southern front, and so the Russo-Ottoman Treaty of Bucharest, in the same year, provided for Russia's withdrawal from almost all of the occupied Ottoman territories. Napoleon's demise three years later ended a complicated phase of international politics but left British and other European concern for limiting Russian expansion into Ottoman territories as a perennial theme.

RIVAL REFORMERS:
ISTANBUL AND CAIRO

In Istanbul, Salim III's reforms evoked a conservative backlash. During 1807 an alliance of Janissaries, *ulama,* and local notables, whose independence was endangered by strengthened central authority, overthrew the sultan and put a weak, conservative member of the Ottoman house on the throne, one who abandoned the New Order. Soon afterward, a Balkan notable, Bayrakhtar Mustafa Pasha, who was bitter over not getting an important position in the central government, embraced the cause of reform and tried to restore Salim. When the latter was murdered, only one member of the ruling dynasty, soon to become Sultan Mahmud II, remained. At first under Bayrakhtar's aegis, the new sultan began to restore the reform program. But the Janissaries again intervened to overthrow the strongman. In the absence of an eligible rival for the throne, the ardently reformist sultan's life was spared, but for most of two decades he dared not take a stand against the powerful conservative groups.

It was left to Muhammad Ali Pasha, who emerged as ruler in Egypt in the aftermath of the French invasion, to carry out the Middle East's first intensive program of modernization. An Ottoman soldier and former tobacco merchant born in Macedonia of Albanian or possibly Turkish extraction, he succeeded to the command of an Albanian regiment sent against the French. A clever, ruthless man of unexcelled cunning (he later had a translation of Machiavelli's writings prepared, only to find out that he had nothing to learn from the seemingly overrated Florentine), Muhammad Ali adeptly played off the rival *mamluk* factions against one another and the Ottoman governor. He gained the support of the populace and their leaders from among the *ulama.* In 1805 they proclaimed him governor, a position that the sultan soon formalized. The *mamluks* retreated to Upper Egypt, and Muhammad Ali finally broke their power in 1811 by inviting their commanders to the citadel in Cairo, where his artillery exterminated them as they passed along a narrow passageway. Repeating the pattern of eighteenth-century *mamluk* beys, Muhammad Ali established his virtual independence in a personal empire centered in Egypt. With no loyalty to Egypt as such, he maintained autocratic control until 1848 and started a dynasty that survived until 1953.

Muhammad Ali's central concern was the development of a powerful army. Depending at first on his Albanian force and other heterogeneous troops, his army invaded the Sudan in the early 1820s. It went primarily to find recruits for a new slave army, otherwise organized along Western lines, following Salim III's example. The beginnings of modern education emerged in the form of a school for officers, a medical school to provide necessary medical care for the troops, and the like, all staffed by French instructors. When the enslaved blacks succumbed to disease, Muhammad Ali sought another source of military manpower and finally fell upon an option that no one seemed to have thought of before—Egyptian peasants. For millennia, the latter had been under the rule of alien military classes who assumed that they were unfit to be soldiers. Using cruel means that resembled the capture of wild animals, the governor's agents conscripted large numbers of Egyptian villagers. Many fled their villages or mutilated their bodies to avoid this fate, but those who were conscripted were molded into the most effective military force in the Middle East. This also began a pattern in which Egyptians—known as "peasants" regardless of social background—provided the common soldiers and eventually some junior officers. Turks and Circassians long remained at the top of the army and the society but tended gradually to melt into the general population.

A broad program of modernization provided the foundation for this military power. In order to squeeze what he could out of the country more efficiently, Muhammad Ali gradually abolished the existing tax-farms and pious foundations (institutions that, as recent research shows, had evolved into a kind of de facto landlordism there a century earlier, unlike in other parts of the Ottoman Empire), thus restoring central control over agriculture. The peasants, in turn, continued to have customary rights to, but not freehold ownership of, particular pieces of land. They could be punished and forced to return if they fled their villages, which many did as a result of severe exploitation. In a pattern of monopoly, the peasants had to sell their produce to the government at artificially low prices that left them ever deeper in debt and impoverishment, while the ruler was able to get handsome profits to pay for his military adventures.

Muhammad Ali opened an important channel for Western influence by sending student missions to France. Perhaps more receptive than the students to what he saw and read there was the *imam* accompanying them, Shaykh Rifa'ah Rafi al-Tahtawi. He left us an exciting account of his experiences and also other works that argue in favor of reopening the gates of *ijtihad* and of popular government—his loyalty to Egypt's regime notwithstanding—and even socialism. Tahtawi has the distinction of being the first Middle Easterner to articulate a strong patriotic sentiment, in this case a purely Egyptian loyalty expressed in the poetic gems scattered throughout his works. In addition, Tahtawi became the director of Muhammad Ali's Translation Bureau, which rendered about two thousand diverse Western books into Arabic.

A new pattern of landlordism eventually emerged as Muhammad Ali granted land to members of his family and to other important people around him. All land remained technically under state ownership at first, with the grants again often in the form of tax-farms, but the emergence of private ownership eventually was formalized.

Besides assuming direct control over the land, the new ruler took various steps to enhance productivity and thus to increase government revenue. New crops, notably long-staple cotton, helped enable Egypt to become increasingly dependent on the sale of agricultural products to Europe. After centuries of deterioration, the irrigation system was greatly improved. Ruthless measures succeeded in settling most of the relatively small bedouin population.

Muhammad Ali made an unsuccessful attempt to industrialize Egypt. He established numerous factories and brutally forced peasants and artisans to work in them. But maintenance of machinery was poor, and a lack of other kinds of power forced reliance on oxen to turn the wheels, which did not work well. Those Europeans who initially felt some apprehension lest Egypt's industry eliminate part of their own export market soon had their fears allayed.

At first Muhammad Ali offered his service to his weak overlord in Istanbul. Even while he was establishing control in Egypt, he was called on for help in suppressing the "Wahhabi" Sa'udi rulers of Najd, who had by now occupied the Hijaz and were uncontrollably raiding into Syria and Iraq, where they attacked the Shi'ite holy places. Under the command of Muhammad Ali's sons, notably the capable Ibrahim, a campaign in Arabia succeeded in conquering most of the peninsula between 1811 and 1820. While the Sa'udis restored their control of central Arabia after the forces from Egypt withdrew, the Hijaz and coastal Yemen remained in Muhammad Ali's empire a little longer.

Then, in 1821, the sultan needed Muhammad Ali's troops in Greece to suppress a rebellion that typified a growing nationalism among Christian Balkan peoples. (A series of revolts starting in 1804 had already led to autonomy for Serbia in 1817.) Promised the governorship of Crete and the Morea, Muhammad Ali succeeded in his mission. But the real arbiters were the powers of Europe, where Ottoman but not Greek atrocities evoked much one-sided moral indignation. Also, Britain and France feared unilateral Russian intervention, and the navies of these three powers joined to destroy the Ottoman and Egyptian fleets in 1827. Muhammad Ali's forces withdrew from Greece, while the sultan was unable to resist a Russian invasion of the Balkans and eastern Anatolia.

Only the apprehension of other European powers about the czar's expansionism induced the Russians to withdraw from most of the occupied territories (while acquiring numerous privileges in the Balkans). Recognition of Greek independence, though within a much smaller territory than today, was left as Istanbul's main concession in the peace treaty signed at Adrianopole (known today by its Turkish name, Edirne) in 1829.

Mahmud II finally was able to carry out reforms that in part were in emulation of his vassal in Cairo. With the end of one war with Russia in 1812, the sultan concentrated on consolidating his control of the empire. This was achieved with the exception of places such as Greece, Egypt, Arabia, and parts of the Fertile Crescent. By 1826, Mahmud II dared create modern military units, thus evoking rebellion by Janissaries and their supporters among the artisans and *ulama*. In turn, he was able to massacre the Janissaries—the "auspicious event," as this break with medievalism came to be known—and to create a new army that was in effect the restoration of Salim's previous attempt. The Bektashi order of dervishes, which was closely associated with the Janissaries, also was banned. The remaining *timars* finally were abolished, and the state took control of pious foundations. There were modifications in provincial administration, while building roads, conducting a census, starting a regular postal service and an official newspaper, and the like helped to bolster central control.

With the creation of a powerful army in mind, Mahmud II started the westernization of education. Schools of engineering and military science (as well as of medicine) emerged, with French and Prussian army officers as instructors. And students were sent to study in France. A program of translating European books ensued. Some European-style schools, even for adolescent boys, began the "bifurcation" of Middle Eastern culture into its indigenous and westernized forms.

Although such fundamental Western institutions as secular law or representative government still had virtually no presence in the Ottoman Empire, Mahmud II began a pattern of superficial westernization. Western nomenclature for government offices came into use. Western-style furniture graced the palace, and the sultan started appearing on the street at various public events like a European king. Not only did he adopt Western clothes and cut his beard to conform to European styles, but he tried to revolutionize the dress of his subjects by legal fiat. Instead of the traditional turbans, a new kind of headdress, the fez, was decreed for nonclerics. This round red hat with a tassel—permitting the Muslim to touch his forehead to the floor during prayer—had previously appeared in North Africa and may have been of European origin, but it eventually caught on so as to become a distinctive part of Middle Eastern attire.

Still, the sultan was no match for his titular subordinate in Cairo, who came close to taking over the empire in the 1830s. Muhammad Ali allied himself with the Shihab amir in Lebanon, and his troops, commanded by Ibrahim Pasha, invaded Syria with ease in 1831. Within two years, they moved on through Anatolia to within 150 miles of Istanbul. Muhammad Ali's armies could almost surely have made him the strongman, or perhaps sultan, of the whole empire except for European intervention.

The challenge of his rebellious vassal forced the sultan into the arms of the czar. The Russian fleet sailed to the Golden Horn, and Russian soldiers got permission to march overland to help defend Istanbul. The Treaty of Hunkiar Iskelesi (1833) established an alliance between Istanbul and St. Petersburg. This treaty obligated the former at Russia's request to close the Straits to the warships of third powers. By implication, Russian warships were to gain access to the waterway, in contrast to the "ancient rule" of the Ottoman Empire excluding all alike. In effect, this constituted a de facto Russian protectorate over the Ottomans and evoked protests from other capitals.

One of Muhammad Ali's initial advantages—being welcomed with open arms in Syria because of his seemingly more orderly administration and emphasis on religious toleration—vanished as the same oppressive methods known in Egypt appeared in Syria and bred rebellion. But when the sultan tried to push the pasha's army back from Syria in 1839, the latter proved his superiority all the more. Perhaps in part because of the fear of Russia's embrace, the Ottoman fleet mutinied and transferred its loyalty to Muhammad Ali.

Again, the European powers decided the outcome, leaving a weakened empire for Muhammad Ali and a sultan no longer dependent on St. Petersburg. Meeting in London in 1840, the representatives of the great powers decided that Muhammad Ali's forces must leave Anatolia and Syria. Austrian and British naval forces temporarily occupied Beirut and encouraged a renewal of the Syrian revolt to force the pasha's hand. In accordance with the "ancient rule," the London Straits Convention of 1841 forbade the use of the Straits to foreign warships, and the czar renounced the Treaty of Hunkiar Iskelesi. In the same year, the sultan awarded a consolation prize to Muhammad Ali: the hereditary governorship of Egypt and the Sudan for his family. Annual tribute to Istanbul was required, but while Egypt continued to be under an Ottoman ruling class and in some respects a meaningful part of the empire, the sultan henceforth had little say over his vassal's affairs. Now that his more grandiose dreams were shattered, Egypt's ruler lapsed into depression and then senility before he died in 1849.

TRADITIONAL ECONOMIES
DISRUPTED

An often overlooked feature of the settlement imposed on Muhammad Ali was the effective extension of the Anglo-Ottoman Commercial Treaty of 1838 to Egypt. With other European states getting the same privileges as Britain, this removed barriers to the importation of goods into Ottoman lands. It hastened the ongoing process whereby industrial goods imported from Europe undermined the older Middle Eastern industries and the guilds that had been such an important aspect of urban life. As for Egypt, where the state monopolies were now banned, this in fact provided a final blow to Muhammad Ali's industrialization program. Throughout Ottoman lands, there were dramatic decreases in the number of factories during this period, matched by equally dramatic increases in foreign trade—possibly fiftyfold during a hundred-year period. Middle Easterners even sometimes became dependent on agricultural goods imported via Europe, as when Western Hemisphere coffee replaced the Yemeni product in many places.

The other side of the coin was the increasing dependence of Middle Eastern countries on exporting agricultural goods and other raw materials for the world market, with the terms of trade always favoring European goods. Self-sufficient peasant villages with hereditary rights to state-owned land made way for the emergence of private ownership in the hands of big landlords and production of cash crops. Although some traditional industries and guilds survived into the twentieth century and village life retained some of its age-old characteristics in less accessible regions, such economic changes generally shattered the older coherence of society. According to one present-day interpretation (that of the "dependency," or "world system," school), it was the emergence of the European-centered world market from about the sixteenth century on, with regions such as the Middle East on the disadvantaged "periphery," that created "underdeveloped" societies. According to this school of thought, today's industrialized countries—the "core"—actually acquired their wealth at the expense of the periphery. Whether or not one accepts this controversial theory, it is clear that a grotesque gap between the standard of living of much of the West and that of what is today called the Third World was emerging by the nineteenth century.

Despite some abortive earlier attempts, the beginnings of modern industries had to await the twentieth century. Some new industries—the production of thread in Bursa for European factories, for example—were developed in the nineteenth century, but by European, especially British, interests. Most European investment—on a large scale later in the nineteenth century—was in raw materials, particularly mines, or in communications, most of all railroads, sometimes with the Ottoman government providing subsidies. European bank loans at high rates of interest also started Istanbul, Cairo, and Tehran on the road to bankruptcy. Thus did the impact of the Western economic tide devastate the Middle East in ways that proved more fundamental than the more obvious political subordination.

RUSSIAN AGGRANDIZEMENT
AND THE EUROPEAN BALANCE
OF POWER

Russian pressures repeatedly led to new collisions with the Ottoman Empire after 1840. Each time other European powers frustrated czarist aggrandizement, but they increasingly took territories for themselves and imposed a kind of collective protectorate on the empire.

In the early 1850s growing rivalry over the holy places in Palestine created a new crisis. Russia claimed the right to protect the sultan's Greek Orthodox subjects, and France asserted the same responsibility for Roman Catholics. Monks of the two faiths sometimes resorted to violence in their rivalry over particular shrines, and this dragged in their foreign patrons. As the Ottomans rejected Russian demands on this issue, the Russians proposed to Britain that "the sick man is dying" and should be partitioned. Perhaps not understanding that Britain firmly opposed the suggestions, the czar's forces invaded the Principalities in 1853. Another Russian army penetrated eastern Anatolia, and the Russian navy obliterated its Ottoman counterpart in the Black Sea. In turn, British and French forces landed in the Straits region to protect the Ottomans. But the major theater of battle came to be the Crimea, with British, French, Sardinian, and Ottoman forces landing there and, after a long siege, eventually taking the city of Sevastopol.

A conference convened in Paris, and the resulting peace of 1856 ended the Crimean War and brought withdrawal of all occupying forces. The Principalities reverted to Ottoman sovereignty but with their autonomy protected by the powers, and a growing sense of Romanian nationalism soon led to their gradual merger. Several

Balkan peoples revolted during the next two decades. No further territorial changes occurred, although autonomy in some cases, such as that of Serbia in 1867, became little less than independence.

The Black Sea was largely neutralized. The Peace of Paris restricted naval activity to light Russian and Ottoman vessels, but another international agreement in 1871 restored Russian rights to maintain a fleet there and allowed other navies to enter the Straits under certain conditions during peacetime. The Peace of Paris also opened the Straits, the Black Sea, and the Danube to merchant ships of all nations.

A new financial dependence matched the Ottomans' military dependence on the great powers. Beginning with the need to finance the Crimean War, the foreign debt got out of hand. By the 1870s, inefficient collection of revenue and a series of bad crops led to a situation in which most of the money was committed to paying the debt. The government could now neither meet civil servants' salaries nor pay interest on loans. Eventually, the powers agreed to a major reduction of the debt and in 1881 set up an Ottoman Public Debt Administration that included European representatives in charge of collecting specific taxes.

A new round of international crises over the Balkans culminated in another Russo-Ottoman War in 1877. Despite some early Ottoman successes, the Russians eventually pushed through the Balkans to the vicinity of Istanbul, where the British fleet again appeared. Another Russian force occupied much of northeast Anatolia. The harsh Peace of San Stefano followed, which forced the sultan to cede parts of the Balkans and of northeastern Anatolia, including Kars, Ardahan, and Batum, to Russia; to accept independence for Serbia and Montenegro; and to give autonomy to an extremely large Bulgaria, still to be Russian-occupied.

The other powers would not stand for such big gains by Russia. An international congress met in Berlin and forced a revised peace that was much less favorable to St. Petersburg. The most significant change was a reduction in Bulgaria's territory. In addition to Serbia and Montenegro, Romania also became independent. The new arrangement put Bosnia and Herzegovina under Austrian administration, although technically they remained Ottoman territories. Britain occupied Cyprus on a similar legal basis.

The few remaining areas of the Balkans still under Ottoman control subsequently were scenes of revolt, including Macedonia and even heavily Muslim Albania in the 1880s. A Greek attempt to take Thessaly in 1897 failed, but a bloody revolt in Crete, aided by the Greek army and involving massacres by all sides, led to intervention by the powers and autonomy for the island, which Greece finally annexed in 1912.

THE TANZIMAT

As for the Ottoman Empire's continuing process of westernization, the death of Mahmud II initiated a period of accelerated reform known as the Tanzimat ("Reorganization"). Extending through the reigns of Abd al-Majid (1839–1861) and Abd al-Aziz

(1861–1876), this in part represented efforts, sincere or otherwise, to satisfy European demands and prevent the further intervention for which abuses provided a rationalization. Consequently, the promulgation of two important documents declaring an end to arbitrary practices, the Noble Rescript of Gulhane in 1839 and the Imperial Rescript of 1856, occurred at the time of great international crises, when the fate of the empire was at the mercy of European power. But, while this was an important catalyst, it was the convictions of a series of devoted reformers, particularly Mustafa Rashid Pasha and later Ali Pasha and Fu'ad Pasha, all of whom recurrently held the grand vizierate and the dominant role in shifting political coalitions, that fundamentally fueled the drive for change.

The principle of equality for all the sultan's subjects, regardless of religion, occupied a prominent place in Tanzimat decrees. The relative tolerance of Islamic practice notwithstanding, this was a radical idea that contradicted the concept of *dhimmis* as protected peoples subject to certain disabilities, and full application was perhaps too much to expect at once. Indeed, opposition to equality came from the *dhimmis* themselves. Some Christian church leaders were wary of losing their special position as millet leaders. And although the end of the *jizyah* (poll tax) on *dhimmis* was welcome, the prospect of being conscripted into the army just like Muslims was not. A compromise that emerged—allowing non-Muslims to opt to pay a special tax equivalent to the *jizyah* in return for their old privilege of exemption from military service—was a reversion to Islamic principles in a disguise that pleased everyone.

Major reforms in the administration of the empire ensued. The abolition of tax-farming was a major promise of the 1839 decree. But the practice was restored two years later. A land law of 1858 that apparently represented the goal of codifying the old categories of ownership turned out to produce tremendously important socioeconomic consequences. Its provision for registration of rights to land led to the acquisition of title by a few people to large tracts of former wasteland. And although the historian Haim Gerber's recent study has questioned the extent to which this was true, the new law also resulted in landlords' getting title to much soil that those who tilled it had always enjoyed usufruct rights to. Many such villagers seemingly were too suspicious of the government to enter the land in the registers in their own names. In any case, the land law slowly brought about the emergence of a landlord class and a sharecropping peasantry.

Among other reforms, this period saw the beginning of efforts to establish municipal government. Also, a law of 1864 provided for a new provincial unit, the vilayet, and a slow move toward a uniform provincial administrative system followed.

New developments in communications spread to the Ottoman Empire. In 1854 the telegraph appeared and steamship companies began to form. Foreign-financed railroads slowly began to connect Ottoman cities. All of this enhanced centralization and accelerated foreign influences.

The gradual secularization of the legal system began at this time. The Noble Rescript, perhaps the Ottomans' first open break with Islamic principles, announced "new rules" as though to defy the concept of an immutable body of law, and no *fatwa* (ruling) by the highest religious authority was sought to legalize it. A criminal code, enacted in 1840, was based on Islamic rules, but a subsequent series of codes, such as the commercial code of 1850, brought a large degree of westernization of law. Published in stages between 1870 and 1876, the Majallah (Digest) codified Hanafite civil law, covering contracts and related matters, thus giving this aspect of Ottoman jurisprudence a European form while retaining Islamic substance. Only the law of personal status was too sacrosanct for tampering. The subsequent legal system reflected the growing duality in the Islamic world between aspects of life governed by Western-style law and those ruled by religious courts.

Modern education gained a new impetus. From the late 1850s on, there was a vast increase in the number of modern elementary schools and an even greater increase in secondary schools. An elite institution, the Lycée of Galatasaray, emerged in 1860. With its instruction in French and its totally Western-style curriculum, this school was to play a central role in the growth of a modern-educated class.

The appearance of a new kind of intelligentsia—in contrast to the graduates of traditional mosque-colleges—pushed modernization in new directions. Private newspapers began to appear in 1840, and they initiated a simplified kind of journalistic Turkish that avoided much of the older pomposity and use of Persian and Arabic vocabulary. Translations from French literature made way for the imitation of European literary styles. Turkish literature from this time on has been labeled more European than Asiatic. Even the drama, a literary genre formerly largely absent in the Islamic world (aside from Shi'ite passion plays, there were shadow plays in Islamic Spain), had a beginning with the plays of Ibrahim Shinasi.

THE YOUNG OTTOMANS
AND THE CONSTITUTION

Some of the new intellectuals began to demand further change. For the first time, reform was not something only pushed from above. The early modernizers had seen the emulation of Western military techniques and then administrative reform as the way to defend the empire. This kind of change, however, only led to further European interference. Now, the idea emerged that other facets of Western societies provided the secret source of their power. The real key to success was thought to be "freedom," limitations on the power of the ruler, and popular control through an elected parliament. Another idea new to the Ottomans was that of love for their ancestral land—a territorial nationalism that encompassed all peoples in the empire—although this idea tended still to be incongruously mixed with the concept of an Islamic *ummah* (community).

Ideas such as these inspired the formation in 1865 of an organization that later became known as the Young Ottoman Society. Shinasi, Ziya Pasha, and, perhaps most important, Namik Kemal were among the writers and journalists who pushed for reform. They even had some support in the Ottoman royal house, and a member of the ruling family in Egypt, Mustafa Fazil Pasha, became a leading Young Ottoman. The latter was apparently miffed over a new rule relating to succession to the

Egyptian throne that left him out, and he hoped instead to head a constitutional government for the whole Ottoman Empire.

The Young Ottomans opposed both the authoritarianism and the secularism of the Tanzimat. They realized that reform had created a highly autocratic, centralized state, in contrast to earlier practices that let many groups participate in political decisions. Also, Islamic injunctions about consultation and the right of the people to approve the ruler (the *bay'ah*)—as well as his limited power under the *shari'ah* that seemed comparable to modern constitutionalism—provided indigenous rationales for the kind of westernization that the Young Ottomans wanted. Superficial, slavish imitation was scorned. This movement has the distinction of being the first that worked to reconcile Islamic and Western civilizations, indeed to embrace much of the deeper aspects of the latter on the ground that they were in accord with a rightly interpreted Islam.

Other forces for a while seemed to push the empire in the direction called for by the Young Ottomans. Sultan Abd al-Aziz's wastefulness got the blame for the hopeless financial situation. And a new conflict with Russia renewed incentive for reform. Student demonstrations brought matters to a head. Midhat Pasha, a capable official who had become known for his effectiveness in implementing administrative reforms in the Balkans and Iraq, came to the fore as the spokesperson for a constitution. A *fatwa* authorized the deposition of Sultan Abd al-Aziz; and another prince, who agreed to support a constitution, eventually ascended the throne as Sultan Abd al-Hamid II.

After a committee headed by Midhat drew it up, the constitution was promulgated by Sultan Abd al-Hamid II. In accordance with its terms, a parliament was elected. To many, the establishment of a European-style parliamentary regime seemed to be on its way, even though the parliament had limited authority and the sultan continued to have much arbitrary power—for example, to banish any person or to dissolve the parliament.

Abd al-Hamid II soon made full use of the constitution's loopholes to create a new absolutism. In 1878 he dissolved the parliament, which did not meet again during his long period of rule. Dismissed from office and exiled, Midhat later got permission to return, only to be imprisoned and finally to be murdered by the sultan's agents. The Young Ottoman movement withered, eventually to be replaced by a new generation of reformers.

ACCELERATED MODERNIZATION AND DESPOTISM

The long reign of Abd al-Hamid II (1876–1909) turned out to be the antithesis of constitutionalism. Instead, tyranny reached its zenith as the suspicious sultan employed spies and informers and as modern communications allowed despotism to penetrate all corners of his domain. Although two plots to overthrow him in 1878 failed, they helped to intensify his suspiciousness and cruelty.

Contrary to what is often believed, Abd al-Hamid II's reign was a period of intensified modernization along the lines of the Tanzimat period. The population continued to grow, with that of Anatolia reaching about twelve million by the early twentieth century. Modern education progressed rapidly as schools of all levels came into existence, and the University of Istanbul (to use its later name) opened in 1900. Censorship sometimes bordered on the ridiculous, such as covering up news of assassinations of foreign heads of state by attributing their deaths to fictitious diseases. Still, more newspapers and other periodicals got their start, and the number of readers vastly increased. Scientific knowledge was disseminated through popular articles written in an increasingly simplified Turkish. Another literary medium, the novel, emerged in Turkish. Railroads tripled their previous length to nearly six thousand kilometers of track by 1913, admittedly still small in comparison with European countries. From 1888 on, the Orient Express provided an unprecedented connection between Istanbul and western European cities. The Hijaz Railway connected Damascus and Madina, financed by contributions from all over the Muslim world at the start of the twentieth century.

The beginnings of a great tragedy for the Armenian people appeared at this time. The Armenians had been regarded as one of the most fortunate groups under Ottoman rule, and they filled many important positions after the growth of nationalism caused the Greeks to lose favor in the early 1800s. But the growth of education and cultural activities among the Armenians also fed their own political nationalism. In addition, Armenian officers in the czar's army were prominent among the invaders of eastern Anatolia in 1877, enhancing the natural appeal of this Christian power as a liberator. Armenian nationalist societies began to engage in terrorist activities, such as holding hostages in a bank in 1896. Such incidents provoked countermeasures by Turks, particularly those increasingly numerous refugees from persecution in places formerly under Ottoman rule. Several thousand Armenians were massacred in the 1890s, but this was only a precursor of even worse events to come. All of this was the nearly inevitable consequence of a Christian separatist nationalism near the heart of the empire among a people who formed only a minority of the population, even in most parts of their traditional homeland.

THE YOUNG TURKS

By the 1890s, a combination of despotism and external threats to the empire helped to inspire a new opposition movement to the sultan among his Turkish subjects. Various intellectuals and again some dissident members of the Ottoman family became active in exile in Europe. Divergent attitudes with regard to issues of Westernization and the question of Turkish nationalism versus a multinational federal empire split the ranks of such people. But these "Young Turks," the name that came to be applied to them although they never used it themselves, were united in demanding the restoration of the constitution and opposing despotic rule. A network of Masonic lodges provided one medium for spreading revolutionary ideas. Opposition groups were also forming among army officers and among those in strategic positions as telegraph operators. In 1907 some older civil and military groups came together to form the Ottoman Committee of Union and Progress (CUP).

In 1908 there was widespread popular unrest in many places, with food short-ages and high prices leading to riots and strikes. Salonica, in Macedonia, became the key to revolution, as a leading CUP army officer, Enver Bey, suspecting a crackdown by the sultan, escaped to the hills and drew increasing numbers of his fellow soldiers to his side. As other troops in Macedonia mutinied against their generals, the sultan gave in to CUP demands for restoring the constitution. Though not officially assum-ing power, the CUP became a major force influencing the state. The next year a re-volt led by *ulama* and their students brought Abd al-Hamid back to power. But soon afterward an "Army of Deliverance" restored CUP influence and removed Abd al-Hamid from the throne in favor of a sultan more amenable to its will. Amid several splits and the appearance of other opposition groups, the CUP increasingly became the real rulers. In fraudulent parliamentary elections in 1912, CUP candidates took nearly all of the seats. Although another group of officers temporarily overthrew the growing despotism of the CUP, the latter again took control in 1913. The hopes for real constitutionalism were finally dashed as the arbitrary will of a CUP triumvirate of three beys (soon elevated to pashas)—Enver, Tal'at, and Jamal—tightened its grip.

The early CUP period found the Ottoman Empire still on the defensive against local nationalism and European imperialism. Tripolitania and Benghazi (i.e., Libya), the last North African territory over which Istanbul exercised even loose control since the establishment of French rule in Algeria (1830) and Tunisia (1881), fell prey to an Italian invasion in 1911. Ottoman troops remained in Libya to aid in the con-tinuing resistance of the Sanusis, a puritanical religious group dating back to the early nineteenth century. Italy also occupied the Dodecanese Islands in the Aegean.

In 1912, four Balkan states—Bulgaria, Greece, Montenegro, and Serbia—joined together to attack their former overlord. Ottoman territory in the Balkans shrank to Istanbul and its immediate hinterland. In a Second Balkan War later in the same year, the Balkan states turned on each other, allowing the Ottomans to enter and retake Thrace and Edirne from Bulgaria, but this hardly represented a basic reversal of fortunes.

With almost all European powers encroaching on Ottoman territories, the one with the cleanest hands seemed to be Germany. All the Ottoman eggs were still not put in the German basket, for as late as 1914 Istanbul looked forward to receiving two warships it had purchased in Britain, and many realized that Britain was their only real hope for restraining the more blatant expansionism of the other powers. But the CUP committed itself increasingly to Germany. Enver, in particular, ever since he served as the Ottoman military attaché in Berlin, was an admirer of the Germans.

From the 1880s on, Berlin was engaged in an avid courtship of Istanbul. Kaiser Wilhelm II visited Istanbul in 1889 and 1898. German capital began pouring in, the most notable example being financing for an Istanbul-to-Baghdad railway, which, with its western connections, might constitute a Berlin-to-Baghdad line and further tie Germany to the Ottoman Empire. Berlin sent a military mission to Istanbul as early as 1883. Following defeats in the wars with Italy and the Balkan states, the Ottomans' concern with improving their armed forces led to further dependence on Germany, with General Liman von Sanders and fifty-two other German officers gaining key positions in the sultan's army in 1913.

TURKISH NATIONALISM

The modern Western concept of nationalism infiltrated the Middle East during the late nineteenth century. According to nationalist thinking, which had dominated Europe for the past hundred years, the individual owed his on her supreme loyalty to a nation. Especially in central and eastern Europe this was often defined along ethnic lines, with separate statehood the goal of those peoples who had not already achieved it.

This was in contrast to the older Middle East concept: Aside from personal loyalty to a ruler and an emotional attachment to a restricted locality, people had identified themselves primarily with the religion to which they belonged. In Islamic doctrine, all Muslims formed one community (*ummah*), regardless of their tribe, language, or race. Ethnic differences had, in practice, been divisive many times throughout the history of Islam, but the multiethnic Ottoman Empire had not been based on the principle of domination by one particular ethnic group. On the other hand, identity never transcended religious divisions.

One alternative for the Ottoman Empire during the nineteenth century was "Ottomanism." This was the idea, urged by liberals, of one Ottoman people without religious or ethnic distinctions. It proposed to solve the problem of identity in keeping with another recent Western idea, equality. But this never really caught on, and even its advocates often expressed contradictory sentiments.

The religious identity still had deep roots and now took the form of pan-Islamism. The Ottoman dynasty began to assert its dubious claim to the title of caliph. And since the Ottoman Empire was the only major Sunni Muslim state retaining any degree of real independence, Muslims outside the empire, particularly those under Western colonial rule, tended to accept the claim. Turning the tables on those who saw Islam as the basis for constitutionalism, Sultan Abd al-Hamid II exploited pan-Islamic sentiment in order to suppress liberalism within Ottoman territory and to assert his leadership in the Islamic world. Though mixed with contradictory ideas, emphasis on pan-Islamism even survived the CUP revolution of 1908.

Turkish ethnic nationalism gained official acceptance after 1908. In addition to the general influence of central and eastern European nationalist movements, the writings of several nineteenth-century European scholars on the pre-Islamic Turks of Central Asia nurtured a new pride in Turkishness. The influx of Turkish refugees from Russia, influenced by the pan-Slav movement, further strengthened the new Turkish ethnic identity, as did the development of Arab separatism. For the first time poets proclaimed the glorious history of the Turks. A Turkish Society, designed to emphasize Turkish greatness, emerged in 1908. A network of local clubs, called the Turkish Hearth, spread after 1912 and with it grew a new pride in Turkish culture.

Since there was no concept of a homeland within boundaries approximating the later Republic of Turkey, this ethnic movement took the form of pan-Turkism. The idea often carried the label pan-Turanism, from *Turan*, a term with strong romantic connotations used for the original Central Asian homeland. The "Turanian" peoples supposedly included Hungarians, Finns, and Mongols too (that is, what we have called Ural-Altaic peoples), but in practice pan-Turanian goals were limited to the Turks. Although at first this was a purely cultural nationalism, it also assumed political aspects and called for the unity of all Turks throughout the world. The Turks of the Russian Empire were perhaps more numerous than those of the sultan's domain, and there were Turkish areas in Iran and China as well. All such Turkish-inhabited areas, according to the new nationalist movement, formed one homeland.

AFGHANI AND MODERNISM

An enigmatic Islamic scholar, Jamal al-Din al-Afghani (1839–1897), appeared in nearly every Islamic capital during the late nineteenth century. Even his origin is unknown. Although the designation "al-Afghani" indicates that he was from Afghanistan, he may have been an Iranian named al-Asadabadi trying to disguise his Shi'ite background. For that matter, some recent historians have questioned his sincerity as a Muslim. Although he sometimes became an advisor to rulers, each time he fell into disfavor. But wherever he went, he spellbound numerous followers with his pan-Islamic appeals—for the solidarity of all Muslims regardless of state or sect against the increasing danger of European imperialism.

Afghani's concerns went much further than pan-Islamism; they extended to the whole problem of the encroachment of modernity on Islamic society. Often considered the founder of "modernist" Islam, Afghani saw that modern ideas and institutions were emerging alongside—and gradually displacing—Islamic ones. Instead of this, he preached the need to integrate the two. Much in the spirit of some medieval Islamic philosophers, Afghani rejected charges that Islam was inconsistent with human reason in general or with modern science in particular. Taking reason as his guide, he insisted that any seeming conflict with religion must be reconciled by reinterpreting the latter. Afghani gave special impetus to the idea that Muslims must reopen the "gates of *ijtihad.*" Otherwise, rigid adherence to what the jurists had settled a millennium earlier would stand in the way of progress and the ability of the Islamic world to defend itself, or else change would leave Islam bypassed and irrelevant. From the point of view of later secularists, who wanted simply to throw out the religious basis of society, such ideas seem like precursors of what in the West came to be called "fundamentalism" (a term that makes little sense in relationship to Islamic movements, for there is no disagreement among Muslims on the issue of the Qur'an being literally the Word of God and thus of the "inerrancy of scriptures," the doctrine that distinguishes fundamentalists from other Christians); but to traditionalists this sounded like dangerous innovation.

EGYPT AFTER MUHAMMAD ALI

The quarter century following the death of Muhammad Ali (in 1849) saw new strides in the development of Egypt under his descendants. But the period turned into one of disappointment and led to bankruptcy, European financial control, and finally occupation in 1882.

Ibrahim Pasha took the reins for a while during his aging father's last days but preceded him in death. Then one of Muhammad Ali's grandsons, Abbas, came to the throne and, contrary to his image as a "reactionary" who let his predecessors' transformations lapse, actually followed in their footsteps with a reasonable degree of enthusiasm, while the next ruler, Sa'id, was greatly enamored of Europeans and favored accelerated modernization and westernization. This outlook continued under Isma'il (1863–1879), the early part of whose reign represented a new high point for the dynasty but then made way for its ruin.

Important changes were now occurring in Egyptian society. More and more land came under perennial (year-round) irrigation,[1] and agriculture came to be dominated by cash crops, especially long-staple cotton, for the world market. Privately owned agricultural estates developed here as elsewhere, but in Egypt the change took place much faster. Big landowners of Circassian origin were part of the picture, but some Egyptian peasants acquired smaller holdings and tended to predominate on a local level as village mayors (*umdas*) appointed by the central government. Especially as the sons of local leaders lost their exemption from military conscription during the reign of Sa'id and began to enter officer ranks, this indigenous landholding class was eventually to assert itself against the Turko-Circassian oligarchy and growing European influence.

Geography made Egypt an increasingly important focus for European ambitions. Britain's need for fast communication with its empire in India was of special importance. Steamships sailed from Britain to Alexandria and from India to Suez, at the northern tip of the Red Sea, in the 1830s; the short overland connection was made by British-built railways in the 1850s.

The old idea of a canal to connect the Mediterranean and the Red Sea now became a reality. Using his long-standing friendship with Sa'id, the French engineer and entrepreneur Ferdinand de Lesseps won a concession in 1854 that made unlimited quantities of Egyptian labor available for the project. Shares in the Suez Canal Company were owned partly by the Egyptian government but mainly by French stockholders. Despite the initial misgivings of the British government and the sultan, the 101-mile Suez Canal was completed and opened to traffic in 1869 amidst an extravagant celebration to which Isma'il invited European royalty.

---

[1] In contrast to basin irrigation, in which water is collected during the annual flood for one crop, perennial irrigation allows Egyptians to raise as many as three crops per year.

Isma'il's reign saw the appearance of a modern veneer. Railroad mileage multiplied, and such innovations as the telegraph were introduced. Street lights and modern buildings gave sections of major Egyptian cities a European look, although the rapid growth of urban population did not take place until after 1880. Banks and new schools, including some for girls, appeared. Isma'il was determined to make the country a "part of Europe."

Perhaps 100,000 Europeans, including Greeks and Italians, lived in Egypt by the 1870s. As in Ptolemaic and Roman days, parts of Alexandria seemed to belong more to a European-oriented Mediterranean world than to Egypt. Such minorities, as well as Armenians, Syrian Christians, Jews, and Copts, were virtually to monopolize the world of commerce and finance for several decades. This paralleled the preponderance of non-Muslims in such fields in other parts of the Ottoman Empire.

The international status of the Muhammad Ali dynasty soared for a while during Isma'il's rule. Expeditions into southern Sudan and East Africa put Egypt alongside European powers in the ongoing competition to partition the continent. (Ethiopia, however, imposed defeats on Egyptian forces twice in the mid-1870s.) The ruler's nominal superior, Sultan Abd al-Aziz, came to Egypt as a guest and granted him a loftier title, "khedive," of Persian origin. A new rule of succession whereby the khedivate passed to the eldest son rather than to the senior member of the dynasty also bolstered Isma'il's prestige. The capitulations remained in force, but in 1873 the consular tribunals made way for mixed courts that included foreign and Egyptian members.

But Isma'il's successes gradually turned sour. The disruption of U.S. cotton exports during the American Civil War put Egyptian cotton at a premium on the world market, but the end of that conflict in 1865 deprived Egypt of this temporary source of prosperity. Meanwhile, khedivial grandiosity cost the country dearly and left it hopelessly in the throes of foreign indebtedness. Isma'il resorted to various desperate measures, including the shortsighted announcement that those who paid three years of taxes in advance would be given partial exemption in the future. Also, he sold Egypt's shares in the Suez Canal Company to the British government, which accordingly acquired a new interest in the country.

The independence of Egypt rapidly made way for European financial control. In 1878, the khedive had to accept an Englishman and a Frenchman in the cabinet as ministers of finance and public works. These "dual controllers" and the malleable Armenian prime minister, Nubar Pasha, took effective power over a large sphere of Egyptian affairs. Also, from 1876 on, a Debt Commission, including representatives of Austria, Italy, Britain, and France, made sure that most of the revenue, now necessarily increased by higher taxation, would be earmarked for payment of the foreign debt.

European control led to growing opposition. Afghani stayed in Egypt during most of the 1870s, and his preaching inspired one brand of resistance. Khedive Isma'il also tried to resist, mainly by encouraging other anti-European forces, and international pressures finally induced the sultan to dismiss him in favor of the more subservient Khedive Tawfiq in 1879.

The nationalist forces also included Egyptian army officers and the Consultative Assembly, which Isma'il established in 1866. Both groups, who barely managed to paper over their other differences by virtue of joint opposition to foreign financial control and to the predominance of Circassians and Turks, tended to represent the new indigenous Egyptian landed class. The Consultative Assembly, composed mostly of village mayors, had little power at first but increasingly attempted to assert itself until the new khedive dissolved it in 1879.

Led by Colonel Ahmad Orabi, Egyptian army officers became the vanguard of the nationalist movement. Besides a more general resentment against foreign control, the ire of this "peasant" party focused on the effects of the new financial stringency brought on by foreign indebtedness. While the Circassians and Turks remained in top ranks, reductions in the size of the army had brought the dismissal of some Egyptian officers. Others found themselves put on half-pay, or else their salaries fell far into arrears. As early as 1879 some officers led a demonstration outside the ministry of finance and insulted Prime Minister Nubar Pasha and Sir Rivers Wilson, the British member of the dual control.

In 1881 there were bigger demonstrations and mutinies by the Orabists. They succeeded in forcing the khedive to reconvene the Consultative Assembly and to dismiss several top persons and in getting their candidates appointed instead. Thus the leader of the Constitutionalists, Sharif Pasha, became prime minister in September, while the pro-Orabist poet-statesman, Sami Pasha al-Barudi, became minister of war. Orabi himself later held the position of minister of war. So far, the nationalists were prevailing at the expense of foreign control; the prospects of the Muhammad Ali dynasty also appeared dim.

The first Egyptian national movement ended with British occupation. Foreign financial interests feared that their loans would not be repaid, and Britain became concerned over the security of the Suez Canal. An Anglo-French naval demonstration near Alexandria accompanied demands that Orabi leave the country and that Egyptian defenses in the Alexandria harbor be dismantled. As the nationalists defied such calls, the mood of the Egyptian people showed in riots against Europeans, and in turn European governments became more agitated. France had formerly taken the most hawkish position but now backed down from intervening. The British proceeded to bombard Alexandria and then to land their forces, among whom Khedive Tawfiq took refuge. The Egyptians were defeated in the Battle of Tal al-Kabir, Orabi was exiled, and a period of British occupation and effective rule began. Still owing nominal allegiance to Istanbul, Tawfiq remained as the obliging puppet of the new conquerors. The British at first expected the occupation to end soon, and repeatedly gave assurances to that effect, but subsequent developments perpetuated it until 1956.

A puritanical religious movement under the leadership of Muhammad Ahmad, proclaimed to be the Mahdi, overthrew Egyptian rule in the Sudan in 1881. For a while, it even seemed possible that the Mahdi would invade Egypt and be joined by a mass revolt of Egyptian peasants. A ten-thousand-member Egyptian force led by General William Hicks was sent against the Sudanese zealots in 1883, only to be wiped out. The garrison at Khartoum, together with General Charles Gordon, who had been sent to evacuate it, was also overrun. It was not until 1896–1898 that Sir Horatio (later Lord) Kitchener, commanding Egyptian troops, suppressed the Mahdist movement. In 1899 the Sudan gained the unusual status of a condominium, called the Anglo-Egyptian Sudan. In reality Britain dominated the country, and Egypt's role in the condominium was essentially a formality. French resentment over the British takeover of Egypt and a barely avoided clash between the two powers in the southern Sudan made way in 1904 for an entente in which Paris acquiesced in the British role in the Nile Valley in return for a free hand in Morocco.

The occupation left Egyptians too dazed to resist. The religious scholar Muhammad Abduh, a disciple of Afghani and an ardent supporter of the Orabi movement, returned to Egypt after a period of exile ready to pursue modernist reform but not a seemingly useless struggle for independence. Avidly receptive to the writings of such Europeans as Tolstoy and Spencer, Abduh expanded on Afghani's emphasis on the need to interpret revelation in the light of reason, going so far as to reject the value of much of the corpus of *hadiths*. As chief mufti of Egypt he issued innovative rulings, and as a member of al-Azhar's supreme council, he pushed for a modernized curriculum. After Abduh's death in 1905, his colleague Rashid Rida dominated the modernist movement but gave it an increasingly conservative tone.

The British "consul-general," Sir Evelyn Baring (soon to become Lord Cromer) assumed real rule over Egypt in 1883. Authoritarian and condescending toward his subjects and allowing them only a nonelective Legislative Council, Lord Cromer—and his successors, including Lord Kitchener from 1911 to 1914—ruled through British "advisors" scattered throughout the Egyptian administration. His greatest success was in straightening out the financial mess by the 1890s. In part, this was the result of other achievements, especially an increase in agricultural productivity. Irrigation was improved by such steps as the construction of a dam at Aswan, in Upper Egypt (not to be confused with the more recent Aswan High Dam). Also, such age-old brutal practices as forced labor for peasants and the use of the whip were gradually abolished.

A new phase of Egyptian nationalism soon became evident. Khedive Abbas Hilmi (1892–1914) was of a different mettle from his predecessor and schemed to undermine British power. He aspired to get French and Ottoman support and also encouraged nationalistic expression. Perhaps the most important nationalist leader was a French-educated journalist, Mustafa Kamil, whose bombastic speeches and articles in his Patriotic party's newspaper expressed an amalgam of Egyptian nationalism and solidarity with the Islamic world. He also emphasized the need for democracy and the adoption of Western civilization. Although he was careful not to violate the law, Kamil was intransigent in demanding an end to the occupation.

Some Egyptians countered the anti-British agitation with what they considered to be a more positive program. Included in this group were Ahmad Lutfi al-Sayyid and his Ummah party, which stood for a purely Egyptian identity and liberal democracy and stressed the importance of education and westernization. This party, which appealed to big landowners, was friendly toward and favored by the British.

The year 1907 brought an event that embittered a previously apathetic peasantry against British rule. Some British officials were hunting pigeons in the village of Dinshaway when one of their bullets hit an Egyptian woman. Indignant villagers attacked the hunters, and the soldiers then fired at Egyptian crowds. This was climaxed by brutal punishment—including four executions—of the Egyptians involved in the incident. Dinshaway long continued to symbolize Egyptian bitterness over the occupation. The Coptic prime minister, Boutros Ghali Pasha (whose grandson, Boutros Boutros-Ghali, became the secretary-general of the United Nations during the 1990s), presided over the largely British tribunal that imposed the sentences. He also later supported an unpopular scheme to prolong the Suez Canal Company's concession for fifty years after its scheduled expiration date (1968). The prime minister was assassinated in 1909 by a Muslim Egyptian. Nationalism thus threatened to disrupt relations between the two religions.

Cairo became a growing center of Arabic culture, with key roles played by Syrian émigrés, mainly Christians, for whom Egypt both before and after the British occupation was a welcome refuge from the more oppressive Ottoman regime. These émigrés were especially important in the proliferation of newspapers during this period. Journalistic requirements tended toward simple writing styles. Poetry flourished at the hands of such writers as Ahmad Shawki, and Western literary forms, such as drama and the novel, began to catch on.

THE FERTILE CRESCENT
AND ARAB NATIONALISM

The nineteenth century brought important developments in the Fertile Crescent, only some of which paralleled the course of other Ottoman regions. Almost for the first time, Istanbul imposed real control in some areas. For example the *mamluk* regime in Baghdad finally succumbed to the central government in 1831, but it was left to the governorship of Midhat Pasha in 1869–1872 to establish real order by suppressing the ever-marauding bedouin tribes. Although the Egyptian route for east-west commerce won out, British steamships became active on the Tigris and Euphrates. Iraq, however, remained a backwater in comparison with the western Fertile Crescent.

Muhammad Ali's occupation was a turning point for Syria. The mosaic of local chiefs made way for an effective government, and the position of non-Muslims was enhanced by their membership on local consultative councils and the removal of some traditional restrictions. The application of the Tanzimat later perpetuated the same tendencies.

By mid-century, there were signs of a literary revival in Syria. This has sometimes been credited to the arrival of American missionaries in 1820, as has subsequent Arab culture and eventual political nationalism. Actually, the revival had already begun in both Syria and Egypt, but such Syrian Christians as the poet Nasif Yaziji and Boutros Bustani, whose accomplishments included an encyclopedia and an Arabic dictionary, worked closely with the Americans. Missionary schools, including the Protestant College, later called the American University in Beirut, and its French Jesuit counterpart, later called the Université Saint-Joseph, continued to be major educational influences.

Mount Lebanon was experiencing traumatic changes. The Druze sect had long predominated in the area, particularly the south; Maronites lived in the north. But, reflecting prosperity derived from the production of silk for the world market, the Maronites were increasing in numbers and moving south. Even the dominant clan, the Shihabs, had taken the unusual step of converting to the Maronite religion, apparently in order to maintain their positions. But as Muhammad Ali's most ardent Syrian collaborators, the Shihab amirs did not long survive the restoration of the sultan's power.

Clashes between Maronites and Druzes began in 1841. The Ottoman response was to partition Lebanon into two districts, but that left an unhappy minority in each place. Trouble broke out in 1857 in the north, ironically with a revolt of Maronite peasants against their Maronite landlords. By 1860 the conflict had spread south and turned into a clear-cut civil war between the two sects, soon overflowing into other parts of Syria, with Muslim mobs attacking Christians in Damascus.

The European powers decided to intervene, and French troops landed in Beirut. In 1861 the Ottoman government proclaimed a special regime for Mount Lebanon that was to last until 1914 and to serve as a precursor to parallel patterns later in the twentieth century. According to this arrangement, the sultan, in consultation with the European powers, appointed a governor, who was assisted by a council representing the various sects.

Syria became the breeding ground for Arab ethnic nationalism, a movement that asserted the unity of Arabic-speaking Christians and Muslims and eventually called for independence from Turkish rule. Christian Arabs played an important role in this movement, especially in its early stages. After all, nationalism was a Western virus that Christians were more susceptible to catching, and the bonds of religion and loyalty to the sultan-caliph continued to unite Turks and Muslim Arabs.

Some beginnings of Arab nationalism appeared in the first half of the nineteenth century, particularly among Christians. Again, the cultural revival and the American missionaries have been given credit for this. Founded in 1857, the Syrian Scientific Society has been described as a manifestation of Arab national consciousness. It was where Ibrahim Yaziji (son of Nasif) read a poem calling on the Arabs to "arise and awake." A secret society established in Beirut in 1875 protested against Turkish rule; some earlier writers—notably George Antonius in his famous book, *The Arab Awakening*—called it the first movement for Arab independence, but this now seems to have been an exaggeration. Such movements apparently represented local particularism, and especially Christian opposition to Ottoman rule, more than Arab nationalism.

However, other evidences of Arab nationalism did appear. In part reflecting resentment over the Ottoman claim to the caliphate, a Muslim Arab from Aleppo, Abd al-Rahman al-Kawakabi, wrote a book extolling the virtues of his people and blaming the Turks for the backwardness of the Muslim world. He called for an Arab caliph but not for a state limited to the Arab-inhabited region. Some suggest that he was working for the khedive, who may have aspired to lead the Arabs. The distinction of having been the first writer to call for Arab independence belongs to Najib Azouri, a Christian Palestinian exiled in Paris and possibly receiving French support. Azouri's book, published in French in 1905, stressed the unity of Muslim and Christian Arabs and called for an Arab sultan as the constitutional ruler of the proposed Arab state and for an Arab caliph, with secular power in the Hijaz, as the head of the Islamic world.

It was not until Turkish nationalism began to supplant older identities in Istanbul that Arab separatism gained any substantial support. To the extent that Ottomanism or pan-Islamism prevailed, Turks and Muslim Arabs continued to feel a sense of unity. But Turkism left the Arabs out or, worse still, posed the threat of assimilation. After an initial period in 1908 when the CUP revolutionaries seemed to have ushered in a spirit of interethnic brotherhood, the pan-Turkism of the new regime revealed itself to the Arabs. The government soon banned the Arab-Ottoman Brotherhood, an organization founded by Arabs in Istanbul to stress the unity of the two peoples. The Young Turks proceeded to try to centralize the empire. They made Turkish the official language. Despite their numerical preponderance, the Arabs were allowed only 60 seats in the newly elected Parliament in comparison to 150 for the Turks.

Arab nationalist societies began to proliferate after the 1908 revolution. Perhaps because its location was conducive to Western influence, Syria was the center of Arab nationalism, but several Iraqi officers in the Ottoman army also joined the movement. One of the most notable of the Arab nationalist societies was al-Ahd ("the Covenant"), consisting of Arab officers under the leadership of the popular Egyptian Major Aziz Ali al-Misri, a hero of the Italo-Ottoman War of 1911. Al-Misri has the distinction of being the only Egyptian to play an important role in the early Arab nationalist movement; at the time, his countrymen were wavering between Egyptian and pan-Islamic identities but rarely thought in terms of Arabism. Arab students in Paris organized another group, al-Fatat ("Youth") in 1911. Both organizations officially called for a dual Arab-Turkish monarchy on the model of Austria-Hungary, but they were turning increasingly toward the goal of full independence. An Arab congress representing various groups met in Paris in 1913; it called for decentralization and for Arabic as the official language in the Arab provinces. Istanbul sent a representative to agree to the demands, but when the CUP did not implement the agreement, the embitterment of Arab nationalists became more intense. Even in 1914, however, there were still only a few Arab nationalists, and Arabs remained overwhelmingly loyal to the empire.

Although distinct from the nationalists, the princes of Mecca were also restive under Turkish rule. As members of the clan of Hashim, to which the Prophet Muhammad belonged, they were known as Hashimites; and as the Prophet's descendants they were *sharifs* ("nobles"). For almost a thousand years Hashimites had filled the office of amir and sharif of Mecca, usually simplified as "Grand Sharif" by Westerners. They were keepers of the holy places, sometimes also controlling the adjacent region, the Hijaz. The Ottomans, after imposing their hegemony over the area in the

1500s, designated amirs from the rival branches of the sharifian family and left the Hijaz largely to them.

Sharif Husayn, the headstrong and ambitious old man who held the office after Sultan Abd al-Hamid II conferred it on him (over CUP opposition) in 1908, felt threatened by centralization. So distrustful was the sultan of Husayn that he had kept him as an involuntary "guest" in Istanbul for the previous fifteen years. Following his appointment Husayn warded off Ottoman control by winning the loyalty of the Hijazi tribes and forced one Ottoman governor to kiss the hem of his garment. He dreamed of higher things—of becoming king of the Hijaz or of all the Arabs, or even heading the whole Islamic world as caliph. But, with a railroad now connecting Madina with the rest of the empire, the central government was becoming a greater threat. The Ottomans were making plans, bitterly opposed by Husayn, to extend the railroad to Mecca.

Arab nationalists in the Fertile Crescent began to think of Husayn as a potential leader. Thirty-five Arab members of the Ottoman Parliament notified him in 1911 of their willingness to "rise with him" against the Turks. Encouraging Husayn's ambition was his impatient son, Amir Abdullah, who wanted to work with the Arab nationalists. When Abdullah, a member of the Ottoman Parliament, passed through Cairo on his way to Istanbul in February 1914, he met Lord Kitchener and inquired whether his father could expect British assistance against the Turks. Kitchener replied that Britain could not interfere in the internal affairs of a friendly power but only laughed when Abdullah pointed to previous intervention in Kuwait, which was also an Ottoman territory. Two months later, when Abdullah was in Cairo on his return trip to the Hijaz, he pursued the matter further with Sir Ronald Storrs, the Oriental Secretary. However, another son of Sharif Husayn, the more cautious Amir Faysal, was still persuading his father to remain loyal to Istanbul.

IRAN: RISE OF THE QAJARS

To resume the story of Iran so abruptly interrupted in the midst of Karim Khan Zand's sway over much of the country, this ruler's achievements reached their zenith with an invasion of Ottoman territories and the occupation of Basrah in 1775. But with his death four years later the Iranians withdrew, and the Zand dynasty also succumbed to intrafamilial conflict.

This made way for the advances of a Turkish tribe, the Qajars, located just south of the Caspian Sea in the region of their future capital, Tehran. Agha Muhammad Khan Qajar, who escaped from detention by the Zands and whose vindictiveness dated back to his childhood castration by Afshar captors, eventually subdued his rivals throughout the country. Reflecting patterns that had recurred since Mongol days, his troops presented him with twenty thousand eyes plucked from his opponents' heads in Kirman. The Qajar forces also built pyramids of human skulls. The new ruler's coronation in 1796 (a year before his assassination) formally inaugurated a dynasty that was to last until 1925. But the peace that the new shah and his successor, Fath Ali Shah (1797–1834), harshly imposed, after so much anarchy, was soon to make way for the accelerated disintegration of a country whose population was perhaps half tribal.

THE IRANIAN *ULAMA* IN OPPOSITION

Besides the emergence of the new ruling dynasty, the later eighteenth century saw important developments in Twelver Shi'ism. The previously important school of thought, the Akhbaris, who rejected *ijtihad,* gave way to the overwhelming predominance of its rival, the Usulis. The latter accept the right of a few leading *ulama,* known as *mujtahids,* to reinterpret Islamic law. According to this doctrine, other people are bound by *taqlid* (imitation), but not in the sense that Sunni Muslims follow the details of one of the centuries-old schools of jurisprudence. Instead, each person voluntarily chooses a living *mujtahid* as his or her *marja-i taqlid* ("source of imitation") on the basis of the *mujtahid*'s great learning. This was quite in contrast with Sunni religious leaders in the Ottoman Empire, who were chosen by and tended to be subservient to the sultan. Sometimes one Twelver *mujtahid* gains preeminence as the sole *marja,* but usually he is only one of several such persons whose authority is accepted by varying proportions of the community. In any case, while the *marja*'s views are not considered infallible, he is at least theoretically in a position to mold religious teachings in a way that would be impossible for Sunni *ulama.*

Much more than under the Safavids, the *mujtahids* tended to reject the legitimacy of the shahs' rule, particularly from the mid-nineteenth century on. This often was matched by a quietist attitude based on the idea that all governments are necessarily illegitimate during the Twelfth *Imam*'s absence. But at other times the prevailing tendency has been to stress the need to work for justice and to oppose tyranny, with less concern sometimes even for the details of Islamic law prior to its future full implementation when the *imam* returns as the Mahdi. Shi'ite passion plays depicting the Umayyad Caliph Yazid versus the martyred Husayn sometimes implied opposition to all tyrants—although the message that generally came through until the late twentieth century was that Husayn's failure demonstrated the futility of revolution—and perpetuated the stress on martyrdom.

Several factors enhanced the *ulama*'s power. These included the location of some of their religious centers in Ottoman-controlled Iraq beyond the shah's reach, the important role they played as funnels for charitable contributions, and their close alliance with merchants. The feebleness of the Qajars was another factor, at times allowing clerics to maintain their own private armies. Also, unlike the Safavids, the Qajars could not legitimize their role by pretending to be descendants of one of the twelve *imams,* and a myth sometimes surfaced that they had fought alongside the Umayyads at Karbala. Iran was thus the only part of the Islamic world in which one could find something like the church-state dualism of medieval Latin Christendom. The Shi'ite "church" was to play a major role during the nineteenth and twentieth centuries as leader of the populace against both tyranny and foreign domination. But while *ulama* opposed particular shahs, especially those accused of subservience to European imperialism, they did not claim the right to rule directly or challenge the idea of monarchy.

EUROPEAN IMPERIALISM IN IRAN

Now wedged between British India and the Russian Empire, which progressively incorporated the Islamic peoples of Central Asia during the nineteenth century, Iran's independence increasingly lost its reality. Britain and Russia repeatedly decided which prince would ascend the throne. Formal independence became largely a product of the two European empires' mutual jealousy. Concerned with protecting its commercial interests and the security of the "road to India," Britain rarely evinced interest in actual territorial aggrandizement at Iran's expense and sometimes even promoted the kinds of reforms that might enable the country to resist blatant expansionism. In a sense Iranians could find satisfaction in the ability of Great Britain (or more precisely of the British colonial government of India, which oversaw matters east of Suez) to check the czars. But although the Iranians often appreciated Britain's position during the nineteenth century, both Britain and Russia eventually earned nearly equal shares of their animosity.

Russian encroachment on Iran became intense in the early nineteenth century. Georgia switched from Iran's to Russia's sphere of control in 1783, but during the next decade Russian and Iranian armies alternately dominated this area. Russian victories in 1812 led to the Treaty of Gulistan (1813), in which Tehran renounced its right to have naval vessels on the Caspian Sea and its claim to Georgia and other former parts of its domain. In reality, Iran's territorial losses were greater than the extent of its military defeat made necessary, for the commander (and governor of Azarbayjan), Abbas Mirza, successfully bargained for Russian support as heir to the throne. He did not live long enough to claim his prize, but as would often happen later in the century, the personal interests of a member of the ruling dynasty took priority over those of Iran.

Further Russian encroachments brought a new war in 1826. Before long the enemy occupied northwestern Iran, including Tabriz. In the resulting Treaty of Turkomanchay (1828), Iran ceded more territories to its northern neighbor (who withdrew approximately to today's border) and agreed to pay a large indemnity. The subsequent broad extraterritorial privileges for Russian subjects, later extended to other powers, further ate into Iran's independence. Led by religious leaders, who had inspired many people with calls for *jihad* during the war, Iranian anger against Russian imperialism—and particularly over the refuge given to a eunuch and two Muslim women of Christian origin, captives of earlier wars—culminated in an attack by the populace on the Russian legation in 1829. Several people were killed, including the minister. In turn, the shah apologized to St. Petersburg and agreed to further indemnities.

Tehran began a persistent pattern of looking for a third imperial power to use as a lever against Russia and Britain. In 1807, following Britain's successful negotiation of a treaty with Iran in 1801, Napoleonic France became the first such state with the conclusion of a Franco-Iranian Treaty of Alliance that seemed to offer France a base for an attack on British India and to give Iran an alternative to Russian encroachment. But Napoleon left the shah out in the cold by entering into an alliance with the czar at Tilsit soon afterward, and the Franco-Iranian treaty made way in 1814 for an Iranian alliance with Britain in the form of the so-called Definitive Treaty. A bribe to Abbas Mirza allowed Britain to abrogate relevant provisions of this treaty fourteen years later, during the Russo-Iranian war.

BEGINNINGS OF IRAN'S
WESTERNIZATION

Defeat evoked some "defensive modernization" in Iran, but to a much smaller extent than in the Ottoman Empire. The introduction under Abbas Mirza's leadership of modern weapons and drill and European instructors—a faint imitation of Ottoman military reforms—seems to have had little positive impact but served mainly to undermine the age-old patterns of tribal cavalrymen. Nasir al-Din Shah's able minister, Amir-i Kabir, attempted a program of reform and industrialization, but he was dismissed in 1851 and later killed, as his popularity seemed to make him a possible rival to the monarch. Nasir al-Din Shah created a Dar al-Funun ("House of Sciences [or Arts]"), a European-style college with European teachers, to train army officers and civil servants. A few students were sent to Europe after 1875 on, and the foreign sectarian schools that were starting had some impact, but educational modernization hardly developed a momentum comparable to that in Ottoman lands.

A printing press appeared in 1812 under Abbas Mirza's aegis, and an official gazette began publication in 1851. The translation of European works and the development of less obscure writing styles also proceeded. The introduction of the telegraph in 1858, followed by an Indo-European Telegraph Line in 1865, helped to open the country to outside influences. Still, Iran's communication system remained relatively primitive, with only eight miles of railroad as late as 1900.

As in other non-European regions, although more slowly than in the Ottoman Empire, the ever-growing world market produced by Europe's Industrial Revolution drew Iran into the role of exporting primary (i.e., nonindustrial) products. The development of widespread private land ownership paralleled this during the late nineteenth century, and landowners concerned with getting large profits from market crops brutally exploited the peasants. Still, the overall impact of modernity, including the world market and medical advances, brought a net improvement in living conditions. This was reflected in the approximate doubling of the population during the period starting in ca. 1774 (several devastating epidemics of cholera notwithstanding) to about 10 million in 1914.

Partly reflecting the slower impact of modernity, craft guilds retained their vitality longer in Iran than in many other places. In an exception to the general trend, considerable development occurred in some handicrafts, especially carpet making, and craft products supplemented the stream of agricultural sales to Russia, India, and Ottoman territories. Some merchants grew increasingly prosperous.

The merchant class spawned new ideas and movements. One such development was that of Sayyid Ali Muhammad, who in 1844 declared that he was the *bab* (door) to the Hidden Imam. The Babis—as his movement came to be known—emphasized equality, world brotherhood, and the importance of education. Soon asserting themselves as an entirely new religion, they attempted to supersede Islam altogether. This new heresy met heavy persecution, especially after several revolts and after one of its adherents tried to assassinate the shah. The main portion of the movement accepted the leadership of a man who called himself Baha Allah. This group, the Baha'is, continued to exist as a small minority in Iran and to engage in worldwide missionary activity, with its center in Acre, in Palestine.

DESPOTISM, NATIONALISM, AND CONSTITUTIONALISM IN IRAN

The country's administration retained brutal features. Tax-farming continued to be a general practice, and the collectors exacted all they could from the peasants. Those villages that resisted paying were sacked and their people massacred or taken captive. Even such practices as keeping hostages from their members could not keep the numerous tribes under control, and the peasants recurrently bore the brunt of this harsh world.

Spendthrift shahs imposed an intolerable drain on the treasury. The reparations to Russia after 1829 and continuing military campaigns created a financial strain; primitive methods of collecting taxes and expenses such as those incurred by a series of royal visits to Europe from 1873 on aggravated the situation.

The sale of concessions to European businesspeople with little regard for the country's overall interests became a quick but shortsighted source of revenue. In 1872 a British subject, Baron Julius de Reuter, obtained exclusive rights to mines, a railway, and a national bank, with the bulk of Iran's revenues designated for payment. In this case Russian indignation brought cancellation. But then in 1890, in return for an annual percentage, the tyrannical Nasir al-Din Shah (1848–1896) granted another English company a monopoly over the production and sale of tobacco.

Such concessions brought on popular anger led by merchants and religious scholars. The former's economic interests were threatened, and the *ulama* were embittered by shahs who seemed to cooperate with the Christian European onslaught against the Islamic world. Following the 1890 concession, the leading *mujtahid,* Hasan-i Shirazi, issued a ruling forbidding the use of tobacco under these circumstances. Iranians showed incredible solidarity in putting aside the practice of smoking until the monopoly was terminated. But the concessionaire had to be compensated, and the government fell deeper in debt to Britain and Russia. Customs receipts were pledged in payment, and the need for efficient collection led to the practice of farming out customs houses to Belgian officials.

Concession hunters continued to find prizes. In 1901 a British subject, William Knox D'Arcy, obtained an oil concession that led to the creation of the Anglo-Persian (later, Anglo-Iranian) Oil Company (AIOC). The first commercial discovery of oil in Iran (or anywhere in the Middle East aside from the Russian-ruled part of Azarbayjan) came in 1907. The British navy switched from coal to Iranian oil by 1914 and gained a controlling interest in AIOC in the same year.

Agitation against foreign penetration and local corruption and absolutism continued to intensify. Afghani came to Iran in 1866 and was later in the forefront of opposition to the tobacco concession. Escaping from Nasir al-Din Shah's agents, Afghani fled to London to direct an opposition newspaper. One of his followers assassinated the shah in 1896.

Another Iranian, Malkom Khan, originally an Armenian Christian but at least formally a convert to Islam, led a wing of the opposition that included many graduates of modern schools. In exile in London, Malkom Khan published a newspaper that strove to simplify and modernize the Persian language and called for an end to corruption and despotism, even for the adoption of secular law.

Though destined not to succeed, a constitutional revolution, fundamentally an expression of the growing Iranian nationalism, seemed for a while to win out over a monarchy whose despotism and ineffectiveness were matched by a readiness to succumb to European imperialism. Beginning in December 1905, two thousand merchants and religious scholars took refuge (*bast*) in a mosque, which custom forbade the government from violating, and demanded various reforms. This occurred again in January 1906, and each time the shah merely pretended to agree to some of the demands as the withdrawal of the merchants from their usual activities brought the economy to a halt. During the following summer, over twelve thousand joined in the *bast*. These included *ulama* in a mosque in Qum, the holy city south of Tehran, and a large number of merchants on the grounds of the British legation. A network of committees throughout Iran supported the demands for reform. The weak Muzaffar al-Din Shah (1896–1907) had no choice but to give in and grant a constitution providing for an elected Consultative Assembly (Majlis) and the principle of ministerial responsibility to that body. As a concession to the vital religious wing of the revolution, the constitution provided for a committee of *mujtahids* to determine whether acts of the new assembly were consistent with the *shari'ah*, but this provision came to be ignored in practice.

IRAN STRANGLED

Aided by the Russians, Muhammad Ali Shah came to the throne in 1907 and conspired to overthrow the constitution. In 1908 the Russian-officered Cossack

Brigade, which dated back to 1879, shelled the Majlis building and declared martial law in an attempt to restore despotic rule. But constitutionalists took control of Tabriz, while many of the religious leaders continued their opposition to autocracy from the Shi'ite holy cities of Iraq. Of course, it is an oversimplification to think of all *ulama* opposing the shah—even more so to imagine that all (or perhaps even most) supported constitutionalism. Deciding that constitutionalism, particularly the idea of popular sovereignty, was a dangerous innovation, one leading *mujtahid,* Fazlullah Nuri, shifted to the shah's camp. He was later executed by temporarily victorious constitutionalists. Ironically, it was the Bakhtiar tribe, led by a chief, Sardar As'ad, who had been influenced by Western ideas while studying in Paris, who turned the tide by occupying Isfahan and Tehran in support of the constitutionalists and permitted the Majlis to convene again in 1909. Britain and Russia allowed Muhammad Ali Shah to be deposed in favor of the twelve-year-old Ahmad Shah. A comeback attempt by the ex-shah from his Russian exile later was nipped in the bud.

Meanwhile, betraying those who saw it as a supporter of constitutionalism and a bulwark against expansionism, Britain agreed with Russia in 1907 on a plan to divide Iran into spheres of influence. Although it did not take away the country's formal independence, the agreement gave Russia a free hand to penetrate the north economically, with the British enjoying similar rights in much of the southeast. Both powers could compete for concessions in a third zone.

In another expression of its tendency to seek ties with a third state, Iran looked to the United States as a country whose hands were free of imperial designs there. An American banker, Morgan Shuster, was recruited to put Iran's finances in order. Supported by the ardently nationalist, intellectual-led Democratic party, Shuster became Treasurer-General and was entrusted with full control over the country's finances. But a financially sound Iran was not acceptable to those who were looking for prey, and in 1911 Russia demanded Shuster's dismissal. The Iranian government had no choice but to comply as the czar's troops occupied Tehran and ended the constitutional regime. The title of Shuster's subsequent book, *The Strangling of Persia,* would vividly describe what was happening.

The constitution and the struggle for independence that motivated it had now lost out. The constitutionalists' efforts to abolish such practices as tax-farming had dissipated. Iran was a country whose only army, aside from anarchic tribes, consisted of the Russian-dominated Cossack Brigade and a pro-British, Swedish-officered gendarmerie. The country seemed destined for formal annexation by the two imperial powers. There were now British troops in the south and Russian troops in the north, with provincial governors their puppets. The Russians and British even manipulated elections in an attempt to keep Iranian nationalists from being elected to the Consultative Assembly. The Democrats, including many now in exile, could only feel agony. Their hope was that another power, Germany, whose imperialism could not seem more than hypothetical despite its recent concession-hunting in the Persian Gulf region, would come to the rescue.

CONCLUSIONS

The 140 years ending in 1914 saw repeated attempts by Middle Easterners to come to terms with a European civilization whose capability grew more and more overwhelming. Much of a European-originated modernity penetrated the region. Westernization started with attempts to modernize armies and seemed to spread uncontrollably into other areas of life. Western-style education took its place alongside the older type of schools to produce a dual civilization, partly indigenous and partly westernized. Western ideas such as democratic and constitutional government took hold, although without much success. The relatively recent development of nationalism in Europe also led to similar movements among Muslim peoples.

Modern technology—the railroad, the telegraph, and such—appeared in the Middle East but penetrated the society at a vastly slower pace than in most of the West. While Japan's uniquely successful modernization allowed it to defeat Russia in 1905, thus inspiring Middle Eastern nationalists with proof that Asians were not inherently weaker than Europeans, the gap between the Middle East and the West continued to grow, leaving the Middle East more vulnerable than ever. Significant population growth everywhere in the Middle East testifies to the improvement of living conditions in some ways. But the irresistible tide of a "world market" where the West's industrial products commanded high prices in exchange for the raw materials of the larger world undermined the latter's own crafts and its social structures and created dependent economies.

None of the many attempts by Middle Eastern rulers to put their houses in order had succeeded. The task would have proved formidable even under the best of circumstances. Now those who were trying to bridge the gap between their own societies and those of the West were themselves beset by a babel of conflicting ideas—narrow traditionalism versus blind imitation; constitutionalism versus autocracy; theocracy versus secularism; religious versus ethnic, dynastic, and local identities—that crippled the effort. With provinces struggling to break away and with European powers rivaling one another in encroaching on the area, successful modernization efforts by Istanbul, Cairo, or Tehran would have provided cause for wonder.

By the late nineteenth century Asians and Africans were rarely free of some form of European domination. European power seemed to be closing in on what little remained of Middle Eastern independence in 1914. Egypt was already a province of the British Empire in all but name. What remained of the Ottoman Empire was receding in the face of continuing European designs. After a remarkable constitutional revolution of 1906, Iran was experiencing renewed strangulation at Russian and British hands.

6

the east engulfed
1914–1920

The summer of 1914 found most of the nations of Europe aligning themselves in two rival warring camps. The peace had long been fragile, and the aspiration of an increasingly powerful Germany to obtain a "place in the sun" alongside Great Britain and France polarized the Great Powers. Then the assassination of Austrian Archduke Francis Ferdinand by Serbian irredentists in June unleased a flood of rivalries. By August Germany and Austria-Hungary, known as the Central Powers, confronted a coalition, the Allies, that included Great Britain, France, and Russia. The Great War or World War I, as the struggle later came to be known, raged for more than four years and involved growing numbers of nations. In comparison with Western nations, Middle Eastern countries possessed little weight to affect the scales. But they found themselves pulled into the war as clients of one Western camp or the other, and in the end they were to be at the mercy of whoever prevailed.

The First World War was a watershed in the relationship between the Middle East and the West. The Ottoman Empire, which had ruled most of the area for four centuries, fell apart as a result of its defeat by European powers and of separatist nationalisms among its peoples. Arabs and Turks, previously united by a common faith and a common government, would henceforth go their separate ways. The political map began to take its contemporary form, with European powers gaining control over most of the fragments of the Ottoman Empire. The end of the war was to leave the Middle East, particularly the Arabs, with new grievances against the West that would remain a major preoccupation for many years. The Arab-Zionist (or Arab-Israeli) conflict, which was further to poison Arab-Western relations, also emerged at this time.

THE OTTOMAN ENTRANCE
INTO THE WAR

The possibility of helping Germany defeat the Allies attracted many Turks. This seemed to be a chance to shake off the capitulations, that is, Western nationals' privileged exemption from Ottoman law and courts. In September 1914, even before it had entered the war, Istanbul unilaterally abrogated these unequal arrangements, but only a victory over the Allies could make this permanent. Some Turkish leaders also hoped to reconquer lost territories, from North Africa to the Balkans. Moreover, it was natural for the Turks to ally themselves with the enemies of Russia, which had habitually encroached from the north and openly hoped to control the Straits and to restore the Ottoman capital city to Orthodox Christendom. Both pan-Turkism and pan-Islamism, which were now at their height, provided further incentives for the Turks to join the Central Powers. In a war against Russia, the Ottomans could hope to liberate the Turkish areas of the Transcaucasus and Central Asia. And pan-Islamism, besides its value in rallying the Muslims of the Ottoman Empire against the Allies, potentially served as a powerful weapon for undermining Western colonialism in such places as India and North Africa, which might lead to the expansion of Ottoman control over these areas.

Many leading Turks, however, admired British and French liberalism. More important, they realized that Britain, despite its occupation of Ottoman territories such as Cyprus and Egypt, had been largely responsible for preserving the Ottoman Empire during the previous century. They perceived that, to the British, the existence of the Ottoman Empire was an important asset to prevent Russian expansion into the eastern Mediterranean and to provide stability in the territories that lay along the vital route to British-ruled India. The British commitment to this longtime policy had already weakened. But to go to war against Britain, especially now that it was allied with Russia, would be an invitation for it to change its policy. And even the German embrace seemed more and more to be a stranglehold.

Yet Istanbul, despite an initial declaration of neutrality, stood alongside Berlin and Vienna. Enver's vanity, ambitiousness, and recklessness made him especially vulnerable to the urgings of German diplomats. Now as the minister of war and increasingly the dominant figure of the CUP triumvirate, he worked to bring the Ottomans into the war and soon overcame the doubts of his colleagues.

The Allies gave momentum to Turkish pro-German sentiment. They rejected Turkish requests for border rectifications in the Balkans and for the abolition of the capitulations. It is possible that an agreement to end the capitulations would have prevented the Ottomans from joining the Central Powers. In addition, the British government, as part of its mobilization for the war, retained two warships that had been built by a British company for the Ottoman navy and were due for delivery. This was a hard blow for the Turks, who were deeply concerned with ending Greek naval supremacy in the Aegean. Voluntary contributions from the Turkish people had paid for the ships, with women even donating their hair, the sale of which would raise cash for this purpose.

Then the Ottomans discovered an alternative to the British ships, although one with fateful consequences. When the war started, two German battle cruisers, the *Goeben* and the *Breslau,* found themselves stranded in the Mediterranean. Barely eluding capture by the British navy, the ships surprised nearly everyone on August 10 by sailing to Istanbul, which had concluded a secret alliance with Berlin eight days earlier. In violation of Turkish neutrality, the ships obtained sanctuary under the pretext that they had been sold to the Ottoman navy. In reality, the Germans had gained control of the Ottoman navy; the two ships adopted Turkish names, and the German officers simply exchanged their hats for fezzes.

With the ships' guns pointed at the Ottoman capital, the choice of war was no longer in Turkish hands. A German general ordered the closure of the Bosporus and the Dardanelles, Russia's vital outlet from the Black Sea to the Mediterranean and to the other Allied powers. In October the Ottoman navy launched an attack on Russian Black Sea ports and sank several Russian ships. Aside from the members of the triumvirate, even the Ottoman cabinet did not know of the attack in advance, but it was too late to turn back as Russia and its allies declared war. In keeping with pan-Islamism, the *shaykh al-Islam* declared the war to be a *jihad.* The incongruity of a *jihad* fought by a junior partner of Christian Germany limited its appeal, though Istanbul spread the fictitious story that Kaiser Wilhelm II had converted to Islam and had, following a pilgrimage (*hajj*) to Mecca, changed his name to Hajji Muhammad Wilhelm.

IRAN AND THE WAR

Encroachment by Britain and Russia had left Iranian independence as little more than a formality when the war started. Although Prime Minister Mustaufi al-Mamalik declared his country's neutrality, most Iranians supported Germany and the Ottomans. If given a chance, Iran would have joined the Central Powers. Prince Ruess, the German minister, assiduously cultivated hatred of British and Russian imperialism. The tribes, who constituted about a fourth of the population, staunchly opposed the Allies. German agents, the most famous of whom was Colonel Wilhelm Wassmus (the so-called German Lawrence), helped to organize tribal rebellions. Religious leaders called for *jihad.* Most of all, the liberal intellectuals, the core of the Democratic party, strongly supported the Central Powers. But many of the leading nationalists were in exile, mainly in Germany, leaving inordinate influence in the hands of opportunists whose sympathies changed with the tides of war.

In November 1915 Prime Minister al-Mamalik was ready to conclude an alliance with Germany. As rumors spread that Russian forces were planning to occupy

Tehran, the prime minister and most of the members of the Majlis slipped out of the capital city to go south to Qum. Those fleeing included not only nationalistic Democrats but also opportunists who, foreseeing a German victory, wanted to end up on the winning side. In fact, thousands of people were soon joining the flight to Qum. There were plans to proceed farther south to Isfahan to establish a temporary capital. Young Ahmad Shah was ready to join the exodus, but as he was getting into his carriage, the British and Russian ministers kept him from leaving, assuring him that Tehran would not come under occupation. This thwarted the nationalist plan to move the capital. However, many pro-German members of the Majlis moved from Qum to Kirmanshah, closer to the Ottoman border. There they established a provisional government and organized a military force of Lur tribespeople.

THE BRITISH PROTECTORATE
IN EGYPT

The guns had barely begun to fire in 1914 when European statesmen started to make plans for disposing of the Ottoman Empire. With the Turks in the enemy camp, the former British policy of upholding the empire was no longer viable. And aside from the need to secure local allies during the war, London had to consider postwar arrangements along the route to India.

Egypt had been under British occupation and de facto rule since 1882 but remained legally under Ottoman sovereignty. London terminated this anomaly in December 1914 and declared Egypt a protectorate. The independent-minded Khedive Abbas Hilmi lost his throne to his more pliable uncle, Husayn Kamil. With the ties to Istanbul now broken, the new Egyptian ruler took the title of sultan.

While the formality of a protectorate changed the reality little, the war made British rule a heavier burden for Egypt. The country was under martial law and became an armed camp for British troops. The assembly of five or more people became illegal, and press censorship was strict. The Legislative Assembly, established in 1913, did not meet after the beginning of the war. Admittedly, Egypt avoided the ravages of war that much of the Middle East suffered. Hostilities on Egyptian territory were limited to Turkish attacks on the Suez Canal, the occupation of a border post in the Western Desert by tribes from Cyrenaica heeding the Ottoman call to *jihad,* and in rare instances the penetration of German warplanes. The British did not force the Egyptians to fight in the war. But they turned to the Egyptian peasantry as a source of labor for building roads and railroads and for digging trenches in the war zones. Local Egyptian officials cooperated with the British by furnishing their quotas of forced laborers. The number of peasants harshly uprooted reached more than a million and a half, some of whom were sent as far away as France. The British also requisitioned animals and fodder, often with inadequate compensation. A few Egyptians benefited financially from the war as a result of the influx of British troops and the soaring cotton prices. But food became scarce and prices more than doubled, while most incomes remained on a prewar level. The poor suffered heavily.

Egyptian resentment against British rule was growing. It spread to the peasantry, who had tended to be apathetic. But the iron hand imposed by the British during the war kept most of this resentment below the surface. Informed Egyptians found some cause for hope in a vague British commitment, when the protectorate was declared, to work for a revision of the capitulations and to hasten the development of self-government. Furthermore, in January 1918, President Woodrow Wilson of the United States, which had entered the war on the Allied side during the previous year, outlined Fourteen Points, including the principle of self-determination, for a future peace settlement. With the other Allies agreeing to accept most of Wilson's proposals, Egyptians were heartened. But without progress toward independence, suppressed Egyptian feelings would explode after the war.

PLEDGE TO THE ARABS

The First World War strengthened Arab nationalism, which had previously had only a few adherents. Arab nationalists could now hope for British assistance against the Turks; and repressive Turkish policies in Syria, evoked by fears of Arab collaboration with the British, multiplied anti-Turkish sentiment.

At the beginning of the war, Enver sent Jamal to command the Fourth Ottoman Army in Syria. Jamal seemed a suitable commander for the Arab region, since his pan-Islamic inclinations might have enabled him to gain the confidence of Muslim Arabs.

But following the failure of his attack on the Suez Canal in 1915, evidence of Arab nationalist sentiment brought out the harshness and despotism of Jamal's personality. He sent scores of leading Syrians into exile and had others, twenty-two in one day, hanged for treason. Jamal was in touch with the Allies, scheming to establish himself as the sultan of a breakaway state, but the need to cover up his own activities made repression of Arab nationalists even more expedient for him.

The war provided a new opportunity for Sharif Husayn to work with the British. Even now he carefully maintained a wait-and-see attitude, while stalling on persistent Ottoman efforts to get his endorsement of the *jihad* and to get him to send Hijazi tribal forces to fight against the Allies. But in January 1915 he learned by chance that Istanbul was planning to depose him.

Amir Faysal also embraced the Arab nationalist cause, removing a major pro-Istanbul influence from Sharif Husayn. Faysal stopped in Damascus in 1915 on his way to Istanbul, where he sought assurances that his father would not be deposed. Meeting with Arab nationalists, Faysal learned that they shared his suspicions of the Allies and would join them only if given firm guarantees of independence. Having failed to obtain satisfaction in Istanbul, Faysal stopped in Damascus again on his way home and became a member of two Arab nationalist organizations, al-Ahd and al-Fatat. While he was away, the leaders of the two societies had drawn up a document stating the terms under which they would agree to join the Allied camp. The Damascus Protocol, as the understanding later came to be known, asked for British recognition of Arab independence, with boundaries specified to include the whole Arabian Peninsula (except for Aden, already under British rule) and the Fertile Crescent, extending north to embrace a narrow region of present-day Turkey as far west as Adana and Mersin, on the Mediterranean coast of Anatolia. In return, the Arab nationalists were willing to conclude a defensive alliance with and grant economic concessions to Britain. Faysal transmitted the Damascus Protocol to his father, who was now also ready to negotiate with the British.

Early in the war, the British began to think about working with the Arabs. An Arab revolt against the Turks, especially if led by the sharif of Mecca, might undermine Istanbul's attempt to rally the world's Muslims, most of whom were under Allied control. Furthermore, some British officials envisaged one or more Arab client states that would replace the Ottoman Empire as their means of securing imperial communications. On instruction from London, Sir Henry McMahon, the British high commissioner in Egypt, began to exchange letters with Sharif Husayn.

The Husayn-McMahon correspondence of July 1915 to March 1916 prepared the way for the Arabs to enter the war on the British side. In return for Arab support against the Turks, the British promised to recognize Arab independence. Husayn accepted a fifteen-year alliance and the obligation to depend on British advisors and to give preference to British economic enterprise. As for the boundaries of the future Arab kingdom, Sharif Husayn asked for the area specified in the Damascus Protocol but later agreed to exclude the Turkish-inhabited region of Mersin and Adana. McMahon, pointing to French interests, also excluded those "portions of Syria lying west of the districts of Homs, Hama, Damascus, and Aleppo"[1] from his promise. Husayn refused to relinquish the Arab claim to this area but agreed to defer a final agreement on the matter until the war was over. Although Iraq was included in the area of Arab independence, Husayn agreed to a temporary British occupation of the southern part of the country.

Another loophole in the British commitment to Husayn was a stipulation that agreements with other Arab chiefs would not be prejudiced. The colonial government of India had entered into treaty relationships with the rulers of Southern Arabia, Kuwait, Bahrain, the Trucial States, and Muscat and Oman during the nineteenth century, making these states essentially British protectorates. Reflecting concerns that sometimes put British officials in New Delhi and Cairo in conflict, the Indian government concluded a similar arrangement with Asir, in the Red Sea coastal region north of Yemen in 1915, as well as one with Qatar, on the Persian Gulf, in 1916. However none of these rulers participated in the Arab revolt.

Aside from Sharif Husayn, the most important potentate in Arabia was Amir Abd al-Aziz (whom Westerners always incorrectly referred to as Ibn Sa'ud), the Sa'udi ruler of Najd, also in the Indian government's sphere of concern. The Sa'udis' hereditary enemies, the Rashidi dynasty of Shammar, in northern Arabia,

---

[1] Whether Palestine, lying to the south of the four specified cities, was part of the excluded area has been a matter of unending debate ever since.

had temporarily driven them into exile in Kuwait in the late nineteenth century, but Abd al-Aziz restored Sa'udi control over his homeland in 1902. By 1913 he had expanded, at Ottoman expense, into the al-Hasa region on the Persian Gulf. Captain W. H. I. Shakespear, the British political agent in Kuwait, traveled to Najd in 1915 for negotiations with the amir but died while participating in a Sa'udi military campaign against the Rashidis. Then Sir Percy Cox, the British political advisor in the Persian Gulf region, continued the talks and formalized an alliance with Abd al-Aziz in December 1915. The Sa'udi amir, unlike Sharif Husayn, did not fight against the Turks during the First World War, but he provided assistance to the Allies by continuing periodically to battle with the pro-Ottoman Rashidis. The latter and Imam Yahya of Yemen were the only rulers in the peninsula to support Istanbul.

THE WAR IN THE ARAB LANDS

Following the conclusion of his correspondence with McMahon, Sharif Husayn launched an Arab revolt against Turkish control on June 5, 1916. The original Arab nationalist plans had called for the mutiny of Arab troops in Syria, joined by a general uprising, but this was thwarted when Jamal, fearing that possibility, transferred Arab units to other fronts and when his repressive actions removed many potential leaders and deterred others. Instead, the revolt, begun in Mecca, was primarily one of Hijazi (and later Transjordanian) tribal forces led by Husayn's sons. But some Syrian and Iraqi officers in the Ottoman army also joined the revolt after deserting or being taken prisoner. In addition to London's subsidies to the tribes, the British navy provided important assistance in the capture of towns along the Red Sea coast, enabling the Arabs to drive the Turks out of much of the Hijaz during 1916.

The Arab revolt seemed to have lost momentum toward the end of 1916, when Allied liaison officers, mainly British but also including a few Frenchmen, arrived in the Hijaz. One of these was an enigmatic and flamboyant young Englishman, Lieutenant (later Colonel) T. E. Lawrence. The Arab forces moved farther north in February 1917. A small group of bedouins, led by Lawrence, rode on to Transjordan, where they recruited a tribal force that in July captured Aqaba, at the northern end of the Red Sea. Turkish forces continued to occupy the city of Madina until the end of the war. They also held the Hijaz Railway, which allowed them to send provisions to Madina, although the Arabs, sometimes led by Lawrence, periodically sabotaged it. However, the Arab revolt undermined the Ottoman call to *jihad*, as well as German plans to establish a submarine base on the Red Sea coast.

The British army in Egypt was now preparing for an offensive into Palestine. Jamal Pasha launched an attack on the Suez Canal in 1915 but was driven off, succeeding neither in disrupting the canal nor in inciting Egypt's Muslims to support their caliph against the British. Smaller Turkish raids on the waterway during 1916 were equally unsuccessful. The major impact of the Turkish threat to the canal was to inspire British wartime diplomacy with an obsession for its security and to accelerate the military buildup in Egypt.

Two British attacks on Gaza in early 1917 failed. But then the capable General Sir Edmund Allenby took command, providing superior leadership and inspiring great confidence in his troops. Allenby's army now cut into Palestine, taking Beersheba in October and Jerusalem in December, and continued to advance northward.

Following the capture of Aqaba, the British brought Faysal and his troops there by ship to form the "right wing" of Allenby's army. The Arab forces, with Faysal and Lawrence, moved north on the eastern side of the Jordan River, though with no spectacular military victories. Some of Lawrence's raids on the Hijaz Railway at this time were notably unsuccessful. The tribes along the way joined Faysal, and as the Turks moved out, Arab governments emerged in various cities. In October 1918 Faysal, at the head of a thousand Arab horsemen, entered Damascus, a city now in a joyous frenzy as the starving Turkish army withdrew. All of Syria was in Allied hands by the end of the month.

Meanwhile, a British invasion was ending Ottoman rule in another Arab land, Iraq. The British navy's new dependence on oil dictated concern for the security of the oil fields of southwestern Iran, adjacent to Iraq. A British force landed at the head of the Persian Gulf in November 1914 and soon occupied Basrah but did not find it easy to push much farther. General Sir Charles Townshend moved twelve thousand troops upriver by boat and reached the town of Kut al-Imara, south of Baghdad. With the Turks besieging the town for 143 days, the British troops, now starving and disease-ridden, surrendered in April 1916. The British eventually made a comeback and pushed the Turks out of the southern two-thirds of Iraq before the war ended, but only with strenuous efforts involving nearly half a million soldiers.

SECRET INTER-ALLIED AGREEMENTS

Meanwhile, the European powers made secret plans, based on their own interests, that ignored the aspirations of Middle Eastern peoples. Russian Foreign Minister Sergei Sazanov proclaimed in a note to the British and French ambassadors in St. Petersburg in March 1915 that "the time-honored aspirations" of his country must now be realized. He asked for the incorporation of the Ottoman capital city and other specified territories adjacent to the Straits into the Russian Empire. In an exchange of notes during the following months, generally known as the Constantinople Agreement, the British and French governments accepted the Russian proposal. This also stipulated that the spheres of influence into which the British and Russians had divided Iran in 1907 would be extended to cover the whole country. According to this agreement, most of the central area would be joined to the British (southeastern) sphere, while Russia obtained liberty of action in its area (the north), which seemed to mean eventual annexation.

The Allies promised southwestern Anatolia to Italy as a postwar prize. The Treaty of London, concluded in 1915 to induce Italy to join the Allied camp, provided that Rome would acquire sovereignty over the Dodecanese Islands and get a "just share" of territory in southwest Anatolia. The St. Jean de Maurienne Agreement, concluded by Britain, France, and Italy in 1917, clarified this ambiguous commitment by allotting the whole southwestern quarter of Anatolia to Italy.

Greece wanted to annex Thrace (European Turkey) and parts of western Anatolia, including the port city of Smyrna, with its large Greek population. During the early part of the war, Great Britain made several offers to Greece. Greek Prime Minister Eleutherios Venizelos, later dismissed from office, was favorable to the Allied cause, but King Constantine supported a policy of neutrality. When Greece entered the war in 1917, after Venizelos had returned to power at the head of an Allied-supported rebellion, there was no promise of territory.

The most important secret commitment was the so-called Sykes-Picot Agreement, concluded by Britain, France, and Russia. Great Britain named Sir Mark Sykes, an Orientalist then serving in the War Office, to negotiate with France on the division of the Ottoman Empire. His French counterpart in the negotiations was François Georges-Picot, a career diplomat who, as a former consul-general in Beirut, was particularly concerned with Syria. Sykes and Georges-Picot reached a tentative agreement in February 1916 concerning the Arab provinces. Then they went to St. Petersburg for talks with Sazanov and concluded a tripartite agreement in May. As for Anatolia, the Sykes-Picot Agreement added the eastern part to the area already reserved for Russian annexation and earmarked much of south-central Anatolia for French administration.

Despite Britain's prior commitment to Sharif Husayn, the Sykes-Picot Agreement provided for partition of the Fertile Crescent. It reserved southern Iraq and the Palestinian port cities of Haifa and Acre for British administration and the Syrian coastal region north of Palestine for French rule. It stipulated that the region between French Syria and British Iraq would be under Arab rule but divided into French and British spheres of influence.

Palestine was a special problem. It was part of the whole region of Syria, for which France had had a concern for several centuries. France saw itself as the protector of the Catholic minority, mainly the Maronites. French cultural interests (including numerous French schools) and investments in Syria were extensive. On the other hand, Russia was concerned with the interests of the Orthodox Church in Palestine. Sazanov adamantly rejected French control over the holy places. And Anglo-French rivalry, despite a rapprochement since 1904, was still alive in matters relating to the Middle East. London was uneasy about the possibility of French control of Palestine, not so much for religious as for strategic reasons. Palestine was important to the British because of its closeness to the Suez Canal. Consequently, the Sykes-Picot Agreement designated a large part of Palestine, including the holy places, for international administration.

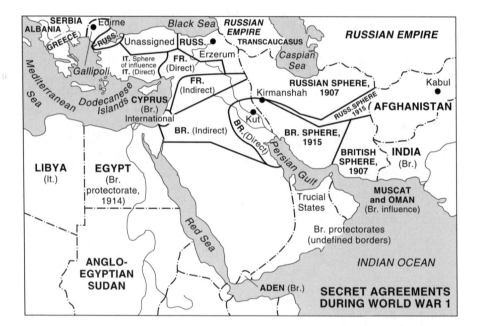

SERBIA Edirne   *Black Sea* *RUSSIAN*
ALBANIA   *EMPIRE*   *RUSSIAN EMPIRE*
GREECE RUSS. Unassigned RUSS.   TRANSCAUCASUS
              IT. Sphere FR.   Erzerum *Caspian*
              of influence (Direct)   *Sea*
Gallipoli IT. (Direct)
                    FR.   RUSSIAN SPHERE,   Kabul
Mediterranean   (Indirect)   1907
              Dodecanese   Kirmanshah   RUSS. SPHERE 1915
Sea   Islands CYPRUS   AFGHANISTAN
                      (Br.)   Kut
              International   BR. SPHERE,
                    BR. (Indirect) BR. (Direct) 1915
                                          Persian Gulf BRITISH INDIA
                                                         SPHERE, (Br.)
LIBYA   EGYPT   1907
(It.)   (Br.   MUSCAT
         protectorate,   Trucial   and OMAN
         1914)   States   (Br. influence)

              Red Sea   Br. protectorates
                                    (undefined borders)

         ANGLO-   *INDIAN OCEAN*
         EGYPTIAN
         SUDAN   ADEN (Br.)   **SECRET AGREEMENTS**
                                        DURING WORLD WAR 1

MAP 8

THE ZIONIST MOVEMENT
AND THE BALFOUR DECLARATION

The claim of European Jews to Palestine now also entered the picture. The Jews had been one of the peoples of ancient Palestine, particularly of Jerusalem and the adjacent area, known as Judea. But by the Hellenistic period emigration, forcible uprooting, and conversion had spread Judaism worldwide. Since Rome's ruthless expulsion of Judea's remaining Jewish population, only a few Jews remained in Palestine, including those in such areas as Galilee. The conquest of Palestine by Muslim Arabs in the seventh century A.D. resulted in immigration by Arabs from Arabia and—undoubtedly of greater importance—in the gradual Arabization of the indigenous Aramaic-speaking population (probably including many people whose ancestors had been Jewish). Palestine became part of a larger and relatively homogeneous Arab world, and so it remained until the twentieth century.

Yet the Jews kept their emotional and religious ties to Palestine, which they called "the Land of Israel." Some modern Jews see themselves as simply a religious group of diverse ethnic origins rather than as a nationality. But Jews have more often identified themselves (and have been identified by others) as a people, "the people of Israel," the supposed "descendants," in "diaspora" (dispersion) or "exile," of the people of ancient Judea. This sense of being a people was perpetuated both by the persecution that the Western Christian world regularly meted out to the Jews and by the autonomy that they and other religions enjoyed in the more tolerant—if not always idyllic—Eastern Islamic world under the millet system. The dream of "returning" to "the Land of Israel" never died. Throughout the centuries, small groups of pious Jews trickled to Palestine. At each Passover, Jews vowed to be "next year in Jerusalem."

A new movement, political Zionism, joined this older religious Zionism toward the end of the nineteenth century. The political Zionists called for the establishment of a Jewish state, or, as they often put it for tactical purposes, a "national home." This more ambiguous term evoked less opposition, particularly among Jewish opponents of Zionism. The new Zionists were modern nationalists, influenced by the other emerging national movements of eastern Europe. Many were not religious at all. Political Zionism was a religious movement only in the sense that membership in the Jewish "nationality" was usually defined in terms of adherence (perhaps only formally) to the Jewish religion. Some highly orthodox Jews rejected it as contrary to Judaism, since they believed that only the Messiah, not the political Zionists, could reestablish the Jewish state. Some early Zionists thought in terms of a Jewish state in any available land, but the majority, in rejecting a British offer made in 1903 of territory in East Africa, would accept only Palestine, a decision that permitted political Zionism to mesh with traditional religious sentiment.

The best-known figure in the early Zionist movement (and to some extent deserving his reputation as its founder) was a brilliant Viennese journalist named Theodor Herzl. He covered the trial in Paris of a Jewish army officer, Colonel Alfred Dreyfus, who was framed on false charges amid obvious manifestations of prejudice, and he became convinced that such discrimination was endemic to Western society. Although Russian persecution of Jews had led to some Zionist colonization in Palestine during the 1880s, political Zionism gained popularity after Herzl's publication of *The Jewish State* in 1896. His powerful personality mesmerized many eastern European Jews, who saw him as a savior. In 1897 Herzl convened the First Zionist Congress in Basel, Switzerland, which adopted a program calling for a Jewish "national home" and established the World Zionist Organization. Yet only a tiny proportion of the Jews of the world were Zionists.

A future Arab-Zionist conflict was in the making. On one side were those Zionists who, though coming from Europe and belonging to Western civilization, thought they were returning to the ancient homeland from which the Romans had driven their forebears. On the other side were the indigenous Arab Palestinians, supported by their fellow Arabs in neighboring countries. The Arab Palestinians saw the Zionists as European intruders—indeed, as another manifestation of Western colonialism—whose stated aspiration to establish a society that would be "as Jewish as England is English" threatened their own right to Palestine. Although supporters of Zionism today reject this interpretation of their movement, since "colonialism" and "imperialism" have become derogatory words (and since Oriental Jews too eventually became Israelis and staunch Zionists), early Zionists were proud of their movement's "colonial" nature. Herzl described the future Jewish state as "a rampart of Europe against Asia."

Up until 1917 Zionism had achieved little. Herzl (who died in 1904) and his successors had, hitherto without success, tried to gain the support of European governments and of the Ottoman Empire. But despite Ottoman opposition to a Jewish national home, more Zionist colonization took place, bringing Palestine's Jewish population—according to the recent estimates of demographic historian Justin McCarthy—from about 10,000 in the 1860s to about 60,000 in 1914. The deportation of Russian nationals as enemy aliens during the war reduced the number to slightly under 59,000 by 1918. The Arab Palestinians numbered nearly 740,000 in 1914, although wartime conditions had reduced them to about 690,000 four years later. Perhaps the most remarkable Zionist achievement was the beginning of a revival of the Hebrew language, which had not been a spoken tongue for more than two millennia, as the common language of the immigrants.

World War I presented a problem for the Zionist movement but also gave it its first great opportunity. Zionists divided along national lines. Some saw the war as a conflict between Russia, the country of pogroms against Jews, and Germany, a country that many Jews had idealized as particularly hospitable to them. Others supported the Allies, foreseeing an Allied victory that would give the British control over Palestine. Most notable among the pro-British Zionists was Chaim Weizmann, an immigrant from Russia and a chemist at Manchester University. Even before the war, Weizmann had developed friendships with key British journalists and politicians, including David Lloyd George and Arthur James Balfour, and had skillfully won their sympathy for Zionism. His discovery of a new method of producing acetone, an ingredient in explosives, contributed to the British war effort, gaining him gratitude and valuable publicity.

It was partly through Weizmann's efforts that the British government offered to support some of the Zionist objectives. Balfour became foreign secretary in 1915, and Lloyd George became prime minister the following year. With these and other pro-Zionists in the Cabinet, a declaration favorable to Zionism was not long in coming. In November 1917 Balfour addressed a letter, every word of which had been carefuliy weighed by the Cabinet, to Lord Rothschild, head of the British Zionist Federation, announcing London's support for "the establishment in Palestine of a national home for the Jewish people." The Balfour Declaration did not offer all that the Zionists wanted. While the members of the British Cabinet may, at least vaguely, have understood "national home" as a step toward eventual Jewish statehood, the declaration carefully avoided mentioning a Jewish state. By using the phrase "in Palestine," the government did not clearly propose all of Palestine as a Jewish national home. Finally, the "civil and religious rights of existing non-Jewish [i.e., Arab] communities" were guaranteed. Yet this was a foundation on which Zionists could later build.

Many writers have tried to explain why Britain issued the Balfour Declaration. The British may have been influenced by guilt over the West's persecution of Jews, by a familiarity with the Old Testament that created a romantic attitude toward Jews, and even by a belief that Zionism was a fulfillment of Biblical prophecy. On a more practical level, British leaders saw the desirability of rallying Jewish support for their side of the war. But their major motivation was strategic. Great Britain wanted a postwar arrangement to secure its vital lines of communication. A Jewish national home, so British leaders reasoned, might become a useful ally on the eastern flank of the Suez Canal.

THE ARAB RESPONSE

The Arabs were shocked when, in the wake of the Balfour Declaration, the new revolutionary regime in Russia revealed the Sykes-Picot Agreement in November 1917. When the news got to Jamal Pasha, he called a meeting of leading people in Damascus and gleefully publicized the fact that the British, after promising Arab independence, had then agreed with France and Russia to partition Arab territories among themselves.

There is some inconclusive evidence that Sharif Husayn had known about the Sykes-Picot Agreement all along and accepted it, but other evidence contradicts this notion. Husayn had been aware of French claims in Syria and had heard rumors of an Anglo-French agreement. But as late as May 1917 Sykes and Georges-Picot traveled to the Hijaz to meet with Husayn, who again rejected French aspirations. And the two men left Husayn with the understanding that French influence would be limited to the Syrian coast, with France merely supplying advisors even there. For Husayn, these terms were more favorable than McMahon's original promises had been. The Arabs have since seen themselves as victims of a betrayal. In any case, the contradictions between the Husayn-McMahon correspondence, the Sykes-Picot Agreement, and the

Balfour Declaration initiated a series of Arab nationalist grievances against the British and the West.

The Allies continued to reassure the Arabs. The British Foreign Office sent a telegram to Husayn in February 1918 claiming that what the Bolsheviks had published were preliminary discussions held before the Husayn-McMahon correspondence. A British statement in June 1918 (Declaration to the Seven) promised Arab nationalists that all territories already liberated by the Arabs would have full independence and that areas liberated by Allied armies would be governed according to "the principle of the consent of the governed." Britain further committed itself to work for the "freedom and independence" of Arab territories then still under Ottoman rule. A widely publicized Anglo-French Declaration of November 1918 stridently denied any aim of imposing foreign control over Arab territories and proclaimed that the Arabs would be allowed to choose their own governments. A British representative sent to the Hijaz in January 1918 told Husayn, to his satisfaction, that Jewish immigration would be permitted only to the extent that it was consistent with the Arab Palestinians' "political and economic freedom." President Wilson's Fourteen Points also seemed to point the way toward Arab Independence.

THE WAR IN NON-ARAB LANDS

The Ottoman Empire, although eventually crushed, proved to be a formidable adversary for the Allies, not only in the Hijaz, Syria, and Iraq, but on other fronts as well. This was more than one might have expected of an underdeveloped Eastern society pitted against some of the greatest industrial powers of Europe, even allowing for the fact that the Allies were exerting their primary effort against Germany at such places as the Marne and Verdun. Although the Ottoman army was already exhausted by the recent Italo-Turkish and Balkan wars and was poorly armed and clothed from the start, it inflicted hundreds of thousands of casualties on the Allies and sometimes defeated them. The training and leadership of German officers helped make this possible, as did supplies from Germany, particularly after Bulgaria's entry into the war on the side of the Central Powers in 1915 facilitated transportation. However, the Turks' main successes were in defending their own territory from impregnable positions against Allied onslaughts.

The Ottoman grip on the Dardanelles and the Bosporus proved unbreakable. Early in the war the Allies decided to land troops on the fifty-two-mile-long Gallipoli Peninsula, on the western side of the Dardanelles, and to proceed from there to Istanbul. For this purpose they (primarily the British, a large proportion of whose troops in fact were Australians and New Zealanders) assembled a great naval armada in the Aegean and made the planned landing in April 1915. The people of Istanbul thought the British forces would soon be there. Women and children were being moved to Anatolia, and a special train was ready to evacuate Sultan Mehmed V and his family.

The Turks thwarted Allied advances in May and in August. Of the half million Allied troops and the 800,000 Ottoman troops participating in the campaign, nearly half on each side were killed or wounded. The heat of summer proved unbearable to the Allied soldiers, accompanied, as it was, by flies and disease, a scarcity of water, and the constant odor of decaying human flesh. In November came snow and sleet, with men freezing to death and dying of influenza. In December the British Cabinet decided to withdraw and end the campaign. The Allied troops were lucky to be able to escape undetected in small boats, leaving behind vast stores of food and equipment for the Turks. The war would probably have ended by 1916 rather than two years later if the Turks had not succeeded in defending the Straits.

Eastern Anatolia and Transcaucasia, the adjacent Russian-ruled area south of the Caucasus Mountains provided another major theater of combat. Transcaucasia is a formidable mountainous area swept by blizzards during much of the year, which might ordinarily have precluded a winter offensive. But Enver became intoxicated by the idea that pan-Turkism was attainable and proceeded to eastern Anatolia with hopes of becoming a great conqueror by personally heading an invasion of Russia. His troops, who attacked in December, were repelled by Russian forces and Armenian volunteer units, and most of his soldiers were killed or froze to death. Enver slipped back to Istanbul, vainly hoping to suppress the news of his failure from his own people. Then the Russian army entered northeastern Anatolia and occupied large areas. By March 1917 the Ottomans had lost 300,000 men on the Russian front. Those who survived were on the verge of starvation.

But the Russian Revolution gave the Turks another chance. The March Revolution, which overthrew the czar, started the disintegration of the Russian army in Anatolia and the Transcaucasus. The October (Bolshevik) Revolution—which brought the Communists to power and resulted in the creation of "Soviet" Russia and eventually of the Soviet Union (or the USSR)—completed the process. Although unexpected, this was not an entirely unearned opportunity for the Turks, as the successful closure of the Straits had been an important factor in undermining the Czarist regime.

Turkish forces again crossed into Transcaucasia. In the Treaty of Brest-Litovsk (February 1918), the new Bolshevik government of Russia made a separate peace with the Central Powers and ceded the Transcaucasian regions of Kars, Ardahan, and Batum, parts of Russia since 1878, back to the Ottoman Empire. However, the peoples of the region (Georgians, Armenians, and Azaris) had taken advantage of the chaos in Russia to establish their independence and form a Transcaucasian Federation. The Turks, for the time being, imposed their terms by force. In the face of the Ottoman invasion, the Federation disintegrated, with the Azaris and other Muslim and Turkish groups generally supporting the Ottoman advance and rallying to form a pan-Islamic army. By September 15, 1918, the Turks had conquered Baku, on the Caspian Sea. With the Muslim Turks across the Caspian attempting to establish their independence from Russia and presumably ready to greet the Ottoman armies as liberators, pan-Turkism seemed to be near realization. But with the Turks losing on the other fronts and now on the verge of surrender, the Transcaucasian victories turned into a mirage.

A gruesome tragedy for the Armenians, who numbered almost two million people in the Ottoman Empire in 1914, accompanied the Turko-Russian phase of the war. Although Armenian leaders shrewdly proclaimed their loyalty, few Ottoman Armenians had any enthusiasm for the Turkish war effort. Thousands of Armenians in Russia eagerly volunteered to fight against the Turks. In this frantic situation, in which the Turks feared their own destruction, the authorities ordered the deportation of all Armenians from Eastern Anatolia, and hundreds of thousands of men, women, and children were subsequently driven for hundreds of miles, with many dying of thirst and starvation along the way. In other cases the Turks simply took groups of Armenians from their villages and slaughtered them. The army systematically massacred a quarter of a million Armenians who had been drafted to form labor battalions. Tal'at, as minister of the interior and later as prime minister, supervised the killings with terrible efficiency. Nearly a million Armenians perished. In turn, Armenians organized to massacre Turks whenever they had the upper hand, as during the Russian occupation of northeast Anatolia. Thousands of Turks, fearing the Armenians, died of hunger or cold as they fled from their homes in the face of Russian advances.

In a less clear-cut battle zone, contending forces fought for control of "neutral" Iran. The Russians augmented their troops in the north and moved closer to Tehran. The Turks occupied parts of western Iran, particularly the northwestern province of Azarbayjan. Fearing that the Central Powers would inspire a rebellion in India, the British established a series of bases in eastern Iran along the Afghan and Indian borders early in the war. Even then, a small group of Turks and Germans eluded capture and crossed the whole breadth of Iran to Afghanistan in an unsuccessful attempt to induce that country to join the Central Powers.

Pro-German tribes took control of southern Iran. The major exceptions, aside from some coastal towns, were the oil fields in the southwest, which the British occupation of southern Iraq safeguarded. Elsewhere in the south, tribesmen assassinated several British consuls and businessmen, leading to a general flight of British officials. However, in 1916 the British dispatched Sir Percy Sykes and a small group of Indian troops to southwestern Iran. Sykes organized a local force known as the South Persia Rifles and restored British control over much of the country during 1917.

Kuchik Khan, an Iranian nationalist and reformer who was determined to end his country's exploitation by Europeans and its own upper class, organized a rebellion in Gilan Province, on the Caspian coast, in 1915. Within two years, the *jangali* ("forest") movement, as his group was known, controlled the thick Gilani woods that are so atypical of the Middle East. They gained a Robin Hood-like fame, robbing the rich to give to the poor. Although Kuchik Khan accepted German and Turkish aid, he was subservient to no one.

THE END OF THE WAR

The Ottoman war effort (except in Transcaucasia) was in a state of collapse by the fall of 1918. The Turkish army had suffered almost 1,500,000 casualties. It had lost the Arab portions of the empire, except for northern Iraq. In September an Allied force advanced from Greece into Bulgaria, which then capitulated, disrupting Turkish access to the Central Powers. Germany and Austria-Hungary would also sue for peace in November. With all hope ended, the Young Turk government resigned, and its leaders, including Enver, Tal'at, and Jamal, hastened to flee from Ottoman territory aboard German ships. Istanbul's bid for peace led to the signing of an armistice, in effect a surrender, on October 31 in the Aegean harbor of Mudros. Among other provisions, the Mudros Armistice called for the disbanding of Ottoman forces and authorized the Allies to occupy any strategic point in the empire whenever any situation threatened their security.

The war had deeply disrupted civilian life in the Middle East. Scarcity brought soaring prices for food and other necessities. The British blockade hindered foreign trade. In Syria and elsewhere, authorities withheld food supplies from certain areas to punish people suspected of disloyalty. In other places, including parts of Iran, nomads were able to plunder at will. With roads unsafe, supplies were unobtainable. Hunger and disease were widespread during the war, leading to massive Western relief efforts. According to very conservative estimates, wartime conditions caused 200,000 deaths in Syria alone. Anatolia's population fell from 12 million in 1914 to 9.5 million at the end of the war. Travelers reported misery everywhere they went. Millions of peasant women toiled in the fields during the war, and most of their husbands never returned. There were hundreds of thousands of orphans, and after the war it was often impossible to determine whether they were Turks or Armenians.

The war set back economic and social progress. Little time or energy remained for such matters. Instead, the rival armies were busy destroying what already existed. Soldiers chopped down ancient olive trees in Syria to obtain fuel for military trains. Russian and Turkish troops in Iran tore down buildings to use their beams as fuel. Railroads were destroyed. The struggle for survival meant delays for many reforms.

But some positive changes occurred. For instance, the Ottoman Law of Family Rights of 1917 brought modifications, favorable to women, in the laws of marriage and divorce. This was the aspect of the traditional Islamic legal system that westernization had previously left untouched. And wartime necessity led to the employment of women by the Ottoman government and by private businesses, freeing them from their traditional seclusion in Eastern society. Women were instrumental in maintaining continuity in the educational system and in establishing new schools. Still another change at this time was the improvement of roads by the various armies. In Iran the British built hundreds of miles of roads over which automobiles could pass for the first time, as well as more than a thousand miles of usable railroads.

Indeed, one cannot ignore the broader effects—whether for better or for worse—of Western armies on the Middle East. The end of the war left about one million British troops there. More than two million British soldiers had served in the area during the war. Admittedly, many of them were Indians and other non-Westerners. But in the long interaction of the two civilizations, neither had ever before made itself so directly and intensely felt in so many of the lands of the other.

Only a shadow of the Ottoman Empire now remained. The loss of the Arab provinces was complete when the Turks relinquished northern Iraq to the British. Much of southern Anatolia also came under British occupation but later was turned over to Italian and French troops. The British also landed at other points on the Anatolian coast. A joint Allied force occupied Istanbul itself. A French general symbolized the Christian West's defeat of the Muslim Turks by riding into the city on a white horse, as Mehmed the Conqueror had done when he took it from the Byzantines in 1453. Local Greeks and Armenians, feeling that their day had come, pushed Turks off streetcars and tore off Turkish fezzes and veils. The Turks were bitter and seemingly helpless. The reactionary Sultan Mehmed VI, who ascended the throne shortly before the end of the war, had reasserted royal authority in pre-1908 fashion and meekly accepted Western protection against nationalists and reformers. He hoped for a permanent British protectorate like the one in Egypt.

The sultan was even ready to acquiesce when the Greeks, former Ottoman subjects who now aspired to create a Hellenic empire on both sides of the Aegean, landed a force (under Allied authority and from Allied warships) at Smyrna in May 1919 and began to penetrate the interior. But most Turks, aside from their contempt for the Greeks, felt that this was a betrayal of the spirit of the Mudros Armistice, since Allied security had not required it. Stories of massacres and plundering by the Greek troops further horrified the Turks. To the Turkish people the Greek occupation was the greatest humiliation of all, and it finally stimulated general resistance against the Allies.

By the end of the war, Iran also was part of the British Empire in all but name. The country was in chaos. In 1915 the British and Russians had planned to complete the partition of Iran. But with the collapse of Russian power in 1917 and the Bolsheviks' subsequent repudiation of previous Russian imperialism, the British had the field to themselves.

THE PEACE CONFERENCE

The Allied leaders met in Paris in January 1919 to tackle the problem of peace settlements with the Central Powers, which had capitulated during the previous autumn. The Allies' primary concern was to devise a settlement with Germany, resulting in the Treaty of Versailles. The Peace Conference imposed separate treaties on the other defeated states, including the Ottoman Empire. Hoping to preserve peace and security and to promote international cooperation, the Peace Conference also established the League of Nations and incorporated its Covenant (constitution) into the Versailles Treaty. Among other provisions, the Covenant established the "mandate system," designed as a compromise between proponents of self-determination and colonialism as a means of governing territories detached from the Central Powers. According to this plan, various territories, all non-Western, that were considered insufficiently prepared for independence would be assigned, as "a sacred trust of civilization," to the tutelage of "advanced [mostly Western] nations."

The Peace Conference contended with a tangled network of conflicting claims to Ottoman territories. The Greeks asked for European Turkey and the Smyrna region. The Italians demanded the share of Anatolia that their allies had promised them in 1917. The Armenians, who had established an independent state in Transcaucasia, presented an exaggerated claim to eastern Anatolia, very little of which had had an Armenian majority even before the recent massacres and deportations. Amir Faysal, astute among Arab tribes but bewildered by European diplomacy, appeared at the conference (officially as the representative of the Hijaz) to present the case for Arab independence. Lawrence, still in Arab dress, came to the conference as Faysal's translator and advisor. He fervently supported Faysal against the French but not against the Zionists, whose interests coincided with those of the British. The Zionists, represented by a delegation headed by Weizmann, asked for a Jewish national home in a Palestine that would have included large parts of present-day Jordan, Lebanon, and Syria and much of Egyptian Sinai. Meeting in London, Weizmann and Faysal had reached an agreement in January for cooperation between a future Jewish national home and the Arabs, but Faysal made this conditional on immediate Arab independence.

The French were suspicious of the British, who, as the main foe of the Ottomans during the war, had emerged as the preponderant power in the Middle East and allowed other Allied nations to participate in the occupation only as a courtesy. Before the Peace Conference convened, Prime Minister Lloyd George persuaded French Premier Georges Clemenceau to accept a revision of the Sykes-Picot Agreement. According to the Lloyd George–Clemenceau Agreement, Palestine would be assigned to Great Britain, instead of being internationalized as the Sykes-Picot Agreement stipulated. Northern Iraq, rather than being part of the area under French influence as the Sykes-Picot Agreement provided, now was assigned to Britain, along with the rest of Iraq. Clemenceau thought that Lloyd George had, as part of the bargain, agreed to full French control over all of Syria, including the interior, which according to the Sykes-Picot Agreement was to be merely a French sphere of influence. The British were torn between their desire to cooperate with France and their reluctance to ignore completely their commitments to the Arabs, not to mention their longstanding rivalry with the French in the area. The French equated demands for Arab self-determination with a British desire to renege on the Sykes-Picot Agreement and to perpetuate their own dominance through Hashimite protégés.

THE SETTLEMENT IN ARAB LANDS

Arab Asia was now a patchwork of independent and foreign-ruled areas. The Ottoman collapse left local dynasties in control of Shammar, Yemen, Asir, Najd, and the Hijaz, over all of which Istanbul's suzerainty had previously been weak or nonexistent. Sharif Husayn had unrealistically assumed the title "King of the Arab Countries" in 1916 but obtained international recognition only as "King of the Hijaz." To the north both Iraq and Palestine were under British occupation. The Syrian coast north of Palestine, at first occupied mainly by British troops, was turned over to French administration in 1919. Arab forces under Amir Faysal in Damascus ruled the interior of Syria.

On the insistence of President Wilson, the champion of self-determination, the Allied leaders agreed to send an international commission to determine the wishes of the former Ottoman provinces. When the other governments failed to carry out this agreement, Wilson sent an American commission, consisting of Henry King, the president of Oberlin College, and Charles Crane, a leading businessman. The King-Crane Commission, which conducted an intensive investigation, found that the Syrians overwhelmingly rejected French control. The Syrians were determined to establish their own independence and refused to accept the severance of any part of their country, including Palestine or Lebanon. They were willing to accept a mandate, preferably American but with British as a second choice, only if this would be limited to temporary aid. The commission accordingly recommended a temporary American or British mandate over a united Syria, with Faysal as king. After interviews with Iraqi leaders, it recommended a similar British mandate for Iraq. Initially favorable to Zionism, the commission was surprised by the extent of Arab opposition to the movement, as numerous conferences with Zionists revealed that they aspired to "a practically complete dispossession of the present non-Jewish inhabitants, by various forms of purchase." The American investigators recommended a rejection of the Zionist program for unlimited Jewish immigration and for a Jewish state. The Peace Conference, however, ignored the commission's report, which was not published until 1922.

Arabs in the Fertile Crescent meanwhile were making plans for independence. A General Syrian Congress, composed of representatives from all parts of geographic Syria, met in Damascus in 1919. In March 1920 the congress declared the independence of a united Syria, with Faysal as the constitutional monarch. A meeting of Iraqi leaders chose Abdullah as their king, even though Iraq was still occupied by British troops.

The Paris Peace Conference disregarded Arab sentiment and Britain's previous commitment to Arab independence. The Allied Supreme Council, representing the leading Allied Powers, met in San Remo in April 1920 and awarded a mandate for Syria and Lebanon to France. It awarded separate mandates for Iraq and Palestine (including Transjordan) to Britain. These were to be "Class A" mandates, a designation restricted to relatively advanced areas whose independence, according to the League of Nations Covenant, was "provisionally recognized subject to the rendering of administrative advice and assistance for a limited time." Some Arabs wondered, however, whether such arrangements would really differ from old-fashioned colonialism. Furthermore, the mandate for Palestine incorporated the words of the Balfour Declaration, which had provided for a Jewish national home. The declaration had heretofore been merely a statement of British policy, without international legal status.

France was now free to uproot the Arab government in Damascus. The French commander in coastal Syria presented an ultimatum to King Faysal, demanding acceptance of the mandate and other terms that would, at best, have reduced the king to a figurehead in a French-dominated country. Faysal, breaking with more intransigent Syrian leaders, accepted the ultimatum at the last minute. This did him no good. Claiming that his reply had arrived too late, French forces moved eastward from the coastal region. The small and poorly armed Syrian army made a futile stand at Maysalun Pass, outside Damascus. The French army quickly prevailed and occupied the Syrian capital. Faysal, his kingdom ended, went into exile. The "Day of Maysalun" came to symbolize the sorrow of Arab nationalists.

THE TREATY OF SÈVRES

Following the San Remo Agreement, the Allies drew up a peace settlement, the Treaty of Sèvres, for the Ottoman Empire. The terms the treaty tried to impose on the Turks (unsuccessfully as it later turned out) were harsh. Istanbul gave up all claims to the Arab provinces. Armenia was to be independent, and President Wilson was designated to determine its boundaries. The treaty gave autonomy to Kurdish-inhabited southeast Anatolia, with the option of complete independence within one year. It permitted Greece to annex most of European Turkey and several Aegean islands and put Smyrna and the adjacent area under a five-year Greek administration, with the possibility of formal annexation to Greece at the end of that period. The Ottomans renounced their title to the Dodecanese Islands in favor of Italy. Britain, France, and Italy signed a separate agreement providing for the division of most of southern Anatolia into spheres of influence, the boundaries of which approximated those established in the secret wartime agreements.

The few remnants of Turkey, after all these truncations, were subjected to restrictions that belied its independence. The treaty continued the capitulations, which the occupying powers had already reimposed. It included humiliating provisions to assure fair treatment of various minorities, and set up a three-power commission, not including Turkey, to exercise extensive financial control. Limiting the Turkish army to fifty thousand soldiers and imposing numerous other military restrictions, the treaty also established an international commission to control the Straits.

NEW ARRANGEMENTS FOR IRAN

The British government was planning to determine Iran's future. The British would not permit an Iranian delegation to attend the Paris Peace Conference, using the excuse of Iranian "neutrality" in the war. But the real reason was that London did not want interference from other powers. Sir Percy Cox became the British minister to Tehran in 1919 and proceeded with negotiations that led to the conclusion in August 1919 of an Anglo-Iranian Treaty providing for a British loan and for British advisors to train the Iranian army. The treaty essentially imposed a protectorate over Iran and thus infuriated nationalists. Although Iran's ratification of the treaty had become uncertain by 1920, the British were so confident about the new arrangement that they were already sending the advisors.

The Communists, despite their attacks on imperialism, now demonstrated that they were not much different from the czars or other powerful European nations. In

1919 the Russians began to extend aid to the now-beleaguered *jangalis* in Gilan Province. Kuchik Khan, as a devout Muslim and Iranian patriot, was reluctant to work with the Soviets, but some of his colleagues eagerly welcomed their help. Then in May 1920, a Soviet force landed on the Caspian coast. Kuchik Khan prayed for guidance, but his colleagues finally persuaded him to conclude an alliance with the newcomers. His worst fears were realized when the Soviets and a few Iranian Communists reduced him to a figurehead and declared a "Persian Soviet Socialist Republic." Having temporarily lost one province, Iranians feared that they would lose the entire country.

CONCLUSIONS

By 1920, Western domination had submerged the Middle East. European powers had parceled out northern Africa and various other lands during the nineteenth century, and more subtle forms of penetration such as the capitulations and spheres of influence had long undermined Ottoman and Iranian sovereignty. Now, however, the victorious Allies were partitioning the Turkish heartland with the acquiescence of a sultan whose capital was under Allied occupation. Arab nationalists, who had joined the Allied side in return for a promise of independence, now found their lands in the Fertile Crescent divided into British and French mandates and the concept of a Jewish national home imposed on Palestine. Iran was seemingly becoming a veiled British protectorate. The British in Egypt, having formally established a protectorate, seemed more determined than ever to stay. Only in the Arabian Peninsula did local rulers retain any kind of independence, and even they were under degrees of British tutelage.

Yet a reaction against Western imperialism was setting in. A mass uprising was underway in Egypt. A determined nationalist resistance movement was gaining momentum among the Turks. Iranians were standing their ground against the Anglo-Iranian Treaty. Iraq was in revolt. Amir Abdullah was threatening to avenge his brother Faysal's expulsion from Syria. Anti-Zionist riots were beginning in Palestine. Even in countries where nationalism appeared to have been crushed during the summer of 1920, it would, in most cases, achieve partial success within the next two years.

7

rebellion, emulation, and reaction 1920–1939

The confrontation with European power and civilization continued to permeate all the concerns of the Middle East during the 1920s and 1930s. This relationship had two aspects. First, Middle Easterners struggled to free themselves from Western domination, which had reached its height by 1920. This fight for independence consumed an inordinate share of the energy of all Middle Eastern peoples. Although nationalism would force Western imperialism to recede in some places during the early 1920s, further Middle Eastern successes came slowly.

A second and perhaps more fundamental concern for a still underdeveloped region continued to be how to catch up with the modern society of the West. Nearly all agreed on the desirability of attaining a higher level of material progress, if only to provide the means for defense against the West. But to what extent was it necessary to adopt nonmaterial facets of Western civilization? Some leaders wanted to make a total transformation of their countries; others sought to preserve or to return to traditional Islamic values. Many wavered or tried to find a middle path between the two extremes.

THE TURKISH STRUGGLE
FOR LIBERATION

The Turks, against seemingly hopeless odds, put up the most valiant resistance and achieved the most conclusive victory in the struggle against Western imperialism. This was partly because the Treaty of Sèvres that the Allies tried to impose on them was so unbearable. But the Turkish nationalist success was also the result of capable military and political leadership. Setting limited goals, Turkish nationalists achieved them by skillfully exploiting rivalries among the European powers and these powers' unwillingness, particularly just after an exhausting war, to risk using their full capabilities, disproportionate to any possible gain, for suppressing a determined people.

A major factor in the repulsion of European rule from Turkey, pointing the way for other Eastern lands, was the leadership of Mustafa Kemal, who later took the name Kemal Atatürk. The brilliance and daring of this iconoclastic young man had enabled the Ottoman army to foil the Allied campaign in Gallipoli in 1915 and had brought his forceful personality to the attention of the Turkish people. Despite Enver's jealousy, Kemal rapidly rose from the rank of lieutenant-colonel to become a general and a pasha. Although he had strongly opposed the alliance with Germany in 1914, he was the only Turkish hero to emerge from the war. And as he returned from the Syrian front to Istanbul in November 1918, he more than anyone else saw that the battle for his homeland must go on, and awaited the chance to act.

Feigning a willingness to accept defeat, Kemal had the good fortune to be sent by the sultan's government to eastern Anatolia as Inspector General of the Ninth Army in 1919. He landed at Samsun, on the Black Sea coast, on May 19, just as the news of the Greek landing at Smyrna four days earlier was readying the Turkish people for struggle. Since the 1918 armistice, local societies for the defense of rights had sprung up in some parts of the Turkish heartland. And, in eastern Anatolia, many army units, victorious in Transcaucasia to the end of the war, remained intact. Kemal's assignment was to demobilize Turkish forces; instead he proceeded to weld soldiers and civilians together into an iron-willed resistance movement. When the government recalled him, he resigned his commission in order to stay in Anatolia. He called two congresses, at Erzerum and Sivas (both in northeastern Turkey), out of which emerged a nationwide revolutionary organization, the League for the Defense of Rights in Anatolia and Rumelia. The congresses adopted a National Pact, which accepted the loss of Arab provinces but insisted on the integrity and independence of the area "inhabited by an Ottoman Muslim majority." (Despite the previous upsurge of Turkish ethnic pride, some members of the two congresses still were not inclined to use the traditionally pejorative word "Turk"; the term "Ottoman Muslim" also had the advantage of including Kurds and various other non-Turks, such as refugees from the Balkans and Russia.)

At one point, the sultan's government seemed ready to work with the nationalists. The sultan's incompetent brother-in-law resigned as prime minister in October 1919. His replacement claimed to lead a "Ministry of Conciliation." Elections were held, resulting in an overwhelming nationalist majority in the Ottoman Parliament, which adopted the National Pact. The Allies reacted by imposing a full-fledged occupation of Istanbul. Scores of nationalist leaders were arrested, some by British troops in the lobby of the Ottoman Parliament, and were exiled to Malta. Those who had avoided arrest now began to steal away at night, making a long trek to Ankara, a remote town protected by the mountain fastness of central Anatolia and yet connected to the outside by railroads and telegraph lines. It was here that Kemal had meanwhile set up the center of Turkish resistance.

Kemal called for the establishment of a new parliament, the Grand National Assembly. This met in Ankara in April 1920 and declared that sovereignty belonged to the nation, as represented in the Assembly. Thus began a fierce struggle, not only against foreign occupation but also against the royalist government in Istanbul, although the nationalists still insisted that they were loyal to the sultan himself, whom they described as being under duress. The Treaty of Sèvres, imposed in July, reinforced nationalist resistance against the Allies and the Ottoman government that had accepted it.

The Kemalists' foremost concern was the Greeks, who advanced deep into Anatolia in 1920. In January of the following year Turkish forces commanded by General Ismet repelled the advance at the Battle of Inönü, and again at a second battle of Inönü in March. But a renewed Greek offensive in July forced the Turks to retreat almost to Ankara. After the Grand National Assembly granted him full dictatorial powers, Kemal took personal command of the army. He proceeded to mobilize the people and resources of the country, requisitioning 40 percent of the cloth, food, and other articles. Turkish women were organized to bring supplies by donkey cart or on their backs over the mountains to the front lines.

Kemal's forces stood against the advancing Greeks at the Battle of the Sakarya River in August and September. After twenty-two days of unceasing ferocity over a sixty-mile front, possibly the longest pitched battle that had ever been fought and certainly one of the most decisive encounters between the Islamic world and Europe, the Greeks finally fell back. The tide had turned. The Greeks were not yet conclusively defeated, but the Turkish nationalist movement acquired new momentum. Kemal gained the rank of field marshal and the title of ghazi, warrior for Islam (implicitly against Christendom). Then a final Turkish offensive in August 1922 drove the Greeks to the sea. Turkish forces entered Smyrna in September, as the enemy troops and thousands of Greek civilians boarded British warships. The Greek section of Smyrna, longtime center of Greek Anatolia, was soon in flames, as though to symbolize the final victory of the Islamic East in the Anatolian Peninsula.

Meanwhile, the Turkish nationalists approached other European powers. After defeating small French forces in eastern Anatolia in 1920, Kemal reached an agreement with France, which had begun to see the Turkish nationalists as a lever against its British rivals, considered to be the real power behind the Greeks. The French had also decided to limit their ambitions to Syria. They withdrew from Anatolia and even agreed to a modification of the Turko-Syrian border in Turkey's favor. Thousands of Armenians, who had collaborated with the French occupiers, fled

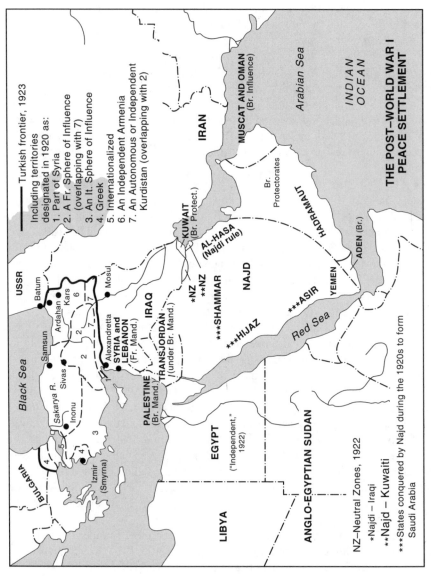

Turkish frontier, 1923

Including territories
designated in 1920 as:
1. Part of Syria
2. A Fr. Sphere of Influence
   (overlapping with 7)
3. An It. Sphere of Influence
4. Greek
5. Internationalized
6. An Independent Armenia
7. An Autonomous or Independent
   Kurdistan (overlapping with 2)

NZ–Neutral Zones, 1922
*Najdi – Iraqi
**Najd – Kuwaiti
***States conquered by Najd during the 1920s to form
Saudi Arabia

**THE POST–WORLD WAR I
PEACE SETTLEMENT**

MAP 9

to the sanctuary of Arab lands. Similarly, the Italians, who resented the Allies' awarding part of southwestern Anatolia to Greece, decided to undermine Anglo-Greek designs by cooperating with the Turks and withdrawing from Anatolia. Both the Italians and the French settled for minor economic concessions. This freed Turkish troops to face the Greeks, and they also acquired large stores of military equipment left behind by the French. A Soviet and Turkish pincers movement defeated the Armenians in northeast Anatolia and the Transcaucasus in 1920, just as President Wilson futilely awarded a large area of eastern Anatolia to them. Although Kemal was anti-Communist, he joined forces with the Soviets, who were also resisting an Allied invasion, and Soviet weapons and other aid gave the Turks another advantage. The Treaty of Moscow, which Ankara and the Soviets concluded in 1921, left Kars and Ardahan, both of which had been under Russian rule from 1878 to 1917, in Turkish hands.

When, following the Greek defeat in Anatolia, the Turkish nationalists turned toward Istanbul and European Turkey, only the British stood in their way. British Prime Minister Lloyd George's government had staked its life on support for the Greeks against what he called the "Asiatic barbarians." Lloyd George saw this not only as an expression of European Christian solidarity but also envisaged an expansionist Greece as a useful protégé on Britain's route to India. But the other Allies backed down. After a short confrontation, during which a war between Britain and Turkey (and possibly Russia) seemed imminent, the British government lost the backing of a war-weary public and also gave in to the Turks. The Armistice of Mudanya allowed the Turks to cross the Straits into Europe and recognized their sovereignty over Istanbul. Lloyd George's resignation was final proof that the Turks had shaken the greatest imperial power of the West and broken the pattern of Europeans' manipulating the East with impunity.

A new Peace Conference met at Lausanne, Switzerland, in November 1922. Months of negotiations ensued, during which General Ismet, now the Turkish prime minister, relentlessly pursued every point, even using his hearing deficiency to wear away the patience of the Allied negotiators. The Treaty of Lausanne, concluded in July 1923, enabled Turkey to achieve essentially the objectives spelled out in its National Pact. Foreign occupation would end. Turkey regained control over the Straits, although with provisions for demilitarization and free access to other nations. It would be free from all the other restrictions, including the capitulations, that the Sèvres Treaty had imposed. Even the loss of the Arab provinces, to which the nationalists had been reconciled from the start, was an advantage in that it helped to create a relatively homogeneous Turkish nation. A separate Greco-Turkish agreement further enhanced this homogeneity, though at the cruel price of uprooting people from their ancestral homelands. It provided for an exchange of over a million Greeks in Turkey for almost half a million Turks living in Greece. Rising from utter defeat, the Turks had snatched their emancipation from Western imperialism. They had also been allowed to keep the lands of the Armenians that they had depopulated and to deprive the Kurds of the right to self rule.

THE EGYPTIAN REVOLUTION OF 1919
AND FORMAL INDEPENDENCE

Egyptians also resisted Western control, though with less clear-cut success than Turkey. Egypt's relative calm during the First World War could not last. Its people were bitter over the imposition of a British protectorate in 1914. The presence of thousands of soldiers from all parts of the British Empire, restriction on civil liberties, wartime shortages, inflation, and forced peasant labor in the war zones all combined to unite the country against colonial domination.

On November 13, 1918, only two days after the Armistice in Europe, a self-appointed three-man nationalist delegation met with Sir Reginald Wingate, the British high commissioner. The delegation (soon generally known by the Arabic word, *wafd*) asked for an end to the protectorate and to martial law. Furthermore, the Wafd requested permission to travel to London to present its demands to the British government. Thus began a new phase in Egypt's struggle for independence and the emergence of the Wafd as the leading political party in this national struggle during the next three decades.

The leader of the Wafd was Sa'd Zaghlul, often regarded as the "father of the Egyptians." The son of a small landowner and mayor of a village in the Egyptian Delta, he studied in traditional religious schools and at al-Azhar, where he became a disciple of Afghani and Abduh. He later studied at the French School of Law, adding a modern, Western-style education to his indigenous, Eastern one. As a collaborator with the British in Egypt, he was highly regarded by Lord Cromer, the British agent, who had him named Minister of Education in 1906. In this and other positions, Zaghlul worked for legal and educational modernization rather than for independence. But as Britain's rule in Egypt became more blatant during World War I, Zaghlul emerged as the nationalist leader.

The movement that Zaghlul led was a liberal, secular, purely Egyptian nationalism. It wanted Egypt's independence under a representative government, with the monarch's powers curtailed and with civil liberties guaranteed for the people. While the old Patriotic party, now in decline, had diluted its Egyptian nationalism with pan-Islamic solidarity, the Wafd's object of loyalty was unambiguously Egypt.

Furthermore, there was no idea of Egypt's being part of a wider Arab nation. The Arab nationalist movement had grown up under fundamentally different circumstances. While Egyptians, resentful of British rule, had sometimes supported the Ottoman sultan-caliph (without actually wanting to be under his control) before the First World War and had seen the Ottoman Empire as a potential safeguard against British colonialism, the Asian Arab nationalists had allied themselves with Britain during the war in order to throw off the Turkish yoke. To many Egyptians, the Arab nationalists were traitors to Islam. And, since the Egyptians typically considered themselves more advanced than the Fertile Crescent Arabs, not to mention those of Arabia, the Allies' promises of independence for Arab Asia, while Egypt had just become a protectorate, were galling.

The only territory outside Egypt that the Wafd wanted to control was the Sudan, which Egyptians had long considered to be an integral part of their country. Nationalist slogans thus called not only for the evacuation of the British from Egypt but also for the unity of the Nile Valley.

To get back to November 1918, the British refused to reconsider the protectorate or even to permit Zaghlul and his colleagues to go to London. In turn, Zaghlul organized a nationwide movement to collect funds and gathered hundreds of thousands of signatures on petitions designating the Wafd as the representative of the Egyptian people. He sought support from foreign representatives in Egypt, appealed to President Wilson, and continued to denounce the protectorate. Prime Minister Husayn Rushdi, though willing to work with the British, had also wanted to head a delegation to London to request greater independence. But by this time Zaghlul had become so unmistakably the spokesperson for the Egyptians that, when Rushdi and his colleague, Adli Yakan, got permission to go, they refused to make the trip without him. They knew that the Egyptian people would think that they were undercutting the authentic national movement and would reject any partial settlement that they might obtain. Finally, on March 8, 1919, the British arrested Zaghlul and some other Wafdist leaders and deported them to Malta in the hope that their absence would calm Egypt.

The British were mistaken. Zaghlul's arrest enraged the Egyptians. There were strikes and student demonstrations in Cairo, and before long, disorder spread to the villages. Sabotage disrupted railroads and telegraph lines, and British soldiers were murdered. For a while most of the country lay outside effective British control. The movement was truly national, as Copts and Muslims, rich and poor, and men and women marched in the streets to demonstrate their support for Zaghlul.

In the hope that a leading general might intimidate the Egyptians, the British government replaced Wingate with Allenby. But Allenby tried to appease the nationalists. Zaghlul was released. Free to go wherever he wished, he proceeded to Paris to put Egypt's cause before the Peace Conference. There he met bitter disappointment, as the victorious Allies, even Wilson, recognized the protectorate. Turbulence in Egypt continued, as Egyptians considered Zaghlul's release a sign of further British concessions.

Britain appointed a commission of inquiry, headed by Lord Milner, to study the situation in Egypt and to make recommendations on new arrangements, but only within the scope of the existing protectorate, which was what the Egyptians had been demonstrating against. The Wafd boycotted the Milner Commission, which arrived in December 1919, and nearly all Egyptians followed its lead. So impressed was the commission with the mood of the country that its report went beyond the mandate given to it. Milner recommended that the protectorate be replaced by an Anglo-Egyptian treaty of alliance that would safeguard British interests. Zaghlul now entered into negotiations with the commission in London, but they could not reach an agreement. Then the Egyptian government sent a delegation to London, headed by Adli Yakan, who was now the prime minister. Adli, too, could not make the compromises demanded by the

British, lest his government be denounced by the Wafd. As new riots broke out in Cairo, the British arrested Zaghlul again and sent him into exile.

Since Britain could not conclude a treaty, Allenby pressed his government into ending the protectorate unilaterally. On February 28, 1922, he formally declared Egypt's independence from Britain. Sultan Fu'ad (who had succeeded to the throne in 1917) took the title of king, and a group of Egyptian legal experts began to draw up a liberal constitution. But the British reserved four matters for their own discretion: (1) the security of British communications; (2) the defense of Egypt against all foreign aggression; (3) the protection of foreign interests and of minorities; and (4) the Sudan. This was acceptable to subservient, pro-British politicians such as Abd al-Khaliq Tharwat, now the prime minister, who had not really wanted complete independence but who had not dared to accept anything less. For many rich Egyptians, who feared that continued anti-British agitation would lead to a social revolution, Allenby's unilateral declaration was quite convenient. But to Egyptian nationalists, 1922 was only the first step toward real independence.

IRAN: A NEW DYNASTY

Meanwhile, the tide of European imperialism was also receding from Iran. The 1919 Anglo-Iranian Treaty had become increasingly repulsive to the Iranian people and to the Majlis, which would have to ratify it. As British public opinion became ever more hostile to foreign military involvements, London chose not to force its will on Iran and gradually withdrew its troops.

Instead, Britain quietly worked to set up a new regime that could effectively govern Iran and preserve its independence from the Soviets. General Riza Khan, who had gained command of the 15,000-member Cossack Division (formerly the Russian-officered Cossack Brigade), was ready to engineer a coup. A shrewd, if uncouth, young man of modest origin and scanty education, Riza ardently wanted to put an end to the anarchy, foreign penetration, and backwardness of his country. For this purpose, he formed an alliance with a leading journalist, Sayyid Ziya al-Din al-Tabataba'i, and proceeded, with some help from British troops and with the British minister facilitating his efforts in a variety of ways, to move his forces to Tehran in February 1921. He took control of the government, becoming commander-in-chief of the army, with al-Tabataba'i as prime minister. Within three months, he squeezed al-Tabataba'i out of power and in 1923 became prime minister. Two years later, Riza Shah Pahlavi, as he was subsequently known, began a new dynasty, called the Pahlavis.

Meanwhile the Russians pulled out of Iran. A Soviet-Iranian Treaty of Friendship, already being negotiated before the 1921 coup, was soon concluded. Tehran recognized Moscow's right to send troops into Iran whenever a third power used its territory to plan an attack on Russia. The Soviets formally repudiated all Russian privileges and concessions in Iran. The troops, from the Azarbayjan Soviet Socialist Republic, for which Moscow claimed no responsibility, withdrew from Iran's Gilan Province. Only then did Tehran ratify the Soviet-Iranian Treaty. It is unclear why the

Soviets renounced their foothold in Gilan. Perhaps they were there primarily to counter British control, and after the British withdrew the Soviets had no reason to stay. There may have been disagreement in Moscow all along on whether to control Gilan at the expense of antagonizing Iran as a whole.

With Soviet troops gone, Riza Khan's forces crushed the *jangali* movement. Its leader, Kuchik Khan, who had broken with the Soviet forces during the fall of 1920 and had even fought against them, had joined forces with them again. When the Soviets withdrew, he fled into the mountains and died of exposure.

IRAQ, TRANSJORDAN, AND THE HASHIMITES

Iraq and Transjordan acquired limited self-government during the early 1920s. The end of the war had left Iraq under British military rule, with acting Civil Administrator Colonel A. T. Wilson (in the absence of Sir Percy Cox, the civil administrator, who was transferred to Iran in 1918) responsible to the military authorities. Wilson headed a largely Anglo-Indian administration and strongly opposed giving self-government to Iraq, as Iraqis became increasingly bitter against British rule. Finally, the tribes of the middle Euphrates rose in rebellion in June 1920, and the Shi'ite religious leaders proclaimed a *jihad*. Soon most of the country was out of Britain's control. The British managed to suppress the insurrection only at great expense. Cox now returned to his position in Baghdad. Seeing the need for some Iraqi participation in the government, he set up a Council of State, with limited power, headed by an Arab Iraqi.

The Hashimites, angry over Faysal's expulsion from Syria, also made trouble for the British. In November 1920 Amir Abdullah, heading a Hijazi force, arrived in southern Transjordan. Originally part of Faysal's Syrian kingdom, Transjordan had been included in the Palestine mandate. But the British established only loose control over the largely desert, tribal area. Abdullah threatened to use this territory as a springboard for an attack on the French in Syria.

Winston Churchill, now the colonial secretary, called together the leading British officials concerned with the Middle East to meet in Cairo in March 1921. The conference worked out a solution to the problems of Iraq and Transjordan. Faysal would become king of the former, while Abdullah would be amir (prince) of the latter. After obtaining the consent of notables in each country, plus popular approval in a carefully managed plebiscite in Iraq, these two sons of King Husayn of the Hijaz took their respective thrones. An Anglo-Iraqi Treaty of Alliance followed in 1922, but among other restrictions on independence, it provided that Iraq, which was still subject to the British mandate, would accept British advice on important matters. Transjordan, now a separate entity but still technically part of the Palestine mandate, would be exempt from the area designated for a Jewish national home, a unilateral British action that angered many Zionists but was legitimized by the mandate document that the League officially adopted in 1922.

FURTHER STEPS TOWARD
INDEPENDENCE

Several Middle Eastern countries gradually won more independence from European control during the late 1920s and the 1930s. The 1922 Anglo-Iraqi Treaty was slightly modified in 1926 and 1927. Another Anglo-Iraqi Treaty, in 1930, substituted a twenty-five-year alliance for the mandate and gave Iraq formal independence. However, among other limiting provisions, the British kept two air bases in the country, the right of transit across Iraqi territory, and the exclusive right to provide military advisors. The treaty went into force in 1932, when Iraq gained admission to the League of Nations. But to increasing numbers of Arabs the Hashimite "Anglo-Arab" monarchies in both Iraq and Transjordan appeared to be mere client regimes dependent on London.

The development of Arab unity was slow. Iraq aspired to be an "Arab Prussia" to undo the largely artificial postwar division of the Arabic-speaking world. Egypt was still preoccupied with its own nationalism, although by the late 1930s it had become more interested in Arab Asia and even other Muslim areas as young King Faruq, who succeeded his father in 1936, dreamed for a long time of becoming caliph. But apart from rudimentary separate nationalisms in other Arab countries (and the more deeply rooted local identity of Lebanon's Maronite Christians), pan-Arabism also faced such obstacles as continuing French rule over Syria and distrust between the Sa'udi and Hashimite families.

Britain's limited grant of independence to Egypt in 1922, with its "four reserved points," did not satisfy the nationalist movement. Egyptians faced further humiliation in 1924, following the assassination in Cairo of Sir Lee Stack, the British governor-general of the Sudan. As British troops occupied the customs house in Alexandria, the Egyptian government bowed to British demands, including the withdrawal of Egyptian troops and civilian officials from the Sudan.

After several unsuccessful attempts to settle Anglo-Egyptian differences, the threat to both sides posed by the Italian invasion of Ethiopia in 1935 induced London and Cairo to compromise. The Anglo-Egyptian Treaty of 1936 officially put an end to the British occupation of Egypt and established an alliance between the two countries. But the treaty actually perpetuated the occupation on a more limited basis by letting Britain keep ten thousand troops in a specified Suez Canal Zone. Even then, British troops retained the right to stay in other parts of Egypt until the Egyptian government provided certain buildings and communications facilities for the Suez Canal Zone. Egypt also agreed to turn over all its means of communication to Britain in case of war. The treaty gave Britain the exclusive right to provide military advisors. The joint administration of the Sudan was confirmed, to be safeguarded by both British and Egyptian troops. Britain renounced its responsibility for foreigners and minorities and agreed to support the termination of the capitulations, which an international conference at Montreux accepted in 1937. Egypt became a member of the League of Nations in the same year.

With Riza Shah effectively controlling Iran and developing its economic and military capacity, Iranian independence gained increasing respect. The powers went along with the shah's termination of the capitulations in his country in 1928. To protect Iranian independence, he avoided borrowing money from abroad and restricted foreign ownership of land and businesses. In a further assertion of national pride, the shah decreed in 1935 that foreign governments must use his country's real name, that is, Iran. Iranian postal officials were ordered to send back mail addressed to "Persia," which was what foreigners had normally called the country. As worldwide depression led to declining royalties from the Anglo-Iranian Oil Company, the shah canceled its concession in 1932 and managed to get a new one the next year, with increased royalties for Iran. The once-customary British and Russian control had become a thing of the past, although it would return in 1941. Yet in the 1930s Iran continued to suspect these powers of trying to undermine its independence and sometimes picked quarrels with them. It was while in search of an outside protector against Britain and the USSR that Iran turned to Nazi Germany, toward which it directed much of its trade during the 1930s. Riza Shah admired the apparent efficiency of Hitler's regime, and some Iranians were flattered to be regarded by German racists as fellow "Aryans."

With its victory over Western imperialism by 1923, Turkey was the one Middle Eastern country that no longer had reason to bear a grudge against the West. Even relations with Greece became normal. The only country whose expansionist policies threatened Turkey was Mussolini's Italy, causing Turkey to conclude a Balkan Entente with Greece, Rumania, and Yugoslavia in 1934. Fear of Italy also provided one motivation for entering into the Sa'dabad Pact, a nonaggression treaty signed by Turkey, Iran, Iraq, and Afghanistan in 1937.

Turkey pursued two territorial claims after 1923. The Treaty of Lausanne had temporarily left Mosul, a province inhabited largely by Kurds that Turkey was then unwilling to renounce, as part of British-mandated Iraq. After the League of Nations Council awarded Mosul permanently to Iraq in 1925, Turkey reacted by reviving its ties with the USSR, with which it concluded a Treaty of Friendship and Neutrality. This reaction proved temporary, for Ankara soon decided that it had too much to lose from a confrontation with London. In a treaty with Iraq and Britain, Turkey settled for 10 percent of the royalties on oil from the Mosul region over a twenty-five-year period. Later on, though, Turkey did obtain Alexandretta, previously the northwestern part of Syria, as will be explained later. Also, an international conference meeting at Montreux in 1936 replaced the Lausanne Straits Convention. Although a complicated set of rules continued to govern navigation through the Bosporus and the Dardanelles, Turkey managed to get rid of several restrictions, including the provision for demilitarization, which had meant that it could not defend a vital part of its own territory.

CONTINUED FRENCH RULE
IN SYRIA AND LEBANON

Syria and Lebanon, which together came to be called the "Levant States" during the period of French rule, faced frustration in their attempts to gain independence. French colonial policy usually allowed little self-government, and the Levant States

were no exception. Martial law prevailed much of the time. Particularly through
the educational system, the rulers attempted to perpetuate French at the expense of
the Arabic language and culture. The separation of Palestine and Transjordan from
the rest of geographic Syria had left a dismembered country, and the French further
divided Syria. To be sure, predominantly Maronite Mount Lebanon wanted France to
protect its long-standing autonomy against Muslim domination. But France increased Lebanon's territory, at Syria's expense, to form a Greater Lebanon containing large numbers of Sunni and Shi'ite Muslims and non-Maronite Christians. This
act antagonized the Syrians and many non-Maronite Lebanese and laid the basis for
future turmoil.

The French even divided up what remained of Syria into the states of Damascus and Aleppo, which however reunited to form the State of Syria in 1925. They
established separatist governments for the predominantly Alawite (a heterodox offshoot of Twelver Shi'ite Islam) district of Latakia and for the mainly Druze (another
Shi'ite offshoot) area near Transjordan. The partly Turkish region of Alexandretta
also obtained a separate government. Thus, in a classic policy of divide-and-rule, the
French played off one religious and ethnic minority against another to facilitate colonial control.

Syria, for most of the time, was tense and hostile to French rule. Beginning
with a Druze uprising, a general revolt spread over the country in 1925. Harsh suppression followed, including two bombardments of Damascus.

Constitutional development was slow. A constitution for Lebanon that provided for limited self-government went into effect in 1926. A Syrian Chamber of
Deputies, elected in 1928, also drew up a constitution. The French first rejected the
proposed document because it refused to accept the mandate or the separation of any
part of geographic Syria from the country but then unilaterally enacted it after omit-
ting the objectionable provisions.

A new sympathy for nationalism in the Levant States emerged in Paris when
the leftist Popular Front government took power in 1936. The fear of Italian imperialism also evoked a spirit of compromise. France proceeded to conclude treaties
(similar to the 1930 Anglo-Iraqi Treaty) with both Lebanon and Syria, providing
for their independence within three years. The Alawite and Druze areas were
to unite with Syria. The Lebanese and Syrian Chambers of Deputies approved
the treaties, but France, with a new government in power, changed its mind. By
1939, it had abandoned the treaties entirely and even suspended the Syrian constitution.

Meanwhile, France acceded in 1937 to Turkish demands to give increasing autonomy to Alexandretta. Elections in the province followed in 1938, after Turkish
troops got permission to share in the maintenance of order, thus raising much doubt
about whether the vote was fair. Although about 60 percent of Alexandretta's population was Arab and presumably pro-Syrian, the Turks won control. With another war
imminent and with France anxious to win Ankara to its side, France ceded Alexandretta to Turkey in 1939, providing a new and lasting grievance for Syria and the
Arabs.

CONFLICT IN PALESTINE

Palestine had not achieved even partial independence by 1939. Moreover, the ethnic makeup of the country was changing as a result of Britain's commitment to building a Jewish national home. During most of the 1920s, the flow of Jewish immigrants from Europe into Palestine was a mere trickle. In 1931 the Jews still formed less than 17 percent of Palestine's population. But the rise of Hitler in Germany in 1933 created a new situation, as German Jews were deprived of their civil rights, their professions, and often their property. Jews throughout Europe were fearful. Few countries were willing to open their doors to large numbers of Jewish refugees from Nazi persecution. The Zionists, for their part, wanted to encourage Jewish immigration to Palestine and discouraged Jews from going elsewhere. In 1935, more than 66,000 Jews, still mainly from eastern Europe, entered Palestine. The Arab population was also rapidly increasing because of a high birth rate. By 1939 the country's population of one and a half million was 30 percent Jewish.

From the start, the British were ready to offer rudimentary self-government, but on terms that seemed totally inadequate to the Arab Palestinians. In 1922 the mandatory government proposed the establishment of a Legislative Council, consisting of two Christians, two Jews, eight Muslims, and ten British governmental officials. This plan would have put ten Arabs and two Jews on the Council, and the Christian Arab Palestinians were no less anti-Zionist than the Muslims. But the Arabs rejected the plan, pointing out that it would give the supporters of the Balfour Declaration—that is, the Jews and the British—a permanent majority. The plan would also have required Arab Palestinians to acquiesce in the concept of a Jewish national home, which they understood to mean an eventual Jewish state. The Jews were unenthusiastic about any development of representative government for Palestine as a whole while they were still a small minority. But the Jewish community (the Yishuv) adroitly indicated its acceptance of the British plan, seemingly confident that it would be rejected by the Arabs and not be implemented. Many Arab Palestinians later believed that their refusal to accept a tactical compromise, which might have eventually given them a greater voice in their country's affairs, had been a mistake. Pointing to the strength of the Zionists and the existence of an international climate favorable to settler societies and colonial rule, others deny that greater moderation would have helped the Arab cause.

The Yishuv had its own political institutions. First of all, there was the World Zionist Organization, to which the British gave responsibility in matters relating to the "ingathering" and settlement of Jews. In 1929 a Jewish Agency for Palestine was set up to take over these functions. The creation of the Jewish Agency, headed by the president of the World Zionist Organization, was supposed to provide representation for "non-Zionist" Jews, who nevertheless could be counted on to support the development of the national home. The Jewish Agency, with diminishing "non-Zionist" representation, soon became virtually indistinguishable from the World Zionist Organization. It even maintained a clandestine military force, the Haganah. In addition, the Yishuv established an Elected Assembly, which chose a National Council and an

Executive to govern the community between sessions. Another vital organization was the General Federation of Trade Unions, or Histadrut, which was closely linked with the Elective Assembly in that the Mapai (Workers) party dominated both institutions. The Histadrut not only represented workers' interests but also ran a health service, a newspaper, schools, and business enterprises.

The British proposed the establishment of an Arab Agency in 1923. But the Arabs refused the offer, indignant at the suggestion that they, who still made up nearly 90 percent of the population, could be treated as merely one of the two Palestinian communities. Each Arab religious group did, however, retain control over its strictly religious affairs, a carry-over of the Ottoman millet system. Thus the Supreme Islamic Council supervised Sunni Muslim schools, law courts, mosques, and religious endowments.

The Palestinian Arabs were not simply against foreign rule. Immigration on such a large scale by a group of people who did not identify with the existing population of the country would have caused disturbances anywhere. In this case, the hostility was compounded by the cultural and political differences between the newcomers, almost all of whom were Europeans, and the indigenous Arab population. The Arabs feared that they would become a minority if Jewish immigration continued. Besides, they believed that the creation of a Jewish state would require their own expulsion from Palestine. Zionist leaders recurrently spoke of the need to "transfer" the Arab population, as recent studies make increasingly clear.

The acquisition of land by the Zionists added another dimension to the struggle for Palestine. The Arab Palestinian peasants, like rural people everywhere, had a deep emotional attachment to the land they tilled, aside from economic dependence on it, but they found themselves without any say in its disposition. Until the nineteenth century, the formal title to land had been vested in the state, although the peasants had customary rights to it and considered it theirs. Under the prevailing *musha* system, plots of land rotated from family to family in each village on an annual basis. The Ottoman Empire, in trying to westernize its legal system, had from 1858 on encouraged registration of titles to land, but the peasants feared that this would enable the government to tax them more heavily and conscript their sons for military service. Many peasants realized that a powerful and wealthy man would not likely be overtaxed, and so they registered their land in the name of some local notable, thereby enhancing his wealth and power. In other cases, peasants did nothing to obtain land titles, which wealthy persons later managed to buy cheaply. While at least one study now casts doubt on how widespread the loss of peasants' rights was, such a process existed to some degree, while rich individuals also began to establish estates on land that had previously been deemed unfit for use or which, in the case of parts of the coastal region, bedouin raids had long made uninhabitable. Whatever the explanation, the result was the same—a landlord class in a position to sell land to outsiders who would not need the services of those who had been accustomed to tilling it. Hence even before the rise of political Zionism, a situation developed that would later facilitate Zionist objectives.

The World Zionist Organization had set up a Jewish National Fund to purchase land in Palestine. One of the goals of the Zionists was to create a "new Jewish man," a worker or, better still, a farmer, unlike the urban middle-class Jews of eastern Europe. Although most of the European Jewish immigrants settled in cities, Zionism—which stressed that anti-Jewish prejudice would end when the Jews become a "normal" people with a country of their own—placed an almost mystical emphasis on establishing ties to the land. Collective Jewish agricultural settlements, the kibbutzim (singular: kibbutz), with their total sharing of land and other property, and the moshavim (singular: moshav), which permitted greater private ownership, developed in Palestine. Arab landowners, particularly those who lived in Damascus and Beirut and found the new political borders inconvenient, were tempted to sell, and many did. Although the Zionists still had bought only about 6 percent of the land (maybe 20 percent of the cultivatible part) by 1948, this land tended to be in the most fertile areas.

As Zionists acquired land, many Arab peasants were uprooted. Arabs could not even stay on the land as tenants or hired labor, since the Jewish National Fund forbade the use of non-Jewish labor (a rule that was sometimes violated in practice). At least in part, this was because the Zionists hoped to create a totally Jewish society, but socialists explained it in terms of opposing the exploitation of cheap labor. In this way, Jewish settlement did not entirely fit the pattern of most other Western settler societies in Africa and Asia, which was based on cheap "native" labor. But the consequences for the Arab Palestinian peasants were even more severe. The fund's rules provided that the land it purchased must remain the inalienable property of the Jewish people. Once Arab-owned land was sold to Zionists, the process was irreversible. Although the fund, with its available capital and Western technical skills, developed much marshland and desert, it also took possession of lush Arab farmland in the Vale of Esdraelon and eastern Galilee. On one occasion, in 1921, the Sursuk family of Beirut sold 50,000 acres, comprising twenty-two Arab villages, to the fund.

Anti-Zionist violence in Palestine became endemic. There were Arab riots in 1920 and 1921. Then in 1929 an incident arising from the construction the previous year of a temporary screen by Jews at the Wailing Wall (the western remnant of Herod's temple, which is also a part of the Haram al-Sharif or Noble Sanctuary, the Islamic holy area) got out of hand, leaving 133 Jews and 116 Arabs dead in various parts of Palestine. The riots took a particularly heavy toll of lives in the small Orthodox Jewish community of Hebron, which had been there long before Zionism but now had to end its existence while continuing to inspire Zionist zealotry as late as the 1990s.

As Jewish immigration increased, a large-scale Arab rebellion broke out in 1936 against the British and the Zionists, turning into a three-year civil war. All Arab Palestinian factions now united to form a Higher Arab Committee led by the mufti of Jerusalem (and president of the Higher Islamic Council), al-Hajj Amin al-Husayni, who had emerged as the leader of the struggle against the British and the Zionists during the 1920s and who gained a reputation—which some historians now say was not entirely deserved, particularly in the early years—for being fiery and intransigent. The Husayni family had been dominant in Jerusalem since Ottoman times. Its main rival, the Nashashibi family, was much more willing to work with the British, in the hope of winning them over from the Zionist side, but it was less influential. Demanding an end to Jewish immigration and land transfers and the establishment of an independent Palestine, the Arabs declared a general strike and an economic boycott of the Yishuv. Emotions flared throughout the Arab world in sympathy with the Arab Palestinians. It was a Lebanese, Fawzi al-Qawuqji, who led the anti-British and anti-Zionist guerrilla campaign in northern Palestine. A zealous Muslim religious leader, Shaykh Izz al-Din al-Qassam, might have inspired many Arabs to resist (and indeed was to serve as a symbol for Islamists in the 1990s) had he not already died in a battle with the British in 1935.

The British found themselves in an impossible situation. The mandate had committed them to virtually irreconcilable principles, and their policies wavered. Their attempt to be impartial antagonized both Zionists and Arabs. Colonial secretary Winston Churchill issued a White Paper in 1922 that reiterated British support for Zionism but reassured Arabs that this would not mean their subordination to the Zionist movement. He stated that the Jewish National Home did not mean a Jewish state and that immigration would be limited by Palestine's "economic absorptive capacity." Following the reports of two British commissions in 1930, the Passfield White Paper announced a policy of setting aside government-owned lands for landless Arab peasants, not for Jewish immigrants, and of henceforth considering Arab unemployment in determining economic absorptive capacity. But following strong protests from Zionists in Britain, Prime Minister Ramsey MacDonald issued a statement that essentially nullified the Passfield White Paper.

Another commission, sent to Palestine in 1936, concluded that conflict between the "predominantly Asiatic" Arabs and the "predominantly European" Zionists was "irrepressible" and proposed a plan for partition: Palestine would be divided into an Arab and a Jewish state, with a smaller international area to include Jerusalem. Some Zionists reluctantly accepted the concept of partition, but the Twentieth Zionist Congress rejected this particular proposal in 1937. The Arabs refused the plan outright, pointing out that almost half the inhabitants of the proposed "Jewish state" were Arabs and that most of the land was Arab-owned. They also objected to the commission's proposal that the bulk of the Arab population be removed from the Jewish state, by force if necessary, and they believed that the influx of Jewish refugees from Europe would lead to further Zionist expansion.

London now decided to make important concessions to Arab Palestinian nationalism. Further attempts to work out a settlement, including three alternate partition plans proposed by another British commission in 1938 and an Arab-Jewish conference in London in February 1939, had come to naught. The Arab rebellion was intensifying, while gathering war clouds in Europe made pacification in Palestine imperative. To many British leaders, it also seemed foolhardy to alienate Egypt and Iraq, two Arab states where Britain had strategic interests. A White Paper of May 1939 stipulated that Jewish immigration to Palestine would not exceed 75,000 during the next five years and that further immigration would require Arab consent.

Land transfers to Jews would be forbidden in some areas and limited in others. After ten years, unless circumstances required postponement, Palestine would obtain its independence—with certain safeguards for the holy places, British interests, and the protection of the various communities—but presumably as a predominantly Arab state with a Jewish minority. Although recent studies refute this interpretation (which insinuates that Arab demands were unjust), the Zionists saw the White Paper as a case of appeasement comparable to Munich and a betrayal of the Balfour Declaration, just at a time when the Jews of Europe were in mortal peril. Nor did it satisfy the Arab Palestinians, whose leaders, including al-Hajj Amin, were in exile. But although it did not guarantee their independence, it gave some of them hope that the British commitment to Zionism was weakening and that the European Jewish tide would finally recede.

OUTRIGHT WESTERNIZATION
IN TURKEY

After leading Turkey to victory over European imperialism, the Ghazi Mustafa Kemal proceeded to implement a drastic "Herodian" program of westernization. In his view, Western civilization was the only one that mattered. He dismissed Islamic civilization as an amalgam of "age-old rotten mentalities" inferior in every way, not just technically, to the West. As a Turkish nationalist he also saw Islamic civilization as something foreign, borrowed from the Arabs, which Turks should now cast off. Unlike later Middle Eastern nationalists, he did not even bother to clothe westernization in the more acceptable guise of modernization.

Kemal aspired to adopt Western civilization as a whole; he believed that one could not acquire it piecemeal. This outlook heavily represented the influence of the writings of the Turkish nationalist sociologist, Ziya Gökalp, who had distinguished between culture, defined as the nonmaterial aspect of life, and civilization, the material aspects. Gökalp, reacting to the failure of earlier reformers to stem the decline of the Ottoman Empire, advocated the adoption of Western civilization. While he wanted the Turkish people to have their own culture, he rejected the one they then had, which he saw as Arab and foreign, in favor of his romantic vision of a pre-Islamic Turkish culture. He believed that this had in many ways been like that of the modern West. To advocate westernization in such areas as emancipating women or secularizing society was really to seek a return to authentic Turkish ways.

In particular, Kemal believed that the ills of the Islamic world were a result of the influence of religion. Himself an agnostic, he rejected religious discipline and indulged in sexual promiscuity and drunkenness, which he sometimes flaunted to show his contempt for the Islamic prohibition of alcohol. He was allegedly not hostile to Islam as such or to religion in general, and he did not contemplate turning his people into non-Muslims. What he opposed was religious influence on society and the brakes it allegedly put on progress. But the distinction was not clear to many Turkish—let alone non-Turkish—Muslims.

Kemal's first priority was to abolish religio-political institutions. This actually began with the 1919 National Pact's attribution of sovereignty to the people, which fundamentally contradicted the Islamic concept of the sovereignty of God, that is, the principle that earthly governments lack supreme legislative authority and must govern within the narrow limits of a revealed body of law. Despite his protests to the contrary, Kemal had also long awaited the opportunity to abolish the sultanate and caliphate. When the Allies invited representatives of both the nationalists and the sultan to the Lausanne Conference, Kemal took advantage of the occasion to push the abolition of the sultanate through the Grand National Assembly. It was not until the following year that he dared prod the Assembly into formally declaring the establishment of a republic, a word that to Muslims still carried an un-Islamic ring. When Sultan Mehmed VI went into exile, Abd al-Majid II succeeded him in the role of caliph. Then in 1924 the Assembly also abolished the caliphate and other such offices, including that of *shaykh al-Islam.* The religious schools and courts disappeared, along with the Ministry of *Waqfs* (religious endowments). In 1928 the reference to Islam as the state religion was deleted from the Constitution.

The Kemalist program of secularization meant a complete revamping of the legal system along Western lines. Previous Ottoman attempts to modernize law had led to the adoption of European-style codes of secular law, partly in substance and partly in form, replacing the immutable God-given law. But the rules of personal status, relating to marriage, divorce, inheritance, and religious endowments, had remained Islamic. The only change in the law of personal status had been the Ottoman Law of Family Rights of 1917, which introduced a few reforms. Kemal rejected any continuation of this gradualist approach. Instead, the Grand National Assembly completely westernized Turkish law by adopting European codes in all fields, including personal status. Among other changes, polygamy became illegal, and men could no longer arbitrarily repudiate their wives; women acquired equal rights in the areas of divorce, child custody, and inheritance (but not in all matters, for the European rules that Kemal copied contained their own inequalities).

The Kemalist period witnessed a whole series of symbolic changes. To be like Europe, Turkey adopted Sunday (and Saturday afternoon) as a weekly holiday (called the *vikend*). Turkish writing took on a "Western" appearance as Arabic letters made way for a slightly modified form of the Latin alphabet. The Qur'an appeared in a Turkish translation, and the call to prayer—which had always been in Arabic throughout the Muslim world—now had to be recited in Turkish. While Middle Eastern men had increasingly adopted Western clothing, they had always kept their traditional headgear. A turban, skullcap, or fez permitted the forehead to touch the floor during prostrations for prayer. For a Muslim to put on a hat with a brim was virtually a symbol of apostasy. Yet Kemal wore such a hat publicly in 1925, and before the gasps ceased, the Assembly outlawed the fez and made wearing hats with brims compulsory. Kemal attempted to discourage women from dressing in an Islamic way, but stopped short of actually forbidding them from doing so. The "international" (Gregorian) calendar replaced the Islamic one. Every Turk was required by law to adopt a family name, something that was still uncommon in the Islamic world. The Assembly awarded the surname Atatürk ("Father of the Turks") to Kemal. General Ismet, his eventual successor, took the name Inönü in commemoration of his victories over the Greeks in 1921. Dervish orders, long an important facet of Turkish life, were outlawed.

Some of Kemal Atatürk's reforms seemed comical to Westerners. Some Muslims took offense at what they considered his superficial aping of "unbelievers'" ways. To Kemal, however, these changes signified Turkey's entrance into the Western world and removed the marks of being Oriental that had prevented its acceptance as a modern country. Embracing the ethnocentrism of the West, he saw these discarded symbols of his own civilization as stigmas of barbarism. As a Turkish nationalist he rationalized that the Islamic influences that he was abolishing were foreign.

In addition, it was possible to show, at times perhaps by forcing the argument, that many of the reforms would have practical benefits for Turkey. For example, the Arabic alphabet did not fit the sounds of the Turkish language. Having Sunday as a day of rest—instead of Friday, which had become widespread, although not required by Islam—would facilitate commerce and communication with Europe. Kemal even pointed out that the fez required more material than the brimmed hat and was too expensive for a poor country. But these were rationalizations, not fundamental reasons, for such drastic changes.

Kemalism included an intense Turkish nationalism that adopted some far-fetched versions of history. Paralleling nationalists in other countries, the Kemalists wanted to purge Turkish, insofar as possible, of words of Arabic and Persian origin, and insisted on calling cities by their Turkish names, as in the case of Istanbul (as opposed to Constantinople), Ankara (rather than Angora), and Izmir (not Smyrna). When they found that some words had no Turkish equivalents, European (mainly French) words had to be substituted. To justify such borrowing, Kemal—and Turkish schoolbooks—propounded a pseudoscientific theory that all languages came from Turkish and consequently that these adopted European words were really Turkish. According to this "sun-language" theory, all past civilizations were the result of Turkish immigration from Central Asia to the Eurasian periphery. Any cultural borrowing could thus be justified as a resumption of some primordially Turkish trait.

Although Kemal's version of Turkish nationalism had an ethnic basis, it lost its former pan-Turkish aspect. It was a devotion to the "Anatolian homeland," that is, the territory essentially within existing boundaries, which had no meaning historically. But by claiming that ancient Anatolian peoples, particularly the Hittites, were also Turks, the Turkish nationalist could annex the whole history of Anatolia to that of his people and thus foster a new territorial identity. Even the one significant linguistic and ethnic minority, the Kurds of eastern Anatolia (whose languages, along with Persian, belong in the Iranian—and the broader Indo-European—family), were euphemistically called "mountain Turks." Non-Turkish Muslims such as Kurds find it easy to be accepted as full-fledged Turks if they are willing to assimilate and adopt Turkish as a replacement for their original tongues.

The formal structure of government, according to the Constitution of 1924, replicated the model of European parliamentary democracy. A basic slogan of Kemalism was "populism," which made "the people" the theoretical source of authority. Populism sometimes took on more specific meanings, such as opposition to economic privilege, which the regime actually did little to combat. In reality, the commitment to westernization dictated suspicion of the traditionalistic masses, and Turkey's government was an authoritarian single-party system dominated by Kemal. The aura he had obtained as the leader of Turkey's liberation, in addition to his personal persuasiveness or charisma, enabled him to rule virtually as he wished. He was not only the president of the Republic but also the leader of the People's Republican Party (the real center of power), which was essentially a continuation of the League for the Defense of Rights under a new name. He was able to select the prime minister, usually Ismet Inönü.

Some writers have said that Kemal's dictatorship was generally not harsh. But perhaps they were not aware of his most brutal actions, notably the extent to which he responded to Kurdish revolts with wholesale slaughter and burning villages. Sometimes vigorous debates took place within the party and the Assembly. And Kemal's ideal form of government was liberal democracy, for which he viewed his period of tutelage as paving the way (but many other dictators have used the same argument). On two occasions, in 1925 and 1930, he allowed opposition parties to form. But each time dissent turned into disorder. Conservative, antisecularist forces still represented the dominant sentiment within Turkey and threatened to undo Kemalist reforms by co-opting any opposition party. Kemal then proceeded each time to restore single-party government. It is doubtful whether he ever really wanted to permit authentic opposition, for at least on one occasion careful analysis reveals that his purpose was to trick dissidents into coming out into the open so he could repress them.

A final principle of Kemalist Turkey was etatism (statism, meaning government control over the economy). Kemal instituted a series of government plans, state banks to promote industrial development, state-owned industries (including government monopolies in some fields), and high protective tariffs. Communist and fascist practices may have influenced him to move in this direction, but practical considerations were more important. Etatism seemed to fill the vacuum left by the departure of the Greeks and the destruction of the Armenians, who had predominated in commerce and industry. Private capital was scarce. The world depression intensified the emphasis on etatism, which the People's Republican party adopted as one of the six principles of Kemalism in 1931, along with nationalism, revolutionism, secularism, populism, and republicanism.

When President Kemal Atatürk died in 1938, he left a deeply changed country. Yet he had not transformed it into a modern nation, certainly not a Western one. The villagers, particularly in eastern Turkey, were still traditional Middle Easterners. The secularizing reforms were not understood and were evaded whenever possible. Marriages in the villages continued to be conducted without regard to the new law, and again and again the Assembly retroactively legalized such unions and legitimized their offspring. When one political leader unintentionally raised his brimmed hat at a meeting, the people in the crowd mistook the act as defiance against westernization and began throwing their own hats to the ground. The country experienced minimal economic development during this period. Neither did it undergo any sort of social revolution, for Atatürk's regime rested on a coalition of urban bureaucrats and rural notables, with the latter group's economic and political position in the villages perpetuated.

It is ironic that, despite Kemal's emphasis on secularism and his rejection of pan-Islam or any special ties with the Islamic world, the Turkish national identity remains more closely bound to Islam than is any other Middle Eastern nationalism. While general usage recognizes the existence of Christian Arabs, most Turks could not conceive of a "Christian Turk," except in the legal sense. Such a person is popularly called a "non-Turkish Turk." At the time of the exchange of populations with Greece during the early 1920s, religion provided the criterion for distinguishing between the two peoples, even in the case of Turkish-speaking Christians and Greek-speaking Muslims. Religion never ceased being an important touchstone for Turkish nationality.

EMULATION OF KEMALISM IN IRAN

With the example of Kemal Atatürk in mind, Riza Shah attempted to westernize Iran, but with even less success. First, whereas Turkey's geographical position had long exposed it to Europe, there were fewer beginnings of westernization in Iran. Second, lacking the aura of heroism that Atatürk had gained from his triumph over European imperialism, Riza Shah was less able to impose unpopular reforms on a conservative population. In addition, the shah's lack of education or exposure to the West hardly prepared him to be a Persian Atatürk. Nor did the political structure he established facilitate changes in Iran similar to those effected by the Turkish single-party regime.

At first, Riza planned to declare Iran a republic. But this evoked so much furor among the *ulama*, who associated a republic with Kemalism, that he backed down and opted to start a new dynasty. As the new shah, he gave lip service to the 1906 Constitution but assumed the role of an autocrat. He became increasingly authoritarian and paranoid. His closest associates were in frequent danger of arrest or murder by his agents. The only organ somewhat analogous to Atatürk's People's Republican Party was the Society to Guide Public Opinion, a propaganda organization inspired by Nazi and fascist models. Established in 1939, it might have developed into an authoritarian party had Riza Shah remained in power.

Riza Shah devoted great effort to reviving a strong Iran that could resist foreign control. The tribes, which had long defied the government in Tehran, were crushed by 1925, as were subsequent tribal revolts. The government forcibly settled some tribes, an action that turned them from proud warriors and herders into poor and dispirited peasants. But at last there was an effective central government. And Riza Shah created a national army, starting conscription as early as 1925. The army, almost 400,000 strong by 1941, was an awesome means for controlling the country, though too poorly armed to ward off an invasion by Britain and the USSR.

Furthermore, the new regime attempted to modernize Iran. Aside from the roads and railroads built by the British during World War I, the country still had a primitive communications system when Riza Shah seized power. One of his greatest achievements was the construction of a Trans-Iranian Railway between 1927 and 1938. This was all the more impressive because the Iranian government refused to finance it with foreign loans but raised the necessary funds from taxes on sugar and tea, two staples in the diet of even the poorest Iranians. By 1941 Iran also had 15,000 miles of new roads. Government monopolies established factories for producing textiles, sugar, and cement, and the construction of a steel mill began in 1929. A modern school system started to develop, at least in the cities and towns. But the new ruler hardly tried to change drab village life or to develop agriculture.

There was no fundamental transformation of Iranian society under Riza Shah's rule. He gave little attention to improving the economic conditions of the masses. While much of the old aristocracy declined, Riza Shah's sale of state lands led to the growth of a new landlord class. The tax that he imposed on staples weighed heavily on the poor, and few of them, least of all the humiliated, impoverished, and embittered ex-nomads, had any admiration for him.

Riza Shah emulated Atatürk's attacks on religious influence and dictated westernization in such matters as clothing. Since there had been virtually no prior westernization of law in Iran, the government began in 1928 to institute a new civil code, based largely on French law except in matters of personal status. Reform in family law followed, including a 1931 statute permitting women to begin divorce proceedings. In another effort to break with the past, in 1935 the shah required men to wear European-style hats. This followed an earlier attempt to replace traditional Islamic headgear with a new "Pahlavi hat." Riza Shah further shocked traditionalists when he gave a tea and ordered officials to bring their wives. In 1936 he outdid Atatürk by forbidding women from wearing Islamic dress in public, particularly the chadour, a tentlike garment that covers the whole body from the top of the head on down. Women who could not bear to expose their faces and figures in a Western manner had no choice but to stay at home, and governmental employees whose wives resisted such immodesty could be fined or even fired. By adopting for his dynasty the name "Pahlavi," the name of an ancient form of the Persian language, Riza Shah stressed his country's ties with pre-Islamic Iran rather than with the Islamic world.

THE ZEALOT APPROACH:
THE ARABIAN PENINSULA

The Arabian Peninsula had long been the area of the Middle East least affected by the modern world. As westernization and secularization proceeded elsewhere in the Middle East, Arabia actually reinforced the Islamic character of its society. In Toynbeean terms, this was the "zealot" approach to an encroaching civilization.

The puritanical "Wahhabi" movement that had been identified with the Sa'udi amirs of Najd since the eighteenth century did not merely stand for traditional Islam against westernization. It insisted on returning to its own version of pristine Islam, uncorrupted by centuries of accretions of non-Islamic practices. To these Unitarians, as they called themselves, traditional reverence for saints and even the marking of graves were anathema. The "Wahhabis" rejected such generally accepted practices as wearing silk, shaving beards, and smoking tobacco. They denounced the laxity of Muslims who drank alcohol or accepted westernized, non-Islamic systems of law, which, in late Ottoman times, had even penetrated the Hijaz. After restoring Sa'udi power in Najd in 1902, Abd al-Aziz gave renewed impetus to this puritanical movement. By creating agricultural settlements he transformed bedouins, who had generally taken religion lightly, into *Ikhwan* (brethren) whose dedication to their strict version of Islam took priority over tribal ties and who fanatically fought for their faith.

King Husayn of the Hijaz had become stubborn and unrealistic in his later years, and this helped to bring about his fall from power. His claim to being "king of the Arab countries" had antagonized other Arab rulers in the peninsula, especially Abd al-Aziz, whose followers considered his rule over the holy places a sacrilege. He had antagonized much of the Islamic world by rebelling against the caliph during World War I. The failure of his regime to protect pilgrims from marauding tribes, as well as abominable health conditions in the holy cities, cost him further support. He was bitter over the partition of the Fertile Crescent, seeing this as a betrayal of Britain's promises to him during the war. The British offered him a treaty of alliance, which might have protected him against the Najdi threat, but only on condition that he accept British policies in Palestine, which he refused to do. Even in 1918 the Sa'udis and the Hashimites were resuming their struggle for mastery of Arabia. When Husayn sent Amir Abdullah to occupy a disputed border oasis in 1919, the Najdis waylaid his force and almost wiped it out. By 1921, Abd al-Aziz had conquered Shammar and part of Asir, the rest of which he made a Sa'udi protectorate in 1926 and then annexed in 1930.

The big prize, though, was the Hijaz. In 1924, following the abolition of the Ottoman caliphate, Husayn climaxed his folly by assuming the title of "caliph" himself. Most of the Islamic world greeted this claim with scorn, and the Najdis began a rapid advance into the Hijaz. Abd al-Aziz's troops entered Ta'if and massacred more than three hundred of its people. Even though Husayn abdicated in favor of his eldest son, Ali, his enemies occupied Mecca and Madina and finished their conquest of the Hijaz by taking Jiddah in December 1925. Adding to his title of sultan of Najd and its dependencies, Abd al-Aziz now also became "king of the Hijaz." He consolidated the two realms as the kingdom of Saudi Arabia in 1932.

But Abd al-Aziz did not prove to be the inflexible fanatic that many Hijazis had feared. The invaders did not repeat their massacre at Ta'if, as Abd al-Aziz kept his most ferocious warriors out of the holy cities. To be sure, he began a stricter enforcement of Islamic law under the supervision of Committees for the Commendation of Virtue and the Condemnation of Vice. The five daily prayers were enforced by police with long canes. He reinstated the practice of cutting off the hands of convicted thieves, as enjoined by the Qur'an. The "Wahhabis" destroyed tombs, including one alleged to be Mother Eve's, although they prudently stopped short of desecrating the Prophet's grave. But, while alcohol and music were forbidden, Abd al-Aziz finally agreed not to destroy the merchants' stocks of tobacco. Once he had reached what were to become the boundaries of his kingdom, he saw fit in 1930 to suppress the fanatical *Ikhwan*. While foreign Muslims were at first appalled by his domination of the holy places, Abd al-Aziz's essential moderation, plus the improved security and health conditions that he instituted, allayed their fears and won their eventual acceptance.

The Sa'udi ruler welcomed the material innovations of the modern West, such as automobiles, medicine, and telephones, despite the opposition of his more rigid followers. Perhaps they realized that once modernity entered the door it could not be stopped. Ever able to think of clever arguments, Abd al-Aziz once convinced some *ulama* that the telephone could not be the work of Satan by using it to carry the words of the Qur'an. He even set up a few small but modern schools.

Even in 1939, however, Saudi Arabia had experienced little westernization. It had a patriarchal government that made no distinction between the private purse of the king and the finances of the state. The monarch was "democratic" in the traditional tribal sense of being accessible to everyone. Indeed, he could not disregard the opinions of tribal and religious leaders or the advice of other members of the royal family. Nevertheless, Abd al-Aziz made all the major decisions himself.

An event took place in 1935 that seemed insignificant at the time, yet would ultimately lead this stronghold of traditionalism to become part of the westernized world. Standard Oil of California (which had been given a concession in 1933 when Abd al-Aziz needed money to supplement his income from a declining pilgrim trade) discovered oil at Dhahran, in the Eastern Province. Little did anyone dream that Saudi Arabia possessed the world's largest oil reserves, which would eventually bring incredible wealth and power but would also undermine an ancient Eastern way of life.

Except for the British-protected states of the Persian Gulf and southern Arabia, Yemen was the only part of the Arabian Peninsula that Abd al-Aziz failed to absorb. His army actually invaded Yemen in 1934 but withdrew after the two countries concluded a mutually satisfactory peace. Abd al-Aziz was too shrewd to try to annex this densely populated country, whose towering mountains and distinctive Zaydi branch of Islam made it virtually impregnable to foreign invaders.

Under Imam Yahya, Yemen survived as a medieval Islamic society. The *imam*, who administered his absolute rule through an oligarchy of *sayyids* (descendants of the Prophet), wanted nothing that the West had to offer. He once proclaimed bluntly that he did "not like alcohol and parliaments and things like that." Yet even he inadvertently paved the way for a republican revolution of 1962 when he sent a young man, Abdullah al-Sallal, to Baghdad for military training and secondhand exposure to Western ways and ideas.

THE MIDDLE ROAD: EGYPT
AND THE FERTILE CRESCENT

Along the spectrum ranging from a Western-inspired secularism to a rigorous adherence to Islam as the basis of society, Egypt and the Fertile Crescent countries came
to occupy a middle ground. Their leaders were Herodians, but gradualists. Constitutions (except in Lebanon, where a multisectarian system emerged) invariably proclaimed Islam to be the official religion. But they also proclaimed the sovereignty of
the nation, thus perhaps unwittingly repudiating the Islamic concept that the ruler is
God's agent for the enforcement of his unchanging law. Indeed, few people realized
that a break with Islamic concepts had occurred. When the Turkish government abolished the caliphate in 1924, a storm of protest ensued throughout the Islamic world,
not least in an Egypt whose constitution had already proclaimed national sovereignty. Egyptians had failed to draw the logical conclusion that this was a rejection
of the authority of the caliph, who was not, according to Islamic doctrine, simply a
spiritual leader but rather the successor to the Prophet Muhammad in his capacity as
ruler of the Islamic community. Representatives from throughout the Islamic world
met in Cairo in 1926 in an effort to restore the caliphate, but national and dynastic rivalries made it impossible to reach any agreement on this subject.

While there was no constitutional obligation in these countries to retain the Islamic *shari'ah*, parliaments trod softly. Thus the earlier pattern persisted, in which
Western-style codes went into effect except in matters pertaining to personal status.
Egypt and Lebanon adopted French-style civil codes; elsewhere, the nineteenth-century Ottoman *Majallah* (European-style codification of Islamic civil law) continued
to prevail. No one gave serious consideration to abolishing the *shari'ah* on the Kemalist pattern, and the only modification of Islamic family law accepted in the Fertile Crescent countries was that which the Ottoman Parliament had enacted in 1917.
The Egyptian Parliament, carefully justifying its actions by eclectically citing rules
from various schools of jurisprudence or from the minority opinions of some legal
scholars, enacted several laws during the 1920s modifying the rules on marriage and
divorce slightly more radically than the Ottoman law of 1917 had done. For example, Egyptian women could now apply to a court for divorce under some circumstances, contrary to the previous rule that allowed only husbands the prerogative of
divorce. The Parliament rejected more radical changes, such as the Egyptian cabinet's proposal in 1927 for restrictions on polygamy.

At first there was an intellectual trend toward greater secularization and westernization. A book by an Egyptian *shari'ah* judge named Ali Abd al-Raziq appeared
in 1925 which went so far as to assert that the caliphate had always been incidental
to Islam and thus that the true Islamic conception of the relationship between religion
and state did not differ from that of the Christian West. A blind Egyptian, Taha
Husayn, who had studied in what he considered to be stultifying traditional mosque-
schools and at al-Azhar before blossoming at the modern Cairo University and at the
Sorbonne, was emerging as the great figure in modern Arabic literature. In a book
published in 1926 on the subject of pre-Islamic Arabic poetry, Taha Husayn funda-

mentally challenged orthodox Islam. Aside from ridiculing certain Islamic doctrines, he attempted to show that some of the supposedly pre-Islamic poetry had actually been written at a later date. Since the Arabic usage in this poetry had been a foundation for the interpretation of the Qur'an, his assertions stirred up a hornet's nest, but other liberal intellectuals came to his defense.

Such writers were obviously out of tune with the masses and with traditionalist *ulama*. Al-Raziq's unorthodoxy lost him his license as a religious scholar. Husayn's book was withdrawn from publication, although it was later printed in a slightly revised form. Even the reformist tradition of Muhammad Abduh, out of which the liberal intellectual movement had branched, developed in a conservative direction. Abduh's successor, Rashid Rida, while continuing to criticize the rigidity of traditional Islamic thinking, urged a return of the Islam of the *Salaf* ("predecessors," i.e., early Muslims). The movement, known as the Salafiyyah, had begun to identify itself with the "Wahhabis," the very antithesis of the liberal camp.

By the mid-1930s, the liberals' position was also less clear-cut. They were beginning to write about religious subjects in tones that seemed to contradict their earlier writings. Although Taha Husayn, in his 1939 *Future of Culture in Egypt*, clearly placed himself among the modernists by proclaiming the need to westernize and even by arguing that Egypt had always been part of Europe, there was a time during the early 1930s when the tone of his own writing typified the conservative trend.

A popular revulsion against westernization culminated in new religious movements, the most notable of which was known as the *Ikhwan al-Muslimin* (Muslim Brethren). Hasan al-Banna, a young Egyptian schoolteacher of strict religious upbringing who had been concerned with religious causes from his youth, founded the movement in 1928. It was a reaction against both Western political domination and the Western influence that had eroded Muslim life. Combining the Herodian and zealot approaches, the Brethren did not blindly reject all innovations. Like the earlier modernist movement, they agreed on the need to rethink Islamic doctrines (i.e., to reopen the gates of *ijtihad*) but nevertheless insisted on interpreting the Qur'an and the *hadiths* strictly. They did not object to modern technology or to such superficial matters as Western-style clothing. Nor did they stand for the seclusion of women, whom they organized as "Muslim Sisters," some of whose members attended the modern universities to prepare for careers as teachers and nurses. They supported Egyptian and Arab nationalism insofar as it opposed Western rule, although in principle they rejected the Western-inspired concept of separate nations that did not include all Muslims. Actually, by stressing ties with the Islamic world, which in practice meant mainly the neighboring Arab lands, the Brethren may have helped bring Egypt into the pan-Arab movement, which is basically a secular, ethnic nationalism. But the Muslim Brethren demanded that society be restored to an Islamic basis, with the Qur'an as the constitution, and the reinstatement of the *shari'ah* in every sphere. The so-called "fundamentalism" of the Brethren resembled that of the "Wahhabis" but was the reaction of a more westernized society. Far from simply being reactionary, the Brethren stressed social justice and sometimes even "Islamic socialism."

The movement appealed to the poor and increasingly to almost all segments of society, in part because it expressed deep-seated popular resentment against Western influence. Success also was the result of the constructive activities that the Brethren organized—hospitals, food for the poor, and even factories—and of the tight hierarchical organization, comparable to that of a totalitarian political party, from cells composed of a few members up to the General Guide (al-Banna), who dominated it. Not least, the movement was the result of Hasan al-Banna's magnetic personality and brilliant mind. The Society of the Muslim Brethren later became still more important; by 1939 it already had grown into a mass organization in Egypt, with a membership numbering in the hundreds of thousands, and it had spread to the Sudan and the Fertile Crescent.

EUROPEAN-STYLE PARLIAMENTARY GOVERNMENT IN THE ARAB WORLD

One Western idea that took hold in Egypt and the Fertile Crescent during this period was parliamentary democracy. Western-style constitutions emerged in Egypt (1923), Iraq (1924), Lebanon (1926), Transjordan (1928), and Syria (1930). Each provided for civil liberties much like those included in Western constitutions. In each case there was some sort of elected parliament and a cabinet headed by a prime minister. Except for Transjordan's, each constitution provided that the cabinet would be responsible to the parliament.

Later Arab radicals have called this system a sham. In reality, parliaments did function in some countries, but they were limited in what they could do and in how truly they represented the people. Much power remained in European hands, even after formal independence. The politics of "independent" Egypt consisted of shifting alliances between the king, the Wafd (the popular political party), and the British. Parliamentary government was even less meaningful in Syria and Lebanon, where the real ruler continued to be the French high commissioner. Furthermore, the Egyptian, Iraqi, and Transjordanian monarchs, rather than being merely formal heads of state, were at the center of the political process. The Egyptian king, for example, had the legal power to dissolve the Parliament, to dismiss a cabinet that had the Parliament's support, and to reject bills passed by the Parliament. He appointed two-fifths of the members of the upper house. The position of the king of Iraq was even stronger; he had the right to appoint all the members of the upper house. The amir of Transjordan appointed six of the twenty members of his country's rudimentary representative body, the Legislative Council, whose powers were merely advisory.

Monarchs went beyond their constitutional authority. The Wafd party, led by Zaghlul until his death in 1927 and then less ably by Mustafa al-Nahhas, won large majorities in each Parliament for which elections were relatively free. But the party controlled the cabinet only for a few short periods. Zaghlul's government, after the Wafd won 90 percent of the seats in the 1924 election, lasted only nine months. The king simply dismissed each Wafdist cabinet, dissolved the Parliament, and installed his own men. Some of the "king's men" organized their own short-lived parties, such as the Unionist party in 1925, headed by Prime Minister Ahmad Ziwar. In 1928 Nahhas was dismissed after heading the government for two months, and the king dissolved the Parliament to rule by decree. After the Wafd won 212 out of 235 seats in the 1929 election, Nahhas became prime minister in January 1930, but King Fu'ad soon replaced him with another of his men, Isma'il Sidqi, who founded the grossly misnamed People's Party. For more than five years, an authoritarian constitution that made the cabinet responsible to the king alone superseded the 1923 Constitution. The Wafd won another free election in 1936, but young King Faruq installed a cabinet in January 1938 that manipulated new elections to the extent that the Wafd won only twelve seats.

Much the same situation prevailed in Iraq, but without any political party analogous to the Wafd. The king (Faysal, up to his death in 1933, and then his son, Ghazi, until he died in a car crash in 1939) ruled through cabinets headed by various handpicked individuals, some of whom headed their own loosely organized parties based on personal loyalties and alliances. The government generally determined who would get elected to the Parliament. The real dynamics of power have been aptly explained in terms of a narrow oligarchy consisting of a few former Ottoman soldiers who participated in the Arab Revolt during World War I and a group of tribal *shaykhs* now turned into landlords. A law passed in 1933 in effect made peasant debtors into serfs by forbidding them to leave the land or to seek other employment.

The typical parliamentary party in these instances was formed by a politician who brought together a group of friends and relatives, with no ideological or popular basis. Egypt's Wafd was the exception, as it represented the nearly unanimous opposition of Egyptians to foreign rule and had a high level of organization throughout the country. In Syria, a National Bloc also opposed foreign rule but was itself a loose association of traditional notables. Such parties were committed to the social status quo. Clandestine ideological parties were also beginning to emerge—small Communist movements, the fascist Young Egypt, and the proto-fascist Syrian Nationalist Party that advocated a pan-Syrian (including the whole Fertile Crescent) as opposed to a pan-Arab or local nationalism. In Iraq, the Ahali (People's) Group of intellectuals that emerged in the early 1930s, though not organized as a political party, advocated a combination of democracy and socialism.

To the extent that Western-style democratic practices worked, they were getting a bad name. Democratically elected majorities, such as the occasional Wafd cabinets, retained the same restrictions on civil liberties that they had complained about when out of power. Neither the Wafd nor any other popularly supported political party cared much to improve the lot of the poor. Politicians gave little thought to land redistribution or to ending the highly regressive system of taxation in a country such as Egypt, in which most peasants lived on the verge of starvation while toiling to enrich their tax-exempt absentee landlords. And "democratic" procedures tended to have undemocratic results; illiterate peasants trooped to the polls to vote as their landlords directed them.

The usual prerequisites for democratic government did not exist. Democracy has rarely lasted long in underdeveloped countries, particularly in those without a substantial middle class. Industrialization in Egypt was beginning under the leadership of local capitalists who established the Bank of Egypt in 1920 to finance industrial projects. Most countries also made some progress in education, public health, and communications. But basic change was discouragingly slow. For example, illiteracy in Egypt only declined from 91 percent in 1917 to 85 percent in 1937, despite a 1923 law calling for free compulsory primary education. Living standards, already low, declined significantly as population grew, and particularly during the depression of the 1930s as prices for agricultural products exported to Europe declined. The gap between rich and poor became wider than ever before.

A tradition of democratic government was also lacking. Admittedly, many Islamic concepts—the spiritual equality of believers, religious toleration, the absence of any rigid caste system, religious law as a limitation on rulers, and even the injunction to rulers to consult their subjects—seem conducive to democratic government. But the reality of Islamic history, at least after the first few years (with some exceptions on the village and tribal levels at times), had been one of autocracy based on military power, without any of the institutions such as elected parliaments that required centuries to take root in the West. This Western tree, when transplanted fullgrown to Middle Eastern soil, produced strange fruit if it did not immediately wither, and few cared to keep it watered.

Iraq's attainment of formal independence was soon followed by the intervention of the army into politics. After the Ahali Group reduced its socialism to a milder reformism, some of its leaders, particularly Hikmat Sulayman, a relatively liberal politician who had joined the movement, began to make contact with nationalist army officers. The dissatisfied officers, mainly younger ones, were led by General Bakr Sidqi, who had gained renown in Iraq from his suppression of a revolt by Nestorian Christian (so-called "Assyrian") refugees who fled from Turkish control during the First World War. Sidqi led a coup d'etat in 1936 that installed him as chief of the General Staff and Sulayman as prime minister. But this coup led to others in 1937 and 1938. The 1938 coup installed General Nuri al-Sa'id in power. Nuri, who already had headed two governments during the early 1930s, had been one of the Iraqi officers serving with Faysal during the First World War and had the reputation for being devoted to the Hashimite house and to cooperation with Britain. The series of coups still had not come to an end, and by 1941, reverting to a centuries-old Middle Eastern pattern, Iraq had experienced seven.

CONCLUSIONS

The two decades preceding the Second World War witnessed profound developments in the Middle East. The Turkish-inhabited core of the former Ottoman Empire reacted violently against humiliations at the end of the First World War and emerged by the early 1920s as the Republic of Turkey. While pushing back European political domination, the Turks, led by President Kemal Atatürk, attempted wholeheartedly to transform their Eastern society and to make themselves a part of the West. Iranian independence also acquired a new reality, as the British stopped trying to impose a semicolonial arrangement on Iran and as Riza Shah tried, though with limited success, to modernize the country along Western lines.

The achievements of the Arab countries were more gradual and limited. Egypt and Iraq had gained formal independence by the 1930s, but Britain retained much control. French rule in Lebanon and Syria did not recede, despite violent resistance. The Arabs of Palestine were being struck by a unique tidal wave from Europe that was threatening to submerge them completely. While a new British policy in 1939 threatened to halt the development of the Jewish national home and gave the Arab Palestinians some hope, the outcome of the Arab-Zionist clash was far from certain. In the Arabian Peninsula a new political order under the aegis of the Sa'udi dynasty was committed to purifying the Islamic character of society. Elsewhere in the Arab world receptivity to westernization varied and vacillated. Experiments with Western-style parliamentary government showed little success. And the westernizing intellectual trend of the 1920s gave way to a more conservative one during the 1930s. At the two extremes, Kemalist Turkey and Saudi Arabia knew whether they wanted to march resolutely westward or to turn toward their own Eastern heritage. But most of the Arab world was divided and unsure of itself and seemed to wander in circles.

8

the retreat of europe
1939–1954

In Europe during the 1930s a storm was rising that would eventually sweep through the Middle East and leave a new situation in its wake. Germany, led by Adolf Hitler, was endlessly making territorial demands. After a futile attempt at appeasement, Britain and France declared war on Germany when it invaded Poland in September 1939. By 1941 this European conflict had turned into a Second World War in which the so-called Axis Powers—Germany, Italy, and Japan—confronted the Allied Powers, chiefly Britain, the USSR, and the United States.

Middle Easterners played a minor role in the Second World War. The area was crucial largely as a terrain for some of the duels of European armies, and European control in the Arab lands and Iran temporarily increased.

Yet the war left European colonial powers enfeebled and Eastern nationalists more resolute. Outright colonial arrangements were largely finished, and nominal independence became more real during the decade following the end of the war in 1945.

The same period witnessed stronger popular demands for social, economic, and political change. Existing regimes that often combined conservative monarchs with landowning cliques deferential to Western hegemony came under attack. The challengers came heavily from a generation younger than the one in power. They represented a "new middle class" of professional people whose standing derived from their modern education, unlike the older, smaller commercial middle class. They often came from relatively poor families and owed their status to their Western-style education. A key element in this new class, and one with the necessary force at its disposal, was young army officers. This was a partially westernized group, one that was relatively unencumbered by tradition and sometimes truly committed to the modernization (though not complete westernization) of society and to ending corruption, social injustice, and the vestiges of Western colonialism.

MIDDLE EASTERN RESPONSES
TO A EUROPEAN WAR

Most Middle Easterners did not consider the European war—and the Allied cause in particular—to be their concern. Aside from Italian-ruled Libya, the European imperial powers that Middle Easterners had resisted (at least after Turkey's and Iran's long-time foe, the USSR, entered the war in June 1941) were on the Allied side. Hitler's expansionism had focused on other regions, and many Middle Easterners looked to the Axis nations as possible deliverers. They often overlooked Germany's deference to an Italian imperialism that might, as the Libyan and East African experience showed, make British and French power seem benevolent by comparison. Although official commitments (still not public) by Berlin and Rome to Arab independence and unity were forthcoming by 1941, Italian designs long inhibited the Germans from making promises to Middle Eastern nationalists. Many also overlooked the Nazi race theory that put most Middle Easterners—Arabs in particular—on the bottom rungs of humanity.

And yet in the period just after September 1939 the Middle East appeared to be on the Allied side. Nearly everyone assumed that the Allies would win, and they were supreme in the Arab world. France tightened its control in the Levant States, suspending the constitution in Lebanon, as it had already done in Syria. The British army was still in the Egyptian Delta, since Egypt had not yet been able to build the roads and other facilities on which Britain's commitment in the 1936 treaty to withdraw to the Suez Canal area was contingent. Egypt broke diplomatic relations with Germany and interned German nationals. Iraq, under Prime Minister Nuri al-Sa'id, did the same, only more enthusiastically. Nuri even wanted to participate in the war against Germany, and the regent, Prince Abd al-Ilah, who ruled in the name of his infant nephew, King Faysal II, was equally pro-British. More nationalistic Iraqis were willing to support Britain only in return for concessions to the Arabs, including a definite commitment to Arab Palestinian independence. These ardent Arab nationalists were strongly influenced by al-Hajj Amin al-Husayni, the exiled Palestinian leader, who now made Baghdad his headquarters. He later took refuge in Iran and eventually in Germany, from where he broadcast anti-Allied messages to the Arab world during the last years of the war. Other Arab Palestinian leaders supported the British, as did Amir Abdullah of Transjordan.

The Jews in Palestine were bitter over the recent White Paper but had nowhere to turn except to the British. Except for a few extremists, they attempted a tightrope act of simultaneously opposing the White Paper and supporting the British war effort. Aside from their fears of extermination in a Nazi-dominated world, the Zionists hoped that support for the war against Germany would woo the British away from their policy. They also hoped to gain military experience that could be effective against the Arabs after the Second World War was over. With this in mind, they petitioned the British authorities to permit the formation of a Jewish division. British fears of inflaming the Arab world blocked this, although a small Jewish brigade was formed late in the war. But thousands of Jews served in the British army, as did smaller numbers of Arab Palestinians. Understandably, few Arab Palestinians were enthusiastic about the British war effort.

Turkey, now led by President Ismet Inönü, no longer had grievances against Britain and France. The Turks were apprehensive about Italian imperialism. The Soviet-German Treaty of Nonaggression of August 1939, in which Moscow switched from bitter opposition to fascism to an agreement with Berlin to partition Eastern Europe, put the Germans in additional bad company in Turkish eyes. In October 1939 Ankara concluded an alliance with London and Paris, committing itself to support the other parties in a war that entered the Mediterranean area, though not if this would involve it in a conflict with the dreaded USSR.

Riza Shah's Iran was pro-German. Traditional anti-British sentiment (and anti-Russian feeling after the German attack on the USSR in June 1941) propelled Iran in this direction, as did the shah's admiration for Hitler's regime and Iran's close commercial relationship with Germany. Increasing numbers of German technicians were in key positions throughout Iran.

Then momentous developments in Europe shattered all expectations. The German army struck in May 1940, and within weeks continental Western Europe was at Hitler's feet. Most of France, including Paris, came under Nazi occupation. The French government, having fled to the city of Vichy, transformed itself into an authoritarian system headed by Marshal Philippe Pétain and made peace with Germany. Only a few "Free French," led by General Charles de Gaulle, escaped to England to continue the struggle. The British army in France was lucky to escape across the English Channel, and months of German bombing of British cities left little doubt that an invasion would follow.

To the peoples of the Middle East, the Axis victories made support for the Allies seem foolhardy. Turkey announced its neutrality. In June 1941, Germany and Turkey concluded a Treaty of Nonaggression, but Ankara rebuffed pressures from both sides to enter the war. Turks were fearful that belligerency would lead to bombing and occupation either by Germans or by Soviet "liberators." Some of them hoped that Germany would destroy the USSR and liberate the Turkic peoples; others simply tended to identify with their old World War I ally. Otherwise, the predominant sentiment continued to be pro-Allied. The country's leaders argued that neutrality was beneficial to the Allies in relieving them of the need to defend Turkey. But Moscow protested that the closure of the Straits handicapped the Soviet war effort and that Turkey's sale of chrome to Germany strengthened the Axis nations. Only as the tide turned toward the Allies would Turkey gradually come over to their side. It would not declare war on Germany until February 1945, and then (like several Arab states) only in order to get an invitation to the San Francisco Conference the following spring, where a new world organization, the United Nations (UN), was to be established.

The defeats of 1940–1941 undermined Britain's position in the Arab world. Aside from the Yishuv, only Transjordan stuck by Britain, although "neutral" Saudi Arabia continued to pursue pro-Allied policies. Nuri's arch-rival, Rashid Ali al-Gaylani, now headed the Iraqi government. Rashid Ali was not pro-Axis per se, but he was coming under the influence of the "Golden Square," four highly nationalistic colonels led by Salah al-Din Sabbagh. Even now, Rashid Ali was willing to bring Iraq into the war on Britain's side in return for immediate independence for Palestine under the rule of its Arab majority. But among other acts of defiance, he refused to sever diplomatic relations with Italy after it entered the war in 1940. Fear of being on the losing side led even Nuri to seek a secret deal with Germany, which, however, suspiciously spurned the reputed British "puppet." When Rashid Ali was temporarily replaced as prime minister, the Golden Square forced his reinstatement in February 1941. Nuri and Abd al-Ilah fled to Transjordan, as the new government planned to use German support to achieve Iraq's and the Arabs' national objectives.

Egypt reaffirmed its alliance with Britain but dragged its feet. The government of Ali Mahir, later replaced under pressure from the British, severed relations with Italy but did not expel Italian diplomats. Although forces crossed the border from Libya and bombed Alexandria, Cairo chose to consider this a "border incident" rather than an invasion and refrained from declaring war until February 1945. King Faruq—apparently in order to ensure more favorable treatment in case of an Allied defeat—secretly wrote to Hitler in April 1941 that he hoped to see the German army liberate Egypt.

THE DESERT WAR

Libya and the western desert of Egypt were becoming a major theater of the war. The Italian army crossed into Egypt from Libya in September 1940, but the British, under the Middle East commander General Sir Archibald Wavell, mounted a counteroffensive in December. By February 1941 Wavell had driven his foe out of Cyrenaica (eastern Libya) as well as Egypt.

But the Germans, commanded by the daring and brilliant General Erwin Rommel, came to their ally's rescue and largely took over the Axis venture in this region. Despite Hitler's low priority for the Middle East, Rommel soon demonstrated his genius with tanks in the desert and got permission to mount a major effort to drive the British out of Egypt and beyond. Until late in 1942 the Allies faced the threat of a great German pincers movement closing in through Egypt and via the Soviet Union to Iran.

The two sides alternately advanced and retreated over vast distances. In May 1942 German forces were sixty miles from Alexandria, and the British grimly contemplated a last-ditch stand on the east bank of the Suez Canal. They were already burning documents in Cairo and preparing for the evacuation of British families. Many of the inhabitants of Alexandria were fleeing.

The British forged their defenses along a line extending south from the little railway station of El Alamein, on the coast west of Alexandria. Two German offensives failed to break through. Then, in October, under the command of General Sir Bernard Montgomery, the reinforced British army began its drive. Rommel was lucky to escape as most of his tanks were wrecked and 55,000 of his soldiers were killed, wounded, or captured. The British now advanced quickly through North Africa, soon meeting the Allied forces that had landed in Morocco and Algeria. The tide had also turned in Russia as the Soviet victory at Stalingrad blocked the other prong of the German pincers. European powers again had determined the fate of the region, with Middle Easterners largely looking on.

ALLIED INTERVENTION

The Allies meanwhile had asserted their power in several Middle Eastern countries. In April 1941 Britain notified Iraq that troops from India would land at Basrah en route to Palestine. In accordance with the Anglo-Iraqi Treaty, Iraq agreed but, once the force had arrived, asked it to move on before other British troops arrived. With Britain rejecting such a restrictive interpretation of Iraq's treaty obligations, Iraqi troops besieged the British air base at Habbaniyyah. Nationalists throughout the Arab world applauded this attack on British imperialism and in some cases headed for Iraq to offer their services. Floods prevented British troops in Basrah from moving northward, but British planes bombed the Iraqi forces on the high ground overlooking the base and drove them back. A British force assembled in Palestine. It crossed to Iraq, together with Transjordan's Arab Legion, a bedouin force commanded by Sir John Bagot Glubb, to relieve the Habbaniyyah base.

The Germans were too busy elsewhere to provide much help to the Iraqis. Arranging with Vichy France to refuel in Syria, they did manage to land about fifty planes at Mosul, in northern Iraq. But this limited aid came too late. By the end of May the British and Transjordanian force had arrived at Baghdad. Rashid Ali, al-Hajj Amin, and their leading supporters fled to Iran. As Abd al-Ilah, Nuri, and the other pro-British politicians returned from exile, the old order got a new lease on life under another British occupation.

Vichy's collaboration with Berlin spelled doom for its rule in Syria and Lebanon. British and Free French forces entered the two countries in June 1941 and soon overcame fierce resistance from the French Army. The Free French commander, General Georges Catroux, announced that Syria and Lebanon would get their independence, and the British, who had insisted on this declaration in order to reassure the Arab world, issued an endorsement.

Riza Shah's pro-German policies provoked a new Anglo-Russian occupation of Iran. The Allies were deeply concerned over the influence of more than two thousand German technicians. Even more, with the Soviets in the Allied camp, the Allies needed Iran as a supply route. Harsh British and Soviet notes in August 1941 demanded in vain the expulsion of the Germans from Iran. Eight days later Soviet forces poured in from the north and the British from Iraq. The Iranian army, Riza's proud accomplishment of two decades, rapidly collapsed. He finally abdicated in favor of his twenty-one-year-old son, Muhammad Riza, and went into exile. An Anglo-Soviet-Iranian Treaty of Alliance provided for withdrawal of foreign troops from Iran within six months after the end of hostilities. The rivalry of politicians in the Majlis replaced the shah's absolutism, but the real powers were again the British (later joined by American troops) in the south and the Russians in the north.

War transformed Egypt into an armed British camp and brought flagrant intervention in its politics. With King Faruq sympathetic to the Axis and with demonstrators cheering for Rommel as he approached the gates, the British decided (paradoxically, in view of Egypt's earlier political history) that it was time for the Wafd to come to power. The Wafd, it was reasoned, had shown no pro-Axis tendencies and was still the only party sufficiently organized and popular to control the mobs and too antiroyalist to work with Faruq against the Allied war effort. In February 1942 the British ambassador, Sir Miles Lampson, presented an ultimatum to the king, threatening "consequences" unless he immediately appointed Mustafa al-Nahhas as prime minister. British tanks then surrounded the palace, and the ambassador and British troops went in to demand Faruq's abdication. Only a shameless plea for "another chance" saved Faruq's throne, with Nahhas heading a new Wafdist government.

IMPACT ON LIFE
IN THE MIDDLE EAST

Fears that the region would again experience the same degree of suffering caused by the First World War failed to materialize. Few Middle Easterners lost their lives in this war. There were food shortages, especially early in the war, but nothing comparable to the starvation in places such as Syria during the First World War. This was partly the result of a unique experiment in regional integration under imperial auspices, the Middle East Supply Centre, established by Great Britain in 1941 and later joined by the United States. The Centre, based in Cairo, allocated scarce resources throughout the Middle East. The presence of foreign troops and wartime demand for Middle Eastern raw materials and manufactured goods even brought prosperity and industrial advance in some places. A few Middle Easterners gained great wealth, although inflation was a severe problem for the poor throughout the region. Prices at least doubled or even tripled in almost every country; they shot up an estimated 699 percent in Iran.

FRANCE'S DEPARTURE
FROM THE LEVANT

The blatant way in which the British intervened in the Arab world during the war necessitated special efforts to prove their good intentions toward Arab aspirations that antagonized both France and the Zionists. In particular, the British could justify their invasion of Syria and Lebanon to Arabs only by working for the two countries' independence.

After the defeat of the Vichy forces, the Free French soon began to qualify their promise of independence. General Catroux took firm control, appointing pliable presidents for the two republics. He specified that the mandate would continue until replaced by treaties, which would have left most important matters still in French hands. This met increasing British objections, French accusations of interference, and at least one threat by de Gaulle to use force against his ally. Only after an acrimonious meeting between British Prime Minister Winston Churchill and de Gaulle in September 1942 did France reluctantly permit elections for the Lebanese and Syrian Chambers of Deputies during the following year.

The elections returned nationalist majorities in both countries. So tarnished was France's image as a dependable protector that even most of the historically pro-French Lebanese Maronites opted to seek independence. With France unwilling to end the mandate without a treaty, the Lebanese decided to act unilaterally while the British were still there to support them. In November 1943 the Lebanese Chamber abrogated references to the mandate in the constitution, claimed all governmental power, and ended the status of French as an official language. The French then arrested Lebanese President Bishara al-Khuri, Premier Riyad al-Sulh, and other ministers and suspended the constitution. As general outrage found expression in strikes and the organization of rebel groups, Britain and the United States protested to France. Britain threatened to use force unless France restored the Lebanese constitution.

France had to give in and release the Lebanese leaders. When the Syrian Chamber made similar changes in its constitution, France did not challenge it. According to an agreement reached in December 1943, France gradually turned over most functions to the Syrian and Lebanese governments during the following year. The two main exceptions were control of the French schools and command of the eighteen thousand locally recruited Special Troops. France continued to insist on the conclusion of treaties to define its privileged position in the two states.

In May 1945, after Germany's surrender, Paris reverted to a hard-line position and made additional demands on Syria and Lebanon. Rioting and attacks on French troops and property ensued. France reacted by bombarding a large part of Damascus, including major public buildings. Churchill, with United States support, sent a note to de Gaulle on May 31 demanding that all French troops return to their barracks, and the local British commander threatened to open fire on the French. With de Gaulle declaring to the British ambassador that London had "insulted France and betrayed the West," France nevertheless gradually withdrew without retaining any special rights. The slow pace of withdrawal, which resulted from a quarrel between Britain and France over whose troops would be the last to leave, led to a UN Security Council debate in February 1946, but all foreign troops were gone from both Syria and Lebanon by the end of the year.

ARAB UNITY AND
THE ARAB LEAGUE

London also sought to conciliate the Arab world by supporting Arab unity, though under the leadership of British clients. Foreign Secretary Sir Anthony Eden announced his government's approval of Arab unity in May 1941. Nuri al-Sa'id came forward the next year with a proposal for a Fertile Crescent union. Amir Abdullah, who would become king of a nominally independent Transjordan in 1946, suggested a similar plan for a united "Greater Syria," to be federated with Iraq. Such plans, however, met opposition from the Hashimites' blood enemies, the Sa'udis, and from an Egypt that saw a united Fertile Crescent as a threat to its primacy in the region, not to mention the apprehension of many Syrians. Egyptian Prime Minister al-Nahhas took the initiative away from the Hashimites by proposing a wider but looser grouping, which led to the formation of the League of Arab States in 1945. This organization, which perpetuated state sovereignty, would henceforth provide a forum for inter-Arab cooperation and quarrels.

THE SHIFT FROM BRITISH
PREDOMINANCE

Victory for Great Britain in World War II left its wealth and energy depleted. It was no longer possible to hold on everywhere, especially as non-Western nationalism was intensifying. And by 1946 the influence of other West European states had nearly vanished from the Middle East (excluding French North Africa).

But the field was not left for local nationalists alone. The American presence in the Middle East was becoming apparent, at least temporarily, even before 1945. The United States' wartime roles in Iran and in the Middle East Supply Centre, as well as the extension of lend-lease (as Washington's wartime aid program was known) to several countries, were cases in point. There was extensive Saudi-United States cooperation during the war, including the construction of a United States air base at Dhahran. Of definite long-range significance was the Arabian-American Oil Company (ARAMCO), a corporation that had grown out of the original Saudi concession to Standard Oil of California. With the participation of other American oil companies, it was becoming an important private operation. United States oil interests in the Arabian Pennisula rivaled those of the British in Iran. Elsewhere, as in Iraq and Kuwait, American oil companies held concessions jointly with British (and sometimes French) firms. Despite the special relationship between the United States and

Britain, it sometimes seemed to the latter that the Americans wanted to eliminate its presence in the Middle East because of either a historic aversion to colonialism or the intention of taking over the British imperial role.

Moscow also was making demands on Turkey and Iran that appeared to various observers either as the legitimate pursuit, at least in part, of important interests or else as the revival of czarist expansionism. In any case, Soviet aspirations would soon be "contained" by the active involvement of the United States.

Nor did British power withdraw from the area entirely. Just as Britain was decolonizing in the Indian subcontinent—access to which was formerly the main reason for concern with such places as Egypt and eastern Arabia—the increasingly vital role of Persian Gulf oil for the British economy made it stubbornly cling to its position in the Middle East. This included oil concessions in the Persian Gulf area; protectorates along the Arabian periphery (and the crown colony of Aden); and the treaty relationships with Egypt, Iraq, and Transjordan that allowed British bases and access.

COMPETITION FOR IRAN
AFTER THE WAR

During the war the Soviet occupation authorities virtually cut off northern Iran from the rest of the country. The agricultural products that normally flowed southward were diverted to the Soviet Union. Iranian troops were unable to enter the north. The Tudeh (Masses) party, a Communist organization under Moscow's patronage, was becoming a powerful force. A Soviet demand in 1944 for an oil concession made the Iranian government apprehensive. On the proposal of Muhammad Musaddiq, an elder statesman known for his integrity, his dedication to his country, his flair for the dramatic, and his longtime opposition to the Pahlavi dynasty, the Majlis made it a crime for any Iranian to engage in negotiations for a foreign oil concession without legislative authorization.

As the six-month deadline for evacuation passed, Soviet troops remained in northern Iran. Under their guidance a "Democratic Republic of Azarbayjan" took shape. With little popular backing, the regime was propped up almost entirely by Soviet power. Another separatist government, the Kurdish Republic of Mahabad, also emerged under Soviet auspices, but with greater popular support, in the Kurdish area of northwestern Iran.

When the clever, energetic seventy-year-old Ahmad Qavam became prime minister in January 1946, the way seemed paved for Soviet success. Qavam, though a landlord, had close ties with the Tudeh party, and many assumed that he would cooperate with Moscow. He brought several members of the Tudeh party into the Cabinet and dismissed key anti-Tudeh officials. Even when Iran's UN representative brought a complaint against the USSR in the Security Council, where his position found strong United States support, the prime minister disavowed his action. But the disavowal was apparently tongue-in-cheek, with Qavam glad to take advantage of the pressure and embarrassment that the UN debate was causing the USSR. Qavam flew to Moscow and concluded an agreement providing for a Soviet withdrawal (but giving autonomy to Azarbayjan) and the establishment of a joint, 51 percent Soviet-controlled oil venture. The oil arrangement, however, was contingent on approval by the Majlis, which Moscow thought was assured.

In fact, Qavam set about organizing his own party, the Democrats of Iran, as a counterweight to the Tudeh. He used a tribal insurrection in the south as an excuse to dismiss the Tudeh members from his cabinet. Following elections, the Majlis, led by Musaddiq, overwhelmingly rejected the Soviet oil agreement. Iranian troops moved to the northwest to suppress the Soviet-backed regimes, which soon collapsed, with their leaders fleeing to Soviet territory amidst an anti-Tudeh campaign. Declarations of American support for Qavam's actions precluded any return of Soviet troops.

Iran was establishing closer ties with the United States and meeting Soviet hostility. United States military credits were forthcoming in 1947. The sending of a United States military mission in 1948 brought reminders from Moscow of its right to intervene in Iran under the 1921 treaty. Hostile diplomatic notes and Soviet propaganda kept the fires going. An American company was employed to advise Iran on carrying out a seven-year plan, and a technical assistance program began in 1950.

TURKEY JOINING
THE ANTI-COMMUNIST WEST

Turkey, still led by President Inönü, became a key focus of Soviet-American rivalry. Before World War II ended, Moscow began making demands on Ankara and denounced the Turko-Soviet Treaty of Friendship in March 1945. In June Soviet Foreign Minister V. M. Molotov called for bases on the Turkish Straits, which had been closed to Soviet ships during the war, and the return of Kars and Ardahan, which had been under Russian control since 1917. Moscow later asked for a revision of the Montreux Straits Convention and the cession of some Turkish territory to Bulgaria.

While the British and American governments initially showed sympathy for the Soviet desire for freer access to the Straits, they supported Turkey in resisting other demands. Soviet propaganda continued against the undemocratic nature of the Turkish government and its failure to join the Allies in the war. Soviet and Bulgarian troops were massed near the Turkish borders. The Turkish army, whose equipment and training had become obsolete as a result of its noninvolvement in World War II and also because of the country's general failure to keep up with European and Western technical and economic advances, was depending on numbers for strength. But three-quarters of a million Turks under arms were imposing a severe strain on the economy.

Turkey had been receiving aid from Britain, whose economic exhaustion now forced its discontinuation. London announced that it could no longer support either Turkey or Greece, where a British-sponsored monarchy was attempting to suppress a Communist guerrilla movement backed by the Soviet bloc.

Washington was deciding to take London's place. In an early application of the "containment" doctrine, President Harry S Truman proposed a program of military and economic assistance to Greece and Turkey in March 1947. With the rapid approval by Congress of what came to be known as the "Truman Doctrine," Turkey soon aligned itself with the United States and the anti-Communist coalition in the emerging cold war. Later in 1947 the United States announced that it would keep naval ships in the Mediterranean, the beginning of the Sixth Fleet that would long remain a powerful American instrument in the area. Turkey later was included in the Marshall Plan for United States aid to Europe. It gained admission to the Council of Europe, an organization of non-Communist states, in 1949. After a delay that hurt the feelings of many Turks anxious to assert that they were "Western," Turkey was allowed to join the North Atlantic Treaty Organization (NATO) in 1951. Although Stalin's successors renounced Soviet demands in 1953, Turkey, now with increased economic and military capability resulting partly from United States aid, remained a staunch member of the anti-Communist Western alliance.

THE RISE OF ISRAEL

During and immediately following World War II, the White Paper continued to form the basis for British policy in Palestine. Regulations laid down in 1941 restricted land transfers to Jews. And just as Nazi Germany was proceeding with the extermination of most of Europe's Jews, the doors to Palestine were almost closed to any who were able to leave Europe and seek refuge there. This helped to placate the Arab Palestinians but exacerbated the Zionist challenge to the British.

Violent opposition to Britain during the first years of the war came only from the most extreme Zionist faction, the Stern Gang (or Lehi). Established by the youthful Abraham Stern, a recent arrival from Poland, this organization carried out terrorist attacks on the British and more moderate Jews. At one point, it called for a "totalitarian" Jewish state allied with Nazi Germany. A larger organization, from which Stern's group had split off, was the Irgun Zvai Leumi (National Military Society), which had grown out of the interwar Revisionist movement founded by Vladimir Jabotinsky that preached a hard-line policy against the Arabs and ardently demanded the inclusion of Transjordan in the Jewish national home. Led by another Polish immigrant, Menachem Begin, the Irgun had initially joined with the Haganah, the largest Jewish military organization, in its policy of wartime "self-restraint." But it also began a terror campaign after the war turned in Britain's favor. While the Jewish Agency condemned such acts, targets of extremist Zionist assassins included Lord Moyne, the British Secretary of State for the Middle East, who was gunned down in Cairo in 1944, and Sir Harold MacMichael, the High Commissioner for Palestine, who survived a similar attempt. Actually, the British government was ready to replace the White Paper with a new policy favoring postwar partition of Palestine when the assassination of Lord Moyne occurred and thus stopped any move in that direction.

The Zionists pursued other clandestine activities. The Haganah, like the Irgun and the Stern Gang, stole arms from British troops in preparation for a postwar confrontation. In an attempt to rescue the remnants of European Jewry, the Jewish Agency helped thousands of illegal immigrants enter Palestine and evade the British authorities.

At a time when Hitler was not yet sure whether emigration or extermination would be used to solve his "Jewish problem," the Germans allowed shiploads of Jews to leave Europe. Germans sometimes cooperated with the Zionists by facilitating the transfer of Jewish property and funds. Dilapidated old vessels, overloaded with suffering human cargo, sailed toward Palestine. Some people perished in shipwrecks on the way. Most of those who reached their destination were denied entry and were instead transferred to the Indian Ocean island of Mauritius or, later, to Cyprus. Nor would other countries accept them. On one occasion, the Jewish Agency blew up a refugee ship (the *Patria*), which resulted in 240 deaths, and gained increased world sympathy by inaccurately presenting the incident as a collective suicide of the people on board. People in austere temporary relocation camps felt the anguish of living in limbo and could hardly comprehend why they were being turned away from Palestine.

Demands for the admission of large numbers of European refugees to Palestine increased the Palestinian Arabs' fears of being uprooted to make room for a Jewish state. They and other critics of Zionism suggested that other countries should accept these unfortunate people and accused Western Christian supporters of Jewish immigration to Palestine of using Zionism to divert refugees from their own shores. Some also maintained that Zionists were callously using the plight of their fellow Jews to achieve political objectives. While non-Jewish public opinion in the United States was averse to admitting more Jews, some anti-Zionists said that this might have been overcome if Zionist leaders had not strongly opposed the creation of any alternative to Palestine.

The Zionist movement took a hard-line stand. The tough and brilliant David Ben-Gurion, a pre–World War I immigrant from Poland, was eclipsing the leadership of the more moderate Weizmann. Leaders such as Ben-Gurion began to see the United States as the center of gravity of a postwar West and its Jewish minority as a vital reservoir of support. An important meeting of American Zionists, which many Zionists from other parts of the world also attended, took place in the Biltmore Hotel in New York in 1942. Dominated by Ben-Gurion, the Biltmore Conference demanded that Palestine be opened for Jewish immigration and that the whole country become an independent Jewish commonwealth. The Jewish Agency later adopted the Biltmore program. A rival but smaller movement among moderate Jews in Palestine, the Ihud (Union) called for Jewish immigration but for a binational Palestine. Although led by such eminent people as Dr. Judah Magnes (the president of the Hebrew University) and the great philosopher and theologian, Martin Buber, the Ihud gained little support.

The end of World War II left a weakened Britain with an intractable problem in Palestine. The Zionist hope that the Labour Party victory in the 1945 elections would change British policies in favor of Jewish statehood was soon dashed. A quarter of a million Jewish survivors of Nazism were waiting in camps in Europe. Although some State Department officials pleaded that support for Zionism would drive an embittered Arab world into the arms of the USSR, American political leaders vied for the votes of Jews and others who favored the Zionist program. Many Christians as well as Jews believed that the Jews had a clear-cut moral or even God-given right to Palestine. The Arab claim to the country rarely seemed to be understood in the Western world. President Truman infuriated London by asking for the immediate admission of 100,000 Jewish refugees into Palestine.

Zionist terrorism increased. The Haganah reached an agreement with the more extreme organizations to coordinate their activities in November 1945. After the Haganah destroyed ten bridges in June 1946, Britain imposed martial law throughout Palestine and arrested seven hundred Zionist leaders. Then the Irgun blew up the King David Hotel, the site of the British civil and military headquarters in Jerusalem, leaving ninety-five people, mainly British, dead.

Britain's attempts to reach a solution were to no avail. In 1946 an Anglo-American Committee of Inquiry proposed the admission of 100,000 Jews to Palestine but not the establishment of a Jewish state. Another Anglo-American commission, composed of Henry Grady and Herbert Morrison, proposed a UN trusteeship with autonomy for predominantly Jewish and Arab provinces, but met rejections from all sides. The British government invited representatives of the Zionists (who refused to attend), Arab states, and Arab Palestinians to a conference in London in September 1946, but again without results.

Faced with a hopeless task, London took the problem to the UN General Assembly in April 1947, although it did not bind itself to carry out the UN recommendation. A UN Special Committee on Palestine (UNSCOP) visited the country and proceeded to draft two alternate proposals. The minority plan called for a federal Palestine, composed of Jewish and Arab areas. The majority plan called for partition, in a complicated checkerboard pattern, into a Jewish and an Arab state and an internationalized area to include Jerusalem. Partition had the support of most Western states, Britain being the major exception. In a short-lived reversal of their traditional anti-Zionist policy, which may have been due to a desire to expel the British from Palestine, even the Soviet Union and the Communist bloc supported the partition plan. The main opposition came from Arab and some other Asian states. Still, a two-thirds vote was not assured, and it was only after the application of considerable pressure on several wavering delegations by Zionists and some of their influential supporters that a partition plan based on the UNSCOP majority report, with minor modifications, gained UN endorsement in late November.

Neither side was satisfied with the UN plan. The Zionists reluctantly announced their acceptance of it as an "irreducible minimum," viewing as essential the creation of a state which European Jewish refugees might freely enter. The Arab Palestinians and the Arab states officially rejected it, pointing out that although the Jews formed only a third of Palestine's population they were awarded 54 percent of the country, including most of the fertile areas (but also most of the Negev desert in the south). They pointed out that the partition lines represented a double standard, drawn so that almost every Jew in Palestine would be within the Jewish state or the international area. On the other hand, the Jewish state would include large areas that were overwhelmingly Arab-populated, and Arabs would constitute almost 50 percent of its overall population. Arabs suspected—as research by some Israeli scholars now confirms—that the Zionist "acceptance" of the partition plan was only tactical in nature and would be followed by attempts to take more territory. Arabs also objected to the fact that the establishment of a Jewish state would split the Arab world geographically and argued that the partition of Palestine was illegal. Their efforts to bring the question before the World Court were not heeded. Behind the scenes, Arab governments were showing a willingness to accept the partition plan. The Transjordanian ruler had long had friendly secret ties with the Zionists and was quite ready to allow them to have a state if he could annex the parts of Palestine left to the Arabs. And as documents the Israeli government published in 1984 show, Egypt at one point was ready to agree to the Jewish state's admission into the Arab League, with the organization's name to be changed to the "Oriental League." The Zionists rejected a last-minute proposal for a three-month truce during which their declaration of independence would be postponed.

The partition plan was never implemented, since a full-scale Jewish-Arab civil war started immediately. Britain announced that it would terminate the mandate on May 15, 1948, and began pulling out its troops in stages. Zionist forces fought against Palestinian guerrillas led by Abd al-Qadir al-Husayni (who was killed in April) and an Arab Liberation Army that crossed over from Syria under Fawzi al-Qawuqji. The Zionists were better armed, especially after the arrival of weapons from Czechoslovakia, and unlike the Arab Palestinians, had a well-established community government. They soon prevailed. Although some Jewish settlements were isolated, the Palestinian Arabs could not take them, while Arab cities and villages fell in rapid succession during April, leaving Jews in control of parts of the proposed Arab state.

Cruelty abounded on both sides. The Irgun, Stern Gang, and Haganah took the Arab village of Dayr Yasin, near Jerusalem, in April. The Haganah then withdrew in favor of the other Zionist forces, who proceeded systematically to slaughter 254 of its inhabitants. Arab forces in Jerusalem retaliated by waylaying a convoy of buses carrying Jewish doctors and nurses to the Hadassah Hospital on Mount Scopus. The Jewish Agency condemned the Dayr Yasin massacre, which, however, helped to remove the basic impediment in the way of a Jewish state by accelerating a mass flight of Arabs from most of Palestine. This impact of Dayr Yasin is what sets it apart from the numerous other massacres of Arabs during 1948, most of which were not revealed until recently.

The departure of a few thousand well-to-do Arabs for safer places soon after the UN partition resolution started the exodus. After the Dayr Yasin massacre, major demographic changes occurred, with virtually the entire population of villages and whole cities, such as Jaffa (and the Arab sector of Haifa), fleeing in terror. Both the

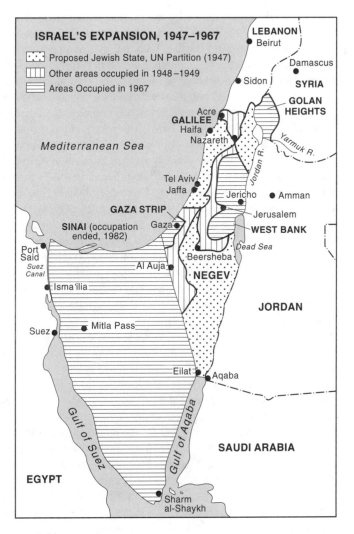

ISRAEL'S EXPANSION, 1947–1967

Proposed Jewish State, UN Partition (1947)

Other areas occupied in 1948–1949

Areas Occupied in 1967

LEBANON
Beirut

Damascus

Sidon

SYRIA

GOLAN
HEIGHTS

Acre

GALILEE

Haifa

Nazareth

Mediterranean Sea

Yarmuk R.

Jordan R.

Tel Aviv

Jaffa

Jericho

Amman

Jerusalem

GAZA STRIP

WEST BANK

SINAI (occupation
ended, 1982)

Gaza

Dead Sea

Port
Said

*Suez
Canal*

Al Auja

Beersheba

NEGEV

Isma'ilia

JORDAN

Suez

Mitla Pass

Gulf of Suez

Gulf of Aqaba

Eilat

Aqaba

SAUDI ARABIA

EGYPT

Sharm
al-Shaykh

MAP 10

eagerness of the Arab elite to escape and the dissemination of information about Jewish terrorism by both sides may have exacerbated the fears of ordinary people. However, there is no viable evidence for later allegations of evacuation orders from Arab leaders, and monitored Arab radio broadcasts reveal consistent Arab warnings not to leave. Documented studies published by Israeli historians in the 1980s further discredit the claim of Arab responsibility for the exodus. Although some rare Jewish leaders urged Arabs to stay, the Irgun and the Stern Gang warned them that other massacres would follow if they did not flee. Later on, the Israeli army also expelled Arabs on a large scale, sometimes in accordance with orders from Ben-Gurion. Most of those who were expelled had not been involved in the fighting, and their villages in many cases had futilely entered into pacts with neighboring Jewish communities.

On May 14, 1948, as the British withdrawal was completed, Zionist leaders announced the establishment of the State of Israel. The armies of the surrounding Arab states had already decided to intervene—at least purportedly—to support the Arab Palestinians. But King Abdullah also wanted to annex as much of Arab Palestine as he could get, an ambition most other Arab leaders hoped to block. Recent studies make it clear that he was in collusion with the Zionists (ironically, his forces fought a few battles against them, achieving the only Arab successes of the war), with whom he agreed to partition the area assigned to the Arab Palestinian state. Egyptian troops moved into the southern Palestine coastal region and also crossed over to the area south of Jerusalem. The Transjordanian Arab Legion entered eastern Palestine (carefully avoiding any encroachment on areas the partition plan had allotted to the Jewish state), assisted by Iraqi contingents on its right flank. The minuscule Lebanese army even entered the war in token fashion, while the Syrians made slight penetrations in the northeast.

The Palestine War provided a unique crucible to demonstrate the weakness of Eastern societies. The Arabs confronted a largely European Jewish society, whose people were highly cohesive, literate, and proficient in modern technology. Middle Eastern nationalists recently had forced other Europeans to give in, but largely because they lacked determination when nationalistic opposition caused them excessive trouble or expense. Only in the case of the Zionists, whose modernity was matched by a fierce willingness to stand up for their objective of a Jewish state (and sometimes believing they had no other alternative), did Middle Eastern peoples face a truly determined European enemy. Characteristic of the gap between the two societies, Israel, with a population of only 650,000 Jews, was able to mobilize more troops than all the Arab states could send against them. Israelis possessed the technical skills to make weapons to supplement the war material that reached them (sometimes smuggled) from the United States and Europe. In addition, the Arab states acted at times as if they distrusted one another even more than they did the State of Israel. And indeed, the main reason for the involvement of most Arab states—notably Egypt—now seems to have been to thwart Transjordan's and Israel's attempt to occupy the area reserved for an Arab Palestinian state. Some recent analysts suggest that the outcome—notably the Israeli success—was never in question.

Despite their lack of preparation, sometimes lacking maps or food supplies except those obtained locally, the Arabs initially had considerable success. But the Israeli army (in effect the Haganah) increasingly prevailed. At one point Egyptian troops were sixteen miles from Tel Aviv, and Transjordanian and Iraqi forces came within ten miles of the sea. But before the Jewish state could be pinched in two, the Israelis were relieved by a UN-sponsored truce on June 11. They effectively used the truce to strengthen their forces, and the second round of fighting, which broke out briefly in July, brought Arab retreats. After small Israeli advances into the northern Negev at the end of September, a full-scale offensive began in October and was renewed in December. By the end of the year, the Israelis had penetrated Sinai and cut off the Egyptian forces in the Gaza region. British pressures forced them to pull back.

Armistice talks began in January 1949 on the island of Rhodes, with Dr. Ralph Bunche, the acting UN mediator, as the intermediary. (The original UN mediator, Count Folke Bernadotte, had been assassinated by members of the Stern Gang in September 1948, following his proposal for a modification of the UN partition plan that would have allotted the Negev to the Arabs and Western Galilee to the Israelis.) The Arab representatives at first refused to deal directly with the Israelis, whose state they did not recognize. An Egyptian-Israeli armistice was the first breakthrough. Another armistice followed with Lebanon. Then came Transjordan, after being driven out of the southern Negev in a last-minute Israeli truce violation and yielding another strip of territory in central Palestine under Israeli pressure, and finally Syria. The UN had already provided a small Truce Supervisory Organization (UNTSO); and an Egyptian-Israeli, a Jordanian-Israeli, a Syrian-Israeli, and a Lebanese-Israeli Mixed Armistice Commission (MAC) were composed of representatives of UNTSO, Israel, and the Arab state concerned. The armistices were viewed as the first step toward a peace settlement, to be facilitated by a UN Palestine Conciliation Commission, composed of United States, French, and Turkish representatives, and by a full-dress conference later in 1949 at Lausanne.

The armistices left Israel in control of about 78 percent of Palestine. And the general Arab exodus had resulted in an overwhelmingly Jewish country. Perhaps 770,000 Palestinians were now huddled in "temporary" refugee camps in surrounding areas, dependent on meager UN rations. Only two small fragments of Palestine were left to the Arabs. The narrow "Gaza Strip" in southwest Palestine, now overflowing with refugees, remained under Egyptian administration. The "West Bank," the portion of east-central Palestine held by Transjordan (from now on simply Jordan), including part of Jerusalem (notably the Old City, containing the holy places), was soon formally annexed, despite denunciations by other Arab states. The Arab-Palestinian diaspora spawned what in some ways might be called a new kind of Zionist movement—in reverse—that would produce endless volumes of poetry and prose expressing its determination to return to its usurped homeland but would long remain unorganized, waiting for the Arab states to defeat Israel.

While Israelis considered their independence a victory against British colonialism in their own ancient homeland, Arabs viewed the Jewish settlers in Palestine as a product of the British mandate. To the Arabs, British opposition to Zionist demands during the last years was just another example of a colonial government opposing the extreme position of a colonial settler population, as later occurred in Rhodesia (now Zimbabwe) or South Africa. To Arabs, the establishment of Israel seemed to represent the ultimate form of colonialism, in which the local non-Western population is displaced by European settlers.

MUSADDIQ'S RISE AND FALL

Let us return to the story of post–World War II Iran. By 1949 Muhammad Musaddiq, although a member of the landed class, had come to symbolize nationalism and reform in the eyes of most Iranians. The main target was the Anglo-Iranian Oil Company (AIOC), which Iranians saw as a surviving instrument of British imperialism. Beginning with his earlier stand against a Soviet oil concession in northern Iran, Musaddiq espoused the slogan "negative equilibrium," which rejected the former practice of balancing privileges granted to Britain and the USSR in favor of denying privileges to any foreign power. Musaddiq's movement, a loosely organized National Front consisting of several political parties, also favored domestic change. Muhammad Riza Shah, largely a figurehead when he first succeeded his father, had asserted his influence to a considerable extent after the end of World War II in an alliance with the landed class that controlled the Majlis, though he later began a much-touted distribution of royal lands to the peasants. The shah had a lot of say in military matters in particular, and Britain and the United States tended to support him as opposed to the Majlis. Also, American military missions were developing close ties with army officers that would prove to be important later on. Musaddiq aspired to weaken the shah's influence, possibly by establishing a republic, and to break the power of the landlords.

Bitterness against the AIOC was growing. Iran had suffered economically for several years and badly needed increased revenues to finance its Seven-Year Plan for development, adopted in 1949. Iranians were shocked to learn that AIOC royalties paid to their own government amounted to little more than a third of the profits and taxes accruing to the British government from Iranian oil. In contrast, Venezuela had obtained the right to share profits on a fifty-fifty basis with the oil companies, an arrangement that spread to Saudi Arabia in 1950. Although in 1949 the AIOC agreed to more favorable terms for Iran, nationalists were not satisfied, and Iranian demands for nationalization became increasingly strident. In March 1951 this culminated in the assassination of Prime Minister Ali Razmara, who favored a compromise agreement, by a member of the radical Fida'iyan-i-Islam, which was roughly comparable to the Muslim Brethren in Egypt.

Musaddiq now came to the fore. Under his leadership, the Iranian Parliament (the Majlis and the recently established Senate) quickly followed up the assassination of Razmara by voting to nationalize the oil industry, as many conservative members dared not go against the tide of pro-Musaddiq public opinion. Soon afterwards

Musaddiq took office as prime minister, and another, more detailed law provided for the implementation of nationalization, with compensation offered to the AIOC. When British technicians refused to work for the newly created National Iranian Oil Company (NIOC), their residence permits were terminated, and they left Iran in October. During his two-year period of leadership, Musaddiq not only stood up against what he perceived to be British economic imperialism but also secured the enactment of domestic reforms. A law passed in August 1952 required landowners to earmark 20 percent of their shares of crops for the peasants' use.

An Anglo-Iranian confrontation ensued, although London accepted the principle of nationalization. Anglo-Iranian negotiations that were held in August 1951—following appeals to the two countries from President Truman and the efforts of his special representative, Averell Harriman—floundered over London's demand for a British role in the actual management of the oil industry. All efforts to reach a settlement failed, including British appeals to the Security Council, which took no action, and to the International Court of Justice, which eventually ruled that it lacked jurisdiction in the case. With Britain applying various kinds of economic pressures, such as freezing Iranian assets, and engaging in intrigues against the Iranian government, Tehran severed diplomatic relations with London in October 1952.

Iran now faced economic hardship. Its people did have the technical skills required to run the oil fields and refineries, but the operations and Iran's main source of income ground to a halt because Western oil companies generally cooperated with the AIOC by refusing to buy Iranian oil. And monarchs in other oil-producing countries in the Middle East destroyed Iran's leverage by increasing their own countries' oil production to meet Western demand.

The Iranian prime minister, who had long been favorable to the United States and expected its support, appealed to President Eisenhower for economic aid in 1953, pointing to the danger from Communism. But Eisenhower—whose administration was fundamentally more anti-Musaddiq than Truman's had been—interpreted this as a threat and refused his request. Actually, the United States position in the Anglo-Iranian dispute, though neutral at first, had been moving increasingly in a pro-British direction. The Tudeh, which until recently had been a fervent opponent of an allegedly United States–backed Musaddiq, was rapidly becoming more and more powerful in the streets; and much to his distress, Musaddiq was coming to depend on it. His support was eroding as several of his opportunistic former allies were breaking with him. Though a devoted liberal democrat, he finally resorted increasingly—if reluctantly—to authoritarian measures. In a rigged plebiscite—which his supporters justified as necessary to prevent the kind of manipulation by landlords that occurs in a "free" election—in early August 1953, the voters overwhelmingly voted to dissolve the Majlis, leaving Musaddiq in sole control.

Later in August, the shah tried to dismiss Musaddiq, appointing a right-wing general, Fazlullah Zahidi, in his place. Musaddiq, amid massive demonstrations in his favor, refused to step down. The shah, now violently attacked in the press, fled Iran.

But the CIA, with some British help, engineered a coup that brought the royalists back. A large, CIA-paid anti-Musaddiq crowd, headed by professional mob leaders and joined by army units, surged out of southern Tehran to overthrow the nationalist government. Allied with the upper class and the United States government, the returning shah gradually established a royal dictatorship. His secret police penetrated everywhere, rounding up anyone who threatened his rule. Six hundred army officers were arrested in 1954 because of alleged links with the Tudeh. Iran came to terms with Western interests by turning over oil production to a consortium of companies (40 percent British and 40 percent United States, a prime case of Americans taking over British privileges) that would technically act as an agent of the NIOC under a fifty-fifty arrangement.

TURKEY BECOMES
A WESTERN-STYLE DEMOCRACY

In Turkey, under President Inönü, the People's Republican Party (PRP) remained the sole center of power. In some ways authoritarianism grew more blatant during the war years. The most notable example was the imposition of a special tax in 1942 on excessive business profits, which had resulted from burgeoning wartime exports. The law specified no tax rate, and special commissions exacted extortionate amounts from members of non-Turkish, non-Muslim minorities. Those who could not pay were sent immediately to labor camps. Only with the decline of Nazi Germany, whose racism had inspired this type of ruthless discrimination, did the Turkish government relax its application of the law and release those who had been arrested.

The end of the war brought a move toward Western-style liberal democracy. With the Nazi-Fascist model gone, many Turks thought it necessary to become a democracy in order to be part of Europe. This move gained support from a prosperous new business class that disliked the statist policy of the single-party regime and from a rural elite—formerly an important component of the Kemalist coalition—that was less committed to secularism and resented the limited land reform instituted in 1945. Backing for change also came from peasants, who typically deplored PRP secularism, although some landlords and their clients among the peasantry still supported the PRP. As Ankara relaxed its policies, new political parties were allowed to form to oppose the government. The Democratic Party, established in 1946 by dissident PRP leaders including Celal Bayar and Adnan Menderes, won a landslide victory in the 1950 elections. Menderes became the new prime minister, with Bayar the largely ceremonial president.

But by 1954 democratic government was facing setbacks. The Democrats enacted laws imposing penalties on journalists whose writing was harmful to the state and allowing the government to dismiss judges, professors, and civil servants without appeal. Once again it became clear that deep-seated patterns of authoritarian rule were hard to erase.

The general standard of living had risen little before 1945, but a substantial improvement took place during the postwar decade. Improvements in education, health, and communications laid the foundation for further economic development. The literacy rate, 30 percent in 1945, had reached 40 percent ten years later. Modernization was rapidly penetrating the villages, especially after the Democrats, with their strong peasant constituency, devoted much attention to rural improvements. Turkey was outstripping most of the Third World in modernization, though at the cost of severe inflation and mounting government indebtedness.

Turkish secularist policies instituted by Atatürk remained on the books but were not so rigidly enforced. In 1948 religious education returned to the schools, and the University of Ankara got a faculty of divinity in 1949. The Democrats, though they did not renounce secularism and even banned the religious Nation Party in 1954, swung back further toward the center. One of their first acts after coming to power was to permit the restoration of the call to prayer in Arabic. They later permitted the reading of the Qur'an on the radio. Interest in Islam increased, as shown by attendance at Friday prayers and the volume of religious publications. Perhaps this was partly a result of a growing realization that westernization did not necessitate outdoing the West in secularism.

THE ARABIAN PENINSULA

The Arabian Peninsula was still the area least affected by westernization and its accompanying ferment. With a fifty-fifty profit-sharing arrangement with ARAMCO in effect after 1950, Saudi oil revenues soon reached a quarter of a billion dollars a year. This brought the country the material trappings of the West and the beginning of the breakdown of "Wahhabi" austerity and puritanism, as evidenced by the conspicuous consumption and corruption of the royal family. There was even some rumbling of discontent among an incipient modern-educated group and among ARAMCO employees. But so far, the Sa'udi dynasty was secure in power. The death of King Abd al-Aziz in 1953 led to the succession of his weak, spendthrift son, Sa'ud, but with another son, the more capable Faysal, designated crown prince. There were faint signs of more modern political patterns, notably the establishment of an advisory Council of Ministers just before Abd al-Aziz's death. But government remained a family affair, with the king's absolutism limited mainly by the need to keep the support of the tribes and his enormous family.

New wealth from oil was also beginning to transform some of the once poor and still (in certain ways) medieval shaykhdoms in the Persian Gulf region. Kuwait, with tremendous revenues for a population of less than half a million, was becoming a welfare state with a patriarchal ruler and a conservative society.

Yemen was one of the world's least modern countries. But it bordered on the British crown colony of Aden, a modernized enclave whose hinterland, the Aden Protectorate, was still a medieval area under British-protected rulers. With thousands of the *imam*'s subjects finding jobs there, Aden had become a window for Western influence. Yemenis in Aden organized a Free Yemen party to plot against despotism in their home country. Revolutionaries assassinated the aged Imam Yahya in 1948, and a member of a dissident branch of the royal family temporarily took power. But after leading loyal tribes in a march on the capital, Yahya's son, the ruthless Ahmad, became the new *imam*.

CONSERVATISM AND UNREST
IN IRAQ

The old order seemed to be well fortified in Iraq. Prince Abd al-Ilah was a dominant figure as the regent until 1953, when King Faysal II came of age, and then informally as his advisor. So was Nuri al-Sa'id, whether or not he happened to be prime minister at the moment. Both were champions of close ties with Britain and of preserving the landed oligarchy.

But unrest was not far below the surface. Demonstrations and strikes were recurrent, sometimes leading to workers' being killed by the police. Several new political parties rose to challenge the oligarchy. In varying degrees they supported social reform or socialism, antiimperialism, democracy, neutralism in the cold war, and Arab unity. These groups gradually had to go underground, and in 1954 Nuri's government forbade all political parties, including the oligarchical factions organized around people such as himself. The Arab defeat in Palestine in 1948 increased dissatisfaction with the ruling group, as did the failure to obtain a more favorable treaty with Britain. A compromise agreement, signed in 1948, only intensified hostility against the government, and massive rioting blocked its ratification. Economic growth accelerated, as 70 percent of the oil revenues resulting from a new fifty-fifty sharing agreement with the Iraq Petroleum Company in 1951 was allocated to a development board. But even this seemingly progressive measure evoked accusations of graft and favoritism and tended to increase popular expectations faster than national income.

JORDAN: ENLARGEMENT
AND CHALLENGE

The aftermath of the Palestine War left Jordan in a state of shock. Formerly a quiet desert principality, it suddenly found itself with a population tripled by annexing the West Bank and by the influx of refugees. The more modern, westernized, aggrieved, and nationalistic Palestinians were a new breed of subjects for the Hashimite ruler. With word getting out that he was ready to make peace with Israel, Abdullah was killed by a Palestinian supporter of al-Hajj Amin al-Husayni in 1951. His son, Talal, succeeded him, but the new king's severe mental disorder—or, as many Arabs believed, his more nationalistic outlook that appeared to be a threat to the British-backed elite—soon forced him to abdicate in favor of his seventeen-year-old son, Husayn. Although a new constitution in 1952 and subsequent amendments created the formal framework of a Western-style parliamentary government, the monarch, strongly supported by bedouin tribes, continued in effective control. The kingdom remained under British tutelage, formalized by a new treaty of alliance in 1948 that allowed Britain to have air bases and the exclusive right to equip and train the Jordanian army, even to provide commanding officers.

INSTABILITY IN SYRIA

Western-style parliamentary institutions in independent Syria were influenced by traditional Middle Eastern social patterns. The conservative representatives of leading families, who dominated the Chamber of Deputies during the late 1940s, formed loosely organized factions that differed on few major issues. With the Arab states competing for Syria's loyalty, the overriding question was inter-Arab alignments. The People's Party, based in Aleppo, favored unity or close ties with Iraq, while the Damascus-based National Party, led by President Shukri al-Quwatli, was generally aligned with the Hashimites' rivals, Egypt and Saudi Arabia.

But new forces were rising. Two young Syrian schoolteachers, the Christian Michel Aflaq and the Muslim Salah al-Din al-Bitar, both of whom had studied in France and first espoused but then rejected Communism, formed an Arab Renaissance (Ba'th) Party. Emphasizing the slogan "unity, liberty, and socialism," the Ba'th was foremost an Arab nationalist party whose main concern was to bring about a revival of Arab greatness. It called for the unification of the Arab world as one state. Organized on a pan-Arab ("national") basis, the Ba'th treated existing states as mere "regions." The Ba'th gained a new base of support in 1953 when the Arab Socialist Party of Akram al-Hourani, a passionate opponent of "feudalism" (that is, big landlords) who had rallied peasants in the region around Hama to his banner, merged with it to form the Arab Renaissance (Ba'th) Socialist Party. Other challenges to the old order included the Syrian Nationalist Party and a small but vocal Communist movement, not to mention many disaffected army officers, often with partisan connections.

The old order soon broke down. Defeat in Palestine, which gave birth to tales of corruption in the Syrian government, provided a catalyst. Colonel Husni al-Za'im, a would-be Syrian Atatürk, overthrew the parliamentary regime in 1949 with CIA support (apparently representing the first such American participation in a Middle Eastern coup). Za'im was pro-Hashimite at first, but after a visit to King Faruq, whose flattering reception dazzled him, he joined the Egyptian-Saudi alignment. Za'im also had secret ties with the Israelis, with whom he was ready to make peace. A second coup brought the pro-Hashimite Colonel Sami al-Hinnawi to power, but the prospect of Syria's subordination to Iraq led to a third coup before 1949 was out. The new strongman, Colonel Adib al-Shishakli, consolidated his power in 1951. However, with discontent building up under al-Shishakli's repressive regime, the army intervened again in 1954, this time to restore parliamentary government. Old-guard politicians, including Syria's first president, Shukri al-Quwatli, returned to office, although the military remained the final arbiter. But the relatively free elections later in 1954 brought into the Chamber a large minority of Ba'thists, who, together with other radical deputies, were to become a powerful force in Syrian politics.

RELIGIOUS BALANCE IN LEBANON

Of all the Arab countries, Lebanon provided Western-style democracy—or perhaps the right word is "quasidemocracy"—with its longest and strongest foothold, although here too local factors shaped its actual working. Lebanon's contact with the West over several centuries had left it a semiwesternized country, and its experience with representative (though hardly democratic) institutions went back to the nineteenth century. Its relatively high per-capita income and literacy rate provided two of the common prerequisites for democratic government. The fears of the various Christian and Muslim sects, none of which had a majority of Lebanon's population, of domination by the others also worked in favor of establishing a representative system.

An informal agreement called the National Pact, concluded by Lebanese leaders in 1943, stipulated some of the rules of sectarian balance. The pact provided that Lebanon would remain independent, thus satisfying the Western-oriented Maronite Christians. They, fearing their own submergence by a union with Syria or the Arab world in general, tended to be Lebanese nationalists. But it also provided that Lebanon would maintain an "Arab face" and would not rely on Western protection. According to a pattern that had already evolved, the president, who was the dominant political figure, was always a Maronite Christian, while the prime minister was a Sunni Muslim. The system of representation in the Chamber of Deputies gave Christians six seats for every five going to the Muslims. The constitution even provided for the allocation of civil service positions according to religious quotas.

There were several sources of potential ferment. The six-to-five ratio was based on a 1932 census taken by the French. The higher emigration rate of Christians and the higher birthrate of Muslims were changing the composition of Lebanon's population, but the politically dominant Christians resisted any new census. The free enterprise system helped to make Lebanon a center for international banking and transit trade. This produced a disproportionately Christian rich class but also a large, heavily Christian middle class. Even the 50 percent of the population engaged in agriculture were perhaps generally better off than most other Middle Eastern peasants. Still, the gap between rich and poor was wide, and there were many destitute (mainly Muslim) peasants in some areas. Some flocked to the outskirts of Beirut in search of employment, often in vain. And many Lebanese, especially the younger ones, disliked the way in which leaders of a few "feudal" families—in traditional Middle Eastern style, despite economic modernization—dominated politics. Growing dissatisfaction with official manipulation of elections and other corruption in the government of President Bishara al-Khuri, who had secured a constitutional amendment exempting himself from the six-year limit on his term of office, caused a temporary alliance of political leaders to form against him in 1952. Following a general strike, al-Khuri stepped down, to be succeeded by Camille Chamoun. But no long-term changes ensued.

THE EGYPTIAN REVOLUTION

Egypt's primary concerns were still to obtain the withdrawal of British forces and the unity of the Nile Valley. The Sidqi-Bevin Agreement of 1946 provided for the evacuation of British troops during peacetime, but its ambiguous language regarding the Sudan led to riots in Egyptian cities and rejection by the Parliament. The British were unwilling to turn the Sudan over to Egypt without Sudanese consent and were in the process of establishing an autonomous government there, which Egyptians saw as a plot to keep the Nile Valley divided. The Sudanese were split on the issue, with the Ashiqqa (Brothers) Party supporting union with Egypt and the Ummah (Nation) Party asking for independence. In accordance with the 1936 treaty, British troops withdrew from most of Egypt during the late 1940s, restricting themselves to the Canal Zone. But Egyptian attempts to end this last remnant of the occupation—including bringing the issue to the Security Council in 1947—were unavailing.

The old order was disintegrating. King Faruq, widely admired when he succeeded his autocratic father in 1936, had dissipated his popularity when he submitted to the British diktat in 1942 and as his growing reputation as a degenerate lecher embarrassed the Egyptian people. The Wafd, having consented to serve British imperialism during the war, was losing its claim to represent the Egyptian people. A former Wafdist, Makram Ubayd, published a *Black Book* of damaging revelations about Wafdist leaders in 1943. Nor was the party willing to respond to the needs of a country of great landlords and landless, diseased, and uneducated peasants; of cities burgeoning with unemployed emigrés from the countryside; and with a population that had outgrown Egypt's resources. The splinter parties and the politicians who led non-Wafdist governments from 1944 to 1950 had even less claim to represent the masses or the reformers.

The old regime faced growing challenges. There were sporadic strikes and demonstrations. Attacks on traditional aspects of society appeared in print, notably the modernist Khalid Muhammad Khalid's *From Here We Start*, published in 1950. In it the author blamed traditional religious leaders for the troubles of the Islamic world. The response of a prominent Muslim Brother, Muhammad al-Ghazzali, in his *The Beginning of Wisdom*, not only rejected Khalid's secular approach but also joined in the attack on traditional *ulama* who are subservient to evil rulers. Marxist and other radical writers went even further in attacking the status quo.

The Muslim Brethren grew increasingly numerous and influential. Some of them resorted to terror bombings and assassinating Egyptian leaders. When Prime Minister Nuqrashi's government outlawed the Brethren in 1948, he soon fell to one of their assassins. Six weeks later, the movement's leader, Hasan al-Banna, was shot to death, with government complicity. The loss of al-Banna, now replaced by Hasan al-Hudaybi, proved to be a grave setback for the Brethren.

As in the case of Syria, Egypt's defeat in Palestine was the main catalyst for change. Revolutionary cells began to form within the Egyptian army, hitherto a royalist preserve. One of these groups called itself the Free Officers. Its leader was the intelligent and persuasive Gamal Abd al-Nasir, who had been active in political demonstrations since childhood and who passionately hoped to restore dignity to his country. The son of a minor government employee descended from Upper Egyptian peasants of moderate means, Nasir's modest background was like that of many of the Free Officers. While the officer corps had formerly been recruited mainly from Egypt's elite, Nasir and his fellow conspirators were among the first graduates of the military academy after it had been opened up to young men of a broader social background in the late 1930s. Having already long talked among themselves about the need to clean up the country, these officers blamed their government for sending them to Palestine unprepared, with defective weapons that high officials had been bribed to procure. Upon returning to Egypt in defeat, they became a formally organized group in 1949.

Anglo-Egyptian differences helped to finish the old regime. General elections in 1950 brought al-Nahhas back at the head of a new Wafdist government, and negotiations with London resumed. But the British refused to accept Egypt's right to the Sudan or to withdraw without leaving ununiformed British technicians behind to maintain the Suez Canal base and assurances of the right to reoccupy it in case of war. The talks ended in failure in October 1951. A last minute Anglo-American-French-Turkish proposal for a multilateral Allied Middle East Command (the first proposal to establish an eastern counterpart to NATO), with Egyptian participation, was bluntly rejected by Cairo as being simply the substitution of a multilateral occupation for the British one. Instead, the Egyptian Parliament unilaterally proclaimed the abrogation of the 1936 treaty and declared Faruq to be king of Egypt and the Sudan. Egyptian guerrillas, mainly organized by the Muslim Brethren, sporadically attacked the British forces in the Canal Zone, and a boycott of the base by Egyptian workers undermined its usefulness.

In January 1952 British forces attacked the Isma'ilia police station, which was accused of aiding guerrillas. Over fifty police officers were killed, and Egyptians were indignant. A mass demonstration in Cairo turned into a frenzied mob bent on burning the hotels, bars, cinemas, and other symbols of Western presence. Before the day was over, much of the modern sector of Cairo was in ashes. The Wafdist government, which had not dared take action against the mob, made way for a series of short-lived cabinets of the king's choosing.

The Free Officers were preparing to take control. They had come to the attention of the king by defeating his candidate for president of the officers' club and electing General Muhammad Nagib, a popular figure with a good-natured, fatherly image, who had been one of Egypt's few heroes in the Palestine War. General Nagib, though not one of the Free Officers, had been contacted by them and endorsed their objectives. The group finally named him their titular leader in order to give it greater standing with a public that had never heard of the thirty-four-year-old Lieutenant-Colonel Nasir. Tipped off that King Faruq was about to arrest them, the Free Officers carried out a quick, almost bloodless coup in the early hours of July 23, 1952. Although they did not declare a republic for almost a year, they forced Faruq to abdicate and to leave Egypt. Pending the formation of a new civilian government, power was placed in the hands of a Revolutionary Command Council (RCC), composed of the leading Free Officers and nominally headed by Nagib, although Nasir pulled the strings from behind the scenes.

A land reform decree of September 1952, the RCC's first major social achievement, chipped away much of the power of the landlord class. Along with other guarantees to peasants, it provided for the confiscation (reimbursed in long-term government bonds) of landholdings in excess of two hundred feddans[1] (with an additional hundred feddans for dependents) and for the sale of small plots to peasants on favorable terms. This merely dented Egypt's large problem of landlessness. The regime's revolutionism seems to have been tempered by its roots in the class of small landowners (of less than fifty acres) that remained dominant on the village level.

The new regime showed its moderation by rapidly settling the dispute with Britain. An agreement in February 1953 accepted the principle of self-determination for the Sudan over a three-year period. Ensuing elections there returned a pro-Egyptian majority, but the Sudanese later disappointed the Free Officers when they opted for independence. An agreement on the Suez Base question followed in 1954, with Britain agreeing to gradual withdrawal, to be completed by June 1956. British forces retained the right to reoccupy the base during a seven-year period in case of an attack by a non–Middle Eastern state on Turkey or any member of the Arab League.

The inclusion of Turkey seemed indirectly to tie Egypt to NATO. Nasir had close ties with United States diplomats and CIA officials and was regarded as basically pro-American and anti-Communist, although neither he nor most other Arabs were primarily concerned with fears of the USSR. But the Egyptian government, already accused of having conceded too much to Western imperialism, still refused to join any anti-Communist defense organization for the time being, if ever. In any case, the United States, following Secretary of State John Foster Dulles's trip to the region in 1953, had decided that such an alliance should start with the countries of the "Northern tier," such as Turkey and Iran, rather than with the Arab world.

Internally, a new authoritarian order was taking shape under Nasir. Political parties received orders to clean out corruption, and then the RCC dissolved them early in 1953. To fill the vacuum and to mobilize support for the regime, Nasir established a Liberation Rally, his first try at creating a single party to bolster his regime. The RCC suspended the 1923 Constitution but promised to restore representative, constitutional government by 1956.

Nasir had to overcome challenges to his leadership. By mid-1953, Nagib held the titles of president, prime minister, and chairman of the RCC, while Nasir held lesser offices. Nagib, encouraged by his popularity, wanted to have power concentrated in his own hands. The RCC rejected his request for a veto power and, fearing a return to the old order, opposed his desire to speed up the return to constitutional government. In February 1954, Nagib resigned. Nasir took over as prime minister and chairman of the RCC, but popular opposition, plus a mutiny in the cavalry corps, brought Nagib back. Then, in an adept maneuver that looked like a complete capitu-

[1] A feddan is 1.038 acres.

lation to Nagib, the RCC announced that it would dissolve itself and permit the restoration of political parties and constitutional government. As Nasir had calculated, those who feared an end to the revolution united in opposition to Nagib. A strike by the pro-Nasir Transport Workers, demonstrations by the Liberation Rally, and other expressions of opposition to the announcement led to Nasir's return as prime minister in April. Still the strongest popular group in Egypt, the Muslim Brethren had gradually turned against the new leader, whose compromise on the Suez Base issue led one Brother to attempt to assassinate Nasir. Suppression of the Brethren ensued, with several thousand arrested and six executed. Following accusations that Nagib was working with the Brethren, the RCC finally deprived him of the already empty title of president in November and put him under house arrest.

ISRAEL: A WESTERN ISLAND?

Israel was in, but not yet of, the Middle East. Immigrants from Europe had built the state. Its culture was European. Some of its indices of modernization paralleled those of Europe. According to UN statistics, in per-capita income, it ranked just below West Germany and the Netherlands but higher than Italy and Austria in the early 1950s. The country was heavily urban and industrialized, but successful reclamation projects were also augmenting the farmland that both Arabs and Jews had long made productive. This progress was achieved despite the flood of destitute Jewish immigrants that roughly doubled the population remaining after the Arab exodus. The Law of the Return, enacted in 1950, guaranteed the right of any Jew to enter Israel and attain citizenship. But in addition to the benefit derived from confiscated Arab property, the influx of foreign public and private assistance had reached a cumulative total of two billion dollars by 1955. This included United States government aid, United Jewish Appeal contributions, the sale of Israel bonds, and the first installments of West German reparations (according to an agreement reached in 1952) for anti-Jewish atrocities. Besides German payments to the Israeli government, there were also German restitution payments to Jewish survivors. With such financial resources, a highly educated and technically proficient population was able to overcome the obstacles of a largely arid and hitherto underdeveloped country, a rapid influx of immigrants, and hostile neighbors.

Israel became a Western-style parliamentary democracy. Competition flourished among numerous political parties. All gained representation in the Knesset (parliament) in proportion to their percentages of the vote in the whole country. The democratic socialist Mapai seemed to be the permanent ruling party, with a plurality in the Knesset that was able to form shifting coalitions with minor parties. Smaller parties included the more leftist and dovish Mapam (from which one faction broke off to form the Ahdut Avodah in 1954), the free enterprise-oriented General Zionists, the rightist and expansionist Herut (a reconstituted Irgun), several religious parties, and a small Communist Party.

Israel was not a wholly Western country. One Middle Eastern element was the remnant of the Arab Palestinians who did not flee in 1948. They numbered 160,000 in 1949, and their high birthrate allowed them, despite Jewish immigration, always to exceed 10 percent of Israel's population. These Arabs mostly became Israeli citizens; and despite its gross neglect of their needs, they sometimes benefited from the country's economic development. But they found themselves in an anomalous position in a state that proclaimed Jewishness as its unifying characteristic and was surrounded by hostile countries whose language, culture, and identity the Arabs shared. Suspected of disloyalty to Israel, they were also subject to special security measures that restricted their movement and placed them under military rule. And a variety of subtle techniques—such as keeping the Arabs dependent on the establishment in obtaining jobs and services—helped to prevent any unified protest movement, despite discrimination in such matters as wages and employment. Much of the Arab population, including some who had taken no part in the 1948 war, found their land confiscated and their villages razed by the government.

A second Orientalizing influence came from the religious parties, which reflected certain similarities between Orthodox Judaism and Islam. Their members in the Knesset were few, but by forming coalitions with them, Mapai gained the majorities necessary to govern. The need to work with such parties made it necessary for a government led mainly by non-observant Jews to make compromises on such issues as enforcing the sabbath, requiring kosher food to be served in government cafeterias and military installations, denying official recognition to Conservative or Reform Judaism, and leaving jurisdiction over marriage and divorce to religious courts and religious law. In a remarkable perpetuation of the Islamic pattern, each religious community in Israel has its own law in matters of personal status, and all Jews, however nonobservant, are thus subject to Orthodox jurisdiction.

A third and more effective factor diluting Israel's European character was the arrival of Middle Eastern Jewish immigrants. Eastern Jews had been little involved in the Zionist movement, but the establishment of Israel made them suspect in Arab eyes. Some became victims of bombings and mob attacks, and many perceived open or subtle discrimination by Arab governments that suspected them of having pro-Israeli leanings. Their future was insecure. Also, there is some evidence that Israeli agents pressured Middle Eastern Jews to move to Israel, even to the point of inciting anti-Jewish actions. Many Oriental Jews were very religious and saw the establishment of Israel as a messianic event that called for their "return." Israel's higher standard of living may have provided another attraction.

The result was the departure of most Jews from Arab countries—and also some from countries such as Iran or even India—for Israel. They often had to leave their property behind or sell it in haste for much less than its real value. After some initial resistance, the Iraqi and Yemeni governments permitted Jews to leave, and only a handful chose not to participate in the airlifts that followed. Jews from other countries left gradually. Between 1948 and 1954 the more than 370,000 Oriental immigrants slightly outnumbered those from Europe. By 1954 nearly 90 percent of the new immigrants were Easterners, and they were still coming. Their high birthrate was fast making them a majority of Israel's Jewish population.

Aside from a common religion, the Occidental—mostly Ashkenazic—and Oriental—largely Sephardic—Jews were complete aliens to each other. Jews from Iraq or Libya were culturally more akin to Arabs than to European Jews. Their typically dark complexion made them seem indistinguishable from Arabs and sometimes resulted in unofficial racial discrimination. Eastern and Western Jews tended to live in separate communities, and intermarriage was rare. Easterners—many of whom could never forget having been sprayed with DDT when they arrived in Israel—tended to fill the most menial occupations. Relatively few rose to positions in the cabinet or Knesset or attended universities.

Israeli efforts to help the Middle Eastern Jews integrate into Israeli society brought discouraging results. Some European Israelis expressed their disdain for Middle Eastern culture. Israel's leaders expressed the hope that the country would not turn into "merely another Levantine state." The effort was directed not at merging the two cultures but at assimilating the Oriental, which stirred resentment. Although the Oriental Jews were loyal to Israel (and typically more anti-Arab than anyone else), they did not feel that they had been fully integrated into the society.

THE CONTINUING ARAB-ISRAELI CONFLICT

The expectation of an Arab-Israeli settlement following the armistices in 1949 gradually waned. The Israelis would not permit large numbers of the Arab Palestinian refugees to return. To do so would have diluted the state's Jewish character. At one point Israel officially agreed to accept the return of 65,000—not 100,000, as was reported—refugees as part of an overall settlement, but it soon backed down—as may have been planned—under pressure from public opinion, although some offers of compensation were made as part of an eventual settlement. At a conference in Lausanne called by the Palestine Conciliation Commission in 1949, Israel and the Arab states accepted the UN partition lines of 1947 as the starting point for negotiations. But Israel later refused to consider any major territorial concessions, arguing that the Arab states' earlier rejection of the partition plan had invalidated it. Even though Ben-Gurion made way for the more conciliatory Prime Minister Moshe Sharett in 1953, the Arab and Israeli positions proved to be basically irreconcilable, partly because Ben-Gurion's supporters still occupied key positions.

Documents made available long afterward show that Arab governments put out secret peace feelers on several occasions during the late 1940s and early 1950s, only to be spurned each time by the Israelis, who opined that a "rush toward peace" was undesirable. Without a settlement that rectified some of their grievances, Arab countries refused to recognize Israel. Invoking the argument that the armistices had not ended the state of war, Egypt claimed (despite a rebuff by the Security Council in 1951) that it could exclude Israeli shipping through the Suez Canal. On the same logic, it denied Israel access to the Straits of Tiran, which, though in Egyptian territorial waters, constituted the entrance to the Gulf of Aqaba and to the new Israeli port of Eilat. Among other arguments, Arabs pointed out that this town was built on the site of a Palestinian village that Israel occupied after the conclusion of the armistice with Egypt. Arab states boycotted Israeli goods and foreign companies that did business with Israel.

The small demilitarized zones along the armistice lines caused further problems. The Israelis gradually took control of the al-Auja demilitarized zone and established armed settlements there. Israel, despite protests from the UN and Syria, also inched in on the Syrian-Israeli demilitarized zone and expelled the Arab inhabitants, evoking recurrent artillery fire from the overlooking Golan Heights in retaliation. At one point, the United States, which had announced a more even-handed, less pro-Israeli policy with the start of the Eisenhower administration, forced Israel (though only temporarily) to stop a drainage project in the demilitarized zone by threatening to cut off aid. Israel argued that the UN representatives' almost consistent support for the Arabs was proof of bias and refused to participate in the Syrian-Israeli MAC from 1951 on.

Violence became commonplace. Arab Palestinians could look across the barbed wire to see their homes occupied by Israelis and the fruit being picked from their trees. Despite precautions by both sides, individuals would slip across the frontier, often in attempts to recover possessions. Sometimes they would get killed or they would kill Israelis or commit acts of sabotage, and the Israelis in turn launched "retaliatory" raids. Several such incursions—carried out by the army's Unit 101, commanded by Ariel Sharon—involved indiscriminate massacres of Arab civilians; the bloodiest one, in 1953, resulted in the killing of sixty-six men, women, and children in the West Bank village of Qibiya.

Arab leaders sometimes put their people off with talk about an eventual "second round." Israeli military strength—already by the early 1950s the drive to acquire nuclear weapons reportedly was on—made it impractical for them to take any real action, although they believed that Israel would eventually seek more territory. Indeed, Ben-Gurion secretly spoke of the need for another "round," and his supporters in the ministry of defense continuously tried to provoke such a development even after Sharett became prime minister. Sharett's diary, which was later published, reveals that, from the start, the purpose of the "retaliatory" raids was to force the Arabs into a war they could not win, as well as to encourage a siege mentality among the Israeli people.

A Tripartite Declaration, issued by the United States, Britain, and France in 1950, bolstered the status quo. The declaration stated that the three countries—at a time when there was no other major power to counter them in the area—would not let a resort to force settle the conflict and that they would cooperate in preventing an Arab-Israeli arms race. Meantime, Israel was secretly beginning to cooperate with the United States in ways that would eventually lead the latter to see it as an important asset in the regional and worldwide struggle for power. Notably, the CIA and its Israeli counterpart, according to recent accounts, started cooperating during 1951.

CONCLUSIONS

Despite European retreats, the predominance of Europe and the West had not yet ended in 1954. Britain still clung to its privileged position in parts of the Arab world, although it finally agreed in 1954 to withdraw from the Suez Base. The intervention of the old European imperial powers was in some ways replaced by the struggle of the United States and the Soviet Union to add the Middle East to their spheres of influence. So far, the Soviets had been "contained." America's role was one of supporting particular regimes (and sometimes subverting those it did not like). It provided economic and military aid, protected economic interests, sought military bases and alliances as part of the containment policy, and pursued policies toward officially sovereign Middle Eastern states that seemed at least outwardly to be a far cry from old-fashioned colonialism. But the superpowers were joined in the Middle East by a local power of European origin: the Zionist movement transmuted into the State of Israel, whose humiliation of the Arab world and displacement of most Arab Palestinians constituted the clearest proof that the Middle East was still weak and, in many ways, backward.

Calls for reform or revolution were being heard almost everywhere. The old order had survived in places such as Iraq. After a brief interlude of radicalism, the Iranian monarch was back in power. In Syria, challenges to old patterns had brought instability. Egypt was in the hands of a junta that was determined to clean out the evils of the old regime, but it was not following a very radical pattern.

Only a few countries were free of the typical ferment. In Yemen and Saudi Arabia, which were a generation behind most of the area, traditionalism was barely challenged by Western influence. In Turkey the old order had disappeared a generation earlier, and the revolutionary party was making way for a new phase. And Israel was a Western island, building dikes in an attempt to keep out the Eastern sea.

9

victories and setbacks
1954–1973

The first part of 1955 was in some ways a turning point for the Middle East and its relationship with the world. Although the Egyptian Revolution was already two and a half years old, Premier (later President) Gamal Abd al-Nasir had only recently consolidated his leadership. So far, the new regime had brought more continuity than change, particularly in foreign affairs. But with the achievement of a long-sought British commitment in 1954 to withdraw troops from the Suez Canal zone, Egypt was to start a new phase in its foreign policy objectives.

Nasir emerged as more than the leader of Egypt. He came to epitomize the struggle of Arabs and sometimes of non-Westerners generally against the remnants of Western colonialism. Turning Egypt's policy toward pan-Arabism, he gained widespread acclaim from nationalists throughout the Arab world as he defied powerful nations. In response to United States and British plans to align Middle Eastern countries on their side in the cold war against the USSR-led bloc, Nasir became a leading proponent of "positive neutralism" or "nonalignment." This was a natural re-action in a region whose grievances had long been mainly against western European (and now increasingly American), not Russian, imperialists. To most Middle Easterners, the cold war appeared to be an intra-Western feud that they should avoid. Moreover, as affronts from members of the anti-Communist bloc continued, one response was to accept support from—which sometimes threatened potentially to become dependence on—the USSR. Such "new middle class" leaders as Nasir were also devoted to relatively radical change at home. Traditional monarchies increasingly felt threatened by radical nationalists and depended all the more on ties with the United States, which their critics deemed neocolonialist. Only in a non-Arab country such as Turkey, where both geography and historic precedent made the USSR appear to be the main threat, was nationalism not largely synonymous with nonalignment. Even in Iran, which had a similar experience with Russian expansionism, underlying nationalist sentiment tended to be directed more immediately against a regime that was widely regarded as a tool of United States domination.

The Arab-Israeli conflict began increasingly to occupy center stage. Israel saw itself as a restored ancient Middle Eastern nation, but to the Arabs it appeared to be a European settler state and an instrument of other Westerners against Middle Eastern peoples. Getting renewed support from some Western countries, Israel sometimes acted in concert with them against Arab nationalism. Continued humiliation at Israeli hands belied the Arabs' ability to cope with the modern world and made their formal independence, once reached, seem like a mirage.

BAGHDAD, BANDUNG, AND GAZA

The first bombshell of 1955 was the announcement in January that Iraq and Turkey were ready to form an alliance, the Baghdad Pact. This was the culmination of efforts from the beginning of the decade to establish a Middle Eastern counterpart to NATO. By the end of the year, Iran, Pakistan, and Great Britain had joined the grouping. The United States responded to the opposition both of Arab nationalists and of the Israelis, who feared a buildup of Arab armies in the alliance, by avoiding formal membership. Still, Washington proceeded to work closely with the organization and to participate in its committees.

Iraq's membership in the Baghdad Pact accentuated its longstanding rivalry with Egypt, and a struggle ensued between the two countries to line up other Arab states on one side or the other. The Baghdad Pact's leading Arab proponent, Iraqi Prime Minister Nuri al-Sa'id, saw it as a great gain, not only against what he believed to be the danger of Communism but also—as he argued—for strengthening Iraq and other potential Arab members against Israel. Nuri could also point out that the pact replaced a bilateral alliance with Britain and allowed that country's air bases to be turned over to Iraq, a gain corresponding to Nasir's success in getting rid of the base in Egypt. But to most of the Arab public, with which the Iraqi leader became more and more out of touch, Nuri again seemed to be showing his true colors as a British agent. The Baghdad Pact ultimately proved to be a major step in undermining the Iraqi monarchy.

Although the Egyptian government was anti-Communist and up to then perhaps still a candidate for membership in such an alliance in the long run, it was angry over the Baghdad Pact. Nasir thought that his government had assurances from Nuri that the pact would not be concluded. To him it seemed to undermine the Arab Collective Security Pact of 1950, which still existed only on paper. More than that,

Nasir saw the Baghdad Pact as a Western attempt to build up Iraq to replace Egypt as the leading Arab state. A bitter radio propaganda war began in which an already un-popular Iraqi regime was highly vulnerable to attack.

In this conflict between pro-Western Iraq and neutralist Egypt, several Arab countries at first hesitated to take sides. Saudi Arabia, because of its old conflict with the Hashimites, and Yemen, because of its conflict with Britain over the Aden colony and protectorate (Southern Yemen), sided with Egypt. For Syria, the pact evoked sus-picion of a move toward a Hashimite-led Fertile Crescent, and a pro-pact govern-ment soon gave way to alignment with Egypt, with the Ba'thist minority in the Syrian Chamber of Deputies exerting more and more influence, and—as archival re-search later revealed—with the CIA and its British counterparts energetically plot-ting a coup that would put a pro-Western regime in power. British-subsidized King Husayn of Jordan was naturally inclined to join with his cousin, King Faysal II of Iraq, and a British mission in December brought offers of military aid as part of Jor-danian membership in the pact. But the scheme was thwarted as demonstrations and riots indicative of the popular Jordanian mood, particularly among a Palestinian ma-jority that eagerly accepted Cairo Radio's encouragement, threatened to bring his regime down. Soon afterward, King Husayn bettered his own nationalist credentials for a while by suddenly dismissing Sir John Bagot Glubb, whose able command of the Arab Legion had nevertheless put the kingdom's independence in question.

A conference of Afro-Asian leaders in Bandung, Indonesia, in April 1955 gave Nasir's leadership a new thrust. He gained recognition as one of the main Afro-Asian leaders, along with Nehru of India, Sukarno of Indonesia, and Chou En-lai of China, and became more conscious of belonging to an Afro-Asian world that shared a strug-gle against Western colonialism. The exclusion of Israel from the conference pointed to gains to be made from working with this wider circle of nations. Although Nasir supported pro-United States positions on some issues at Bandung, the dominant trend among his fellow Afro-Asian leaders in favor of positive neutralism reinforced his own inclination in that direction.

On February 28, shortly before the Bandung meeting, the conflict with Israel suddenly loomed large for Egypt. The heretofore generally quiet Israeli-Egyptian armistice line blew up as hit-and-run Israeli forces crossed into the Gaza Strip to de-stroy the pumphouse that supplied drinking water to Gaza, killing thirty-eight peo-ple. David Ben-Gurion had just returned from his short-lived retirement on a kibbutz to replace Pinhas Lavon as Israel's minister of defense. (Ben-Gurion would later be-come prime minister again.) The Gaza raid signaled a renewed militancy that was de-signed to provoke another war, already planned for the following year. Even during the previous lull, Israel had continued to violate the demilitarized zone, while Egypt still denied Israeli ships access to the Suez Canal. In late 1954 Israel tested the Canal closure, and one of its ships was confiscated by Egyptian authorities. And an Israeli had recently been killed by an "infiltrator" from the Gaza Strip.

Another event of the previous year was of even greater importance as part of the background of the Gaza raid. In July 1954 Israeli agents appeared in Cairo and Alexandria to firebomb the United States Information Service libraries and other

American and British buildings in the expectation that Egypt would be blamed. Israel hoped that the consequent disruption of Egyptian relations with the two Western countries would reverse British plans to withdraw from the Canal Zone. But the Israeli agents were apprehended before they could carry out their mission. The hanging of two of them in Cairo on January 27, 1955, on seemingly incredible charges provided Israel with one justification for the Gaza raid. The story, however, was confirmed six years later, as responsibility for the unsuccessful "security operation," the so-called Lavon affair, became a heated issue in Israeli politics. More relevant to the Gaza raid was the fact that the "security" failure brought Lavon's fall and put Ben-Gurion in office again, although debate still rages in Israel over whether it was Lavon or Ben-Gurion's protégés in the Defense Ministry who planned the operation.

SOVIET ARMS FOR EGYPT

The Gaza raid was only the beginning of a series of Israeli incursions during 1955–1956. The Egyptian army was so hopelessly weak that Cairo Radio once resorted to reporting a fictitious victory to save face with the public. Nasir proposed that each side pull its troops back one kilometer from the line to avoid incidents, and although the suggestion met Israeli scorn, Egyptian troops moved back unilaterally. But the Egyptian response to the Gaza raid also had a less pacifistic side, as the army began to train Palestinians as *fida'iyin* ("self-sacrificers") to carry out sabotage and terrorist raids in Israel. The renewed violence created a climate in which the proposals of an American representative for sharing the waters of the Jordan River, though acceptable to everyone on a technical level, were rejected by Arab governments.

Another Egyptian response was a renewed interest in building up the army. Egypt had hoped to get American arms once the conflict with Britain was settled, but aside from pro-Israeli pressures at home, the United States at this time tended to be irritated with neutralism. This was at the height of the cold war, and many Americans perceived their cause as one of righteousness against the "evils" of Communism. Reflecting a common attitude toward those nations that refused to "stand up and be counted," Secretary of State John Foster Dulles once declared that neutralism was indeed "immoral." While the sale of American arms to neutralist Egypt was not denied outright, the proposed terms of payment were such that Cairo could not accept.

With some reluctance Egypt now approached the USSR, and an arms deal (at first said to be with Czechoslovakia) that stunned many governments in the anti-Communist camp was announced in September. Since Stalin's death in 1953 Moscow had reversed its former ideological rigidity in favor of a new willingness to work with antiimperialist, non-Communist ("national bourgeois") regimes, such as Nasir's, in Africa and Asia. This support for such regimes, some of which had formerly been condemned as "fascist," carried with it an increasing amount of criticism for Israel. With the arms deal, the USSR seemed to have achieved a major coup by leapfrogging the Baghdad Pact countries to a position of potential influence farther south.

For Egypt, too, the arms deal seemed to be a big achievement. No longer would Arab states have to wait meekly for the British, French, and Americans ("the arms monopoly") to mete out weapons. By playing their Russian card, Arab states could hope to make their independence more real, although some of them also possibly feared that they risked falling under Soviet control.

These events gave Nasir a new stature in the Arab world. He was not now perceived, as he had been a year earlier, as one who had unduly compromised with London. As a result of the arms deal and subsequent bold acts, he came to be idolized by increasing numbers of Arabs. Perhaps this was true in other Arab countries even more than at home, where he was also seen as the first authentic Egyptian to lead the country since Pharaonic times. Despite his authoritarianism, he gained wide acceptance as a real representative of the Arab masses. Not only did he seem to be sweeping away much in Egypt's society that younger nationalists detested, but the Baghdad Pact had also made him the symbol of opposition to Nuri al-Sa'id and others accused of subservience to colonialism. The acquisition of Soviet arms gave Arabs new hope that the rights of the Palestinians could be restored by the "new Salah al-Din," and some Israelis also began to fear that the Arabs had found their great leader. It was largely in response to acclaim for him in other Arab countries that Nasir began to give more emphasis than ever to the idea that Egypt was an integral part of one Arab nation.

THE HIGH DAM

After showing initial irritation over the arms deal, the United States decided to counterbalance the USSR's new position of influence by instituting a dramatic program of its own. The Egyptian government had already decided to seek aid for building a massive High Dam at Aswan, in southern Egypt, to be 365 feet high and two and one-half miles long. By saving surplus water when the Nile was high, the dam would create an artificial lake in southern Egypt and the northern Sudan. In addition to providing a major source of hydroelectric power, the dam was supposed to enable Egyptians to increase their irrigated land to meet the demands of a rapidly increasing population. In December 1955 the United States, Great Britain, and the World Bank offered to help finance the project, with Washington and London to provide $70 million for the first stage. This offer was conditional on a commitment from Cairo to accept certain restraints on its economic policies. For example, the Egyptian government would be unable to obtain other foreign loans without the World Bank's permission. Despite the high priority Egypt gave to this project, it was reluctant to accept such limitations on its independence and consequently delayed its response.

On July 19, 1956, the Egyptian ambassador in Washington nevertheless informed Dulles of his country's acceptance of the offer. But Dulles replied that the United States had changed its mind, offering the excuse that the Egyptian economy was too weak to support the project. Besides insulting the Egyptians, this explanation was unconvincing, since there was no more basis for it than when the offer was made. The real reason was more complicated, involving the opposition of Israel's supporters and of American cotton farmers who feared an increase in Egyptian production as a result of the dam. Some United States allies also argued that none of them was getting such a big aid program and that Egypt was thus being rewarded for its neutralism. Although Nasir played down reports that the USSR was willing to help with the dam, American policymakers thought they detected "blackmail" and wanted to call Moscow's bluff. A more immediate reason was one of Egypt's recent actions in keeping with a neutralist policy, namely its recognition in May of the Communist regime in China. This was done partly because that country appeared to be an alternative source of military aid in the event the USSR agreed with the United States, as had been suggested, on a joint arms embargo of the area. But recognition of Beijing was anathema to the United States; although Britain and Israel had already recognized the regime, U.S. officials pointed out that this had occurred before the 1950 "aggression" in Korea.

The news that Dulles had reneged came to Nasir while he was flying with Nehru to Cairo from Yugoslavia, where they had met with their fellow neutralist, Marshal Tito. To Nasir, Dulles's action seemed like a slap in the face and perhaps an attempt to undermine his government. He did not wait long before responding in a way that would allow him to recoup his prestige.

THE SUEZ CRISIS

Nasir's dramatic response to Dulles's action came on July 26, during the celebration of the fourth anniversary of the overthrow of King Faruq. Evoking wild applause from the crowd and a mixture of joy and apprehension from opponents of Western colonialism in general, Nasir announced that Egypt had nationalized the Suez Canal Company, indeed that Egyptian authorities were taking full control of it at that moment. The Canal Company, a private corporation operating in Egyptian territory and incorporated under Egyptian law but with the shares owned by the British government and by French investors, seemed to be a remnant of European colonialism. The completion of the British withdrawal from the Suez base a month earlier made the company the next logical object of Egypt's antiimperialism. Although the concession was due to expire in 1968 in any case, Nasir had already thought of the possibility of nationalizing the company before that time. The Aswan Dam episode made this imperative for him.

Nasir now became a bogeyman for much of the West, and his "seizure" of the canal became a rallying cry for some who had already determined to crush him for other reasons. The British and the French were heavily dependent on the waterway, especially for oil shipments, and feared that Egyptian control jeopardized it. More generally, they saw Nasir as a threat to their remaining colonial and semicolonial arrangements throughout the Middle East and Africa. British Prime Minister Anthony Eden was particularly concerned with destroying the "Egyptian dictator," whom he compared to Hitler. Eden was so obsessed with the appeasement of Hitler at Munich in 1938 that he was unable to deal with the Suez situation rationally. It also seems that Eden's enmity toward Nasir went back to his mistaken belief that the Egyptian leader was the real "culprit" in King Husayn's dismissal of Glubb Pasha and was bolstered by a general tendency to see Cairo Radio's "Voice of the Arabs" as the sole cause of Arab nationalism and anticolonialism.

France had its own reason for wanting to crush Nasir. A revolt had broken out in Algeria in 1954, which increasingly threatened French rule and the position of the dominant European settler minority. Arabs in general sympathized with their Algerian "brothers," and Egypt gave the rebels some aid. But the French convinced themselves that Nasir was the cause of all their trouble and that the road to victory in Algeria went via Cairo. Unlike Britain, the French had little to lose in the Arab East, and from 1954 on, a Paris–Tel Aviv axis emerged. With United States encouragement, French armaments poured into Israel, which was awaiting the right moment to attack Egypt.

The "Suez Crisis" persisted through the summer and fall of 1956, as Britain, France, and Israel prepared for war against Egypt. As the argument ran, nationalization of the Canal Company was a gross violation of the Constantinople Convention of 1888, which provided that the canal would be open to the ships of all nations. When others pointed out that ownership of the Canal Company did not necessarily have anything to do with the right to use the canal (and Egypt continued to reaffirm its commitment to the Constantinople Convention), Eden in turn repeatedly scorned such "legal quibbles." Egyptian promises to compensate the stockholders, the major legal requirement for nationalizing foreign-owned property, were ridiculed. In fact, Egypt would not have had any real choice in the matter of compensation, for London, Paris, and Washington had immediately responded to nationalization by freezing Egyptian financial assets, which were more than sufficient to cover the cost of the Canal Company.

Most Westerners assumed that a "backward" country such as Egypt could not run the Canal and that this would make Egyptian guarantees of its accessibility to them useless. Britain and France, in effect, attempted to sabotage the waterway by withdrawing all pilots of their nationalities, but they were surprised when the operation ran more efficiently than ever with drastically reduced personnel. Such a great success was a source of pride to Egypt, although it was in large part due to the inherent ease of operating a sea-level canal, with no locks. Looking for another provocation, Britain and France were also frustrated by Nasir's willingness to allow their ships through the canal and thus to refuse to present a *casus belli* even when they refused to pay.

While the USSR and most of the Afro-Asian states supported Egypt, the United States joined its allies in criticizing the nationalization of the canal. But the United States also opposed the use of force. Dulles and President Eisenhower earned Eden's enmity first by delaying any action. A series of conferences of major maritime nations, held in London, failed to bring about a solution. The First London Conference, in August, proposed an international board to run the canal, but Egypt adamantly rejected this. A Second London Conference, in September, proposed to set up a Suez Canal Users' Association (SCUA) to operate the waterway from ships positioned at each end. The SCUA was set up, but Eden was angered to discover that Dulles was still opposed to having it "shoot its way through."

SUEZ-SINAI WAR

A series of secret meetings of British, French, and Israeli officials worked out other plans. These called for an Israeli attack on Egypt, with French planes to provide air cover in case Egypt retaliated by trying to bomb Israeli cities. Then, feigning innocence, London and Paris would issue an ultimatum to the two belligerents, demanding that they withdraw ten miles from each side of the canal to protect it from danger and allow an Anglo-French force to act as a buffer. Israel was not expected to have penetrated that far into Egypt anyway, thus making the planned demands for "withdrawal" by the two sides completely asymmetrical. Since Egypt could not fail to reject such a proposal, British and French forces would then take the "safety" of the canal into their own hands by forcibly occupying it. The three states adamantly denied that any kind of collusion had occurred, but official revelations a decade later removed all doubt.

Events at first went according to plan for the three allies. A series of incidents on the Israeli-Jordanian frontier helped to camouflage Israel's intentions until its forces, commanded by Chief of Staff General Moshe Dayan, struck into the Gaza Strip and the Sinai on October 29 and simultaneously parachuted in to occupy the strategic Mitla Pass in west-central Sinai. Most of the Egyptian forces normally stationed there had withdrawn to face an expected invasion of the Canal Zone. Although Egyptians fought well in the few cases when they were able to put up resistance, even against overwhelming odds and without air cover, Israel routed them without difficulty. Almost all of Sinai was soon under Israeli control. Nearly three decades later, Israeli participants in the invasion revealed that their forces massacred large numbers of Egyptian prisoners of war. Egyptian reinforcements were at first sent against the invader but then got orders to return when the Anglo-French ultimatum, presented according to plan, made their presence vital in the Canal Zone. On November 1, Britain and France began bombing Egyptian bases, airports, and other points, but the two powers failed to land their forces at Port Sa'id, at the northern end of the Canal, until November 5. Again Egyptian troops proved helpless, although popular resistance in Port Sa'id slowed the invasion slightly.

At the UN the United States joined with the USSR in condemning the invasion. Washington was angry with its allies for having acted behind its back and saw this as a kind of outright aggression that could not be condoned without making America's proclaimed principles patently hollow. Soviet hints of retaliation against London and Paris and broadcasts referring to "volunteers" had less impact than did American opposition. While an Anglo-French veto stalled action in the Security Council, a special session of the General Assembly called for a cease-fire and withdrawal of troops. The Suez invasion ground to a halt on November 7, when British and French forces were still only twenty miles south of Port Sa'id. The canal was closed temporarily as a result of damage during the hostilities, particularly by a ship that Egypt purposely sank to delay the invasion. An American offer to provide oil to the two countries at a time of impending scarcity—and financial help to bolster the now-endangered British pound—provided a major inducement for them to quit. The establishment of a UN Emergency Force (UNEF), ultimately to consist of seven thousand people, also facilitated withdrawal, which was complete by the end of the year.

Israel resisted calls for withdrawal and stayed on for a while in the Gaza Strip and at Sharm al-Shaykh, which commands the entrance to the Gulf of Aqaba. This evoked criticism from the United States and a possibility of UN economic sanctions. Finally, with a United States endorsement of its right to use the Gulf of Aqaba, Israel ended the occupation in March 1957, and the territorial status quo ante was restored. The UNEF patrolled the armistice line, although its presence was dependent on continued Egyptian permission, as Israel never permitted the force on its side of the line. The UNEF was not designed for fighting, but by separating the two sides it helped to keep the Egyptian-Israeli frontier quiet for a decade. Its units also guarded Sharm al-Shaykh, thus preventing Egypt from closing the Gulf to Israeli ships again. Israel's access to the waterway became its only tangible gain from the invasion, although this demonstration of its military power renewed its self-confidence.

NASIR'S UPSURGE AFTER SUEZ

The victor of Suez was Arab nationalism and its symbol, President Nasir. Britain had been discredited, and its remaining quasi-colonial positions shrank. Even in Jordan, October elections, the only relatively free ones that the country had ever had, resulted in a nationalist, Nasirite parliament and cabinet, headed by Prime Minister Sulayman Nabulsi. The aftermath of the tripartite attack on Egypt also brought the abrogation of the Anglo-Jordanian Treaty, with Jordan turning to Egypt, Syria, and Saudi Arabia to replace the British subsidy. Admittedly, Nasir's army had been crushed, but that did not discredit him with Arab nationalists, for no poor, ex-colonial country could be expected to stand up against such odds. While in the past, the British had been able to bring down Egyptian governments, now it was Eden, not Nasir, who fell from power as a result of Suez. Further, less than two years would pass before the challenge of Arab nationalism, particularly in Algeria but with the Suez episode in the background, sufficed to bring down the whole Fourth French Republic.

Although the United States saved Egypt from defeat, the American position was not enhanced. Many Arabs gave more credit to the USSR's empty threats against their enemies and to its continuing military and economic aid to nationalist Arab governments. Although Arabs gave Washington credit for opposing aggression in this case, they were not satisfied with other United States actions. Arab nationalists pointed out that, while the United States was helping the aggressors recover from the shambles they had brought upon themselves, it continued to freeze Egyptian financial assets. Egypt was not even able to obtain polio vaccine from the United States at this time. Trials in Syria that revealed a United States–British–Iraqi plot to overthrow the government also helped cancel out the gratefulness that other American policies might have earned.

When Dulles spoke of the new power "vacuum" in the Middle East, Arabs were angered. President Eisenhower announced a plan to help Middle Eastern countries fill this "vacuum" by giving military and economic assistance and even by offering to send troops if needed against the danger of "international Communism." But Arab nationalists interpreted this as a crusade against Arab nationalism and neutralism and as an attempt by the United States to replace Britain as the dominant power in the region. While Turkey and Iran endorsed the Eisenhower Doctrine, as this policy was labeled, even the conservative Arab regimes, except for those of Lebanon and Libya, refused to do so openly.

After Suez, a bitter conflict ensued between neutralist and pro-Western regimes. In the face of a growing challenge by nationalists that could be counterbalanced only by United States support, King Sa'ud of Saudi Arabia was weaned away from his ties with Egypt. Even when the Sa'udi royal family forced the inept, wasteful king to turn over much of his power temporarily to his reputedly pro-Nasir brother, Prince Faysal, in 1958, the resulting budgetary reforms were not matched by lessening opposition to revolutionary forces. Also, King Husayn of Jordan dismissed the Nabulsi government and nipped an army coup in the bud as the American Sixth Fleet made a show of force for him in the eastern Mediterranean. The kingdom's former British subsidy turned out to be replaced by an American, not an Arab, one. This included payments from the CIA that were kept secret for two decades. The threat of Nasirite revolution caused the Sa'udi and Hashimite monarchs to put their old rivalry aside in a new royalist solidarity.

The nationalistic government of Syria was the center of much Western and conservative Arab wrath. With some reputedly pro-Soviet figures taking important positions in the government, the Western news media and Western governments exaggerated the imminence of a Communist takeover there. The United States was still devoted to replacing this government (the attack on Egypt the previous fall caused the earlier plan to unravel), and documents later pretty much confirmed what then seemed to be wild accusations by the Syrian government about CIA plots during 1957. As Turkish troops were mobilized on the Syrian border, the United States concocted a plan for Jordan and Iraq to invade their neighbor. But even conservative Arab governments grew nervous about the project. King Sa'ud began to mediate between Turkey and Syria, and the crisis cooled off.

Syrian leaders' fear of Communism and even more of "reactionaries" now began to reinforce their long-standing emotional commitment to "one Arab nation." Various Syrian calls for unity with Egypt culminated in a mission to Cairo in January 1958 that asked for immediate union. President Nasir was skeptical of such an unplanned merger and refused to agree except on his own strict terms. These included the establishment of a unitary rather than a federal state and the abolition of all Syrian political parties, including the Ba'th. The latter, though unsympathetic to Nasir before 1955, had come to see him as fully embodying their own cause. Syrian

Ba'thists believed that even with their party disbanded, they would have a predominant position in any unified Arab state, and so they agreed to Nasir's terms.

After a plebiscite in February, a United Arab Republic (UAR) came into being, with Syria and Egypt transformed into the northern and southern regions of the new state. Ecstasy reached a high point among Arab nationalists. Nasir was now and afterward simply "the President" (*al-Ra'is*) to Arabs everywhere. When he visited Damascus in 1958, the exultant mood seemed to be one of expecting all "artificial" inter-Arab borders to vanish, and with them the regimes propped up by "imperialists." While the Yemeni *imam* sought protection from nationalist criticism by joining with the UAR to form a nominal United Arab States, the Hashimite monarchs of Jordan and Iraq tried to rival Nasir's union by establishing their own loose "Arab Federation," with Nuri as its first prime minister. However, few people took this seriously.

The Arab nationalist mood combined with domestic politics to produce a crisis in Lebanon during 1958. Many Arab nationalist Lebanese (mainly Muslims) went to Damascus to celebrate Nasir's visit and were swept away by emotion. Still, neither they nor Nasir envisaged that Lebanon would give up its independence. There was also growing resentment among Muslims against domination by what had been a bare majority of Christians but was by then undoubtedly a minority. And many Lebanese were embittered by several of President Camille Chamoun's actions, including his failure to break off diplomatic relations with Britain and France during their attack on Egypt. His endorsement of the Eisenhower Doctrine was another mark against him. In addition, Chamoun and the CIA manipulated parliamentary elections in 1957 to get his protégés elected, and some of the defeated politicians, Muslims and Christians alike, were now angry. With his own supporters predominating in the Chamber, the Lebanese president was reputed to have plans to push through a constitutional amendment allowing him to be elected for a second term.

The assassination of a pro-Nasir journalist in May 1958 brought the crisis to a head. Barricades appeared throughout Lebanon as pro-Chamoun and anti-Chamoun forces fought a desultory civil war. The army, under General Fu'ad Shihab, also a Maronite, stood aside. The conflict was widely presented in much of the outside world in grossly oversimplified terms as one between Christians and Muslims, although even some of the traditional Maronite leaders, including the patriarch of the Maronite Church, aligned themselves with the so-called "Muslim" camp. Some arms were smuggled from the UAR (Syria) to the anti-Chamoun forces, but this was only a minor factor in the struggle.

As the Lebanese crisis heightened, Iraq took center stage on July 14. Part of the army received orders to move to Jordan to bolster King Husayn, but there was reason to suspect that this was a prelude to intervention in Syria and Lebanon. As units commanded by General Abd al-Karim Qasim and Colonel Abd al-Salam Arif passed close by Baghdad on their way, they seized the opportunity to overthrow the government, the realization of a goal that had previously emerged in discussions with civilian nationalist leaders. The army quickly took control, while the streets of Baghdad witnessed pent-up fury against a generally hated regime. King Faysal and his uncle,

Abd al-Ilah, were shot to death, apparently as the latter tried to resist the soldiers sent to arrest them. The royal family was exterminated. Nuri attempted to escape in a woman's garb but was killed on the spot when the crowd discovered who he was. His body was dragged through the streets and torn apart. With this response to "reaction" and "imperialism," Baghdad soon announced its withdrawal from the Baghdad Pact, whose name was changed to the Central Treaty Organization (CENTO).

As Arab nationalists celebrated the Iraqi Revolution in the expectation that Baghdad would soon join the UAR, the anti-Communist camp was appalled. Turkey apparently wanted to invade Iraq and to restore the old regime but was restrained by the United States. British troops flew into Jordan to bolster the king's position. And in response to Chamoun's appeal for help, American marines landed in Lebanon to protect it from an "international Communism" that was almost entirely a product of the imagination as far as that country was concerned. But American forces took no active part in the civil war. Instead, the United States helped to bring about a compromise settlement, with Shihab elected president, and some of the former rebels joining the new cabinet. Little basic change occurred in the Lebanese political system, although the Eisenhower Doctrine was repudiated and relations with Cairo were normalized. The new president strove to strengthen governmental authority at the expense of local oligarchs, who however won out over his "Shihabist" approach a decade later.

NASIR'S DOMESTIC REFORMS

While Nasir's Egypt led the way against colonialism and Arab disunity, it also adopted revolutionary policies that inspired emulation elsewhere. Economic and social development received increasing attention. Provision of schools, medical care, and potable water for the rural population became high priorities, and the country proceeded to make small dents in the miserable conditions that had prevailed for so long. But disease and illiteracy were not easy to wipe out. Even in 1970 only 53 percent of the school-age children were enrolled in school, but this represented a considerable achievement in comparison with 20 percent in 1950. Industrialization became another major goal, and projects such as constructing a steel mill at Helwan, near Cairo, were implemented with Soviet assistance. By 1970 industry contributed 38 percent of the GNP, compared with 21 percent in 1950. Land reclamation got attention, with the High Dam, which was completed between 1960 and 1970 with Soviet aid, overshadowing all other efforts. Two successive five-year plans, adopted in 1960, set the unrealistic goal of doubling the GNP by the end of the decade, but economic development proceeded at a respectable rate of about 6 percent a year during the early 1960s. Official attempts to encourage birth control had little effect; the population increased at a rate of over 2.5 percent a year, which meant that much of the economic gain was eaten up.

With the effort to increase the "national pie" came attempts to divide it more equally. The mild reforms in the years following the 1952 coup made way for more radical change in the early 1960s. The word *socialism* came increasingly into the official vocabulary, although the only industries nationalized during the 1950s were those owned by enemy nationals during the Suez War. Brussels's intervention in the newly independent Congo (now Zaire) in 1960 also resulted in the nationalization of Belgian-owned property in Egypt. The Bank of Egypt was nationalized in 1960.

July 1961 saw the promulgation of a whole set of "socialist laws" establishing "Arab socialism" and a "socialist, cooperative, democratic society." These nationalization measures, together with others that followed in the early 1960s, turned most large businesses into state enterprises, while 51 percent government ownership was imposed on others. The socialist laws also gave employees a share of the profits and representation on boards of directors. Among numerous leveling measures was a highly progressive income tax, which—at least on paper—took 90 percent of incomes exceeding ten thousand pounds. Land reform was also extended, with the maximum ownership set at one hundred acres in 1961 and reduced to half that amount in 1969. While a shortage of foreign exchange and government control over imports largely kept foreign-produced luxury goods out of the country, subsidies helped the poor to buy basic foods.

But the extent of leveling can be exaggerated. While dire poverty still prevailed among most of the people, a privileged few flaunted their wealth or else kept much of it out of sight awaiting what, from their point of view, might be a better day. Some landowners partly evaded land reform by dividing their estates among members of the family, and preserved much of their local influence. New privileged groups emerged, such as army officers and technocrats managing state factories, and they resisted leftist pressures to make the revolution more thorough.

The nationalist and socialist measures undermined the position of some minority groups. Small foreign minorities such as the Greeks largely vanished as their members returned to their home countries. With the Arab-Israeli conflict putting their loyalty in question, almost all the Egyptian Jews left Egypt. Several thousand who had not obtained Egyptian nationality were expelled during the Suez War, along with other enemy aliens. Since the minorities, including Copts, were on the whole relatively privileged economically, they sometimes felt that socialism was directed against them. They were generally less antiimperialist and tended not to identify with Arab nationalism and thus were unenthusiastic about official policies. Attempts to correct the Muslim majority's underrepresentation in desirable positions also evoked grumbling about alleged discrimination by members of minority groups.

The doctrine and practice of Arab socialism developed pragmatically. For example, the 1961 socialist laws were in large part a response to the problem of carrying out an economic plan when business was under private ownership. But the laws also represented a strong "democratic" bias in the leadership, in the socioeconomic but not the political sense. Communism was rejected, and, in line with methods that varied from benign autocracy to extreme repressiveness, Communists sometimes were given harsh treatment. The Marxist doctrine of class struggle came in for particular criticism from the regime. But individual Marxists were tolerated and given positions in the press and elsewhere after the outlawed Communist Party agreed to disband in 1965.

In an attempt to tie the doctrine to the people's previous heritage, Arab socialism was said to be derived from Islam. Nasir sometimes proclaimed that all religions teach socialism and cited numerous egalitarian aspects of Islamic teachings and of early Islamic practice to demonstrate his point.

Nasir's revolution contrasted with Atatürk's in that it did not involve an attack on religion. Yet Nasir was a secularist to a large extent. Together with many Arab nationalists, he emphasized an Arab nationalism that incorporated Muslim and Christian Arabs, although some non-Muslims tend to interpret this as a disguised form of Islamic identity. He downplayed religion in foreign policy, as in failing to support his fellow Muslims in the Cyprus and Indo-Pakistani conflicts. The Muslim Brotherhood was feared perhaps more than any other movement. Members of this group allegedly were caught plotting to kill the president in 1965, and some executions followed. One of the people who went to the gallows was the widely revered Islamist, Sayyid Qutb, who ushered in an idea that more moderate Muslim Brothers found too extreme, namely that Egypt had returned to a state of *jahiliyyah,* that is, had forsaken Islam. But Nasir showed respect for Islam and justified his policies as being in accord with it. His government used religious leaders as a communications channel and prepared sermons for delivery in the mosques. Religion was a required subject in the schools, with each child instructed in his or her own faith. At the same time the government instituted reforms in the thousand-year-old al-Azhar University, particularly by adding modern subjects to its curriculum. There was no attempt to replace religious law in matters of personal status, and only a few substantive reforms ensued in these matters. But religious courts were abolished in 1956, leaving the regular courts to apply the law of all sects.

The regime of the "Free Officers" set about establishing governmental institutions. When the transition period expired in 1956, a constitution was drawn up and submitted to a plebiscite. Its approval by more than 99 percent of the voters was typical of elections in this and other authoritarian regimes. The election of Nasir, without opposition, by a similar percentage provided still another example. A political movement called the National Union, in effect a single political party, also came into existence in 1956, and after a delay caused by the Suez crisis, a National Assembly was elected during the next year from a limited number of approved candidates. The establishment of the UAR in 1958 led to the adoption of a new constitution, with an enlarged National Assembly and National Union. The breakup of the UAR required still another try, and the National Union made way for an Arab Socialist Union (ASU) in 1962. A "National Congress of Popular Forces" approved a charter that elucidated the regime's official ideology in the same year, while a new constitution, still deemed provisional, was adopted in 1964.

These institutions proved to be of limited importance. The National Assembly, half of whose members had to be peasants and workers according to the 1964 constitution, acted as an independent legislative body only to a minor extent and usually gave automatic approval to the regime's proposals. There were attempts to breathe some life into the ASU, for example, by excluding "reactionary" elements and by creating an inner category of vanguard members. Its local committees did, in fact, provide a basis for popular participation, but it gained little effectiveness as an organization for mass mobilization and participation on the national level. The leadership was unable to rule through the ASU, and instead, so-called centers of power continued to exist in the society. Notably, the army, whose officers now became a pampered elite, was under the largely independent control of Field Marshal Abd al-Hakim Amir until 1967. Amir, who had the unswerving loyalty of most officers, was also Nasir's close friend and associate, but it was later revealed that the relationship between the two men became tense during the mid-1960s and that the president, fearing an army coup, was powerless to deal with him. Leftists argued that such a weak political order should make way for a more effective ASU, with a clearer ideology, in order to facilitate a real social transformation.

NASIR'S DECLINE

Nasir's position in the Arab world reached its peak in the summer of 1958 and then began to descend. After Iraq's revolution, there was a widespread expectation that it would join the UAR and that other revolutions and an ever larger unity would follow. But subsequent events showed that Arab unity was hard to attain. Iraq's Qasim was determined to keep power himself, not to turn it over to Nasir, and the ardently pro-Nasir Arif soon fell out of favor; at one point he received a death sentence, which, however, was never carried out. The bitter propaganda war between Iraq and the UAR soon resumed. In order to counter the Nasirites, who were bloodily suppressed when they revolted in Mosul in April 1959, Qasim began to depend on Communist support. Then the Communists' excesses, particularly a massacre in Kirkuk in July 1959, led the government to suppress them too, but no lasting rapprochement with the UAR was possible while Qasim was in power.

As the euphoria of union wore off, Syria proved to be another disillusionment for Nasir. The Nasirite-Ba'thist honeymoon ended when the Ba'thists discovered that they would not be allowed to provide the brains for the new state. Conservative candidates were even allowed to defeat Ba'thists in the northern region in the National Assembly elections of 1959. Ba'thist leaders began to resign from the government. In turn, power became increasingly centralized, and Nasir's popularity in Syria was partially eroded, though not destroyed. To some Syrians, the union began to seem more like annexation to Egypt. Then, when the socialist measures were introduced in July 1961, conservative Syrians were bitter, and a group of conservative Syrian army officers staged a coup in September that restored the country's independence. Despite an initial impulse to restore Cairo's control, Nasir decided that it would be wiser not to risk an Arab civil war and thus acquiesced in the breakup. But, in order to keep the dream of union alive, Egypt retained the name "UAR" for another decade.

UPS AND DOWNS, 1961–1967

With the breakup of the UAR, Egyptians were disillusioned with the other Arabs. Reflecting a temporary tendency to avoid Arab entanglements, Nasir blamed himself for having dealt with "reactionaries," or what he called his former policy of "unity of ranks," and announced a new policy of "unity of purpose"—that is, of working only with other "progressives," none of which at the moment was in control of any Arab government outside Egypt. But other radical regimes soon emerged, beginning with the achievement of Algerian independence in 1962.

In September 1962, Imam Ahmad of Yemen died. He had also turned against Nasir after the adoption of Arab Socialism, and his reputedly more "progressive" son, Badr, succeeded him. It was then that antimonarchical army officers, led by Abdullah al-Sallal, took control and established a republic. Numerous reforms were instituted, ranging from abolition of slavery to ending the dominance of the *sayyid* ruling group (descendants of the Prophet Muhammad) who had monopolized the bureaucracy. But the *imam* escaped and rallied some Zaydi tribespeople to his side in the rough, mountainous north.

Faced with the threat of counterrevolution, the new regime asked for Egyptian help. With a certain degree of anti-"reaction" zeal, Nasir sent troops to Yemen, while Saudi Arabian funds kept the *imam*'s opposition alive. As the Egyptians became bogged down in a seemingly interminable conflict in an impossible, unfamiliar terrain, Egypt chose to commit increasingly large numbers of soldiers—70,000 by 1967—in the hope of finally prevailing. The intervention in Yemen at first seemed to be an opportunity to emerge from isolation in the Arab world, but now it was wasting Egyptian energy and funds. It was partly for this reason that the country's economic growth began to slow down. With Egypt sometimes strafing the Saudi side of the border in southern Arabia, there seemed to be danger of an all-out Egyptian-Saudi war.

The Arab socialist threat helped to bring modest reform to Saudi Arabia. With King Sa'ud epitomizing wastefulness and corruption, even some members of his family showed their opposition by moving to revolutionary Cairo. Then the royal family, backed by a *fatwa* (ruling) from high religious authorities, forced Sa'ud to abdicate in favor of his brother Faysal in 1964. Despite his earlier pro-Nasir reputation, King Faysal now became the leading Arab opponent of revolution. His greater ability and his efforts to curb waste made him more effective in this role than his deposed brother. The institution of some social reforms, including the abolition of slavery, blunted Nasir's antireactionary propaganda.

The year 1963 also brought new coups in Syria and Iraq. In each case, Ba'thist-dominated governments were established and, in order to get the stamp of Nasir's approval, proceeded to negotiate an agreement to establish a new UAR. But the agreement soon fell apart as Egypt and the two Ba'thist regimes exchanged diatribes.

Arif, the nominal president of Iraq after the Ba'thist takeover, assumed real control through a coup of his own in November of the same year and entered into close relations with Egypt. Iraq and Egypt even agreed to proceed gradually toward unity, but this too was eventually dropped. In fact, Egypt had no enthusiasm for such a union, particularly in light of the Kurdish revolt in northern Iraq, led by Mulla Mustafa Barzani from 1961 on.

In many ways, the radical regimes that henceforth dominated Syria and Iraq were to parallel Nasir's Egypt. They too were committed to Arab socialism and thus decreed large-scale nationalization measures, although the Iraqis toned down their initial enthusiasm for this policy in favor of an emphasis on "prudence" in the mid-1960s. These were also authoritarian governments brought to power by and continuously dependent on the army. In each case there was some attempt to create a single-party regime, with the Ba'th in Syria and an Arab Socialist Union in Arif's Iraq. The main difference was that the Iraqi and Syrian regimes were long unable to create stability, partly because there was no one with Nasir's stature or charismatic appeal, but also because both countries were deeply divided along sectarian and regional lines. In the case of Iraq, the perennial Kurdish struggle for autonomy undermined national leaders, who were unable to deal with it effectively. A constant danger of coups kept each country from concentrating on basic problems, and repeated purges of army officers drained the defense capability.

INTENSIFICATION OF THE ARAB-ISRAELI CONFLICT IN THE MID-1960S

During this time the Palestine question had not gone away. The number of aggrieved Arab Palestinians continued to grow, while Israel was further consolidated by gradual immigration and by economic development, although by 1966 the country was experiencing increasing unemployment and emigration. The former patterns of Israeli party politics continued, with Mapai (later to form the core of a broader Labour Party) the dominant coalition partner in each government. Ben-Gurion retired in 1963 but continued to bedevil his successor, Prime Minister Levi Eshkol, with accusations of weakness and to quarrel over who was responsible in the Lavon affair. He and a few of his cohorts, including Dayan, led their own breakaway party for a while.

From time to time "retaliatory" raids continued to be launched against Jordan and Syria. Because of the presence of the UNEF, the Egyptian frontier remained quiet. But the arms race intensified. Israel obtained weapons from France and other Western countries, while Soviet supplies to Egypt continued. Israel launched a guided missile in 1961, and Egypt offered high salaries to European scientists to help it match the Israeli achievement. Since most of these were West Germans, this led to an Israeli propaganda campaign against "Nazis" in Egypt. The Israeli Secret Service started sending letter bombs to the scientists, and this helped to undermine Egypt's missile project.

An Israeli project to divert water from the Jordan River to irrigate land in the Negev desert was scheduled for completion in 1964. This provided an issue that brought the Arabs together for a while. Citing Israeli military power and Arab weakness, President Nasir continued to reject calls for the restoration of Palestinian rights by force. Now he hosted a series of Arab summit conferences to deal with the Jordan River problem. As he relaxed his antimonarchical policy for about a year, a show of Arab solidarity ensued. A plan to divert the Jordan's tributaries in Lebanon and Syria was adopted. This was really a tacit agreement to acquiesce in Israel's action by limiting the Arabs' usage to the share that the earlier American proposals had allotted to them. But, since other Arab leaders, such as the Syrians, were involved in formulating this policy, they could not blame Nasir for being so "soft" on Israel.

The 1964 summit conference also agreed to establish a Palestine Liberation Organization (PLO). Some Arab leaders, beginning in 1959, had proposed an entity to represent the Palestinians. Again leaders such as Nasir seemed to go along with calls for militancy, but the PLO was really designed to be ineffective. It established a small Palestine Liberation Army (PLA) in the Gaza Strip which, however, was kept under Egyptian supervision. Ahmad Shuqayri, who became the head of the PLO, was known to be inept and capable only of loud talk, which aided Israeli propaganda. But most Arab leaders seemed to be glad to substitute talk for action. Another, more authentic Palestine resistance group, Fatah (a reverse acronym in Arabic for "Movement for the Liberation of Palestine"), which may have existed informally on a small scale even in the 1950s, also emerged under the leadership of a popular Cairo-educated engineer, Yasir Arafat.

By this time radical Arab governments were recurrently colliding with the anti-Communist West. France was an exception, as the end of the Algerian War permitted it gradually to improve its relationship with the Arab world, although the de facto Franco-Israeli alliance was not repudiated until 1967. Prodded by the United States, West Germany provided arms to Israel from the early 1960s on, and most Arab countries broke diplomatic relations with Bonn in 1965 because of its recognition of the Jewish state. Guerrilla warfare against British rule flared up in Aden, with Egypt aiding the Front for the Liberation of Southern Yemen (FLOSY). Egypt also broke off relations with Britain in 1965 because of its refusal to take action against the white minority government in Rhodesia.

United States–Egyptian relations, which had become unusually amicable during the administration of President John F. Kennedy, deteriorated after Lyndon Johnson succeeded to the presidency in 1963. Johnson seemed to detest nationalist leaders such as Nasir, and several incidents helped to increase the strain. In 1964 some Egyptian officials organized a demonstration in Cairo of black African students against United States policy in the Congo. The demonstration got out of hand, with the students burning the American Information Library. Although Cairo apologized for this incident, Egyptian policy in Yemen and conflict with pro-American "reactionaries" further disrupted relations with the United States. When the Saudi and Iranian monarchs proposed an Islamic summit conference in December 1965, Nasir attacked it as an attempt to create a new "reactionary" alliance against "progressive" regimes, and the conservative-revolutionary conflict intensified. With coups backed by the CIA in countries such as Indonesia and Ghana, Nasir got the impression that Washington was working to destroy radical nationalist regimes throughout the Third World. In his eyes the cutoff of American wheat sales to Egypt in 1966 was confirmation. For Nasir the establishment of a United States–backed rightist dictatorship in Greece in April 1967 seemed to provide another warning of things to come elsewhere in the region.

In February 1966 a new faction of the Ba'th took control of Syria. A physician, Nur al-Din Atassi, became president, with General Salah al-Jadid the real strongman. Disproportionately representing the minority Alawite community, a traditionally underprivileged group living in the coastal region north of Lebanon, this new breed of Ba'thists was more Marxist than pan-Arabist and espoused a newly militant antiimperialism and anti-Zionism. One of its new approaches was to allow Fatah to carry out commando raids on Israel from Syrian territory, though the raiders usually crossed into Israel via Jordan, whose Palestinian population and long armistice line facilitated such acts. The new Syrian leaders were basically more anti-Nasir than were their predecessors, but Cairo entered into a security treaty with Damascus in order to be in a position to restrain it from rash acts.

THE 1967 WAR

The Arab-Israeli conflict exploded again in November 1966 as Israeli forces crossed into the West Bank of Jordan to destroy the village of al-Samu in retaliation for guerrilla raids. Israel received the strongest condemnation ever from the Security Council, with warnings of action if such an attack occurred again. While Arabs considered this and other UN resolutions inadequate responses to aggressive attacks, Israelis branded them one-sided and hypocritical. The Palestinians were in turmoil, and King Husayn, unable to protect them, again seemed endangered by revolution.

The crisis continued into 1967. Israeli leaders repeatedly threatened to invade Syria to topple its government if it did not stop supporting guerrillas. In April, Israeli jets crossed into Syrian airspace to engage in a dogfight that downed several Syrian planes. There were reports of Israeli troops concentrating near the Syrian frontier. Meanwhile, Nasir's Arab critics broadcast statements ridiculing him for posing as a great Arab leader while hiding behind the "skirts" of the UN. It was obvious that the UNEF would make it difficult for Egypt to come to the aid of Syria if the latter was attacked.

With this in mind Egyptian authorities asked the UNEF on May 16 to pull back from some sections of the armistice line. Secretary-General U Thant recognized that the force had no legal right to stay without Egypt's permission but gave President Nasir the choice of having it stay where it was or seeing it completely withdrawn from Egyptian territory. Nasir chose the latter alternative, and Israel rejected a request to allow the force to move over to its side. As the UNEF units left Sharm al-Shaykh, Egypt announced the closure of the Gulf of Aqaba to Israeli shipping, an act that no one expected Tel-Aviv to tolerate willingly. For Egypt, this seemed to be the removal of the last "fruit of [the 1956] aggression," and Nasir's prestige soared again in the Arab world. But an Israeli armed attack on Egypt appeared increasingly likely.

The Egyptian army went on full alert, and large-scale reinforcements moved into the Sinai. Israel then began to call up its reserves, as a general expectation of war emerged. Prime Minister Eshkol's cabinet was enlarged to include all Israeli parties except the Communists. Even the Herut party of Menachem Begin, then normally regarded as a fringe group by more moderate Israelis, joined the government. On popular demand Dayan became minister of defense, a development which seemed to be a signal that force would be used.

The Israeli public was led to expect an Egyptian attack, although several generals, including the chief of staff, General Yitzhak Rabin, later admitted that there had been no basis for this. But while American and Israeli military experts knew that the Egyptian army was hopelessly weak (especially with its best forces tied down in Yemen), much of the Israeli public began to feel threatened with destruction. Correspondingly, some Palestinians experienced a euphoric feeling that the day of their return might be near. This was particularly true after King Husayn flew to Cairo on May 30 to end his feud with President Nasir and to conclude an alliance.

There were threats on all sides. Much of the world's press stressed President Nasir's threat to make any war started by his foe a total one, in which the destruction of Israel as a state would be the aim. What was often omitted from these reports was his promise not to start a war. In any case, contrary to his former opinion, he seems to have decided that his armed forces were adequate to ward off an Israeli attack or, if not, that Israel would only occupy a little territory and then be pressured by the UN to withdraw. As the major powers warned both sides not to start a war, it was announced that the American and Egyptian vice presidents would visit each other's capitals on June 7, and there was reason to think that a compromise was in the offing. Perhaps, aside from having restored his leadership in the Arab world, Nasir believed that the cards then in his hands would allow him to impose on Israel at least some Arab demands regarding Palestinian refugees and territory it still held in excess of what the UN had allotted twenty years before. But this was the sort of settlement that Israel was not prepared to tolerate.

Instead, Israel saw a chance to end the Arab-Israeli conflict on its own terms and delivered a devastating surprise attack on Egypt on June 5. The Egyptian air force hardly knew what was happening before the enemy virtually destroyed it on the ground. With no air cover, Egyptian troops in the bleak Sinai desert were quickly routed and fell back in disarray. Thousands were captured and then turned loose without shoes or water to try their luck trekking across the burning sand. In 1995, Israeli sources revealed that their forces had gunned down many of the Egyptian prisoners after they surrendered. Jordan and Syria entered the war against Israel, and several other Arab states sent token contributions, but their forces were quickly repelled. In the Security Council, the United States, despite President Johnson's later expression of regret that Israel had started the fighting (others say he provided a "green light"), opposed Soviet demands for a quick cease-fire and withdrawal. Finally, a cease-fire was voted without any mention of withdrawal. Israel, however, went ahead with a campaign against Syria.

On June 11, six days after the battles had started, the cease-fire became effective. Israel now occupied territories more than three times its own size. These included what had up to now been left of Arab Palestine (the West Bank of Jordan, including Arab Jerusalem, and the Gaza Strip) and all of Sinai and southwestern Syria (the Golan Heights). A new group of refugees emerged, as roughly 400,000 fled or were expelled from the West Bank and the Gaza Strip, although not—as in the case of other territories in 1948—to an extent that undid the Palestinian Arab character of these areas. However, during and soon after the fighting, the Golan Heights, including the city of Qunaytra, were nearly cleared of their population of about 140,000. Sunken ships blocked the Suez Canal, and the Israelis occupying its eastern bank refused to allow the Egyptians to reopen it for seven years.

THE AFTERMATH OF THE 1967 WAR

Israeli jubilation was matched by the Arabs' despair. Not only had they been proven inept and weak and found an unbearable situation imposed on them, but the authority of their leaders was also undermined. Admitting his acceptance of full blame for the "setback," Nasir announced his resignation from the presidency. But, aside from an unending affection for their leader, millions of Egyptians united to deprive the Israelis of the joy of having ousted him. Nasir responded to the overwhelming popular plea by agreeing to stay in office until the Arabs' humiliation could be removed. Any real hope for economic growth had to be put aside indefinitely. Several Egyptian generals were tried and punished for negligence. Amir was dismissed and was arrested after being caught plotting a coup. He killed himself soon after. Student demonstrators called for reforms and more severe punishment for the generals, and Nasir supported some of their demands. He announced attempts to strengthen the ASU and—among other changes—brought several university professors into the government.

Zionism appeared to the world as a uniquely successful movement. Jewish immigration to Israel, even from the United States to a minor extent, began to swell again. With a growth rate of 10 percent a year, an economic boom was on, and the inhabitants of the newly occupied territories increasingly provided the manual labor. For a short while after the June war most Israelis assumed that peace was imminent, but the "telephone call" from Cairo that Dayan and others said they expected did not come. In any case, Israel had come to be rated as a military power of no mean dimensions. The idea that it was an important "strategic asset"—as some had long argued, particularly after the 1956 war—gained increasing importance in Washington, complementing the influence of the pro-Israeli forces in domestic politics.

Israel at first announced that it had no territorial aspirations and that it only wanted to force the Arabs to accept its right to exist in peace. But Arab suspicions were gradually confirmed as Israel began to talk about the necessity of "secure boundaries" and about areas that would not ever be evacuated. Arab Jerusalem was unilaterally annexed under the guise of "unifying" the city, and calls by the Security Council for rescission of this action were to no avail. A call for the return of the new refugees brought compliance in a handful of cases, obstructionism, and the eventual dropping of the issue. Israelis soon started planting settlements in the new territories.

Widespread sympathy for Israel throughout the world, much of which believed that the Arabs had provoked the war (or, at first, actually believed the Israeli claims that Arabs had fired the first shots), was gradually to diminish.

Before long most of the Arab states reluctantly began to acquiesce in the existence of Israel in order to concentrate on getting it to withdraw from newly occupied territories. An Arab summit meeting in Khartoum in August 1967, boycotted by militant Syria, agreed to try for a diplomatic solution but also attempted to avoid criticism from hard-liners by proclaiming a policy of "no negotiations, no peace, no recognition." The Khartoum meeting also brought an agreement by Nasir to withdraw from Yemen. To many people's surprise, the Yemeni regime survived, though with Sallal making way for another group of republican leaders. Some former royalists eventually joined the government, which veered in a conservative direction. The rift between "progressives" and "reactionaries" throughout the Arab world narrowed as the new circumstances forced Egypt to concentrate on the problem of Israel rather than on opposing monarchies. Egypt, Jordan, and Syria became the recipients of subsidies from oil-rich Saudi Arabia, Kuwait, and Libya.

A compromise plan, Security Council Resolution 242, was adopted in November 1967. While calling for an end to belligerency and for mutual recognition, the resolution also rejected "acquisition of territory by war" and reaffirmed the principle of "territorial integrity." It specifically called on Israel to withdraw from "occupied territories," although the failure of the English version, unlike the others, to specify "the" territories soon became the basis for an Israeli argument that withdrawal did not have to be complete. But while interpreting it in different ways, Israel, Egypt, and Jordan (and later Syria and the PLO) accepted the resolution as the basis for a settlement. In any case, American opposition prevented the adoption of any binding UN resolution demanding unilateral withdrawal—as in 1957—without an overall peace settlement.

For Arab monarchies Egypt's defeat may have seemed to provide a reprieve from Nasirite radicalism. But the resultant bitterness of Arab nationalists sometimes worked against status quo forces. When Southern Yemen won its independence in December 1967 the Nasir-supported FLOSY lost out, but to a more radical, Marxist group, the National Liberation Front. There was even an abortive coup in Saudi Arabia in 1969. The Iraqi government of President Abd al-Rahman Arif, who succeeded after his brother's accidental death in 1966, succumbed to a Ba'thist coup in 1968. The new Iraqi regime, headed by President Ahmad Hasan al-Bakr, adopted a militant, nationalistic stance that for several years often put it at odds with virtually the whole Arab world. Ba'thist Iraq, with which some of the original Syrian leaders of the party aligned themselves, persistently collided with the Ba'thist regime in Syria, where a pragmatic faction of the party, led by another Alawite, Hafiz al-Asad, came to power in a military coup in 1970.

In 1969 both the Sudan and Libya experienced military coups led by young, idealistic army officers, Ja'far al-Numayri in the Sudan and Mu'ammar al-Qadhdhafi in Libya. For these men Nasir was still the great Arab hero to be emulated. Among other results of the Libyan coup, the major United States air base at Wheelus Field had to be evacuated. The quixotic Qadhdhafi, who tended to see the world in terms of good and evil, began to push for Arab unity. He appeared to others either as a mad fanatic or else as a breath of fresh air, an island of naive virtue in an opportunistic world. One of Nasir's close associates described the Libyan leader as "scandalously pure," and Nasir once told him that he reminded him of himself as a youth. And while Numayri ultimately proved to be a conventional, even conservative figure, Qadh-dhafi never lost his ardor.

Another result of the 1967 war was Egypt's and Syria's increased dependence on the USSR. A massive Soviet resupply effort restored lost equipment, and Soviet advisors and trainers helped to correct demonstrated deficiencies. Facilities in Egypt-ian and Syrian ports opened to the Soviet navy, which became a potential challenge to the United States Sixth Fleet in the Mediterranean for the first time. Most Arab states severed diplomatic relations with the United States, which Egypt accused of participating in the June 5 attack. Nasir eventually admitted that this had been a mis-take, but it was later revealed that the United States did participate in the war, not by actually bombing Egyptian targets but by carrying out vital "damage assessment" flights that enabled the Israelis to know what targets to strike a second time. Contin-uing United States support for Israel prevented any improvement of relations with most Arab states. As the United States provided Israel with sophisticated weapons and aircraft, including Phantom fighter-bombers, many began to see the Arab-Israeli conflict as simply a theater of Soviet-American rivalry.

With Arab armies discredited, Palestinians increasingly began to believe that they must depend on themselves to defeat Israel. Fatah increased its commando raids and became the symbol of Arab resistance. After it inflicted severe casualties, with the Jordanian army's cooperation, on Israeli raiders at the village of Karamah in 1968, the guerrilla movement began to attract droves of volunteers. Fatah's new prestige also brought it control over the PLO, now essentially an umbrella for vari-ous guerrilla groups. Arafat became the head of the PLO as well as of Fatah.

Other guerrilla organizations outdid Fatah in militancy. George Habash, a Palestinian Christian pediatrician and former leader of the (Nasirite) Arab National Movement, now turned to Marxism-Leninism. Habash headed the Popular Front for the Liberation of Palestine (PFLP), which called for revolution in the Arab world as a prelude to liberating his own country. The PFLP, which later spawned several breakaway groups, became known for its spectacular terrorist activities against Is-raeli interests throughout the world and particularly for airplane hijacking. Both the outright radical groups such as the PFLP and the more widely based Fatah, which unites individuals of diverse political philosophies, called for the defeat of Israel and its transformation into a "secular democratic Palestine." They were calling for Jews and Arabs to live together, a goal that Israelis usually dismissed with derision as be-ing patently insincere. (The Palestinian National Charter only specified those Jews who lived in Palestine before the "Zionist invasion," but various Palestinian leaders later broadened this to include other Israeli Jews.)

Various moves to settle the conflict gained no headway. Such were the efforts of the UN representative Gunnar Jarring of Sweden, as well as Big Two and Big Four meetings. Sporadic battles raged along the cease-fire lines, and Israeli shelling destroyed Egyptian cities on the western side of the Suez Canal and forced their people to flee. Hoping to evoke international pressure for a settlement, Egypt began a "War of Attrition" in the form of regular artillery fire across the canal in 1969. Israel, in turn, completed a seemingly invulnerable series of fortifications known as the Bar-Lev line and eventually escalated the conflict to the level of "deep penetration" raids that reached military and civilian targets near Cairo. Only when Egypt obtained the most up-to-date surface-to-air missiles, manned by Soviet technicians, did the deep penetration raids stop, although the war continued in the canal area for a while.

In July 1970 Egypt and Israel, the latter now led by Prime Minister Golda Meir, accepted a United States plan for a temporary cease-fire and increased efforts by Jarring to work out a settlement. This precipitated a massive round of hijackings by the PFLP. King Husayn, in turn, brutally suppressed the resistance movement in his territory. The guerrillas had become a threat to his rule and to his plans for peace with Israel.

After "Black September," as the month of their defeat came to be known, the Palestinian guerrillas were barred from Jordan, whose regime became for a while a pariah in the Arab world. With United States and Israeli threats of intervention on the king's behalf, Arab talk about helping the guerrillas came to naught, a short-lived Syrian crossing into northern Jordan notwithstanding. There also were unsuccessful attempts by the small, predominantly Maronite Lebanese army to suppress the guerrillas in 1969, but, in the years after "Black September," Lebanon became the main focus of Palestinian resistance.

As Nasir frantically engaged in inter-Arab peacemaking during the Jordanian-Palestinian crisis of 1970, he suffered a fatal heart attack. Unprecedented mourning, only partly organized by the government, demonstrated that his popularity among Egyptians and other Arabs had outlived all his reverses, and the Arab world seemed to have suffered another heavy blow.

One of Nasir's oldest associates, Anwar al-Sadat, who was vice president at the time, automatically succeeded to the presidency. With a reputation as a bumbling protégé of Nasir, Sadat was hardly expected to last long. For his potential rivals he seemed to be an ideal choice as an interim chief of state precisely because he was not a real contender. But a series of masterful political tactics soon demonstrated that he had always been underrated. As an early step in consolidating his position (and allegedly foiling a conspiracy against himself), Sadat purged his regime of members of a generally more leftist, pro-Soviet faction led by Vice Premier Ali Sabri, who had been a main proponent of a strong one-party system when he headed the ASU in the mid-1960s. Sadat increasingly gave his own stamp to the regime. With the voices that had pushed with little success for deeper revolutionary transformation now muted, Sadat's regime began to turn to the right and to favor the interests of the emerging privileged classes.

Sadat loosened Egyptian ties with the USSR. Although an Egyptian-Soviet Treaty of Friendship and Cooperation, concluded in 1971, paradoxically appeared to be a further shift from nonalignment to an openly pro-Soviet role, this only camouflaged increasing disenchantment with Moscow. Egyptians tended to see the Russians as overbearing and as being unwilling—especially in the context of an emerging Soviet-American détente in the early 1970s—to provide the kind of weapons required to end the "no war, no peace" situation. In 1972 Sadat suddenly expelled most of the Soviet advisors, not only to end a situation that leading public figures in Egypt saw as putting their country's independence in question but also in the hope that the United States would now adopt a less pro-Israeli stance and work for an acceptable settlement.

Sadat was bewildered when Washington's policy did not change. Although the Israeli victory had stirred up radical forces and made the Arabs more dependent on the USSR, the United States apparently had begun to see Israel more than ever as an invincible instrument ("strategic asset") to keep the Arab world in line. A powerful Israel seemed to mesh well with the Nixon Doctrine, already announced by President Richard Nixon in 1969, according to which the United States' Asian allies would be armed to act as its regional police. Following this approach, a settlement of the Arab-Israeli conflict was less desirable than a continuation of an Israeli-imposed peace. And some observers believe that both Washington and Tel Aviv had concluded that by waiting a few more years they could obtain better terms for the latter in a settlement.

While not openly rejecting the Nasir era, Sadat turned Egypt gradually away from its revolutionary orientation. Some pro–United States figures who had been imprisoned or exiled under Nasir were now given important positions, and some previously sequestered property reverted to its original owners. Harsh attacks on Nasir's policies began to appear openly in print. Sadat showed continuity with his predecessor's policy for a while by agreeing to establish a loose, and eventually meaningless, Federation of Arab Republics with Libya and Syria. But he also began to put emphasis on friendship with and aid from an increasingly rich Saudi Arabia, while he and Qadhdhafi began to grow wary of each other. There was an accelerating trend from Arab to Egyptian nationalism. In response to emotional Libyan appeals for a full merger of the two countries, Sadat dragged his feet and eventually put off Qadhdhafi with an agreement in principle to unite, but without any timetable.

After declaring 1971—and then 1972—the "year of decision" in the conflict with Israel Sadat became an international laughingstock when nothing happened. Although he once said that his generation of Arabs could not be expected to establish diplomatic relations with Israel, he went to considerable lengths to express his willingness to make peace, but without results. For example, when Jarring addressed identical notes to Egypt and Israel in 1971 proposing an Israeli withdrawal from all of Sinai in return for a peace agreement, Sadat readily accepted. But Israel angrily ended all dealings with the UN representative.

Israel became more and more famous for derring-do that made the Arabs look hopelessly inept. An Israeli assassination squad entered Beirut in 1973 and was able to kill several PLO officials without getting caught. With more conventional commando raids largely ruled out after the guerrillas' demise in Jordan, small Palestinian groups increasingly resorted to international terrorism to publicize their cause. Thus the world was stunned in 1972 when a group representing a minuscule Palestinian faction called Black September took eleven Israeli athletes hostage during the Olympic Games in Munich in an attempt to force the release of Palestinian prisoners in Israel; a West German rescue attempt ended with the killing of the captives and most of the captors. Each Palestinian action brought massive reprisals in the form of air raids on guerrilla bases and refugee camps in Lebanon. Israeli and Palestinian agents sought out and assassinated each other in Western Europe. To the Arabs Israeli arrogance seemed incomparable when a Libyan civil airliner that accidentally veered into the airspace over the Sinai in 1973 was shot down, resulting in over a hundred deaths. Also, the governing Labour Party in the upcoming elections, scheduled for October 1973, ran on a platform calling for increased Israeli settlements in the occupied territories. A final Egyptian plea to the Security Council in June met the rebuff of a United States veto. Aside from growing diplomatic support from black African countries and some weakening of Israel's support in Western Europe, the Arab cause seemed hopeless.

IRAN: SEEMING UPSURGE
AND SIMMERING OPPOSITION

The absolute monarchical pattern that had emerged in Iran by 1955 was further consolidated during the subsequent two decades. The continuing existence of the 1906 Constitution made little difference in practice. The "king of kings and light of the Aryans," Muhammad Riza Shah Pahlavi, ruled entirely through his loyal servants, keeping them tame by playing one off against another and encouraging each to outdo the others in corruption so he could use such behavior against whomever he pleased whenever this suited his purposes. The electoral process tolerated only rival supporters of the shah. In 1957 he tried to create a two-party system by fiat, even assigning politicians arbitrarily to the ruling party and the equally pro-shah "opposition." The parliamentary elections of 1960 were so notoriously corrupt that the embarrassed shah decided to hold new ones. Ruthless security forces, including the secret police agency, the State Security and Intelligence Organization (Savak), ferreted out those of questionable loyalty and subjected them to imprisonment and torture.

In an effort to preempt a revolution from below, and with the Kennedy administration's nudging, the shah launched his own "White Revolution." Pressure from Washington brought to power during much of 1961–1962 a reformist cabinet headed by Ali Amini, about whom the shah had strong misgivings. In 1963 the program was submitted to a referendum and won the expected 99 percent approval. The key feature of the program was land reform, which, as subsequently enacted, required owners to sell holdings in excess of one village to the government for resale in small plots to cultivators. A second phase provided for further division of estates, although owners were allowed alternatives, such as mechanization and new forms of tenancy. There was a later trend toward large-scale "agribusiness." The government succeeded in presenting itself as enlightened and progressive in much of the Western world. Indeed, a few peasants, mostly those who already were relatively well off, gained from the land reform, but the overwhelming majority did not. The ouster of the ardently reformist minister of agriculture, Hasan Arsanjani, in March 1963 deprived the forces of change of much of the momentum that had existed, while the Johnson administration's generally uncritical attitude toward the shah was another factor.

Iran was closely aligned with the United States. Membership in the Baghdad Pact and endorsement of the Eisenhower Doctrine, as well as the acceptance of over $600 million in U.S. economic and military aid between 1953 and 1967, were matched by hostile Soviet radio propaganda and Soviet support for the exiled leaders of the Tudeh party.

In the early 1960s Iran began to normalize its relationship with the USSR. This in part represented a delayed response to Moscow's disavowal, following Stalin's death in 1953, of its post–World War II expansionism. Tehran's announcement in 1962 that it would not allow the United States to establish missile bases on its territory provided a signal that began the normalization process. Soviet-Iranian cooperation emerged in certain fields, such as in the USSR's construction of a steel mill in Isfahan in return for Iranian natural gas. The shah later even purchased some military equipment from the USSR. Largely reflecting the worldwide easing of cold war tensions, this did not invoke any real shift from Tehran's pro–United States position.

The shah kept aloof from Arab causes. There was always strong anti-Israel sentiment at the popular level, and the regime usually supported the Arabs in UN votes and in other superficial ways. But Tehran never considered the Arab-Israeli conflict its concern and recognized Tel-Aviv as early as 1950. The shah's announcement a decade later that he was ready to exchange diplomatic representatives with Israel precipitated a break in Egyptian-Iranian relations that lasted another ten years. Occasional references by Arabs to the right of their brethren in Khuzistan (adjacent to Iraq) to self-determination, Iran's long-standing claim to Bahrain (dropped only in 1970), the shah's aspiration to dominate the Persian Gulf (now tellingly renamed the "Arab" Gulf by the countries bordering on the other three sides), and a special fear of the influence of radical Arab regimes with close ties to the USSR propelled Iran into a de facto alliance with Israel. Iranian army officers and Savak got Israeli training, and Iran became Israel's major source of oil. Savak and its Israeli and Turkish counterparts allegedly formed an organization for close cooperation in the intelligence field in the late 1950s. On the other hand, Tehran-Baghdad relations were especially bitter by the early 1970s, with Iran in 1969 renouncing the 1937 treaty that recognized Iraq's title to most of the Shatt al-Arab, the river that forms part of the boundary between the two countries. Iran and Israel provided support for Iraqi Kurdish rebels.

Iran began to assert its hegemony in the Persian Gulf and even to extend its power into the Indian Ocean. The withdrawal of British forces from the Gulf in 1971 and the emergence of several independent Arab amirates provided an important fillip for this Iranian aspiration. Meeting with the shah in 1972, President Nixon assured him of the availability of unlimited quantities of conventional armaments. Now the shah's forces, soon bloated by the purchase of massive amounts of such military equipment, could fill the vacuum the British withdrawal created in the Gulf in a way that made Iran a prime example of the kind of regional police envisaged in the Nixon Doctrine. Among other actions in keeping with the new role, Iranian forces, in collusion with the departing British, seized three islands belonging to the emerging United Arab Emirates (UAE) in 1971 and evoked increased resentment in the Arab world. An Iranian expeditionary force managed to suppress a leftist, Southern Yemeni–supported revolt in Oman's Dhufar Province during the mid-1970s. The apprehensiveness of conservative Arab countries such as Saudi Arabia (sometimes described as constituting, with Iran, "the twin pillars" of United States policy in the Gulf) was numbed by a common concern with combating revolutionaries and Soviet influence.

The shah's military power was made possible by dramatic growth of oil revenues. This allowed the Plan Organization—the agency set up in 1949 to take charge of developmental efforts—to carry out a series of economic plans seemingly with unusual success. American economic aid ended in 1967, not as a punishment but rather marking a completed mission. During the decade starting in 1963 Iran registered a real growth rate of more than 10 percent a year, and the annual per-capita income reached $500. Among other indices of economic change, less than half the work force was engaged in agriculture by the early 1970s; but from another point of view this demonstrated the extent to which neglect of agriculture was pushing peasants off the land into fast-growing urban slums. Tehran's population in 1973 was 3.3 million, more than double its size a decade earlier. Technical and managerial weakness notwithstanding, industry was gaining diversity, though not efficiency.

When in 1971 the shah held a gala celebration of the alleged 2,500th anniversary of the Iranian monarchy, it was in the spirit of an approaching resurgence of greatness going back to the Achaemenids. Others, however, discerned a megalomaniacal and insecure ruler dedicated to his own personal grandeur, piling up weapons like toys at his people's expense. Critics of the regime claimed that the Iranian people gained nothing from the new wealth. While gains indeed went disproportionately to the wealthy and intensified class divisions, a wide section of society was apparently experiencing improvements during this period. However, social advancement did not match the rising per-capita income, and studies that take into account infant mortality, life expectancy, and literacy rates reveal an Iran whose material well-being during the early 1970s was no higher than Egypt's and India's and was lower than Turkey's and Syria's.

Most outside observers failed to comprehend the strength of opposition to the regime. The great majority of the people did not identify with it, and its achievements were not popularly perceived as national achievements. Indeed, Iranians mostly thought of the shah as a puppet of the United States, although some specialists argue that an initial dependence made way for a more normal alliance during the 1960s. The monarchy's identification with pre-Islamic Iran flew in the face of religious people who traced their spiritual lineage to the early Muslims rather than to the Sassanians.

Much in the tradition of their involvement in opposition to autocracy and foreign domination in 1890 and 1906, the Iranian *ulama* led a serious challenge to the shah's rule in the early 1960s. In 1963 a leading religious scholar (and *marja-i taqlid* of millions), Ayatullah Ruhullah Khumayni, fiercely denounced the regime, and his subsequent arrest ignited a large-scale uprising that the army was able to suppress but which foreshadowed bigger results to come. Again, in October 1964, Ayatullah Khumayni attacked the government following the adoption of a bill exempting United States military advisors and their dependants from the jurisdiction of Iranian courts. Many Iranians viewed this as shameless servility toward the United States and, in effect, a renewal of the old capitulations. Again, massive riots ensued, with thousands of people shot in the streets, but at the time the revolt proved abortive. Khumayni was arrested and sent into a foreign exile that lasted until 1979.

The regime succeeded in picturing Khumayni's movement as purely reactionary, opposing land reform and female suffrage. Indeed, many *ulama* had previously opposed the land reform program, partly because of the effects it had on the pious endowments they administered. But Khumayni never raised these issues. Far from being an ally of the landlords, he spoke on behalf of the "downtrodden" and against the "dwellers in palaces." He also attacked the regime's ties with Israel. In fact, he represented a radical faction within the *ulama,* as shown by his later untraditionalist open rejection of the monarchy in favor of an "Islamic Republic" or even by his teaching of a usually disfavored subject such as philosophy.

Older opposition movements such as the National Front and the Communist Tudeh party waned, but new ones arose. Some, like that of the sociologist Ali Shari'ati, called for a socialist society based on a reinterpreted Islam. For example, Shari'ati argued that the story of Cain and Abel symbolized the class struggle. New Marxist groups, including the People's Fida'iyin and the militantly Islamic socialist People's Mujahidin, arose among youths in the early 1970s and turned to sporadic guerrilla warfare against the regime. Several attempts to assassinate the shah were foiled. But the regime kept the strong support of the upper class, the army, and the police, and temporarily won the backing or at least the passive acceptance of parts of the middle class either by providing lucrative jobs or by making opposition look foolhardy.

TURKEY: A SICK MAN AGAIN?

If Iranian fortunes rose in some respects during this period, the earlier Turkish success story turned sour. The Democratic government continued to overspend on development and on the army during the late 1950s; inflation and balance of payments deficits became rampant. But as modern, educated, urban groups became increasingly disenchanted with the government's economic policies and its relaxation in the face of Islamic resurgence, the rural Turkish majority was won over by these policies and also by Democratic support for agriculture and such rural improvements as road building. In a situation of growing polarization of public opinion, Prime Minister Adnan Menderes won the adulation of the less westernized elements and sometimes even was hailed as a prophet and worker of miracles. If he was the first Turkish leader to have any claim of heading a Western-style democracy, this was being eroded as more and more ardent opposition brought more repression. Legislation allowing the government greater authority to restrict the press, the closing of some newspapers, new rules restricting political campaigns, and arbitrary violations of the tenure of judges and university professors undermined the constitutional system. Democratic victories registered in successive elections for the Grand National Assembly (GNA) seemed to represent a built-in rural majority, and an increasingly tyrannical one. The army was even ordered to hinder the movement of the revered old national hero and People's Republican Party (PRP) leader, Ismet Inönü, during a speaking campaign in 1960.

The actions against Inönü helped bring the crisis to a head. Student demonstrations brought on martial law and the closing of the universities. Then the war college cadets marched in protest. On May 27, 1960, the army stepped in, and a thirty-eight-member junta, the National Unity Committee, headed by General Cemal Gürsel, took power. A "High Court of Justice," established to try 601 officials of the previous government, found most of them guilty of violating the Constitution and other charges. Twelve people, including Menderes, were subsequently executed.

The Turkish army's brutality was matched by an unusual inclination to return to its barracks. The failure of two attempted coups in 1962 by army officers favoring continued military rule showed that this was not the dominant trend. A Constituent Assembly wrote a new constitution, which set up a system of checks and balances, including a bicameral GNA (National Assembly and Senate) and restraints on legislative power protected by a Constitutional Court. This was intended to limit the tyranny of the democratically elected majority in the future. The Constitution was approved in a national referendum in 1961, although the mere 60 percent majority it received seemed to be a warning that much of the Turkish nation remained loyal to the now-proscribed Democratic party. It is possible that the junta's determination to go ahead with Menderes's execution was bolstered by a realization that his popularity would otherwise eventually bring him back to power. But with the army continuing to serve as the watchdog, the Second Turkish Republic restored the electoral, constitutional process.

A Turkish age of trouble lingered on. With the general elections of October 1961 giving the PRP the largest number of seats in the GNA, Inönü headed a new government based on a shifting coalition of parties, which at first oddly included the new Justice Party. The latter, which was supported heavily by rural voters (except in the most conservative regions in the east, where minor parties flourished), was essentially the successor to the Democrats. In 1965 the Justice Party got an absolute majority in the GNA, and its leader, Süleyman Demirel, became prime minister. By 1969 a tendency of the parties to splinter made him again dependent on a shaky coalition.

By this time Turkey was rife with conflict. Militant groups grew on both the extreme right and the extreme left, and also among the Kurdish minority. Class divisions came to the fore as guerrillas engaged in terrorism, and the government seemed unable to cope with them or with the deeper social and economic problems coming from burgeoning cities and landless peasantry in some areas. In 1971 the top military officers intervened again in a "coup by communiqué" that led to a government of army-backed technocrats headed by a former PRP member, Nihat Erim. Martial law and other restrictions on civil liberties followed. But weak coalition governments soon emerged again, with a new polarization of the conservative Justice Party and the PRP. The latter was now led by the journalist Bülent Ecevit, and it began to assume the role of a left-of-center, social democratic party favoring labor unions and land reform. It then seemed to be reduced to a permanent minority position.

Turkish foreign policy gradually shifted away from its total identification with the United States–led camp. The waning of the cold war and the Soviet Union's renunciation of its post–World War II demands facilitated a degree of normalization of relations with that country, as demonstrated by growing trade and official visits. The alliance with the United States lost some of its former centrality as other issues evoked anti-American sentiment. The problem of Cyprus, with its roughly 18 percent Turkish population living amid a Greek majority, gained attention during the late 1950s, with Turkey resisting any plan for *Enosis* ("union") of Cyprus and Greece. The island gained independence from Great Britain in 1960 under a compromise formula forbidding *Enosis* and with cumbersome procedures designed to protect the Turks from unlimited majority rule, but the scheme soon proved unworkable. The possibility of Turkish military intervention in Cyprus evoked a harsh, threatening letter from President Johnson in 1964. This caused much bitterness in Turkey toward the United States, whose attempts during the early 1970s to have that country ban the growth of opium brought additional resentment. No one could take Turkey's allegiance for granted any more, although its continuing alignment with the United States still had a solid base in public opinion. No major party favored withdrawing from NATO or adopting nonalignment.

A BRIGHT SPOT: OIL

While large countries such as Turkey and Egypt continued to endure poverty, oil provided unprecedented riches for those bordering on the Persian Gulf. An industrial world that had become increasingly dependent on oil slowly was growing aware of an approaching "energy crisis" by the 1970s. Saudi Arabia alone possessed one-fourth of the world's proven oil reserves, and its goodwill was coming to be recognized as essential in order to prevent a severe shortage in the future. The effective use of oil as a political weapon in the Arab-Israeli conflict began to seem more feasible than before, although most oil-importing nations still were not ready to worry much about such a possibility.

Oil had long been a bonanza for some Middle Eastern countries. A small underpopulated state such as Kuwait now had a per-capita income exceeding that of any Western country. It combined a nearly absolute monarchy (a freely elected parliament—representing only 3 percent of the population—notwithstanding) and a traditional social structure with an enviable modern welfare state. The impact of oil revenues on countries such as Iraq and Saudi Arabia already was significant, though still far from Kuwait's fairy-tale version. Saudi Arabia's annual oil revenue reached

$5 billion in 1973, but fewer than 11,000 pupils—including only 700 girls—were enrolled in secondary schools. In terms of the literacy rate, average life expectancy, and the like, it was one of the world's most underdeveloped countries.

From the late 1950s on, oil exporters were subject to unfavorable trends. A few large Western companies controlled the industry. The world was experiencing an "oil glut," and the bargaining power of producer governments was nearly nil. With Iran's experience during the early 1950s in mind, even radical regimes were long afraid of considering nationalization. The companies were able to lower at will the "posted prices" on which payments were based. Such a reduction in 1960 evoked the formation of an Organization of Petroleum Exporting Countries (OPEC) for collective bargaining, but for another decade only a few minor gains were registered.

Then a convergence of several factors brought the first breakthrough in the early 1970s. The closing of the Suez Canal as a result of the Israeli occupation of the Sinai cost the world billions of dollars in extra shipping costs. This also made North African oil particularly attractive to Europe. By now, both Algeria and, even more so, Libya were important producers, although their resources were minor in comparison with those of the Persian Gulf countries. The temporary accidental disruption of the pipeline crossing Syria in 1970, at a time of increased demand for oil in Europe, gave the North African countries extra leverage. And this was soon after the militantly nationalistic regime of Qadhdhafi came to power. With Libya holding out for higher prices and using nationalization as a threat, the companies succumbed. In 1971 negotiations in Tehran between OPEC and the oil companies brought a general increase of $0.33 in the posted price. Subsequent increases raised the posted price per barrel of oil, which was (depending on the variety) $1.80 in 1970, to $2.59 by early 1973. Revised arrangements also began to give producer countries greater control. The Libyan government took over some of the operations in 1971, and Baghdad nationalized the Iraq Petroleum Company in 1972. The consortium of Western companies set up in 1954 turned over full control of the industry to the Iranian government in 1973 in return for a privileged position as contractor and buyer. Other countries began to get "participation" agreements, whereby they obtained partial, but gradually increasing, ownership of the oil operations.

CONCLUSIONS

From 1955 on, Middle Eastern peoples confronted the remnants of Western colonial rule and undertook serious efforts to modernize. Phrases such as "positive neutralism," "nonalignment," "Arab socialism," "five-year plan," and "Palestinian resistance" epitomized the continuing domestic and international struggle. By the early 1970s, the last outposts of formal colonialism were gone, but weakness perpetuated more subtle kinds. The wealth that a few countries now received from oil was matched by the seemingly insurmountable economic problems of more populous countries. There was little indication of progress in developing viable political orders, and internal and intraregional conflict held back the area. Even Turkey, one

Middle Eastern country that had previously seemed to find its way, suffered severe economic and political maladies.

The Arabs' encounters with Israel exposed their weakness more than ever. The occupation of additional territory and displacement of more people intensified bitterness not only against Zionism but also against those Western nations that, in a crunch, seemed to the Arabs always to apply a double standard to them. The conflict seemed interminable as Arabs refused to accept the unbearable terms of their seemingly invincible foe.

10

the crossing and after
1973–1996

On October 6, 1973, Egyptian and Syrian artillery broke the calm of "no war, no peace" in the Arab-Israeli confrontation. Few imagined that the Arabs would dare fight what experience had shown to be an unbeatable enemy. Even the Israelis and the CIA failed until nearly the last minute to take obvious Syrian and Egyptian war preparations seriously. The offensive came at an unlikely time, during the Muslims' holy month of Ramadan. It took the name "Operation Badr," after the historic victory of the early Muslims over their Meccan persecutors. This was also the holiest day of the Jewish calendar, Yom Kippur ("The Day of Atonement").

The Egyptians had skillfully planned for a time when the light of the moon and the water currents in the Suez Canal would be optimal for an offensive. Egyptian commandos had already slipped over to the other side to close off the pipes through which burning napalm was supposed to pour into the water if an army ever tried to cross. After the artillery cleared the way, Egyptian troops began to cross the canal in rubber boats and then over the pontoon bridges that they quickly put into place. High-pressure water hoses washed away the mountains of sand that the Israelis had piled up as a further barrier, and the Bar-Lev line began to crumble. Simultaneously, the Syrian army moved into the Golan Heights.

An already surprised world was incredulous when it discovered that the Egyptian and Syrian armies had not been immediately crushed. Early victories reported by the Israelis that much of the world tended to take at face value turned out to be just as fictitious as Arab accounts had been in 1967. Using Soviet-made antitank and antiaircraft weapons, the Syrians temporarily retook most of the Golan Heights, while Egyptian forces recovered a strip of territory all along the eastern side of the canal. The Arabs themselves were amazed to see that they had achieved more in a short time than they had ever thought possible. Their main purpose had been to stir the world from its apathy in order to stimulate movement toward a diplomatic settlement of the conflict, and they hoped that success in occupying small beachheads would be sufficient for this. The Egyptians eventually pushed farther in an attempt to take the strategic mountain passes. It is sometimes argued that only a lack of confidence prevented them from moving on successfully to this objective while the initial momentum of surprise made it possible. Indeed, some Israeli leaders panicked as the Arabs seemed momentarily to pose a threat to their existence. According to one Israeli account, Golda Meir wept as a distraught Moshe Dayan proposed that his country surrender. But there also are reports that the Israelis at one point were getting ready to use nuclear weapons.

WHOSE VICTORY?

If the October War[1] destroyed the assumption of Israeli invincibility, it hardly brought an Arab military victory. After mobilizing their reserves, the Israelis at first concentrated on driving the Syrian army back to the former cease-fire line. Then they pushed on to occupy a salient that ended less than twenty miles from Damascus, now in range of Israeli artillery fire. For a while, the prospect of an occupation of the Syrian capital seemed real, although it is likely that long-range dangers of holding such areas, with their hostile populations, would in any case have induced the Israelis to steer clear of this. But the Syrians avoided a disorderly rout and managed to hold a defensive line. A still viable Syrian army, aided by contingents from such countries as Morocco, Iraq, and Jordan, was able to keep fighting as the enemy began to concentrate on its southern front.

The tide of battle also turned in the Suez Canal area as a massive airlift of weapons from the United States—allegedly designed in part to make resorting to the nuclear option unnecessary—restored the capability of the Israeli army. The USSR resupplied the Egyptians and Syrians. With a tank battle of legendary proportions raging in the Sinai, the Israelis found a gap in the Egyptian center, between the Second Army in the north and the Third Army in the south. Before their enemy realized what was happening, a few Israeli tanks slipped through and crossed to the western side of the Suez Canal. Wreaking havoc on Egypt's antiaircraft defense from the rear, the Israeli force began to grow as more troops and heavy weapons crossed over. The Security Council ordered a cease-fire on October 22, but the Israelis kept up their offensive for several more days. After the United States rejected a Soviet suggestion

---

[1] Pro-Israeli writers usually call this the "Yom Kippur War," while Arabs and their supporters use the term "Ramadan War." More neutral terms include both "Fourth Arab-Israeli War" and "October War."

that the two powers send in a joint force to stop the fighting, the seeming prospect of a unilateral Soviet intervention on Egypt's side was checkmated when United States armed forces throughout the world went on alert. The Israeli-occupied area on the western bank, which now extended all the way to the Gulf of Suez, covered more square miles than did the Egyptian-held parts of Sinai. Egypt's First Army, defending the capital, was depleted, and the road to Cairo seemed to offer a relatively easy challenge to the Israelis. The Egyptian Third Army was nearly surrounded, and supplies were cut off.

While the Israelis had again won militarily, the October War was an Arab victory in some ways. At least the Arabs felt that they had regained their honor, for no one now disputed that they too could fight. Egypt's success completed the process whereby Sadat became not just Nasir's interim successor but a leader in his own right. The possibility of a greater victory for the Arabs in the future no longer seemed far-fetched to the rest of the world, and Arabs tended to forget about the actual military outcome of the October War. Sadat later pointed out that he had missiles aimed at enemy cities. While this may have helped deter the Israelis from further advances, the use of such missiles would have also brought retaliation and unbearable losses for Egypt. But, aside from the fact that it forced diplomatic overtures for peace, the "Crossing" appeared as a great, historic turning point to the ebullient Arabs and to the increasingly pessimistic Israelis. The "Crossing" came to refer to not just one amphibious operation, but also symbolically conveyed the idea that Arabs had, or were about to, catch up with the modern world. To others, though, the "Crossing" was from Nasir's era to Sadat's; from the perspective of many Arabs, the latter seemed paradoxically to become one of capitulation to forces so long defied.

The Israelis began to feel that suddenly everything was going wrong. Over 2,500 Israelis were killed in the 1973 war, far fewer than the number of Arab losses but too many for the state's small population to take without severe trauma. The period between 1967 and 1973 seemed like a dream that turned into a nightmare. The Israelis were still determined, and a post-1973 military buildup gave them a new edge. But they now seemed less sure that they could survive in the long run. It became well known, though not fully admitted officially, that they had developed nuclear weapons, which could be used in a dire situation. But it was assumed that some Arab states also would get these weapons, making a future war mutually suicidal. Tel-Aviv's dependence on the United States became more obvious during the 1973 war. American aid, mainly military, eventually surpassed $3 billion a year, and Israelis knew that this could be used as leverage, especially if their intransigence seemed to threaten the oil supply.

While some Western countries continued to strongly support Israel, it increasingly took on the role of an international pariah. Even West European countries were now so wary of antagonizing the Arabs—and also genuinely critical of Israeli policies—that only the rightist dictatorship in Portugal, soon overthrown, allowed American planes resupplying Israel to use its airspace. Virtually all black African governments that had not already done so broke off relations with Israel in the aftermath of the 1973 war. In part, this was in response to the importance of Arab oil and the large amounts of Arab economic aid made possible by higher oil prices. But it was also a result of an increasing tendency to see Israel as a European settler state, a Middle Eastern version of South Africa. Growing Israeli–South African cooperation—particularly in military matters, including the joint production of nuclear weapons—was widely presented as evidence of a basic affinity between the two societies. Reflecting the new voting strength of non-Western countries, the UN General Assembly officially declared Zionism to be a form of racism in 1975, evoking bitter rejection by the United States and a few other Western governments. It often seemed likely that Israel would be excluded from the General Assembly, but Washington's opposition kept this from happening.

Economic woes ate away at Israeli morale. The inflation rate leaped upward, exceeding 130 percent in 1980 and jumping past the 1,000 percent mark during some months in the mid-1980s. Only the adoption of austerity measures in 1985 brought inflation down to more moderate levels, but at the expense of creating unemployment in its place. Public opinion polls showed that large portions of the population favored a more authoritarian type of government. The possibility of vastly increased immigration from the USSR provided a gleam of hope for a while. But continuing Soviet restrictions and a growing tendency for Jewish emigrants to settle elsewhere brought disappointment. In fact, Israel began to experience a net loss of emigrants over immigrants. Only in 1989, as the emigration of Soviet Jews escalated and as their admission to the United States began to face restrictions, did the Israeli dream of having a substantial influx of immigrants begin to come true. This created corresponding fears among the Palestinians that more extreme Zionist plans for absorbing the occupied territories could be implemented. Although Israel repeatedly was able to behave with great arrogance toward a divided Arab world, few Israelis expected that what were to them the heady years between 1967 and 1973 would ever resume.

Israeli politics were subject to increasing strains. The Arab minority grew to over 17 percent of the population and identified more and more with Palestinian nationalism. Arabs may have formed a slight majority in Galilee by the 1980s. Reflecting resentment against attempts to "Judaize" the area by confiscating their land, and against governmental neglect, Arabs in Israel increasingly voted for the small Communist party and then, by the late 1980s, for Islamists. Within the Jewish community, blame for being caught napping in 1973 became another divisive factor, although a commission appointed to study the situation relieved the Israeli leaders of blame. In any case, popular dissatisfaction led Prime Minister Meir and Defense Minister Dayan to resign. Meir's successor as prime minister, Yitzhak Rabin, also had to resign when it was revealed that he had an illegal foreign bank account, and other scandals began to surface.

The hawkish right-wing Likud, the successor to a series of parties whose origin went back to Herut and the terrorist Irgun (and Revisionist Zionism) emerged as the largest political bloc. The old Irgun leader, Menachem Begin, became prime minister after the 1977 elections. Support for the Likud by the Oriental Jews (by now a majority of the Jewish population—immigration from the USSR and its successor states in the 1990s would make this no longer true—but with average per-capita income less than half as high as those of European background) was a major factor in its success. The Orientals expressed their discontent with the Labour government, but they continued—though somewhat less so after another election four years later—to suffer from their usual underrepresentation in the Cabinet and the Knesset. Whereas before the "earthquake" election of 1977 the Labour alignment had seemed to provide the permanent core for government coalitions, the best it was able to do during the late 1980s was to participate with the Likud in "governments of national unity." Orthodox religious parties grew in influence and were able to exert increasing leverage on the formation of coalition governments; secular Jews demonstrated hostility to them to the extent that violence broke out on some occasions. Particularly divisive was the religious parties' demand for legislation narrowing the definition of the word "Jew." This threatened to undermine support for Israel among American Jews, some of whom would have been excluded on grounds of having been converted by non-Orthodox rabbis. The Israelis were also polarized by such issues as the Lebanon War of 1982, which evoked protests by hundreds of thousands but enjoyed the ardent backing of even larger numbers on the right wing.

MOVES TOWARD ARAB-ISRAELI PEACE

A series of steps toward peace emerged from the October War. Although the United States gave unprecedented help to Israel during the war, it also realized that an overwhelming Israeli victory would in the long run not serve anybody's purposes. Fearing Soviet involvement, the United States pressured the Israelis to allow supplies to reach Egypt's beleaguered Third Army via a regular corridor. Secretary of State Henry Kissinger flew from capital to capital trying to work out agreements on troop disengagement. In January 1974 an Egyptian-Israeli agreement provided for an Israeli withdrawal to a line several miles east of the Suez Canal, with limited force zones and a new United Nations Emergency Force in between. A similar agreement between Israel and Syria, also concluded through Kissinger's shuttle diplomacy, brought an Israeli withdrawal from its newly occupied salient and from another narrow slice of territory, including the city of Qunaytra. The Israelis, however, utterly obliterated that city just before returning it. In another round of shuttle diplomacy, Kissinger arranged for a further minor Israeli withdrawal on the Sinai front in 1975.

Sadat began to calculate that he had much to gain by strengthening ties with the United States, which would be able to pressure Israel into a settlement. Egypt became the leading recipient of American economic aid, which soon exceeded $1 billion a year, and eventually rose to over $2 billion. An "opening" to the United States and other capitalist countries also was expected to draw massive private investment, although an uncertain political situation and a cumbersome bureaucracy helped to prevent this from occurring. Correspondingly, relations with the USSR deteriorated, and the supply of weapons dried up. With Moscow refusing to reschedule the payments on Cairo's $5 billion debt, Sadat unilaterally renounced the Treaty of Friendship and Cooperation. As a result he forfeited any opportunity to get Soviet weapons again, and the United States also was unwilling to provide much military aid to a frontline Arab state in the conflict with Israel. The Egyptian military capacity kept deteriorating while the USSR built the Syrian and Iraqi armies to new levels. However, the United States would begin a massive arms supply to Egypt after the latter made peace with Israel in 1979.

A Geneva Conference, jointly chaired by the United States and the USSR, opened briefly in December 1973 to move toward a comprehensive Arab-Israeli settlement. But the Conference never reconvened, partly because Israel and the United States preferred to keep the USSR out of the picture and also to work toward separate peace between Israel and particular Arab states that would leave the former in a position to settle the Palestinian problem on its own terms. In any case, the unwillingness of the United States and Israel to allow PLO participation in a peace conference, which was now otherwise generally being called for, became another big roadblock. While Americans talked about the "peace process," critics of United States policy saw this as a euphemism for bypassing the road to real peace.

The dominant elements in the PLO now expressed their willingness to establish a Palestinian authority in the West Bank and the Gaza Strip. Except for small "rejectionist" groups such as the PFLP (long supported by Libya and Iraq), Palestinian leaders relegated their goal of a unified, nonsectarian Palestine to a distant "dream." The PLO continued to object to UN Security Council Resolution 242's failure to call for a Palestinian state. Until the late 1980s, it did not officially commit itself in advance to peace with Israel, but there were indications that such a stance would emerge as part of a settlement.

In 1974 an Arab summit conference in Rabat, Morocco, unanimously proclaimed the PLO to be the "sole legitimate representative" of the Palestinian people. Jordan no longer claimed to represent the West Bank, at least not openly. But Israel, backed by the United States, adamantly refused to negotiate with the PLO on the ground that the latter is a "terrorist" organization, which negates the Jewish state's "right to exist." In any case Israel rejected the idea of establishing a Palestinian state. For some Israelis, including the Likud bloc, the West Bank ("Judea and Samaria," as they call it) is an integral part of the ancient—and thus the modern—Jewish homeland and cannot be given up. The Labour alignment generally was willing to return part of the area (annexation of which would endanger Israel's Jewish character in the long run) to Jordan, but not to a separate Palestinian state.

CONFLICT WITHIN
THE ARAB WORLD

The unprecedented Arab unity of October 1973 soon gave way to new levels of inter-Arab conflict. The 1975 Egyptian-Israeli disengagement agreement embittered some Arabs, particularly Syria and the Palestinians, for Egypt seemed to be deserting its allies in order to recover what it could of its own territories. Rivalry between the two Ba'thist regimes in Damascus and Baghdad also intensified. By contrast, Iraq and non-Arab Iran established normal relations in 1975. Baghdad accepted Iranian sovereignty over part of the Shatt al-Arab in return for an end to Tehran's help for the troublesome Kurdish rebellion. This revolt, the renewal of which the United States and Iran had promoted in 1974, not with the goal of actually allowing the Kurds to achieve their objectives but in order to weaken militant Iraq, immediately collapsed. With Qadhdhafi aspiring to inherit Nasir's mantle as an Arab leader and resenting Sadat's conciliatory attitude toward Israel and coolness toward Arab nationalism, Libya strengthened its ties with the USSR, and a bitter antagonism began to color relations between Egypt and Libya. Mutual subversion became rife, and Sadat launched an indecisive air attack on Libyan forces in 1977.

Lebanon became a maelstrom of local and inter-Arab conflict. Right-wing Maronite Lebanese, notably the Phalangists, resented the growing Palestinian presence in the country and blamed it for Israeli attacks. Other Lebanese, mainly Muslims, aspired to end the domination of the Christian minority and also identified with the Palestinian cause. Two largely Muslim "belts of misery"—the southern, eastern, and northern parts of the country and a crescent of slums around Beirut enlarged by flights of Shi'ites from Israeli raids in the south—formed around the prosperous, largely Christian sections. Beginning in 1975 civil war pitted rightist Maronites against a "leftist" coalition of Palestinians and Lebanese—mostly Muslims but also including many Christians, especially non-Maronites. The war left almost 100,000 dead by the early 1980s. Syrian troops intervened in 1976, not to impose defeat on the rightists, as might have been assumed, but rather to act as mediators. In fact, the Syrians saved the rightists from defeat and allowed them to brutally overwhelm some armed Palestinian refugee camps. With Saudi pressure to end the crisis, Syrian troops soon became the core of an Arab League peacekeeping force, and in effect Damascus's hegemony over the country was accepted. The rightists continued to control part of the country, and Israel refused to permit the Arab force to enter the south, where the war between Maronite rightists and Palestinians continued. Reacting to guerrilla raids, Israel occupied much of the area in 1978. In response to international pressures, the invaders withdrew in favor of a UN peacekeeping force but also left a buffer zone controlled by rightist clients, the South Lebanon Army (SLA). Lebanon continued to witness chaos periodically, with Syrian forces sometimes clashing with rightists. Even greater violence arose among various leftist and Palestinian factions and among rival rightist groups. Also, Israeli incursions into the south continued from time to time. But worse was to come from 1982 on.

AN EGYPTIAN-ISRAELI PEACE

In the Arab-Israeli arena, the new administration of United States President Jimmy Carter in 1977 at first seemed ready for a comprehensive settlement involving some kind of Palestinian "homeland." In October, Washington and Moscow accordingly agreed to reconvene the Geneva Conference. But Sadat, who apparently had been approached indirectly by the Israelis with suggestions of a separate settlement that would enable him to get the Sinai back, was eager to assure himself a central role in negotiations and wanted a quick settlement that would allow him to concentrate on Egypt's severe economic problems and to consolidate his alliance with the United States. In November, he consequently initiated a new kind of "electric shock" diplomacy by announcing his willingness to visit Israel. Responding to the invitation that immediately followed, he flew there to speak before the Knesset. With most of the Arab world fearing a sellout, an anti-Sadat "Steadfastness Front" (Syria, Libya, Algeria, South Yemen, and the PLO but not still ultramilitant and anti-Syrian Iraq) was unable to foil his plans, and oil-rich monarchies seemed for a while quietly to accept the new tactic by continuing their aid.

A meeting of Sadat, Begin, and Carter at Camp David, Maryland, in September 1978 managed to work out a framework for a future peace treaty that would gradually return all of Sinai to Egypt in return for fully amicable relations between the two longtime foes. Israel also committed itself to negotiate with Egypt, Jordan, and local Palestinian leaders (but not the PLO) with regard to establishing autonomy and an end to the military government (though not the military presence) in the West Bank and Gaza Strip. The agreement committed Israel then to try to move toward a settlement of the final status of these territories within another five-year period. The nature of the settlement—whether these areas would be annexed to Israel, become an independent Palestinian state, or whatever—was not specified in advance.

Most Arab governments believed that a separate peace between Egypt and Israel would leave the latter in a position to offer a settlement on its own terms as the only alternative to the status quo. In response to the Camp David agreements the Steadfastness Front announced its intention to bring Sadat down, and a summit meeting of all other Arab League members condemned his policy and agreed to impose sanctions if he concluded a peace treaty. Even conservative oil-rich regimes, such as that of Saudi Arabia, on which Egypt was heavily dependent for economic aid, started to show their anger. Perhaps the ongoing revolution in Iran—which was moving it into the anti-Israel camp—made them fear that they too would be vulnerable if they supported policies that went against the nationalist and Islamic grain. In what some observers saw as potentially further counterbalancing the loss of Egypt to the anti-Israel camp, Iraq and Syria began to patch up their old differences and to talk about a future merger. However, the rapprochement soon made way for greater antagonism than ever between the regimes in Damascus and Baghdad.

Some Israelis foresaw that relinquishing the Sinai would be a prelude to pressures for withdrawal from the other occupied areas and feared a piecemeal achievement of Arab objectives. They argued that Israel was being induced to give up tangible benefits—the Sinai's strategic depth and its oil (hereafter available only at market prices), as well as removing settlements and air bases at great expense—in return for friendly relations with Egypt that might be illusory or might simply evaporate in the future.

After repeated setbacks, intensive diplomatic efforts in March 1979 succeeded in concluding an Egyptian-Israeli peace treaty and a framework for the future settlement of the status of the West Bank and Gaza Strip, basically along the lines agreed on at Camp David. A decision of other Arab states to suspend Egypt's membership in the Arab League (whose headquarters were moved to Tunis) and to sever economic and diplomatic relations with Cairo initiated a new phase of inter-Arab animosity. New levels of United States military and economic aid to both Egypt and Israel emerged, and Sadat was accused by his enemies of trying to replace Iran as Washington's policeman in a tacit alliance with Israel.

For a while, Sadat's new approach seemed to evoke widespread popular backing in Egypt, based on a resurgence of local (as opposed to pan-Arab) nationalism and also on the hope that peace would bring prosperity. Still, growing resentment against an alleged new role as a United States surrogate and against the separate peace, particularly as the promise of prosperity failed to bear fruit, began to strengthen militantly anti-Sadat forces, especially those with an Islamic cast.

With both local Palestinian leaders and the Jordanian government refusing to participate, subsequent Egyptian-Israeli negotiations on establishing autonomy for the West Bank and Gaza Strip provided little to vindicate Sadat's approach in the Arab world. The Israelis argued that they had never accepted the principle of autonomy for the area, but only for its "inhabitants." Israeli proposals called for an administrative council that would have no legislative or judicial authority. Arab East Jerusalem, excluded from the Israeli definition of the West Bank, was to be denied representation on such a council. Israel refused to consider ending its now-accelerated policy of establishing Jewish settlements, including some on land that continued to be expropriated from Arab owners. Nor would it allow any autonomous authority the right to control water resources—already being drained away from Palestinian villages by the deep wells that only the new settlers were permitted to drill—or to control public land. Any possibility of independence, even at the end of the transition period, was utterly rejected as the Israeli government insisted that it had a historic and God-given right to the territories and that they were vital to its security.

Palestinians spoke with contempt of proposals that made South African bantustans (all-black enclaves with limited self-government but with bogus independence) seem appealing in comparison. Backed by growing world opinion that blamed Israeli intransigence, Cairo also considered such proposals unworthy of consideration. Tensions recurrently flared up in the occupied Palestinian territories, as Israeli troops sometimes fired on student demonstrators and sent local officials into exile, detained people without trial, and razed the homes of the families of those accused of supporting "terrorists." Indeed, both Palestinians and Israelis became victims of the other side's terrorist attacks. Egypt sometimes temporarily broke off the autonomy talks to protest against Israeli policies, as in the case of Israel's formal declaration in 1980 that the whole of Jerusalem was the Israeli capital. The failure of an expected Labour Party victory to materialize in the 1981 Israeli elections ended the only hope for a breakthrough in the negotiations, although no major group in Israel appeared willing to accept complete withdrawal from the occupied territories or the establishment of a Palestinian state. On a bilateral level the Egyptian-Israeli "peace process" continued, with an exchange of ambassadors coming on schedule, and the withdrawal from Sinai was completed in 1982. At least for the foreseeable future, Egypt was outside the circle of Israel's enemies, who thus could offer no credible military challenge. But the Israeli desire for truly friendly relations with Egypt—as in the development of trade, tourism, and joint economic projects—was unattainable while other Arabs remained under occupation.

REVOLUTION IN WORLD ECONOMICS

In 1973 the Arabs supplemented their new military power with economic leverage. In order to induce the world to put pressure on Israel during and after the October War, Arab oil exporters announced that they would reduce production in stages until the occupation of Arab territories ended. Only those countries adopting stands favorable to the Arab position were to be exempt from the consequences of this action. A total boycott was declared against the United States because of its aid to Israel. It is unclear to what extent the producers really carried out such actions. In any case, there were "leaks," and the boycott and cutback ended early in 1974, without the final objective being achieved, but real or imagined fuel shortages in many countries made them take the Arabs seriously. Utterly dependent on Middle Eastern oil, Japan and Western Europe countries fell in line with demands that they proclaim their support for a complete Israeli withdrawal.

A byproduct of the use of the oil weapon was a sudden jump in prices that made the increases of the early 1970s seem small in comparison. For a while shortages produced by the cutback caused oil to be auctioned off at as much as $20 a barrel. From now on, OPEC was able to dictate prices without having to negotiate with the companies. Oil that went for $2.59 a barrel in early 1973 sold for $11.65 a year later. Price hikes continued from time to time but were minimized by the resistance of some Arab monarchies, particularly Saudi Arabia, whose small population and high level of production evoked less need for increases than was true of countries such as Iran or Algeria. Also, fearing adverse economic consequences for the non-Communist world (and despite the danger of further alienating more nationalistic elements), the Saudi regime was in a position to increase production and thus undermine price increases set by other OPEC members.

The price per barrel was scheduled to reach $14.55 in 1979 (cheaper than five years earlier if one considers inflation), when revolution in Iran—until then second only to Saudi Arabia in oil exports—and resultant cuts in production generated a new series of price explosions. By the end of 1980 the cost per barrel ranged from $32 to $41, as economic forces seemed for a while to make collective price-setting almost redundant. However, as Saudi Arabia increased its production and as high prices helped bring decreasing demand, the ensuing glut forced prices down. OPEC settled on a common price of $34 per barrel for its "benchmark" grade late in 1981.

Prices plunged as low as $10 per barrel in 1985, as Saudi Arabia refused to continue its "swing producer" role. An OPEC agreement on production quotas in

1988 tried to maintain the price at $18 per barrel, but without much success as some countries persistently sold extra oil in violation of the agreement. Major producers with small populations were insulated from dire consequences (and, in the case of such a state as Kuwait, had massive investments in Western countries). But others, such as Iran and Algeria, faced financial hardship. In July 1990, Iraq, whose military spending during the war with Iran had left it heavily in debt, mobilized troops on its border with Kuwait, whose cheating was driving oil prices down. The threat succeeded in bringing prices back up, and the OPEC meeting that convened soon afterward set new quotas aimed at establishing a price of $21 per barrel. But this proved to be a mere prelude to more dramatic events the following month.

Even with setbacks, the ironic phenomenon of rich but underdeveloped countries remained. Countries such as Kuwait and the UAE that long enjoyed the distinction of having the world's highest per capita GNPs still found themselves listed by the World Bank among the "high-income economies" in the late 1980s, with per capita GNPs in the $15,000 range, a little lower than that of the United States. Saudi Arabia's figure of $6,200 put it alongside Spain and Ireland, as well as Israel, the only non-oil-producing country in the Middle East that reached a comparable economic level.

Other Middle Eastern states remained poor. Admittedly, Egypt had an annual per capital GNP ($680 in 1987) that was double that of a truly poor nation such as India. The Middle East did not have such extremely poor countries (unless areas on the periphery, such as Afghanistan or Somalia, are included). Turkey had a per capita GNP of $1,210 in 1987, while Syria's and Jordan's were in the $1,500 range. There were millions of unemployed or underemployed people of rural origin in the slums of Turkish or Egyptian cities. These people had been pushed out by the utter hopelessness of life in their overpopulated native villages. Cairo's population, for instance, approached 10 million by the late 1970s. For these unfortunates, figures on national per capita GNPs provide a notoriously superficial indication of well-being, particularly in light of the highly unequal distribution of wealth. The oil exporters provided a new source of aid, along with jobs and remittances, that brought noticeable increases in the standard of living for wide sectors of society throughout the region. The "temporary" workers from poor countries, including two million Egyptians and two million other Arabs, thus came to make up a majority of the population in some Persian Gulf countries during the early 1980s. But that source of livelihood too dried up to a great extent with the end of the boom in the producer countries, with the resulting hardship providing a new impetus for Islamist movements.

The rich realized that money alone would not solve their own problems. The benefits could last only if they were used to finance the difficult and uncertain process of economic development. Materials, machinery, expertise, and often most of the labor force were imported for building infrastructures—roads, airports, harbors, and such—and for developing industries. Saudi Arabia's fifth five-year plan (for 1989–1994) brought the total amount spent on development to slightly under $1 trillion.

Success was not assured, as industrialization was not simply a matter of building. Skills and modern habits were hard to come by. Even literacy, still limited to a minority of the adult population in most countries, could not be bought in the short run, although billions of dollars were being invested in schools and universities. A country that recently had had only a few literate people, Saudi Arabia had 1.5 million pupils enrolled in school by 1980. In terms of life expectancy, literacy, and infant mortality (which may be deemed meaningful indicators), Middle Eastern oil producers, arguably with the exception of Kuwait, still ranked clearly as underdeveloped countries, but by the 1980s they were no longer in the category of least developed.

WEAK POLITICAL ORDERS

Even less did money buy viable political orders. Most absolute monarchies gained a new lease on life as a result of the new wealth, but some only for a short time. In Saudi Arabia, for example, economic opportunities turned many heads away from political opposition. And potential challengers were restrained by the firm clutch of a gigantic royal family, whose perhaps three thousand princes filled many key positions. But the continuation of the past legitimacy of a regime controlled by one family was unlikely in a society being so rapidly exposed to modern developments such as urbanization and literacy. More people become politically relevant under such circumstances, and modern structures allowing for participation—either on a competitive basis or in a single-party system—seemed to be a prerequisite to effectiveness and stability. Signs soon appeared that the new wealth indeed was undermining the regime. A modern educated group—the so-called "new middle class"—grew and demanded opportunities of a professional and a political nature, and pious Muslims reacted against rampant materialism, inequality, and corruption, as well as the kingdom's perceived role as a United States client. To many, the Saudi regime no longer remained a true Islamic government, despite its revivalist origins and its continuing enforcement of the *shari'ah*. According to critics of the royal family, all the strict Islamic rules enforced on the ordinary people were violated within palace walls. In keeping with the quasi-democratic ideals of early Islam, the idea was taking hold that both kingship and extremes of economic inequality are un-Islamic.

The Saudi regime underwent a terrible shock in November of 1979, as the Islamic year 1400 began, when armed rebels took over the Grand Mosque in Mecca, the seat of the Ka'bah. Led by a fervent Wahhabi in the tradition of the Ikhwan movement that King Abd al-Aziz suppressed in the 1920s, Muhammad al-Utaybi, the rebels denounced the Saudi family's corruption and deviation from Islam. They may have planned uprisings in other parts of the kingdom. Saudi troops were able to subdue and kill the rebels only after more than two weeks had passed, allegedly with the use of nerve gas, as recommended by French forces whose aid Riyadh desperately invited (for Muslims, a desecration of the holy site, from which nonbelievers are supposed to be excluded). The choice of this location as the site of rebellion helped to discredit the rebels, but not entirely, and stories are told of young men passionately awaiting an opportunity to join them. Both this and riots among the Shi'ite population of Saudi Arabia's Eastern Province in late 1979 and early 1980 helped to intensify doubt about the stability of the monarchy.

In the absence of a consensus based on strong liberal democratic traditions, of a strong sense of national identity, and of appropriate socioeconomic conditions, Western-style representative systems scarcely seemed to offer a real alternative. Those in Turkey and Lebanon had succumbed at least temporarily to chaos and military intervention (domestic or external) by 1980. The continuing vitality of elective, parliamentary procedures in Israel, a society established by immigrants from Europe, was an exception that confirmed the rule. Aside from the fact that the majority of Palestinians were refugees, Israel could not claim to be a democracy while retaining control over the Arab-inhabited Gaza Strip and West Bank short of becoming a binational state, which was hardly thinkable to many Israelis. As for Iran, the aftermath of the revolution provided some signs of a new synthesis of populist Islam and Western-originated democracy, and the new regime showed strength based on institutional procedures and widespread legitimacy that were absent in other countries. But, while elections and parliamentary debate as well as an innovative set of checks and balances demonstrated unusual vitality, the limits of free political competition grew narrow, while violent opposition evoked repression.

The Middle East has had little more success in attempts to establish viable radical authoritarian regimes based on single parties that involved the masses in a controlled way and provided new legitimate structures. Southern Yemen, whose Marxist ideology and Leninist-inspired Yemen Socialist Party (previously the National Liberation Front) emerged from one of the few popular revolutions in the area, at first seemed to provide a possible exception. But it too increasingly showed that it was a personalistic regime—one in which civil war became the arbiter of leadership in 1986. Weakened by the diminishing of the Soviet role in the area, Southern Yemen provided a rare example of Arab (or, at least, Yemeni) unity by merging with Northern Yemen in 1990. As for Libya, Qadhdhafi at first began an ASU on the Egyptian model but later turned to a unique kind of direct democracy involving a hierarchy of People's Congresses from the local level up. But his unwillingness to let the committees work freely dictated controls by "revolutionary committees" that stripped the whole structure of any meaning. Regimes established by military coups have had trouble transmuting themselves into anything more than shaky dictatorships resting on force. Charismatic leadership sometimes has provided a temporary basis for legitimacy, as in Nasir's case, but transferring this to permanent institutions has proved more difficult.

The Ba'thist regimes of Iraq and Syria were cases in point, although both showed some signs of having become true single-party regimes. (In each case, the Ba'th was united with some minor parties in a "national front.") It is notable that a nonmilitary party leader, Saddam Husayn, emerged as the dominant personality in the post-1968 Iraqi regime and finally assumed the presidency in 1979. He ruled through a party with an organization of devoted cadres that reached all facets of the society, including the army. At long last, the first parliamentary elections since the 1958 coup occurred in 1980; they allowed a limited choice but at least provided a start with the kind of symbolic act that helps to legitimatize real single-party regimes. Among the regime's successes in truly transforming the society was a compulsory literacy program in the late 1970s that made major strides. But continued repressiveness, including the execution of several of the new president's associates in 1979 on charges of plotting a coup and reports of hundreds of other executions in later months, pointed to underlying instability. Kurdish separatism boiled over in the 1980s in an alliance with Iran. For a while Baghdad seemed to be losing control of this part of the country and resorted to large-scale use of chemical weapons, including the mass killing of much of the population of the Kurdish town of Halabjah in 1988, and a dispersal of many Kurds to areas outside Kurdistan. By contrast, the regime's repressive apparatus prevented a similar revolt from emerging among the Shi'ites, whose location in the nonmountainous south made them easier to control. But the regime's leaders and following seemed largely limited to the Arab Sunni minority. Indeed, the leadership was essentially a personalistic clique hailing from one place, the town of Tikrit. Despite continuing revolutionary rhetoric, increasingly pragmatic policies made way for the emergence of a privileged class in both Iraq and Syria.

The Ba'thist regime in Syria shared the remarkable longevity and superficial stability of its Iraqi rival. The former's weaknesses were equally obvious. Corruption was on the upsurge, and widespread opposition of Islamists and others to the Alawite-dominated regime evoked increasing repression. The Muslim Brethren—membership in which became a capital offense—led a series of uprisings beginning in 1979, starting with an attack on the largely Alawite military academy in Aleppo that led to hundreds of deaths of people connected with the regime and to the execution of many of its opponents. The year 1982 saw a full-scale "fundamentalist" Sunni revolt in Hama that the army was able to suppress only by destroying much of the city and by killing thousands of people. Rival regional centers and sectarian diversity (despite a large Sunni majority) had always made Syria a difficult country to govern. President Asad was heavily dependent on the military, particularly on the mainly Alawite special forces headed by his corrupt brother, Rif'at Asad, until 1984. That year the latter went into exile following a struggle for succession among commanders of various forces that pushed the country to the edge of civil war, as the president was temporarily hospitalized.

Sadat's Egypt seemed to regress from the limited political development in Nasir's time. For a while Sadat permitted more freedom of expression than formerly existed, especially for rightists. Competitive—though clearly rigged—elections took place, but within limits that barred comparison with a true parliamentary system. Sadat began by allowing three "platforms" within the ASU—including small leftist and rightist "opposition" groups—to criticize his own majority faction. He permitted the three groups to act as separate political parties from 1976 on, and others, including a New Wafd, later joined them. In January 1977, violent riots broke out, directed heavily against the growing symbols of economic privilege and sparked by International

Monetary Fund proposals for removing subsidies on basic foodstuffs. Following the riots, a decree, backed by 99.4 percent of the voters in a plebiscite, made strikes and demonstrations punishable by hard labor. In 1978 the New Wafd decided to disband (it came back later). The leftist National Progressive party temporarily suspended its "mass political activities" after Sadat obtained a 98.27 percent affirmative vote in a referendum proposing that pro-Soviet and prerevolutionary parties be banned. He later announced the formal abolition of the ASU in favor of a National Democratic Party. Presumably this party would be guaranteed an overwhelming majority of the vote, while some minor parties would continue on the periphery. With Egypt's number of millionaires and even the extent of corruption allegedly exceeding their levels under King Faruq, Sadat did not seem to be following either the Western democratic or the revolutionary, mobilizational road to political development. The regime had become essentially a personal autocracy backed by the military and the police, as well as by affluent classes glad to be rid of Nasirite radicalism.

"Fundamentalist" Islamic organizations gained strength, particularly among Egyptian youths. University student bodies came under their control. Ultramilitant groups emerged, a case in point being one the authorities dubbed the "Society Making Accusations of Unbelief and Calling for Separation" (Takfir wa al-Hijrah). This organization earned this name by virtue of its insistence that most Egyptians were no longer real Muslims and had returned to the state of *jahiliyyah*, and its corresponding call for the few remaining faithful to isolate themselves as a prelude to restoring Islam. Moderate groups included the Muslim Brethren, who now seemed willing to work within the existing system and anxious to participate in elections. They also seemed supportive of private enterprise, rather than repeating calls for Islamic socialism.

Growing resentment against Sadat's domestic and foreign policies threatened to bring down the regime during the early 1980s. In September 1981, Sadat ordered the arrest of over 1,500 people, including former cabinet ministers and other prominent individuals. Accused of "religious fanaticism," they actually were a diverse group, only some of whom were religious zealots. Accusing the USSR of conspiring with his opponents, Sadat expelled the Soviet ambassador and the last remaining Soviet technicians.

Then on October 6, during the military parade celebrating the anniversary of the "Crossing," participants in the parade gunned down Sadat as he watched from the reviewing stand. The assassins were associated with an organization called "al-Jihad," which called for struggle against allegedly apostate rulers, and seemed to hope that their action would spark a revolution. They failed in that objective, as security forces suppressed the small-scale revolts that ensued in parts of Upper Egypt. But the popular reaction to Sadat's death was telling. While the First World, especially the American audience to whom he had played, joined in bereavement unprecedented for any foreign leader, the majority of his own people surprised many outsiders by showing little grief.

Sadat's vice president and handpicked successor Hosni Mubarak, a former air force commander, quickly took over the presidency with the usual, ritualistic 98.5

percent vote of approval. Many of the people Sadat had arrested were immediately released by Mubarak, and some were invited to the palace and interviewed on television. The regime won the backing of many of Sadat's opponents. Mubarak showed some signs of greater sensitivity to the gap between rich and poor and took action against certain symbols of conspicuous wealth and corruption with which Sadat had been associated. He even arrested the late president's brother, who had used his personal ties to enrich himself. Mubarak also tried to seem less accommodating than Sadat in dealing with Israel, although he was careful not to endanger the final stage of withdrawal from Sinai. This—despite growing Israeli reluctance—occurred on schedule in April 1982. Mubarak managed not only to hold on to the peace treaty with Israel, but also gradually throughout the 1980s to win back Egypt's acceptance into the ranks of Arab states.

The nature of the regime did not change much under Mubarak, whose low-key approach contrasted with Sadat's flamboyance. The new president did not seem so blatantly authoritarian. And yet real power remained in his hands, as he continued to be reelected without opposition, but—perhaps a measure of the much-touted democratization—now getting only 97.1 percent of the vote. Parliamentary elections became more competitive, but the government used vote rigging and other, more subtle means to guarantee that the opposition parties did not win anything approaching a majority of seats.

Symptoms of a potentially revolutionary situation continued to appear. Strikes, as in 1989, and riots were recurrent. For example, conscripted security forces, whose members were paid $4 a month, mutinied in 1986 and went on rampage for days against symbols of luxury before the army could get them under control. Perhaps it was the rioters' utter destructiveness that prevented them from sparking a wider revolt. Emergency laws in effect since 1967 continued to be invoked against opposition movements, most of which took on religious tones.

ISLAMIC RESURGENCE: THE ZEALOT APPROACH

The 1970s and 1980s saw increasing signs of Islam's vitality as a political force. In the first place, it was an expanding faith, largely because of the Muslims' continuing high birthrate at a time when modernization was increasing life expectancy. By 1990 the Muslims of the world numbered about a billion. As a case in point, some population projections gave the USSR—whose breakup soon afterward virtually nobody would have believed possible—a Muslim majority in less than a century. Immigration was rapidly making Muslims the biggest non-Christian group in Western Europe and America. Conversion to Islam was continuing in Africa and—now often in less heterodox forms than before—among black Americans.

Seemingly reversing the earlier trend toward secularization, Middle Eastern Muslims more and more asserted their Islamic identity. Many women in various countries who had looked on their mothers' or grandmothers' clothing as antiquated

292   The Crossing and After/1973–1996

began to return to wearing scarves and long dresses, often inaccurately described as "the veil" since face coverings usually were not a part of such Islamic dress.

Governments began to show new concern with shoring up their Islamic credentials. Qadhdhafi's regime in Libya—itself a target of Islamist opposition—supplemented its pan-Arabism with pan-Islamic—but in some ways unorthodox—tendencies from the start and also, along with the Sudan and Pakistan, restored some Islamic rules. Moves in Egypt to reinstate the death penalty for defection from Islam were rejected, and a new law in 1977 even imposed a few limitations on polygamy and easy divorce for men. But respect for religious sentiment was demonstrated by such actions as limiting the sale of alcoholic drinks and a constitutional amendment declaring the *shari'ah* the main source of Egyptian law. In fact, conservative regimes such as Sadat's encouraged the new trend as a weapon against leftists only to have it come back against them in a radical, populist, egalitarian form. The Islamist movement remained diverse, with some elements committed to the socioeconomic status quo and supported by wealthy businesspeople and the Saudi regime.

Numerous reasons for the seeming religious upsurge were suggested. Some pointed out that this was a worldwide phenomenon and, in a local context, extended to groups such as Copts too. Correspondingly, there were occasional violent incidents that pointed to a growing tension in Muslim-Coptic relations. Indeed, while Muslims and Christians sometimes remained united under an Arab nationalist banner, they faced enemies such as Israeli Jews and Lebanese Maronites who defined themselves in a sectarian way that may have encouraged emulation in their own camp. The conflict with Israel, notably over the issue of Jerusalem, was especially conducive to being seen in religious terms.

In some ways there was nothing new in this visibility of religion. Intersectarian identities always were fragile, and the masses had been most effectively moved by appeals to religion. The return to religion involved many dangers, including the alienation of secularists and Balkanization along sectarian lines, but it also promised to be more effective than secular nationalism precisely because it did not cut across the grain of deep-seated feelings. The Egyptian army's replacement of uninspiring secular slogans with "God is great" is said to have been one factor in the successful crossing of the Suez Canal in 1973. And while traditional values had a special appeal to people whose lives were disrupted by rapid change, the influx of millions of villagers into urban slums—and also the spread of literacy and of the mass media's impact—helped to politicize strata of the population for whom secularism always had been alien. Perhaps the secular elements of society were getting more numerous in the period of "Islamic resurgence," but the nonsecular masses were becoming more prominent and politically relevant. They also were reacting against increasing non-Islamic influences via television and the cinema as well as the physical presence of large numbers of Westerners and the existence of secular (including Marxist) movements and regimes.

Both successes and failures may have encouraged a religious upsurge. Defeat by Israel in 1967 left some Arabs with feelings that there was nowhere else to turn and sometimes that God would not have deserted them if they had been more faithful. Some governments, such as Nasir's, began to mute their secularism. Then, with the failure of secular movements to solve the area's problems and, after Nasir's death, the absence of another charismatic figure of comparable stature (before Khumayni's rise), religious fervor waited to fill the vacuum. Finally, many took the military and economic successes starting in 1973 as renewed proof of God's favor. This was a reversal of the centuries-old situation in which the course of history demoralized Muslims by flying in the face of the success that the faithful were supposed to experience. Still, the perception of continuing imperialist control and increased corruption, tyranny, and social injustice turned heads to radical movements, and those who phrased their calls for revolutionary change in Islamic terms possessed an enormous advantage.

IRAN'S ISLAMIC REVOLUTION

Iran provided special circumstances that enabled the zealot approach to find a remarkable manifestation. For the first time in the modern Middle East, a national government succumbed to a mass revolution, one that was largely unique up to that time in the twentieth century non-Western world in not being based on a Western ideology. Despite its partly traditionalist garb, Iran's upheaval showed some signs of portending the only truly revolutionary change the area had known.

Iran's undreamt-of riches after the oil price increases of 1973 evoked unprecedented grandiosity on the part of the shah's regime. Suddenly money was available to increase the allotment for the recently adopted five-year plan from $36 billion to $69 billion. By 1978 the average annual per capita GNP exceeded $2,000. Funds for the military especially burgeoned, as the armed forces grew to nearly half a million. Military purchases from the United States alone amounted to over $20 billion in six years.

Pardoxically, these riches provided a catalyst that hastened the shah's undoing. Military spending by a regime with which the populace had never identified only bred resentment, as did the influx of over 100,000 Westerners as technicians and advisors. Waste and corruption abounded. The country's infrastructure could not handle the flood of imports, and backlogs in ports brought shortages and delays in massive projects. Shortages of funds forced cutbacks in the wild spending in 1975. By contrast, relatively little was being spent on social development, with the literacy rate not surpassing 50 percent and with Tehran, its population swollen to over five million, lacking such amenities as a sewer system. Neglect of agriculture increased the need to import food. Most of all, overspending spawned uncontrollable inflation that reached 50 percent a year. The rich gained, but the plight of the majority actually worsened.

The opposition grew more active and ultimately encompassed the vast majority of the population. The government admitted to holding a few thousand political prisoners; the opposition put the figure at 100,000. According to one interpretation, short-lived liberalization in response to the Carter administration's emphasis on hu-

294 The Crossing and After/1973–1996

man rights whetted Iranian appetites for more freedom, while the regime quickly returned to former practices in the apparent belief that Washington was not seriously concerned with applying its declared principles to Iran.

Again, the Iranian *ulama* provided the opposition with its most potent leadership. The regime could hardly prevent people from going to the mosque, which thus provided a vital and unsurpassed communication network. When mullas[2] retold the stories of Umayyad depotism and of the battle of Karbala (the lesson of which historically had been the futility of resisting tyranny but which Ayatullah Ruhullah Khumayni and other radicals cited as the model for revolution), it was as though they were speaking in a well-understood code about their own time. For the masses, the inveterate opposition of Khumayni, now exiled at the mosque-college at Ali's grave in Najaf (Iraq), remained the most powerful influence. Diverse antishah leaders made their way to Najaf, and tape cassettes of Khumayni's sermons eluded the censors and were bootlegged in Iranian bazaars, keeping alive the call for revolution.

Riots broke out in Qum in January 1978 after the Iranian press published libelous accusations against Ayatullah Khumayni. Unrest soon spread over the whole country. The popular anger intensified as the army shot into the crowds, which produced a claim (undoubtedly exaggerated) that there were sixty thousand martyrs. A general strike brought oil production to a virtual halt and, with it, an end to the regime's economic prop.

A military government, headed by a loyal general, tried to restore order with martial law. Announced reforms, such as forbidding members of the royal family from engaging in business activities, which had provided lucrative opportunities for corruption, were to no avail. Neither was an attempt to name scapegoats, as in the arrest of Amir Abbas Hoveida, longtime prime minister and key figure in the shah's inner circle. Instead, the number of demonstrators against the regime—often crying "Death to the shah!"—swelled to several million.

By the beginning of 1979 the shah's position had deteriorated so far that he left the country ("on vacation") in a last-ditch attempt to stave off full-scale revolution. Before going, the shah instructed his generals to follow the advice of a visiting American general, Robert Huyser, with regard to the feasibility of a military coup. Shapur Bakhtiar, the only leader of the National Front now willing to play such a role, took the helm as prime minister. He instituted several changes, ranging from the abolition of Savak to banning the sale of oil to Israel and South Africa, but failed to appease the opposition. Most Iranians were satisfied with nothing less than the return of Khumayni, whose last months in exile were spent in France. He was no longer welcomed by an Iraqi regime anxious to preserve its rapprochement with the shah and fearful of an Islamic revolution that might not be limited to Iran. In France, Khumayni had freer access to other enemies of the Pahlavis and the advantage of coverage by the world's news media. For a while, Iranian airports were closed to keep him from returning.

---

[2] Mullas are ordinary *ulama,* as opposed to *mujtahids* (those qualified to exercise *ijtihad*). Top *mujtahids* are given the unique Shi'ite title of Ayatullah, literally "sign" (*ayat*) "of God" (*Allah*). The word *ayat* also refers to verses in the Qur'an.

The old regime finally disintegrated as Imam[3] Khumayni (to use the title that his followers increasingly were bestowing on him) flew to Iran in February 1979 amidst the rapturous response of millions. With common soldiers joining the crowds, whole army units attacking forces still loyal to the monarchy, and top commanders declaring the army's neutrality, Bakhtiar fled to rally counterrevolutionary forces abroad. The *imam* was able to designate Mahdi Bazargan, a French-educated engineer and leader of the moderate, liberal antishah Freedom Front, as the new prime minister in a prudent prelude to a later acceleration of the revolution.

Paralleling the moderate formal government were local committees and a Revolutionary Council, mostly representing the more militant *ulama*-dominated Islamic Republican party. Revolutionary Guards supplemented—and checked likely counterrevolutionary tendencies in—the largely shattered armed forces. Revolutionary tribunals carried out hasty trials that brought the executions to an estimated total of at least a thousand within the next eighteen months. Included were many members of the old elite who had not fled, as well as lesser individuals found guilty of torture and other crimes.

A militantly religious political system emerged. A plebiscite replaced the monarchy with an "Islamic Republic." A new constitution, approved by 98.2 percent of the voters, established a governmental structure—with a president, prime minister, and Consultative Assembly—that in many ways did not depart from modern Western patterns. (In each case, large numbers of people boycotted the election.)

Other provisions of the new constitution gave an Islamic character to the government. A Council of Guardians, with members chosen for six-year terms (partly by the Consultative Assembly) and not limited to the *ulama*, was given authority to determine whether proposed laws were contrary to Islam. (However, the very concept of law made by people was a deviation from Islamic traditionalism.) Another provision was unique, reflecting Khumayni's radical version of the Twelver doctrine of the role of the *ulama*—that is, his call for the guardianship of the *faqih* ("jurist"; *fiqh* specialist)—during the absence of the Twelfth Imam. Thus the office of *faqih* emerged, with Khumayni designated to hold this position for life. He was to be replaced on his death only if another generally accepted candidate emerged; otherwise his function would be filled by a collective Leadership Council. The *faqih* (or the Leadership Council) was to stand above the rest of the governmental system in that he had authority to appoint half the members of the Council of Guardians and all the top judicial personnel, to dismiss the president in certain situations, to declare war, and to command the armed forces.

This essentially institutionalized the de facto charismatic authority already possessed by the *imam*. Seemingly uncorruptable and content to live the simplest life, devoid of all luxuries, he exercised his influence sporadically and with seeming

---

[3] Despite possible messianic overtones, this does not mean that he was considered to be one of the twelve *imams*. That is, far from claiming that Khumayni was the Mahdi (Twelfth *Imam*), representatives of his movement spoke of creating conditions favorable to the Mahdi's return.

reluctance as he chided those in charge for their weakness or for failing to revolutionize the society fast enough.

A reinstituted Islamic order reversed much westernization and secularization. The execution of adulterers and prostitutes reemerged, at least sporadically, as did a ban on alcoholic beverages. Women were told to dress "modestly," evoking futile protests from westernized middle-class circles as Islamic dress for women (usually the black chador that encompasses all but face and hands) became a requirement in public. (Men, too, faced restrictions in dress, as organizations of zealots sometimes painted the arms of those wearing short sleeves, and neckties—a symbol of privileged, *ancien régime* status—also had to be shunned.) Women were not relegated to the traditional seclusion, for chador-clad women could be seen demonstrating and even carrying guns. But such actions as the suspension of the 1975 law modifying the unequal status of men in matters of marriage and divorce—some of the provisions later were reinstated—seemed to many to represent a backward step for women.

Even those Western observers who were sympathetic with the Iranian Revolution found cause for concern. Many of its excesses could be dismissed as nearly inevitable aspects of revolutionary turmoil and foreign invasion, even as being mild in comparison with what had happened in other such situations. But the populist regime in some ways seemed to inherit the repressive methods of the shah's dictatorship; what had been known as Savak was revived under a new name and employed many of the same people. Although non-Muslim minorities were guaranteed the right to practice their religion and even had representation in the Consultative Assembly in proportion to their numbers, many were naturally unhappy with the religious nature of the regime. Some individuals who were considered apostates from Islam or were under suspicion of working with Western powers suffered accordingly. The Baha'i minority, the legitimacy of whose religion the *ulama* always rejected, was dismissed as a mere political group and denied the rights of other religious minorities. There were allegations that the Baha'is were facing outright persecution.

A new kind of nonalignment—one that stressed "true independence" in contrast to what was seen as the servility of most Third World regimes to one or both superpowers—reversed the shah's foreign policies. Military cooperation with the United States and the existence of electronic surveillance bases on the Soviet border were ended. With Tehran's withdrawal from CENTO, the organization finally disappeared. More importantly, the new regime renounced Iran's role as a "surrogate" of the United States in the Persian Gulf region. In economic matters, Iran was no longer inclined to restore oil production to levels desired by importers, levels that would deplete its own reserves too rapidly. Preferential sales to the oil consortium ended. The mood was one of defying both superpowers, but suspicion was directed especially against the United States, independence from whose intervention seemed inseparable from ending the royalist order.

A new crisis in relations with the United States from November 1979 on threatened severe dangers for Iran, but also accelerated its revolution. When the ex-shah, now dying of cancer, left his most recent refuge in Mexico for medical treatment in the United States, many Iranians believed that a plot was underway to restore him to power, as had happened in 1953. Militant students took control of the United States embassy in Tehran (the "den of spies," as they called it) and held the American diplomatic and consular personnel hostage, demanding the ex-shah's return for trial and the restoration of the billions of dollars he was accused of embezzling. Declaring the United States to be the "Great Satan," Imam Khumayni endorsed the students' action and ultimately left the matter to the Consultative Assembly, then still not elected. After decades of foreign intervention in their domestic affairs, few Iranians were impressed by talk about international law.

The students failed to achieve their declared objectives. But they became another important center of power in Iran and helped to fuel the radicalization of the revolution. One of the first results of the embassy takeover—and perhaps its real motivation—was the resignation of the moderate Bazargan government. This helped to propel the revolution to another stage. Immediately before the embassy takeover, Bazargan had met with top American officials in Algiers, and the radicals' fear that the moderates were gradually enabling Washington to restore its influence seems to have helped to spark the students' action. And the resultant outside threats served to unify the country behind the new regime.

Such a blatant violation of diplomatic immunity threatened dangerous repercussions for Iran. The International Court of Justice demanded release of the hostages, and the UN Security Council condemned Iran's action. The United States froze $12 billion in Iranian assets and in April 1980 attempted a rescue operation that turned into a fiasco. The prisoners were finally freed in January 1981 in return for the immediate release of about one-fourth of the frozen assets, with other financial claims to be arbitrated. But Iran obtained only a vague, unmeaningful commitment from Washington to facilitate the return of the former royal family's wealth.

Revolutionary Iran combined an emphasis on pan-Islamic solidarity with rhetoric about supporting the "dispossessed" throughout the world. The country appeared to totally reject nationalism in the name of Islamic universalism, although some observers argued that a kind of de facto Iranian nationalism was emerging under the surface. Iran severed relations with South Africa and Israel. Arafat was received with great emotion in Tehran, and Khumayni fervently supported the Palestinian cause. The former Israeli mission in Tehran was turned over to the PLO, and Israel began to fear that Iranian troops would eventually be encamped with the Arabs on its eastern frontier.

The Islamic Republic's radicalism, with its widespread popular appeal transcending Iran's borders, found itself at odds with other types of regimes. It did, however, reject exporting the revolution by force unless attacked first. The subversive call went out to all Muslims (Khumayni always downplayed sectarian differences) but appealed especially to Shi'ites. Khumayni's appeal among Iraq's Shi'ite majority terrified the Baghdad regime. The Shi'ite majority in Bahrain and those in Saudi Arabia's Eastern Province—and also Sunnis in the Sudan, Gaza, and elsewhere—frightened their governments by demonstrating in favor of the Iranian Revolution. Sadat's Egypt, where the dying ex-shah found his last refuge, became another avid enemy of the new regime and the source of CIA-supported radio broadcasts calling for its overthrow.

With the end of the monarchy, divisions began to appear among the makers of the revolution. Imam Khumayni seemed to retain the overwhelming loyalty of the poor classes (the "dispossessed"). But secularist liberals and generally the upper middle class often deemed the Islamic Republic worse than the shah's regime. Having failed to understand the significance of the politicized masses and their radical clerical leadership (thinking Khumayni was just a symbol), middle-class opponents of the shah now complained that the revolution had been "stolen" from them. Marxist groups, which Khumayni sometimes strongly condemned, also posed a future threat to the Islamic direction of the revolution. Although the Tudeh party and the "Majority Section" of the People's Fida'iyin continued—until 1983—to back Khumayni, some other Marxist groups, but mainly the non-Marxist People's Mujahidin, clashed with the Revolutionary Guards. Also, the radical aspects of the new regime were not to the liking of many *ulama*, and none of the other leading *mujtahids* really supported Khumayni. Supporters of the basically conservative Ayatullah Shari'at-Madari, the leading *marja-i taqlid* of Azarbayjan and some other areas, clashed with the followers of the *imam* at times, and Shari'at-Madari was kept under house arrest until his death. The long-standing separatist sentiment of ethnic minorities, such as Turkomans and Khuzistani Arabs, came into the open. Most of all, the Kurds were in rebellion (with Iraq and Iran said to be subverting those in each other's territory), and suppression ensued.

With an explosion of competitive politics, diverse centers of power emerged among those who worked under the umbrella of the Islamic Republic with the *imam*'s blessing. Such for a while was Abu al-Hasan Bani-Sadr, a relative pragmatic, French-educated economist who advocated a combination of Islam and socialism and won the first presidential election because word was out that the *imam* preferred him. On the other hand, the Islamic Republican Party got overwhelming control of the Consultative Assembly and gradually won out in a growingly bitter conflict with Bani-Sadr, who was impeached by the Consultative Assembly and then dismissed from office by the *imam* in June 1981.

Attempts to overthrow the government periodically came to light. A large-scale plot, involving parts of the military and calling for bombing the *imam*'s residence, was aborted in July 1980. A cacophony of counterrevolutionary groups emerged among exiled members of the old elite. Despite a plea from Khumayni to remain at home as a thinker and writer, Bani-Sadr fled to France with Mas'ud Rajavi, leader of the People's Mujahidin, to add another voice in opposition to the *imam*. A subsequent terror campaign by the Mujahidin decimated the leadership of the Islamic Republican Party (killing seventy-four leaders of the party in one explosion) but was unable to unseat it. Instead, the opposition appeared to be largely crushed by an accelerated reign of terror—though still on a small scale compared with that of the

French Revolution—that brought the number of executions since the revolution to at least the four thousand mark by 1982.

Generally described as opposing modernization, the Islamic revolutionaries obviously condemned much of what the royalist regime had meant by that term, especially westernization and secularization. They also—at least in principle at first—rejected excessive urbanization, concentration on prestigious industrial projects, and the like. But their emphasis on economic equality and the goal of improving conditions of life was in line with more sophisticated concepts of modernization. They seemed to favor the development of agriculture and small-scale industries, improvements in medical care, emphasis on vocational education and teacher training, the extension of literacy, rural electrification, and other programs that arguably represent much of the essence of real modernization. Organizations known as "*jihad* brigades" concentrated on bringing modern improvements to villages. There was no opposition to modern technology.

Many of the steps—and the rhetoric—of this revolution might have been labeled *socialist* had current Islamic radicals been inclined to use such Western terminology. Banks and insurance companies were nationalized, as were many industries. Wages for most workers dramatically increased, while salaries for those in higher-level jobs shrank. Peasants began to take over large landholdings, with some local committees declaring that all land belongs to God.

The extent of eventual land reform and redistribution of wealth in general remained unclear. The parliament and the Islamic Republican Party were divided on such economic issues. The radicals tended to predominate, especially after the 1988 parliamentary elections, in which voters responded to Khumayni's call to elect those who favored the poor. But the Council of Guardians had rejected most of the radical legislation, such as nationalization of foreign trade and more thoroughgoing land reform. Khumayni, who at times also had seemed to oppose more extreme socialist tendencies, went so far in his support of radical change in 1988 as to issue a statement declaring that an Islamic state has the right to suspend the most basic rules of religion. But following his death the next year came a new leadership, including his successor as *faqih*. Hujjat al-Islam (sometimes elevated to Ayatullah) Ali Khamana'i, and newly elected President Hashemi Rafsanjani. The powers of the president were now enlarged, and the new government tended to lean toward pragmatism and moderation on economic and other issues.

Despite divisions on economic issues, support for the "dispossessed" colored all the regime's pronouncements. Indeed, the backing of the overwhelming majority of the poor provided the main hindrance to those who wanted to overthrow it. The *imam*'s followers demonstrated their devotion in an incredible outpouring of grief when he died in 1989. The largest mass of humanity that had ever been present at a Middle Eastern funeral (apparently outdoing even that of Nasir) nearly turned to chaos, with people trying to touch the corpse. This came after nearly a decade of hardship resulting from what the Iranians called the "imposed war," in which they had succeeded in their original defensive goals but failed in their subsequent attempt to overthrow the regime that had started the war.

RENEWED SUPERPOWER
INVOLVEMENT

While the Iranian crisis was in full swing in December 1979, a crisis in Afghanistan provided a new strand to complicate the international relations of the region. Soviet troops entered the country in full force; their number a few months later was put at 85,000. The Soviets came supposedly on the invitation of the year-old Communist government, which incongruously was immediately replaced by another Afghan Communist faction. There were diverse interpretations of the Soviet action. Some saw it as a basically defensive move, considering that the faction the Soviets over-threw was the more extreme one whose antireligious fervor threatened to bring about its overthrow by militantly Islamic rebels. As this view sometimes goes, the Soviets were threatened not only by a potentially hostile regime in Afghanistan but also by the possibility that this would infect the growing numbers of Soviet Muslims, some of whom were ethnically related to those in Afghanistan.

Others, however, saw a new Soviet aggressiveness, with the invasion of Afghanistan being a step (perhaps via an eventually disintegrating Iran) into the Persian Gulf and Indian Ocean area. Some noted the existence of Soviet facilities and bases in Ethiopia and South Yemen and large numbers of Soviet troops in Transcaucasia, near the Iranian border. Observers pointed to a possible motive of depriving the United States and its allies of oil. A CIA report that projected an end to the Soviets' self-sufficiency in that vital resource within the next few years also colored the reaction to Soviet moves, although later United States government studies increasingly showed this to be fallacious.

Whatever the USSR's motive, it suddenly found itself widely condemned in the Islamic world. Iran was preoccupied with its conflict with the United States, but even while the new crisis in Soviet-American relations led the USSR to veto sanctions against Iran in the Security Council, it too condemned the invasion of Afghanistan and gave some aid to the Afghan rebels. The rebels also were to get much financial help from Saudi Arabia. Sadat's Egypt became a major source of weapons and training for them, and perhaps three million Afghans took refuge in Pakistan and two million in Iran. Washington seemingly also was restrained from taking vindictive actions against Iran, which might have played into Soviet hands. Only a few Middle Eastern countries, such as South Yemen and Syria, whose renewed ties with the USSR were evidenced by increased arms shipments and a treaty of cooperation, generally failed to condemn the Soviet action.

The United States began increasingly to flex its muscles in the Indian Ocean region. South Yemen's close relationship with the USSR and its clash with North Yemen early in 1979 had already brought American military aid to the latter with official expressions of a new willingness to be involved in the region. Now the Iranian pillar of United States policy was gone, and regimes of other vital oil producers were left impotent in the face of new, if largely internal, dangers. Then the passions aroused by the hostage crisis, together with the Soviet move into Afghanistan, helped overcome America's post Vietnam War reluctance to become militarily involved. A large-scale United States naval buildup occurred in the Indian Ocean, and agreements were negotiated for base facilities in Somalia, Kenya, Oman, and Egypt, while joint maneuvers of the American and Egyptian air forces ensued from bases near Cairo. Washington also accelerated its plans to develop a Rapid Deployment Force, whose name was later changed to the United States Central Command, especially designed for large-scale operations in the Middle East. The Carter Doctrine of 1980 defined any outside attempt to control the Persian Gulf as "an assault on the vital interests" of the United States that, if necessary, would be countered by the use of "military force."

With the beginning of President Ronald Reagan's administration in 1981, Washington stepped up its campaign against the alleged Soviet threat to the Middle East. Proclaiming the goal of "strategic consensus," the new administration in effect called on all Middle Eastern governments—Arab and Israeli alike—to give priority to the common danger that should, in its view, reduce every other issue to relative insignificance. But the reality of intraregional and intrastate dynamics soon got in the way of such an outlook, as we shall see.

The Reagan administration relegated settlement of the Palestine problem to the back burner, although later events would make for some further involvement in the "peace process." Israel came more openly than before to be proclaimed a great strategic asset of the United States in the region, and the two countries concluded an agreement providing for various kinds of military cooperation. The new administration promised not to criticize Israel. Spokespersons for the administration even proclaimed that previously condemned Israeli acts, such as building settlements in the occupied territories and raiding Lebanon, were not illegal.

Libya and Syria were pictured by Washington as extensions of the USSR in a region whose internal dynamics were played down. Libya, with which Egypt and the Sudan were engaged in mutual subversion during the early 1980s, became singled out as the greatest *bête noire*. The Reagan administration apparently gave high priority to the overthrow of the Qadhdhafi regime, which turned out to be a frustratingly elusive goal. The climax of the campaign against Qadhdhafi came in the form of a massive United States air raid on Libyan cities in 1986—condemned by most of the world, with such countries as France and Italy refusing to allow the raiding planes to use their airspace—in response to allegations that Tripoli had supported certain terrorist operations in Europe. Even this action failed in its goal of killing or even overthrowing the Libyan leader, although he was sobered.

Washington increased its commitments to other Middle Eastern states. Pakistan—bordering on Soviet-occupied Afghanistan and, in return for large amounts of petrodollars, a potentially important protector of the Saudi regime against revolution—gained much American economic and military aid, while Egypt got increased military credits. Besides increasing its ties with other Arab monarchies in the Persian Gulf region by forming a Gulf Cooperation Council, Saudi Arabia apparently hoped to be able to depend on military support from several conservative regimes against any internal threat. In what has been dubbed the "Reagan Codicil" to the Carter Doctrine, the United States president issued assurances that his country would not allow the Saudi monarchy to be overthrown. Despite recurrent opposition from the pro-Israel lobby, the United States sold billions of dollars worth of arms—including AWACS—to Saudi Arabia. In the fifteen-year period ending in mid-1989, Saudi Arabia imported $75 billion worth of weapons from various countries, while its total military expenditures amounted to $200 billion.

Meanwhile, United States–provided Stinger missiles helped the Afghan rebels to make the Soviet presence in Afghanistan too costly. The Soviet forces withdrew in 1989, but the widely expected quick overthrow of the Afghan regime failed to occur. The United States had intervened elsewhere in the Middle East during the 1980s—with ignominious results in Lebanon, whose intraregional and interstate dynamics clearly went against the grain of Washington's idea that it was involved primarily in an action against Soviet influence. American intervention in the Persian Gulf met with more success in the short run in containing Iran's Islamic Revolution and in building up Iraq. The revolution in Iran was directed against the influence of both superpowers, with the United States and the USSR basically on the same side. In fact, the USSR was by this time surprisingly losing its superpower status altogether, and the specter of its dominating the world could no longer provide the rationale for United States involvement in the Middle East. And yet the United States presence as a protector of regimes allied with it and as a supporter of Israel remained intact.

THE FIRST PERSIAN GULF WAR

The immediate threat to stability at the beginning of the 1980s came from within the region as Iraq launched a major armed invasion of Iran in September 1980. The messianic appeal of the Islamic revolution to many Iraqis provided a main reason for the conflict. Soon after the revolution in Iran the two regimes began to clash militarily and to subvert each other, with some Iranian leaders calling for revolt against Iraq's "unbeliever" regime and Iraq backing Arab separatists in southwest Iran. Iraq also expelled thousands of Shi'ites, especially those of Iranian origin, across the border; hundreds were executed, including the Shi'ite religious leader Ayatullah Muhammad Baqir al-Sadr. Iranian counterrevolutionaries such as General Ghulam Oveissi gathered in Iraq to join in action against the Islamic Republic. Formerly isolated within the region by its doctrinaire radicalism, the Iraqi regime increasingly forged a de facto alliance with the monarchies against the threat of Islamic revolution.

Iraq also saw what looked like a unique opportunity to replace the shah's Iran as the dominant power in the Persian Gulf and even to become the leader of the Arab world. Egypt, which previously had overshadowed Iraq, now was conveniently excluded from the inter-Arab arena by virtue of its peace treaty with Israel. The Iraqi army grew to 280,000, seemingly unchallenged in the Gulf region now that the Iranian military had fallen apart through desertions, absence of trained officers, and the unavailability of spare parts for and proper maintenance of weapons and equipment. Since the drop in Iran's oil production, Iraq had replaced it as the second largest exporter, gaining immense financial capacity. With Iraq having discarded its image as a Soviet client since 1978 and with the hostage crisis continuing, there was no likelihood that the United States would actively oppose an attack on Iran. In fact, Iranians generally believed, though perhaps erroneously, that the United States masterminded the attack. There is some reason to believe that the United States and Israel helped to induce the attack by providing Iraq with an exaggerated picture of Iran's weakness.

The goals of overthrowing Iran's Islamic Republic before its contagion could overwhelm Arab regimes and of establishing Iraqi primacy in the region overshadowed specific, announced objectives. The latter included the restoration of Iraqi sovereignty over the Shatt al-Arab to the Iranian shore, that is, a reversal of the humiliating concession to the shah in 1975; Iraqi control over a disputed border area; the return of three islands occupied by Iranian forces in 1971 to "Arab sovereignty" (presumably to the UAE); and autonomy for Iran's Kurdish and Arab regions.

The Iraqis succeeded in occupying some Iranian territory. Perhaps two million Iranians became refugees. But military experts were stunned by the fierce resistance of the ill-trained Revolutionary Guards. The expected quick Iraqi victory turned into a long war. Nothing could have been better calculated to unite Iranians, including opponents of the regime who saw the homeland threatened. For weeks the Iranian city of Khorramshahr defied repeated Iraqi announcements that it had fallen. The other cities of Khuzistan came under attack but refused to give way and provided a continuing series of "miracles" for the revitalized Islamic regime.

The Iraqi regime found the Iranian Kurdish rebels to be allies but failed to gain the expected backing of Khuzistan's Arabs. Meanwhile, appeals from Iran—including taped broadcasts by the "martyred" Ayatullah Baqir al-Sadr—provided a potential threat to Baghdad, although the expected Shi'ite revolt never materialized during this conflict. The populist regime in Iran was able to survive great hardships as financial reserves vanished, but a financially solvent Iraqi government feared that discontent would get out of hand if its people were asked to sacrifice much. Also, President Husayn dared not launch offensives that would risk heavy casualties on his side for fear that his people would turn on him.

As for the Iranians, fervent believers in their revolution provided "human waves" willing to sacrifice themselves. By the latter part of 1981, they seemed clearly to be winning; March of the following year saw them inflict major losses on the Iraqis and push them back several miles. Iraqi forces fled from Khorramshahr in disarray in April 1982, leaving Iranian territory now nearly free of enemy occupation. With the benefit of hindsight, everyone realizes that if Iran had agreed to end the war then its remarkable victories would have provided a tremendous boost for its revolutionary ideology. Saddam Husayn's regime probably could not have survived the blow it had received. But confident of greater victory and talking about an eventual citizen "Army of Twenty Million" men and women, revolutionary Iran refused to consider the kind of compromise peace that the regime in Baghdad now desperately wanted. Iran insisted on reparations, the right of expellees to return to Iraq, and even the overthrow of the regime that started the war. Horrified by the Islamic Republic's military momentum and by its calls for exporting the revolution, supporters of the status quo saw an allegedly Iranian-backed abortive coup in Bahrain in 1981 as an omen of things to come in the Gulf region.

The war threatened to spread. The Arab monarchies gave more or less open diplomatic and financial support to Iraq, and Jordan's port of Aqaba became a back-door supply route. Some Jordanian "volunteers" joined Iraqi forces in 1982. American radar aircraft (AWACS) were flown to Saudi Arabia to guard against an enlarged war. But Iraqi attempts to evoke Arab solidarity by portraying the conflict as one between Arabs and Persians had only mixed success on the popular level. Many Arabs saw Khumayni as an Islamic rather than merely as an Iranian or even a Shi'ite leader, although his enemies did have some success in reviving anti-Shi'ite feelings, especially in the Gulf region. Revolutionary-minded Arabs also tended to blame the Iraqi regime for having attacked the "wrong enemy"—in fact, a new ally against Israel.

Syria's renewed enmity toward Iraq and—at least at first—Jordan pulled it into the Iranian camp. Syrian forces massed on the Jordanian border in late 1980, perhaps partly to prevent Jordanian troops from entering the war against Iran but also in an attempt to induce King Husayn to stop aiding Muslim Brethren guerrillas in Syria and to restrain him and other Arab leaders from reneging (as rumor had them about to do) on the 1974 Rabat declaration that the PLO is the sole representative of the Palestinians. Libya, whose rapprochement with Syria was symbolized by an unpromising announcement in 1980 of plans to unite, strongly favored Iran. So seemingly did Algeria and South Yemen in less obvious ways in the beginning.

Although revolutionary Iran was now the most fervent of Israel's enemies and very supportive of the PLO, the latter also had important ties with Iraq and would have found it risky to embrace Iran at the expense of alienating conservative Arab regimes, and of course Iraq itself. In any case, the PLO had long aspired to a two-state solution of the Palestine problem, which was complicated by Iran's commitment to totally defeating Israel. While at first the PLO's Arafat concentrated futilely on trying to mediate between the warring parties, his relationship with Iran deteriorated, leaving only some radical, peripheral Palestinian organizations allied with it. Oddly, the longtime Israeli policy of supporting forces on the non-Arab periphery of the Middle East continued in the form of arms sales to what had now become its worst enemy, Iran. The logic of this action was the belief that the Islamic revolution was a temporary phenomenon and that continuing arms sales would facilitate restoring ties with a future, postrevolutionary regime. Also, by keeping Iran and Iraq fighting each other, Israel could feel safer for the time being. There are reports that Saddam Husayn put out feelers for peace with Israel and sought the latter's support but was spurned. Adding to the irony is the fact that in the meantime Iranian-backed guerrillas in Lebanon in the mid-1980s were giving Israel what might be considered its first defeat.

Egypt's Sadat, whose assassination did not occur for more than a year after this war started, at first ridiculed his opponents for being in such disarray, but he and his successor firmly backed Iraq and even presented the contingency of intervening militarily if the Arab countries in the Gulf ever faced being overwhelmed. Such a need for Egypt's help provided an important motive for its readmission into the Arab fold after the Egyptian-Israeli peace settlement.

Following its recovery of Khorramshahr in 1982, Iran began to plan a counter-invasion of Iraq. It mobilized forces of up to half a million on the frontier. These soldiers became famous for their "human wave" tactics to confront an entrenched Iraqi army that continued to increase in size and to acquire more advanced weapons. One estimate puts Iraq's total spending on weapons at $102 billion during the war—weapons worth $23.5 billion from the USSR and $17 billion from France. The latter had developed important economic ties with Iraq in the 1970s and feared major financial losses if a pro-Iranian Islamic regime replaced that of Saddam Husayn. Iraq had become the world's biggest arms importer. Restoring relations with the United States, it became the recipient of credits from that country to finance vital food purchases. Later revelations showed that much of this had been secretly diverted to buying arms. Iran, by contrast, found it increasingly difficult to acquire weapons as its potential victory in the war posed a threat to the clients of the major powers. For a while Iran received some American weapons in line with a secret strategy in Washington—terminated when revealed in 1987—of cultivating moderates in Tehran and encouraging them to use their influence to get pro-Iranian guerrillas in Lebanon to release Western hostages.

Iraq constructed oil pipelines across Saudi Arabia and Turkey to replace the sea route that Iran had closed at the beginning of the war and the pipeline to the Mediterranean, which Syria had closed. Iraq also hoped to use French-made Super Etendard bombers and Exocet missiles to weaken Iran by attacking its oil facilities and shipping in the Persian Gulf. But for years Iraqi pilots amazed foreign military observers with their ineptitude. Iranian forces, whose only advantage was superior commitment, seemed gradually to be wearing down an enemy whose superiority in arms was now estimated to be eight to one. Outside observers tended to be convinced that total defeat of Iraq would come sooner or later. Such a view was confirmed when, in 1986, Iranian forces slipped across the Shatt al-Arab to occupy the Fao Peninsula at Iraq's southern tip and entrenched themselves so firmly that successive Iraqi offensives failed to retake it. Meanwhile, several Iranian offensives penetrated into Iraq, nearly severing the main road between Baghdad and Basrah. Iran penetrated the outskirts of now largely deserted Basrah early in 1987 but failed to capture it. Iranian-backed Kurdish rebels also were finding Baghdad's authority evaporating in Kurdistan.

Iranian-Saudi hostility heated up as large contingents of Iranians participated in the pilgrimage to Mecca each year and used the occasion to proselytize for their revolution. The pro-Khumayni pilgrims carried banners condemning Israel and the United States, implicitly directed against the Saudis as an American client state and an indirect ally of Israel. The Iranians and their supporters among the pilgrims—some of whom allegedly smuggled weapons into the country—recurrently clashed with the Saudi police. In 1987, this friction culminated in a massacre of over four hundred pilgrims. The circumstances remain clouded by contradictory reports, but it is clear that, whether or not some of them attacked the police, many were shot down and did not merely die in a stampede, as the Saudis claimed. In order to shore up his religious credentials in the face of Iran's challenge, King Fahd began to encourage his subjects to address him as the "servant of the two holy sanctuaries." This change came as Tehran talked about the need to liberate the holy places and as pro-Tehran Muslims organized conferences and other activities expressing their concern over the sites' alleged desecration by the Saudis.

As Iraq attacked oil shipments from Iran, the logical response of the latter was to retaliate against shipments from the technically "neutral" Gulf monarchies. Iran thus attempted to pressure the Gulf states into ending their massive financial aid to Iraq ($50 billion, according to one estimate, in addition to $30 billion from other countries) that made its war effort possible. Apparently in order to force the hand of the United States, Kuwait entered into an agreement with the USSR whereby the Soviet flag would fly over Kuwaiti vessels, thereby inhibiting Iran from bombing them. This action frightened Washington, which in 1987 offered instead to provide its own flag to the amirate's ships, making it necessary for an increased United States naval force to protect the "reflagged" vessels. American officials spoke of defending the "freedom of the seas," although in fact it was shipping from Iran, which the United States did not protect, that was mainly under attack. With the United States intervening in this way, small Iranian speedboats engaged in a new kind of guerrilla warfare against its naval forces. The United States in turn bombed Iranian oil facilities and destroyed much of the Iranian navy. The Iranians failed in their attempt to turn the Gulf into a "new Vietnam" (or "Lebanon"), in which American public opinion would force a withdrawal as the buildup of naval forces, joined by ships from other Western countries, turned into one of the biggest armadas of all times. In fact, the hardest blow to the United States came from Iraq. Its missiles—whether by accident or by design—destroyed an American vessel, the USS Stark, oddly evoking both increased anti-Iranian feelings in the United States and the further buildup of a fleet that served essentially as an extension to the Iraqi army.

Iran was suffering heavily from a war in which the casualties (perhaps a total of a million) had been mainly on its side. Its forces and its Kurdish allies faced accelerated use of the mustard and nerve gas that Saddam Husayn had resorted to almost from the beginning. Iranian cities now endured massive attacks by Scud missiles that Iraq had acquired from the USSR and then upgraded to increase their range. Meanwhile, Tehran faced widespread blame throughout the world for not heeding a UN Security Council call to end the war, as well as increasingly effective efforts of various powers to prevent it from purchasing arms. Iran considered this action highly unfair in light of the UN's failure to condemn Iraq for starting the war and of what it considered the right of a victim of aggression to overthrow its perpetrator. But blows to morale kept coming, as United States naval forces destroyed an Iranian civilian aircraft flying over the Gulf in the regularly designated flight corridor, which resulted in the deaths of all 290 passengers. The United States said the incident was a mistake; this apparently was true, although evidence points to trigger-happiness, prompted by the tense situation, as part of the explanation. Wherever the blame lies, the incident intensified Iran's feeling of helplessness.

Meanwhile, 1988 saw Iranian military setbacks that further destroyed morale. Elite Iraqi troops (Republican Guards)—with the United States, according to at least one source, providing the plans and satellite intelligence—suddenly retook Fao in April. The following summer an Iraqi military force advanced a few miles into western Iran, temporarily occupying some towns. These areas were left in the control of the increasingly discredited People's Mujahidin, which had moved its base from France to Iraq to participate in the war against the Islamic regime, but whose force was immediately destroyed once its allies withdrew. Faced with the argument that the Islamic revolution might not be able to survive such continued suffering, Imam Khumayni now relented—comparing his decision to taking poison—and agreed to stop the war. With the UN sending in a peacekeeping force, the cease-fire soon took hold, and the two war-weary countries seemed not to contemplate renewing the conflict. Issues such as the exchange of prisoners and sovereignty over the Shatt al-Arab prevented any movement toward a peace settlement, although the early months of 1990 finally offered signs of progress as the two countries began to cooperate within OPEC in an effort to get oil prices increased.

LEBANON: INVASION AND CHAOS

Conflict in Lebanon seemed about to get out of hand during 1981, as rightists built a road connecting the main area under their control with their supporters in the town of Zahlah, in eastern Lebanon. This move threatened to upset the status quo in the rightists' favor. In subsequent clashes between Syrian forces and the Lebanese rightists, Israeli warplanes intervened to shoot down Syrian helicopters. Syria, in turn, installed surface-to-air missiles in Lebanon, allegedly contrary to earlier understandings, thereby threatening Israeli supremacy in the skies. Despite initial anti-Syrian statements, the United States assumed a mediatory role in the crisis. Israeli promises to destroy the missiles were not fulfilled, meaning that Syria had won this round of mutual bluff.

In July 1981 Israel accelerated its conflict with recently strengthened Palestinian forces in southern Lebanon. An artillery war between Israel and the PLO raged for days; Israel escalated it by carrying out an air raid on Beirut, with United States–supplied weapons, that killed about three hundred people. Washington condemned the Israeli raid and further delayed shipments of warplanes, already held up following condemnation of an Israeli raid that destroyed the nuclear reactor that Iraq had completed with French assistance. Dealing with the PLO via Saudi Arabia, the United States also helped to arrange a cease-fire. It remained effective for nearly a year, although—as Israel faced renewed condemnation and even the temporary suspension by Washington of the new agreement on "strategic cooperation" following its annexation of the Golan Heights in December—it soon became widely known that a bigger Israeli attack on Lebanon was impending.

And indeed, apparently with a United States "green light," Israel ended the months of relative quiet by launching a full-scale invasion in June 1982. Its main goal was to destroy the PLO in order to have a free hand in imposing its will on the West Bank and Gaza Strip. The PLO, lacking even air cover, was no match for the Israeli military (about which pundits were debating whether it was number three or only number four in the world) and was quickly overrun in southern Lebanon. The Israelis also devastated the outdated Syrian air force in large-scale duels. Although Israel initially announced that its forces would only penetrate twenty-five miles into Lebanon, General Sharon moved on and began to besiege West Beirut.

The city endured two months of massive bombing from the air and bombardment from the ground, with one aim being the assassination of Arafat and other Palestinian leaders. Although they could have occupied West Beirut, the Israelis— especially in light of opposition to the war at home—were anxious to avoid the losses that a house-by-house invasion would impose on them. And so, with United States intercession, a plan was worked out whereby a Western multinational force would oversee the evacuation of PLO and some Syrian troops by sea. This was accomplished in August.

The Israelis saw the opportunity to create a new Lebanon under the leadership of the Phalangists, who had been in touch with them and welcomed the invasion. Phalangist leaders, notably the party's founder, Pierre Jumayyil, were heretofore regarded as too extreme in their commitment to continuing Maronite supremacy to be taken seriously as presidential candidates. However, with Israeli troops occupying much of the country and the Phalangists' enemies seemingly forever subdued, the parliament chose as president Jumayyil's son Bashir, commander of the main Phalangist militia (the Lebanese Forces) and champion of the most extreme tendencies. But before he could take office, a bomb blew up the Phalangist headquarters and killed him. His brother, Amin Jumayyil, regarded as a much more moderate Phalangist, was elected in his place. Even many Muslim Lebanese, particularly from the old establishment (now making their own comeback after years of being overshadowed by radical leaders), were optimistic that their demands for a readjustment of the sectarian power balance would occur. The Muslims were disappointed in this regard, but the whole Israeli plan for a Lebanon more firmly in Maronite hands was beginning to unravel.

With Western troops withdrawing after the evacuation of the PLO forces, the Israeli response to the assassination was to renege on the commitment to the United States not to occupy a now virtually defenseless West Beirut. Israeli troops moved up to the edge of the Sabra and Shatila refugee camps and sent Phalangist forces inside. As the Israeli troops waited outside, the Phalangists predictably carried out a two-day orgy of indiscriminate massacres that shocked the world when it became known and evoked large-scale protests even from more moderate elements in Israel. International pressures forced Prime Minister Begin to relent and appoint a commission to investigate the massacres, resulting in such actions as General Sharon's removal from the post of Defense Minister (but not from the cabinet).

The Israeli occupation turned out to be the catalyst for the emergence of Shi'ite influence in Lebanon. Some Shi'ites—now by far the largest sect in the country, but the most disadvantaged—had initially been glad to see the defeat of Palestinian forces, whom they blamed for Israeli retaliatory raids. But an occupation that lasted long was bound to turn the Israelis into bitter enemies. The awakening had begun several years earlier as an Iranian religious scholar of Lebanese ancestry, Imam Sayyid Musa al-Sadr, inspired his coreligionists with calls for ending their passivity; his disappearance in 1978 had added to his charisma by seemingly assimilating him at least subconsciously to the Shi'ites' chiliastic doctrine of the Absent Imam. Actions of the Phalangist regime such as the destruction of the destitute Shi'ites' shanties as winter was coming in 1982—some were quipping that it was now illegal to be poor—helped make way for rebellion.

Resistance to Israel was sparked in October 1983, when its troops rudely—having virtually no understanding of the country—broke through a gathering of Shi'ites in a Lebanese town celebrating the martyrdom of Husayn at Karbala. This became a kind of resistance that the Israelis had never imagined before, as Shi'ite guerrillas began to attack and kill them, turning Lebanon into their nightmare. With no Arab regime turning its hand to resist the Israeli invasion in 1982, only Iran—which had recently liberated Khorramshahr and was talking about marching on to Karbala and then to Jerusalem—sent troops. They came in the form of a few hundred Revolutionary Guards, whose presence in Syrian-controlled areas of eastern Lebanon encouraged the emergence of a radical Shi'ite Lebanese organization. Known as the Party of God, this and other loosely affiliated groups, with their willingness to sacrifice themselves for the cause, provided the most effective resistance. Unwilling to take continuing losses, the Israelis finally withdrew from Lebanon, except for a narrow "security belt" along their northern frontier where a few Israeli troops continued to advise the SLA. In 1983, Begin was so depressed over what he had gotten Israel into the year before (as well as by the death of his wife) that he retired from politics. Yitzhak Shamir, a member of the triumvirate that had led the former Stern Gang, took his place as prime minister, as Begin mysteriously went into seclusion.

The Israelis had already withdrawn several miles south of Beirut in 1983. By turning Druze areas in the Shuf (east of Beirut) over to the Phalangists, they incited a fierce communal battle, with the Druze resisting subjection and threatening to take a strategic point overlooking Beirut, and with American naval forces intervening with massive bombardment of the Shuf from the sea that embittered many Lebanese and other Arabs and Muslims. The international force, particularly the Americans, which had returned to Beirut following the Sabra and Shatila massacres, more and more came to be seen as participants in the conflict rather than as true "peacekeepers." The United States became a target of attacks, with its embassy in Beirut and then its Marine barracks (as well as that of the French contingent) blown up by Shi'ite guerrillas willing to sacrifice themselves by driving truckloads of bombs into these structures. The international force soon withdrew altogether.

Throughout the following years, Lebanon descended further and further into chaos and economic ruin that made the years of civil war before 1982 seem benign in comparison. The strands of conflict crisscrossed one another as the Syrian regime—whose massive acquisition of more advanced Soviet weapons allowed it to grow in influence, even to hope for Syrian "strategic parity" with Israel, before Moscow began to limit its support during the latter part of the decade—aspired to dominate the PLO, using renegade Palestinian groups to fight pro-Arafat Palestinians. Damascus also backed the (Shi'ite) Amal, which warred with the Palestinians, brutally besieging their refugee camps during the late 1980s and also struggling against the Party of God. This latter group increasingly dominated Shi'ite-populated South Beirut and less successfully challenged Amal in southern Lebanon, putting a strain on the Syrian-Iranian alliance. Although the Party of God, which also aspired to liberate Palestine, supported the Palestinians against Amal, the PLO—committed to a peaceful, two-state settlement of the Palestine conflict and tied to anti-Iranian Arab regimes—later backed Amal against the Shi'ite zealots.

Continuing resistance to the Israelis evoked from them an "iron fist" policy that put hundreds of Palestinians and Lebanese in Israeli prisons. Radical Shi'ite factions captured several Westerners. On one occasion, a group hijacked an American airplane for use in bargaining for the release of those in prison in Israel and in Kuwait, where Shi'ite guerrilla attacks were carried out against the regime. The Phalangists similarly captured some Iranian diplomats and sometimes fought fiercely among themselves, as in the case of the conflict over an attempt by some of their leaders to back an accommodation with Syria in 1987 that evoked a revolt by other Phalangists. Radical Palestinian splinter groups carried out several spectacular international terrorist attacks and were accused of having Syrian backing.

The Lebanese army, which United States funding and training had helped to rebuild, disintegrated during 1984, when the Jumayyil regime tried to use it against the militias. Hope for a Phalangist-dominated Lebanon then disappeared, providing a final reason for the multinational force to withdraw. The Lebanese government finally abrogated the agreement it had reached with Israel in May 1983, which though not termed a peace treaty would have made Lebanon a veritable Israeli vassal. Israel's withdrawal was contingent on a withdrawal by Syria, which refused to cooperate. In Lebanon there emerged a "government of national unity," whose ministers represented mutually antagonistic factions. Real control over the country remained in the hands of the militias and of the Syrian and Israeli forces, with Israeli raids continuing from time to time.

When Jumayyil's term as president expired in 1988, what was left of the parliament (elected in 1972) could not agree on a successor. What ensued for several months was the existence of two rival premiers as the outgoing president appointed a Maronite general, Michel Aoun, to the post, challenging the authority of Premier Salim al-Huss. Imagining unrealistically that intensified conflict would bring Western intervention on his side, and enjoying massive provision of arms by Iraq (which saw this as a way of weakening Syria), Aoun launched artillery attacks against Syrian forces, bringing retaliation and devastation.

In 1989, an Arab League committee eventually helped bring about a meeting of the Lebanese parliament in Ta'if (Saudi Arabia) and the selection of a new president, along with acceptance of adjustments in the old sectarian balance, which some would dub the "Second Lebanese Republic." This in turn brought about a terrible intra-Maronite war as General Aoun rejected the settlement on the ground that it failed to end the Syrian presence. Fierce battles between the Phalangists (Lebanese forces) and Maronite troops loyal to General Aoun left vast destruction in East Beirut (and its mountain hinterland), which had mostly remained an oasis of calm and prosperity throughout the previous years. Many observers believed that the Maronites themselves had finally finished off their own leading role in the country.

INTIFADAH

The 1980s saw all the old roadblocks continuing to stand in the way of resolving the Palestine question. Hawkish Israelis sometimes noted that only the absence of formal annexation masked the fact that the "green line" (the pre-1967 frontier) was disappearing. A prominent Israeli, Meron Benvenisti, sized up the situation in terms of a "Second Israeli Republic" having emerged. He called it a "Herrenvolk democracy," because a now-permanent sector of the population—most of the Palestinians—lacked citizenship, suffrage, and other rights.

In the absence of momentum for a comprehensive settlement, various proposals by Israel and the United States failed to find acceptance. Such was the case with Israel's attempt in the early 1980s to rely on a few Palestinians, regarded as collaborators by others, to form "village leagues" to counter the PLO's leadership and to implement a new kind of "civilian administration." In the aftermath of the 1982 war, a new United States initiative, the Reagan Plan, called for negotiations aimed at the return of parts of the occupied areas to Jordan. But that went nowhere in the face of Palestinian commitment to self-determination under PLO leadership and opposition to Hashimite rule, as well as outright rejection by Israel. In 1985, the PLO and Jordan (the former hoping for a loose confederation between the latter and a future Palestinian state) agreed on a joint approach to negotiations, but this fell apart a year later. For a while, Washington and the Labour Party sector of Israel's leadership urged a return to the Geneva Conference approach, though only as a formality to legitimize separate peace talks. The Likud adamantly opposed even this limited comprehensive approach.

Many had begun to predict that the Palestinians' hopelessness was about to make way for civil war in the occupied territories. But everyone seemed to be surprised when a minor incident—in addition to an Arab summit meeting that won praise in the Western world by explicitly consigning the Palestine issue to the back burner in favor of confronting the threat to Arab regimes posed by the Iranian revolution—ignited an uprising in December 1987. The form the uprising (*intifadah*, literally a "shaking off") took seemed even more remarkable, as Palestinian youths eschewed guns and bombs in favor of throwing stones and sometimes using slings against the Israeli "Goliath." National and local committees representing various factions coordinated a much broader set of activities, including strikes, boycotts of Israeli goods, and nonpayment of taxes. The Palestinians also attempted to become self-sufficient in foodstuffs and the like, rather than passively resigning themselves to collaboration and dependence while waiting for others to liberate them. Still more remarkable was the way in which the Intifadah seemed to rage on endlessly, in the face of stepped-up arrests, detentions, closing of schools and universities, expulsions, and destruction of houses. By 1990, there were over seven hundred deaths from Israeli bullets and over two hundred collaborators killed by their fellow Palestinians. The Israelis were unable to control the situation and found themselves the focus of much world outrage as their attempts to suppress the Intifadah continued.

The Intifadah created new pressures on all sides to move toward a settlement. Autocratic regimes in the Arab world feared the spread of the Intifadah to their own populations and thus generally suppressed demonstrations in support of the Palestinians. With King Husayn finally renouncing his kingdom's claim to the West Bank, PLO Chairman Arafat was so anxious to get peace talks started that in 1988 he and the Palestine National Council (PNC), whose declaration of an independent Palestine gained recognition from many countries, gave up "cards" they had long insisted on saving for negotiations. The PNC succumbed to demands for recognizing Israel's "right to exist" and renouncing "terrorism" in order to get the United States to start a "dialogue" with the PLO. The dialogue ensued but continued to disappoint those who thought it would lead to anything. The year 1989 saw proposals from Prime Minister Shamir for the occupied territories to elect representatives, who in turn would negotiate a settlement. However, he made it clear that the only acceptable end result would be annexation to Israel, with Palestinians to be given autonomy but excluded from citizenship and representation in the Jewish state. Egypt and the United States, whose Bush administration showed some signs of being less supportive of Israel than had Reagan's, tried to narrow the differences. But no agreement was attainable even on the question of which Palestinians would meet with Israeli representatives to discuss the procedure for elections. By mid-1990, as Israel got a new Likud-led cabinet that excluded the Labour alignment in favor of ultrarightist parties, Palestinian despair was on the increase. The PLO leadership's moderate stance was subjecting it to contempt in Palestinian ranks, especially among the growing Islamist movement. When a small Palestinian guerrilla organization in June 1990 carried out an abortive raid on Tel-Aviv's beaches that the Israeli government claimed had been aimed at civilians (that is, constituting terrorism), the United States broke off dialogue with the PLO, whose leadership the raid apparently had intended to undermine.

With the Israeli government moving farther to the right, there was much expectation of increased violence, perhaps involving mass expulsion of the Palestinian population ("another 1948") since more and more Israelis openly talked about the "transfer" option. The accelerating immigration of Soviet Jews, as well as reduced Soviet backing for countries such as Syria and Libya, renewed the hopes of hawkish Israelis. But Arab regimes—particularly Iraq's—were seemingly pulled into a renewed confrontation. Iraq had a huge army and chemical weapons that promised to counter Israel's nuclear arsenal, and it threatened massive retaliation if Israel attacked any Arab country. Closely allied with Iraq was Jordan, which feared being overrun by a wave of Palestinian expellees. The specter of a sixth Arab-Israeli war increasingly haunted the world.

TURKEY: CONTINUING TROUBLES

Though in some ways aloof from its neighbors' affairs, Turkey shared in many of their troubles. The People's Republican Party leader, Bülent Ecevit, became premier after the October 1973 elections. This was made possible only by an incongruous, shaky coalition with the (Islamist) National Salvation Party that epitomized the beginning of increased political instability. But the premier's prestige soared as he dealt forcibly with a new phase of the Cyprus problem during the following summer. When pro-*Enosis* army officers took control of Cyprus with the connivance of the rightist Greek military dictatorship, Turkey invaded the largely Greek-populated island and occupied the northern 40 percent of it. Ecevit soon resigned in the belief that new elections would follow and give his party a majority, but Justice Party leader Suleyman Demirel surprised him by mustering enough support to form his own government.

The invasion of Cyprus was a great boost for Turkish national pride. Reminiscent of the 1920s, Turkish victories produced 200,000 Greek refugees. Both this situation and conflicting claims to the mineral resources of the Aegean aggravated tensions between Turkey and Greece.

With the invasion of Cyprus, a new United States–Turkish rift emerged. Citing the use of United States–supplied weapons in the operation, Congress banned future United States arms shipments to Turkey, which in turn closed important United States intelligence bases near the Soviet border. Ankara also improved its ties with Moscow, and the two governments signed a nonaggression pact in 1978. Still, the Turks refrained from carrying out threats to withdraw from NATO or otherwise to loosen ties with the United States-led bloc. With the ongoing revolution in Iran making the United States more conscious of Turkey's importance, Congress lifted the arms embargo in 1978, allowing the bases to be reopened.

Turkey's internal problems seemed to snowball as it faced higher oil prices. Also, the economic slowdown in Western Europe in the mid-1970s resulted in the layoffs of thousands of "guest workers," whose remittances were a major source of foreign exchange for Turkey. Inflation increased to a rate of 118 percent a year by 1980, and balance-of-payments problems brought recurrent devaluation of the Turkish lira. Foreign debt exceeded $15 billion by 1980, while industries operating at 55 percent of capacity resulted in an unemployment rate of 20 percent. The slum population grew at a rate of 6 percent a year, and the per capita GNP seemingly declined during the late 1970s.

As extreme factions grew on both left and right, riots and terrorism tore the country apart. Calculations in 1980 put the number of deaths at about three thousand during the previous two years. The toll reached two hundred a month by the first half of 1980. Whole towns temporarily established their independence, and nighttime control of large sections of the cities fell into the hands of urban guerrillas. This sometimes took on a religious dimension; the leftists came disproportionately from the roughly 8 percent Alawite minority in eastern Anatolia, while the rightists were largely Sunnis. Martial law prevailed in much of the country after December 1978, and international human rights groups began to report "widespread and systematic torture." Weak coalition cabinets—Ecevit formed a new government in 1978 but made way for Demirel after the next year's elections—were unable to deal with the problem effectively.

During 1980 the generals issued several warnings to the political parties to unite to solve the country's problems. Finally, that September the army engineered another coup, and a junta headed by General Kenan Evren took control. Martial law extended to the whole country, and thousands of people, including members of the Grand National Assembly and the top civilian leaders, came under arrest. Ruthless measures by the military regime caused the number of political killings to plunge. The country experienced an economic upturn as production and exports increased and as the rate of inflation fell.

An appointed Consultative Assembly drew up a new Constitution that got a 91 percent "yes" vote in a referendum in 1982, thus initiating the Third Turkish Republic. The Constitution aimed at establishing a more powerful president and put Evren in that office (without an election) for a seven-year term. With the checks and balances of the Second Republic blamed for the government's weakness, the pendulum swung in the opposite direction, as in the emergence in the Third Republic of a unicameral Grand National Assembly. There also was an attempt to minimize divisiveness in the new body by denying representation to parties winning less than 10 percent of the total vote, and awarding those votes to the big parties. Furthermore, the military sponsored the Nationalist Democracy Party (NDP), which it expected to dominate the parliament. The old parties were banned and their leaders were denied the right to participate in politics.

The military was disappointed to see the NDP—which later dissolved itself—defeated in the 1983 parliamentary elections. Among the two other parties allowed to contest the election, the business-oriented Motherland Party of Turgut Özal, whose policies as minister of economic affairs under the military regime had gained credit for the economic upturn, won a majority. Özal headed all governments until 1989, when the parliament picked him to succeed Evren as president. (He would enlarge the powers of this office.) Oddly, this came at a time when the Motherland Party had suffered major losses in local elections. With a major attempt under Özal to privatize an economy in which much of Atatürk's statism had survived, Turkey experienced considerable economic growth oriented toward exporting manufactured goods. It also suffered from revived inflation, unemployment, and a big foreign debt, and it experienced considerable unrest on the part of workers whose trade union activity the government severely restricted.

Although the prospect of renewed military intervention could not be excluded, the electoral process gained ground during the 1980s. More political parties gradually got permission to contest elections. Some parties essentially were the old ones under new names, and they were even formally headed by wives of veteran leaders, the ban on whose official leadership of their parties ended in 1987. But, aside from remaining restrictions on unions and universities, the large—if declining—numbers of political prisoners, the extensive use of torture, the continuing state of emergency in the Kurdish region even after martial law there and elsewhere gradually ended, and the denial of cultural rights to the Kurds (whose language the government attempted to ban) gave "democracy" a certain hollow ring.

The Turkish elite still aspired to have their country accepted as part of Europe. With Ankara's application for membership in the European Community still not accepted on grounds of its poor human rights record, it continued to hope for eventual admission as democracy gained increasing reality. But however authentic the Europeans' concerns were, there was much reason to believe that they also were motivated by a perception of Turkey—whose "guest workers" (estimated at 1.8 million in the European Community during the late 1980s), like other Middle Easterners and Africans, specialized in the menial jobs Europeans were unwilling to take and had become an object of prejudice in countries such as Germany—as fundamentally a Middle Eastern, not a European, country.

THE SECOND PERSIAN GULF WAR

The second half of 1990 saw Ba'thist Iraq, following a decade of bolstering the West's client monarchies, come full circle to play the role of challenger to the status quo again. New alignments emerged as the West and its local collaborators collided with President Husayn and those in the Arab, Islamic, and Third worlds who saw him as the champion of unprecedented resistance to a renewed colonial crusade. Husayn emerged as the West's new *bête noire* or, like Musaddiq and Nasir before him, as the "new Hitler"; his fresh atrocities (only some of which, as in the case of the widely hyped story about Iraqis throwing Kuwaiti babies out of incubators, turned out to be fabrications) were supplemented by a rediscovery of the worse, if heretofore ignored, ones he had committed when the West was at his side.

Following Kuwait's acquiescence in Iraq's demand in July to stop exceeding its oil production quota, a financially troubled Baghdad that accused the amirate of continuing to engage in economic war against it kept troops massed on the frontier. Further Iraqi goals included cancellation of the loans of at least $10 billion that had helped to finance the war with Iran and compensation for the alleged excessive exploitation of the Rumaylah oil field, only the southern tip of which extends into Kuwait. Not getting compliance and seemingly facing little threat of action by other powers even as clear indications of an impending military move were observed (the United States ambassador to Baghdad personally assured President Husayn that Washington was neutral in this inter-Arab rift, creating one basis for later accusations that her country had set a trap), the Iraqi army quickly occupied the city-state on August 2 as the amir fled. Reasserting the old claim that Kuwait was a part of Basrah Province during Ottoman times that the British had illegally separated from the motherland, Baghdad soon declared that the amirate had been transformed into an Iraqi province as word spread of harsh suppression of opposition, as well as of massive looting, and as much of the Kuwaiti population went into exile.

The world's reaction to the invasion, especially that of the United States, proved far stronger than Baghdad had imagined. As even the USSR (needing economic help now that the Cold War was over and apparently hoping for toleration of its own repressiveness in places such as Lithuania) and China (aspiring to ease the isolation the West had imposed on it because of recent human rights abuses) went along with United States proposals, the UN Security Council called for withdrawal and ordered a blockade of Iraq. Meanwhile, United States naval forces began to prevent vessels from sailing in and out of that country and of occupied Kuwait. The oil pipelines across Turkey and Saudi Arabia were closed down, drying up Iraq's source of income.

To many, the situation seemed to dictate that Iraq move its forces on to occupy Saudi Arabia in order to get out of the fix in which it found itself, for then it would control so much of the world's oil that economic sanctions would not be feasible. And its bargaining power in setting oil prices would be dramatically enhanced. Whether Iraq contemplated such a move or not, United States officials convinced the Saudis to allow American troops to enter the kingdom, the very sort of eventuality that they and other United States clients in the peninsula—who preferred that their superpower patron stay just "over the horizon"—had long resisted because of the extent to which such a presence would undermine their legitimacy.

The biggest deployment of United States forces since World War II followed as a desperate Baghdad reacted by turning thousands of Westerners for months into "human shields" to protect industrial and military sites. The force, located mainly in Saudi Arabia, near the border with Kuwait and Iraq, grew to well over 400,000 by January of the following year. Together with contributions of Arab, Muslim, and Western European countries (especially Britain, which sent 40,000 troops) designed to make it appear to be a truly multinational effort, the force reached a total of 680,000. By that time, the United States, inexplicably to many, shifted from its original stance of defending Saudi Arabia ("Desert Shield") to one of driving the occupiers out of Kuwait ("Desert Storm")—as well as destroying the military power of Iraq, the specter of whose development of nuclear weapons was given wide publicity, and perhaps overthrowing its regime—without waiting for the embargo to work.

Washington got the Security Council to set January 15, 1991, as the deadline for Iraq's withdrawal, after which force would be authorized. And indeed only one day passed after the deadline before Iraq found itself subjected to the most massive series of air strikes that the world had ever known and by planes and missiles so advanced that it scarcely dared to contest them. Instead it awaited a ground attack, apparently in the hope that the deeply dug-in defenders could impose such losses on the invaders that a continuation of the battle would prove politically infeasible for them at home, possibly enhancing President Husayn's prestige as one who so valiantly stood up to Western imperialism. Husayn may have believed that even a limited military defeat would turn into a political victory. Apparently convinced that Washington was determined to destroy him and his military power whether his forces withdrew from Kuwait or not, the Iraqi leader possibly calculated that if the United States and its coalition partners won the war, their reward would be to find themselves in a gigantic future quagmire.

Shortly after the invasion of Kuwait, a majority of the members of the Arab League voted to condemn Iraq and to send forces to Saudi Arabia. Morocco, Syria, and Egypt sent a few thousand troops each—5,000, 15,000, and 40,000 respectively. Within the Arab world, President Mubarak took the lead in opposing Baghdad. He saw an opportunity to gain increased Western and Arab aid (Washington canceled a $7 billion military sales debt, while loans of an equal amount were forgiven by the oil-exporters) and hoped to gain a key political role for Egypt in the Persian Gulf region. In addition, he apparently was angered by the Iraqi leader's misleading promises to him not to invade Kuwait, as well as by alleged offers of a personal bribe.

President Asad was eager for the opportunity to strike a blow against his old Iraqi enemy and seemed to see this as a chance to strengthen ties with the West and the oil-rich monarchies at a time of decreased Soviet backing. The Syrian president hoped to obtain favorable terms for his country in peace negotiations with Israel, while giving the United States and Israel reason to look the other way as he took advantage of Baghdad's preoccupation with the situation closer to home to consolidate Syrian hegemony in Lebanon. Syrian troops crushed General Aoun's forces in October 1990, massacring several hundred of them after they surrendered. With the various militias disbanding in Beirut, a tenuous peace emerged within the city but still did not extend to the whole country.

Iraq's leader sought to undermine the Arab regimes' role in the United States–led coalition by presenting himself as a spokesperson for the Palestine cause and turning the conflict into an Arab-Israeli war. The summer and fall of 1990 saw Iraqi suggestions that relinquishing Kuwait might be a possibility if Israel also pulled out of the territories it had occupied since 1967 (and if Syria withdrew from Lebanon, et cetera). For a while it seemed possible that a compromise could be reached if the United States would only agree to the convening of an Arab-Israeli peace conference, but Washington rigidly rejected any "linkage" between the two issues or any other compromise.

Iraq let it be known that it would respond to any United States assault by attacking Israel, which, if the latter responded, would put anti-Baghdad Arab regimes under great pressure at home to withdraw from the coalition in order to avoid the anomalous position of being partners of the Jewish state in an Arab-Israeli war. And indeed when the attack on Iraq came, its highly inaccurate Scud missiles (without the chemical warheads that many expected) began to rain down on Tel Aviv as well as Saudi Arabia, hitting residential areas but inflicting few casualties. In order to avoid doing a favor to Iraq—and facing pleas from Washington—the Israelis refrained from immediate retaliation and turned the whole matter into a public relations victory for themselves. The United States—which had distanced itself from the Jewish state earlier in the crisis, as in backing a Security Council resolution condemning it after a massacre of Palestinians at the Haram al-Sharif—rushed Patriot missiles and American military personnel for the first time ever to Israel to shoot the Scuds out of the sky. Later reports cast doubt about the actual effectiveness of the defensive weapons. Germany responded to revelations that its corporations had helped Iraq acquire chemical weapons by extending military aid to Israel, which now dared ask the United States for an additional $13 billion—including $10 billion in loan guarantees—over the next five years to repair damage and facilitate the settlement of immigrants from the USSR.

Even without Israeli retaliation, such rulers as Mubarak began to face fierce protests, notably from Islamists, against their alignment with the forces attacking another Arab country. Protests increased as weeks passed and accounts grew of the continuing merciless destruction of Iraq's military and strategic sites and its infrastructure, and increasingly of the civilian deaths—sometimes in the hundreds from one bombing—and injuries and widespread deprivation. Iraq's Husayn emerged as a great popular hero in places such as Syria, Jordan, Yemen, Sudan, and the Maghrib. Some democratization in Tunisia and especially Algeria, as well as in Jordan, made it hard for governments not to reflect such sentiment. Regimes in Muslim countries such as Pakistan, which had sent a few troops to join the anti-Iraq coalition, began to fear the popular anger.

Many Palestinians saw their livelihoods in Kuwait disrupted by the invasion. Yet the beleaguered Iraqi leader came to be widely admired among them for the way he stood up to the United States and Israel. The PLO did not endorse the occupation of Kuwait (and there are reports that Arafat privately pleaded with, even yelled at, the Iraqi president to withdraw), but in the Arab League it refused to vote to condemn Baghdad (the procedures did not allow either negative votes or abstentions). After all, the PLO had always tried to avoid antagonizing Arab governments, but now, as Arafat maintained friendly ties with Iraq, he and the Palestinians generally won the enmity of the rich monarchies that had previously provided much aid.

The Intifadah intensified. With Israeli-Palestinian violence increasing, people in the occupied territories were at least temporarily stopped from working in Israel, while the drastic drop in remittances from the Gulf added to the economic plight. The beginning of war saw Palestinians subjected to a curfew that amounted to a general house arrest.

Saddam Husayn emerged momentarily not only as the champion of Palestinian rights but of the poor Arabs generally who resented autocratic, corrupt, pro-Western oil monarchies and the great divide that had emerged between themselves and a few in the Persian Gulf states that seemed so crudely addicted to palaces, big cars, and discos. More ironically in light of his past secularism, Husayn resorted to a zealot stance, calling for a *jihad* against the Saudi regime and the United States and other non-Muslim forces that many saw as desecrators of the holy soil of Arabia.

The crisis had devastating effects in many places. With the embargo ending their employment, hundreds of thousands of now impoverished Asians and others who, in many cases, had lived in Kuwait for decades, poured into Jordan, often barely surviving in refugee camps in the desert. Others who had been used to big incomes returned to poverty in places such as Egypt. Responding to pro-Baghdad sentiment among resident Yemenis, the Saudis suddenly forced hundreds of thousands of them to return home.

The Yemeni government seemed to lean toward Baghdad. Riyadh had already been troubled about the emergence of a united Yemen on its border earlier in 1990, especially one with potential territorial claims on it, not to mention the dangerous example of Yemen's elected parliament.

Few places were more shaken than Jordan, where popular support for Iraq was especially strong. According to one interpretation, the king—who had recently asked to be called Sharif Husayn—may have dreamed momentarily of recovering his great grandfather's domain, the Hijaz. In any case, he found himself circumscribed by a democratically elected parliament (dominated by Islamists) and a relatively free press that riots had forced him to accept a year earlier, following decades of royal dictatorship. While continuing his amicable relationship with Baghdad and striving assiduously to avert war, he nevertheless saw no alternative—especially with the United States Navy preventing Iraq-bound cargo from entering Aqaba—to participating in the sanctions against a neighbor that had become his primary trading partner, resulting in brutal economic consequences for his kingdom. Still, the Saudis made economic war on Jordan by cutting off the oil and other aid they had formerly supplied. Many feared that Israeli involvement in the war against Iraq would destroy Jordan, which put troops on alert and declared that it would resist any intrusion into its territory. It was also widely known that many in Israel favored the creation of a Palestinian state in Jordan to relieve them of pressure to withdraw from the West Bank and Gaza, as well as the "transfer" of the Palestinians from these territories. As the popular rage heightened over the continuing destruction of Iraq, King Husayn came down verbally on the side of the Iraqis. Later there were reports from Israelis that he had been in contact with them during this time, confirming suspicions that verbal solidarity with fellow Arabs was essentially a maneuver to save his throne.

Some of the most dramatic reverberations of the crisis involved Iran. Finding himself threatened from another direction, President Husayn immediately sought to take the pressure off his Iranian flank and suddenly accepted virtually all of Tehran's terms for a peace settlement, including its claims vis-à-vis the Shatt al-Arab. Iraqi forces withdrew from the small portions of Iran they had occupied, and prisoners of war on each side returned home. When the war started, the response of much of Iraq's air force was to take refuge in Iran, where it was announced that the planes would be impounded for the duration of the conflict. Iran also saw an opportunity to emerge from the isolation long imposed on it by the Western world. And seeing itself threatened by Iraq's annexation of Kuwait, it condemned the move and joined in the embargo, whose consequences however, large-scale smuggling across the border helped to ameliorate.

But Iran also saw itself and the region threatened by the presence of the United States forces in the Arabian Peninsula. Ayatullah Khamana'i, apparently with the danger of permanent United States bases in mind, called for a *jihad* against this presence. Iranians seemed overwhelmingly to sympathize with their fellow Muslims in Iraq who were being bombed by the Americans, who they continued to believe were the real villains behind Baghdad during the First Persian Gulf War. Many observers suspected that eventually Iran—perhaps after Saddam Husayn's defeat—would be pulled into the sort of antiimperialistic struggle favored by hard-line revolutionaries. Although President Rafsanjani rejected an alliance with Iraq now as "suicidal," there was speculation that an Israeli entry into the war would cause Iran to reconsider its neutrality.

Many in the region saw Washington as exercising a cynical double standard and as manipulating the United Nations for its own purposes. They interpreted its talk of a New World Order not to mean the initiation of the rule of law but rather as renewed imperial domination. There was a widespread belief that a permanent United States military presence in the Persian Gulf region was in the offing, even that the whole Kuwaiti affair had been used for this purpose. While Iran seemed to favor authentic cooperation by states in the region to maintain order, talk by United States officials about a future "security arrangement" seemed to hark back to the Baghdad Pact of the 1950s and to mean an organization through which Washington would control the area's oil and maintain its hegemony.

Eager to find a new role as an asset to the West that would justify enlarged military and economic aid (many Turks were also dreaming of scenarios in which they could revive their old claim to Iraq's Mosul region and possibly annex northern Cyprus), President Özal of Turkey took a strong stand against Baghdad. This evoked protests from opposition parties—who feared getting involved in a conflict with a neighboring country and also rejected Özal's enlargement of the role of the presidency—and even resignations by some members of the cabinet and the chief of staff. But, as the disruption of trade with Iraq cost his country billions of dollars, Özal proceeded to mass 100,000 troops on the Iraqi frontier and to make United States air bases in Turkey available for attacking Iraq.

NEW WORLD ORDER

When the ground attack on Iraqi positions started on February 24, 1991, it turned out to be hardly a war at all. Despite all the weapons that Iraq had acquired, the contest pitted the most advanced technology of the West against a Third World society and demonstrated how far the latter had to go in order to gain equality. American soldiers called the campaign a "cake walk" and talked of "shooting fish in a barrel." Expecting an amphibious assault and one coming overland directly north to Kuwait, the Iraqi forces found the enemy using its "left hook" to attack on their right (western) flank. But relentless bombing had already broken their spirit, and Baghdad undoubtedly had long been willing to withdraw from Kuwait, an option that Washington and its allies found unacceptable because it would have left the Iraqi military basically intact. When the invasion came, Iraqi soldiers surrendered in droves, although in some cases gigantic tractors literally buried them alive in their trenches before they had an opportunity to do so. Iraqi troops retreating from Kuwait on the highway to Basrah and attempting to salvage weapons and loot found themselves subjected to napalm attacks and were asphyxiated and incinerated by "fuel-air explosives." This left the highway littered with charred bodies in such a horrible manner that the fear of revulsion at home may have provided one reason for Washington to end the hostilities sooner than expected—immediately following the liberation of Kuwait and only 100 hours after the ground attack started.

Much of southern Iraq temporarily was under occupation, while—according to some estimates—100,000 Iraqis had died. The destruction of sewage-treatment plants, power plants, bridges, and the like promised to bring further suffering and death. Although in fact repairs of the infrastructure ensued with remarkable success during the following months, a UN report on civilian damage in March 1991 described what had happened as "near apocalyptic" and as having returned the country to the "preindustrial age."

It was not only Iraq that suffered. Before retreating, the Iraqis set fire to the Kuwaiti oil wells, and it was several months before the inferno, with its incalculable damage to the environment, could be extinguished. Kuwait was a shambles. The Arab Monetary Fund put the total cost of the conflict to the Arab world, not including environmental damage or new obstacles to future economic development, at $676 billion.

As for Iraq, the war proved to be only the beginning of its tribulation. Harsh terms were imposed on it. The Security Council called for the destruction of its biological and chemical weapons and an end to the development of nuclear arms, with UN inspection teams carrying out on-site investigations. Parts of future oil revenues were designated to pay reparations to countries suffering damages during the war. A UN commission determined the boundary with Kuwait in ways that gave Iraq less access to the sea than ever before. Occasionally there were further military actions against Iraq, with American cruise missiles hitting targets there twice during 1993, once in response to restrictions put on UN inspectors and again as punishment for an alleged plot to assassinate former President Bush.

And all the while the economic sanctions remained in place. There were repeated offers to allow limited oil sales, with part of the revenue—under close international supervision—going to pay for essential food and medicines. But throughout the early 1990s the regime rejected such an arrangement, while signs that Baghdad was withholding information about armaments remained the basis for refusing to end the sanctions altogether. As a result, the ordinary people—including the opponents of the regime—suffered terrible deprivation, often scrounging to sell whatever they owned in order to survive. A UN study conducted in 1995 estimated that well over half a million Iraqi children had died as a result of the economic warfare. Many ordinary Iraqis felt that they were the victims both of a regime they would like to be rid of and of a Washington-influenced UN that was punishing them rather than the regime itself. In 1996 Baghdad finally accepted UN terms that would allow oil sales of $2 billion during succeeding six-month periods, which it was hoped would end some of the worst hardship, but no end to the sanctions was in sight.

Many people found it surprising that the Second Persian Gulf War ended with Saddam Husayn still in power and with much of his military largely intact. There was even more surprise over the failure of the United States and its partners to come to the aid of those Iraqis who, in response to calls from Washington to do so, tried

322   The Crossing and After/1973–1996

to overthrow him immediately afterward. A massive insurrection erupted in the predominantly Shi'ite south, and another revolt occurred the same spring in the Kurdish north. But the Americans and their allies did nothing to help the rebels, and there are accusations that various kinds of indirect support to the regime helped it accomplish its bloody suppression. It seems that while Washington wanted the Iraqi army to overthrow Saddam Husayn and install a new dictator, it feared the kind of popular rebellions likely to result in a Lebanon-style civil war that would pull outsiders in and turn the defeat of Iraq into an Iranian rather than an American victory in the long run, destabilizing the United States-backed monarchies. The Americans and their allies looked on passively as the Iraqi army used helicopters brutally to suppress the rebels, wreaking massive destruction (including much damage to the Shi'ite holy sites in Najaf and Karbala) in places that the foreign assault had left untouched. They could point out that the recently concluded cease-fire agreement had allowed the use of helicopters (while banning fixed-wing aircraft), but although the inclusion of such a provision may have been an oversight on the part of Iraq's foes, it seemed to mesh with the intent of Washington and its partners not to encourage popular revolts.

The mass flight or expulsion of the Kurdish population as the Iraqi military overran the north horrified much of the world. Perhaps as many as two million people fled into the mountains to be stranded in snow and rain, seeking refuge in Turkey and Iran. Fearing an influx of more Kurds, the Turkish authorities brutally used rifle butts and such in an effort to force them back. Iran was more generous in giving them refuge, doing what it could to help them without the benefit of the international relief agencies that rushed to Turkey. After so many people had perished and the finger of shame could no longer be ignored, Washington declared much of northern Iraq a "no-fly" zone and later totally banned the Iraqi military from the area.

Coalition troops temporarily entered Iraqi Kurdistan to create a "safe haven," and eventually the refugees returned to what was left of their homes. With international guarantees, the Iraqi Kurds were able to establish their de facto independence, holding free elections in 1992 which seemed to provide a model of democracy for the region as the Kurdish Democratic Party and the Patriotic Union for Kurdistan were able to create a broadly based government. But intra-Kurdish violence soon dissipated most of the optimism, and it was widely understood that none of the countries in the region, all of which feared similar independence movements among Kurds on their sides of the border, would tolerate the emergence of a full-fledged independent Kurdish state. And Turkey, which provided the base from which the United States protected the Iraqi Kurds but was occupied with a Kurdish revolt of its own, repeatedly sent its forces into northern Iraq to strike at Kurdistan Workers Party (PKK) guerrillas, who had fled from repression at home to establish bases there. A massive Turkish force invaded northern Iraq during 1994 and remained for several months to destroy the PKK forces and caused much suffering among the Iraqi Kurds as well. This also led to conflict between Iraqi Kurds and the guerrillas, as the latter sometimes uprooted the population in areas suitable for resisting the Turkish army, not to mention the fact that the presence of these outsiders was what evoked Ankara's military campaign.

The regime in Baghdad continued to suppress rebels in the south, despite the creation of a "no-fly zone" there in 1992. The objective was being achieved, in part, by draining the marshes and thus destroying the distinctive ancient culture for which they provided the environment.

The revolts of the Kurds and the Shi'ite Arabs seemingly evoked fears among the Arab Sunnite core of Iraq that helped to solidify the regime's hold. Sporadic plots in the military failed. Although cracks in the power structure sometimes seemed ominous, particularly with the appearance in 1995 of conflict within Saddam Husayn's family (on which he had increasingly relied during the early 1990s), Husayn was able to demonstrate the extent of his control soon afterwards by mobilizing a high level of participation in an "election" that gave him the customary nearly unanimous backing for a new term. The opposition groups whose representatives met in Beirut in March 1991 were too diverse to work together to bring the regime down.

Still a "democracy" and showing impressive economic progress in its continued drive for export-driven industrialization (for which a customs union agreement with the EU in 1995 seemed to open up new opportunities), while low wages, unemployment, inflation, and massive deficit spending were reducing the standard of living, Turkey engaged in cruel suppression of its own large Kurdish minority. In the early 1990s the Özal administration allowed the Kurds limited cultural freedom, but a more conservative policy on this issue soon reemerged, particularly after Demirel's True Path Party (TPP) gained at the expense of the Motherland Party in the 1991 elections. Demirel went on to head a new government and then to be elevated to the presidency two years later, with another TPP leader, Tansu Çiller, becoming the first female prime minister of a Middle Eastern Muslim country. With the revolt of the PKK accelerating in the Southeast and the state of emergency continuing there, the Turkish army carried out a harsh campaign that by 1995 brought about the destruction of 2,200 Kurdish villages, the devastation of much of the country's forests, and the uprooting of 2.5 million people. There were reports of extensive use of torture and killings by death squads, while leading writers who criticized the war on the Kurds faced criminal charges. Even some Kurdish members of the parliament were sentenced to prison.

The immediate aftermath of the Second Persian Gulf War coincided with the demise of the Soviet Union, leaving one military superpower at least momentarily dominant in the Middle East and the world. Some said that in fact both superpowers had lost the Cold War and that the decline of the United States—either in absolute terms or at least relative to the rising power of others—was underway. But for the moment there was a degree of American hegemony in the Middle East which at least one writer compared to the position of Great Britain immediately after World War I. Washington portrayed this "new world order" as one of peace, justice, and democracy, but many people in the Middle East perceived that they were now being subjected to an informal American empire which selective application of these principles would bolster while denying justice to peoples such as the Palestinians and democracy to the subjects of American client monarchs. As one Arab writer saw the matter, the balance of terror had made way for the "terror of imbalance."

Throughout the Middle East and much of the world, agencies such as the International Monetary Fund that were dominated by the United States and other industrial powers were increasingly pushing the idea of "structural adjustment." This involved reducing the role of government in the economy by eliminating state ownership and subsidies that were intended to protect the poor but which allegedly produced inefficiency and corruption. While there was a promise that this would attract investment by multinational corporations looking for cheap labor and lower standards to produce goods for an increasingly globalized market, few Middle Eastern countries saw gains as the suffering of the poor tended to increase.

The New World Order seemed at least for a while to consolidate the position of American client regimes. Now there seemed to be an idea that the United States would protect them, while in any case the recent conflict with Iraq at least temporarily created cracks in the old popular sense of solidarity that regimes had needed to placate, thus making it seem less necessary to appear to support Arab and Islamic causes, particularly concerning Palestine.

The widespread expectation that the democratization recently experienced by much of the world would extend to the Middle East generally failed to be realized. The expulsion of Iraqi forces from Kuwait made way for arbitrary arrests, torture, disappearances, and other human rights violations there. The Palestinians whose presence dated back to 1948 were accused of having collaborated with the Iraqis and found themselves largely expelled from the amirate, as were many members of the Bedoon ("Without") group, that is, people who, despite their residence in Kuwait for generations, were stateless. Kuwaitis, especially those who had engaged in resistance, hoped that their solidarity with the amir during the occupation would earn them the right to a more democratic government but instead saw their ruler attempting to reinstate autocracy. Demands for the restoration of parliament finally bore fruit, and if the electorate represented a larger proportion of the population than the three percent allowed to vote in the past, this was largely by virtue of the recent expulsion of many of those who lacked the franchise. But a lively parliament dominated by the opposition stood in the way of the amir's autocratic inclinations, even if power remained fundamentally in his hands.

Little democratization occurred elsewhere. Although the legalization of political parties in Jordan would seem to represent an advance in this direction, it was accompanied by other changes in the electoral system that brought overrepresentation of the East Bankers, particularly the bedouins who had traditionally supported the monarchy. And as many Palestinians refrained from voting in the elections held in 1993 amid renewed restrictions imposed by the regime, the king was able to get a compliant parliament. The move toward peace with Israel amid growing popular opposition seemed to dictate further emasculation of the limited democracy.

The recently revised Lebanese democratic system got on track. Most of the militias were dissolved. And elections for a new parliament took place in 1992. But all of this was within the framework of the continuing Syrian military presence which many Lebanese saw as making their country a protectorate, a relationship that the Treaty of Fraternity, Cooperation, and Coordination of May 1991, with its provision for joint committees to oversee the country's affairs, seemed to formalize. Objecting to this situation (and to their overall loss of predominance), most of the Maronites boycotted the 1992 elections.

Meanwhile, the Party of God continued to resist the Israeli occupation of the "security zone" in southern Lebanon. This recurrently evoked harsh retaliation, including an air invasion in July 1993 that brought massive destruction of the southern third of the country and forced a temporary flight northward of almost the whole population of this region. Only those too sick or old to do otherwise stayed behind to die from the shelling.

The limited cease-fire worked out in 1993 that allowed continued resistance against the Israeli occupation but forbade attacks on Israel itself or on civilians in Lebanon broke down in April 1996. Retaliating against the killing—unintentionally, it was claimed—of Lebanese children by Israeli artillery, the Party of God launched rocket attacks on a settlement at the northern tip of Israel. This was during an electoral campaign in Israel in which Prime Minister Peres's government was trying—unsuccessfully, as the outcome of the subsequent election proved—to demonstrate to the voters that it was not too soft in the face of Likud accusations. And so another massive attack on Lebanon took place, with that country bombarded for weeks from land, air, and sea. The attacks reached as far as the suburbs of Beirut and eastern Lebanon this time, but again concentrated on the south. About one-half million people fled northward as the highway that was essential to their escape was bombarded. With the attacks directed at civilian targets, the Party of God remained largely unscathed and indeed continued to retaliate against Israeli territory during the whole campaign.

All the while, Washington refused to condemn the Israeli action. It found itself alone with Israel voting against a resolution mildly criticizing the latter in the UN General Assembly. Washington and Tel Aviv apparently hoped that the suffering would turn the Lebanese people against the guerrillas, whose resistance was evoking the attacks and also would force Damascus to rein them in. The Americans ironically justified the campaign as being necessary to keep an Israeli government committed to "peace" in power, and their diplomats were busy trying to get Damascus to accept Tel Aviv's terms. But worldwide outrage over what was happening—notably over the killing of Lebanese civilians, including on one occasion more than a hundred people who were taking refuge in a UN compound (a report of the world organization concluded that it was deliberate)—proved frustrating to the Peres government and its American backers. The result was another limited cease-fire, pretty much the status quo ante except for a provision for an international monitoring committee, allowing the war between the Party of God and the Israeli occupiers to continue. Remarkably, the attacks failed to turn the Lebanese against one another and actually seemed to create a new kind of solidarity across sectarian lines.

Although the Second Persian Gulf War enhanced the long-term American military presence in the Persian Gulf, the monarchical regimes remained circumspect about having large American land forces on their soil. Reports that the United States Central Command would move its headquarters to Bahrain (the home of the American Fifth Fleet) turned out to be premature, as this was too likely to create outrage among nationalist and Islamist circles. But enlarged naval forces, large stores of prepositioned weapons in various Gulf monarchies, the continued presence of air force planes and military personnel (nearly five thousand in 1996) in Saudi territory, and regular military exercises, together with the conclusion of formal defense agreements with some Gulf states, made for an American presence in the region unlike anything that had existed before the war. The movement of Iraqi troops toward the Kuwaiti border in 1994 brought a renewed American buildup in the Gulf. It was not clear whether this would protect these regimes in the long run, particularly against the opposition of their own people that the American presence might exacerbate. Plans that were announced in March 1991 for Syrian and Egyptian forces to remain in the Gulf monarchies fell through as such protectors loomed as potential future threats to the regimes and as Iran voiced opposition to the scheme.

Israel lost much of its pariah status. More and more countries—including India and China, as well as increasing numbers of Muslim and African states—established diplomatic relations with Israel, often calculating that this would gain them favor with Washington. With economic pressure applied to countries such as India and with the former Socialist bloc having disappeared (and with some Arab representatives absent or not voting), Washington was able to get the General Assembly to annul the declaration that Zionism is a form of racism. With its per capita income reaching $16,000 a year (about the same as Great Britain's) by the mid-1990s, Israel's economy was growing rapidly, and its backers could point to the prevalence of luxuries that now made it a "rich country."

But some observers believed that Israel would not be a winner in the post-Cold War world. The Second Persian Gulf War had demonstrated that it was a liability, and a main fear of the American-led coalition was that it would undermine them by joining in the attack on Iraq. And the end of the Cold War carried with it the demise of the idea that Israel was a strategic asset in the conflict with the Soviet Union. On the other hand, those who believed that support for the Jewish state had always undermined the American position in the area by driving the Arabs into Soviet arms foresaw an American foreign policy driven by domestic considerations that would now be less inhibited than ever before in its backing for it. And some supporters of Israel seemed to be preparing a new rationale for continuing United States backing: that it was on the front lines of a new world conflict in which the "Red menace" had made way for a "Green" one, that is the "Islamic threat."

In any case, the move toward a peace settlement gained new momentum in the immediate aftermath of the Second Persian Gulf War as Washington saw the need to vindicate the position of those Arab regimes that had played such a crucial role in defeating Iraq. With an arrangement worked out whereby Palestinians from the West Bank and the Gaza Strip would participate technically as part of the Jordanian delegation but in close consultation with the PLO, a peace conference met for one day in Madrid in October 1991, and a series of bilateral meetings between the Israelis and their neighbors followed, as well as multilateral meetings on "regional" issues. For months there was little progress, and Prime Minister Shamir allegedly confided to other Israelis that he was planning to drag his feet for ten years, after which there would be so many settlers in the occupied territories that it would be too late for anyone to push for withdrawal. And indeed the Bush administration embittered the Israelis and their supporters by calling for an end to the establishment of new settlements. For a while Washington refused to approve $10 billion in United States government loan guarantees that the Israelis said were necessary to provide housing for the influx of Jewish immigrants from the former Soviet Union unless the construction of settlements stopped. And it seems that the prospect of loan guarantees served as a carrot to Israeli voters in the June 1992 elections, leading—along with other forces, including the votes of pragmatic new immigrants from the former Soviet Union—to gains by the Labour party that allowed Rabin to head a new coalition government, with the Likud in the opposition for the first time since 1977. Although the Rabin government refused to stop building settlements that already were in progress or to refrain from establishing what it called "strategic"—as opposed to "political"—settlements, Washington gave in and approved the loan guarantees.

Soon thereafter the Israelis found a new administration in Washington, headed by President Bill Clinton, that seemed committed to them to an unusual degree. For example, the Clinton administration appointed a reputed Likud-leaning individual long associated with the main pro-Israel lobby organization, AIPAC, as its main advisor on Middle Eastern affairs (he later became the ambassador to Tel Aviv). The United States sometimes demonstrated more hawkish pro-Israeli positions than those of the Israeli government itself. Thinking that it had found an issue that even a country at peace with Israel could not be faulted for, Egypt had to back down in the face of American opposition in 1995 after initially leading a movement to make the renewal of the Nuclear Nonproliferation Treaty conditional on Israel's adherence to it. Initial expectations in the early 1990s that American aid to Israel would gradually be reduced were followed by Clinton's assurance that the high levels of assistance would continue "for years to come" and might even be increased, and it was left to a few Israelis to discuss the possibility of flaunting their affluence by requesting a reduction of one billion dollars a year.

Meanwhile, Islamist forces were giving the Intifadah a more violent turn, and the Israelis were finding it difficult to deal with. The emergence of a small group known as Islamic Jihad, inspired by the Iranian Revolution, may have provided an important ingredient in the Intifadah in the first place, while the heretofore more passive Muslim Brotherhood responded by forming a new organization, the Movement for Islamic Resistance (Hamas, "Zeal"), whose military wing included Izz al-Din Qassam Brigades that attacked the occupiers. Everything the Israelis did in their attempts to destroy this new militancy seemed to fail. For example, they arrested over 400 alleged Islamist leaders, including prominent professional people, and expelled them across the northern frontier of the Israeli-occupied area of Lebanon in December 1992, where with the assistance of Lebanese Islamists they set up tents on the side of a hill for more than a year. This new resistance movement showed signs of eclipsing the role of the PLO (which also had lost important financial backing from Gulf monarchies), thus giving Arafat an incentive to work out a deal with the Israelis.

The breakthrough came as a big surprise in 1993 with news that secret negotiations between the Israelis and the PLO in Oslo had borne fruit. After reaching an agreement on mutual recognition (though asymmetrically of Israel's "right to exist" as a state in return for the PLO's right to represent the Palestinian people, not to establish a state), the two sides formally signed a Declaration of Principles at the White House in Washington in September, with Rabin reluctantly shaking Arafat's hand. According to the new arrangement, details of which later were worked out, Israeli military forces would withdraw from the Gaza Strip and from Jericho to allow a Palestinian Interim Self-Governing Authority to take charge, although Israel would still have control of its settlements, access to roads, and control over the external border even for these small areas. Arafat indeed was able to set up his administration in the two areas during the following year and—despite many delays that set back the original timetable—gradually to take over various functions in other parts of the West Bank (excluding East Jerusalem, the determination of whose status was left for a later stage). The Israelis finally redeployed their forces from most of the major population centers in the West Bank, as originally agreed, in time to allow elections for a Council to take place in January 1996, and for Arafat to be elected as president of the transitional authority. Talks began later in that year that were supposed to work out a permanent settlement by December 1999.

It was far from clear whether the end of the Palestinian-Israeli conflict was indeed at hand. Right-wing Israeli settlers and their backers from the Likud feared that a Palestinian state would emerge. And indeed one of the first major setbacks the "peace process" had to overcome occurred when a settler in Hebron took matters into his own hands by carrying out a massacre of Muslims praying in the Ibrahimi Mosque in 1994. The assassination of Rabin by another right-wing Israeli the next year portended further problems for Israeli-Palestinian peace, although it temporarily discredited the hawkish faction and brought Peres, who was even more committed to peace than his predecessor, to the prime ministership. Repeated Israeli assassinations of Palestinian Islamist leaders and suicide attacks on Israeli civilians by members of Hamas also kept setting back support for the arrangement. The first months of 1996 saw an unprecedented flurry of such killings, which seemed at least temporarily to be turning the Israeli voters against the arrangement with the Palestinians (one that had produced new heights of personal insecurity for Israelis). Indeed, this contributed to the defeat of Peres by his Likud rival, Benjamin Netanyahu, in the direct elections for prime minister later that year and to the formation of a coalition government consisting of the Likud and other right-wing parties that were highly critical of the direction that the "peace process" had been taking. Arafat, who had been forced to walk a tight rope between suppressing those who insisted on still resisting the Israelis and not destroying his credibility among his own people, was left with little room for optimism.

Although realism often tempered this feeling (there were some indications that the political wing of Hamas would eventually agree to work within the framework the PLO had accepted), many Palestinians saw Arafat as having become a collaborator who could hope to win further concessions only to the extent that he satisfied continuing Israeli demands and whose role was to do the Israelis' "dirty work" (Israelis sometimes spoke of him as their "enforcer") in return for backing him. There were those who argued that a process had been put in place that would make it difficult for the Israelis eventually to reject Palestinian independence, but others were not so sure. The latter argued that even if the end result turned out to be formal Palestinian independence—which they said still might not be more than a "bantustan"—the Israelis were openly committed to keeping East Jerusalem and other parts of the West Bank. Arafat's critics saw him as having given his stamp of legitimacy to the occupation— the bulk of the West Bank was still under direct occupation—and as having agreed to work within its framework without any guarantee of satisfactory results.

At least for a while concessions by each side encouraged reciprocity. The Palestine National Council in 1996, apparently in a futile attempt to help Peres and the Labour Party win the elections, finally abrogated the clause in its charter (already long out of keeping with its policies) adopted three decades earlier calling for the liberation of the whole of Palestine. Soon thereafter the Labour Party rewarded Arafat with a formal withdrawal of its opposition to the possibility of a Palestinian state. But Netanyahu's victory in the election created despair among those on both sides that wanted such a two-state settlement. It was not even necessary for Netanyahu to renounce the agreements that his Labour Party predecessors had already made with the Palestinians, for, aside from the fact that it was the PLO itself that was involved, the commitments to them scarcely went beyond the "autonomy" in an unspecified part of the occupied territories that Israel had agreed to in the days of Begin.

Meanwhile, "peace" had brought more violence than ever before, and Palestinians in the West Bank and Gaza were suffering renewed deprivation. The menial jobs in Israel on which they had long become so dependent now were being lost as each act of violence invited the closing of the frontier and as the Israelis imported alternative cheap labor from Eastern Europe and the Far East. The Israelis continued to build their settlements, to confiscate land, and to mete out collective punishments such as destroying the homes of Palestinian terrorists' relatives that they did not apply in the case of Israeli terrorists and to seal off Palestinian communities. In the early months of 1996 the towns and villages were subjected to harsh isolation from one another and from the outside, and the resulting loss of employment brought the condition of those in the occupied territories to a new low. Many were complaining about the way the new Palestinian authority, having to satisfy Israeli demands to suppress opposition to the "peace process," was violating human rights.

The move toward Arab-Israeli peace gained on other fronts. Jordan made peace with Israel in 1994, with the king publicly demonstrating great zeal for friendly ties. Some other Arab states curtailed the longtime boycott of Israel or established low-level diplomatic ties with it, while various meetings were taking place to discuss regional economic cooperation (and causing fears on the part of many Arabs of Israeli economic domination). With Syria moving toward accepting peace with Israel and with the latter, while the Labour government was in power, seemingly edging toward an agreement to withdraw totally from the Golan Heights, there was widespread expectation that a Syrian-Israeli (and with it a Lebanese-Israeli) peace treaty would eventually materialize. But with the Likud adamantly opposing the return of the Golan Heights to Syria, Netanyahu's victory in 1996 seemed to exclude such a possibility in the short run.

With hardly any other form left for protest to take against corruption, injustice, authoritarianism, and American and Israeli domination, the New World Order evoked renewed Islamist resistance. Islamist organizations increasingly were able to provide medical and charitable services to the poor that otherwise would not have been available at a time when structural adjustment was producing much hardship. And guerrillas could be reassured that if they died in a holy endeavor their families would be taken care of by the militant organizations they were working with. When elections approached being free in various countries, Islamist gains recurrently surprised both the local elites and Western observers, while more militant, revolutionary Islamist movements—sometimes augmented by the zeal of those who had participated in the war against the Soviets in Afghanistan, ironically with American backing and thus evoking the term "blowback"—engaged in warfare against existing regimes (and, in an extreme case, constructed bombs designed to wreak havoc on New York City).

Especially when regimes blocked Islamist participation in politics, violence often was the result. Egypt, where moderate Islamist groups in fact existed openly and were able to get limited representation in the People's Assembly, experienced something bordering on civil war during the early 1990s. The militant Islamists for a while resorted to threats against foreign tourists, an important prop for the economy and thus of the existing regime. By 1995 the regime—whose fraudulent practices in the general elections that year and new restrictions on the press seemed to provide further signs of decay—was extending its repression to the moderate Muslim Brethren.

Algeria seemingly was becoming a democracy in the early 1990s. But when the main Islamist party, the FIS—after winning in local and regional elections in 1991—stunned its rivals with the extent of its success in the first stage of national elections the next year and seemed to be ready to win a big majority in the parliament, the military intervened (with much Western backing, especially from France) and cancelled the contest. The Islamists turned to guerrilla warfare against the new dictatorship, and the bloody repression that ensued left thousands dead.

The monarchies of the Arabian Peninsula seemed to be increasingly vulnerable to Islamist opposition. Both the cost of the Second Persian Gulf War and the continuing general lag in oil prices meant that the abundance of petrodollars that had bolstered the rulers' power now was making way for governmental debt and cutbacks on spending—the classic recipe for revolution. Massive arms purchases—$30 billion worth by Saudi Arabia during 1991–1994 alone, sixty percent of this from the United States—added to the financial problems without contributing much, on the basis of past experience, to defense against these regimes' internal and external enemies. Perhaps the fear of cutting further into the oil sales of such countries provided one important reason for not ending the sanctions against Iraq. And some observers believed that the renewed ties to the United States that were supposed to protect them actually were providing the "friendly fire" that ultimately would bring them down. The Saudis were putting growing numbers of dissidents in jail, while computers and fax machines in the hands of expatriates were providing new means for attacking the regime. An explosion set off by Islamist rebels at the United States military mission in Riyadh in 1995—for which four Saudis (including three veterans of the Afghanistan conflict) later were beheaded—killed several American military personnel engaged in training the Saudi National Guard. In June 1996 a truck bomb killed nineteen—and wounded many more—American air force personnel in Dhahran. With such American forces seeming to constitute a vital prop for the regime, they had become the logical target of revolutionaries and of those who generally were angry about Washington's policies in the area.

Demands in Bahrain during the mid-1990s (particularly among the large Shi'ite majority that was subject to much discrimination) for the restoration of the parliament that the regime dissolved two decades earlier evoked repression. This led to riots and bombings early in 1996 that threatened to bring down the autocratic and corrupt ruling family. The Bahraini regime reported later that year that it had foiled an organized plot to overthrow it and blamed Iran for allegedly providing aid and training to the conspirators.

Even in Turkey, where "structural adjustment" was causing much hardship, including inflation and unemployment, Islamism showed signs of finally being about to reverse Atatürk's policies. The Welfare Party (WP, successor to the former National Salvation Party) won control of numerous municipalities, including Istanbul and Ankara, in local elections in 1994. Then the WP came out on top in the general elections of December 1995, getting 21.3 percent of the vote and 158 of 550 seats in the parliament. With the failure of an initial attempt of secular parties to maintain a viable coalition, WP leader Necmettin Erbakan reached an agreement with the TPP in June 1996 designating him as the new prime minister, with Çiller to be assistant prime minister and minister of foreign affairs. A coalition between such incompatible partners seemed to have little chance of lasting long or, if it did, of allowing the WP to make profound changes. But many people believed that being in office might allow Erbakan's party to gain increasing numbers of votes in the future, although it was likely that the military (whose commitment to secularism extended to dismissing officers who showed such signs of being religious as making the *hajj* or allowing their wives to wear head scarves) would intervene again to prevent any democratic reversal of Atatürk's changes if indeed this ever became imminent.

While the Turkish Islamists were critical of their country's alliance with the West generally, they were particularly hostile to the once-secret relationship with Israel that now was both enlarged and more open. A major Turkish-Israeli agreement concluded in 1996 provided for renewed collaboration—apparently after Damascus and Athens (the two Aegean countries had recently gone to the brink of war over an uninhabitable island) signed a pact on military cooperation that Ankara saw as a threat. The collaboration included intelligence sharing, military training in each other's territory, Israeli training for Turkish troops, and joint military exercises. Syria, which was giving refuge to Kurdish leaders from Turkey and allegedly allowing the PKK to train in the parts of Lebanon it controlled, saw the agreement as providing for a kind of encirclement of itself that posed a dire danger. A bomb, apparently planted by Turkey, that exploded in Damascus early in 1996 caused additional concerns for Syria. Iran saw the Turkish-Israeli agreement as leading to a new base for attacking it. And the Israelis and the Turkish military saw the Islamists as a threat to their continuing relationship.

Wherever Islamist forces gained ground, their opponents tended simplistically to blame Iranian support. And while the Iranian leadership leaned more and more in a pragmatic direction—and arguably was acting more in an Iranian nationalist fashion than as zealous missionaries of Islamic revolution—it continued to maintain links with and to provide inspiration to those who challenged the status quo. One exception was its policy toward Afghanistan, where the fall of the communist regime in 1992 made way for a patchwork of feuding factions; there it was Saudi Arabia and Pakistan that supported the militant factions, including the ultra-zealous—and anti-Shi'ite—Student (Taliban) Militia that was trying to unify the country in the mid-1990s, while the Iranians backed the moderate regime in Kabul. Tehran generally was demonstrating pragmatism in the newly independent Muslim republics of the former Soviet Union, where it was competing with Ankara and others for influence. It was trying to maintain normal relations with the Arab monarchies of the Persian Gulf. But as far afield as Bosnia, where Serbs were engaged in genocide against the Muslims, it was Revolutionary Iran that most eagerly sent aid—partly, as it turned out, with the tacit approval of the United States—in the form of military training and weapons and small contingents of Revolutionary Guards. Iran established strong ties with the Islamic regime in the Sudan, where the revolt in the non-Muslim south was leading to atrocities on all sides. It continued to inspire various revolutionary movements and by the 1990s clearly had become the main center of opposition to Israel, although there were indications that it would pragmatically acquiesce if Syria made peace. The relationship with Iraq remained tense—and sometimes violent—after the Second Persian Gulf War, with Iran aiding the rebels and opening its doors to those who fled. Iranian planes also retaliated against guerrilla raids by bombing People's Mujahidin bases in Iraq during 1993.

Revolutionary Iran was experiencing its own problems at home. The decline in oil revenues and the cost of the First Persian Gulf War had cut deeply into the country's economy. There was also the cost of supporting refugees, mainly from Iraq and Afghanistan; statistical reports on refugees gave Iran the distinction of having more, in absolute terms, than any other country in the world. With severe inflation and unemployment creating discontent, the regime confronted rioters in various places in 1992, particularly in Mashhad. Although at least a significant minority of the population apparently continued strongly to support the regime, there were many reports of a backlash against it that led to a loss of interest in Islam, even stories of a few individuals in extreme cases who were subjecting themselves to persecution by committing apostasy (that is, embracing Christianity). As for leadership within Shi'ism, the regime tried to get the Jurist, Ayatullah Khamana'i—whose credentials as a *mujtahid* were questionable—accepted as the sole *marja-i taqlid,* but gave up in the face of resistance in many places to a government trying to interfere in what historically had been a personal matter. The division persisted between the now-predominant pragmatists and the radicals, some of whom were excluded from the 1992 parliamentary election on the ground that they had flunked an examination on Islam, but that chamber remained a lively center of debate on the government's policies. There appeared to be some tension in the relationship between Khamana'i and President Rafsanjani, with the former apparently leaning more in the direction of pushing for social justice internally and opposing the status quo externally, although no break between them took place.

Compared to most of the countries in the area, Iran's regime had a somewhat democratic character, with one of Rafsanjani's opponents in the presidential election of 1993 allowed to get nearly a quarter of the vote. But with only a little over half of the qualified voters bothering to participate, it seemed that revolutionary fervor had faded. Parliamentary seats were highly contested (and there was a high rate of turnover with each election), although the Council of Guardians excluded forty percent of the would-be candidates in the 1996 races, which—without producing a clear majority for either side—pitted two main factions against each other, namely the pragmatic, market-oriented Servants of Construction that backed Rafsanjani's policies versus the zealous Militant Clergy Association, allied with the Speaker of the parliament, Ali Akbar Natiq-Nuri.

Contrary to the image in the Western world of Iran having returned to the past, there were some signs of a synthesis of Islam and modernity that sharply contrasted this country with conservative Islamic countries. As a case in point, the Iranian parliament included several female deputies, and there were women in other official positions. The president's daughter, Fa'izah Rafsanjani, proved to be such a popular candidate in Tehran in the 1996 parliamentary elections that there was some talk about her as a possible successor to her father, who was constitutionally prohibited from seeking election to a third term. And going back to the latter days of Imam Khumayni's guardianship, the country was making serious efforts to push birth control, something that conservative Muslims elsewhere strongly opposed, and participated in the conference on population in Cairo in 1994 that some Muslim governments boycotted. Working within the limits of Islamic law, various efforts were being made to improve the position of women in matters of marriage and divorce.

But for Washington, Tehran represented a threat to the status quo and was branded a "rogue nation" and a supporter of "terrorism." Iranians responded to such epithets by hurling the word "outlaw" back at the United States. The Clinton administration declared a policy of "dual containment" against both Iraq and Iran, and in 1994 it banned Americans from engaging in economic ties with Iran. Washington tried, with little success, to pressure the rest of the world to follow its lead in this punitive policy. By contrast, Japan and the countries of Europe were meeting Iranian pragmatism with a policy of "constructive engagement." Washington was devoting special effort to preventing Iran from strengthening its military forces and particularly from acquiring nuclear weapons. In 1995 President Clinton signed a bill passed by Congress allocating $18 billion to be used to overthrow the Iranian government.

New United States legislation the following year carried the economic warfare a step further—and threatened to antagonize much of the world—by banning American dealings with foreign companies that invested in Iran or Libya.

CONCLUSIONS

From 1973 on, the Middle East began to assume a shape that few could previously have foreseen. The gap between Arabs and Israelis—and perhaps more broadly between the Middle East and the West—showed signs, at least for a while, of closing. For some the military "Crossing" of the Suez Canal and the increased oil prices momentarily symbolized a beginning of the swing of the pendulum of history back to the East. Corresponding to elation on the Eastern side, some Westerners began to open dusty copies of Spengler's *The Decline of the West* or even to issue exaggerated pronouncements about an Islamic East that, figuratively speaking, was prevailing in a second Battle of Tours.

In truth, the Middle East was an underdeveloped area suffering from centuries of subordination and still struggling to bridge the gap between itself and a West that for centuries had undergone accelerated modernization. It was still the Middle East that found itself subjected to varying kinds of Western domination, not vice versa. The fact that the whole Arab world was still unable to defeat the minuscule state of Israel and that even within that country those of Western origin remained dominant most clearly demonstrated the continuing civilization gap. The advantages of oil wealth accrued mainly to a few countries, not including most of the ones with large populations. Even those who became rich could not buy modernity overnight, and a tragic possibility loomed that all the money would be squandered sometime in the twenty-first century, before the area achieved a modern technological level. The quest of Middle Eastern nations for viable political orders promised to be even more arduous than that for economic development, and internal and interstate conflict threatened to destroy everything. Furthermore, a fundamental indicator of how far the Middle East had to go was that what military successes it had achieved were largely with weapons imported from Western countries such as the United States and the USSR. An even deeper measure may be the relative meagerness of recent Middle Eastern productivity in cultural and scientific fields. Reflecting its Western origins, Israel alone surpassed the whole Arab world in scientific publication by more than a two-to-one ratio.

As the limited assertions of Middle Eastern interests by Western client rulers such as Sadat and the shah brought disappointments, more militant responses to Western hegemony emerged. The Iranian revolution and parallel zealot movements posed a new kind of challenge to Western political, economic, and cultural supremacy. These movements, as well as less political Islamist responses, belied the old assumption that the modernization of the world was inevitably bringing about its westernization. So far, accelerated chaos and destruction in many parts of the region overshadowed everything else. Internecine conflict left Middle Eastern peoples still subordinated but made way for new challenges both by zealots and—if only for a short time—by such a ruthless Herodian as Saddam Husayn, who also resorted to zealot slogans as the 1990s began with an unprecedented assault on his country that was coming to be seen on the popular level within the region as a newly intensified Western colonialism.

As the decade passed, the Middle East—unlike some parts of the Third World—seemed to lag further behind the West than ever before, while the end of the Cold War left it at the mercy of the victorious superpower and its local clients. Many felt the need to come to terms with the new reality, which to those secularists who found it unacceptable seemed preferable to any alternative offered by the Islamists, whose zealot approach acquired unprecedented momentum as the vehicle of protest.

bibliographical essay
selected works in english

For more thorough bibliographical materials, the reader may want to refer to Claude Cahen, *Jean Sauvaget's Introduction to the History of the Muslim East: A Bibliographical Guide* (Berkeley and Los Angeles: University of California Press, 1965; reprint, Westport, CN: Greenwood Press, 1984); R. Stephen Humphreys, *Islamic History: A Framework for Inquiry,* 2d ed. (Princeton, NJ: Princeton University Press, 1991); and J. D. Pearson, *Index Islamicus, 1906–1955* (London: Mansell, 1958) and subsequent five-year supplements, as well as *The Quarterly Index Islamicus* (London). Also see *The Middle East: Abstracts and Index* (Pittsburgh).

For criticisms of conventional scholarship, see Edward Said, *Orientalism* (New York: Pantheon Books, 1978). For essays replying to Said, see Bernard Lewis, *Islam and the West* (Oxford and New York: Oxford University Press, 1993). Also see Asaf Hussain et al., eds., *Orientalism, Islam and Islamists* (Brattleboro, VT: Amana Books, 1984), and Patricia Springborg, *Western Republicanism and the Oriental Prince* (Austin: University of Texas Press, 1992). Also on Western attitudes, see Norman Daniel, *Islam and the West: The Making of an Image,* 2d ed. (Oxford: Oneworld Publications, 1993).

Relevant journals include the *International Journal of Middle East Studies* (New York) and the *Middle East Journal* (Washington, D.C.). Among the best publications on current developments are *Middle East Report* (Washington, D.C.) and *Middle East International* (London).

GEOGRAPHY AND WORLD HISTORICAL PERSPECTIVE

General geographical works include Alasdair Drysdale and Gerald Blake, *The Middle East and North Africa: A Political Geography* (New York: Oxford University Press, 1985), and Colbert C. Held, *Middle East Patterns: Places, Peoples, and Politics,* 2d ed. (Boulder, CO: Westview Press, 1994).

For the Middle East in world historical perspective, see William McNeill, *The Rise of the West* (Chicago: University of Chicago Press, 1963). Invaluable insight may be gained from Arnold Toynbee's works, notably *A Study of History,* 12 vols. (New York: Oxford University Press, 1933–1961), also available under the same title in a two-volume abridgment by D. C. Somerville (New York: Oxford University Press, 1947–1957). I also especially recommend the *Journal of World History* (Honolulu).

ISLAMIC HISTORY: GENERAL WORKS

For an unsurpassed history of a central part of the Islamic world, see Albert Hourani, *A History of the Arab Peoples* (Cambridge, MA: The Belknap Press of Harvard University Press, 1991). As for general treatments of Islamic history, P. M. Holt et al., *The Cambridge History of Islam,* 2 vols. (Cambridge: Cambridge University Press, 1970), is indispensable. Marshall Hodgson, *The Venture of Islam,* 3 vols. (Chicago: University of Chicago Press, 1974), is a monumental work. Also see Ira M. Lapidus, *A History of Islamic Societies* (Berkeley: University of California Press, 1988). Another excellent work is Bertold Spuler, *The Muslim World: A Historical Survey,* 4 vols., trans. by F. R. C. Bagley (Leiden, Netherlands: E.J. Brill, 1960–1981).

For rulers and dates, see Clifford Bosworth, *The Islamic Dynasties: A Chronological and Genealogical Handbook* (Chicago: Aldine, 1967). A variety of useful materials may be found in Jere Bacharach, *A Middle East Studies Handbook,* 2d ed. (Seattle: University of Washington Press, 1984).

A new edition of the *Encyclopaedia of Islam* (Leiden, Netherlands: E.J. Brill, 1954–) is in progress. The first eight volumes have been published. The old edition (Leiden, Netherlands: E.J. Brill, 1913–1938), reprinted as *E.J. Brill's First Encyclopaedia of Islam,* 9 vols. (1987), is still useful. Although it focuses on modern topics, an even more valuable reference for a wide range of students of Islam and the Islamic world is John L. Esposito, ed., *The Oxford Encyclopedia of the Modern Islamic World,* 4 vols. (New York and Oxford: Oxford University Press, 1995).

First-rate introductory material may be found in Trevor Mostyn, executive ed., and Albert Hourani, advisory ed., *The Cambridge Encyclopedia of the Middle East and North Africa* (New York: Cambridge University Press, 1988). Also see Reeva Simon et al., eds., *Encyclopedia of the Modern Middle East,* 4 vols. (New York: Macmillan, 1995).

FROM MUHAMMAD TO THE MONGOLS
AND MAMLUKS

The following works deal mainly with this period: Gustav von Grunebaum, *Classical Islam: A History, 600–1250* (Chicago: Aldine, 1970); Philip Hitti, *History of the Arabs,* 9th ed. (New York: St. Martin's Press, 1976); Hugh Kennedy, *The Prophet and the Age of the Caliphates: The Islamic Near East from the Sixth to the Eleventh Centuries* (New York: Longman, 1986), Bernard Lewis, *The Arabs in History,* 6th ed. (New York and Oxford: Oxford University Press, 1993); H. U. Rahman, *A Chronology of Islamic History, 570–1000 CE* (Boston: G. K. Hall, 1989); J. J. Saunders, *A History of Medieval Islam* (London: Routledge & Kegan Paul, 1965); and Joseph Schacht and C. E. Bosworth, eds., *The Legacy of Islam,* 2d ed. (Oxford: Clarendon Press, 1974).

Some important medieval Arabic historical materials are increasingly becoming available in English translation. Most of the 38 volumes of *The History of al-Tabari (Ta'rikh al rusul wa'l muluk),* translated by various scholars and edited by Ehsan Yar-Shater, have already appeared (Albany: State University of New York Press, 1987–). Also see Masudi, *Meadows of Gold: The Abbasids,* trans. and ed. by Paul Lunde and Caroline Stone (London: Kegan Paul International, 1989). Excerpts from a wide range of sources may be found in Bernard Lewis, ed. and trans., *Islam from the Prophet Muhammad to the Capture of Constantinople,* 2 vols. (New York: Walker and Walker, 1974; reprint, New York: Oxford University Press, 1984.) Also see Eric Schroder, ed., *Muhammad's People: A Tale by Anthology* (Portland, ME: Bond Wheelwright, 1955).

For socioeconomic matters, see E. Ashtor, *A Social and Economic History of the Near East in the Middle Ages* (Berkeley and Los Angeles: University of California Press, 1976); Richard W. Bulliet, *Conversion to Islam in the Medieval Period: An Essay in Quantitative History* (Cambridge: Cambridge University Press, 1979); Richard W. Bulliet, *Islam: The View from the Edge* (New York: Columbia University Press, 1994); Richard W. Bulliet, *The Patricians of Nishapur: A Study in Medieval Islamic Social History* (Cambridge, MA: Harvard University Press, 1972); M. A. Cook, ed., *Studies in the Economic History of the Middle East from the Rise of Islam to the Present* (London: Oxford University Press, 1970); Ann K. S. Lambton, *Continuity and Change in Medieval Persia: Aspects of Administrative, Economic and Social History, 11th–14th Centuries* (Albany: State University of New York Press, 1988); Bernard Lewis, *Race and Slavery in the Middle East* (New York and Oxford: Oxford University Press, 1990); Maurice Lombard, *The Golden Age of Islam,* trans. by Joan Spencer (New York: American Elsevier, 1975); and Andrew W. Watson, *Agricultural Innovation in the Early Islamic World* (Cambridge: Cambridge University Press, 1983). Also see S. D. Goiten, *A Mediter-*

ranean Society: The Jewish Communities of the Arab World as Portrayed in the Documents of the Cairo Geniza, 4 vols. (Berkeley and Los Angeles: University of California Press, 1967–1983).

Works on cities include L. Carl Brown, ed., *From Madina to Metropolis: Heritage and Change in the Near Eastern City* (Princeton: Darwin Press, 1973), and A. H. Hourani and S. M. Stern, eds., *The Islamic City: A Colloquium* (Oxford: Bruno Cassirer; Philadelphia: University of Pennsylvania Press, 1970).

On the topic of women, see Leila Ahmed, *Women and Gender in Islam: Historical Roots of a Modern Debate* (New Haven, CN and London: Yale University Press, 1992), and Nikki R. Keddie and Beth Baron, eds., *Women in Middle Eastern History: Shifting Boundaries in Sex and Gender* (New Haven: CN: Yale University Press, 1991).

On the Prophet's life, the beginner may want to consult W. Montgomery Watt, *Muhammad: Prophet and Statesman* (London: Oxford University Press, 1961). Watt also has written two more detailed studies: *Muhammad at Mecca* (Oxford: Clarendon Press, 1953; reprint, London: Billing, 1965) and *Muhammad at Medina* (Oxford: Clarendon Press, 1956; reprint, Karachi, Pakistan: Oxford University Press, 1981). Also see Martin Lings, *Muhammad: His Life Based on the Earliest Sources,* 2d ed. (Cambridge: Islamic Texts Society, 1991), and Maxime Rodinson, *Muhammad* (New York: Pantheon Books, 1980). An important medieval biography is also available in English translation: A. Guillaume, trans., *The Life of Muhammad: A Translation of Ibn Ishaq's Sirit Rasul Allah* (Lahore, Karachi, and Dacca: Oxford University Press, Pakistan Branch, 1955). Also see Nabia Abbot, *Aisha, the Beloved of Mohammed* (Chicago: University of Chicago Press, 1942; reprint, New York: Arno Press, 1987).

The "Wars of Apostasy" are covered in Elias Shoufani, *Al Riddah and the Muslim Conquest of Arabia* (Toronto: Toronto University Press, 1973). On the subsequent conquests, see Philip Hitti's translation of Ahmad al-Baladhuri's work: *The Origins of the Islamic State* (New York: Columbia University Press, 1916; reprint, Beirut: Khayats, 1966). Also on the early Islamic period: Khalifa Yahya Blankinship, *The End of the Jihad State: The Reign of Hisham 'Abd al-Malik and the Collapse of the Umayyads* (Albany: State University of New York Press, 1994); Fred McGraw Donner, *The Early Islamic Conquests* (Princeton, NJ: Princeton University Press, 1982); G. R. Hawting, *The First Dynasty of Islam* (Carbondale: Southern Illinois University Press, 1987); John W. Jandora, *The March from Medina: A Revisionist Study of the Arab Conquests* (Clifton, NJ: Kingston Press, 1989); and J. Wellhausen, *The Arab Kingdom and Its Fall* (Calcutta: University of Calcutta; reprint, Beirut: Khayats, 1966).

For a synthesis of chronicles, see Sir William Muir, *The Caliphate* (London: J. Grant, 1915; reprint, New York: AMS Press, 1975).

M. A. Shaban is the author of three controversial revisionist studies: *Islamic History,* A.D. 600–750 (A.H. 132): A New Interpretation* (Cambridge: Cambridge University Press, 1971); *Islamic History: A New Interpretation, vol. 2:* A.D. 750–1055 (A.H. 132–448) (Cambridge: Cambridge University Press, 1976); and *The Abbasid Revolution* (Cambridge: University Press, 1970).

Works on the Abbasids include N. Abbot, *Two Queens of Baghdad* (Chicago: University of Chicago Press, 1946; reprint, London: Saqi Books, 1986); Muhammad Ahsan, *Social Life Under the Abbasids* (London: Longman, 1979); Elton L. Daniel, *The Political and Social History of Khurasan Under Abbasid Rule, 747–820* (Minneapolis: Bibliotheca Islamica, 1979); Hugh Kennedy, *The Early Abbasid Caliphate: A Political History* (Totowa, NJ: Barnes & Noble, 1981); Jacob Lassner, *The Shaping of Abbasid Rule* (Princeton, NJ: Princeton University Press, 1980); Guy Le Strange, *Baghdad Under the Abbasid Caliphate* (Oxford: Clarendon Press, 1924); and Guy Le Strange, *Lands of the Eastern Caliphate,* 2d ed. (New York: Barnes & Noble, 1966).

Works on regional dynasties include C. E. Bosworth, *The Ghaznavids* (Edinburgh: Edinburgh University Press, 1963); Marshall Hodgson, *The Order of the Assassins* (The Hague: Mouton, 1955); Hafizullah Kabir, *The Buwayhid Dynasty of Baghdad* (Calcutta: Iran Society, 1964); Bernard Lewis, *The Assassins,* 2d ed. (New York: Oxford University Press,

1987); and De Lacy O'Leary, *A Short History of the Fatimid Khalifate* (New York: Dutton, 1928).

For a thorough recent work on the crusades that also deals with related aspects of the area, see Kenneth Setton, ed., *A History of the Crusades,* 6 vols. (Madison: University of Wisconsin Press, 1969–1989). Also see Sir Steven Runciman, *A History of the Crusades,* 3 vols. (New York: Cambridge University Press, 1951, 1952, 1954), as well as Francesco Gabrieli, ed. and trans., *Arab Historians of the Crusades* (Berkeley and Los Angeles: University of California Press, 1984); Philip K. Hitti, trans., *An Arab-Syrian Gentleman and Warrior in the Period of the Crusades: Memoirs of Usama Ibn-Munqidh* (Princeton: NJ: Princeton University Press, 1929; paperback edition, 1987); and Amin Maalouf, *The Crusades Through Arab Eyes,* trans. by Jon Rothschild (London: Zed Books, 1984). Works on related matters include Andrew Ehrenkreutz, *Saladin* (Albany: State University of New York Press, 1972); Stephen Humphreys, *From Saladin to the Mongols* (Albany: State University of New York Press, 1977); and Malcolm Cameron Lyons and D. E. P. Jackson, *Saladin: The Politics of Holy War* (Cambridge and New York: Cambridge University Press, 1984).

An old-fashioned chronology of the Mamluk and earlier periods may be found in Stanley Lane-Poole, *A History of Egypt in the Middle Ages,* 5th ed. (London: Methuen, 1936; reprint, London, Frank Cass, 1968). For a similar work, see Sir William Muir, *The Mameluk or Slave Dynasty of Egypt, 1260–1517 A.D.* (London: Smith, Elder, 1896; reprint, New York: AMS Press, 1973). More recent studies include Robert Irwin, *The Middle East in the Middle Ages: The Early Mamluk Sultanate, 1250–1382* (Carbondale: Southern Illinois University Press, 1986); Carl F. Petry, *Protectors or Praetorians?: The Last Mamluk Sultans and Egypt's Waning as a Great Power* (Albany: State University of New York Press, 1994); and Carl F. Petry, *Twilight of Majesty: The Reigns of the Mamluk Sultans al-Ashraf, Qaytbay and Qansuh al-Ghawri in Egypt* (Seattle: University of Washington Press, 1994).

Another leading student of the Mamluks is David Ayalon, author of *Gunpowder and Firearms in the Mamluk Kingdom,* 2d ed. (London: Cass, 1978) and *Studies on the Mamluks of Egypt (1250–1517)* (London: Variorum Reprints, 1977). For a penetrating study of Mamluk Syria, see Ira Lapidus, *Muslim Cities in the Later Middle Ages* (Cambridge, MA: Harvard University Press, 1967; rev. and abridged ed., 1984). An account of the period's greatest catastrophe may be found in Michael Dols, *The Black Death in the Middle East* (Princeton, NJ: Princeton University Press, 1977). For another aspect of the Mamluk sultanate, see Carl F. Petry, *The Civilian Elite of Cairo in the Late Middle Ages* (Princeton, NJ: Princeton University Press, 1981). Also see Jonathan Berkey, *The Transmission of Knowledge in Medieval Cairo: A Social History of Islamic Education* (Princeton, NJ: Princeton University Press, 1992). A recent study of the relationship between the two powerful states of this time is Reuven Amitai-Preiss, *Mongols and Mamluks: The Mamluk-Ilkhanid War, 1260–1281* (New York and Cambridge: Cambridge University Press, 1995).

For a broad perspective, I recommend Janet L. Abu-Lughod, *Before European Hegemony: The World System A.D. 1250–1350* (New York and Oxford: Oxford University Press, 1989).

On the use of gunpowder weapons, see Robert Elgood, *Firearms of the Islamic World in the Tareq Rajab Museum, Kuwait* (London: I.B. Tauris, 1995).

IRAN: GENERAL STUDIES

Some major books on Iran bridge the ancient and Islamic periods. Under the editorship of different scholars *The Cambridge History of Iran,* 8 vols.—most of which have now appeared—(Cambridge: Cambridge University Press, 1968–) is of special value. Ehsan Yarshater, ed., *Encyclopaedia Iranica* (London: Routledge & Kegan Paul, 1982–)—six volumes now are available—is another valuable work. An important study is Ann Lambton, *Landlord and Peasant in Persia* (London: Oxford University Press, 1953; reprint, London: I.B. Tauris, 1991). For a short history of ancient and early Islamic Iran, see Richard Frye, *The Heritage of Persia,* 2d ed. (London: Sphere Books, 1976).

ISLAM: RELIGION AND INSTITUTIONS

General books on Islam include Roger Du Pasquier, *Unveiling Islam,* trans. by T. J. Winter (Cambridge: Islamic Texts Society, 1992); John Esposito, *Islam: The Straight Path,* 2d ed. (New York: Oxford University Press, 1988); Malise Ruthven, *Islam in the World* (New York: Oxford University Press, 1984); Annemarie Schimmel, *Islam: An Introduction* (Albany: State University of New York Press, 1992); and David Waines, *An Introduction to Islam* (Cambridge and New York: Cambridge University Press, 1995). For works by Muslims, see Abd al-Rahman Azzam, *The Eternal Message of Muhammad* (New York: Devin-Adair, 1964); Gai Eaton, *Islam and the Destiny of Man* (Cambridge: Islamic Texts Society, 1994); Sayyed Hossein Nasr, *Islamic Spirituality: Foundations* (New York: Crossroads, 1987); and Fazlur Rahman, *Islam,* 2d ed. (Chicago: University of Chicago Press, 1979). Anthologies of primary materials, with introductory comments, include Arthur A. Jeffrey, ed., *A Reader on Islam* (The Hague: Mouton, 1962; reprint, Salem, NH: Ayers, 1987); F. E. Peters, *A Reader on Classical Islam* (Princeton, NJ: Princeton University Press, 1994); Andrew Rippin and Jan Knappert, eds., *Textual Sources for the Study of Islam* (Chicago: University of Chicago Press, 1991); W. Montgomery Watt, trans., *Islamic Creeds: A Selection* (Edinburgh, U.K.: Edinburgh University Press, 1994); and John Alden Williams, ed., *The Word of Islam* (Austin: University of Texas Press, 1994).

There are numerous English translations of the Qur'an. See, for example, Ahmed Ali, trans., *Al-Qur'an: A Contemporary Translation* (Princeton, NJ: Princeton University Press, 1988) or *The Qur'an: The First American Version,* trans. and commentary by T. B. Irving (al-Hajj Ta'lim 'Ali) (Brattleboro, VT: Amana Books, 1985). Also see W. Montgomery Watt and Richard Bell, *Bell's Introduction to the Qur'an* (Edinburgh: Edinburgh University Press, 1970; paperback ed., 1977).

As for the second source of Islamic practice, see John Burton, *An Introduction to the Hadith* (Edinburgh: Edinburgh University Press, 1994).

On another important aspect of Islam, see Tor Andre, *In the Garden of Myrtle: Studies in Early Islamic Mysticism,* trans. by Birgitta Sharpe (Albany: State University of New York Press, 1987); Julian Baldick, *Mystical Islam: An Introduction to Sufism* (New York: New York University Press, 1989); or Annemarie Schimmel, *Mystical Dimensions of Islam* (Chapel Hill: University of North Carolina Press, 1975).

On sectarianism, see Said Amir Arjomand, ed., *Authority and Political Culture in Shi'ism* (Albany: State University of New York Press, 1988); Farhad Daftary, *The Assassin Legends: Myths of the Isma'ilis* (London: I.B. Tauris, 1994); Husayn Jabri, *Origins and Early Development of Shi'a Islam* (London: Longman, 1979); Bernard Lewis, *The Origins of Ismailism* (Cambridge: University Press, 1940); Moojan Momen, *An Introduction to the Shi'a Islam: The History and Doctrine of Twelver Shi'ism* (New Haven, CN: Yale University Press, 1985); Matti Moosa, *Extremist Shi'ites: The Ghulat Sects* (Syracuse, NY: Syracuse University Press, 1988); Sayyed Hossein Nasr et al., eds., *Expectations of the Millennium: Shi'ism in History* (Albany: State University of New York Press, 1989); Sayyad Hossein Nasr et al., eds., *Shi'ism: Doctrines, Thought, and Spirituality* (Albany: State University of New York Press, 1979; paperback ed., 1986); or David Pinault, *The Shiites: Rituals and Popular Piety in a Muslim Community* (New York: St. Martin's Press, 1992).

Works on jurisprudence include N. J. Coulson, *A History of Islamic Law* (Edinburgh: Edinburgh University Press, 1964); John L. Esposito, *Women in Muslim Family Law* (Syracuse, NY: Syracuse University Press, 1982); Nicholas Heer, ed., *Islamic Law and Jurisprudence* (Seattle: University of Washington Press, 1991); Majid Khadduri and Herbert Liebesny, eds., *Law in the Middle East* (Washington, D.C.: Middle East Institute, 1955); Joseph Schacht, *An Introduction to Islamic Law* (London: Oxford University Press, 1964); and Bernard G. Weiss, *The Search for God's Law: Islamic Jurisprudence in the Writings of Sayf al-Din al-Amidi* (Salt Lake City: University of Utah Press, 1992).

On modern developments, see Sayed Hassan Amin, *Middle East Legal Systems* (Glasgow: Royston, 1985); J. N. D. Anderson, *Islamic Law in the Modern World* (New York: New York

University Press, 1959); Sir Norman Anderson, *Law Reform in the Muslim World* (Atlantic Highlands, NJ: Humanities Press, 1976); Daisy Hilse Dwyer, ed., *Law and Islam in the Middle East* (New York: Bergis and Garvey, 1990); Herbert Liebesny, *The Law of the Near and Middle East: Readings, Cases, and Materials* (Albany: State University of New York Press, 1975); and Ann Elizabeth Mayer, ed., *Property, Social Structure, and the Law in the Modern Middle East* (Albany: State University of New York Press, 1985).

Another recommended book is Ignac Goldziher, *Introduction to Islamic Theology and Law,* trans. by Andras and Ruth Hamori (Princeton, NJ: Princeton University Press, 1981). Also broader in scope is Majid Khadduri, *The Islamic Conception of Justice* (Baltimore: Johns Hopkins University Press, 1984).

On government, see Sir Thomas Arnold, *The Caliphate,* 2d ed. (New York: Barnes & Noble, 1965); Tareq Y. Ismael and Jacqueline Ismael, *Government and Politics in Islam* (New York: St. Martin's Press, 1985); Ann K. S. Lambton, *State and Government in Medieval Islam* (New York: Oxford University Press, 1981); and P. J. Vatikiotis, *Islam and the State* (London: Croom Helm, 1987).

An important political phenomenon is analyzed in Patricia Crone, *Slaves on Horses: The Elaboration of Islamic Polity* (Cambridge: Cambridge University Press, 1980), and Daniel Pipes, *Slave Soldiers and Islam: The Genesis of a Military System* (New Haven, CN: Yale University Press, 1981).

Works on political theory include Erwin Rosenthal, *Political Thought in Medieval Islam* (Cambridge: Cambridge University Press, 1962), and W. Montgomery Watt, *Islamic Political Thought* (Edinburgh: Edinburgh University Press, 1968).

On the *dhimmis,* see A. S. Tritton, *The Caliphs and Their Non-Muslim Subjects* (London: Oxford University Press, 1931; reprint, London: Frank Case, 1970). Also see Mark R. Cohen, *Under Crescent and Cross: The Jews of the Middle Ages* (Princeton, NJ: Princeton University Press, 1994); S. D. Goiten, *Jews and Arabs: Their Contacts Through the Ages* (New York: Schocken Books, 1974); Bernard Lewis, *The Jews of Islam* (Princeton, NJ: Princeton University Press, 1984); Steven M. Wasserstrom, *Between Muslim and Jew: The Problem of Symbiosis Under Early Islam* (Princeton, NJ: Princeton University Press, 1995); and Marion Woolfson, *Prophets in Babylon: Jews in the Arab World* (London: Faber and Faber, 1980).

More comprehensive studies of institutions include Maurice Gaudefroy-Demombynes, *Muslim Institutions* (London: Allen & Unwin, 1950); Reuben Levy, *The Social Structure of Islam* (Cambridge: Cambridge University Press, 1965); and Gustave von Grunebaum, *Medieval Islam,* 2d ed. (Chicago: University of Chicago Press, 1953). For later developments, see Nikki Keddie, ed., *Sufis, Scholars, and Saints: Muslim Religious Institutions Since 1500* (Berkeley and Los Angeles: University of California Press, 1972).

The notion that Islam has been detrimental to economic progress is countered in Maxime Rodinson, *Islam and Capitalism* (Austin: University of Texas Press, 1978). Also see John Esposito, ed., *Islam and Development* (Syracuse, NY: Syracuse University Press, 1980).

ISLAMIC CIVILIZATION

Anthologies of translations include Arthur Arberry, ed., *Aspects of Islamic Civilization as Depicted in the Original Texts* (Ann Arbor: University of Michigan Press, 1967); John R. Hayes, ed., *The Genius of Arab Civilization: Sources of Renaissance,* 2d ed. (Cambridge, MA: MIT Press, 1983); and John Williams, ed., *Themes of Islamic Civilization* (Berkeley and Los Angeles: University of California Press, 1971). Also see Gustave von Grunebaum, *Medieval Islam,* 2d ed. (Chicago: University of Chicago Press, 1953), and Tarif Khalidi, *Classical Islam: The Culture and Heritage of the Golden Age* (Princeton, NJ: The Darwin Press, 1985).

Studies of art and architecture include K. A. C. Cresswell, *A Short Account of Early Muslim Architecture,* revised and supplemented by James W. Allan (Aldershot, U.K.: Scholar Press, 1989); Oleg Graber, *The Formation of Islamic Art,* 2d ed. (New Haven, CN: Yale University Press, 1987); Oleg Graber, *The Mediation of Ornament* (Princeton, NJ: Princeton University Press, 1992); Ernst Kuhnel, *Islamic Art and Architecture* (Ithaca, NY: Cornell University Press, 1966); and David Rice, *Islamic Art* (New York: Praeger, 1965).

On philosophy and theology, start with Oliver Leamon, *An Introduction to Medieval Islamic Philosophy* (Cambridge: Cambridge University Press, 1985), or W. Montgomery Watt, *Islamic Philosophy and Theology* (Chicago: Aldine, 1962). For a more thorough treatment, see Majid Fakhry, *History of Islamic Philosophy,* 2d ed. (New York: Columbia University Press, 1983). Good translations can be found in Ralph Lerner and Muhsin Mahdi, eds., *Medieval Political Philosophy* (New York: Free Press, 1963). On an important theologian, see W. Montgomery Watt, *Muslim Intellectual: A Study of Al-Ghazzali* (Chicago: Aldine, 1963).

As for Ibn Khaldun, most readers would benefit from starting with Charles Issawi, ed., *An Arab Philosophy of History,* 2d ed. (Princeton, NJ: Darwin Press, 1987). Also see Ibn Khaldun, *The Muqaddimah,* 3 vols., trans. by Franz Rosenthal, 2d ed. (Princeton, NJ: Princeton University Press, 1967).

THE OTTOMAN EMPIRE TO MODERN TIMES

Stanford J. Shaw, *History of the Ottoman Empire and Modern Turkey, Vol. I: Empire of the Gazis: The Rise and Decline of the Ottoman Empire, 1280–1808* (Cambridge: Cambridge University Press, 1976), is a basic work. Still, Sir Edward S. Creasy, *History of the Ottoman Turks* (London: R. Bentley, 1854–1856, reprint, Beirut: Khayats, 1961), is not entirely superseded. For the early period an excellent work is Halil Inalcik, *The Ottoman Empire: The Classical Age, 1300–1600* (New York: Praeger, 1973).

On Ottoman institutions, see H. A. R. Gibb and Harold Bowen, *Islamic Society and the West: A Study of the Impact of Western Civilization, Vol. One: Islamic Society in the Eighteenth Century,* 2 parts (London: Oxford University Press, 1950). Also see P. M. Holt, *Egypt and the Fertile Crescent, 1516–1922* (Ithaca, NY: Cornell University Press; London: Longmans, 1966). On trade, see Huri Islamoglu-Inan, ed., *The Ottoman Empire and the World-Economy* (New York: Cambridge University Press, 1987).

THE SAFAVIDS AND IRAN
TO THE LATE EIGHTEENTH CENTURY

On the Ottomans' contemporaries, see Roger Savory, *Iran Under the Safavids* (Cambridge: Cambridge University Press, 1980). Also see John Perry, *Karim Khan Zand: A History of Iran, 1747–1779* (Chicago: University of Chicago Press, 1979).

THE MODERN MIDDLE EAST: GENERAL

On the eighteenth century, see Nehemia Levtzion and John O. Voll, eds., *Eighteenth Century Renewal and Reform in Islam* (Syracuse, NY: Syracuse University Press, 1987) and Thomas Naff and Roger Owen, eds., *Studies in the Eighteenth Century Islamic History* (Carbondale: Southern Illinois University Press, 1977). For the next century, an excellent collection of specialized studies may be found in William Polk and Richard Chambers, eds., *Beginnings of Modernization in the Middle East* (Chicago: University of Chicago Press, 1968).

Surveys of the modern Middle East include Lois A. Aroian and Richard P. Mitchell, *The Modern Middle East and North Africa* (New York: Macmillan, 1984); Emory C. Bogle, *The Modern Middle East: From Imperialism to Freedom, 1800–1958* (Upper Saddle River, NJ: Prentice Hall, 1996); and William Cleveland, *A History of the Modern Middle East* (Boulder, CO: Westview Press, 1994). M. E. Yapp is the author of two books: *The Making of the Modern Near East, 1792–1923* (London and New York: Longman, 1987), and *The Near East Since the First World War* (London and New York: Longman, 1991). Also see Albert Hourani et al., *The Modern Middle East: A Reader* (Berkeley and Los Angeles: University of California Press, 1993). For an innovative approach, see Haim Gerber, *The Social Origins of the Modern*

Middle East (Boulder, CO: Lynne Rienner Publishers, 1987). Also see Cyril E. Black and L. Carl Brown, *Modernization in the Middle East: The Ottoman Empire and Its Afro-Asian Successors* (Princeton, NJ: Darwin Press, 1992).

Works on economic history include Charles Issawi, ed., *The Economic History of the Middle East, 1800–1914* (Chicago: University of Chicago Press, 1966); Charles Issawi, *The Fertile Crescent, 1800–1914: A Documentary Economic History* (New York: Oxford University Press, 1988); Y. Hershlag, *Introduction to the Modern Economic History of the Middle East* (Leiden, Netherlands: E.J. Brill, 1980); and Roger Owen, *The Middle East in the World Economy, 1800–1914* (London: Methuen, 1987; rev. paperback ed., London: I.B. Tauris, 1993). The lives of ordinary people are portrayed in Edmund Burke III, *Struggle and Survival in the Modern Middle East* (Berkeley and Los Angeles: University of California Press, 1993).

J. C. Hurewitz, ed., *The Middle East and North Africa in World Politics,* 2 vols. 2d ed. (New Haven, CN: Yale University Press, 1975, 1977), is an essential collection of documents. A second important work on diplomatic history is M. S. Anderson, *The Eastern Question, 1774–1923* (New York: St. Martin's Press, 1966). For a comparison of nineteenth- and twentieth-century diplomacy, see L. Carl Brown, *International Politics and the Middle East: Old Rules, Dangerous Game* (Princeton, NJ: Princeton University Press, 1984).

The following works focus on the international relations of the World War I period: Briton Cooper Busch, *Britain, India, and the Arabs, 1914–1921* (Berkeley and Los Angeles: University of California Press, 1971); David Fromkin, *A Peace to End All Peace: Creating the Modern Middle East, 1914–1922* (New York: Henry Holt, 1989); Harry Howard, *The King-Crane Commission* (Beirut: Khayats, 1963); Harry Howard, *The Partition of Turkey* (Norman: University of Oklahoma Press, 1931; reprint, New York: F. Fertig, 1969); Elie Kedourie, *England and the Middle East, 1914–1921,* 3d ed. (London: Mansell; Boulder, CO: Westview Press, 1987); Marian Kent, ed., *The Great Powers and the End of the Ottoman Empire* (London: George Allen & Unwin, 1984); Jukka Nevakivi, *Britain, France, and the Arab Middle East, 1914–1920* (London: Athlone Press, 1969); and Howard Sachar, *The Emergence of the Middle East, 1914–1924* (New York: Knopf, 1969).

Later decades are covered by Uriel Dann, ed., *The Great Powers in the Middle East 1919–1939* (New York: Holmes and Maier, 1988); Lukaz Hirshowitz; *The Third Reich in the Arab East* (Toronto: University of Toronto Press, 1966); Wm. Roger Louis, *The British Empire in the Middle East 1945–1951: Arab Nationalism, the United States, and Postwar Imperialism* (Oxford: Oxford University Press, 1984); Elizabeth Monroe, *Britain's Moment in the Middle East, 1914–1956,* 2d ed. (Baltimore: Johns Hopkins University Press, 1981); and Howard Sachar, *Europe Leaves the Middle East, 1936–1954* (New York: Knopf, 1972). Also see Yehoshua Porath, *In Search of Arab Unity, 1930–1945* (London: Frank Case, 1986).

For broad studies of recent international relations, see Bahgat Korany and Ali E. Hillaal Dessouki, eds, *The Foreign Policies of Arab States,* 2d ed. (Boulder, CO: Westview Press, 1991); Fawaz A. Gerges, *The Superpowers and the Middle East: Regional and International Politics, 1955–1967* (Boulder, CO: Westview Press, 1994); Adel Safty, *From Camp David to the Gulf: Negotiations, Language and Propaganda & War* (Montreal and New York: Black Rose Books, 1992); Avi Shlaim, *War and Peace in the Middle East: A Concise History,* 2d ed. (New York: Penguin Books, 1995); and Stephen W. Walt, *The Origins of Alliances* (Ithaca, NY, and London: Cornell University Press, 1987).

On the United States' role, see Naseer Aruri, *The Obstruction of Peace: The U.S., Israel, and the Palestinians* (Monroe, ME: Common Courage Press, 1995); George Ball, *Error and Betrayal in Lebanon* (Washington, D.C.: Foundation for Middle East Peace, 1984); Noam Chomsky, *The Fateful Triangle: The U.S., Israel and the Palestinians* (Boston: South End Press, 1984); Stephen Green, *Living by the Sword: America and Israel in the Middle East: 1968–87* (London: Faber, 1988); Stephen Green, *Taking Sides: America's Secret Relations with a Militant Israel* (New York: William Morrow, 1984); Donald Neff, *Fallen Pillars: U.S. Policy Toward Palestine and Israel Since 1945* (Washington, D.C.: Institute for Palestine

Studies, 1995); William B. Quandt, *Peace Process: American Diplomacy and the Arab-Israeli Conflict Since 1967* (Washington: Brookings Institution; Berkeley and Los Angeles: University of California Press, 1993); Cheryl A. Rubenberg, *Israel and the American National Interest: A Critical Examination* (Urbana: University of Illinois Press, 1986); Steven L. Spiegel, *The Other Arab-Israeli Conflict: Making America's Middle East Policy from Truman to Reagan* (Chicago: University of Chicago Press, 1985); William Stivers, *America's Confrontation with Revolutionary Change in the Middle East, 1948–1983* (New York: St. Martin's Press, 1986); William Stivers, *Supremacy and Oil: Iraq, Turkey, and the Anglo-American World Order, 1918–1930* (Ithaca, NY: Cornell University Press, 1982); Michael W. Suleiman, *The Arabs in the Mind of America* (Brattleboro, VT: Amana Books, 1988); Michael W. Suleiman, ed., *U.S. Policy on Palestine from Wilson to Clinton* (Normal, IL: Association of Arab-American University Graduates, 1995); and Seth P. Tillman, *The United States in the Middle East: Interests and Obstacles* (Bloomington: Indiana University Press, 1982). Also see Paul Findley, *They Dare to Speak Out* (Westport, CN: Lawrence Hill, 1985), and Edward Tivnan, *The Lobby* (New York: Simon and Schuster, 1987).

As for the other former superpower, see Hashim S. H. Behbehani, *The Soviet Union and Arab Nationalism, 1917–1966* (London: Kegan Paul International, 1986), and Galia Golan, *Soviet Policies in the Middle East: From World War II to Gorbachev* (Cambridge and New York: Cambridge University Press, 1990). Also see Moshe Efrat and Jacob Bercovitch, eds., *Superpowers and Client States in the Middle East: The Imbalance of Influence* (London and New York: Routledge, 1991), and Alan R. Taylor, *The Superpowers and the Middle East* (Syracuse, NY: Syracuse University Press, 1991).

On oil, see Abbas Alnasrawi, *Arab Nationalism, Oil, and the Political Economy of Dependency* (New York: Greenwood Press, 1991); Kate Gillespie and Clement M. Henry, eds., *Oil in the New World Order* (Gainesville: University Press of Florida, 1995); and Daniel Yergin, *The Prize: The Epic Quest for Oil, Money and Power* (New York: Simon & Schuster, 1991).

As for politics, two recent systematic works are available: James A. Bill and Robert Springborg, *Politics in the Middle East,* 4th ed. (New York: HarperCollins, 1994), and Roger Owen, *State, Power and Politics in the Making of the Modern Middle East* (London and New York: Routledge, 1992). For political economy, see Alan Richards and John Waterbury, *A Political Economy of the Middle East* (Boulder, CO: Westview Press, 1990). Also see Fouad Ajami, *The Arab Predicament,* 2d ed. (New York: Cambridge University Press, 1992); Michael Hudson, *Arab Politics: The Search for Legitimacy* (New Haven, CN: Yale University Press, 1977); and Giacomo Luciani, *Nation, State and Integration in the Arab World,* 4 vols. (London and New York: Croom Helm, 1987–1988). A shorter version of Luciani's work was published as *The Arab State* (Berkeley and Los Angeles: University of California Press, 1990).

A regularly updated source of information is *The Middle East and North Africa, 1996,* 42d ed. (London: Europa Publications, 1995). For a detailed record, see Ami Ayalon, ed., *Middle East Contemporary Survey* (Boulder, CO: Westview Press, annual).

MODERN INTELLECTUAL
AND RELIGIOUS DEVELOPMENTS

For a penetrating short analysis, see Bernard Lewis, *The Shaping of the Modern Middle East* (New York and Oxford: Oxford University Press, 1994). An essential work is Albert Hourani, *Arabic Thought in the Liberal Age, 1798–1939,* 2d ed. (Cambridge and New York: Cambridge University Press, 1983). Other studies include Ibrahim Abu-Lughod, *The Arab Rediscovery of Europe* (Princeton, NJ: Princeton University Press, 1963); Ra'if Khuri, *Modern Arab Thought: Channels of the French Revolution to the Middle East,* trans. by Ihsan 'Abbas, ed. by Charles Issawi (Princeton, NJ: Kingston Press, 1983); and Hisham Sharabi, *Arab Intellectuals and the West: The Formative Years, 1875–1914* (Baltimore: Johns Hopkins University Press, 1970). Works dealing with diverse ideas are Anouar Abdel-Malek, ed., *Contemporary Arab*

Political Thought (London: Zed Books, 1989); Leonard Binder, *Islamic Liberalism: A Critique of Development Ideologies* (Chicago: University of Chicago Press, 1988); Issa J. Boullata, *Trends and Issues in Contemporary Arab Thought* (Albany: State University of New York Press, 1989); and Majid Khadduri, *Political Trends in the Arab World: The Role of Ideas and Ideals in Practice* (Baltimore: Johns Hopkins University Press, 1970; reprint, Westport, CN: Greenwood Press, 1983). Translations of important writings may be found in Kemal Karpat, ed., *Political and Social Thought in the Contemporary Middle East,* 2d ed. (New York: Praeger, 1982).

Recent works on modern Islamic movements and issues include Said Amir Arjomand, ed., *From Nationalism to Revolutionary Islam: Essays on Social Movements in the Contemporary Near and Middle East* (Albany: State University of New York, 1984); Mohamed Arkoun, *Rethinking Islam: Common Questions, Uncommon Answers,* trans. and ed. by Robert D. Lee (Boulder, CO: Westview Press, 1994); Edmund Burke III and Ira M. Lapidus, eds., *Islam, Politics, and Social Movements* (Berkeley and Los Angeles: University of California Press, 1988); Juan R. I Cole and Nikki R. Keddie, eds., *Shi'ism and Social Protest* (New Haven, CN: Yale University Press, 1986); R. Hrair Dekmejian, *Islam in Revolution: Fundamentalism in the Arab World* (Syracuse, NY: Syracuse University Press, 1985); John J. Donahue and John L. Esposito, eds., *Islam in Transition: Muslim Perspectives* (New York: Oxford University Press, 1982); Hamid Enayat, *Modern Islamic Political Thought* (Austin: University of Texas Press, 1982); John L. Esposito, *Islam and Politics,* 3d ed. (Syracuse, NY: Syracuse University Press, 1991); John L. Esposito, *The Islamic Threat: Myth or Reality,* 2d ed. (New York and Oxford: Oxford University Press, 1995); John L. Esposito, ed., *Voices of Islam Resurgent* (New York: Oxford University Press, 1982); Michael Gilsenan, *Recognizing Islam: Religion and Society in the Modern Middle East* (London: I.B. Tauris, 1990); Yvonne Yazbeck Haddad, ed., *The Islamic Impact* (Syracuse, NY: Syracuse University Press, 1984); Metin Heper and Raphael Israeli, eds., *Islam and Politics in the Modern Middle East* (New York: St. Martin's Press, 1984); Martin Kramer, *Shi'ism, Resistance and Revolution* (Boulder, CO: Westview Press, 1981); Chibli Mallat, *The Renewal of Islamic Law: Muhammad Baqer as-Sadr, Najaf and the Shi'i International* (Cambridge and New York: Cambridge University Press, 1993); Ann Elizabeth Mayer, *Islam and Human Rights: Tradition and Politics,* 2d ed. (Boulder, CO and San Francisco: Westview Press; London: Pinter Publishers, 1995); Henry Munson, Jr., *Islam and Revolution in the Middle East* (New Haven, CN: Yale University Press, 1988); Sayyed Hossein Nasr, *Traditional Islam in the Modern World* (London: Kegan Paul International, 1987); Farhad Nomani and Ali Rahnema, *Islamic Economic Systems* (London: Zed Books, 1994); Daniel Pipes, *In the Path of God: Islam and Political Power* (New York: Basic Books, 1983); James P. Piscatori, *Islam in a World of Nation-States* (New York: Cambridge University Press, 1986); James P. Piscatori, ed., *Islam in the Political Process* (New York and Cambridge: Cambridge University Press, 1983); Fazlur Rahman, *Islam and Modernity: Transformation of an Intellectual Tradition* (Chicago: University of Chicago Press, 1981); Emmanuel Sivan, *Radical Islam: Medieval Theology and Modern Politics* (New Haven, CN: Yale University Press, 1985); Barbara Freyer Stowasser, ed., *The Islamic Impulse* (London: Croom Helm, 1987); John Obert Voll, *Islam: Continuity and Change in the Modern World,* 2d ed. (Boulder, CO: Westview Press, 1994); Robin Wright, *Sacred Rage: The Wrath of Militant Islam,* 2d ed. (New York: Simon & Schuster, 1986); and Sami Zubaida, *Islam: The People and the State: Political Ideas and Movements in the Middle East* (London and New York: I.B. Tauris, 1993).

Analyses of various nationalisms may be found in William Haddad and William Ochsenwald, eds., *Nationalism in a Non-National State: The Dissolution of the Ottoman Empire* (Columbus: Ohio State University Press, 1977). Despite some shortcomings, George Antonius's readable *The Arab Awakening* (London: H. Hamilton, 1938; reprint, New York: Capricorn Books, 1965) is still a good place to start on the rise of Arab nationalism. Important works that correct Antonius on some points include C. Ernest Dawn, *From Ottomanism to Arabism* (Urbana: University of Illinois Press, 1973) and Zeine Zeine, *The Emergence of Arab Nation-*

alism, 3d ed. (Delmar, NY: Caravan Books, 1973). Also see A. A. Duri, *The Historical Foundation of the Arab Nation: A Study in Identity and Consciousness,* trans. by Lawrence I. Conrad (London and New York: Croom Helm, 1988); Tawfic E. Farah, ed., *Pan-Arabism and Arab Nationalism: The Continuing Debate* (Boulder, CO: Westview Press, 1987) and Sylvia Haim, ed., *Arab Nationalism, An Anthology* (Berkeley and Los Angeles: University of California Press, 1962). A recent important addition is Rashid Khalidi et al., eds., *The Origins of Arab Nationalism* (New York: Columbia University Press, 1991). On a rival movement, see Daniel Pipes, *Greater Syria: The History of an Ambition* (Oxford and New York: Oxford University Press, 1991).

SOCIETY AND CULTURE

Recent works on Middle Eastern society and culture include Daniel Bates and Amal Rassam, *Peoples and Cultures of the Middle East* (Englewood Cliffs, NJ: Prentice Hall, 1983); Halim Barakat, *The Arab World: Society, Culture, and State* (Berkeley and Los Angeles: University of California Press, 1993); Dale F. Eickelman, *The Middle East: An Anthropological Approach,* 2d ed. (Englewood Cliffs, NJ: Prentice Hall, 1989); and Samih K. Farsoun, *Arab Society: Continuity and Change* (London: Croom Helm, 1985).

For a comprehensive work, see Lois Beck and Nikki Keddie, eds., *Women in the Muslim World* (Cambridge: Harvard University Press, 1978). Also see Selma Botman et al., *Women in the Middle East* (London: Zed Books, 1987); Nawal El-Saadawi, *The Hidden Face of Eve: Women in the Arab World* (London: Zed Books, 1980); Elizabeth Warnock Fernea, ed., *Women and the Family in the Middle East: New Voices of Change* (Austin: University of Texas Press, 1985); Valentine M. Moghadam, *Modernizing Women: Gender and Social Change in the Middle East* (Boulder, CO and London: Lynne Rienner Publishers, 1993); and Sherifa Zuhur, *Revealing Reveiling: Islamist Gender Ideology in Contemporary Egypt* (Albany: State University of New York Press, 1992).

An invaluable encyclopedia of ethnic groups is Richard Weekes, ed., *Muslim Peoples: A World Ethnographic Survey,* 2 vols., 2d ed. (Westport, CN: Greenwood Press, 1984). Also see Milton J. Esman and Itamar Rabinovich, eds., *Ethnicity, Pluralism, and the State in the Middle East* (Ithaca, NY: Cornell University Press, 1988).

Several broad studies of the Kurds have appeared during the 1990s. See John Bulloch and Harvey Morris, *No Friends but the Mountains: The Tragic History of the Kurds* (Oxford and New York: Oxford University Press, 1992); Gerard Chaliand, *The Kurdish Tragedy,* trans. by Philip Black (London: Zed Books, 1994); Gerard Chaliand, *A People Without a Country: The Kurds and Kurdistan,* trans. by Michael Pallis (New York: Olive Branch Press, 1993); Nader Entessar, *Kurdish Ethnonationalism* (Boulder, CO: Lynne Rienner Publishers, 1992); Philip Kreyenbroek and Christine Allison, eds., *Kurdish Culture and Identity* (London: Zed Books, 1996); Philip G. Kreyenbroek and Stefan Sperl, eds., *The Kurds: A Contemporary Overview* (New York and London: Routledge, 1992); Sheri Lazer, *Martyrs, Traitors, and Patriots: Kurdistan after the Gulf War* (London: Zed Books, 1996); and Martin Van Bruinessen, *Agha, Shaikh and State: The Social and Political Structures of Kurdistan* (London: Zed Books, 1992).

MODERN TURKEY

A comprehensive study is Stanford J. Shaw and Ezel Kural Shaw, *History of the Ottoman Empire and Modern Turkey, Vol. II: The Rise of Modern Turkey, 1808–1975* (Cambridge: Cambridge University Press, 1977). Two essential studies of the impact of the West are Niyazi Berkes, *The Development of Secularism in Turkey* (Montreal: McGill University Press, 1964) and Bernard Lewis, *The Emergence of Modern Turkey,* 2d ed. (London: Oxford University Press, 1968). Also see Feroz Ahmad, *The Making of Modern Turkey* (London: Routledge, 1993); Charles Issawi, ed., *The Economic History of Turkey, 1800–1914* (Chicago: University of Chicago Press, 1980); Resat Kasaba, *The Ottoman Empire and the World Economy: The Nineteenth Century* (Albany: State University of New York Press, 1988); Sevket Pamuk, *The Ottoman Empire and European Capitalism, 1820–1913: Trade, Investment, and Production* (New York: Cambridge University Press, 1987); and Erik Zurcher, *Turkey: A Modern History* (London: I.B. Tauris, 1993). Works on selected periods include Roderic Davison, *Reform in the Ottoman Empire, 1856–1876* (Princeton, NJ: Princeton University Press, 1963); Serif Mardin, *The Genesis of Young Ottoman Thought* (Princeton, NJ: Princeton University Press, 1962); Ernest Ramsaur, *The Young Turks* (Princeton, NJ: Princeton University Press, 1957); and Erik Jan Zurcher, *The Unionist Factor: The Role of the Committee of Union and Progress in the Turkish National Movement, 1905–1926* (Leiden, Netherlands: E.J. Brill, 1984). On nationalism, see D. Kushner, *The Rise of Turkish Nationalism, 1876–1908* (London: Frank Cass, 1977).

For an interesting biography, see Lord Kinross, *Ataturk* (London: Weidenfeld and Nicolson, 1964). More recent works include Ali Kazancigil and Ergun Ozbudun, eds., *Ataturk: Founder of a Modern State* (Hamden, CN: Archon Books, 1981); Gunsel Renda and C. Kortepeter, eds., *The Transformation of Turkish Culture: The Ataturk Legacy* (Princeton, NJ: Kingston Press, 1986); and Vamik D. Volkan and Norman Itzkowitz, *The Immortal Ataturk: A Psychobiography* (Chicago: University of Chicago Press, 1984). Another development during this period is covered in Robert Olson, *The Emergence of Kurdish Nationalism and the Sheikh Said Rebellion, 1880–1925* (Austin: University of Texas Press, 1989).

On later decades, see Feroz Ahmad, *The Turkish Experience in Democracy, 1950–1975* (Boulder, CO: Westview Press, 1977); William Hale, *The Political and Economic Development of Modern Turkey* (New York: St. Martin's Press, 1981); and Ergun Ozbudun, *Social Change and Political Parties in Turkey* (Princeton, NJ: Princeton University Press, 1976). Richard Robinson, *The First Turkish Republic* (Cambridge: Harvard University Press, 1963), is a general treatment of the period from Ataturk to 1960. Also see Walter F. Weiker, *The Modernization of Turkey: From Ataturk to the Present Day* (New York: Holmes and Meier, 1981).

The following works focus on the 1980s and 1990s: Clement H. Dodd, ed., *Turkish Foreign Policy: New Prospects* (Cambridge: The Oethen Press, 1992); Graham E. Fuller and Ian O. Lesser, *Turkey's New Geopolitics: From the Balkans to Western China* (Boulder, CO: Westview Press, 1993); Metin Heper and Ahmet Evin, eds., *Politics in the Third Turkish Republic* (Boulder, CO: Westview Press, 1994); Caglar Keyder, *State and Class in Turkey: A Study in Capitalist Development* (London: Verso, 1987); Andrew Mango, *Turkey: The Challenge of a New Role* (New York: Praeger, 1994); Huseyin Ramazanoglu, ed., *Turkey in the World Capitalist System: A Study of Industrialization, Power and Class* (Brookfield, VT: Gower, 1985); Philip Robins, *Turkey and the Middle East* (New York: Council on Foreign Relations Press, 1991); Dankwart A. Rustow, *Turkey: America's Forgotten Ally* (New York: Council on Foreign Relations, 1987); Irwin C. Schick and Ertogrul Ahmet Tonak, *Turkey in Transition: New Perspectives* (New York and Oxford: Oxford University Press, 1987); and Frank Tachau, *Turkey: The Politics of Authority, Democracy, and Development* (New York: Praeger, 1984).

MODERN IRAN

General works include Ervand Abrahamian, *Iran Between Two Revolutions* (Princeton, NJ: Princeton University Press, 1980); Michael E. Bonine and Nikki Keddie, eds., *Modern Iran: The Dialectics of Continuity and Change* (Albany: State University of New York Press, 1981); Richard Cottam, *Nationalism in Iran*, 2d ed. (Pittsburgh: University of Pittsburgh Press, 1979); John Foran, *Fragile Resistance: Social Transformation in Iran from 1500 to the Revolution* (Boulder, CO: Westview Press, 1993); M. Reza Ghods, *Iran in the Twentieth Century* (Boulder, CO: Lynne Rienner Publishers, 1989); and Nikki Keddie, *Roots of Revolution: An Interpretative History of Modern Iran* (New Haven, CN: Yale University Press, 1981).

On foreign affairs, see Rouhollah Ramazani's *The Foreign Policy of Iran: A Developing Nation in World Affairs, 1500–1941* (Charlottesville: University Press of Virginia, 1966) and

Iran's Foreign Policy, 1941–1973 (Charlottesville: University Press of Virginia, 1975). James A. Bill's *The Eagle and the Lion: The Tragedy of American-Iranian Relations* (New Haven, CN: Yale University Press, 1988) is of special importance. Also see Richard W. Cottam, *Iran and the United States: A Cold War Case Study* (Pittsburgh: University of Pittsburgh Press, 1988), and Nikki R. Keddie and Mark Gasiorowski, eds., *Iran, the Soviet Union and the United States* (New Haven, CN: Yale University Press, 1990).

Specifically for the Qajar period, Hamid Algar's *Religion and State in Iran, 1785–1906* (Berkeley and Los Angeles: University of California Press, 1969) is indispensable. Also see Said Amir Arjomand, *The Shadow of God and the Hidden Imam: Religion, Political Order and Societal Change in Shi'ite Iran from the Beginning to 1890* (Chicago: University of Chicago Press, 1984); Mangol Bayat, *Iran's First Revolution: Shi'ism and the Constitutional Revolution of 1905–1909* (Oxford and New York: Oxford University Press, 1991); and Guity Nashat, *The Origins of Modern Reform in Iran, 1870–80* (Urbana: University of Illinois Press, 1982). Other important studies include Ann K. S. Lambton, *Qajar Persia: Eleven Studies* (Austin: University of Texas Press, 1987), as well as Nikki Keddie's *Modern Iran: Religion, Politics and Society* (London: Frank Cass, 1979) and *Religion and Rebellion in Iran* (London: Frank Case, 1966). Also see Vanessa Martin, *Islam and Modernism: The Iranian Revolution of 1906* (Syracuse, NY: Syracuse University Press, 1989).

The following works deal mainly with the inter-War period: Amin Banani, *The Modernization of Iran, 1921–1941* (Stanford, CA: Stanford University Press, 1961), and Donald Wilber, *Riza Shah Pahlavi* (Hicksville, NY: Exposition Press, 1975).

On the Musaddiq period, I especially recommend James A. Bill and Wm. Roger Louis, eds., *Musaddiq, Iranian Nationalism, and Oil* (Austin: University of Texas Press, 1988). Other books include Farhad Diba, *Mohammed Mossadegh: A Political Biography* (London: Croom Helm, 1986); Mostafa Elm, *Oil, Power and Principle: Iran's Oil Nationalization and Its Aftermath* (Syracuse: Syracuse University Press, 1994); Homa Katouzian, ed., *Musaddiq's Memoirs: The End of the British Empire in Iran* (London: JEBHE, National Movement of Iran, 1988); and Sepehr Zabih, *The Mossadegh Era: The Roots of the Iranian Revolution* (Chicago: Lake View Press, 1982).

On the Muhammad Riza Shah period, see James Bill, *The Politics of Iran* (Columbus, OH: Merrill, 1972); Mark J. Gasiorowski, *U.S. Foreign Policy and the Shah: Building a Client State in Iran* (Ithaca, NY: Cornell University Press, 1991); Fred Halliday, *Iran: Dictatorship and Development,* 2d ed. (Baltimore: Penguin, 1979); Eric J. Hooglund, *Land and Revolution in Iran, 1960–1980* (Austin: University of Texas Press, 1982); Marvin Zonis, *The Iranian Political Elite* (Chicago: University of Chicago Press, 1971); and Marvin Zonis, *Majestic Failure: The Fall of the Shah* (Chicago and London: University of Chicago Press, 1991).

The revolutionary period is dealt with by Hooshang Amirahmadi and Nader Entessar, eds., *Iran and the Arab World* (New York: St. Martin's Press, 1992); Hooshang Amirahmadi and Monoucher Parvin, *Post-Revolutionary Iran* (Boulder, CO: Westview Press, 1989); Mohammed Amjad, *Iran: From Royal Dictatorship to Theocracy* (Westport, CN: Greenwood Press, 1989); Said Amir Arjomand, *The Turban for the Crown: The Islamic Revolution in Iran* (New York: Oxford University Press, 1988); Shaul Bakhash, *The Reign of the Ayatollahs: Iran and the Islamic Revolution* (New York: Basic Books, 1984); John L. Esposito, ed., *The Iranian Revolution: Its Global Impact* (Gainesville: University Press of Florida, 1990); Graham E. Fuller, *The "Center of the Universe": The Geopolitics of Iran* (Boulder, CO: Westview Press, 1991); Mohamed Heikal, *Iran: The Untold Story* (New York: Pantheon Books, 1981); Shireen T. Hunter, *Iran After Khomeini* (New York: Praeger, 1992); Shireen T. Hunter, ed., *Iran and the World: Continuity in a Revolutionary Decade* (Bloomington: Indiana University Press, 1990); Asaf Hussain, *Islamic Iran: Revolution and Counter-Revolution* (New York: St. Martin's Press, 1985); Nikki Keddie and Eric Hooglund, eds., *The Iranian Revolution and the Islamic Republic,* 2d ed. (Syracuse, NY: Syracuse University Press, 1986); David Menashri, ed., *The Iranian Revolution and the Muslim World* (Boulder, CO: Westview Press, 1990); Mohsen M. Milani, *The Making of Iran's Islamic Revolution: From Monarchy to Islamic Republic,* 2d ed. (Boulder, CO: Westview Press, 1994); Mansoor Moaddel, *Class, Politics, and Ideology in the Iranian Revolution* (New York: Columbia University Press, 1995); R. K. Ramazani, ed., *Iran's Revolution: The Search for Consensus* (Bloomington: Indiana University Press, 1989); and R. K. Ramazani, *Revolutionary Iran: Challenge and Response in the Middle East* (Baltimore: Johns Hopkins University Press, 1986).

The role of the *ulama* in politics is covered in Shahrough Akhavi, *Religion and Politics in Contemporary Iran* (Albany: State University of New York Press, 1980); Michael Fischer, *Iran: From Religious Dispute to Revolution* (Cambridge, MA: Harvard University Press, 1980); and Roy Mottahedeh, *The Mantle of the Prophet: Religion and Politics in Iran* (New York: Pantheon, 1985). Also see Nikki R. Keddie, *Religion and Politics in Iran: Shi'ism from Quietism to Revolution* (New Haven, CN: Yale University Press, 1983). The only acceptable translation of Ayatullah Khumayni's writings is *Islam and Revolution—Writings and Declarations of Imam Khomeini,* trans. and annotated by Hamid Algar (Berkeley, CA: Mizan Press, 1981; London: Kegan Paul International, 1985).

Books on the war with Iraq include John Bulloch and Harvey Morris, *The Gulf War* (London: Methuen, 1990); Dilip Hiro, *The Longest War* (London: Grafton Books, 1990; New York: Routledge, 1991); Farhang Rajaee, *The Iran-Iraq War: The Politics of Aggression* (Gainesville: University Press of Florida, 1994); and W. Thom Workman, *The Social Origins of the Iran-Iraq War* (Boulder, CO: Lynne Rienner Publishers, 1994).

MODERN IRAQ

A recent survey is Phebe Marr, *The Modern History of Iraq* (Boulder, CO: Westview Press, 1985). Specialized papers may be found in Abbas Kelidar, ed., *The Integration of Modern Iraq* (New York: St. Martin's Press, 1979). Also see Reeva S. Simon, *Iraq Between the Two World Wars: The Creation of a Nationalist Ideology* (New York: Columbia University Press, 1986). An important work on the pre-1958 period is Hanna Batatu, *The Old Social Classes and the Revolutionary Movements of Iraq* (Princeton, NJ: Princeton University Press, 1978); also see Robert A. Fernea and Wm. Roger Louis, eds., *The Iraqi Revolution of 1958: The Old Social Classes Revisited* (London: I.B. Tauris, 1991), and Liora Lukitz, *Iraq: The Search for National Identity* (London: Frank Cass, 1995).

On the recent period, see Amatzia Baram, *Culture, History and Ideology in the Formation of Ba'thist Iraq, 1968–89* (New York: St. Martin's Press, 1991); Amatzia Baram and Barry Rubin, eds., *Iraq's Road to War* (New York: St. Martin's Press, 1993); CARDRI [Committee Against Repression and for Democratic Rights in Iraq], *Saddam's Iraq: Revolution or Reaction* (London: Zed Books, 1989); Marion Farouk-Sluglett and Peter Sluglett, *Iraq Since 1958: From Revolution to Dictatorship* (London: KPI, 1987; reprint, London: I.B. Tauris, 1990); Fran Hazelton (for CARDRI), ed., *Iraq Since the Gulf War: Prospects for Democracy* (London: Zed Books, 1994); Bruce W. Jentleson, *With Friends Like These: Reagan, Bush, and Saddam, 1982–1990)* (New York: Norton, 1994); Efraim Karsh and Inari Rautsi, *Saddam Hussein: A Political Biography* (New York: Free Press, 1991); and Samir al-Khalil, *Republic of Fear: The Politics of Modern Iraq* (Berkeley and Los Angeles: University of California Press, 1989; reprint, New York: Pantheon, 1990).

On particular ethnic or sectarian groups, see Michael M. Gunter, *The Kurds of Iraq: Tragedy and Hope* (London: St. Martin's Press, 1993); Yitzhak Nakash, *The Shi'is of Iraq* (Princeton, NJ: Princeton University Press, 1994); and Joyce N. Wiley, *The Islamic Movement of Iraqi Shi'as* (Boulder, CO: Lynne Rienner Publishers, 1992).

THE ARABIAN PENINSULA

St. John Philby wrote numerous books on Saudi Arabia, for example, *Arabian Jubilee* (New York: The John Day Company, 1953) and *Sa'udi Arabia* (London: Benn, 1955). Other works include Mordechai Abir, *Saudi Arabia in the Oil Era: Regimes and Elites: Conflict and Cooperation* (Boulder, CO: Westview Press, 1988); Said K. Aburish, *The Rise, Corruption and*

Coming Fall of the House of Saud (New York: St. Martin's Press, 1995); Jacob Goldberg, *The Foreign Policy of Saudi Arabia: The Formative Years, 1902–1918* (Cambridge, MA: Harvard University Press, 1986); Christine Moss Helms, *The Cohesion of Saudi Arabia* (Baltimore: Johns Hopkins University Press, 1980); David Howarth, *The Desert King: The Life of Ibn Saud* (New York: McGraw-Hill, 1964); Joseph Kostiner, *The Making of Saudi Arabia, 1916–1936: From Chieftaincy to Monarchical State* (Oxford and New York: Oxford University Press, 1993); Leslie McLoughlin, *Ibn Saud: Founder of a Kingdom* (London: St. Martin's Press, 1992); Nadav Safran, *Saudi Arabia: The Ceaseless Quest for Security* (Cambridge, MA: Harvard University Press, 1985); Gary Troeller, *The Birth of Saudi Arabia* (London: Frank Cass, 1976); Peter W. Wilson and Douglas F. Graham, *Saudi Arabia: The Coming Storm* (Armonk, NY: M.E. Sharpe, 1994); and R. Bailey Winder, *Saudi Arabia in the Nineteenth Century* (London: Macmillan, 1965).

On the now-united Yemens, see Robert D. Burrowes, *The Yemen Arab Republic: The Politics of Development, 1962–1986* (Boulder, CO: Westview Press, 1987); Fred Halliday, *Revolution and Foreign Policy: The Case of South Yemen, 1967–1987* (Cambridge and New York: Cambridge University Press, 1990); Tareq Y. Ismael and Jacqueline S. Ismael, *The People's Democratic Republic of Yemen: Politics, Economics and Society* (Boulder, CO: Westview Press, 1986); Joseph Kostiner, *The Struggle for South Yemen* (New York: St. Martin's Press, 1984); Helen Lackner, *P.D.R. Yemen: Outpost for Socialist Development in Arabia* (London: Ithaca Press, 1985); John E. Peterson, *Yemen: The Search for a Modern State* (Baltimore: Johns Hopkins University Press, 1982); B. R. Pridham, ed., *Contemporary Yemen: Politics and Historical Background* (New York: St. Martin's Press, 1985); and Manfred W. Wenner, *The Yemen Arab Republic: Development and Change in an Ancient Land* (Boulder, CO: Westview Press, 1991).

On various Arabian states, see F. Gregory Gause III, *Oil Monarchies: Domestic and Security Challenges in the Arab Gulf States* (New York: Council on Foreign Relations Press, 1994); Fred Halliday, *Arabia Without Sultans* (New York: Vintage Books, 1974); and Khaldoun Hassan al-Naqeeb, *Society and State in the Gulf and Arab Peninsula: A Different Perspective* (London and New York: Routledge, 1990).

On the small Gulf states, see Calvin H. Allen, *Oman: The Modernization of the Sultanate* (Boulder, CO: Westview Press, 1987); Abdul-Reda Assiri, *Kuwait's Foreign Policy: City-State in World Politics* (Boulder, CO: Westview Press, 1990); Briton Cooper Busch, *Britain and the Persian Gulf, 1894–1914* (Berkeley and Los Angeles: University of California Press, 1967); Jill Crystal, *Kuwait: The Transformation of an Oil State* (Boulder, CO: Westview Press, 1992); Jill Crystal, *Oil and Politics in the Gulf: Rulers and Merchants in Kuwait and Qatar* (Cambridge and New York: Cambridge University Press, 1990); Jacqueline S. Ismael, *Kuwait: Dependency and Class in a Rentier State,* 2d ed. (Gainesville: University Press of Florida, 1993); Joseph A. Kechichian, *Oman and the World: The Emergence of an Independent Foreign Policy* (Santa Monica, CA: Rand, 1995); Robert Landon, *Oman in the Late Nineteenth Century and After* (Princeton, NJ: Princeton University Press, 1967); Fred H. Lawson, *Bahrain: The Modernization of Autocracy* (Boulder, CO: Westview Press, 1989); Malcolm C. Peck, *The United Arab Emirates: A Venture in Unity* (Boulder, CO: Westview Press, 1986); Patricia Risso, *Oman and Muscat: An Early Modern History* (New York: St. Martin's Press, 1986); Ian Skeet, *Oman: Politics and Development* (New York: St. Martin's Press, 1992); and Rosemarie Said Zahlan, *The Making of the Modern Gulf States: Kuwait, Bahrain, Qatar, the United Arab Emirates and Oman* (London and Boston: Unwin Hyman, 1989).

MODERN EGYPT

A detailed, if uneven, account is P. J. Vatikiotis, *The History of Egypt from Muhammad Ali to Sadat,* 3d ed. (Baltimore: Johns Hopkins University Press, 1986). There are two good, if less thorough, works: Arthur Goldschmidt, Jr., *Modern Egypt: The Formation of a Nation-State* (Boulder, CO: Westview Press, 1988) and Afaf Lutfi al-Sayyid Marsot, *A Short History of*

Modern Egypt (New York: Cambridge University Press, 1985). For an important specialized study see Kenneth M. Cuno, *The Pasha's Peasants: Land, Society, and Economy in Lower Egypt, 1740–1858* (Cambridge and New York: Cambridge University Press, 1993). Two important collections of papers are P. M. Holt. ed., *Political and Social Change in Modern Egypt* (London: Oxford University Press, 1968) and Gabriel Baer, *Studies in the Social History of Modern Egypt* (Chicago: University of Chicago Press, 1969).

A broad analysis of modern Egyptian intellectual developments is Nadav Safran, *Egypt in Search of Political Community: An Analysis of the Intellectual and Political Evolution of Egypt, 1805–1952* (Cambridge, MA: Harvard University Press, 1961). Also see Charles Adams, *Islam and Modernism in Egypt* (London: Oxford University Press, 1933; reprint, New York: Russel, 1968); Jamal Ahmad, *The Intellectual Origins of Egyptian Nationalism* (London: Oxford University Press, 1960); Malcolm Kerr, *Islamic Reform: The Political and Legal Theories of Muhammad 'Abduh and Rashid Rida* (Berkeley and Los Angeles: University of California Press, 1961); and Donald Malcolm Reid, *Cairo University and the Making of Modern Egypt* (Cambridge and New York: Cambridge University Press, 1990).

A study that challenges some older notions is Peter Gran, *Islamic Roots of Capitalism: Egypt, 1760–1840* (Austin: University of Texas Press, 1979). For two previously neglected eighteenth-century rulers, see Daniel Crecelius, *The Roots of Modern Egypt: A Study of the Regimes of 'Ali Bey al-Kabir and Muhammad Bey Abu al-Dhahab, 1760–1775* (Minneapolis: Bibliotheca Islamica, 1981). On a slightly longer period, see Huseyn Efendi, *Ottoman Egypt in the Age of the French Revolution,* trans. by Stanford J. Shaw (Cambridge, MA: Harvard University Press, 1964), and Christopher Herold, *Bonaparte in Egypt* (New York: Harper & Row, 1962).

Studies of the subsequent period include Juan R. I. Cole, *Colonialism and Revolution in the Middle East: Social and Cultural Origins of Egypt's 'Urabi Revolution* (Princeton, NJ: Princeton University Press, 1993); Fred H. Lawson, *The Social Origins of Egyptian Expansion During the Muhammad Ali Period* (New York: Columbia University Press, 1992); Afaf Lutfi al-Sayyid Marsot, *Egypt in the Reign of Muhammad Ali* (New York: Cambridge University Press, 1984); and Helen Rivlin, *The Agricultural Policy of Muhammad 'Ali in Egypt* (Cambridge, MA: Harvard University Press, 1961). Also see F. Robert Hunter, *Egypt Under the Khedives, 1805–1879: From Household Government to Modern Bureaucracy* (Pittsburgh: University of Pittsburgh Press, 1984), and Ehud R. Toledano, *State and Society in Mid-Nineteenth-Century Egypt* (New York: Cambridge University Press, 1990). Works dealing with the development of imperial interests include David Landes, *Bankers and Pashas: International Finance and Economic Imperialism in Egypt* (Cambridge, MA: Harvard University Press, 1958).

British-occupied Egypt is dealt with in Afaf Lutfi al-Sayyid Marsot, *Egypt and Cromer* (London: John Murray, 1968); Timothy Mitchell, *Colonising Egypt* (New York: Cambridge University Press, 1988); and Robert Tignor, *Modernization and British Colonial Rule in Egypt, 1882–1914* (Princeton, NJ: Princeton University Press, 1966).

Jacques Berque, *Egypt: Imperialism and Revolution* (New York: Praeger, 1967) is a massive study. On the anti-British struggle, see Mahmud Zayid, *Egypt's Struggle for Independence* (Beirut: Khayats, 1965). On the old regime, see Eric Davis, *Challenging Colonialism: Bank Misr and Egyptian Industrialization, 1920–1941* (Princeton, NJ: Princeton University Press, 1982); Marius Deeb, *Party Politics in Egypt: The Wafd and Its Rivals, 1919–1939* (London: Ithaca Press, 1979); Afaf Lutfi al-Sayyid Marsot, *Egypt's Liberal Experiment, 1922–1936* (Berkeley and Los Angeles: University of California Press, 1977); Janice J. Terry, *The Wafd, 1919–1952: Cornerstone of Egyptian Political Power* (London: Third World Center for Research and Publishing, 1982); and Robert L. Tignor, *State, Private Enterprise, and Economic Change in Egypt, 1918–1952* (Princeton, NJ: Princeton University Press, 1984). Also see Gudrun Kramer, *The Jews in Modern Egypt, 1914–1952* (Seattle: University of Washington Press, 1989).

For a thorough study, see Richard Mitchell, *The Society of the Muslim Brothers* (London:

Oxford University Press, 1969). On later movements, see J. G. Jansen, *The Neglected Duty: The Creed of Sadat's Assassins and Islamic Resurgence in the Middle East* (New York: Macmillan, 1986), and Giles Kepel, *Muslim Extremism in Egypt: The Prophet and the Pharaoh*, trans. by Jan Rothschild (Berkeley and Los Angeles: University of California Press, 1986).

Joel Beinin and Zachary Lockman, *Workers on the Nile: Nationalism, Communism, Islam, and the Egyptian Working Class, 1882–1954* (Princeton: NJ: Princeton University Press, 1987), provides a thorough, documented analysis of an important facet of society. On another sector, see Nathan J. Brown, *Peasant Politics in Modern Egypt* (New Haven, CN: Yale University Press, 1990).

For a general survey, see Derek Hopwood, *Egypt: Politics and Society, 1945–1981* (Winchester, MA: Allen & Unwin, 1982). Raymond William Baker, *Egypt's Uncertain Revolution Under Nasser and Sadat* (Cambridge, MA: Harvard University Press, 1978), is an analysis mainly of the Nasir period. John Waterbury, *The Egypt of Nasser and Sadat: The Political Economy of Two Regimes* (Princeton, NJ: Princeton University Press, 1983), is a thorough study of Egypt under both Nasir and Sadat. See also Joel Gordon, *Nasser's Blessed Moment: Egyptian Free Officers and the July Revolution* (Oxford and New York: Oxford University Press, 1992).

For analytical studies of Nasir's Egypt, see Kirk J. Beattie, *Egypt During the Nasser Years: Ideology, Politics, and Civil Society* (Boulder, CO: Westview Press, 1994); R. Hrair Dekmejian, *Egypt Under Nasir: A Study in Political Development* (Albany: State University of New York Press, 1971); and, from an Egyptian leftist's point of view, Anouar Abdel-Malek, *Egypt: Military Society* (New York: Random House, 1968). Also see Mahmud Hussein, *Class Conflict in Egypt: 1945–1970* (New York: Monthly Review Press, 1973). Biographies of Nasir include Anthony Nutting, *Nasser* (New York: Dutton, 1972) and Robert Stephens, *Nasser: A Political Biography* (New York: Simon & Schuster, 1971). Nasir's foreign policy is covered by Tawfig Y. Hasou, *The Struggle for the Arab World* (London: Routledge and Kegan Paul, 1985); Malcolm Kerr, *The Arab Cold War: Gamal 'Abd al-Nasir and His Rivals, 1958–1970*, 3d ed. (London: Oxford University Press, 1971); and A. I. Dawisha, *Egypt in the Arab World, 1952–1970: The Elements of a Dynamic Foreign Policy* (New York: Halsted Press, 1977).

On the Suez Crisis of 1956, see Keith Kyle, *Suez* (New York: St. Martin's Press, 1991); Wm. Roger Louis and Roger Owen, eds., *Suez 1956: The Crisis and Its Consequences* (Oxford: Clarendon Press, 1989); Donald Neff, *Warriors at Suez: Eisenhower Takes America into the Middle East* (New York: Linden Press, 1981); and Mordechai Bar-On, *The Gates of Gaza: Israel's Road to Suez and Back, 1955–1957* (New York: St. Martin's Press, 1995). Also see Benny Morris, *Israel's Border Wars 1949–1956: Arab Infiltration, Israeli Retaliation, and the Countdown to the Suez War* (Oxford and New York: Oxford University Press, 1993).

Mohamed Hassanein Heikal, an Egyptian journalist closely associated with Nasir, has written several books that provide important insight. These include *The Cairo Documents* (New York: Doubleday, 1973), *Cutting the Lion's Tail: Suez Through Egyptian Eyes* (London: Andre Deutsch, 1986), *The Road to Ramadan* (New York: Ballantine Books, 1975), and *The Sphinx and the Commissar: The Rise and Fall of Soviet Influence in the Middle East* (New York: Harper & Row, 1979).

Works on the post-Nasir period include Raymond William Baker, *Sadat and After: Struggles for Egypt's Soul* (Cambridge, MA: Harvard University Press, 1990); Mohamed Heikal, *Autumn of Fury: The Assassination of Sadat* (New York: Random House, 1983); Raymond A. Hinnebusch, Jr., *Egyptian Politics Under Sadat: The Post-Populist Development of an Authoritarian-Modernizing State* (Boulder, CO: Lynne Rienner Publishers, 1988); David Hirst and Irene Beeson, *Sadat* (London: Faber and Faber, 1981); Thomas W. Lippman, *Egypt After Nasser: Sadat, Peace and the Mirage of Prosperity* (New York: Paragon House, 1989); Anthony McDermott, *Egypt from Nasser to Mubarak: A Flawed Revolution* (London: Croom Helm, 1988); Ghali Shoukri, *Egypt: Portrait of a President, 1971–1981; The Counter-*

Revolution in Egypt, Sadat's Road to Jerusalem (London: Zed Books, 1978); Robert Spring-borg, *Mubarak's Egypt: Fragmentation of the Political Order* (Boulder, CO: Westview Press, 1989); Charles Tripp and Roger Owen, eds., *Egypt under Mubarak* (London and New York: Routledge, 1990); and Malak Zaalouk, *Power, Class and Foreign Capital in Egypt: The Rise of the New Bourgeoisie* (London: Zed Books, 1989).

Important studies of the social foundations of the post-1952 regime include Hamied Ansari, *Egypt: The Stalled Society* (Albany: State University of New York, 1986), and Leonard Binder, *In a Moment of Enthusiasm: Political Power and the Second Stratum in Egypt* (Chicago: University of Chicago Press, 1978).

ZIONISM, PALESTINE, ISRAEL, AND THE ARAB-ISRAELI CONFLICT

Charles D. Smith, *Palestine and the Arab-Israeli Conflict,* 3d ed. (New York: St. Martin's Press, 1996), and Mark Tessler, *A History of the Israeli-Palestinian Conflict* (Bloomington and Indi-anapolis: Indiana University Press, 1994), are the most comprehensive accounts. For a more succinct study, see Deborah J. Gerner, *One Land: Two Peoples: The Conflict over Palestine,* 2d ed. (Boulder, CO: Westview Press, 1994). See also Ibrahim Abu-Lughod, ed., *The Transforma-tion of Palestine,* 2d ed. (Evanston, IL: Northwestern University Press, 1987); Fred J. Khouri, *The Arab-Israeli Dilemma,* 3d ed. (Syracuse, NY: Syracuse University Press, 1985); Walter Laqueur and Barry Rubin, eds., *The Israel-Arab Reader: A Documentary History of the Middle East Conflict,* 5th rev. ed. (New York: Penguin, 1995); Donald Neff, *Warriors Against Israel* (Brattleboro, VT: Amana Books, 1988); Donald Neff, *Warriors for Jerusalem: Six Days That Changed the Middle East* (New York: Linden Press, 1984); Ritchie Ovendale, *The Origins of the Arab-Israeli Wars* (New York: Longman, 1984); John Quigley, *Palestine and Israel: A Challenge to Justice* (Durham, NC: Duke University Press, 1990); Itamar Rabinovich, *The Road Not Taken: Early Arab-Israeli Negotiations* (Oxford and New York: Oxford University Press, 1991); Bernard Reich, ed., *Arab-Israeli Conflict and Conciliation: A Documentary His-tory* (Westport, CN: Greenwood Press, 1995); Maxime Rodinson, *Israel: A Colonial Settler State?* (New York: Monad Press, 1973); Maxime Rodinson, *Israel and the Arabs* (New York: Pantheon, 1968); Nadav Safran, *From War to War: The Arab-Israeli Confrontation, 1948–1967* (Indianapolis: Pegasus, 1969); Edward W. Said, *The Question of Palestine* (New York: Times Books, 1979); and Edward W. Said and Christopher Hitchens et al., *Blaming the Victims: Spu-rious Scholarship and the Palestine Question* (New York: Verso, 1987).

For important articles on all aspects of the conflict, see Ian S. Lustick, ed., *Arab-Israeli Re-lations: A Collection of Contending Perspectives and Recent Research,* 10 vols. (Hamden, CT: Garland, 1994).

On the pre-1948 period, see J. C. Hurewitz, *The Struggle for Palestine* (New York: Norton, 1950; reprint, New York: Schocken Books, 1976); Robert John and Sami Hadawi, *The Pales-tine Diary,* 2 vols. (New York: New World Press, 1971); Walid Khalidi, ed., *From Haven to Conquest: Readings in Zionism and the Palestine Problem until 1948* (Beirut: Institute for Palestine Studies, 1971); Justin McCarthy, *The Population of Palestine: Population History and Statistics of the Late Ottoman Period and the Mandate* (New York: Columbia University Press, 1990); Ylana N. Miller, *Government and Society in Rural Palestine, 1920–1948* (Austin: University of Texas Press, 1984); Kenneth W. Stein, *The Land Question in Palestine, 1917–1939* (Chapel Hill: University of North Carolina Press, 1984); and Christopher Sykes, *Crossroads to Israel* (New York: World Publishing Company, 1965; reprint, Bloomington: In-diana University Press, 1973).

There is an important body of "revisionist" writings on 1948. See especially Benny Morris, *The Birth of the Palestinian Refugee Problem, 1947–1949* (New York: Cambridge University Press, 1987), and Benny Morris, *1948 and After: Israel and the Palestinians* (Oxford: Claren-don Press, 1990), as well as Simha Flapan, *The Birth of Israel* (New York: Pantheon, 1988);

Ilan Pappe, *The Making of the Arab-Israeli Conflict, 1947–1951* (London: I.B. Tauris, 1994); and Tom Segev, *1949: The First Israelis* (New York: Free Press, 1986). See also Walid Khalidi, ed., *All That Remains: The Palestinian Villages Occupied and Depopulated by Israel in 1948* (Washington, D.C.: Institute for Palestine Studies, 1992), and Michael Palumbo, *The Palestinian Catastrophe: The 1948 Expulsion of a People from Their Homeland* (London and Boston: Faber and Faber, 1987).

On the occupied areas, see Ziad Abu-Amr, *Islamic Fundamentalism in the West Bank and Gaza: Muslim Brotherhood and Islamic Jihad* (Bloomington and Indianapolis: Indiana University Press, 1994); Naseer Aruri, ed., *Occupation: Israel over Palestine,* 2d ed. (Belmont, MA: Association of Arab-American University Graduates, 1989); Yoram Binur, *My Enemy, My Self* (New York: Doubleday, 1989); Robert O. Freedman, ed., *The Intifada: Its Impact on Israel, the Arab World, and the Superpowers* (Gainesville: University Press of Florida, 1991); David Grossman, *The Yellow Wind,* trans. by Haim Watzman (New York: Farrar, Straus and Giroux, 1988); F. Joost R. Hilterman, *Behind the Intifada: Labor and Women's Movements in the Occupied Territories* (Princeton, NJ: Princeton University Press, 1991); Robert Hunter, *The Palestinian Uprising: A War by Other Means,* 2d ed. (Berkeley and Los Angeles: University of California Press, 1993); Zachary Lochman and Joel Beinin, eds., *Intifada: The Palestinian Uprising Against Israeli Occupation* (Boston: South End Press, 1989); David McDowall, *Palestine and Israel: The Uprising and Beyond* (Berkeley and Los Angeles: University of California Press, 1989); Shaul Mishal and Reuben Aharoni, *Speaking Stones: Communiques from the Intifada Underground* (Syracuse, NY: Syracuse University Press, 1994); Jamal R. Nassar and Roger Heacock, *Intifada: Palestine at the Crossroads* (New York: Praeger, 1990); and Michael Palumbo, *Imperial Israel: The History of the Occupation of the West Bank and Gaza* (London: Bloomsbury Press, 1992.

Broader studies of the Palestinians include Helena Cobban, *The Palestinian Liberation Organization: People, Power and Politics* (New York: Cambridge University Press, 1984); Sami Hadawi, *Palestinian Rights and Losses in 1948: A Comprehensive Study* (London: Saqi Books, 1988); Walid Khalidi, *Palestine Reborn* (London and New York: I.B. Tauris, 1992); Baruch Kimmerling and Joel S. Migdal, *Palestinians: The Making of a People* (New York: Free Press, 1993); Ann Mosley Lesch, *Arab Politics in Palestine, 1917–1939* (Ithaca, NY: Cornell University Press, 1979); Muhammad Y. Muslih, *The Origins of Palestinian Nationalism* (New York: Columbia University Press, 1989); Khalil Nakhleh and Elia Zureik, eds., *The Sociology of the Palestinians* (New York: St. Martin's Press, 1980); Philip Mattar, *The Mufti of Jerusalem: Al-Hajj Amin al-Husayni* (New York: Columbia University Press, 1992); Jamal R. Nasser, *The Palestine Liberation Organization: From Armed Struggle to the Declaration of Independence* (New York: Praeger, 1991); Yehoshua Porath, *The Emergence of the Palestinian National Movement, 1918–1929* (London: Frank Cass, 1973); Yehoshua Porath, *The Palestinian Arab National Movement, from Riots to Rebellion, Vol. II, 1929–1939* (London: Frank Cass, 1978); William B. Quandt et al., *The Politics of Palestinian Nationalism* (Berkeley and Los Angeles: University of California Press, 1973); and Pamela Smith, *Palestine and the Palestinians, 1876–1983* (New York: St. Martin's Press, 1984).

Works on Israel include Yossi Beilin, *Israel: A Concise Political History* (New York: St. Martin's Press, 1993); Benjamin Beit-Hallahmi, *The Israeli Connection: Who Israel Arms and Why* (New York: Pantheon, 1987); Ian Black and Benny Morris, *Israel's Secret Wars: History of Israel's Intelligence Services* (New York: Grove Weidenfeld, 1991); Andrew and Leslie Cockburn, *Dangerous Liaison: The Inside Story of the U.S.-Israeli Covert Relationship* (New York: HarperCollins, 1991); S. N. Eisenstadt, *The Transformation of Israeli Society: An Essay in Interpretation* (Boulder, CO: Westview Press, 1985); Boaz Evron, *Jewish State or Israeli Nation?* (Bloomington and Indianapolis: Indiana University Press, 1995); Robert O. Freedman, ed., *Israel Under Rabin* (Boulder, CO: Westview Press, 1995); Seymour M. Hersh, *The Samson Option: Israel's Nuclear Arsenal and American Foreign Policy* (New York: Random House, 1991); Benjamin M. Joseph, *Besieged Bedfellows: Israel and the Land of Apartheid* (Westport, CN: Greenwood Press, 1988); Efraim Karsh and Gregory Mahler, eds., *Israel at the*

Crossroads: The Challenge of Peace (London and New York: British Academic Press, 1994); Keith Kyle and Joel Peters, eds., *Whither Israel? The Domestic Challenges* (London: Royal Institute of International Affairs, 1993); Ian Lustick, *For the Land and the Lord: Jewish Fundamentalism in Israel* (New York: Council on Foreign Relations, 1988); Camille Mansour, *Beyond Alliance: Israel in U.S. Foreign Policy* (Washington, D.C.: Institute for Palestine Studies, 1994); Amos Oz, *In the Land of Israel* (New York: Harcourt Brace Jovanovich, 1983); Dan Raviv and Yossi Melman, *Friends in Deed: Inside the U.S.-Israel Alliance* (New York: Hyperion, 1994); Bernard Reich and Gershon R. Kieval, *Israel: Land of Tradition and Conflict,* 2d ed. (Boulder, CO: Westview Press, 1993); Bernard Reich and Gershon R. Kieval, eds., *Israeli Politics in the 1990s: Key Domestic and Foreign Policy Factors* (New York: Greenwood Press, 1991); Howard Morley Sachar, *A History of Israel from the Rise of Zionism to Our Time* (New York: Knopf, 1976); Howard Morley Sachar, *A History of Israel, Vol. II: From the Aftermath of the Yom Kippur War* (New York: Oxford University Press, 1987); and Tom Segev, *The Seventh Million: The Israelis and the Holocaust,* trans. by Haim Watzman (New York: Hill and Wang, 1993).

The literature on the Zionist movement includes Shlomo Avineri, *The Making of Modern Zionism: The Intellectual Origins of the Jewish State* (New York: Basic Books, 1981); Bernard Avishai, *The Tragedy of Zionism: Revolution and Democracy in the Land of Israel* (New York: Farrar, Strauss Giroux, 1985); Benjamin Beit-Hallahmi, *Original Sins: Reflections on the History of Zionism and Israel* (New York: Olive Branch Press, 1993); Lenni Brenner, *The Iron Wall: Zionist Revisionism from Jabotinsky to Shamir* (London: Zed Books, 1984); Lenni Brenner, *Jews in America Today* (London: Al Saqi Books, 1986); Lenni Brenner, *Zionism in the Age of the Dictators* (London: Croom Helm, 1983); Mitchell Cohen, *Zion and State: Nation, Class and the Shaping of Modern Israel* (New York: Basil Blackwell, 1987); EAFORD and AJAZ, *Judaism or Zionism: What Difference for the Middle East?* (London: Zed Books, 1985); Roberta Strauss Feuerlicht, *The Fate of the Jews: A People Torn Between Israeli Power and Jewish Ethics* (New York: Times Books, 1983); Simha Flapan, *Zionism and the Palestinians* (London: Croom Helm, 1979); Ilan Halevi, *A History of the Jews: Ancient and Modern,* trans. by A. M. Barrett (London: Zed Books, 1987); Ben Halpern, *The Idea of the Jewish State,* 2d ed. (Cambridge, MA: Harvard University Press, 1969); Arthur Hertzberg, ed., *The Zionist Idea: A Historical Analysis and Reader* (Garden City, NY: Doubleday, 1957); Abdul Wahhab Kayyali, ed., *Zionism, Imperialism and Racism* (London: Croom Helm, 1978); Baruch Kimmerling, *Zionism and Territory: The Socio-Territorial Dimensions of Zionist Politics* (Berkeley: Institute of International Studies, 1983); Walter Laqueur, *A History of Zionism* (New York: Schocken Books, 1976); Walter Lehn, in association with Uri Davis, *The Jewish National Fund* (London: Kegan Paul International, 1988); Nur Masalha, *Expulsion of the Palestinians: The Concept of "Transfer" in Zionist Political Thought* (Washington, D.C.: Institute for Palestine Studies, 1992); Amnon Rubinstein, *The Zionist Dream Revisited: From Herzl to Gush Emunim and Back* (New York: Schocken Books, 1984); Dan V. Segre, *A Crisis of Identity: Israel and Zionism* (New York: Oxford University Press, 1980); Alan Taylor, *Prelude to Israel* (New York: Philosophical Library, 1959); Alan Taylor, *The Zionist Mind: The Origins and Development of Zionist Thought* (Beirut: Institute for Palestine Studies, 1974); Roselle Tekiner et al., eds., *Anti-Zionism: Analytical Reflections* (Brattleboro, VT: Amana Books, 1988); David Vital, *The Origins of Zionism* (Oxford: Clarendon Press, 1975); David Vital, *Zionism: The Crucial Phase* (Oxford: Clarendon Press, 1987); and David Vital, *Zionism: The Formative Years* (Oxford: Clarendon Press, 1982).

MODERN SYRIA, LEBANON, AND JORDAN

Surveys include John Devlin, *Syria: Modern State in an Ancient Land* (Boulder, CO: Westview Press, 1983); Derek Hopwood, *Syria 1945–1986: Politics and Society* (London and Boston: Unwin Hyman, 1988); Robert Olson, *The Ba'th and Syria: From the French Mandate to the Era of Hafiz al-Assad* (Princeton, NJ: The Kingston Press, 1982); Tabitha Petran, *Syria*

(New York: Praeger, 1972); and A. L. Tibawi, *A Modern History of Syria, Including Lebanon and Palestine* (New York: St. Martin's Press, 1969). See also Richard T. Antoun and Donald Quataert, eds., *Syria: Society, Culture, and Polity* (Albany: State University of New York Press, 1991), and Youssef M. Choueiri, ed., *State and Society in Syria and Lebanon* (New York: St. Martin's Press, 1993).

Works on specific periods in the twentieth century include Alasdair Drysdale and Raymond A. Hinnebusch, *Syria and the Middle East Peace Process* (New York: Council on Foreign Relations Press, 1991); A. B. Gaunson, *The Anglo-French Clash in Lebanon and Syria, 1940–45* (New York: St. Martin's Press, 1987); Raymond A. Hinnebusch, *Authoritarian Power and State Formation in Ba'thist Syria: The Political Economy of Rural Development* (Boulder, CO: Westview Press, 1989); Raymond A. Hinnebusch, *Peasant and Bureaucracy in Ba'thist Syria* (Boulder, CO: Westview Press, 1989); Philip S. Khoury, *Syria and the French Mandate: The Politics of Arab Nationalism, 1920–1945* (Princeton, NJ: Princeton University Press, 1987); Eberhard Kienle, *Ba'th v. Ba'th: The Conflict Between Syria and Iraq, 1968–1989* (London: I.B. Tauris, 1990); Eberhard Kienle, ed., *Contemporary Syria: Liberalization Between Cold War and Cold Peace* (London: British Academic Press, 1994); Moshe Ma'oz, *Asad: The Sphinx of Damascus: A Political Biography* (New York: Grove Weidenfeld, 1988); Moshe Ma'oz and Avner Yaniv, eds., *Syria Under Assad: Domestic Constraints and Regional Risks* (New York: St. Martin's Press, 1986); Itamar Rabinovich, *Syria Under the Ba'th, 1963–1966* (New York: Halsted Press, 1966); Patrick Seale, *Asad: The Struggle for the Middle East* (Berkeley and Los Angeles: University of California Press, 1988); Patrick Seale, *The Struggle for Syria: A Study of Post-War Politics, 1945–1958* (New York: Oxford University Press, 1965); Nikolaos van Dam, *The Struggle for Power in Syria: Sectarianism and Tribalism in Politics, 1961–1978* (New York: St. Martin's Press, 1979); and Zeine Zeine, *The Struggle for Arab Independence*, 2d ed. (Delmar, NY: Caravan Books, 1977).

On Lebanon, see Fouad Ajami, *The Vanished Imam: Musa al-Sadr and the Shi'a of Lebanon* (Ithaca, NY: Cornell University Press, 1986); John Bulloch, *Final Conflict: The War in Lebanon* (London: Century, 1983); Helena Cobban, *The Making of Modern Lebanon* (Boulder, CO: Westview Press, 1985); Marius Deeb, *The Lebanese Civil War* (New York: Praeger, 1980); Yair Evron, *War and Intervention in Lebanon: The Israeli-Syrian Deterrence Dialogue* (Baltimore: Johns Hopkins University Press, 1987); Wade R. Goria, *Sovereignty and Leadership in Lebanon, 1943–1976* (London: Ithaca Press, 1986); Dilip Hiro, *Lebanon—Fire and Embers: A History of the Lebanese Civil War* (New York: St. Martin's Press, 1990); Michael Hudson, *The Precarious Republic* (New York: Random House, 1968; reprint, Boulder, CO: Westview Press, 1985); Amnon Kapeliouk, *Sabra & Shatila: Inquiry into a Massacre*, trans. by Khalil Jahshan (Belmont, MA: Association of Arab-American University Graduates, 1984); Samir Khalaf, *Lebanon's Predicament* (New York: Columbia University Press, 1987); Rashid Khalidi, *Under Siege: P.L.O. Decisionmaking during the 1982 War* (New York: Columbia University Press, 1986); Walid Khalidi, *Conflict and Violence in Lebanon: Confrontation in the Middle East* (Cambridge, MA: Harvard University Center for International Affairs, 1980); Sean MacBride et al., *Israel in Lebanon: The Report of the International Commission* (London: Ithaca Press, 1983); Augustus Richard Norton, *Amal and the Shi'a: Struggle for the Soul of Lebanon* (Austin: University of Texas Press, 1987); Tabitha Petran, *The Struggle over Lebanon* (New York: Monthly Review Press, 1987); Itamar Rabinovitch, *The War for Lebanon, 1970–1983* (Ithaca, NY: Cornell University Press, 1984); Kamal Salibi, *Crossroads to Civil War: Lebanon, 1958–1975* (Delmar, NY: Caravan Books, 1976); Kamal Salibi, *A House of Many Mansions: The History of Lebanon Reconsidered* (Berkeley: University of California Press, 1989); and Kamal Salibi, *The Modern History of Lebanon* (New York: Praeger, 1965).

Books on Jordan include Naseer H. Aruri, *Jordan: A Study in Political Development (1921–1965)* (The Hague: Martinus Nijhoff, 1972); Uri Bar-Joseph, *The Best of Enemies: Israel and Transjordan in the War of 1948* (London: Frank Cass, 1987); Uriel Dann, *King Hussein and the Challenge of Arab Radicalism: Jordan, 1955–1967* (New York: Oxford

University Press, 1989); Uriel Dann, *Studies in the History of Transjordan, 1920–1949: The Making of a State* (Boulder, CO: Westview Press, 1984); Robert B. Satloff, *From Abdullah to Hussein: Jordan in Transition* (Oxford and New York: Oxford University Press, 1994); Avi Shlaim, *Collusion Across the Jordan: King Abdullah, the Zionist Movement, and the Partition of Palestine* (New York: Columbia University Press, 1988); and Mary C. Wilson, *King Abdullah, Britain and the Making of Jordan* (New York: Cambridge University Press, 1988).

THE SECOND PERSIAN GULF WAR AND "THE NEW WORLD ORDER"

Books on the crisis of 1990–1991 now occupy much library space. Examples include Phyllis Bennis and Michel Moushabeck, eds., *Beyond the Storm: A Gulf Crisis Reader* (New York: Olive Branch Press, 1992); Herbert H. Blumberg and Christopher C. French, eds., *The Persian Gulf War: Views from the Social and Behavioral Sciences* (Lanham, MD: University Press of America, 1994); Haim Bresheeth and Nira Yuval-Davis, eds., *The Gulf War and the New World Order* (London: Zed Books, 1991); Lawrence Freedman and Efraim Karsh, *The Gulf Conflict 1990–1991: Diplomacy and War in the New World Order* (Princeton, NJ: Princeton University Press, 1993); Dilip Hiro, *Desert Shield to Desert Storm: The Second Gulf War* (New York: Routledge, 1992); James Piscatori, ed., *Islamic Fundamentalism and the Gulf Crisis* (Chicago: American Academy of Arts and Sciences, 1991); and Micah L. Sifry and Christopher Cerf, eds., *The Gulf War Reader: History, Documents, Opinions* (New York: Times Books, 1991).

Works on the "New World Order" of the 1990s with specific reference to the Middle East include Tareq Y. Ismael and Jacqueline S. Ismael, *The Gulf War and the New World Order: International Relations of the Middle East* (Gainesville: University Press of Florida, 1994), and Cynthia Peters, ed., *Collateral Damage: The New World Order at Home and Abroad* (Boston: South End Press, 1992).

index